Criminal Procedure

LAW AND PRACTICE

Seventh Edition

Rolando V. del Carmen

Sam Houston State University

THOMSON
WADSWORTH

Australia • Brazil • Canada • Mexico • Singapore • Spain
United Kingdom • United States

THOMSON

★

TM

WADSWORTH

Criminal Procedure:
Law and Practice, **Seventh Edition**
Rolando V. del Carmen

Senior Acquisitions Editor, Criminal Justice:
 Carolyn Henderson Meier
Editorial Assistant: *Rebecca Johnson*
Technology Project Manager: *Amanda Kaufmann*
Marketing Manager: *Terra Schultz*
Marketing Assistant: *Jaren Boland*
Marketing Communications Manager: *Linda Yip*
Project Manager, Editorial Production: *Jennie Redwitz*
Creative Director: *Rob Hugel*
Art Director: *Vernon Boes*

Print Buyer: *Doreen Suruki*
Permissions Editor: *Joohee Lee*
Production Service: *Melanie Field*
Text Designer: *Cheryl Carrington*
Copy Editor: *Lura Harrison*
Cover Designer: *Bill Stanton*
Cover Images: Left: *Thinkstock/SuperStock;*
 right: *Bob Daemmrich/The Image Works*
Compositor: *Integra Software Services*
Text and Cover Printer: *West Group*

Printed in the United States of America
1 2 3 4 5 6 7 10 09 08 07 06

ExamView® and ExamView Pro® are registered trademarks of
FSCreations, Inc. Windows is a registered trademark of the
Microsoft Corporation used herein under license. Macintosh and
Power Macintosh are registered trademarks of Apple Computer, Inc.
Used herein under license.

© 2007 Thomson Learning, Inc. All Rights Reserved. Thomson
Learning WebTutor™ is a trademark of Thomson Learning, Inc.

Library of Congress Control Number: 2006924109
ISBN 0-495-00600-9

Thomson Higher Education
10 Davis Drive
Belmont, CA 94002-3098
USA

For more information about our products, contact us at:
Thomson Learning Academic Resource Center
1-800-423-0563
For permission to use material from this text or product, submit
a request online at **http://www.thomsonrights.com.**
Any additional questions about permissions can be submitted by
e-mail to **thomsonrights@thomson.com.**

This book is dedicated to my wife, Josie, my daughter, Jocelyn, and to the many graduate and undergraduate students I have had over the years from whom I have learned so much.

About the Author

Rolando V. del Carmen is Distinguished Professor of Criminal Justice (Law) in the College of Criminal Justice, Sam Houston State University. He received a Bachelor of Laws degree (the equivalent of a J.D. degree) from the Philippines, a Master of Comparative Law (M.C.L.) from Southern Methodist University, a Master of Laws (LL.M.) from the University of California at Berkeley, and a Doctor of the Science of Law (J.S.D.) from the University of Illinois at Champaign-Urbana. He has authored numerous books and articles on law and criminal justice. His latest book is *Juvenile Justice: The System, Process, and Law* (with Chad Trulson), published by Thomson Wadsworth. He lectures nationally and internationally on various law-related topics. His *Criminal Procedure: Law and Practice* (Wadsworth) has been translated into Japanese, Korean, and Chinese and is used extensively in those countries. A recipient of many national and state awards, he has the distinction of having received all three major awards given annually by the Academy of Criminal Justice Sciences during its annual national convention: the Academy Fellow Award (1990), the Bruce Smith Award (1997), and the Founder's Award (2005). He has taught numerous graduate and undergraduate classes in law and has been a mentor and friend over the years to his many students.

Brief Contents

Contents

Part 2   Levels of Proof and the Exclusionary Rule

Part 3   Searches and Seizures of Persons

Part 5   Identifications, Confessions, and Admissions

Part 6   Constitutional Rights and the Consequences of Police Misconduct

Preface

Law can be complex, boring, and tedious. It can also be confusing and frustrating, particularly when no clear guidelines are given by court decisions or statutes (as is often the case). These realities must be recognized and accepted as an integral, albeit disturbing, part of criminal justice. The confusion and frustration are experienced not only by students and law enforcement personnel but also by judges, lawyers, and other professionals. The imperfections of the criminal justice system, as embodied in laws and court decisions, are a matter of public knowledge, particularly among those directly affected by crime.

There is no perfect system in society's quest for *criminal justice*, a term best understood as justice for the suspect or defendant, the victim, and the community. Given the swirl of emotions surrounding any criminal act, one wonders whether justice itself is attainable to the satisfaction of all, particularly to the victim and the accused. The search for justice is almost always a zero-sum game in that satisfaction for one is at the expense of the other.

In the search for justice, judges, prosecutors, defense lawyers, and court personnel have developed terms and concepts that are part of the criminal justice process. Law enforcement officers must learn and understand them. Any law-oriented text written primarily for students and in-service personnel must present legal terms and concepts clearly and precisely without oversimplification. This text presents criminal procedure in a format and language that meet the needs of non-lawyers and yet preserve the meaning of law as it should be applied.

Although paths to learning are varied and no single system works well for everyone, legal material tends to be learned and retained best through mastery of concepts reinforced by examples. As frequently as possible, this text defines a concept and then further clarifies it with an example. No two situations in law enforcement are ever exactly alike, and this underscores the need for students to apply legal principles to actual situations that sometimes involve great personal risk. If legal concepts are understood well, their application to field situations becomes easier. Memorizing a legal definition may be helpful, but it is much less important than understanding and applying it to real-life situations in law enforcement.

Although the United States is composed of fifty-two different court jurisdictions (the fifty states, the federal government, and the District of Columbia), criminal procedure rules apply nationwide and transcend state boundaries. Unlike substantive criminal law, which varies from state to state, criminal procedure is "nationalized" or "constitutionalized" through U.S. Supreme Court decisions and is therefore binding in all jurisdictions. For example, the *Miranda v. Arizona* decision applies to all states and the federal government in all cases of custodial interrogation.

Nevertheless, variations in procedures abound, particularly where such variations do not violate constitutional rights. This is because the Constitution, as interpreted by the courts, merely sets the minimum procedures that must be followed so that a suspect or a defendant can be assured of fairness from law enforcement agencies and the courts. Variations are evident in processing minor offenses where the stakes for the defendant and the government are not high and where societal peace and order are not threatened.

This text, however, is written for a national audience, not for any particular state or jurisdiction. Consequently, it is not enough for police officers to know the content of this text. Knowledge of specific state law, court decisions, or agency policy is a must in law enforcement. In case of doubt and where an actual case exists, readers should read their own state statutes or consult a knowledgeable lawyer for authoritative guidance.

The Seventh Edition

Organization

There are no major organizational changes in the seventh edition. However, the order of Chapters 12 and 13 from the sixth edition has been reversed: "Constitutional Rights of the Accused during the Trial" is now Chapter 12, and "Legal Liabilities and Other Consequences of Police Misconduct" is now Chapter 13.

Part 1 is the Introduction. Chapter 1 discusses the court system, court cases, and sources of rights. Knowledge of criminal procedure starts with understanding how state and federal courts are structured and work because the product of police work is processed in these courts. What the police do often is reviewed by the courts that have the final say on whether police behavior was legal or illegal. It is also important that the reader at this early stage becomes familiar with the U.S. Constitution and other sources of rights that limit what the police can do to suspects and defendants. Chapter 2 presents an overview of the criminal justice process. The overview familiarizes the reader with the criminal procedure landscape and facilitates understanding of subsequent chapters that deal with details and how criminal procedure ends.

Part 2 presents two chapters basic to criminal procedure, acquainting the reader with knowledge of probable cause, reasonable suspicion, and the exclusionary rule. *Probable cause* is a term around which the constitutionality of police searches and seizures of persons and things revolve. Without probable cause, searches and seizures of persons and things are unconstitutional. *Reasonable suspicion* gives the police legal ground to act in stop and frisk cases, but it is a lower degree of certainty than probable cause. Both legal concepts must be mastered by law enforcement agents if conviction of a suspect or a defendant is to result. The exclusionary rule is designed to inhibit police excesses in search and seizure cases.

It provides that evidence illegally obtained by law enforcement officers is not admissible in court during a trial. These basic concepts in Part 2 are allied closely and must be learned well by the police so their arrests, searches, and seizures can lead to a conviction.

Part 3 deals with searches and seizures of persons. Chapter 5 discusses stop and frisk and stationhouse detention. Chapter 6 deals with arrests, use of force, and responses to terrorism. These discussions probe the extent of the power of the police under the Fourth Amendment when dealing with people. The use of force by the police during an arrest, discussed in Chapter 6 and not discussed in previous recent editions of this text, is included here because it is a current and important topic in modern-day policing. Illegal use of force is one of the most frequent types of lawsuits filed against law enforcement officers and agencies. Officers must know the limits of the use of force—otherwise, serious consequences ensue.

The topic of responses to terrorism is difficult to neatly categorize in a criminal procedure text because it is new and evolving. It is included in Chapter 6 because the detection, apprehension, and detention of terrorism suspects by law enforcement agencies (usually federal) is a major concern in the fight against terrorists. It does not justify a separate chapter because its relationship to police work needs refining, but not discussing terrorism in a criminal procedure text is an unjustified omission because of the growing involvement of state and local police in this effort, its centrality to national security, and the heightened attention given by the U.S. government to this widespread international concern.

Part 4 addresses searches and seizures of things. It is an important part of policing, but it is not as crucial as searches and seizures of persons. Unless properly organized and separately discussed, this aspect of policing can be confusing. Some textbooks discuss arrests of persons and searches and seizures of things together. Other than the presence of probable cause, however, these aspects of police work have different rules. Confusion also results if searches and seizures of motor vehicles are discussed together with seizures of things, as is done in many texts. These two types of searches (things and motor vehicles) are covered by the Fourth Amendment, but they have different rules and are best addressed separately. Part 4 closes with a discussion of searches and seizures that are not fully protected by the Fourth Amendment. These searches are best discussed in this section, but deserve a separate chapter (Chapter 9) because they do not come under the panoply of Fourth Amendment protection and are governed by different rules.

Part 5 covers pretrial identifications and confessions and admissions. Chapter 10, "Lineups and Other Means of Pretrial Identification," and Chapter 11, "Confessions and Admissions: *Miranda v. Arizona*," go together because they are closely related (although their sequence can be interchanged; confessions and admissions can precede pretrial identifications). *Miranda v. Arizona* is arguably the most recognizable case ever decided by the U.S. Supreme Court in criminal procedure. It forms the core of any discussion on the admissibility of confessions and admissions and strongly influences day-to-day police work. It logically belongs to the latter part of the book and prior to a discussion of the constitutional rights of the accused.

Part 6 addresses two topics of differing importance to law enforcement. Chapter 12 familiarizes officers with the constitutional rights of the accused during a trial. Although of peripheral importance to policing (because the trial takes place usually after the police have done their work and the evidence has been submitted to the prosecutor), it helps acquaint officers with the basic constitutional rights during a trial of those they apprehend. This completes an officer's knowledge of the rights guaranteed to anyone who comes in contact with the criminal justice system. Without a good knowledge of a defendant's constitutional rights during a trial, the police merely see the front end of their work and not how their work is completed by the prosecutor and the court and how the rights of suspects are protected at that stage of the criminal justice process.

Chapter 13, "Legal Liabilities and Other Consequences of Police Misconduct" is discussed last because it affects the totality of police work. Officers must realize that there are legal pitfalls in policing and that they must be well aware of them if they are to avoid being sued. This topic needs to be included in a text on criminal procedure because it governs how the police must deal with suspects, defendants, and the general public in the course of their work and the consequences that flow from illegal police behavior. Lawsuits filed against law enforcement agents and agencies have arguably greatly influenced modern-day policing and reshaped law enforcement policies and practices. The topic of legal pitfalls rightfully belongs in a criminal procedure text if the police are to be aware not only of how they are to do their work properly but also of the consequences if they misuse or abuse their power and authority.

Chapter-by-Chapter Revisions

The seventh edition features updated and enhanced coverage in virtually every chapter. Overall, twenty-seven new Supreme Court cases decided since the last edition of the text was published in 2003 have been added. Also added is brand-new coverage of such key topics as how to brief a case; the right to and expectation of privacy; the use of force; problems with eyewitness identification; brain fingerprinting; death-qualified juries; and more. In response to feedback from reviewers, the material has also been reorganized a bit; for example, immigration and border searches are now covered in Chapter 9 alongside other searches and seizures that are not fully protected by the Fourth Amendment, and the order of Chapters 12 and 13 has been reversed to follow a more chronological path. And perhaps most significantly, we have included a complete update of our discussions of the USA Patriot Act and racial profiling. Other key changes to the seventh edition include:

Chapter 1, "The Court System, Court Cases, and Sources of Rights," now includes the "How to Brief a Case," which was previously relegated to an appendix.

Chapter 2, "Overview of the Criminal Justice Process," now includes coverage of the appeal process, previously introduced in Chapter 1.

Chapter 3, "Probable Cause and Reasonable Suspicion," includes the 2003 case *Maryland v. Pringle*, in which the police officer involved had probable cause to arrest the front passenger of a car from which baggies of cocaine were recovered between the back-seat armrest and the back seat. From the facts of the case, it was an "entirely reasonable inference that any or all of the car's occupants had knowledge of and exercised dominion and control over the cocaine."

Chapter 4, "The Exclusionary Rule," includes discussion of two new cases:

- *Brown v. Illinois* (1975): The defendant's statement did not come under the "purged taint" exception of the exclusionary rule and was inadmissible. "The question whether a confession is the product of a free will under *Wong Sun* must be answered on the facts of each case."
- *United States v. Patane* (2004): The Fifth Amendment self-incrimination clause contains its own exclusionary rule.

Chapter 5, "Stop and Frisk and Stationhouse Detention," now features two case briefs. The new case of *Hiibel v. Sixth Judicial District Court of Nevada* (2004) now joins *Terry v. Ohio*.

Chapter 6, "Arrests, Use of Force, and Responses to Terrorism," now includes discussion of the use of force as well as up-to-the-minute coverage of the USA Patriot Act and the latest related court decisions:

- *Tennessee v. Garner* (1985): It is constitutionally reasonable for a police officer to use deadly force when the officer has probable cause to believe that the suspect poses a threat of serious physical harm either to the officer or to others.
- *Hamdi v. Rumsfeld* (2004): Due process requires that a U.S. citizen who is detained for allegedly fighting against the United States in Afghanistan as an enemy combatant must be given a meaningful opportunity to contest the factual basis for his detention before a neutral decision maker.
- *Kaupp v. Texas* (2003): Seizure by the police of a person occurs within the meaning of the Fourth and Fourteenth amendments only when "taking into account all of the circumstances surrounding the encounter, a reasonable passenger would feel free to decline the officers' request or otherwise terminate the encounter."
- *Rasul v. Bush* (2004): Courts in the United States have the power to hear cases challenging the legality of the detention of foreign nationals captured abroad in connection with the fighting in Afghanistan and their detention in Guantanamo Bay.
- *Thornton v. United States* (2004): Officers may search a vehicle as an area of immediate control after a lawful arrest even if the initial contact and arrest of the suspect took place outside the vehicle.

Chapter 7, "Searches and Seizures of Things and Electronic Surveillance," includes two all-new sections: "The Right to Privacy: A Constitutional Right?" and

"The Meaning of 'Reasonable Expectation of Privacy.'" Electronic surveillance is now addressed in this chapter, as are many new relevant cases:

- *Board of Education of Independent School District No. 92 of Pottawatomie County et al. v. Earls* (2002): A random drug testing policy that applied to all middle and high school students participating in any extracurricular activity, not just athletics, was held constitutional.
- *Groh v. Ramirez* (2004): A search warrant that does not comply with the requirement that the warrant particularly describe the person or things to be seized is unconstitutional.
- *Illinois v. Caballes* (2005): A dog sniff conducted during a lawful traffic stop that reveals no information other than the location of an illegal substance that no individual has any right to possess does not violate the Fourth Amendment.
- *Muehler v. Mena* (2005): Detaining occupants of the premises in handcuffs and for a certain period of time while executing a search does not necessarily violate the Fourth Amendment prohibition against unreasonable searches and seizures.
- *Thornton v. United States* (2004): Officers may search the passenger compartment of a vehicle after a lawful arrest even if the suspect was not in the vehicle when arrested.
- *United States v. Banks* (2003): After knocking and announcing their presence and intention to search, 15 to 20 seconds is sufficient time for officers to wait before forcing entry into a home to execute a search warrant for drugs.
- *United States v. Flores-Montano* (2004): "The government's authority to conduct suspicionless inspections at the border includes the authority to remove, disassemble, and reassemble a vehicle's fuel tank."

Chapter 8, "Motor Vehicle Stops, Searches, and Inventories," includes a new case brief on *United States v. Ross*, as well as a number of new case discussions:

- *Illinois v. Caballes* (2005): A dog sniff conducted during a lawful traffic stop that reveals no information other than the location of a substance that no individual has any right to possess does not violate the Fourth Amendment.
- *Illinois v. Lidster* (2004): Police checkpoints set up to obtain information from motorists about a hit-and-run accident are valid under the Fourth Amendment.
- *Thornton v. United States* (2004): Officers may search the passenger compartment of a vehicle as an area of immediate control after a lawful arrest even if the initial contact and the arrest did not take place in the vehicle.
- *United States v. Benitez* (10th Cir. 1990): The consent to search in motor vehicle searches does not have to be verbal.

Chapter 9, "Searches and Seizures Not Fully Protected by the Fourth Amendment: Plain View, Open Fields, Abandonment, and Border Searches," now covers border searches and includes two new case briefs on *Horton v. California* and *Oliver v. United States*.

Chapter 10, "Lineups and Other Means of Pretrial Identification," includes coverage of problems with eyewitness identification, Breathalyzer™ tests, hair samples, and brain fingerprinting. It also includes a case brief on *United States v. Wade* and discussion of the Wisconsin Supreme Court decision *Wisconsin v. Dubose,* in which the Wisconsin Supreme Court concluded, from a study of the extensive research on eyewitness identification, that eyewitness testimony is often "hopelessly unreliable."

Chapter 11, "Confessions and Admissions: *Miranda v. Arizona*," features a new case brief on *Missouri v. Seibert*, in addition to the following new cases:

- *Fellers v. United States* (2004): The proper standard to be used when determining whether statements made by a defendant after an indictment are admissible in court is the Sixth Amendment right to counsel, not the Fifth Amendment right against self-incrimination.
- *Kaupp v. Texas* (2003): A confession must be suppressed if obtained during a detention where officers did not have probable cause and where the detention amounted to the functional equivalent of an arrest.
- *Missouri v. Seibert* (2004): Giving the *Miranda* warnings after the police obtain an unwarned confession violates the *Miranda* rule; therefore, statements made after the *Miranda* warnings are given are not admissible even if these statements repeat those given before the *Miranda* warnings were read to the suspect.
- *United States v. Patane* (2004): Failure to give the *Miranda* warnings does not require the suppression of the physical fruits of a suspect's unwarned but voluntary statements.
- *Yarborough v. Alvarado* (2004): In determining whether a suspect is "in custody" for purposes of giving the *Miranda* warnings, a police officer does not have to consider a suspect's age or previous history with law enforcement.

Chapter 12, "Constitutional Rights of the Accused during the Trial," previously Chapter 13, includes case briefs on *J. E. B. v. Alabama* and *Lockhart v. McCree*, coverage of death-qualified juries, and several new cases:

- *Iowa v. Tovar* (2004): If a defendant says that he or she wishes to plead guilty without the assistance of counsel, the trial judge does not need to spell out all the possible consequences before accepting the plea.
- *Johnson v. California* (2005): "Permissible inferences of discrimination were sufficient to establish a prima facie case of discrimination under *Batson*, shifting the burden to the state to explain adequately the racial exclusion by offering permissible race-neutral justifications for the strikes."

- *Ring v. Arizona* (2002): A finding by the judge of aggravating circumstances (which the judge was authorized to do under Arizona death penalty law) after a jury trial was "the functional equivalent of an element of a greater offense than the one covered by the jury's guilty verdict," and therefore violated the defendant's right to a jury trial.
- *Smith v. Massachusetts* (2005): A judge's acquittal of a defendant midway through a trial by jury prohibited the judge from reconsidering that acquittal later in the trial.
- *Wiggins v. Smith* (2003): The defendant's Sixth Amendment right to effective counsel in a death penalty case was violated by his lawyer's failure to conduct a reasonable investigation into his social history and mitigating factors.
- *Yarborough v. Gentry* (2003): The lawyer's closing argument in a case, in which he admitted some of the defendant's shortcomings, did not deprive the defendant of effective assistance of counsel, because the summation brought out several key points.

Chapter 13, "Legal Liabilities and Other Consequences of Police Misconduct," previously Chapter 12, includes a new case brief on *Town of Castle Rock v. Gonzales* and several new cases:

- *Brosseau v. Haugen* (2004): "If the law at that time (of the incident) did not clearly establish that the officer's conduct would violate the Constitution, the officer should not be subject to liability, or indeed, even the burdens of litigation."
- *Chavez v. Martinez* (2004): A Section 1983 case succeeds only if there is a proven violation of a constitutional right or of a right guaranteed by federal law.
- *Groh v. Ramirez* (2004): An officer is not entitled to qualified immunity if it is clear to a reasonable officer that his or her conduct was unlawful in the situation he or she confronted.
- *Town of Castle Rock v. Gonzales* (2005): The wrongful failure by the police to arrest a husband who violated a domestic relations court restraining order does not amount to a violation of a constitutional right under the Fourteenth Amendment Due Process Clause and therefore does not result in civil liability under federal law.

The cut-off date for U.S. Supreme Court cases used in this edition is May 1, 2006. Cases decided by the Court subsequent to this date will be included in future editions.

Learning Tools

We have included a number of devices in the seventh edition to facilitate learning. In addition to the chapter outlines, objectives, and introductions, which serve as a roadmap for students, each chapter features lists, tables, and examples to bring the material to life. And for the first time, in the seventh edition we have not only integrated case briefs within the actual chapters where they can be of greatest use to students but also accompanied them by actual excerpts from the courts' decisions. Additionally, the seventh edition features a unique chapter-opening summary of the key cases related to that chapter's subject. "The Top 5 Important Cases in _____" is located near the beginning of most chapters, and these sections spotlight which cases, among the many in the chapter, are most important. Other important learning devices include:

- New "You Be the Judge" sections at the end of most chapters that introduce two cases decided recently by the U.S. Court of Appeals, some of which have been appealed to the U.S. Supreme Court.
- Marginal case references and end-of-chapter summaries, review questions, key terms, and unique "Holdings of Key Cases" sections combine to make the book more useful as a study and review tool.
- Appendices include the Constitution of the United States; a guide to being an effective trial witness; and information on how to search for cases at FindLaw.

Ancillaries

To further enhance your study of criminal procedure, the following supplements are available to qualified adopters. Please consult your local sales representative for details.

For the Student

Crime and Evidence in Action CD-ROM This engaging simulation provides an interactive discovery of criminal investigations and features three in-depth crime scene scenario cases that will allow students to analyze crime scene evidence and then make decisions that will affect the outcome of the case. Each case allows the student to take on various roles, from scene investigation (including forensics) to arrest, the trial, incarceration, and even parole of the convicted felon. Students are encouraged to make choices as the case unfolds and conduct interactive investigative research in a simulated setting. This CD-ROM may be bundled with the text at a discount. 0-534-61524-4

Crime Scenes: An Interactive Criminal Justice CD-ROM Recipient of several *New Media Magazine Invision Awards,* this interactive CD-ROM allows students to take on the roles of investigating officer, lawyer, parole officer, and judge in excitingly realistic scenarios! This CD-ROM may be bundled with the text at a discount. An *Instructor's Manual* is also available. 0-534-21491-3

Mind of a Killer CD-ROM *Mind of a Killer* explores the psyche of a serial killer. The CD-ROM contains over 80 minutes of video, 3-D simulations, three textbooks, an extensive mapping system, a library, and much more. 0-534-50705-0

Careers in Criminal Justice 2.0 Interactive CD-ROM This engaging self-exploration provides an interactive discovery of careers in criminal justice. The CD-ROM provides personalized results from a self-assessment of interests to help steer students to careers based on their profile. Students gather information on various careers, from job descriptions and salaries to employment requirements and sample tests. Actual video profiles of criminal justice professionals bring the experience of working in the system to life. 0-534-56869-6

Careers in Criminal Justice: From Internship to Promotion, Fifth Edition by J. Scott Harr and Kären M. Hess This supplemental book helps students develop a job-search strategy through resumes, cover letters, and interview techniques. It also provides students with extensive information on various criminal justice professions, including job descriptions, job salary suggestions, and contact information. 0-534-62620-3

Wadsworth's Guide to Careers in Criminal Justice, Third Edition by Carol Mathews of Century College This 96-page booklet helps students review the wide variety of careers in the criminal justice field. Included are job descriptions, salary suggestions, and contact information. 0-495-13038-9

InfoTrac® College Edition Student Guide for Criminal Justice This 24-page booklet provides detailed user guides for students that illustrate how to use the InfoTrac College Edition database. Special features include login help, a complete search tips cheat sheet, and a topic list of suggested keyword search terms for criminal justice. 0-534-24719-9

For the Instructor

Instructor's Resource Manual with Test Bank by Craig Hemmens of Boise State University This manual offers you learning objectives, key terms, lecture outlines, discussion questions, supplemental lecture ideas, student activities and projects, and additional resources for instructors. Also included is a test bank of over 800 questions in multiple-choice, true/false, fill-in-the-blank, and essay formats with a full answer key. 0-495-12876-7

ExamView® Create, deliver, and customize tests and study guides (both print and online) in minutes with this easy-to-use assessment and tutorial system. ExamView offers both a Quick Test Wizard and an Online Test Wizard that guide you step-by-step through the process of creating tests, while the unique WYSIWYG capability allows you to see the test you are creating on the screen exactly as it will print or display online. You can build tests of up to 250 questions using up to 12 question types. Using ExamView's complete word-processing capabilities, you can enter an unlimited number of new questions or edit existing questions. 0-495-12877-5

The Wadsworth Criminal Justice Video Library

So many exciting, new videos and DVDs . . . so many great ways to enrich your lectures and spark discussion of the material in this text. Please see our current offerings and review/use policies at cj.wadsworth.com/videos. The Wadsworth Video Library includes selections from a variety of sources and programs, including:

ABC News Video Whatever you're looking for in the way of video support—short, high-interest clips from current news events or classic, historic raw footage going back forty years—you can find it in our ABC News videos! Perfect for use as discussion starters or to enrich your lectures and spark interest in the text material, these videos provide students with a new lens through which to view the past and present, one that will greatly enhance their knowledge and understanding of significant events and open up to them new dimensions in learning. Clips are drawn from such programs as *World News Tonight, Good Morning America, This Week, PrimeTime Live, 20/20,* and *Nightline,* as well as numerous ABC News specials and material from the Associated Press Television News and British Movietone News collections. Your Thomson Wadsworth representative will be happy to provide a complete listing of videos and policies.

CNN® Today: Criminal Justice Video Series Integrate the up-to-the-minute programming power of CNN and its affiliate networks into your course with these short, high-interest clips. Segments are available on a wealth of cutting-edge topics, including corporate crime, the death penalty, prison rape, DNA evidence, medical marijuana, the DC snipers, international criminal courts, sex offender registries, the Internet and child porn, video game violence, hate crimes against Arab-Americans post 9/11, and many more. Order any of these CNN tapes for your classes today:

- Introduction to Criminal Justice: Vol. V: 0-534-56833-5; Vol. VI: 0-534-57354-1; Vol. VII: 0-534-68698-5
- Criminology: Vol. VI: 0-534-53547-X; Vol. VII: 0-534-53548-8; Vol. VIII: 0-534-63699-3

Court TV Videos One-hour videos featuring provocative, high-profile, and seminal court cases as well as key topics that affect our legal system. Available videos include "Police Force: What Killed Malice Green?" "Cyber Crime," "*Florida v. Wuornos,*" "Punishment: Cruel and Unusual," and many others. Over thirty videos are available, each of which follows a case from start to finish.

Wadsworth Custom Videos for Criminal Justice These videos, produced by Films for the Humanities and Social Sciences, feature five- to fifteen-minute clips on current topics that are deep enough to spark a great classroom discussion but brief enough to leave time in your class session for other exercises. Topics covered include twenty-first-century crime fighting, adult punishment for minors, three-strikes laws, new advances in forensics, sex offender registries, and more!

- Vol. II on VHS: 0-534-57335-5; Vol. II on DVD: 0-495-18950-2
- Vol. III on VHS: 0-495-12998-4; Vol. III on DVD: 0-495-18951-0

PLUS Videos from the A&E American Justice Series, Films for the Humanities, and More The A&E videos focus on high-interest topics and cases and feature episodes from A&E's *American Justice* series. Topics include life as a public defender, the challenges facing homicide detectives, juvenile justice, and unusual defenses criminals have tried to use. Or choose from hundreds of Films for the Humanities videos of varying length on such current topics as domestic violence, terrorism, juvenile courts, victim issues, white-collar crime, life after prison, and more. Some videos are less than ten minutes in length and provide ideal lecture launchers. Other videos are longer (up to one hundred minutes) and can be used to start a deeper classroom discussion. *Your Thomson Wadsworth representative will be happy to provide details on our video policy by adoption size.*

Acknowledgments

The changes in the seventh edition were made primarily in response to written suggestions by the book reviewers of the sixth edition. All of the reviewers are highly respected colleagues who currently teach courses in criminal procedure, a number of whom are currently using this book. The reviewers of this and all previous editions include: Kevin Behr, Coastal Bend College; Beth Bjerregaard, University of North Carolina at Charlotte; Don Bradel, Bemidji State University; Jerry Burnette, New River Community College; William Castleberry, University of Tennessee at Martin; Edward Donovan, Metropolitan State College of Denver; Robert Drowns, Metropolitan State University; Catherine Eloranto, Clinton Community College; Jack Enter, Georgia State University, Atlanta; Lorie Fridell, Florida State University; James Hague, Virginia Commonwealth University; Robert Hardgrave, Jr., University of Texas at Austin; William Head, Texas Christian University, Fort Worth; Craig Hemmens, Boise State University; Thomas Hickey, Castleton State College; Louis Holscher, San Jose State University; Tom Hughes, University of Louisville; Martrice Hurrah, Shelby State Community College; William D. Hyatt, Western Carolina University; W. Richard Janikowski, University of Memphis; Judith Kaci, California State University at Long Beach; Raymond Kessler, Sul Ross State University; Dave Kramer, Bergen Community College; Pamela Moore, University of Texas at Arlington; Patrick Mueller, Stephen F. Austin State University; Gary Neumeyer, Arizona Western College; Robert Pagnani, Columbia-Greene Community College; Robert Peetz, Midland College; Robert Reinertsen, Western Illinois

University; Ray Richards, San Jacinto College; Steve Rittenmeyer, Western Illinois University at Macomb; Clifford Roberson, California State University at Fresno; Lore Rutz-Burri, Southern Oregon University; Joseph Schuster, Eastern Washington State College at Cheney; Pamella Seay, Edison Community College; Caryl Lynn Segal, University of Texas at Arlington; Mark Stevens, North Carolina Wesleyan College; Greg Talley, Broome Community College; Roger Turner, Shelby State Community College; Segrest N. Wailes, Jackson State University; and Alvin Zumbrun, Catonsville Community College. Their suggestions have guided the revision of this book and have doubtless shaped this book's format and content. To these esteemed colleagues and thoughtful contributors, I am deeply grateful. I must also point out that some of the legal case briefs used in this textbook are based, with modification, on a book titled *Briefs of Leading Cases in Law Enforcement*, by Rolando V. del Carmen and Jeffery T. Walker (Anderson Publishing/LexisNexis), which is now in its sixth edition.

This and the previous editions would not have been possible without the help of friends and colleagues. Thanks are due to the following colleagues and friends for their contributions: Jerry Dowling and Phillip Lyons of Sam Houston State University; John Scott Bonien, Senior Assistant Attorney General of the state of Washington; Michael S. Vaughn of Sam Houston State University; Jeffery Walker of the University of Arkansas at Little Rock; David Carter of Michigan State University; Craig Hemmens of Boise State University; and Tom Hickey of the University of Tampa.

The hundreds of undergraduate and graduate students I have had the privilege of teaching over the years inspired the writing of this book. From them I learned so much about the law and how student knowledge of legal material can be facilitated and enhanced.

I owe a debt of gratitude to the following administrators in the College of Criminal Justice: Richard H. Ward, former Dean and Director; Wes Johnson, Associate Dean; and Janet Mullings, Assistant Dean. They made the vast resources of the Criminal Justice Center available for this revision. The staff at the Criminal Justice Center have been very helpful, particularly Jillian Harris and Connie Alvarez. Sam Swindell, my research assistant who is a lawyer and has had extensive experience practicing law, and who is now a Ph.D. student at Sam Houston, did all the work on the new feature "You Be the Judge" and also checked the accuracy of the legal citations. To him I owe special thanks.

I thank the personnel at Thomson Wadsworth who were true professionals throughout the revision of this book and who did a terrific job. They are: Carolyn Henderson Meier, Senior Acquisitions Editor; Rebecca Johnson, Editorial Assistant; Terra Shultz, Marketing Manager; Amanda Kaufmann, Technology Project Manager; Jennie Redwitz, Senior Content Project Manager; Melanie Field, production service; Lura Harrison, copy editor; and Cheryl Carrington, designer.

This book derives its strength from the efforts of a lot of people, but the author should and does stand alone in accepting blame for its shortcomings. Feedback from readers is welcome and deeply appreciated—it will help ensure better future editions. To those who provide feedback, I say—thanks.

I hope the goal of somehow demystifying the law so it can effectively guide the conduct of present and future law enforcement officers has somehow been accomplished in this text. Policing a free society is never easy; it typifies a collaborative effort between the police and the public. I hope this book contributes to achieving that goal—in the interest of society and for the benefit of those law enforcement officers who risk their lives daily so the rest of us can enjoy safety and peace.

Rolando V. del Carmen
Distinguished Professor of Criminal Justice (Law)
College of Criminal Justice
Sam Houston State University

Chapter **1** The Court System, Court Cases, and Sources of Rights

What You Will Learn

- The United States has a dual court system—federal and state.
- Court decisions are binding only in that court's territorial jurisdiction.
- Some criminal cases can be tried in both federal and state courts.
- There are distinctions between *jurisdiction* and *venue*.
- Briefing decided cases is a good way to understand a court decision.
- The Internet is an easily accessible source of court decisions.
- There are four sources of legal rights.
- Approaches to the incorporation controversy can be classified into four positions.
- The term *rule of law* has many meanings.

CASE BRIEF

Duncan v. Louisiana (1968)

Introduction

In this chapter, we focus on the structure of federal and state court systems in the United States.

Criminal cases in the United States may be tried in federal and state courts if the act constitutes violation of the laws of both jurisdictions. However, most criminal cases are tried in state courts, because maintaining peace and order is primarily the responsibility of state and local governments. Important topics include the territorial effect of judicial decisions, the principle of judicial precedent based on stare decisis, the extent of federal and state jurisdiction, the principle of dual sovereignty, the legal concepts of

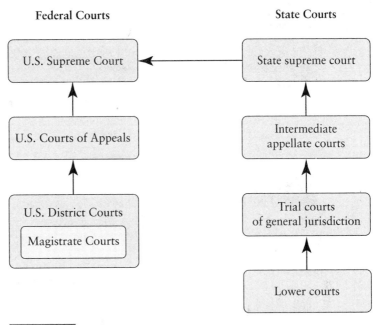

Federal Courts State Courts

Figure 1.1 The Dual Court System: Simplified Flowchart

jurisdiction and venue, and the various sources of individual rights. The chapter discusses the incorporation controversy—how it developed and what role it plays in determining which constitutional rights now also extend to an accused in state prosecutions. It ends with a discussion of the rule of law.

The Structure of the Court System

The United States has a **dual court system**, meaning that there is one system for federal cases and another for state cases (see Figure 1.1). The term *dual court system* is, however, misleading. The United States has fifty-two separate judicial systems, representing the court systems in the fifty states, the federal system, and the courts of Washington, D.C. But because these systems have much in common, they justify a general grouping into two: federal and state.

The Federal Court System

Article III, Section 1 of the U.S. Constitution provides that

> The judicial Power of the United States shall be vested in one supreme Court, and in such inferior Courts as the Congress may from time to time ordain and establish. The Judges, both of the supreme and inferior Courts, shall hold their Offices during good Behavior, and shall, at stated Times, receive for their Services a Compensation, which shall not be diminished during their continuance in office.

The highest court in the federal court system is the U.S. Supreme Court. (*Note:* Whenever the word *Court* is used with a capital *C* in this text, the reference is to the U.S. Supreme Court. The word *court* with a lowercase *c* refers to all other courts on the federal or state levels.) It is composed of a chief justice and eight associate justices, all of whom are nominated and appointed by the president of the United States with the advice and consent of the Senate (see Table 1.1).

A federal law passed in 1869 fixed the number of U.S. Supreme Court justices at nine, but this number can be changed by law. Supreme Court justices enjoy life tenure and may be removed only by impeachment, which very rarely occurs. The Court is located in Washington, D.C., and always decides cases **en banc** (*as one body*), never in small groups or panels (*in division*). Six justices constitute a quorum, but the votes of five justices are needed to win a case. The Court meets to hear arguments and decide cases beginning on the first Monday in October and continues sessions usually through the end of June of the following year. Court cases are argued and decisions are announced during this time, although the Court holds office throughout the year. Members of the U.S. Supreme Court are called justices. All others, from the U.S. Court of Appeals down to the lower courts, are called judges.

The Court has **original jurisdiction**, meaning the case is brought to the Court directly instead of on appeal, over certain cases as specified in the Constitution. Most cases reach the Court, however, either on *appeal* or on a *writ of certiorari*. A third way—by certification—is rarely used; and a fourth method—through a writ of error—was discontinued in 1928.[1] The Court reviews cases on appeal because it must. In reality, however, the Court does not have to consider a case on appeal on its merits, because it can avoid full consideration by saying that the case "lacks substantial federal question" to deserve full consideration by the Court.

A high majority of cases (85–90%) get to the Supreme Court from the lower courts on a *writ of certiorari,* which is defined as "an order by the appellate court which is used when the court has discretion on whether or not to hear an appeal."[2] In writ of certiorari cases, the **rule of four** applies, meaning that at least four justices must agree for the Court to consider a case on its merits. If the case fails to obtain four votes for inclusion in the Court docket, the decision of the court where the case originated (usually a federal court of appeals or a state supreme court) prevails.

Between eight and nine thousand cases reach the Supreme Court each year from various federal and state courts, but the Court considers only a limited number (88 cases in 2001–2002, 73 cases in 2002–2003, 79 cases in 2003–2004, and 87 cases in 2004–2005) on their merit. The rest are dismissed *per curiam,* meaning that the decision of the immediate lower court in which the case originated (whether it is a state supreme court, a federal court of appeals, or any other court) is left undisturbed.

Not accepting a case does not imply that the Supreme Court agrees with the decision of the lower court. It simply means that the case could not get the votes of at least four justices to give it further attention and consider it on its merits. The public perception that only the most important cases are accepted and decided by the Supreme Court is not necessarily true. Cases generally get on the Supreme

■ Table 1.1 United States Supreme Court Justices
(as of February 15, 2006)

Name	Age	Home State	Appointed by	First Day	Prior Positions
John Roberts (Chief Justice)	50	Maryland	George W. Bush	9/29/05	Circuit Judge, Court of Appeals for the District of Columbia Circuit (2003–2005); Private practice (1993–2003); Deputy Solicitor General of the United States (1989–1993); Private practice (1986–1989)
John Paul Stevens	85	Illinois	Gerald Ford	12/19/75	Circuit Judge, Court of Appeals for the Seventh Circuit (1970–1975); Private practice (1948–1970)
Antonin Scalia	69	Virginia	Ronald Reagan	9/26/86	Circuit Judge, Court of Appeals for the D.C. Circuit (1982–1986); Professor, University of Chicago Law School (1977–1982)
Anthony Kennedy	69	California	Ronald Reagan	2/18/88	Circuit Judge, Court of Appeals for the Ninth Circuit (1975–1988); Professor, McGeorge School of Law, University of the Pacific (1965–1988); Private practice (1963–1975)
David Souter	66	New Hampshire	George H. W. Bush	10/9/90	Circuit Judge, Court of Appeals for the First Circuit (1990–1991); Associate Justice, Supreme Court of New Hampshire (1983–1990)
Clarence Thomas	57	Georgia	George H. W. Bush	10/23/91	Circuit Judge, Court of Appeals for the D.C. Circuit (1990–1991); Chairman, Equal Employment Opportunity Commission (1982–1990)
Ruth Bader Ginsburg	72	New York	Bill Clinton	8/10/93	Circuit Judge, Court of Appeals for D.C. Circuit (1980–1993); General Counsel, American Civil Liberties Union (1973–1980)
Stephen Breyer	67	Massachusetts	Bill Clinton	8/3/94	Chief Judge, Court of Appeals for the First Circuit (1990–1994); Circuit Judge, Court of Appeals for the First Circuit (1980–1990); Professor, Harvard Law School (1967–1980)
Samuel Alito	55	New Jersey	George W. Bush	1/31/06	Circuit Judge, Court of Appeals for the Third Circuit (1990–2006); Professor, Seton Hall University School of Law (1999–2004); U.S. Attorney for the District of New Jersey (1987–1990); Deputy Assistant Attorney General (1985–1987); Assistant to the Solicitor General (1981–1985)

Source: "Supreme Court of the United States," *Wikipedia, the Free Encyclopedia* (*http://en.wikipedia.org/wiki/ Supreme_Court_of_the_United_States*). Modified by the author.

Court docket because at least four justices voted to include the case. The standard used for inclusion is left to individual justices to decide.

Next to the Supreme Court in the federal judicial hierarchy are the U.S. courts of appeals, officially referred to as the United States Court of Appeals for a particular circuit (see Figure 1.2). As of 2005, these courts had 179 judgeships located in thirteen judicial "circuits." Of these thirteen circuits, twelve are identified by region, including one solely for the District of Columbia. The thirteenth circuit is the Court of Appeals for the Federal Circuit, which has jurisdiction throughout the country on certain types of cases based on subject matter. Each circuit (other than that for the District of Columbia and the Federal Circuit) covers three or more states. For example, the Fifth Circuit covers the states of Texas, Mississippi, and Louisiana, whereas the Tenth Circuit includes the states of Utah, Wyoming, Colorado, Kansas, New Mexico, and Oklahoma. The District of Columbia has a whole circuit unto itself.

Each court has six or more judges, depending upon the circuit's caseload. The First Circuit has six judges, whereas the Ninth Circuit has twenty-eight (see Figure 1.3). Judges of the courts of appeals are nominated and appointed by the president of the United States for life, with the advice and consent of the Senate, and can be removed only by impeachment. Unlike the Supreme Court, courts of appeals may hear cases as one body (en banc) or in groups (in divisions) of three or five judges.

Occupying the lowest level in the hierarchy of federal courts are the district courts, the trial courts for federal cases. The federal government has 646 federal judgeships located in ninety-four judicial districts in the United States, Guam, Puerto Rico, and the Virgin Islands. Each state has at least one judicial district, but some states have as many as four. Judges are nominated and appointed by the president of the United States for life, with the advice and consent of the Senate, and can be removed only by impeachment. In practice, the senior U.S. senator from that state makes the recommendation for the appointment if he or she belongs to the president's political party.

Also under the federal system are the U.S. magistrate courts, established primarily to relieve district court judges of heavy caseloads. They are presided over by U.S. magistrates (formerly called U.S. commissioners) and have limited authority, such as trying minor offenses and misdemeanor cases in which the possible penalty is incarceration of one year or less. They are also empowered to hold bail hearings, issue warrants, review habeas corpus petitions, and hold pretrial conferences in civil and criminal cases. Unlike other federal court judges, whose offices are created by Article III (the Judiciary Article) of the Constitution, the offices of federal magistrates are created by the Congress of the United States. Magistrates are appointed by federal court judges in that district and are not guaranteed life tenure.

The State Court System

The structure of the state court system varies from state to state. In general, however, state courts follow the federal pattern. This means that states have one state supreme court that makes final decisions on cases involving state laws and provisions of the

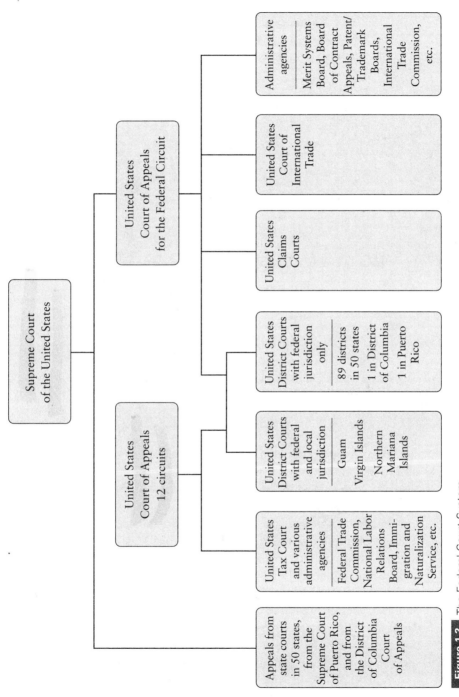

Figure 1.2 The Federal Court System

The following describes the figure (read from the rotated layout):

- **Supreme Court of the United States**
  - **United States Court of Appeals — 12 circuits**
    - Appeals from state courts in 50 states, from the Supreme Court of Puerto Rico, and from the District of Columbia Court of Appeals
    - United States Tax Court and various administrative agencies
      - Federal Trade Commission, National Labor Relations Board, Immigration and Naturalization Service, etc.
    - United States District Courts with federal and local jurisdiction
      - Guam
      - Virgin Islands
      - Northern Mariana Islands
    - United States District Courts with federal jurisdiction only
      - 89 districts in 50 states
      - 1 in District of Columbia
      - 1 in Puerto Rico
  - **United States Court of Appeals for the Federal Circuit**
    - United States Claims Courts
    - United States Court of International Trade
    - Administrative agencies
      - Merit Systems Board, Board of Contract Appeals, Patent/Trademark Boards, International Trade Commission, etc.

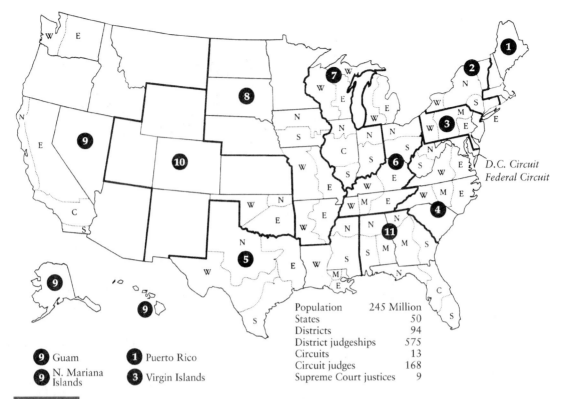

Figure 1.3 Geographical Boundaries of U.S. Courts of Appeals and District Courts

Source: Russell Wheeler and Cynthia Harrison, *Creating the Federal Judicial System*, 2nd ed. (Washington, D.C.: Federal Judicial Center, 1996), p. 26.

state constitution. Texas and Oklahoma, however, have two highest courts—one for civil cases and the other for criminal cases. State courts decide nearly every type of case but are limited by the provisions of the U.S. Constitution, their own state constitutions, and state law.

Below the state supreme court in the state judicial hierarchy are the intermediate appellate courts (see Figure 1.1). Only thirty-five of the fifty states have intermediate appellate courts. Where such courts do not exist, cases appealed from the trial courts go directly to the state supreme court. Each state has trial courts with general jurisdiction, meaning that they try civil and criminal cases. They go by various names, such as circuit court, district court, or court of common pleas. New York's court of general jurisdiction is called the supreme court. Although these courts are of general jurisdiction, some states divide them according to specialty areas, such as probate, juvenile, and domestic relations.

At the base of the state judicial hierarchy are lower courts, such as county courts, justice of the peace courts, and municipal courts. They have limited jurisdiction in both civil and criminal cases and also decide cases involving local ordinances passed by county or city governments.

The Territorial Effect of Judicial Decisions

The jurisdiction of every U.S. court is limited in some way. One type of limitation is territorial or geographic. A judicial decision is authoritative and has value as precedent for future cases only within the geographic limits of the area in which the deciding court has jurisdiction. Consequently, U.S. Supreme Court decisions on questions of federal law and the Constitution are binding on all U.S. courts because the whole country is under its jurisdiction. Decisions of federal courts of appeals are the last word within circuits if there is no Supreme Court action. The First Circuit Court of Appeals, for example, settles federal issues for Maine, Massachusetts, New Hampshire, Rhode Island, and Puerto Rico, the areas within its jurisdiction (see Figure 1.3). When a district court encompasses an entire state, as is the case in Maine, its decision on a federal law produces a uniform rule within the state. However, in a state such as Wisconsin, where there are multiple districts, there can be divergent and even conflicting decisions even on the district court level.

The same process operates in the state court systems, but in one regard state supreme court decisions are recognized as extending beyond state borders. Because the Constitution declares the sovereignty of the states within the area reserved for state control, the court of last resort in each state is the final arbiter of issues of purely state and local law. For example, the meaning that the California Supreme Court gives to a state statute or a municipal ordinance will be respected as authoritative even by the U.S. Supreme Court, unless it involves a constitutional question—in which case the U.S. Supreme Court becomes the final arbiter.

The existence of a dual court system and the limited jurisdictional reach of the vast majority of courts make it highly probable that courts will render conflicting decisions on a legal issue. The appellate process provides a forum for resolving these conflicts if the cases are appealed. If no appeal is made, the conflict remains. For example, a federal district court in the Southern District of Ohio may rule that jail detainees are entitled to contact visits, whereas another federal district court in the Northern District of that state, on a different case, may rule otherwise. However, this inconsistency will be resolved only if the federal appellate court for Ohio decides the issue in an appealed case.

Despite the territorial or geographic limitations of court decisions, there are important reasons why decisions from other jurisdictions should not be ignored. First, there may be no settled law on an issue in a given area. When the issue has not been decided previously by a local court (known as a *case of first impression*), the local federal or state court will probably decide it on the basis of the dominant, or "better," rule that is being applied elsewhere. The second reason is that law is evolving, not stagnant. Over time, trends develop in the law. When a particular court senses that its prior decisions on a point are no longer in the mainstream, it may consider revising its holding, especially if the issue has not been settled by the U.S. Supreme Court. The decisions in other jurisdictions may enable lawyers to detect a trend and anticipate what local courts might do in the future.

Judicial Precedent (Stare Decisis)

Stare decisis is a Latin term that literally means "to abide by, or adhere to, decided cases." Courts generally adhere to stare decisis: When a court has laid down a principle of law as applicable to a certain set of facts, it will follow that principle and apply it to all future cases with similar facts and circumstances. The judicial practice of stare decisis leads to **judicial precedent**, meaning that decisions of courts have value as precedent for future cases similarly circumstanced. These terms are often used interchangeably because they vary only slightly in meaning. The principle of stare decisis ensures predictability of court decisions, whereas judicial precedent is a process courts follow as a result of stare decisis. Judicial precedent is made possible by stare decisis.

A decision is precedent only for cases that come within that court's jurisdiction. For example, the decisions of the Fifth Circuit Court of Appeals are valued as precedent only in the states (Texas, Louisiana, and Mississippi) within the territorial jurisdiction of the court. By the same token, the decisions of the Florida Supreme Court are precedent only in cases decided by Florida courts. U.S. Supreme Court decisions are precedent for cases anywhere in the United States. For example, the case of *Miranda v. Arizona* is precedent for cases involving custodial interrogation, so all cases decided in the United States on that issue must be decided in accordance with *Miranda*. Variations do occur, however, because the facts of cases differ. Therefore, the Court can refine, modify, or expand the *Miranda* doctrine. Moreover, judicial precedent can be discarded at any time by the court that decided it. *Miranda* has been modified and refined by the Court a number of times in subsequent cases (see Chapter 11, "Confessions and Admissions"). Although it is unlikely, the Court could also abandon the *Miranda* doctrine at any time or prescribe a different rule, depending on what the Court determines is required by the Constitution. All that is needed to overturn a judicial precedent are the votes of at least five justices of the Court.

The most binding kind of precedent is that set by cases decided by the U.S. Supreme Court. The decision of any court, however, can set a precedent. Sometimes, lower courts do not follow a precedent set by a higher court. In these cases, the appellate court can reverse the lower court decision on appeal.

Federal versus State Jurisdiction

The rule that determines whether a criminal case should be filed and tried in federal or state court is, generally, if an act is a violation of federal law, the trial will be held in a federal court; if the act is a violation of state law, the trial will be held in a state court. A crime that violates both federal and state laws (such as kidnapping, transportation of narcotics, counterfeiting, or robbery of a federally insured bank) may be tried in both federal and state courts if the prosecutors so desire. For example, if X robs the Miami National Bank, X can be prosecuted for the crime of robbery under Florida law and for robbery of a federally insured bank under federal law. The prosecutions are for the same act but involve two different laws. There is no double jeopardy, because of the concept of **dual sovereignty**, which means that federal and state governments are each considered sovereign in their own right.

The much-publicized Oklahoma City bombing cases provide actual examples. The two defendants in that crime were convicted in federal court. Timothy McVeigh was given the death penalty and subsequently executed. The other defendant, Terry Nichols, was also convicted in federal court and given life imprisonment with no hope of parole. He was later tried in an Oklahoma state court, convicted of 161 state murder charges, and sentenced to life times 161. This did not constitute double jeopardy because of the concept of dual sovereignty.

Defendants can also be tried in two different states for essentially the same crime, if the crime or an element thereof was committed in those states. The cases of John Allen Muhammad and John Lee Malvo, the two snipers who terrorized the Maryland–Washington, D.C.–Virginia areas in October 2002, provide another example. Accused of shooting nineteen people and killing thirteen, they were tried and punished in federal court as well as in state courts in places where the shootings and other crimes took place. Whether the state can and will try a defendant again depends on state law and the discretion of the prosecutor. The government that first obtains custody of the suspect is usually allowed to try him or her first. In most cases, this is the state.

Although the federal government can try the defendant for the same offense, it usually refrains from doing so if the defendant has been convicted and sufficiently punished under state law. The state would do likewise if the sequence were reversed, although some states have laws against state prosecution for a criminal act that has been prosecuted by the federal government.

HIGHLIGHT

Multiple Prosecutions, No Double Jeopardy

The concept of dual sovereignty is alive and well in the United States. It will likely be used more frequently in the immediate future in cases involving international terrorism and high-profile domestic cases.

Dual sovereignty holds that the federal government and the states are separately sovereign and therefore may prosecute offenders separately for crimes committed within their jurisdictions. Multiple prosecutions may be characterized as vertical or horizontal. *Vertical prosecutions* take place when a crime is prosecuted in both federal and state courts. *Horizontal prosecutions* happen when a crime is prosecuted in two states where elements of the crime took place and when the act is punished by the penal codes of those states. In either case, there is no double jeopardy, and therefore the prosecutions are constitutional.

Multiple prosecutions serve several functions: making sure the defendant does not go free if acquitted in one jurisdiction; seeking a more severe penalty if the sentence imposed in the first jurisdiction is not deemed sufficient; and serving as a public expression of outrage over the severity or heinousness of the crime. As the country faces the daunting prospect of more acts of terrorism (as in the case of September 11, 2001) and the continued prospect of appalling violence (as in the 2002 case of the two snipers who left fourteen people dead and five others wounded in various states and Washington, D.C.), the concept of dual sovereignty and multiple prosecutions will serve as ways whereby, in the minds of most people, justice is properly served.

Note, however, that, although successive prosecutions by separate sovereignties are constitutional, they may be prohibited by state law or internal agency policy. Moreover, a prosecutor may not want to file the case, even if he or she can, because of the expense involved or if "justice has been served," perhaps because the defendant has been sufficiently punished. In high-profile cases, however, prosecutors from other jurisdictions may want to try the defendant regardless of the verdict and punishment in other jurisdictions. For example, although Terry Nichols was sentenced to life in prison by the federal government in the Oklahoma City bombing case, the State of Oklahoma tried him again under state law so he could be given the death penalty. He did not get the death penalty but was sentenced to life times 161 by the Oklahoma state court.

Jurisdiction versus Venue

The terms *jurisdiction* and *venue* can be confusing. Sometimes used interchangeably, they nevertheless represent very different concepts. **Jurisdiction** refers to the power of a court to try a case. A court's jurisdiction is defined by the totality of the law that creates the court and limits its powers; the parties to litigation cannot vest the court with jurisdiction it does not possess. Defects in the subject matter jurisdiction of a court (for example, when a civil case is tried in a criminal court, which does not have the authority to try it) cannot be waived by the parties and can be raised at any stage of the litigation, including on appeal.

Frisbie v. Collins (1952)

See Appendix C for information on how to find cases in this chapter on FindLaw.com.

To render a valid judgment against a person, a court must also have jurisdiction over that person. The fact that a defendant has been brought to court against his or her wishes and by questionable methods does not invalidate the jurisdiction of the court. In *Frisbie v. Collins,* 342 U.S. 519 (1952), the Court ruled that an invalid arrest is not a defense against being convicted of the offense charged. In that case, while living in Illinois, the accused was forcibly seized, handcuffed, blackjacked, and then taken back to Michigan by law enforcement officers. The Court ruled that the power of a court to try a person for a crime is not impaired by the fact that the person has been brought within the court's jurisdiction through forcible abduction. The Court said, "It matters not how a defendant is brought before the court; what matters is that the defendant is before the court and can therefore be tried."

Another case involved former Panamanian dictator General Manuel Noriega. In December 1989, the U.S. government sent troops to Panama, who arrested Noriega and then flew him to Florida to face narcotics trafficking charges. Noriega protested, claiming that U.S. courts had no jurisdiction over him because the Panama invasion, which led to his arrest, violated international law. The U.S. courts ruled, however, that the method of arrest did not deprive the courts of jurisdiction. Noriega was tried in the United States, convicted, and sentenced to forty years in prison.[3]

The concept of **venue** is place oriented. The general rule is that cases must be tried in the place where the crime was committed, where a party resides, or where another consideration justifies a trial in that place. Legislation establishes mandatory venue for some types of cases and preferred venue for others. In criminal cases, the trial is usually held in the place where the crime was committed, but the venue may be changed and the trial held in another place for causes specified by law. This change is made to ensure the accused of a fair and impartial trial in cases that have had such massive pretrial publicity or strong community prejudice as to make it difficult to select an impartial jury. The motion for a change of venue is usually filed by the defendant. The decision of a trial judge to grant or deny the motion is seldom reversed on appeal.

Court Cases

Court cases, particularly those decided by the U.S. Supreme Court, are important because they constitute case law and set precedents for cases decided by lower courts throughout the country. Where can you go to read Court decisions in full? Various law publications either in the library or on the Internet publish the full decisions. To use these sources, you must know the basics of case citations, which provide the road map for where to find court cases. Next, we will look at how to understand case citations and sources on the Internet.

Case Citations

Case citations indicate where a case may be found in the vast firmament of legal publications. For example, if a reader wants to read the U.S. Supreme Court decision in the case of *Mapp v. Ohio*, he or she needs the official case citation, which is 367 U.S. 643 (1961). This means that *Mapp v. Ohio* is found in Volume 367 of the *United States Reports*, starting on page 643, and it was decided in 1961. If a reader wants to read the California Supreme Court decision in the case of *Peterson v. City of Long Beach*, he or she should have the citation, which is 155 Cal Rptr 360 (1979). The reader can then go to volume 155 of the *California Reporter* and start reading the case on page 360. The case was decided in 1979. The citation does not indicate the number of pages the case covers; all it indicates is the page where the case starts.

Court cases may be published by official government sources or by private publishers. The better practice is to use the official government source for citation purposes, although private publications' citations may also be used when the official government source is unavailable or if there is no official government publication. For example, *Mapp v. Ohio* is also found in 81 S.Ct. 1684 (the *Supreme Court Reporter* is not a government publication) and 6 L.Ed.2d 1081 (the *Lawyers' Edition* is not a government publication). However, the better practice is to use 367 U.S. 643 (1961) because it is the official case citation.

Here are examples of case citations, some government and others private, and what they mean:

- U.S. (*United States Reports*)—The official source of U.S. Supreme Court decisions; published by the U.S. government; reports only U.S. Supreme Court cases
- S.Ct. (*Supreme Court Reporter*)—Reports U.S. Supreme Court decisions; published by West Publishing Company, a private publisher

- CrL (*Criminal Law Reporter*)—Reports U.S. Supreme Court decisions; published by the Bureau of National Affairs, Inc., a private publisher
- L.W. (*United States Law Week*)—Reports U.S. Supreme Court decisions; published by the Bureau of National Affairs, Inc.
- F.2d (*Federal Reports, Second Series*)—Reports decisions of the federal courts of appeals (thirteen circuits); published by West
- F.Supp (*Federal Supplement*)—Reports most decisions of federal district courts throughout the United States; publishes only a small percentage of cases decided by federal district courts, most federal district court cases are not published at all; published by West
- P.2d (*Pacific Reporter, Second Series*)—Reports state court decisions in the Pacific states; one of seven regional reporters that publish state court cases; the other six are *Atlantic Reporter* (A), *Northeastern Reporter* (N.E.), *North Western Reporter* (N.W.), *Southeastern Reporter* (S.E.), *Southern Reporter* (S), and *South Western Reporter* (S.W.); all published by West
- Cal Rptr (*California Reporter*)—Publishes California state court appellate-level cases; the various states have similar series

Internet Sources

In addition to printed sources, law cases are now also available on the Internet. Here are some of the free Internet sources:

- For U.S. Supreme Court decisions: Type in the case title (as in *Miranda v. Arizona*) at google.com or yahoo.com. Or, go to *http://www.findlaw.com/casecode/supreme.html*, and then click on Supreme Court Decisions "by year." Click the year the case was decided. You will then see Court decisions alphabetically arranged. Note, however, that these means of Internet access may change.[4]
- For United States Courts of Appeals decisions:

  Decisions of the First Circuit: *www.ca1.uscourts.gov*
  Decisions of the Second Circuit: *www.law.touro.edu/2ndcircuit*
  Decisions of the Third Circuit: *www.ca3.uscourts.gov*
  Decisions of the Fourth Circuit: *www.ca4.uscourts.gov*
  Decisions of the Fifth Circuit: *www.ca5.uscourts.gov*
  Decisions of the Sixth Circuit: *www.ca6.uscourts.gov*
  Decisions of the Seventh Circuit: *www.ca7.uscourts.gov*
  Decisions of the Eighth Circuit: *www.ca8.uscourts.gov*
  Decisions of the Ninth Circuit: *www.ca9.uscourts.gov*
  Decisions of the Tenth Circuit: *www.kscourts.org/ca10*
  Decisions of the Eleventh Circuit: *www.ca11.uscourts.gov/opinions.htm*

Decisions of the D.C. Circuit: *www.cadc.uscourts.gov*
Decisions of the Federal Circuit: *www.fedcir.gov*

- For decisions of federal district courts: Some federal district courts have their own websites. If you do not have a federal district court's website, you can go to *http://www.law.cornell.edu* (Cornell Legal Information Institute; or to *http://www.uscourts.gov/links.html* (Federal Judiciary website).[5]

- If you are a student, your institution may have access to Academic Universe, an excellent source of federal and state cases on all levels. Instructions for accessing Academic Universe vary from one institution to another.

- Other legal sources are available on the Internet for a fee. The most popular are VersusLaw, Westlaw, and Lexis. VersusLaw is recommended for nonlawyers as the best legal site for a fee because it is simple and less expensive to use. It is inexpensive and has no specific minimum period of time. It contains federal and state court opinions on various levels. At some universities, Westlaw Campus is available to students and is a great and convenient source of materials for legal research.

How to Brief a Case

Case briefs help readers understand court cases better and are used extensively as a learning tool in law schools and in the practice of law. Students read a case, break it into segments, and then reassemble it in a more concise and organized form to facilitate learning.

To familiarize readers with the basics of case briefing, a sample case brief is presented here. There is no agreement among scholars on how a case should be briefed for instructional purposes. The elements of a brief ultimately depend on the preferences of the instructor or of the student doing the briefing. The sample brief given here is as simple as it gets. Some briefs are more complex; they include dissenting and concurring opinions (if any), comments, case significance, case excerpts, and other elements an instructor or student might deem necessary.

The basic elements of a simple case brief are

1. Case title
2. Citation
3. Year decided
4. Facts
5. Main issue
6. Court decision
7. Holding

The case of *Minnesota v. Dickerson* could be briefed in the following way. (For comparison, read the original of this case on the Internet.

1. **Case title:** *Minnesota v. Dickerson*
2. **Citation:** 508 U.S. 366
3. **Year decided:** 1993

Note: In your brief, the above elements go in this order: *Minnesota v. Dickerson,* 508 U.S. 366 (1993). This means that the case of *Minnesota v. Dickerson* is found in volume 508 of the *United States Reports,* starting on page 366, and it was decided in 1993.

4. **Facts:** During routine patrol, two police officers spotted Dickerson leaving an apartment building that one of the officers knew was a "crack house." Dickerson began walking toward the police but, upon making eye contact with them, reversed direction and walked into an alley. Because of his evasive actions, the police became suspicious and decided to investigate. They pulled into the alley and ordered Dickerson to stop and submit to a pat-down search. The search revealed no weapons, but one officer found a small lump in Dickerson's pocket, which he examined with his fingers and determined, after the examination, that it felt like a lump of cocaine in cellophane. The officer then reached into Dickerson's pocket and retrieved the lump, which turned out to be a small plastic bag of crack cocaine. Dickerson was arrested and charged with possession of a controlled substance.

Note: The facts section can be too detailed or too sketchy, both of which can be misleading.

In general, be guided by this question: What minimum facts must be included in your brief so that somebody who has not read the whole case (as you have) will nonetheless understand it? That amount of detail required is for you to decide—you must determine what facts are important or unimportant. Keep the important, but weed out the unimportant.

5. **Main issue:** Was the seizure of the crack cocaine valid under stop and frisk? No.

Note: The issue statement must always be in question form, as here. The issue statement should not be so broad as to apply to every case even remotely similar in facts or so narrow as to be applicable only to the peculiar facts of that case. Here are some examples: Are police seizures without probable cause valid? (*too broad*) Are police searches based on reasonable suspicion valid? (*too broad*) Is police seizure of something that feels like a lump in a suspect's pocket valid? (*too narrow*) Was the seizure of the crack cocaine valid under stop and frisk? (*just about right*) Some cases have more than one issue. If these issues cannot be merged, they must be stated as separate issues.

6.   **Court decision:** The U.S. Supreme Court affirmed the decision of the Minnesota Supreme Court that held the seizure to be invalid.

Note: The court decision answers two questions: Did the court affirm, reverse, or modify the decision of the immediate lower court (in this case the Minnesota Supreme Court) where the case came from? and What happened to the case? Sometimes students confuse this with the holding of the case. The difference is that the court decision is a brief statement that tells you what happened to the case on appeal and what the court said is to be done with it. In this briefed case, the case ends because the lower court decision was affirmed. It would have been different had the court ordered that the case be "reversed and remanded." The case would then have gone back to the lower courts.

7.   **Holding** (sometimes also known as the *doctrine* or the *ruling*): A frisk that goes beyond that allowed in *Terry v. Ohio* in stop and frisk cases is not valid. In this case, the search went beyond the pat-down search allowed by *Terry* because the officer "squeezed, slid, and otherwise manipulated the packet's content" before knowing it was cocaine. The evidence obtained is not admissible in court.

Note: State in brief, exact, clear language what the court said. In some cases, the holding may be taken verbatim from the case itself, usually toward the end. The holding is the most important element of the case because it states the rule announced by the court. The holding becomes precedent, which means the same rule is applicable to future similar cases to be decided by the courts.

Sources of Rights

The rules governing criminal proceedings in the United States come from four basic sources: constitutions (federal and state), statutes, case law, and court rules.

Constitutions

Both the federal and state constitutions act as sources of rules that protect the rights of individuals.

The Federal Constitution The U.S. Constitution contains the most important rights available to an accused in a criminal prosecution. These safeguards are enumerated in the **Bill of Rights**, which are the first ten amendments to the U.S. Constitution. The constitutional rights set forth in the Bill of Rights are the minimum rights of individuals facing criminal prosecution.

They can be expanded, and an accused can be given more rights by state constitutions and by federal and state law. The constitutions of the various states also contain provisions designed to protect the rights of individuals in state criminal proceedings. These rights are similar to those enumerated in the Bill of

Rights, but they apply only to a particular state. For example, most state constitutions guarantee the right to counsel and cross-examination and prohibit self-incrimination.

The following list contains the federal constitutional provisions most often used in law enforcement cases, and the rights they guarantee.

- **Amendment I:** "Congress shall make no law respecting an establishment of religion, or prohibiting the free exercise thereof; or abridging the freedom of speech, or of the press; or the right of the people peaceably to assemble, and to petition the Government for a redress of grievances." Freedom of religion, freedom of speech, freedom of the press, freedom of assembly, and freedom to petition the government for redress of grievances are all rights guaranteed under the First Amendment. Police problems that might run afoul of First Amendment rights include dispersal of groups practicing religion in public places (airports, downtown intersections, malls); limitations on the use of public places by speakers to advocate ideas or to protest government policies; limiting access by the press to evidence of crime or to ongoing investigations; enforcing juvenile curfew ordinances; and disallowing public gatherings, parades, or meetings without a valid permit. What the police can and cannot do constitutionally in these instances can be a complex and difficult problem.

- **Amendment II:** "A well-regulated Militia, being necessary to the security of a free State, the right of the people to keep and bear Arms, shall not be infringed." The right to keep and bear arms is guaranteed under the Second Amendment. Police problems under the Second Amendment include enforcement of prohibitions against the carrying of arms by a member of the public and enforcement of laws that limit access to or possession of firearms by probationers or parolees.

- **Amendment IV:** "The right of the people to be secure in their persons, houses, papers, and effects, against unreasonable searches and seizures, shall not be violated, and no Warrants shall issue, but upon probable cause, supported by Oath or affirmation, and particularly describing the place to be searched, and the persons or things to be seized." Protection against unreasonable search and seizure (including arrest) is guaranteed under the Fourth Amendment. The limits imposed by the Fourth Amendment are of crucial significance in police work. This is the most important constitutional right in policing because it involves detentions, stops, arrests, and searches of people, motor vehicles, and places. Several chapters in this book address issues stemming from the constitutional prohibition of unreasonable searches and seizures. Violations of this right can lead to police criminal or civil liability.

- **Amendment V:** "No person shall be held to answer for a capital, or otherwise infamous crime, unless on a presentment or indictment of a Grand Jury, except in cases arising in the land or naval forces, or in the

Militia, where in actual service in time of War or public danger, nor shall any person be subject for the same offense to be twice put in jeopardy of life or limb, nor shall be compelled in any criminal case to be a witness against himself, nor be deprived of life, liberty, or property, without due process of law; nor shall private property be taken for public use, without just compensation." The Fifth Amendment guarantees the right to a grand jury indictment for a capital or other serious crime, protection against double jeopardy, protection against self-incrimination, and prohibits the taking of life, liberty, or property without due process of law. Violation of the privilege not to incriminate oneself is the biggest issue for law enforcement under the Fifth Amendment. Chapter 11 on the *Miranda* case addresses many of those issues.

- **Amendment VI:** "In all criminal prosecutions, the accused shall enjoy the right to a speedy and public trial, by an impartial jury of the State and district wherein the crime shall have been committed, which district shall have been previously ascertained by law, and to be informed of the nature and cause of the accusation; to be confronted with the witnesses against him; to have the compulsory process for obtaining witnesses in his favor, and to have the Assistance of Counsel for his defence." The right to a speedy and public trial, the right to an impartial jury, the right to be informed of the nature and cause of the accusation, the right to confront witnesses, the right to summon witnesses, and the right to the assistance of counsel are all guaranteed under the Sixth Amendment. The constitutional rights guaranteed under the Sixth Amendment are primarily limitations on what the courts can do during trial. Police issues, however, may arise in connection with the right to counsel—as when the police question a suspect without counsel or do not provide counsel during a police lineup.

- **Amendment VIII:** "Excessive bail shall not be required, nor excessive fines imposed, nor cruel and unusual punishments inflicted." Protection against excessive bail and cruel and unusual punishment are guaranteed under the Eighth Amendment. The rights under the Eighth Amendment usually do not involve the police. The prohibition against excessive bail involves the court, and the prohibition against cruel and unusual punishment usually applies during sentencing and when a defendant is in jail or prison. The beating of suspects by the police and the use of brutal methods to obtain confessions are punished under criminal law or sanctioned as violations of the constitutional right to due process and equal protection but not under the prohibition against cruel and unusual punishment.

- **Amendment XIV:** "All persons born or naturalized in the United States and subject to the jurisdiction thereof, are citizens of the United States and of the State wherein they reside. No State shall make or enforce any law which shall abridge the privileges or immunities of citizens of the United States; nor shall any State deprive any person of life, liberty, or property, without due process of law; nor deny to any person within its jurisdiction the equal protection of the laws." The right to due process and to equal protection are guaranteed under the Fourteenth Amendment. This amendment is a frequent source of problems in policing. The right to due process means that people must be treated with fundamental fairness. The right to equal protection requires that people be treated alike unless there is justification for treating them differently. The enforcement of these rights can lead to a number of problems for the police who must deal with the public daily and under myriad conditions. For example, beating up a suspect can be a violation of the right to due process, whereas applying different policing standards to minority and nonminority areas can be a violation of the right to equal protection.

State Constitutions In addition to the federal Constitution, all fifty states have their own constitutions. Many state constitutions have their own bills of rights and guarantees of protection against deprivation of rights by state government. The provisions of these constitutions must be consistent with the provisions of the federal Constitution, or they may be declared unconstitutional if challenged in court. The provisions of state constitutions or state law sometimes give defendants more protection than those allowed under the federal Constitution. The general rule is that, if a state constitution or a state law gives a defendant *less* protection than the U.S. Constitution provides, that limitation is unconstitutional and the U.S. Constitution prevails. But if provisions of the state constitution or state law give a defendant *more* protection than the U.S. Constitution provides, that grant of protection by the state prevails. For example, assume that a state constitution, for some unlikely reason, requires a defendant to testify even when the result is self-incrimination. This provision would be declared unconstitutional, because it contravenes the provisions of the Fifth Amendment.

By contrast, the U.S. Supreme Court has ruled that trustworthy statements obtained in violation of the *Miranda* rule may be used to impeach (challenge) the credibility of a defendant who takes the witness stand (*Harris v. New York,* 401 U.S. 222 [1971]). However, if a state's constitution (as interpreted by state courts) or state law prohibits the use of such statements to impeach the credibility of a witness, they cannot be used in that state.

Harris v. New York (1971)

Statutory Law

Federal and state laws frequently cover the same rights mentioned in the U.S. Constitution but in more detail. For example, an accused's right to counsel during trial is guaranteed by the U.S. Constitution, but it may also be given by federal or state law and is just as binding in court proceedings. Moreover, the right to counsel given by law in a state may exceed that guaranteed in the federal Constitution. The right to a lawyer during probation revocation hearings, for instance, is not constitutionally required, but many state laws give probationers this right. The right to jury trial is not constitutionally required in juvenile cases, but it may be given by state law.

State law often determines the procedure the police must follow and available remedies if these procedures are breached. For example, state law may provide that motor vehicles cannot be stopped by the police unless they have probable cause (U.S. Supreme Court decisions allow the stopping of motor vehicles based on reasonable suspicion, a lower degree of certainty). Or, state law may bar pursuits by the police of motor vehicles except in rural areas and only when the suspect is likely to have committed a serious crime that poses an imminent danger to the public. If this is the state law, the police are bound by that limitation on their authority even though the U.S. Supreme Court considers the prohibited practice constitutional.

Case Law

Case law is the law promulgated in cases decided by the courts. When deciding cases, the courts gradually develop legal principles that become law. This law is called *unwritten* or *judge-made* law, as distinguished from laws passed by legislative bodies. Written laws often represent the codification of case law that has become accepted and is practiced in a particular state.

Case law is sometimes confused with common law. The two are similar in that neither kind of law is a product of legislative enactment but has evolved primarily through judicial decisions. They differ in that **common law** originated from the ancient and unwritten laws of England. Although later applied in the United States, common law is generally derived from ancient usages and customs or from the judgments and decrees of the courts recognizing, affirming, and enforcing those usages and customs. Although common law and case law both result from court decisions, common law usually does not have value as precedent in a state, particularly in criminal cases. By contrast, case law has value as precedent within the territorial jurisdiction of the court that issued the opinion. The differences may be summarized as follows:

Case Law	Common Law
Sources are U.S. Court decisions	Sources are the ancient and unwritten laws of England
Court decisions may be new or old	Ancient cases
Authoritative, but only within the territorial jurisdiction of that court	May or may not be authoritative in a certain jurisdiction, usually depending on provisions of state law
May evolve or changes with a new decision	Is set, does not change

Court Rules

Various rules have developed as a result of the courts' supervisory power over the administration of criminal justice. Federal courts have supervisory power over federal criminal cases, and state courts have similar power over state criminal cases. The rules promulgated by supervisory agencies (such as some states' supreme courts) have the force and effect of law and therefore must be followed. For example, the highest court of some states may promulgate regulations that supplement the provisions of those states' laws on pleading and procedure. They cover details that may not be included in the states' codes of criminal procedure.

The Incorporation Controversy: Does the Bill of Rights Apply to the States?

Over the years, one issue affecting individual rights has been litigated in federal courts. That issue is the **incorporation controversy**, or whether the Bill of Rights in the U.S. Constitution (referring to Amendments I–X) protects against violations of rights by the federal government only or whether it also limits what state and local government officials can do. For example, the Fourth Amendment states, in part, "The right of the people to be secure in their persons, houses, papers, and effects, against unreasonable searches and seizures, shall not be violated." Does this limitation apply only to federal officials (such as FBI agents, who are thereby prohibited from making unreasonable searches or seizures), or does it also apply to the conduct of state and local officials (such as police officers)?

Background

The most important safeguards available to an accused in the United States are found in the Bill of Rights. These ten amendments were ratified as a group and made part of the U.S. Constitution in 1791, two years after the Constitution itself was ratified by the original thirteen states. Initially, the Bill of Rights was viewed as limiting only the acts of federal officers, because the Constitution itself limited only the powers of the federal government, not the states. State and local officers originally were limited only by provisions of their own state constitutions, state laws, or local ordinances.

In 1868, the Fourteenth Amendment was passed. Section 1 of that amendment states, in part, "No State shall make or enforce any law which shall abridge the privileges or immunities of citizens of the United States; nor shall any State deprive any person of life, liberty, or property, without due process of law; nor deny to any person within its jurisdiction the equal protection of the laws." This provision clearly applies to the states ("No State shall make or enforce . . .") and has two main clauses: the due process clause and the equal protection clause. The **Due Process Clause** of the Fourteenth Amendment has been interpreted over the years by the U.S. Supreme Court as "incorporating" most of the provisions of the Bill of Rights, giving rise to the incorporation controversy. Therefore, although the fundamental rights granted by the Bill of Rights were originally meant to cover only violations by federal officers, the wording of the Fourteenth Amendment (specifically, the Due Process Clause) has been interpreted by the Court, in various cases over the years, to prohibit violations of rights by either federal or state officers. In other words, those rights that are incorporated under the Fourteenth Amendment apply to state as well as federal criminal proceedings.

Approaches to Incorporation

The question of what constitutional rights are to be incorporated into the Due Process Clause of the Fourteenth Amendment (and therefore held applicable to the states) and what are not is an issue decided by the U.S. Supreme Court. Over the years, various justices have taken differing approaches to the incorporation controversy. These approaches can be classified into four "positions": selective incorporation, total incorporation, total incorporation plus, and the case-by-case approach. (Read the *Duncan v. Louisiana* Case Brief to see an example of how the U.S. Supreme Court incorporates a right.)

CASE BRIEF: An Example of How the Supreme Court Incorporates a Right

Duncan v. Louisiana, 391 U.S. 145 (1968)

Facts: Duncan was convicted in a Louisiana court of simple battery (a misdemeanor punishable under Louisiana law by a maximum sentence of two years in prison and a $300 fine). Duncan requested a jury trial, but the request was denied because under Louisiana law jury trials were allowed only when hard labor or capital punishment could be imposed. Duncan was convicted and given 60 days in jail and fined $150. He appealed to the U.S. Supreme Court, claiming that the state's refusal to give him a jury trial for a crime punishable by two or more years of imprisonment violated his constitutional right.

Issue: *Was the state's refusal to give the defendant a jury trial for a crime that carried a two-year imprisonment as the maximum sentence a violation of the constitutional right to a jury trial in the Sixth Amendment as incorporated through the Due Process Clause of the Fourteenth? Yes.*

Supreme Court Decision: A crime punishable by two years in prison, although classified under Louisiana law as a misdemeanor, is a serious crime, and therefore the defendant is entitled to a jury trial.

Case Significance: The *Duncan* case made the right to trial by jury applicable to the states in cases in which the maximum penalty is two years' imprisonment, regardless of how state law classifies the offense. Although *Duncan* did not clearly state the minimum, a subsequent case (*Baldwin v. New York,* 399 U.S. 66 [1972]) later held that any offense that carries a potential sentence of more than six months is a serious offense, so a jury trial must be afforded on demand. This requirement applies even if the sentence actually imposed is less than six months.

Excerpts from the Decision: The test for determining whether a right extended by the Fifth and Sixth Amendments with respect to federal criminal proceedings is also protected against state action by the Fourteenth Amendment has been phrased in a variety of ways in the opinions of this Court. The question has been asked whether a right is among those "fundamental principles of liberty and justice which lie at the base of all our civil and political institutions," whether it is "basic in our system of jurisprudence," and whether it is "a fundamental right, essential to a fair trial." The claim before us is that the right to trial by jury guaranteed by the Sixth Amendment meets these tests. The position of Louisiana, on the other hand, is that the Constitution imposes upon the States no duty to give a jury trial in any criminal case, regardless of the seriousness of the crime or the size of the punishment which may be imposed. Because we believe that trial by jury in criminal cases is fundamental to the American scheme of justice, we hold that the Fourteenth Amendment guarantees a right of jury trial in all criminal cases which—were they tried in federal court—would come within the Sixth Amendment's guarantee. Since we consider the appeal before us to be such a case, we hold that the Constitution was violated when appellant's demand for jury trial was refused.

Since the mid-1920s, most U.S. Supreme Court justices have taken the **selective incorporation** approach. This selectiveness in the choice of rights to be incorporated has led to another name for this approach, the "honor roll" position. This approach asserts that only those rights considered "fundamental" should be incorporated under the Due Process Clause of the Fourteenth Amendment to apply to state criminal proceedings. Other criteria used by the Court in deciding whether to incorporate a right are (1) whether a right is among those "fundamental principles of liberty and justice which lie at the base of our civil and political institutions," (2) whether it is "basic in our system of jurisprudence," and (3) whether it is a "fundamental right essential to a fair trial." Regardless of the phrase used, selective incorporationists claim that the Due Process Clause of the Fourteenth Amendment requires only fundamental fairness in state proceedings, not the automatic "lock, stock, and barrel" application of all provisions of the Bill of Rights. Selective incorporation has been the predominant approach since the Court began hearing incorporation cases.

Justices who have taken the second approach—**total incorporation**—argue that the Fourteenth Amendment's Due Process Clause should be interpreted as incorporating all the rights given in the first ten amendments to the U.S. Constitution. This position was enunciated by Justice Hugo Black, who wrote in a concurring opinion in 1968, "I believe as strongly as ever that the Fourteenth Amendment was intended to make the Bill of Rights applicable to the states" (*Duncan v. Louisiana,* 391 U.S. 145 [1968]). His is a blanket and uncomplicated approach: It proposes to incorporate, "lock, stock, and barrel," all the provisions in the Bill of Rights.

Duncan v. Louisiana (1968)

The third approach—**total incorporation plus**—is an extension of total incorporation. It proposes that, in addition to extending all the provisions of the Bill of Rights to the states, other rights ought to be added, such as the right to clean air, clean water, and a clean environment. Justice William O. Douglas, an activist jurist, was the main advocate of this approach, but over the years it has failed to gain converts in the Court.

The fourth approach—**case-by-case incorporation**—advocates an examination of the facts of a specific case to determine whether there is an injustice so serious as to justify extending the provisions of the Bill of Rights to that particular case. It is otherwise known as the "fair trial" approach, because the standard used is whether the accused obtained a fair trial. It differs from the selective incorporation approach in that selective incorporation focuses on whether a specific right (such as the right to counsel) should apply to the states. By contrast, the case-by-case approach more narrowly focuses on the facts of a specific case to decide whether *that particular case,* given its peculiar facts, should come under the Due Process Clause.

The problem with the case-by-case approach is that the application of the Bill of Rights becomes unpredictable and totally dependent on the facts, so a particular case has little or no value as precedent.

Rights Held to Be Fundamental and Incorporated

The Court has defined *fundamental rights* as those "of the very essence of a scheme of ordered liberty" and "principles of justice so rooted in the traditions and conscience of our people as to be ranked as fundamental" (*Palko v. Connecticut,* 302 U.S. 319 [1937]). These rather vague, though lofty, phrases really mean that the Court will determine on a case-by-case basis whether a particular right should be incorporated.

Palko v. Connecticut (1937)

In specific cases, the Court (using the selective incorporation approach) has held that the following provisions of the Bill of Rights apply in both federal and state proceedings:

- First Amendment provisions for freedom of religion, speech, assembly, and petition for redress of grievances (*Fiske v. Kansas,* 274 U.S. 380 [1927])
- Fourth Amendment protections against unreasonable arrest, search, and seizure (*Wolf v. Colorado,* 338 U.S. 25 [1949]; *Mapp v. Ohio,* 367 U.S. 643 [1961])
- Fifth Amendment protection against self-incrimination (*Malloy v. Hogan,* 378 U.S. 1 [1964])
- Fifth Amendment prohibition against double jeopardy (*Benton v. Maryland,* 395 U.S. 784 [1969])
- Sixth Amendment right to counsel (*Gideon v. Wainwright,* 372 U.S. 335 [1963])

- Sixth Amendment right to a speedy trial (*Klopfer v. North Carolina,* 386 U.S. 21 [1967])
- Sixth Amendment right to a public trial (*In re Oliver,* 333 U.S. 257 [1948])
- Sixth Amendment right to confrontation of opposing witnesses (*Pointer v. Texas,* 380 U.S. 400 [1965])
- Sixth Amendment right to an impartial jury (*Duncan v. Louisiana,* 391 U.S. 145 [1968])
- Sixth Amendment right to a compulsory process for obtaining witnesses (*Washington v. Texas,* 388 U.S. 14 [1967])
- Eighth Amendment prohibition against cruel and unusual punishment (*Robinson v. California,* 370 U.S. 660 [1962])

In incorporating a right, the Supreme Court expressly states that a fundamental right in the Bill of Rights is made applicable to the states through the Due Process Clause of the Fourteenth Amendment. For example, in *Duncan v. Louisiana,* 391 U.S. 145 (1968), the Supreme Court ruled that the right to trial by jury, guaranteed to defendants in federal trials under the Sixth Amendment, must also be given to defendants in state courts because of the Due Process Clause of the Fourteenth Amendment. Hence, that right is deemed guaranteed.

Rights Not Incorporated

Although the following rights are required in federal proceedings, the states do not have to grant an accused these rights unless they are required by the state constitution or state law: [6]

- The Second Amendment right to keep and bear arms
- The Third Amendment prohibition against quartering soldiers
- The Fifth Amendment right to indictment by grand jury
- The Seventh Amendment right to trial in civil cases
- The prohibition against excessive bail and fine

Nationalization of the Bill of Rights

Through a process of selective incorporation using the Fourteenth Amendment's Due Process Clause, people facing federal or state criminal charges now enjoy the same rights, except the rights to grand jury indictment and to protection against excessive bail and fines. In effect, the Bill of Rights is now applicable throughout the United States; it has become "nationalized." It makes no difference whether an accused is tried in New York, Illinois, California, or any other state or by the federal government—the accused's basic rights are now the same because of incorporation. As a result, in no other field of law are the rights of individuals in the United States as similar as they are in the processing of an accused.

The Judicial Review Doctrine

Marbury v. Madison
(1803)

Courts in the United States exercise **judicial review**, defined as "the power of any court to hold unconstitutional and hence unenforceable any law, any official action based on a law, or any other action by a public official that it deems to be in conflict with the Constitution."[7] The doctrine of judicial review is not explicitly found in the Constitution but was set by the Court in the case of *Marbury v. Madison* (5 U.S. 137 [1803]), considered by most scholars to be the most important case ever decided by the Court. The facts of the case and the politics involved are complex, but they centered around the issue of whether the Congress of the United States could add to the original jurisdiction given to the Court by the Constitution. In a unanimous opinion penned by Chief Justice John Marshall, the Court held that "an act repugnant to the Constitution is void," adding, "It is emphatically the province and duty of the judicial department to say what the law is. Those who apply the rule to particular cases, must of necessity expound and interpret that rule. . . . A law repugnant to the Constitution is void; . . . courts as well as other departments are bound by that instrument."[8]

The judicial review doctrine applies to laws passed by Congress, state legislatures, ordinances passed by municipalities, and acts of public officials. For example, in 1998 the city of Indianapolis, Indiana, established checkpoints on Indianapolis roads in an effort to interdict unlawful drugs. Vehicles passing through those checkpoints were stopped even though there was no individualized suspicion of wrongdoing.

The city conducted six roadblocks over a period of four months, stopping 1,161 vehicles and arresting 104 motorists. Out of those arrests, fifty-five were for drug-related crimes, while forty-nine were for offenses unrelated to drugs. This practice was challenged in court as unreasonable and intrusive upon individual rights. On appeal, the Court held that this automatic stopping of motor vehicles in the absence of individualized suspicion of wrongdoing violated the Fourth Amendment prohibition against unreasonable searches and seizures (*Indianapolis et al. v. Edmond et al.*, 531 U.S. 32 [2002]).

Indianapolis et al. v.
Edmond et al. (2002)

The doctrine of judicial review has significant implications in law enforcement. It means that laws passed by legislative bodies can and will be reviewed by the courts in a proper case and will be declared unenforceable if found to be against the Constitution. For individual law enforcement officers, it means that whatever they do can be challenged in court and, if held to have violated individual constitutional rights, can result in the imposition by the court of civil or criminal sanctions.

The Rule of Law

The concept of the "rule of law" goes back to the days of ancient Greece and has different meanings to different people.[9] Since the tragic events of September 11, 2001, the concept of the rule of law has generated more interest and has been the subject of debate about its proper meaning. In the words of philosopher–writer George Fletcher,

> Of all the dreams that drive men and women into the streets, from Buenos Aires to Budapest, the "rule of law" is the most puzzling. We have a pretty good idea what we mean by "free market" and "democratic elections." But legality and the "rule of law" are ideals that present themselves as opaque even to legal philosophers.[10]

A recent writer maintains that, at one end, the concept is associated with adherence to laws that have been passed by legislatures, regardless of how just or unjust they may be. On the other end, it is associated with the concept of justice and derives its validity from the "morality of the laws that rule." Under this concept, mere passage of laws by the legislature is not enough. The law passed must be just.[11] Some people equate the rule of law with the "supremacy of the law," whereas others associate it with "obedience to the law." A legalistic view, meaning adherence to court decisions, is reflected in former Vice President Al Gore's reaction when he lost the *Bush v. Gore* presidency case. He said, "I strongly disagree with the Supreme Court decision and the way in which they interpreted and applied the law. But I respect the rule of law, so it is what it is."[12]

Perhaps the best-known meaning of the **rule of law**, however, is that which holds that no person is above the law, that every person, from the most powerful public official down to the least powerful individual, is subject to the law and can be held accountable in the courts of law for what they do. In the words of David Hume, the phrase means "a government of laws and not of men."[13] That phrase also highlights one of the main distinctions between a democratic and a totalitarian society. In a democratic society, even the most powerful public official or private person can be held fully accountable under the law for what he or she does; in a totalitarian society, the ruler enjoys boundless power and can do whatever he or she pleases without accountability in any court of law.

Rule of law, with its opaque (meaning "hard to understand or to explain") nature, is important in today's climate of law enforcement on two levels. On one level, the terror brought about by the events of 9/11 has led and will further lead to the passage of laws that curtail the rights and liberties of citizens and noncitizens. Should the Constitution be interpreted to accommodate the immediate needs of a changing time, and should laws passed by legislatures that seek to protect the public from external threats be afforded greater constitutional protection by the courts? On another level, police accountability in the United States is closely tied to the concept of the rule of law. In many countries, the police are immensely powerful, and accountability for their actions barely exists. In the United States, criminal and civil liabilities (discussed in Chapter 13) are an ever-present reality in policing and represent the highest point of police accountability. Law enforcement officers, from the police chief to the newly hired police recruit, can be and are held criminally and civilly liable for what they do. The public considers this accountability a classic example of the fact that no person in this country, not even one wearing a badge of authority, is above the law. This is the most notable difference

Table 1.2 Criminal and Civil Cases Compared

	Criminal	Civil
Who files	Government	Usually a private person or entities
Purpose	To seek punishment for the crime committed	To seek monetary damage and/or an injunction for violation of a duty or obligation
What must be proved	That a crime has been committed and That the defendant committed the crime	Existence of a legal contractual duty or obligation and A breach of that duty or obligation resulting in harm
Proof required to win	Guilt beyond a reasonable doubt (about 95% certainty of guilt)	Preponderance of evidence (more than 50% certainty)
Bill of Rights	Limits conduct of government officials	Does not apply to conduct of private persons
Lawyers	Prosecutor for the government; private lawyers, government-supplied lawyers, or public defender for defendant	Own lawyer(s) for each side
If trial by jury	Usually a unanimous jury vote for conviction or acquittal	Usually a nonunanimous jury vote
Defendant's presence in court	Required, with exceptions	Not required
Testimony	Accused cannot be forced to testify in court	Defendant can be forced to testify in court
Appeal	Defendant can appeal a conviction; government cannot appeal an acquittal except on questions of law, if allowed	Either side can appeal

between "policing a free society" and law enforcement in a totalitarian country. The rule of law is a concept law enforcement officers in the United States must fully understand and adhere to if they are to perform their tasks properly and constitutionally.

The cases discussed in this chapter are mostly criminal cases. There are differences between criminal and civil cases which must be understood. These differences are summarized in Table 1.2.

Summary

- The United States has a dual court system, meaning it has two levels of courts—federal and state.

- If an act violates federal law, it is tried in federal court; if it violates state law, it is tried in state court. If an act violates both federal and state laws, it can be tried in both courts.

- *Judicial review* is "the power of any court to hold unconstitutional and hence unenforceable any law, any official action based on a law, or any other action by a public official that it deems to be in conflict with the Constitution." *Judicial precedent* means that decisions of courts have value as precedent for future cases similarly circumstanced.

- *Jurisdiction* is the power of a court to try a case; *venue* is the place where the case is tried.

- The incorporation controversy is about whether the Bill of Rights protects against violations of rights by the federal government only or also limits actions of state and local government officials. The four approaches to incorporation are selective incorporation, total incorporation, total incorporation plus, and the case-by-case approach.

- *Rule of law* is difficult to define, but it generally means that no person is above the law, that every person, from the most powerful public official down to the least powerful individual, is subject to the law and can be held accountable in the courts of law for what he or she does.

Review Questions and Hypothetical Cases

1. "The United States has a dual court system." Explain what that means.

2. "The general rule is that a case is accepted by the U.S. Supreme Court for decision only if that case has nationwide significance." Is that statement true or false? Defend your answer.

3. "A court decision is effective only within a limited jurisdiction." What does that mean? Give an example.

4. "Every criminal act can be prosecuted in both federal and state courts." Is this statement true or false? Explain your answer.

5. Distinguish between judicial review and judicial precedent.

6. How does jurisdiction differ from venue?

7. What does this case citation mean: *Duncan v. Louisiana,* 391 U.S. 145 (1968).

8. How can you find the U.S. Supreme Court decision in *Miranda v. Arizona,* 384 U.S. 436 (1966), on the Internet?

9. What is the incorporation controversy? How did it originate?

10. Distinguish between selective incorporation and case-by-case incorporation.

11. What is the rule of law? Why is it important in policing?

12. Assume you are a lawyer arguing a case in the Fifth Circuit Court of Appeals in New Orleans on the issue of whether or not prisoners can be required to cut their hair short and to have a haircut every month. Your client, an inmate in prison in Louisiana, wants the right to have his hair long. The Fifth Circuit has not decided a case on the same issue, but your legal research shows that the Ninth Circuit Court of Appeals (for California and other states in that circuit) has already decided that issue, saying that prison inmates have a right to have long hair. Will the decision of the Ninth Circuit be of any use to you when arguing your case before the Fifth Circuit? Justify your answer.

13. Despite airport precautions, X hijacked an airplane in Chicago and forced the pilot, crew, and passengers to fly to New York. Upon reaching New York, X shot the pilot before giving up and surrendering to the New York police. X was later prosecuted for various crimes stemming from the hijacking. Cases were filed against X in Chicago, the New York state court, and the New York federal court. X claims that he could be tried only in a state court in Illinois. Will X's claim succeed? State the reasons for your answer.

14. Y, an undocumented alien, was caught speeding in Phoenix. When Y was stopped by the police, they found 5 pounds of cocaine in his car, located in the passenger side of the car and open to view by the police. Y was arrested, brought to a local magistrate, and bail was set for half a million dollars. Y appealed. You are the appellate court judge. Will you uphold Y's contention that his bail is excessive? Give reasons for your answer.

Key Terms

Go to the Criminal Procedure 7e website for flash cards that will help you master the definitions of these terms.

Bill of Rights, 17
case-by-case incorporation, 25
case citation, 13
case law, 21
common law, 21
dual court system, 3
dual sovereignty, 11

Due Process Clause, 22
en banc decision, 4
incorporation controversy, 22
judicial precedent, 10
judicial review, 27
jurisdiction, 12
original jurisdiction, 4

rule of four, 4
rule of law, 28
selective incorporation, 24
stare decisis, 10
total incorporation, 24
total incorporation plus, 25
venue, 12

Holdings of Key Cases

See Appendix C for information on how to find cases in this chapter on FindLaw.com.

(*Note:* U.S. Supreme Court cases are easily accessible through the Internet. Go to google.com or yahoo.com, and then type in the case title [as in *Miranda v. Arizona*]. Or, go to *http://www .findlaw.com/casecode/supreme.html*, and then click on Supreme Court Decisions "by year." Click the year the case was decided. You will then see court decisions alphabetically arranged. Note, however, that these means of Internet access may change.)

***Duncan v. Louisiana,* 391 U.S. 145 (1968)**
A crime punishable by two years in prison, although classified under Louisiana law as a misdemeanor, is a serious crime. Therefore, the defendant is entitled to a jury trial.

***Frisbie v. Collins,* 342 U.S. 519 (1952)** An invalid arrest is not a defense against being convicted of the offense charged.

***Harris v. New York,* 401 U.S. 222 (1971)**
Trustworthy statements obtained in violation

of the *Miranda* rule may be used to impeach the credibility of a defendant who takes the witness stand.

***Indianapolis et al. v. Edmond et al.,* 531 U.S. 32 (2002)** Automatic stopping of motor vehicles, absent individualized suspicion of wrongdoing, violates the Fourth Amendment prohibition against unreasonable searches and seizures.

***Marbury v. Madison,* 5 U.S. 137 (1803)** A law that is repugnant to the Constitution is void. This case established the judicial review doctrine.

***Palko v. Connecticut,* 302 U.S. 319 (1937)**
The Due Process Clause of the Fourteenth Amendment applies to the states and therefore incorporates those provisions of the Bill of Rights that are "of the very essence of a scheme of ordered liberty" (*http://laws.findlaw.com/us/ 302/319.html*).

Recommended Readings

Larry Gist. *Texas roulette justice: An analysis of sentencing discretion.* South Texas Law Review 695–706 (2001).

Susan N. Herman and Lawrence M. Solan. *Jury in the twenty-first century: An interdisciplinary symposium.* 66 Brooklyn Law Review 1–19 (2001).

Joseph L. Hoffman. *Plea bargaining in the shadow of death.* Fordham Law Review 2313–2391 (2001).

Peter Margulies. *Battered bargaining: Domestic violence and plea negotiations in the criminal justice system.* South California Review of Law and Women's Studies 153–185 (2001).

Ric Simmons. *Re-examining the grand jury: Is there room for democracy in the criminal justice system?* Cleveland State Law Review 829–862 (2000).

Notes

1. Henry J. Abraham, *The Judicial Process,* 7th ed. (New York: Oxford University Press, 1998), p. 198.
2. Henry C. Black, *Black's Law Dictionary,* 5th ed. (St. Paul, MN: West, 1979), p. 1443.
3. *Time Magazine,* December 14, 1998, p. 44.
4. See *World's Leading Law Internet Sites* (Rockville, MD: Surfless Publications), p. 12.
5. Stephen Elias and Susan Levinkind, *Legal Research: How to Find & Understand the Law,* 9th ed. (Berkeley, CA: Nolo Press, 2001), p. 9/20.
6. J. W. Peltason, Edwin Corwin, and Sue Davis, *Understanding the Constitution,* 15th ed. (Fort Worth, TX: Harcourt College Publishers, 2000), p. 214.
7. Abraham, p. 300.
8. Ibid., pp. 342–343.
9. Ronald A. Cass, *The Rule of Law in America* (Baltimore, MD: The Johns Hopkins University Press, 2001), p. 1.
10. As quoted in Cass, p. 1.
11. Cass, p. 2.
12. *Houston Chronicle,* November 16, 2002, p. 24A.
13. As quoted in Cass, p. 2.

Chapter 2

Overview of the Criminal Justice Process

What You Will Learn

- The procedures used when processing suspects and defendants can be divided into three stages: before trial, during trial, and after trial.

- Before trial, the procedure follows this sequence: filing of the complaint, arrest, booking, appearance before a magistrate, setting of bail, preliminary examination, decision by the prosecutor to charge, grand jury indictment or the filing of an information by the prosecutor, arraignment, and plea by the defendant.

- The procedure during trial starts with the selection of jurors, followed by opening statements, the presentation of the cases for the prosecution and the defense, rebuttal evidence, closing arguments, defense motions prior to the verdict, the judge's instructions to the jury, jury deliberation, and a verdict of guilty or not guilty.

- The two main procedures after trial are sentencing and appeal.

- Even while a defendant is serving time in jail or in prison, access to the court is always available by way of a habeas corpus petition.

- Although criminal procedure is governed by the Bill of Rights, procedures differ from one jurisdiction to another.

Introduction

The Procedure before Trial

    The Filing of a Complaint
    The Arrest
    Booking at the Police Station
    Initial Appearance before a Magistrate after the Arrest
    The Setting of Bail
    The Preliminary Hearing
    The Decision by the Prosecutor to Charge
    Grand Jury Indictment versus Information
    The Arraignment
    The Plea by the Defendant
    Plea Bargains

The Procedure during Trial

    The Selection of Jurors
    Opening Statements by the Prosecution
    Opening Statements by the Defense
    Presentation of the Case for the Prosecution
    Presentation of the Case for the Defense
    Rebuttal Evidence
    Closing Arguments
    Defense Motions Prior to the Verdict
    The Judge's Instructions to the Jury
    Jury Deliberation
    The Verdict—Guilty or Not Guilty

The Procedure after Trial

    Sentencing
    Appeal
    Habeas Corpus

Beware: The Procedure in Your Jurisdiction May Differ

    Application to Felony Cases
    Variation among States
    Variation within a State
    Theory versus Reality

CASE BRIEF
_____

Santobello v. New York (1971)

Introduction

Criminal procedure is the process followed by the police and the courts in the apprehension and punishment of criminals—from the filing of a complaint by a member of the public or the arrest of a suspect by the police, up to the time the defendant is sent to jail or, if convicted, to prison. It highlights the sometimes difficult conflict between the constitutional rights of a suspect or defendant and the power of government to maintain peace and order and ensure public safety.

That conflict must be resolved through prescribed rules; criminal procedures are those rules. Although sometimes offered as one course in law schools, criminal procedure and criminal law differ in that criminal procedure prescribes the process whereby a suspect or defendant is eventually found guilty or innocent, whereas criminal law defines what acts are punishable by the federal government or the states. One is process; the other is substance.

Criminal laws differ in detail and terminology from one state to another, but criminal procedure is basically similar from one jurisdiction to another. This is because criminal procedure is mostly a product of U.S. Supreme Court decisions. The main source of rights in criminal procedure is the Bill of Rights (the first ten amendments to the Constitution). Through a process of incorporation, the rights enumerated in the Bill of Rights have been made applicable to criminal proceedings anywhere in the country; hence, basic criminal procedure has been made uniform nationwide in its application. In sum, it has been "nationalized."

In addition to the Bill of Rights, there are other sources of rights for the defendant. The state constitutions, federal and state laws, case law, and court rules are all other sources. These other sources may result in variations from one jurisdiction to another, but they can give more rights to a suspect only by limiting the actions of the police or the courts. These sources cannot deprive a suspect of any right given by the Bill of Rights; they can only add to them. For example, the U.S. Supreme Court has held that it is constitutional for police to stop motor vehicles based on reasonable suspicion. State law, however, may prohibit such stops unless there is probable cause, thus expanding the rights of suspects. Another example: the Constitution does not require confessions by suspects to be in writing to be admissible in evidence. State law, however, may exclude oral confessions unless they are in writing or supported by other evidence. If there is a conflict between other sources of rights and the Bill of Rights, the latter prevails because what the Bill of Rights guarantees are minimum rights that cannot be diminished by state law, police agency policy, or by other rules or regulations.

This chapter presents an overview of the criminal justice process from a legal perspective. The procedure is divided into three time frames: before trial, during trial, and after trial (see Figure 2.1). In the great majority of cases, an arrest triggers criminal justice procedures against the accused. In some cases, however, the procedure is initiated through the filing of a complaint that leads to the issuance of a warrant by a judge or magistrate. Procedure during trial starts with the selection of jurors and ends with a court or jury verdict. If the accused is found guilty, the sentencing phase follows, after which the defendant may appeal the conviction and sentence. The chapter concludes with some words of caution concerning the difference between theory and practice in criminal justice procedures.

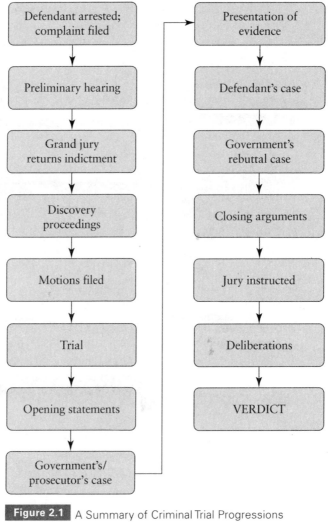

Figure 2.1 A Summary of Criminal Trial Progressions

Source: http://www.uscourts.gov

The Procedure before Trial

The procedure before trial begins with the filing of a complaint, followed by the arrest, booking, first appearance, setting of bail, preliminary examination, decision to charge, grand jury indictment or information, arraignment, plea, and plea bargaining. This section looks at what happens at each stage.

The Filing of a Complaint

A **complaint** is a charge made before a proper law enforcement or judicial officer alleging the commission of a criminal offense. It may be filed by the offended party or by a police officer who has obtained information about or witnessed the criminal act. The

```
STATE OF MISSOURI    )
                     ) ss.
COUNTY OF CLINTON    )

        IN THE ASSOCIATE CIRCUIT COURT OF CLINTON COUNTY, MISSOURI

STATE OF MISSOURI,                          )
                      Plaintiff             )
                                            )
      -vs-                                  )       Case No.
                                            )
                                            )
                      Defendant             )

                        C O M P L A I N T

_____, being duly sworn, deposes and states that in

the County of Clinton, State of Missouri, heretofore, to-wit:  on or about

_____, one _____, in violation

of Section 570.120, RSMo, committed the Class A misdemeanor of passing bad checks

punishable upon conviction under Sections 558.011.1(5) and 560.016, RSMo, in that the

defendant, with purpose to defraud, issued a check in the amount of $_____,

drawn upon the _____, dated _____,

payable to _____, knowing that such check would not

be paid.

     Affiant further states that he has actual personal knowledge of the facts, matters and
things above set out and is a competent witness thereto.

                                   _____
                                   Plaintiff

Subscribed and sworn to before me this _____ day of _____, 20 ____.

                                   _____
                                   Clerk of the Associate Circuit Court
```

Figure 2.2 Complaint Form

Source: Complaint form for Clinton County, State of Missouri

complaint serves as a basis for issuing an arrest warrant. If the accused has been arrested without a warrant, the complaint is prepared and filed at the defendant's initial appearance before the magistrate, usually by the arresting officer (see Figure 2.2).

The Arrest

An **arrest** is the taking of a person into custody for the purpose of criminal prosecution or interrogation. There are two kinds of arrest: arrest with a warrant and arrest without a warrant. In *arrest with a warrant,* a complaint has been filed and presented to a judge, who has read it (see Figure 2.3) and found probable cause (as defined in

STATE OF
RHODE ISLAND
AND
PROVIDENCE
PLANTATIONS

AFFIDAVIT AND ARREST WARRANT

AFFIDAVIT

AFFIANT	AGENT OF			
DEFENDANT	ADDRESS NO.	STREET	CITY/TOWN	STATE

AFFIDAVIT

Your affiant upon oath states that he has reason to believe and does believe that grounds for issuance of an arrest
warrant exists and states the following facts on which such belief is founded:

IF SPACE IS NOT SUFFICIENT,
CHECK (X) HERE AND
☐ ATTACH ADDITIONAL
INFORMATION

AFFIANT

X

SUBSCRIBED AND SWORN TO BEFORE ME AT (CITY/TOWN)	DATE	JUDGE OR DISTRICT COURT, JUSTICE OF SUPERIOR COURT OR ANY OTHER AUTHORIZED OFFICER
		X

ARREST WARRANT

STATE. EX REL	CITY/TOWN	COUNTY	DATE OF BIRTH	DIVISION RHODE ISLAND DISTRICT COURT	WARRANT DATE
VS. DEFENDANT		ADDRESS NO.	STREET	CITY/TOWN	STATE

TO ANY AUTHORIZED OFFICER: Affidavit (and complaint) having been made to me under oath, and as I am satisfied that there
is probable cause for the belief therein set forth that grounds for issuing an arrest warrant exists, you are hereby commanded to
arrest the defendant forthwith and to bring him before a judge of this court without unnecessary delay.

BAIL	SURETY	DATE SIGNED	JUDGE OR DISTRICT COURT, JUSTICE SUPERIOR COURT OR ANY AUTHORIZED OFFICER
$	☐ with ☐ without		X

RETURN OF SERVICE

I have apprehended the within named defendant and have presented him/her before the court as herein commanded.

SERVICE	MILEAGE	DATE OF RETURN	AUTHORIZED OFFICER
$	$		X

POLICE COPY

Figure 2.3 Affidavit and Arrest Warrant Form

Source: Affidavit and Arrest Warrant form, Providence Plantation, State of Rhode Island

Chapter 3) to justify the issuance of an arrest warrant. In contrast, *arrest without a
warrant* usually happens when a crime is committed in the presence of a police officer or, in some jurisdictions, by virtue of a citizen's arrest for certain offenses. As many
as 95 percent of all arrests are made without a warrant. This rate is significant and
requires that the officer must be convinced of the presence of probable cause before
making the arrest. This belief is later established in a sworn complaint or testimony.

Statutes in many states authorize the use of a citation or summons rather
than an arrest for less serious offenses. A **citation** is an order issued by a court or
law enforcement officer requiring the person to whom the citation is issued to
appear in court at a specified date to answer certain charges. A **summons** is a
writ directed to the sheriff or other proper officer requiring that officer to notify

the person named that he or she must appear in court on a day named and answer the complaint stated in the summons. Citations and summonses have the advantage of keeping a person out of jail pending the hearing. They also save the police officer the time and paperwork that go with arrest and booking. In either case, if the person fails or refuses to appear in court as scheduled, a bench warrant may be issued. A **bench warrant** is defined as a "process issued by the court itself, or 'from the bench,' for the attachment or arrest of a person; either in case of contempt, or where an indictment has been found, to bring in a witness who fails to obey a subpoena."[1]

The *Miranda* warnings (discussed in Chapter 11) need not be given every time an officer makes an arrest. The warnings do not have to be given by the officer after an arrest unless the arrested person is asked questions by the officer that tend to incriminate. In many cases, however, the officer simply makes the arrest and does not ask questions, particularly when the arrest is made with a warrant. The officer in these cases does not have to ask questions; all he or she does is take the suspect to a lockup or jail for detention. In many jurisdictions, the *Miranda* warnings are given when the suspect appears before a judge or magistrate.

Booking at the Police Station

Booking consists of making an entry in the police blotter or arrest book indicating the suspect's name, the time of arrest, and the offense involved. Prior to this, the arrestee is searched for weapons or any evidence that might be related to a crime, and his or her belongings are inventoried. If the offense is serious, the suspect may also be photographed and fingerprinted. Before or after booking, the suspect is usually placed in a "lockup," which is a place of detention run by the police department (usually in major cities), or in jail in smaller cities or communities where no lockups are necessary. In most jurisdictions, the arrestee is allowed a telephone call, usually to a lawyer or a family member. In some jurisdictions, the arrestee is allowed to post a predetermined amount of bail for minor offenses on a promise that he or she will appear in court at a particular time. If bail is not posted or is denied, the person is kept under detention until such time as he or she can be brought before a magistrate.

Initial Appearance before a Magistrate after the Arrest

In some states, this step is known as *presentment,* or *arraignment on the warrant.* Most states require that an arrested person be brought before a judge, magistrate, or commissioner "without unnecessary delay." What that means varies from state to state, depending on state law or court decisions. In federal and most state proceedings, a delay of more than six hours in bringing the suspect before the magistrate is one factor to be considered in determining whether any incriminating statements made by the accused were in fact voluntary. Other jurisdictions do not specify the number of hours but look at the surrounding circumstances and decide on a case-by-case basis whether the delay was unnecessary.

Once before a magistrate, the arrestee is informed of his or her rights. This procedure may include giving the *Miranda* **warnings**, which have five components:

1. You have a right to remain silent.
2. Anything you say can be used against you in a court of law.
3. You have a right to the presence of an attorney.
4. If you cannot afford an attorney, one will be appointed for you prior to questioning.
5. You have the right to terminate this interview at any time.

The suspect is also informed of such other rights as may be given by statute. These vary from state to state and may include the right to a preliminary hearing, confrontation, and a speedy trial; the right not to incriminate oneself; and the exclusion in court of illegally obtained evidence.

Many jurisdictions require magistrates to give the *Miranda* warnings when the suspect is brought in, but the warnings must also be given by the arresting officer if he or she questions the suspect prior to the appearance before a magistrate. Failure to issue the warnings makes the suspect's statements inadmissible in court. Conversely, if the officer does not need to ask the suspect any questions (as would usually be the case in arrests with a warrant), the *Miranda* warnings need not be given. The officer arrests the person named in the warrant and brings him or her before a magistrate or judge.

If the charge is a misdemeanor, the arrestee may be arraigned while before the magistrate and required to plead to the pending charge. Many misdemeanor cases are disposed of at this stage through a guilty plea or some other procedure. If the charge is a felony, the arrestee ordinarily is not required to plead to the charge at this time. Rather, he or she is held for preliminary examination on the felony charge.

The Setting of Bail

Bail is defined as the security required by the court and given by the accused to ensure that the accused appears before the proper court at a scheduled time and place to answer the charges brought against him or her. In theory, the only function of bail is to ensure the appearance of the defendant at the time set for trial. In practice, bail has also been used as a form of **preventive detention** to prevent the release of an accused who might otherwise be dangerous to society or whom the judge might not want to release. The Court has upheld as constitutional a provision of the Federal Bail Reform Act of 1984 that permits federal judges to deny pretrial release to persons charged with certain serious felonies, based on a finding that no combination of release conditions can reasonably ensure the community of safety from such individuals (*United States v. Salerno,* 481 U.S. 739 [1987]).

United States v. Salerno (1987)

See Appendix C for information on how to find cases in this chapter on FindLaw.com.

By statute in a number of states, the magistrate or judge before whom the proceedings are pending may free the accused through **release on recognizance (ROR)**, meaning, without monetary bail. This usually happens when the accused has strong ties in the community and seems likely to appear for trial. If he or she fails to do so, an arrest warrant may be issued.

The Preliminary Hearing

An accused charged with a felony is usually entitled to a **preliminary hearing** (called a *preliminary examination* or *examining trial* in some states), to be held before a magistrate within a reasonably short time after arrest. Preliminary hearings closely resemble trials, but their purpose is more limited, and the hearing magistrate is generally not the judge who will preside over the actual trial in the case. Representation by counsel and cross-examination of witnesses are allowed. The preliminary hearing is usually the first chance for the defense to know what evidence the prosecution has and the strength of the case against the accused. Because guilt beyond reasonable doubt is not required during the preliminary hearing, the prosecution does not have to present all the evidence it has. On the other hand, the defense does not have to present anything if it so chooses, because, regardless of what it does, the judge can set the case for trial anyway if probable cause is established.

Preliminary hearings are usually held for three main purposes:

1. *Determination of probable cause.* The primary purpose of the preliminary hearing is to ascertain whether there is probable cause to support the charges against the accused. If not, the charges are dismissed. This process keeps unsupported charges of grave offenses from coming to trial and thereby protects people from harassment, needless expenditure, and damage to their reputations.

   What is the maximum time an arrested person can be detained without a probable cause determination? A 1991 Supreme Court decision is instructive because it sets a tentative limit. The Court held that detention of a suspect for forty-eight hours without any probable cause hearing is presumptively reasonable. If the time to a hearing is longer than that, the burden of proof shifts to the police to prove reasonableness. But if the time to a hearing is shorter, the burden of proof to establish unreasonable delay shifts to the detainee (*County of Riverside v. McLaughlin*, 500 U.S. 44 [1991]). A subsequent case held *McLaughlin* applicable to all cases that had not been decided at the time of the *McLaughlin* decision (*Powell v. Nevada*, 511 U.S. 79 [1992]).

   County of Riverside v. McLaughlin (1991)

   Powell v. Nevada (1992)

2. *Discovery.* **Discovery** is a procedure used by either party in a case to obtain necessary or helpful information that is in the hands of the other party. It is initiated by one side through a motion filed in court seeking discovery of specific evidence the other side might have, such as recorded statements, the results of physical examinations or scientific tests, experiments, and other physical evidence. The items subject to discovery are generally specified by law, court rules, or court decisions. The purpose of discovery is to take the element of surprise out of the trial by making each side lay its cards on the table and ensuring that each is aware of the strengths and weaknesses of the other, so realistic decisions can be made.

Although used extensively in civil cases, the scope of discovery in criminal cases is one-sided in favor of the defense because the accused can invoke the guarantee against self-incrimination and refuse to turn over relevant evidence to the prosecution. For example, Prosecutor X has a constitutional obligation to disclose *exculpatory* (that which tends to establish innocence) evidence to the defense, whereas Defense Lawyer Y does not have any obligation to disclose *incriminatory* (that which tends to establish guilt) evidence to the prosecution, unless waived, because such is a right given to the accused by the Fifth Amendment to the Constitution.

3. *Decision on "binding over."* Some states use the preliminary hearing to determine if the accused will be "bound over" for a grand jury hearing. In these states, there must be a finding of cause at the preliminary examination before a grand jury hearing will be held. Other states use the preliminary examination to determine whether the accused should be bound over for trial, bypassing grand jury proceedings altogether.

In some cases, a preliminary examination is not required:

1. *When an indictment has been handed down prior to the preliminary hearing.*
2. *If the grand jury has previously returned an indictment (usually because the case was referred to it before arrest).* The grand jury proceedings constitute a determination that there is probable cause and thus that the accused should stand trial.
3. *When a misdemeanor is involved.* In most jurisdictions, preliminary hearings are not required in misdemeanor cases, because only lesser penalties are involved. The accused goes directly to trial on the complaint or information filed by the district attorney.
4. *When there is a waiver of the preliminary hearing.* The accused may voluntarily give up the right to a preliminary examination. For example, a plea of guilty to the charge generally operates as a waiver of the preliminary examination. The accused is bound over for sentencing to the court that has jurisdiction over the crime.
5. *As a result of any of three actions in federal cases.* In federal cases, a preliminary hearing is required unless the defendant waives it or is instead indicted, if the federal prosecutor charges the defendant with a felony or a misdemeanor and prefers to use an information, or if the defendant is accused of a misdemeanor and consents to hold a trial before the magistrate judge.[2] In sum, there are exceptions in both state and federal jurisdictions to the holding of a preliminary hearing.

After the preliminary hearing, the magistrate may do any of the following:

1. *Hold the defendant to answer.* If the magistrate finds probable cause, naming facts that would lead a person of ordinary caution or prudence to entertain a strong suspicion of the guilt of the accused, the

accused is "held to answer" and bound over for trial in a court having jurisdiction over the offense charged.

2. *Discharge the defendant.* If the magistrate does not find probable cause, the defendant is discharged.

3. *Reduce the charge.* Most states allow the magistrate to reduce a felony charge to a misdemeanor on the basis of the results of the preliminary hearing. This enables grand juries and higher courts to avoid being swamped with cases that really belong in the lower courts.

The Decision by the Prosecutor to Charge

There is discretion in all areas of criminal justice, but particularly in policing and prosecution. After a suspect is taken into custody, or even before that, the police usually have discretion to charge or not to charge him or her with an offense. As the seriousness of the offense increases, the discretion of the police decreases. For example, the police have almost no discretion to charge or not to charge the suspect with an offense in homicide cases. Minor traffic offenses, however, may be disposed of by the police "on the spot." The prosecutor also exercises immense discretion.

In most states, the prosecutor is not under the control of any superior other than the electorate. This discretion is most evident in the prosecutor's decision to charge or not to charge. In the words of former attorney general and U.S. Supreme Court Justice Robert Jackson, "[T]he prosecutor has more control over life, liberty and reputation than any person in America."

In most cases, the prosecutor has the final say about whether a suspect should be prosecuted. If the prosecutor decides to charge even though the evidence is weak, a suspect can do little else but go to trial and hope for an acquittal. In words attributed to Edward Bennett William, a well-known lawyer, "A prosecutor can indict a ham sandwich." Conversely, if the evidence is strong but the prosecutor declines to charge, there is little anyone can do legally to persuade the prosecutor to charge. Even after a suspect has been charged, the prosecutor may file a **nolle prosequi** motion, which seeks a dismissal of the charges. Such a motion is almost always granted by the court.

Grand Jury Indictment versus an Information

A criminal prosecution is initiated by the filing of an accusatory pleading in the court having jurisdiction. Prior to the filing, the accused will have appeared before a magistrate to be informed of his or her rights and to post bail. The accused also will have had a preliminary examination to determine whether there is probable cause for him or her to be bound over for trial. However, the prosecution formally commences when the government files an indictment or information. An **indictment** is a written accusation of a crime filed by the grand jury and signed by the grand jury foreperson, whereas an information is a criminal charge filed by the prosecutor without the intervention of a jury. The Court has long held that indictment by a grand jury is

Art. 19.01. Appointment of jury commissioners; selection without jury commission.

(a) The district judge, at or during any term of court, shall appoint not less than three, not more than five persons to perform the duties of jury commissioners, and shall cause the sheriff to notify them of their appointment, and when and where they are to appear. The district judge shall in the order appointing such commissioners, designate whether such commissioners shall serve during the term at which selected or for the next succeeding term. Such commissioners shall receive as compensation for each day or part thereof they may serve the sum of Ten Dollars and they shall possess the following qualifications:

1. Be intelligent citizens of the county and able to read and write the English language;

2. Be qualified jurors in the county;

3. Have no suit in said court which requires intervention of a jury;

4. Be residents of different portions of the county; and

5. The same person shall not act as jury commissioner more than once in any 12-month period.

(b) In lieu of the selection of prospective jurors by means of a jury commission, the district judge may direct that 20 to 75 prospective grand jurors be selected and summoned, with return on summons, in the same manner as for the selection and summons of panels for the trial of civil cases in the district courts. The judge shall try the qualifications for and excuses from service as a grand juror and impanel the completed grand jury in the same manner as provided for grand jurors selected by a jury commission.

SOURCE: Texas Code of Criminal Procedure, 2005–2006.

Hurtado v. California (1884)

not a constitutional requirement (*Hurtado v. California*, 110 U.S. 516 [1884]). In states using the grand jury system, an indictment is usually required in felony offenses, but an information is sufficient in misdemeanors.

A **grand jury** hearing, in which a decision is made whether to charge a suspect with an offense, is not a right guaranteed under the U.S. Constitution in all criminal prosecutions. Amendment V of the Bill of Rights simply provides that "No person shall be held to answer for a capital or otherwise infamous crime, unless on a presentment or indictment of a Grand Jury. . . ." Many states today use it, some on an optional basis, but it is required in all federal felony prosecutions and in nineteen states. It is a peculiar institution in that "it belongs to no branch of the institutional government" (the executive, the legislative, or the judiciary) and is intended to "serve as a buffer or referee between the government and the people who are charged with crimes" (*United States v. Williams*, 504 U.S. 36 [1992]).

United States v. Williams (1992)

Federal rules of criminal procedure provide that "when the public interest so requires, the court must order that one or more grand juries be summoned."[3] Federal rules further provide that the court may select alternate jurors who must have the same qualifications and be selected using the same procedure as that for regular jurors. Alternate jurors, when needed, will replace the regular jurors in the same sequence in which they were selected, and they are subject to the same challenges as the regular jurors.

The grand jury proceedings start when a **bill of indictment**, defined as a written accusation of a crime, is submitted to the grand jury by the prosecutor. Hearings are then held before the grand jury, and the prosecutor presents evidence to prove the accusation. Traditionally, the hearings are secret, because the charges may not be proved, and hence it would be unfair to allow their publication. For the same reason, unauthorized persons are excluded, and disclosure of the proceedings is generally prohibited. The accused has no right to present evidence in a grand jury proceeding; however, the accused may be given an opportunity to do so at the discretion of the grand jury. A person appearing before the grand jury does not have a right to counsel, even if he or she is also the suspect. The reason is that the grand jury proceeding is merely an investigation, not a trial. Clearly, the rights of a suspect are minimal during a grand jury proceeding, despite the fact that he or she has a lot at stake. In the words of one former prosecutor, "Technically, an indictment is a written accusation, a piece of paper stating that the grand jury has accused a person of certain crimes. But on a more immediate level, the filing of an indictment in court informs a defendant and the rest of the world that the state thinks it has enough evidence to convict the person at trial. It is an act that ruins careers and reputations."[4]

If the required number of grand jurors (usually twelve) believes that the evidence warrants conviction for the crime charged, the bill of indictment is endorsed as a "true bill" and filed with the court having jurisdiction. The bill itself constitutes the formal accusation. If the jury does not find probable cause, the bill of indictment is ignored and a "no bill" results. In some states, witnesses (as opposed to the prospective defendant) who testify before the grand jury receive complete immunity from criminal charges arising out of the case. In federal court, however, a witness receives grand jury immunity only if immunity is given beforehand by the government.

An **information** is a written accusation of a crime prepared by the prosecuting attorney in the name of the state. The information is not presented to a grand jury. In most states, prosecutors have the option to use an information in all cases instead of a grand jury indictment. Five states require an indictment only in death penalty or life imprisonment cases.[5] To safeguard against possible abuse, most states provide that a prosecution by information may be commenced only after a preliminary examination and commitment by a magistrate or after a waiver thereof by the accused. The "probable cause" needed in every grand jury indictment is thus assured by the reviewing magistrate.

The information filed by the prosecutor must reasonably inform the accused of the charges against him or her, giving the accused an opportunity to prepare and present a defense. The essential nature of the offense must be stated, although the charges may follow the language of the penal code that defines the offense.

The Arraignment

At a scheduled time and after prior notice, the accused is called into court for an **arraignment**, in which he or she is informed of the charges and asked to plead. The accused's presence during arraignment is generally required, except in minor offenses. If the accused has not been arrested, or if he or she is free on bail and does not appear, a bench warrant, or **capias**—a warrant issued by the court for an officer to take a named defendant into custody—will be issued to compel his or her appearance. An exception in many states provides that an accused charged with a misdemeanor may appear through a lawyer at the arraignment. In some jurisdictions, the arraignment is also the first time an accused is asked whether or not he or she is guilty of the offense charged.

In federal courts, the arraignment consists of "(1) ensuring that the defendant has a copy of the indictment or information; (2) reading the indictment or information to the defendant or stating to the defendant the substance of the charge; and then (3) asking the defendant to plead to the indictment or information."[6]

The Plea by the Defendant

A **plea** is an accused's response in court to the indictment or information that is read in court. There are generally three kinds of pleas in modern criminal justice practice: nolo contendere, not guilty, and guilty. Some states add a fourth plea: not guilty by reason of insanity. In federal courts and some states, defendants may enter a conditional plea. In federal cases, this means "a defendant may enter a conditional plea of guilty or nolo contendere, reserving in writing the right to have an appellate court review an adverse determination of a specified pretrial motion. A defendant who prevails on appeal may then withdraw the plea."[7]

A Nolo Contendere Plea
A **nolo contendere plea** literally means *no contest*. The defendant accepts the penalty without admitting guilt. The effect of this plea is the same as that of a guilty plea, but the defendant may benefit because the plea cannot be used as an admission in any subsequent civil proceeding arising out of the same offense. For example, suppose X pleads nolo contendere to a criminal charge of driving while intoxicated. This plea cannot be used as an admission of guilt in a subsequent civil case brought against X by the injured party to recover damages. The injured party must independently prove X's liability and not simply rely on the nolo contendere plea.

By contrast, had X pleaded guilty to the charge of driving while intoxicated, the plea could have been used by the injured party in a civil case. The guilty plea automatically establishes X's civil liability, relieving the plaintiff of the burden of proving it. Nolo contendere pleas are permitted in federal courts and in the courts of about half the states, usually for nonserious offenses and at the discretion of the judge.

Even where such pleas are permitted, however, the accused generally does not have an absolute right to make the plea. It can be made only with the consent of the prosecution or with the approval of the court. It is also generally used only for misdemeanor offenses, although some states allow its use even for felonies.

A Plea of Not Guilty
If the defendant pleads not guilty, the trial is usually scheduled to take place within two to three weeks. The delay is designed to give both the prosecution and the defense time to prepare their cases. When the defendant

refuses to plead, or when the court is not sure of the defendant's plea, the court will enter a not guilty plea. Between the filing of the not guilty plea and the start of the trial, the defense lawyer often files a number of written motions with the court. One of the most common is a *motion to suppress* evidence that allegedly was illegally seized. The motion requires a hearing at which the police officer who made the search testifies to the facts surrounding the seizure of the evidence and the court determines whether the evidence was, in fact, illegally obtained. Another common motion is a *motion for a change of venue,* which is often made when there has been prejudicial pretrial publicity against the accused.

A Plea of Guilty When a defendant pleads guilty, the record must show that the plea was voluntary and that the accused had a full understanding of its consequences; otherwise, the plea is invalid (*Boykin v. Alabama*, 395 U.S. 238 [1969]). By pleading guilty, the defendant waives several important constitutional rights (such as the right to trial by jury, the right to confront witnesses, and protection against self-incrimination). Therefore, it is necessary to make sure that the accused knew exactly what he or she was doing and was not coerced into making the plea. In many states, the judge is required by law to inform the defendant that a guilty plea means he or she is waiving a lot of rights that inhere in a trial, as well as the right to be convicted based on guilt beyond reasonable doubt. Other states go further and require that the prosecutor present evidence in court of the defendant's guilt and have it entered into the record.

An **Alford plea** is a guilty plea in which the defendant claims innocence yet pleads guilty for other reasons. For example: X, a defendant, has been in jail for six weeks pending trial because he cannot afford to post bail. X is charged with a misdemeanor, which carries a penalty of one month in jail. Although X claims innocence, he pleads guilty, knowing that, if credited with the time he has already served in jail, he will immediately be set free. The Court has ruled that an Alford plea is valid because all that is required for a valid guilty plea is a knowing waiver of the rights involved, not an admission of guilt (*North Carolina v. Alford*, 400 U.S. 25 [1970]). In the same case, the Supreme Court also ruled that it is constitutional for a judge to refuse to accept a guilty plea from a defendant if that defendant continues to maintain his or her innocence. The judge, therefore, has the option to accept or reject an Alford plea. A plea of guilty that represents an intelligent and informed choice among alternatives available to the defendant is valid even if it is entered in the hope of avoiding the death penalty (*Brady v. United States,* 397 U.S. 742 [1970]).

Most jurisdictions allow the withdrawal of a guilty or nolo contendere plea if valid reasons exist. For example, federal courts allow a defendant to withdraw a guilty or nolo contendere plea in two situations: "(1) before the court accepts the plea, for any reason or no reason; or (2) after the court accepts the plea, but before it imposes sentence if the court rejects a plea agreement, or the defendant can show a fair or just reason for requesting the withdrawal."[8]

In a recent case, the Court ruled that a waiver by the accused of the right to counsel at the plea state is considered "knowing and intelligent," and therefore

Boykin v. Alabama (1969)

North Carolina v. Alford (1970)

Brady v. United States (1970)

valid, if the trial court informs the accused of the nature of the charges, the right to have counsel regarding the plea, and the possible punishments that come with such a plea (*Iowa v. Tovar*, 541 U.S. 77 [2004]).

Iowa v. Tovar (2004)

Plea Bargains

A **plea bargain** is the popular name given to the process in which a defendant agrees to plead guilty to an offense in exchange for a lower charge, a lower sentence, or other considerations. This section looks at how plea bargains work and the legal issues involved.

How Plea Bargains Work Noted authors LaFave, Israel, and King identify three forms of plea bargaining:[9]

(1) an arrangement whereby the defendant and prosecutor agree that the defendant should be permitted to plead guilty to a charge less serious than is supported by the evidence;

(2) an agreement whereby the defendant pleads "on the nose," that is, to the original charge, in exchange for some kind of a promise from the prosecutor concerning the sentence to be imposed; and

(3) an arrangement whereby the defendant pleads guilty "to one charge in exchange for the prosecutor's promise to drop or not to file other charges."

Not all guilty pleas are the result of plea bargaining. Many people plead guilty for other reasons without bargaining with the prosecutor. Conversely, not all plea bargains result in a guilty plea; the terms may be unacceptable to either side or to the judge. Some forms of "inducement" may be inherently unfair or coercive; a plea obtained by such means is involuntary and therefore invalid. For example, a threat to prosecute the accused's spouse as a codefendant (despite a lack of evidence) would invalidate the plea because of improper pressure.

Plea bargains take many forms and are struck just about anywhere, in mostly informal settings—the hallway of a courthouse, out on the street, or in the office of the prosecutor or judge. It most cases, plea bargaining takes place between the prosecutor and the defense lawyer with or without the presence of the accused. In some, it is in the presence of a judge, whereas in other cases, the judge does not want to know what is taking place until the results are presented in court. The following scenario described by a former New York City prosecutor portrays a disturbing, yet often realistic, backdrop for plea bargaining:[10]

> Prison for a trial that might easily be six months. The message was loud and clear: take my reasonable offer of five days or you're going to rot in Riker's [a detention center in New York] fighting the issues. The defendant's eyes bug out; half-heartedly he pleads guilty. Strong-arming defendants into a plea was rough justice, but it kept the number of dispositions up, the number of "bodies in the system" down, and sped cases along to a conviction.

Plea bargains are controversial. In the words of a former prosecutor, "The general public tends to regard plea bargaining as too lenient. The defense bar and others of like mind think it too coercive."[11] Despite imperfections and persistent criticisms, plea bargaining is here to stay and is considered a necessity for the criminal justice system. Without it, prosecutions become more lengthy and expensive. The American Bar Association says that plea bargaining exists because of four "practical" reasons:[12]

- Defendants can avoid the time and cost of defending themselves at trial, the risk of harsher punishment, and the publicity a trial could involve.
- The prosecution saves the time and expense of a lengthy trial.
- Both sides are spared the uncertainty of going to trial.
- The court system is saved the burden of conducting a trial on every crime.

Legal Issues in Plea Bargains

1. *Should a prosecutor's promise to a defendant to induce a guilty plea be kept?* If a plea is based to any significant degree upon the prosecutor's promise, that promise must be fulfilled. If not, either the agreement or promise is specifically enforced or the plea may be withdrawn.

Santobello v. New York (1971)

In *Santobello v. New York* (404 U.S. 257 [1971]), the state of New York indicted Santobello on two felony counts. After negotiations, the prosecutor in charge of the case agreed to permit Santobello to plead guilty to a lesser offense and agreed not to make any recommendation as to the sentence to be imposed. Santobello then pleaded guilty, but during sentencing a few months later, a new prosecutor asked for the maximum sentence to be imposed. The judge imposed the maximum, but he later maintained that the request was not the reason the maximum sentence was imposed and that he was not influenced by it. The defendant moved to withdraw his guilty plea, but the request was denied by the judge.

On appeal, the Supreme Court ruled that, once the trial court accepts a guilty plea entered in accordance with a plea bargain, the defendant has a right to have the bargain enforced. Therefore, the judge must decide either to enforce the agreement or to allow the defendant to withdraw the guilty plea (see the *Santobello* Case Brief).

To avoid the undesirable result of the *Santobello* case, most prosecutors tell the accused what they will or will not recommend for a possible sentence in exchange for a guilty plea, but they stipulate that the judge is not legally obligated to honor that recommendation. In many states, the judge is required to ask the parties in open court about the terms of the plea bargain. If the terms are unacceptable, the judge enters a not guilty plea for the defendant and then tries the case. One study found that about 30 percent of the time judges asked the defendant if promises other than the plea-bargaining agreement had been made. The same study showed that in 65 percent of the cases judges asked defendants if any threats or pressures had caused them to plead guilty. Judges rejected only 2 percent of the guilty pleas encountered in the study.[13]

2. *Is the defendant entitled to a lawyer during the plea-bargaining process?* Under the Sixth Amendment, the defendant is entitled to a lawyer at all critical stages of the criminal justice process. Clearly, plea bargaining is a critical stage of the criminal justice process; therefore defendants are entitled to counsel unless counsel is waived. LaFave, Israel, and King,[14] however, raise the issue of the role of the defense lawyer as the process goes on, saying: "What if, for example, the prosecutor improperly meets with defendant in the absence of defense counsel and engages in plea bargaining with him but the plea of guilty subsequently entered by the defendant is pursuant to a bargain which defendant's counsel was aware of and had discussed with defendant prior to the entry of his plea?" Is the plea bargain valid? Court decisions on that issue are unclear.

3. *How much evidence should the prosecutors disclose in plea bargaining?* The answer is that the government does not have to disclose everything for the agreement to be valid. In a recent case, the Court reiterated its holding in previous cases, saying that "the Constitution does not require the Government to disclose material impeachment evidence prior to entering a plea agreement with a criminal defendant," adding that "the Constitution, in respect to a defendant's awareness of relevant circumstances, does not require complete knowledge, but permits a court to accept a guilty plea, with its accompanying waiver of various constitutional rights, despite various forms of misapprehension under which a defendant might labor" (*United States v. Ruiz*, 536 U.S. 622 [2002]).

United States v. Ruiz (2002)

4. *What constitutes an involuntary plea?* An involuntary plea violates a defendant's constitutional rights; therefore, it may be withdrawn at any time. However, what constitutes an involuntary plea is a difficult issue and must be determined by the court on a case-by-case basis. Federal procedure permits a voluntary guilty plea to be withdrawn only before sentencing is imposed—except that the court may permit a withdrawal after sentencing "to correct manifest injustice." Some states follow the federal procedure, and others simply do not allow the withdrawal of voluntary pleas.

5. *Should plea bargaining be prohibited by law?* Plea bargaining is controversial; nonetheless, only a few jurisdictions have abolished it. Among them are Alaska and some counties in Louisiana, Texas, Iowa, Arizona, Michigan, and Oregon.

    Plea bargains may be prohibited by state law or by agency policy prescribed by chief prosecutors or judges. The predominant view is that, because they reduce the number of cases that come to trial, plea bargains are an essential and necessary part of the criminal justice process. Most authors agree that around 90 percent of cases that reach the courts are eventually resolved through guilty pleas. It is assumed that "the system can function only if a high percentage of cases are disposed of by guilty pleas and . . . this will happen only if concessions are granted to induce pleas." It is further assumed that "a reduction from 90 percent to 80 percent in guilty pleas requires the assignment of twice the judicial manpower and facilities— judges, court reporters, bailiffs, clerks, jurors and courtrooms."[15]

In sum, despite its negatives, plea bargaining generally benefits the state, the defendant, and the criminal justice system. Its results may not achieve ideal justice (whatever that means), but the practice is here to stay.

CASE BRIEF: The Leading Case on Plea Bargaining
Santobello v. New York, 404 U.S. 257 (1971)

Facts: The state of New York indicted Santobello on two felony counts. After negotiations, the assistant district attorney in charge of the case agreed to permit Santobello to plead guilty to a lesser offense and agreed not to make any recommendation as to the sentence. Santobello then pleaded guilty, but during sentencing a few months later, a new assistant district attorney asked for the maximum sentence to be imposed. The judge imposed the maximum but later maintained that the request was not the reason the maximum was imposed and that he was not influenced by it. The defendant moved to withdraw his guilty plea, but the request was denied.

Issue: *May a plea be withdrawn if the prosecution fails to fulfill all its promises, even if the result would have been the same if the prosecution had kept its promise? Yes.*

Supreme Court Decision: Once the court has accepted a guilty plea entered in accordance with a plea bargain, the defendant has a right to have the bargain enforced. If the prosecution does not keep the bargain, a court should decide whether the circumstances require enforcement

of the plea bargain or whether the defendant should be granted an opportunity to withdraw the guilty plea. In this case, the broken promise (although not maliciously broken) by the prosecutor to make no sentencing recommendation pursuant to a guilty plea is sufficient to vacate the judgment and remand the case back to the trial court.

Case Significance: *Santobello* gives reliability to the bargaining process in that the defendant can now rely on the promise of the prosecutor. If the defendant relied on that promise as an incentive for pleading guilty and the promise is not kept, the guilty plea can be withdrawn.

Excerpts from the Decision: Disposition of charges after plea discussions is not only an essential part of the process but a highly desirable part for many reasons. It leads to prompt and largely final disposition of most criminal cases; it avoids much of the corrosive impact of enforced idleness during pretrial confinement for those who are denied release pending trial; it protects the public from those accused persons who are prone to continue criminal conduct even while on pretrial release; and, by shortening the time between charge and disposition, it enhances whatever may be the rehabilitative prospects of the guilty when they are ultimately imprisoned.

However, all of these considerations presuppose fairness in securing agreement between an accused and a prosecutor. It is now clear, for example, that the accused pleading guilty must be counseled, absent a waiver. Fed. Rule Crim. Proc. 11, governing pleas in federal courts, now makes clear that the sentencing judge must develop, on the record, the factual basis for the plea, as, for example, by having the accused describe the conduct that gave rise to the charge. [1] The plea must, of course, be voluntary and knowing and if it was induced by promises, the essence of those promises must [404 U.S. 257, 262] in some way be made known. There is, of course, no absolute right to have a guilty plea accepted. A court may reject a plea in exercise of sound judicial discretion.

This phase of the process of criminal justice, and the adjudicative element inherent in accepting a plea of guilty, must be attended by safeguards to insure the defendant what is reasonably due in the circumstances. Those circumstances will vary, but a constant factor is that when a plea rests in any significant degree on a promise or agreement of the prosecutor, so that it can be said to be part of the inducement or consideration, such promise must be fulfilled.

On this record, petitioner "bargained" and negotiated for a particular plea in order to secure dismissal of more serious charges, but also on condition that no sentence recommendation would be made by the prosecutor. It is now conceded that the promise to abstain from a recommendation was made, and at this stage the prosecution is not in a good position to argue that its inadvertent breach of agreement is immaterial. The staff lawyers in a prosecutor's office have the burden of "letting the left hand know what the right hand is doing" or has done. That the breach of agreement was inadvertent does not lessen its impact.

The Procedure during Trial

During the trial, several procedures take place. The jury is selected; the prosecutor and defense counsel make opening statements; the prosecution and defense present their cases, rebuttal evidence is presented; the two sides make closing arguments; the defense motions for acquittal prior to the verdict; the judge instructs the jury; and the jury deliberates and returns with a verdict. This section looks at what happens during each of these actions.

The Selection of Jurors

A **venire** is a group of prospective jurors assembled according to procedures established by state law. Twenty-three of the fifty states use the voter registration list as the sole source of names for jury duty. Ten states and the District of Columbia use a merged list of voters and holders of driver's licenses.[16] The jury commissioner then sends letters of notification to the prospective jurors with instructions to

Table 2.1 Compensation of Trial Jurors per Day in Selected States*

Arkansas	$15.00–$35.00
Connecticut	$50.00
Iowa	$10.00
Kansas	$10.00
Kentucky	$5.00
Louisiana	$12.00–$25.00
Maine	$10.00
Massachusetts	$50.00
Michigan	$15.00
Minnesota	$30.00
Mississippi	$15.00–$40.00
Montana	$13.00
Nebraska	$35.00
New Jersey	$5.00
New Hampshire	$10.00
North Carolina	$12.00–$30.00
Oklahoma	$20.00
Oregon	$10.00–$50.00
Texas	$6.00 first day, then $40.00 after that
Utah	$18.50–$49.00
Washington	$10.00–$25.00

*Compiled by the author from state laws, as of 2005. Some states reimburse mileage, parking fees, and other expenses; other states increase the compensation per day if the trial lasts longer than a specified number of days.

report at a specific time and place for possible jury duty. Most states have various statutory exemptions from jury duty, the most common of which are undue hardship, bad health, and status as an officer of the court. Many states by law also exempt people in specific occupations, such as doctors, dentists, members of the clergy, elected officials, police officers, firefighters, teachers, and sole proprietors of businesses.[17]

Jurors are not paid much per day while serving. A study of state statutes shows a low of $5.00 in Kentucky to a high of $10.00 to $50.00 in Oregon (see Table 2.1). Jury selection, particularly in high-profile cases, can last a long time. For example, the jury in the O. J. Simpson case took 10 weeks to choose.

The types of jurors lawyers choose for trials has become an issue in itself. Ideally, jurors in any trial must be impartial, meaning they are not prone to either convict or acquit. In reality, however, neither side wants impartial jurors. Both the prosecutor and the defense want jurors who are sympathetic to their side. The use of consultants by both sides has become common in high-profile criminal cases. For example, both the defense and the prosecution used consultants to choose jurors in the celebrated O. J. Simpson trial and the Menendez brothers trials. There is nothing unconstitutional about this practice, and, unless prohibited by state law, "loading up the jury" will continue—at least in cases in which either or both sides can afford to hire jury consultants. Jurors' names are usually made public, but some states allow the use of anonymous jurors in cases where the chance of possible retaliation against them is high.

Prospective jurors may be questioned to determine whether there are grounds for challenge. This process is known as **voir dire**, meaning *to tell the truth*. In federal courts, the trial judge usually asks the questions, although the judge may permit counsel to conduct the examination or submit questions for the judge to ask the jury. In most state courts, lawyers themselves ask the questions. Some judges conduct a multiple voir dire, a practice whereby a judge selects several juries at one time for future trials. There are two types of challenges to prospective jury members: challenge for cause and peremptory challenge.

Challenge for Cause
A **challenge for cause** is a dismissal of a juror for causes specified by law. Although the causes vary from state to state, some typical causes follow:

1. The person is not a qualified voter in the state or county.
2. The person is under indictment for or has been convicted of a felony.
3. The person is insane.
4. The person is a prospective witness for either party in the case.
5. The person served on the grand jury that handed down the indictment.
6. The person has already formed an opinion on the case.
7. The person is biased for or against the defendant.

Peremptory Challenge
A **peremptory challenge** is a dismissal of a juror for reasons that do not need to be stated. Such challenges are made entirely at the discretion of each party. The number of peremptory challenges allowed varies from one state to another and may also depend upon the seriousness of the offense. The more serious the offense, the more peremptory challenges may be allowed. For example, the prosecution and the defense may be allowed six peremptory challenges each in misdemeanor cases and twelve in felony cases. For capital offenses, the number may go as high as sixteen or twenty. Peremptory challenges have been identified as a reason that minorities are underrepresented in trial juries. Recent Supreme Court decisions hold that peremptory challenges based on race or gender are unconstitutional, if such challenges are, in fact, admitted by the lawyer (which is unlikely) or proved by the opposing party.

As noted earlier, there are two types of juries: grand juries and trial juries. This section discusses trial juries, but Table 2.2 compares the two types to enhance your understanding of them.

Table 2.2 Grand Juries and Trial (Petit) Juries Compared

Grand Jury	Trial Jury (also known as Petit Jury)
Usually composed of sixteen to twenty-three members with twelve votes required for an indictment	Usually consists of twelve members, with a unanimous vote required for conviction
Choice usually determined by state law, with "jury of peers" not a consideration	Usually chosen from voter registration list and driver's license rolls, with "jury of peers" a consideration
Does not determine guilt or innocence: function is to return indictments or conduct investigations of reported criminality	Decides guilt or innocence and, in some states, determines punishment
Retains the same membership for a month, six months, or one year: may return several indictments during that period	A different jury for every case
Hands down indictments based on probable cause	Convicts on the basis of evidence of guilt beyond a reasonable doubt
May initiate investigations of misconduct	Cannot initiate investigations of misconduct

Opening Statements by the Prosecution

The prosecutor's opening statement acquaints the jury with the nature of the charge against the accused and describes the evidence that will be offered to sustain the charge. Opinions, conclusions, references to the character of the accused, argumentative statements, and references to matters on which evidence will not be offered are out of place, and the defense may object to them.

Opening Statements by the Defense

Opinions differ about the tactical value of having the defense make an opening statement. Some argue that, in making an opening statement, the defense risks assuming the burden of proving something in the minds of the jury. Others note that failure to make a statement may imply a weak or nonexistent defense. It is generally considered best for the defense to make its opening statement after the prosecution has presented its entire case; in some jurisdictions, it can be made only at that time.

Presentation of the Case for the Prosecution

After opening the case, the prosecutor offers evidence in support of the charge. Although the prosecutor may introduce physical evidence, most evidence takes the form of the testimony of witnesses. Witnesses are examined in the following order:

- Direct examination (by the prosecutor)
- Cross-examination (by the defense lawyer)
- Redirect examination (by the prosecutor)
- Re-cross examination (by the defense lawyer)

Theoretically, this cycle can continue, but the judge usually puts a stop to the examination of witnesses at this stage. The general rule is that lawyers for the prosecution or the defense cannot ask leading questions of witnesses they present, but they are allowed to ask leading questions during cross-examination of the opposing lawyer's witness. A *leading question* is one that suggests to the witness the desired answer. For example:

> Leading question for the prosecution witness on direct examination: "You saw the accused stab the victim, didn't you?"

> Leading question for the defense witness on direct examination: "The accused never stabbed the victim, did he?"

The prosecutor presents evidence to prove her case beyond a reasonable doubt. Evidence can be classified into two types: direct and circumstantial. *Direct evidence* is based on actual personal knowledge or observation by the witness. An example is testimony by the witness that he saw the defendant shoot the victim. *Circumstantial evidence,* by contrast, results from deductions and inferences drawn from certain facts. Examples are the accused's fingerprints were found at the scene of the crime or the gun that killed the victim belongs to the accused. The public perception is that direct evidence is stronger than circumstantial evidence, but this is not always true. For example, incriminating DNA evidence in rape cases, circumstantial evidence, is compelling and difficult to overcome by the defense. Conversely, some studies show that eyewitness testimony, a form of direct evidence, can be highly unreliable.

Presentation of the Case for the Defense

When the prosecution has rested, the defendant or the defendant's lawyer opens the defense and offers supporting evidence. Witnesses are examined in the order noted, with the defense lawyer conducting the direct examination and the prosecutor cross-examining the witness.

The defense may choose not to present any evidence if it believes that the prosecution failed to establish its case beyond a reasonable doubt. The rule in criminal cases is that the prosecution must establish its case on its own and cannot rely on a weak defense. If the prosecution fails to establish guilt beyond a reasonable doubt, the defense does not have to do anything to win an acquittal. The problem, however, is that guilt beyond a reasonable doubt is subjective, meaning that what may not amount to guilt beyond a reasonable doubt in the mind of the defense lawyer may in fact have established guilt beyond a reasonable doubt in the minds of jurors or the judge. Most lawyers take the safer course and present evidence on behalf of the accused. After presenting all the evidence, the defense rests its case.

Rebuttal Evidence

After both sides have presented their main case, each has an opportunity to present **rebuttal evidence**, which is evidence to destroy the credibility of witnesses or any evidence relied on by the defense—and vice versa. Cross-examination seeks to destroy the credibility of witnesses, but direct contrary evidence is often more effective. It is particularly so when the defense has an alibi, meaning that the accused maintains that he or she was not at the scene of the crime at the time it was committed.

Closing Arguments

In most jurisdictions, the prosecution presents its closing argument first; the defense replies; and the prosecution then offers a final argument to rebut the defense. The prosecution is given two presentations because it bears the heavy burden of proving guilt beyond a reasonable doubt. Closing arguments are limited to evidence or issues brought out during the trial.

The Prosecution's Argument
The prosecution summarizes the evidence and presents theories on how the jury should view the evidence to establish the defendant's guilt. The prosecutor is given a lot of discretion about what he or she says during the summation. However, the comments cannot include improper remarks, to which the defense may object and which (if serious enough) may even lead to a mistrial, new trial, or reversal on appeal. For example, suppose that during the summation, the prosecutor suggests that the defendant's failure to testify is evidence of his guilt. This is prosecutorial misconduct that is a strong ground for a mistrial, because it violates the defendant's right against self-incrimination.

The Defense's Argument
The closing argument by the defense is an important matter of tactics and strategy. Generally, the defense emphasizes the heavy burden of proof placed on the prosecution—namely, proof of the defendant's guilt beyond a reasonable doubt on all elements of the crime charged. The defense then stresses that this obligation has not been met, so the defendant must be acquitted. Neither the prosecutor nor the defense counsel is permitted to express a personal opinion about the defendant's innocence or guilt. It is improper, for example, for a defense lawyer to tell the jury, "I am personally convinced that my client did not commit the crime." The facts as presented must speak for themselves without the lawyer's interjecting his or her own beliefs.

Defense Motions Prior to the Verdict

The defense can file various motions prior to jury deliberations and verdict. A **motion** is a request made orally or in writing, asking the judge for a legal ruling on a matter related to a case. The most common are motions for acquittal, a directed verdict of acquittal, and a mistrial.

A Motion for Acquittal
In most cases, the defense moves for a judgment of acquittal at the close of the prosecution's case on grounds of failure to establish

a **prima facie case**, meaning that the prosecution failed to establish its case by sufficient evidence; hence, a reasonable person could not conclude that the defendant is guilty. A prima facie case can be overthrown by evidence presented by the defense, but if a prima facie case has not been established, then the defendant must be acquitted without the defense having to present its case. For example: After the prosecution completes its case, the lawyer for Defendant X, charged with murder, presents a motion for acquittal, alleging that the prosecution failed to introduce sufficient evidence to convince a reasonable person that a murder occurred. If the motion is denied by the judge (as it usually is), the defense proceeds with its case and the defendant can renew the motion to acquit at the close of the case.

A Motion for a Directed Verdict of Acquittal At the close of the presentation of evidence in a jury trial, the defendant may make a **motion for a directed verdict of acquittal**—again on the grounds that the prosecution failed to introduce sufficient evidence concerning the offense charged. A few states do not permit a motion for a directed verdict, on the theory that the right to a jury trial belongs to the prosecution as well as to the accused, so the judge cannot take the case away from the jury. However, most states allow the judge to direct a verdict of acquittal as part of the court's inherent power to prevent a miscarriage of justice through conviction on insufficient evidence.

Motions for acquittal or for a directed verdict of acquittal are based on the legal tenet that in a criminal case all elements of the offense—and not just the issue of guilt or innocence—must be proved by the prosecution beyond a reasonable doubt. If the prosecution fails to do this (for example, fails to establish beyond a reasonable doubt that the defendant was present at the scene of the crime), the defense does not have to present its own evidence to win an acquittal.

A Motion for a Mistrial Improper conduct at trial constitutes grounds for a *mistrial*, in which the trial is declared invalid before it is completed. If granted, the defendant can be tried again. A **motion for a mistrial** is usually filed by the defense and is made prior to jury deliberations. Grounds for a mistrial include such errors as the introduction of inflammatory evidence and prejudicial remarks by the judge or the prosecution.

The Judge's Instructions to the Jury

The trial judge must instruct the jury properly on all general principles of law relevant to the charge and the issues raised by the evidence. In some states, judges do this after the closing arguments; other states give judges the option of doing so before or after the closing arguments. For example, in the O. J. Simpson trial, Judge Lance Ito gave his jury instructions before the closing arguments.

Included in these instructions are the elements of the particular offense and the requirement that each element and the defendant's guilt be proved beyond a reasonable doubt. Most states empower the trial judge to comment on the evidence, but some states forbid such comment—leaving the assessment of the nature and credibility of the evidence to the jury. In most criminal cases, the parties—especially defense counsel—will ask the court that certain instructions be used. The court must decide whether to give, refuse, or modify the instructions proposed by the parties; decide which additional instructions it will give; and advise counsel of its decision. Often the judge holds an informal conference on instructions with the prosecutor and defense counsel, but the decision on what instructions to give rests with the judge. Any errors in the instructions can be challenged on appeal.

Jury Deliberation

The foreperson of the jury is usually elected by the jury members immediately after the jury has been instructed by the judge and has retired from the courtroom to start its deliberations. The foreperson presides over the deliberations and gives the verdict to the court once a decision has been reached.

Jury deliberations are conducted in secret, and jurors are not subject to subsequent legal inquiry, regardless of their decision. However, nothing prevents a juror from later voluntarily discussing the details of the deliberation. Jurisdictions differ about whether the jury—during the trial and/or during deliberations—should be **sequestered** (kept together or allowed to return to their respective homes at night or during weekends). Sequestration is most often imposed in sensational cases in which chances of jury tampering or misbehavior are high. Most states permit the trial judge to order sequestration at his or her discretion.

HIGHLIGHT

What Is a Death-Qualified Jury?

The question: Assume you are opposed to the death penalty. Can you be disqualified from being a juror in a death penalty case?

The answer: That depends on how strongly you oppose the imposition of the death penalty. In *Witherspoon v. Illinois,* 391 U.S. 510 (1968), the U.S. Supreme Court held that jurors cannot be removed, even if by state law, merely because of general scruples against capital punishment. Doing that denies the accused of the right to an impartial jury. However, the Court added that a juror may be excluded "for cause" if it is "unmistakably clear" that he or she would automatically vote against the death penalty if sought by the prosecutor or if the juror could

not be impartial in the determination of the defendant's guilt.

In *Lockhart v. McCree,* 476 U.S. 162 (1986), the Court affirmed this ruling in *Witherspoon* when it held that removal for cause of jurors whose attitudes toward the death penalty would "prevent or substantially impair the performance of their duties at the punishment phase" is constitutional and does not violate the Sixth Amendment right of the accused to an impartial jury.

The result of these two cases is a death-qualified jury, meaning a jury that is conviction-prone because those unalterably opposed to it are removed "for cause." A death-qualified jury is constitutional, says the Court.

The Verdict—Guilty or Not Guilty

A jury or judge's **verdict** is the pronouncement of guilt or innocence—"guilty" or "not guilty." In some states, a third verdict is "not guilty by reason of insanity"—in which case a civil proceeding follows to have the defendant committed to a mental institution. In federal and most state trials, the jury vote for conviction or acquittal must be unanimous. This section looks at what happens when there is a hung jury, a less-than-unanimous vote, an acquittal, and a guilty verdict. It also examines the phenomenon of jury nullification.

Hung Juries Failure to reach a unanimous vote either way results in a **hung jury** and a mistrial. The length of time a jury must deliberate before a hung jury is declared is determined by the judge. If the judge dismisses the jury because it cannot agree on the result, the case may be tried again before another jury. There is no double jeopardy, because the first jury did not agree on a verdict. There is no constitutional limit on the number of times a defendant can be tried again if the trial results in a hung jury, but prosecutors usually take into consideration whether a conviction can realistically be obtained and the expense of retrying the case.

Apodaca v. Oregon (1972)

Johnson v. Louisiana (1972)

Less-than-Unanimous Votes In *Apodaca v. Oregon* (406 U.S. 404 [1972]), the U.S. Supreme Court held that state laws providing for a less-than-unanimous vote for conviction are constitutional and will be upheld—at least in the case of a required 10-to-2 vote. In *Johnson v. Louisiana* (406 U.S. 356 [1972]), it held that a law providing for a 9-to-3 jury vote for conviction is also constitutional.

Burch v. Louisiana (1979)

The U.S. Supreme Court has decided that a state law providing for a six-member jury in all criminal cases, except those involving the death penalty, is valid. Unlike those of twelve-member juries, the verdicts of six-member juries must be unanimous (*Burch v. Louisiana*, 441 U.S. 130 [1979]). But the Court has also decided that five-person juries are unconstitutional because they would not permit effective group discussion; would diminish the chances of drawing from a fair, representative cross-section of the community; and might impair the accuracy of fact finding (*Ballew v. Georgia*, 435 U.S. 223 [1978]). Most states, however, provide for twelve-member juries in felony trials (*Williams v. Florida*, 399 U.S. 78 [1970]).

Ballew v. Georgia (1978)

Williams v. Florida (1970)

"Not Guilty" After the jury has announced its verdict, the defendant has a right to have the jury polled. The jury must then express its vote in open court either as a group or individually. A not guilty verdict does not necessarily mean that the defendant did not commit the offense; it can simply mean that the defendant may have committed the offense but the prosecutor did not prove it beyond a reasonable doubt. Regardless of the reason, a verdict of acquittal terminates the case immediately and sets the defendant free.

"Guilty" After a guilty verdict, the defendant may file a motion for a new trial. The motion asks the trial court to set aside the verdict and give the defendant another chance to prove his or her innocence. This usually happens under a variety of circumstances when subsequent events or newly discovered evidence requires that the defendant be given a new trial "in the interest of justice." States have laws governing the granting of new trials. In federal courts, the rules provide that any motion for a new trial must be based on newly discovered evidence and be filed within three years after the verdict or finding of guilty. A habeas corpus motion (discussed later) is in essence a motion for a new trial. It alleges that a prisoner's constitutional rights were violated during the trial but that those violations were not discovered then and could not have been included in the appeal.

The similarities and differences between a motion for a mistrial and a motion for a new trial can be summarized as follows:

Motion for a Mistrial	Motion for a New Trial
Filed by the defense	Filed by the defense
If granted, the accused can be tried again	If granted, the accused can be tried again
Usually alleges violations of the defendant's rights during the ongoing trial	Usually alleges violations of the defendant's rights before or during the trial
Filed before the judge or jury renders a verdict of innocence or guilt	Filed after a judge or jury renders a guilty verdict
Usually filed during the trial	May be filed months or years after the trial
Filed before the defendant starts serving the sentence	May be filed while defendant is serving the sentence

Jury Nullification **Jury nullification** occurs when a jury decides a case contrary to the weight of the evidence presented during the trial. This means that the jury acquits the defendant or convicts the defendant of a lesser offense despite the evidence presented; in essence, the evidence and the verdict point in opposite directions. Jury nullification usually occurs when the jury believes that applying the law, as justified by the evidence presented during trial, would result in an injustice. It has long been a part of the American criminal justice process and is traditionally seen as a shield against prosecutorial excesses by the government.

An observer points out that jury nullification usually takes place in two instances: (1) when the jury sympathizes with a guilty defendant (an example is a husband who kills his wife who suffers from a painful and terminal disease), and (2) when the law is controversial or morally debatable (examples are prostitution laws or marijuana possession, regardless of the circumstances).[18] The Court held in *United States v. Powell* (469 U.S. 57 [1984]) that juries have the power to engage

United States v. Powell (1984)

in jury nullification. In *Duncan v. Louisiana* (391 U.S. 145 [1968]), the Court wrote that the function of a jury is to "guard against the exercise of arbitrary power."

Concerns about possible jury nullification arise primarily as a result of controversial verdicts in high-profile cases, including the O. J. Simpson trial and the first Menendez brothers trial, both of which resulted in acquittals. Jury nullification is difficult to prove or disprove because of subjectivity in interpreting whatever evidence may be presented. For example, some members of the American public felt that the evidence in the O. J. Simpson case (he was accused of murdering his ex-wife, Nicole, in California) established his guilt beyond a reasonable doubt, and therefore he had to be convicted. Others—including the jury—believed, however, that no guilt beyond reasonable doubt was established, and therefore the defendant deserved acquittal. It is hard to say that one side is right and the other side is wrong, because "guilt beyond reasonable doubt" is ultimately a matter of personal opinion.

If a jury decides to acquit a defendant regardless of the evidence presented, charges based on the same offense cannot be brought again, because of the prohibition against double jeopardy. Jury nullification, abhorrent though the results may be to some people, is a final act to which there is no legal recourse and that has long been a part of the American jury system.

The Procedure after Trial

After the trial, if the defendant is convicted, sentencing, appeals, and habeas corpus petitions take place. This section looks at what happens during each of these actions.

Sentencing

Sentencing is the formal pronouncement of judgment by the court or judge on the defendant after conviction in a criminal prosecution, imposing the punishment to be inflicted.[19] Sentences may be in the form of a fine, community-based sanctions, probation, jail time (usually for misdemeanors), prison time (usually for felonies), and the ultimate form of punishment—death. Except for death, these sentences are not mutually exclusive. For example, an offender can be given jail or prison time and then later released on probation. Or, community-based sanctions can be included in a probation sentence. The sentence to be imposed is set by law, but judges or juries are given discretion to impose minimum or maximum terms.

In most states, sentences are imposed by the judge only, but, in a few states, the defendant may choose to be sentenced by the judge or the jury after a jury trial. In capital cases, states generally require that no death sentence be imposed unless by a jury of twelve members after a jury trial. Some states and the federal government follow sentencing guidelines, curtailing the judicial discretion inherent in indeterminate sentencing; other jurisdictions do not have sentencing guidelines and leave a lot more discretion to judges.

Sentencing usually does not immediately follow a guilty verdict, particularly for serious offenses. This is because many states require that a presentence investigation report (PSIR) be prepared to help determine the proper sentence.

The PSIR is either required by law or ordered by the judge; it is usually prepared by a probation officer or the probation department. The last part of a PSIR often contains a recommendation by the probation officer of the sentence in view of all the circumstances surrounding the case and the defendant.

In plea-bargained cases, the sentence is imposed by the judge, but most judges merely follow the sentence agreed on by the prosecutor and the defense lawyer or the accused. Although the sentencing power is associated with and assigned to the judge, the actual sentence imposed is the result of several influences. First, the legislature determines the fixed or maximum and minimum penalty to be imposed. The prosecutor and defense lawyer usually determine the sentence in plea-bargained cases. For serious offenses, the probation officer, who is ordered by law or the judge to conduct a PSIR, usually recommends a sentence in the report. Whatever prison term is set by the judge is subject to the provisions of the parole law in states that use determinate sentencing. Parole boards thus have a say about how long an inmate stays in prison. Finally, in practically all states, the governor can issue a pardon or a commutation of the sentence.

In states where juries may impose the sentence at the option of the accused, juries usually determine guilt or innocence and, for a verdict of guilty, decide on the sentence at the same time. Some states, however, have a **bifurcated procedure**, in which the guilt-innocence stage and the sentencing stage are separate. In those states, after a defendant is found guilty, the jury receives evidence from the prosecution and the defense concerning the penalty to be imposed. The rules of evidence are relaxed at this stage, so evidence not heard during the trial (such as the previous record of the accused and his or her inclination to violence) may be brought out. The jury deliberates a second time to determine the penalty.

Most states give the sentencing power to the judge, even when the case is tried before a jury. After receiving a guilty verdict from the jury, the judge usually postpones sentencing for a couple of weeks. The delay enables him or her to hear post-trial motions (such as a motion for a new trial or a directed verdict) and to order a probation officer to conduct a presentence investigation. The judge has the option to use the PSIR in any manner, including accepting or disregarding it completely. Despite controversy, most states now allow the defense lawyer or the accused to see the PSIR, thus affording an opportunity to rebut any false or unfair information it may contain.

Appeal

After the sentence is imposed, there is usually a period of time (such as thirty days) during which the defendant may appeal the conviction and sentence to a higher court. There is no constitutional right to appeal, but all states grant defendants that right by law or court procedure. In some states, death penalty appeals go straight from the trial court to the state supreme court, bypassing state courts of appeals.

In other states, appeals in death penalty cases are automatic and need not be filed by the defendant.

Theoretically, any criminal case may go as high as the U.S. Supreme Court on appeal, as long as either federal law or constitutional issues are involved. In reality, however, the right is generally limited by the *rule of four*—the Court's practice of deciding an appealed case on its merits only if four out of the nine Court members favor doing so. Out of the thousands of cases brought to the Court each year, comparatively few are actually heard on their merits. If the Court refuses to hear a case, the decision of the immediately lower court (whether it is a state supreme court or a federal court of appeals) holds. In cases that do not involve any federal issue—as when an appeal is based solely on a state constitutional provision or a state law, with no reference to any federal law or constitutional right—decisions by state supreme courts are final and unappealable. If an appeal succeeds and the conviction is reversed, the defendant can be tried again for the same offense, because by appealing a conviction a defendant is deemed to have waived his or her right to protection against double jeopardy. The decision whether to prosecute again is made by the prosecutor. However, if the conviction is reversed on appeal because there was not enough evidence to support a conviction, there cannot be a new trial.

Does every error during trial result in the reversal of a conviction on appeal? The answer is no. For example, in the course of a complex murder trial, the judge makes numerous rulings on issues that can be second-guessed on appeal. These rulings can range from a defense motion to object to a question asked by the prosecutor to a prosecutor's motion to sequester the jury. The judge might make mistakes when making a decision for the prosecution or for the defense. The general rule is that errors made by the judge (or by the prosecutor or the defense lawyer) during trial do not result in a reversal of a conviction if the error is deemed **harmless**. But if the error is deemed *harmful,* the conviction is reversed. The appellate court determines, from the totality of the facts of the case, whether the error is harmless or harmful. Usually, if there is enough evidence to establish guilt beyond reasonable doubt despite the error, the error is deemed harmless. There are certain errors, however, that are automatically considered harmful to the accused because they violate basic rights. For example, an error made by the judge in not assigning a lawyer to the defendant when a lawyer should have been assigned is deemed harmful even if the defendant would have been convicted anyway.

The appeals court may affirm, reverse, or reverse and remand the decision of the lower court. **Affirmation** means that the decision of the lower court where the case came from is upheld. **Reversal** means that the decision of the lower court where the case came from is overthrown, vacated, or set aside by the appellate court. A **reverse-and-remand decision** is less final than an outright reversal of the lower court decision in that the lower court's decision is reversed but the lower court has an opportunity to hear further arguments and to give another decision in the case.

If a defendant wins a reversal on an appeal, the case may be tried again without violating the constitutional prohibition against **double jeopardy**—being punished more than once for the same offense. This is because the right to protection against double jeopardy is waived by the defendant if he or she appeals. In appealed convictions, the defendant is essentially saying, "Give me a new trial; there was something wrong with my conviction." This constitutes a waiver of the right to protection against double jeopardy.

Habeas Corpus

If the convicted defendant is still incarcerated, and the appellate process has been exhausted, he or she can file a writ of habeas corpus alleging that the incarceration is unconstitutional and invalid. **Habeas corpus** (a Latin term that literally means *you have the body*) is a writ directed to any person detaining another (usually a sheriff or a prison warden), commanding that person to produce the body of the prisoner in court and to explain why detention is justified and should be continued. It is a remedy against any type of illegal restraint by the government and is frequently called the Great Writ of Liberty. Habeas corpus is always available to anyone deprived of freedom, although successful filings are rare. It is usually filed in the court where the defendant was tried. This helps explain why habeas cases seldom succeed.

A writ of habeas corpus is distinguished from an appeal primarily in that a writ is usually filed to secure a person's release from prison after appeals on the conviction have been exhausted and after the defendant has started serving time. It is a separate proceeding from the criminal case that led to the conviction. The main difference between an appeal and a habeas corpus case can be illustrated as follows: Suppose X is charged with, tried for, and convicted of murder in California. The murder case is *"State of California v. X."* Right after conviction, X may appeal her conviction through the California courts and up to the U.S. Supreme Court (if a federal or constitutional question is involved). Suppose X has exhausted her appeals and her conviction has been upheld by the appellate courts. X must now serve time in a California prison. While serving time, X obtains or discovers evidence that the jury in her trial was tampered with by the prosecution. X can no longer file an appeal, because that process has long been exhausted. But she can file a writ of habeas corpus seeking her release. The title of the case will be *"X v. Y"*; Y is the director of the California prison that is detaining her. Even if X wins her release, however, she may be tried again for the same offense. Her filing of a habeas case constitutes a waiver of her right to protection against double jeopardy because she is, in essence, saying, "Give me a new trial; the first one was unconstitutional or invalid." Table 2.3 highlights the main differences between an appeal and habeas corpus petitions.

In the past, habeas corpus was used as a procedure whereby death row offenders postponed the imposition of the death penalty. This was done through the filing of habeas cases serially (one after the other), each of which took years to reach the Court even if it eventually failed. The Court has since decided that prisoners' allegations in habeas cases should all be contained in one case and that a time limit should be placed on the filing of habeas cases. In short, prisoners are now given

Table 2.3 Appeal and Habeas Corpus Compared

Appeal	Writ of Habeas Corpus
A direct attack upon the conviction	A collateral attack, meaning a separate case from the criminal conviction
Part of the criminal proceeding	A civil proceeding
Purpose is to reverse conviction	Purpose is to secure release from prison
Filed only after conviction	May be filed anytime a person is deprived of freedom illegally by a public officer, before or after conviction, with some exceptions
Accused has been convicted but may be free on bail	Person is serving time or is detained illegally: cannot be filed if person is free
Based on any type of error made during the trial	Based on a violation of a constitutional right, usually during the trial
Must be undertaken within a certain period of time after conviction, otherwise the right of action lapses	Right of action does not lapse, may be filed even while person is serving time in prison
All issues must be raised from the trial record	New testimony may be presented

one chance to file a habeas case. Failure to include allegations in that case precludes the prisoner from raising the same allegations later. There are, however, exceptions to this rule, particularly in death penalty cases when guilt or innocence is at issue and the prisoner can prove that he or she could not have raised that issue when the first habeas case was filed.

Beware: The Procedure in Your Jurisdiction May Differ

The procedures described thus far are the most typical ones. Figure 2.4 summarizes the criminal justice process as presented in this chapter. Although the procedures described so far refer primarily to criminal cases involving felonies, this chart is broader; it includes misdemeanors and cases involving juvenile offenders. These cases are processed more informally and expeditiously. This figure acquaints readers with the totality of the criminal justice process, from beginning to end and as applied to all types of offenses.

This next section looks at exceptions in which the procedures discussed in this chapter may not apply: misdemeanors, variations among states' laws, variation within states' laws, and the difference between theory and reality.

Application to Felony Cases

The procedure just outlined applies mainly to felony cases. Misdemeanors and petty offenses are usually processed in a simpler and more expeditious way. Whether a crime is a felony or a misdemeanor depends on the law of the state and so can vary from one state to another. Generally, a **felony** is a crime punishable by death or

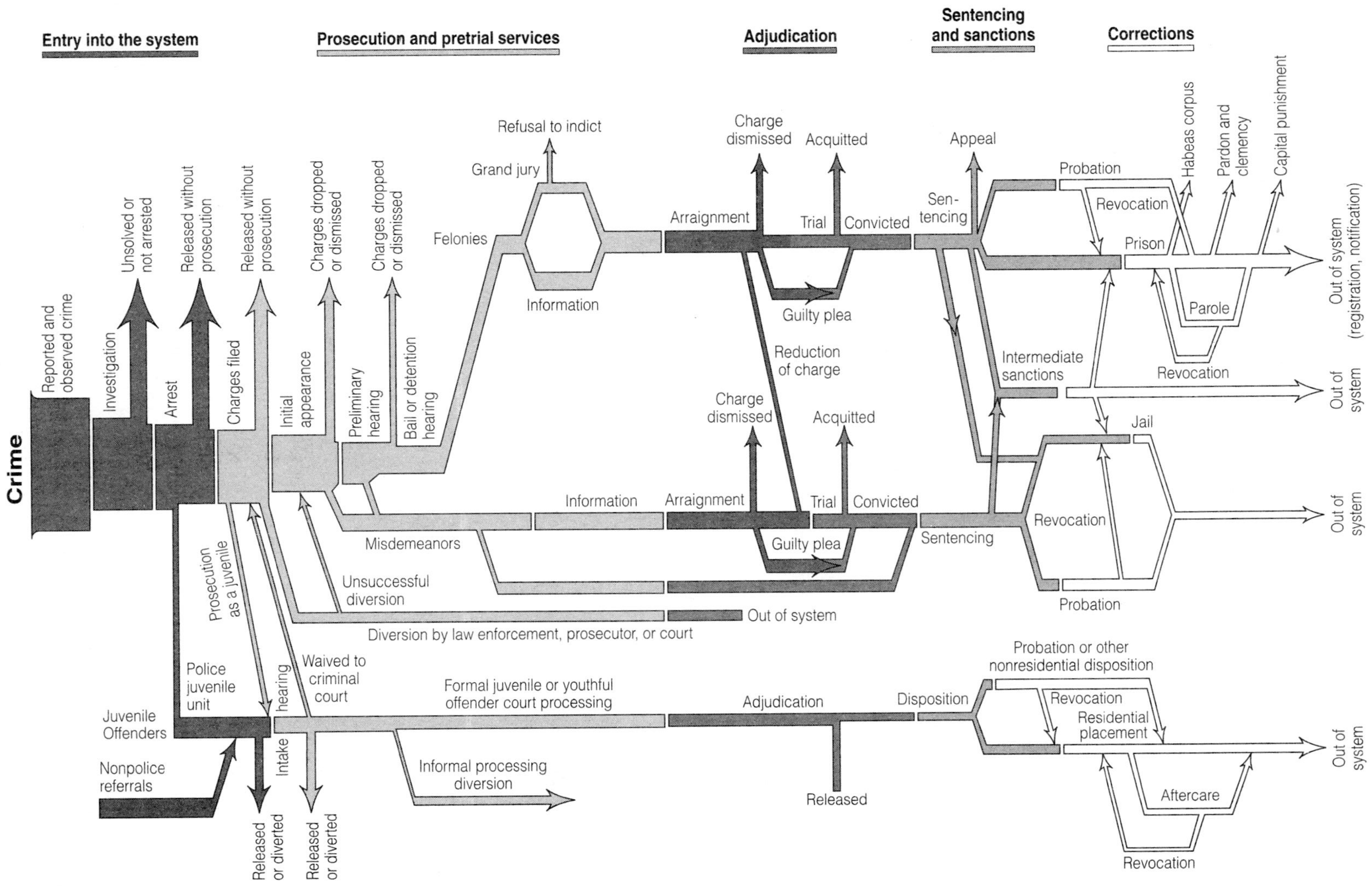

Figure 2.4 A Detailed View of the Criminal Justice Process

Entry into the system

Crime

Reported and observed crime

Investigation

Unsolved or not arrested

Arrest

Released without prosecution

Released without prosecution

Juvenile Offenders

Nonpolice referrals

Police juvenile unit

Prosecution as a juvenile

Prosecution and pretrial services

Charges filed

Initial appearance

Charges dropped or dismissed

Preliminary hearing

Charges dropped or dismissed

Bail or detention hearing

Felonies

Grand jury

Refusal to indict

Information

Misdemeanors

Unsuccessful diversion

Diversion by law enforcement, prosecutor, or court

Waived to criminal court

Intake hearing

Released or diverted

Released or diverted

Formal juvenile or youthful offender court processing

Informal processing diversion

Adjudication

Information

Arraignment

Charge dismissed

Acquitted

Trial

Convicted

Guilty plea

Reduction of charge

Arraignment

Charge dismissed

Acquitted

Trial

Convicted

Guilty plea

Out of system

Adjudication

Released

Sentencing and sanctions

Appeal

Sentencing

Sentencing

Disposition

Probation or other nonresidential disposition

Corrections

Probation

Revocation

Prison

Habeas corpus

Pardon and clemency

Capital punishment

Parole

Revocation

Intermediate sanctions

Jail

Revocation

Probation

Out of system (registration, notification)

Out of system

Out of system

Residential placement

Revocation

Aftercare

Revocation

Out of system

imprisonment in a state prison (as opposed to imprisonment in a local jail) or a crime for which the punishment is imprisonment for more than one year. Examples in most states are murder, rape, robbery, and burglary. All other criminal offenses are generally considered **misdemeanors**. Examples of misdemeanors are traffic violations, theft of small amounts, or parking violations.

Variation among States

The procedure just discussed applies in federal court and in most state courts. However, there are differences from state to state, and the terms used may vary. For example, some states use the grand jury for charging a person with a serious crime, whereas others do not use a grand jury at all. Some states allow jury trial for all offenses, whereas others impose restrictions. As long as a particular procedure is not required by the U.S. Constitution, states do not have to use it. Although criminal procedure has largely been "nationalized," discretion still abounds, particularly when it is not considered a violation of fundamental rights.

Variation within a State

Likewise, there may be variations in procedure among different courts in a given state even though all are governed by a single state code of criminal procedure. Thus, the procedures used in, say, the courts of San Francisco to process felony or misdemeanor offenses may not be exactly the same as those of Los Angeles. Differences exist because of the idiosyncrasies and preferences of judicial personnel or long-standing practices peculiar to a jurisdiction. For example, some jurisdictions hold preliminary hearings in all cases, whereas others hardly ever hold preliminary hearings. Some jurisdictions refer misdemeanor cases to a grand jury; others do not. Certain cities may hold a suspect for a maximum of forty-eight hours without a hearing; other cities hold night court to ensure that detainees are given a hearing almost immediately. Variations in procedure are tolerated by the courts as long as they are not violations of the law or of basic constitutional rights.

Theory versus Reality

The procedures just outlined, as well as those found in codes and textbooks, are the prescribed procedures. But there may be differences between the ideal (prescribed) procedure and reality (the procedures actually used by local criminal justice agencies). Many agencies have their own "convenient" and "traditional" ways of doing things, which may be at odds with procedures prescribed by law or court decisions. Nevertheless, these procedures continue to be used, either because of ignorance or because they have not been challenged. In some cases, courts tolerate certain practices as long as they do not grossly compromise the constitutional and statutory rights of the accused.

Summary

Criminal procedure is divided into three stages: before trial, during trial, and after trial. The sequence is as follows:

1. Procedure before trial

   ■ *Filing of complaint.* By offended party or a police officer

   ■ *Arrest.* With or without a warrant; sometimes a citation or summons is used instead of an arrest

   ■ *Booking.* Recording the suspect's name, time of arrest, and offense; inventorying belongings; photographing and fingerprinting

   ■ *Appearance before a magistrate without unnecessary delay.* Accused is made aware of his or her rights

   ■ *Bail.* Set by the magistrate, or the defendant is released on his or her own recognizance

   ■ *Preliminary examination.* Usually held for determination of probable cause, discovery purposes, or determination to bind over

   ■ *Decision to charge.* Prosecutor has the discretion to charge or not to charge

   ■ *Indictment or information.* Indictment—a charge made by the grand jury; information—a charge filed by the prosecutor; an indictment is required in most states for serious offenses

   ■ *Arraignment.* Accused appears before a judge, is informed of the charges, and is asked for a plea

   ■ *Plea.* Nolo contendere, not guilty, or guilty

2. Procedure during trial

   ■ *Selection of jurors.* Use of voir dire; types of challenges are for cause and peremptory

   ■ *Opening statements.* By prosecution and defense, both summarizing the evidence they will present and their version of the case

   ■ *Presentation by prosecution.* Offers evidence supporting the charge

   ■ *Presentation by defense.* Offers evidence for the accused

   ■ *Rebuttal evidence.* Evidence presented by either side to destroy the credibility of witnesses or evidence presented by the other side

   ■ *Closing arguments.* By the prosecution and then by the defense

   ■ *Judge's instructions to jury.* Includes the elements of the offense charged and the caution that each element must be proved beyond a reasonable doubt

   ■ *Jury deliberation.* Jurors may be sequestered at the option of the judge

   ■ *Verdict.* Pronouncement of guilt or innocence

3. Procedure after trial

   ■ *Sentencing.* Punishment handed down by judge or jury

   ■ *Appeal.* Allowed within a certain period of time

   ■ *Habeas corpus.* May be filed any time during incarceration; the petitioner seeks release from incarceration, alleging that the incarceration is illegal or unconstitutional

Review Questions and Hypothetical Cases

1. Define criminal procedure. Distinguish it from criminal law.

2. Distinguish between a grand jury and a trial jury. If you had a choice, would you prefer to serve as a grand juror or a trial juror? Why?

3. How does an indictment differ from an information? When is one used and not the other?

4. M is charged with sexual assault. Assume you are a defense lawyer for M. Will you ask for

a preliminary examination for your client or not? Justify your answer.

5. What is a plea bargain? Are you in favor of or against plea bargaining? Support your position.

6. Distinguish between the two types of jury challenges. Which type is more conducive to racial and gender discrimination against jurors, and why?

7. "Every error in a criminal trial causes a reversal of a defendant's conviction on appeal." Is that statement true or false? Justify your answer.

8. Identify five differences between an appeal and a writ of habeas corpus.

9. Criminal procedure is governed by U.S. Supreme Court decisions, yet variations exist from one jurisdiction to another. Why, and are they valid?

10. X, a student, was charged with speeding and reckless negligence. The incident caused a lot of damage to another car owned by a faculty member. X is given a choice by the local judge to plead either nolo contendere or guilty. You are X's lawyer. Which plea would you recommend for X, and why?

11. Y pleaded guilty to burglary after having been promised by the prosecutor that he would get probation. The judge sentenced Y instead to a year in jail. Can Y withdraw his guilty plea? State reasons for your answer.

12. Z was accused of murder, convicted, given the death penalty, and sent to death row. Z appealed his conviction and sentence to the state supreme court. Ten months later, the state's highest court turned down Z's appeal. A year later, Z's lawyer obtained reliable information and proof that the main witness against Z gave false testimony during the trial. What remedy, if any, does Z have? Why are other remedies not available?

Key Terms

Go to the Criminal Procedure 7e website for flash cards that will help you master the definitions of these terms.

Holdings of Key Cases

See Appendix C for information on how to find cases in this chapter on FindLaw.com.

(*Note:* U.S. Supreme Court cases are easily accessible through the Internet. Go to google.com or yahoo.com, and then type in the case title (as in *Miranda v. Arizona*). Or, go to *http://www.findlaw.com/casecode/supreme.html*, and then click on Supreme Court Decisions "by year." Click the year the case was decided. You will then see court decisions alphabetically arranged. Note, however, that these means of Internet access may change.)

Apodaca v. Oregon, **406 U.S. 404 (1972)** State laws providing for a less-than-unanimous vote for conviction are constitutional, at least in the case of a required 10-to-2 vote.

Ballew v. Georgia, **435 U.S. 223 (1978)** Five-person juries are unconstitutional because they would not provide effective group discussion; would diminish the chances of drawing from a fair, representative cross-section of the community; and might impair the accuracy of fact-finding.

Boykin v. Alabama, **395 U.S. 238 (1969)** When a defendant pleads guilty, the record must show affirmatively that the plea was voluntary and that the accused had a full understanding of its consequences. Otherwise, the plea is invalid.

Brady v. United States, **397 U.S. 742 (1970)** A plea of guilty that represents an intelligent choice among alternatives available to the defendant—especially when represented by competent counsel—is not involuntary simply because it is entered in the hope of avoiding the death penalty. If otherwise voluntary and informed, the plea is valid.

Burch v. Louisiana, **441 U.S. 130 (1979)** Unlike those of twelve-member juries, the verdicts of six-member juries must be unanimous.

County of Riverside v. McLaughlin, **500 U.S. 44 (1991)** Detention of a suspect for forty-eight hours without any probable cause hearing is presumptively reasonable. If the time to the hearing is longer than that, the burden of proof shifts to the police to prove reasonableness. But if the time to the hearing is shorter, the burden of proof to establish unreasonable delay rests on the person detained.

Duncan v. Louisiana, **391 U.S. 145 (1968)** The function of a jury is to "guard against the exercise of arbitrary power."

Hurtado v. California, **110 U.S. 516 (1884)** Indictment by a grand jury is not a constitutional right.

Iowa v. Tovar, **541 U.S. 77 (2004)** For a waiver by the accused of the right to counsel at the plea stage to be valid, it suffices that the trial court inform the accused of the nature of the charges, the right to have counsel regarding the plea, and the possible punishment that comes with such a plea.

Johnson v. Louisiana, **406 U.S. 356 (1972)** A law providing for a 9-to-3 jury vote for conviction is constitutional.

North Carolina v. Alford, **400 U.S. 25 (1979)** A guilty plea is not invalid simply because the defendant does not admit guilt or even continues to assert innocence, provided that there is some basis in the record for the plea. All that is required for a valid guilty plea is a knowing waiver of the rights involved, not an admission of guilt.

Powell v. Nevada, **511 U.S. 79 (1992)** The decision in *County of Riverside v. McLaughlin,* 55 U.S. 4413 (1991), which said that the detention of a suspect for forty-eight hours is presumed to be reasonable, is not retroactive.

Recommended Readings

Larry Gist. *Texas roulette justice: An analysis of sentencing discretion.* South Texas Law Review 695–706 (2001).

Susan N. Herman and Lawrence M. Solan. *Jury in the twenty-first century: An interdisciplinary symposium.* 66 Brooklyn Law Review 1–19 (2001).

Joseph L. Hoffman. *Plea bargaining in the shadow of death*. Fordham Law Review 2313–2391 (2001).

Peter Margulies. *Battered bargaining: Domestic violence and plea negotiations in the criminal justice system*. South California Review of Law and Women's Studies 153–185 (2001).

Candace McCoy. *Plea bargaining as coercion: The trial penalty and plea bargaining reform*. 50 The Criminal Law Quarterly 1/2: 67–107 (April 2005).

Ric Simmons. *Re-examining the grand jury: Is there room for democracy in the criminal justice system?* Cleveland State Law Review 829–862 (2000).

Notes

1. Henry C. Black, *Black's Law Dictionary*, 6th ed., abridged (St. Paul, MN: West, 1991), p. 107.
2. Federal Rules of Criminal Procedure, Legal Information Institute, *http://www.law.cornell.edu/rules/frcrmp/Rule5_1.htm*.
3. Ibid., Rule 8(a).
4. David Heilbroner, *Rough Justice* (New York: Pantheon Books, 1990), p. 197.
5. Steven L. Emanuel, *Emanuel Law Outlines: Criminal Procedure*, 22nd ed. (New York: Aspen Law & Business, 2001), p. 348.
6. Supra note 2, Rule 10(a).
7. Supra note 2, Rule 11.
8. Ibid.
9. Wayne R. LaFave, Jerold H. Israel, and Nancy J. King, *Criminal Procedure*, 3rd ed. (St. Paul, MN: West, 2000), p. 956.
10. Supra note 4, p. 147.
11. George Fisher, former prosecutor, in "Plea Bargain, by Dirk Olin, *New York Times Magazine*, September 9, 2002, p. 29.
12. "How Courts Work: Steps in a Trial," *http://www.abanet.org/publiced/courts/pleabargaining.html*.
13. Bureau of Justice Statistics, Report to the Nation on Crime and Justice (Washington, D.C.: U.S. Government Printing Office, 1983), p. 65.
14. Supra note 9, pp. 983–984.
15. Supra note 9, p. 957.
16. Supra note 13, p. 67.
17. Ibid.
18. Comments from Reviewer 6, anonymous as of this writing, of the revision of this book. The author thanks the reviewer for these observations.
19. Supra note 1, p. 1528.

3 Probable Cause and Reasonable Suspicion

What You Will Learn

- Law enforcement officers must be thoroughly familiar with the concept of probable cause.

- There is a legal and a practical definition of probable cause.

- The definition of probable cause is the same in various areas of law enforcement work, but the focus may differ.

- It is better to have a warrant when making arrests or seizures.

- Probable cause can be established in three ways.

- Reasonable suspicion is based on the "totality of circumstances" and not simply on a single factor.

- Reasonable suspicion has a lower degree of certainty than probable cause.

The Top 5 Important Cases in Probable Cause and Reasonable Suspicion

Brinegar v. United States (1949):
Probable cause is more than bare suspicion; it exists when the facts and circumstances within the officers' knowledge and of which they had reasonably trustworthy information are sufficient in themselves to justify "a man of reasonable caution" in the belief that an offense has been or is being committed.

Spinelli v. United States (1969):
"Innocent-seeming activity and data" and a "bald and unilluminating assertion of suspicion" in an affidavit are not to be given weight in a magistrate's determination of probable cause. An officer may use credible hearsay to establish probable cause, but an affidavit based on an informant's tip must satisfy the two-pronged *Aguilar*-test.

Michigan v. Summer (1981):
The general rule is that every arrest, as well as every seizure having the essential attribute of a formal arrest, is unreasonable unless supported by probable cause.

United States v. Leon (1984):
Five-month-old information from an informant is "stale" and cannot be used to establish probable cause. In this case, an informant supplied information that he had witnessed a sale of drugs at the suspect's residence approximately five months earlier and had at that time observed a shoe box containing a large amount of cash that belonged to the suspect.

United States v. Arvizu (2002):
"In making reasonable-suspicion determinations, reviewing courts must look at the totality of the circumstances of each case to see whether the detaining officer has a particularized and objective basis for suspecting legal wrongdoing."

CASE BRIEFS

Spinelli v. United States (1969)
Alabama v. White (1990)

Introduction

If there is one legal term with which police officers must be thoroughly familiar, it is *probable cause*. This term is used extensively in police work and often determines whether the police acted lawfully. If the police acted lawfully, the arrest is valid and the evidence obtained is admissible in court. Without probable cause, the evidence will be thrown out of court. In *Michigan v. Summers* (452 U.S. 692 [1981]), the Supreme Court stated, "The general rule is that every arrest, and every seizure having the essential attributes of a formal arrest, is unreasonable unless it is supported by probable cause."

The probable cause requirement in police work is based on the Fourth Amendment to the U.S. Constitution, which states, "The right of the people to be secure in their persons, houses, papers, and effects, against unreasonable searches and seizures, shall not be violated, and no Warrants shall issue, but upon probable cause. . . ."

Michigan v. Summers (1981)

See Appendix C for information on how to find cases in this chapter on FindLaw.com.

Another important legal term used in policing is *reasonable suspicion*. With reasonable suspicion, police can stop and frisk, but it cannot be the basis for a valid arrest. Although we know that reasonable suspicion has a lower degree of certainty than probable cause, the two terms are sometimes difficult to distinguish because both can be subjective, meaning that what is probable cause or reasonable suspicion to one police officer or judge may not be that to another. Determinations of probable cause and reasonable suspicion during trial are made by the trial court, but these decisions can be reviewed by appellate courts if the case is appealed. Most determinations, however, are initially made by law enforcement officers at the scene of the crime or when they make a warrantless arrest.

Not all contacts or encounters with the police, however, require probable cause or reasonable suspicion. They are needed only when the contacts involve an unreasonable search or seizure. The courts determine what is an unreasonable search or seizure. Police do not need probable cause or reasonable suspicion to ask questions of witnesses to a crime or to set up roadblocks to detect drunk driving. Subsequent chapters in this text discuss more extensively when contacts or encounters with the police require probable cause or reasonable suspicion and when they do not.

Probable Cause

Probable cause has both legal and practical meanings. This section examines the variety of ways probable cause is defined, determined, and established.

Probable Cause Defined

Probable cause has been defined by the Supreme Court as more than bare suspicion; it exists when "the facts and circumstances within the officers' knowledge and of which they had reasonably trustworthy information are sufficient in themselves to warrant a man of reasonable caution in the belief that an offense has been or is being committed." The Court added, "The substance of all the definitions of probable cause is a reasonable ground for belief of guilt . . ." (*Brinegar v. United States*, 338 U.S. 160 [1949]). In the words of one observer: The Court measures probable cause by the test of *reasonableness*, a necessarily subjective standard that falls between mere suspicion and certainty. Facts and circumstances leading to an arrest or seizure must be sufficient to persuade a reasonable person that an illegal act has been or is being committed. Always, the test involves the consideration of a particular suspicion and a specific set of facts. Hunches or generalized suspicions are not reasonable grounds for concluding that probable cause exists.[1]

Brinegar v. United States (1949)

Some states use such terms as *reasonable cause* or *reasonable grounds* instead of probable cause. Regardless of the term used, the meaning is the same.

A "Man of Reasonable Caution"

The original term **man of reasonable caution** (some courts use "reasonable man" or "ordinarily prudent and cautious man") does not refer to a person with training in the law, such as a magistrate or a lawyer. Instead, it refers to the average "man on the street" (for instance, a mechanic, butcher, baker, or teacher) who, under the same circumstances, would believe that the person being arrested had committed the offense or that items to be seized would be found in a particular place.

United States v. Ortiz (1975)

Despite this, however, the experience of the police officer must be considered in determining whether probable cause existed in a specific situation. In *United States v. Ortiz,* 422 U.S. 891 (1975), the Court ruled that "officers are entitled to draw reasonable inferences from these facts in light of their knowledge of the area and their prior experience with aliens and smugglers." Given their work experience, training, and background, police officers are better qualified than the average person in the street to evaluate certain facts and circumstances. Thus, what may not amount to probable cause to an untrained person may be sufficient for probable cause in the estimation of a police officer because of his or her training and experience. This is particularly true in property or drug cases, in which what may look like an innocent activity to an untrained person may indicate to a police officer that a criminal act is taking place.

Maryland v. Pringle (2003)

This concept of a "man of reasonable caution" was reaffirmed by the Court in the more recent case of *Maryland v. Pringle,* 540 U.S. 366 (2003), when the Court said: "To determine whether an officer had probable cause to arrest an individual, we examine the events leading up to the arrest, and then decide 'whether these historical facts, viewed from the standpoint of an objectively reasonable police officer amount to' probable cause." Therefore, the term "man of reasonable caution" is best interpreted using the standard of an "objectively reasonable police officer." This phrase is the most specific the Court has been in the many cases it has interpreted the meaning of the term.

HIGHLIGHT

The Legal versus the Practical Definition of Probable Cause

Legal Definition: Probable cause exists when "the facts and circumstances within the officers' knowledge and of which they had reasonably trustworthy information are sufficient in themselves to warrant a man of reasonable caution in the belief that an offense has been or is being committed."

Practical Definition: Probable cause exists when it is more likely than not (more than 50 percent certainty) that the suspect committed an offense or that the items sought can be found in a certain place.

A Practical Definition—More than 50 Percent Certainty

For practical purposes, probable cause exists when an officer has trustworthy evidence sufficient to make "a reasonable person" think it more likely than not that the proposed arrest or search is justified. In mathematical terms, this implies that the officer (in cases of arrest or search without a warrant) or the magistrate (in cases of arrest or search with a warrant) is more than 50 percent certain that the suspect has committed the offense or that the items can be found in a certain place. Despite the degree of certainty that the phrase "more than 50 percent" conveys, the Court itself has repeatedly cautioned against quantification (using numbers) when determining probable cause. In *Maryland v. Pringle,* 540 U.S. 366 (2003), the Court said:

> The probable-cause standard is incapable of precise definition or quantification into percentages because it deals with probabilities and depends on the totality of circumstances. We have stated, however, that "[t]he substance of all the definitions of probable cause is a reasonable ground for belief of guilt, and that the belief of guilt must be particularized with respect to the person to be searched or seized."

The Court then added that "on many occasions, we have reiterated that the probable-cause standard is a 'practical non-technical conception' that deals with 'the factual and practical considerations of everyday life on which reasonable and prudent men, not legal technicians, act.'" Therefore, it must be stressed that although the phrase "more than 50%" is convenient and, to many, extremely helpful in determining probable cause, the Court itself does not use it in its decision. It is therefore a layperson's term rather than a precise legal concept courts use.

The Definition of Probable Cause Is the Same in All Areas of Police Work

Probable cause is required in four important areas of police work: (1) arrests with a warrant, (2) arrests without a warrant, (3) searches and seizures of property with a warrant, and (4) searches and seizures of property without a warrant. An arrest is, of course, a form of seizure—but a seizure of a person, not of property. For practical purposes, other aspects of the criminal justice process, such as grand jury proceedings or preliminary hearing determinations, might have their own interpretation of probable cause, but police work uses the same definition as the Court uses.

Both the legal and the practical definitions of probable cause are the same in all phases of police work—whether it involves arrests with or without a warrant or searches and seizures of property with or without a warrant. It is also the same definition whether the search involves persons, property, or motor vehicles. But there are important differences in focus, as discussed later.

Arrest of Persons versus Search and Seizure of Property

In cases of *arrest,* the probable cause concerns are whether an offense has been committed and whether the suspect did, in fact, commit the offense. In contrast, in cases of *search and seizure of property,* the concerns are whether the items to be seized are connected with criminal activity and whether they can be found in the place to be searched. It follows, therefore, that what constitutes probable cause for arrest may not constitute probable cause for search and seizure—not because of different definitions but because the officer is looking at different aspects. For example, suppose a suspect is being arrested in her apartment for robbery, but the police have reason to believe that the stolen goods are in her getaway car, which is parked in the driveway. In this case, there is probable cause for arrest but not for a search of the apartment, except for a search that is incidental to the arrest.

With a Warrant versus without a Warrant

In arrests and seizures with a warrant, the determination of probable cause is made by the magistrate to whom the complaint or affidavit is presented by the police or victim. In this case, the officer does not have to worry about establishing probable cause. However, such a finding of probable cause by the magistrate is not final. It may be reviewed by the judge during the trial, and if probable cause did not, in fact, exist, the evidence obtained is not admissible in court. In some jurisdictions, the absence of probable cause in a warrant must be established by the defendant through clear and convincing evidence—a difficult level of proof for the defendant to establish and certainly higher than probable cause.

By contrast, in arrests and searches and seizures without a warrant, the police officer makes the initial determination of probable cause, usually on the spot and with little time to think. This determination is subject to review by the court if challenged at a later time, usually in a *motion to suppress* evidence before or during the trial. Moreover, a trial court's determination of probable cause can be reviewed by an appellate court if the case is appealed. The important function of the courts in making the final determination whether probable cause exists is best summarized in a statement written by Justice Frankfurter in an earlier decision, *McNabb v. United States* (318 U.S. 332 [1943]), which says:

> A democratic society, in which respect for the dignity of all men is central, naturally guards against the misuse of the law enforcement process. Zeal in tracking down crime is not in itself an assurance of soberness of judgment. Disinterestedness in law enforcement does not alone prevent disregard of cherished liberties. Experience has therefore counseled that safeguards must be provided against the dangers of the overzealous as well as the despotic. The awful instruments of the criminal law cannot be entrusted to a single functionary. The complicated process of criminal justice is therefore divided into different parts, responsibility for which is separately vested in the various participants upon whom the criminal law relies for its vindication.

Two consequences arise from the absence of probable cause in search and seizure cases. First, the evidence obtained cannot be admitted in court during the trial, hence possibly weakening the case for the prosecution. Second, the police officer may be sued in a civil case for damages or, in extreme cases, subjected to criminal prosecution.

The Supreme Court has expressed a strong preference for the use of a warrant in police work. Because the affidavit has been reviewed by a neutral and detached magistrate, the issuance of a warrant ensures a more orderly procedure and is a better guarantee that probable cause is, in fact, present. In reality, however, most arrests and searches are made without a warrant under the numerous exceptions to the warrant requirement.

The Advantages of Obtaining a Warrant

Police officers are advised to obtain a warrant whenever possible for two basic reasons.

First, there is a presumption of probable cause because the affidavit or complaint has been reviewed by the magistrate who found probable cause to justify issuing a warrant. The arrest or search and seizure is therefore presumed valid unless the accused proves otherwise in court through clear and convincing evidence. But it is difficult for the accused to overcome the presumption that the warrant is valid. If the finding of probable cause is reviewed during the trial, the court's remaining task is simply to determine if there was a substantial basis for the issuing magistrate's finding of probable cause, not to look at specific factual allegations (*Illinois v. Gates,* 462 U.S. 213 [1983]).

A second advantage is that having a warrant is a strong defense in civil cases for damages brought against the police officer for alleged violation of a defendant's constitutional rights. For example, suppose a police officer is sued for damages by a person who alleges that she was arrested without probable cause. If the arrest was made by virtue of a warrant, the officer will likely not be held liable (with some exceptions) even if it is later determined in the trial or on appeal that the magistrate erred in thinking that probable cause existed. Magistrates and judges who err in the issuance of warrants are not civilly liable for damages because they have judicial immunity. The only exception to a warrant's being a valid defense in civil cases for damages is when an officer serves a warrant that is clearly invalid due to obvious mistakes that he or she should have discovered, such as the absence of a signature or failure to specify the place or person subject to the warrant.

Determining Probable Cause

In searches and seizures without a warrant, probable cause is determined by the officer initially. In searches and seizures with a warrant, the initial determination is made by the magistrate who issued the warrant. Both determinations are reviewable by the trial court or by an appellate court if the case is later appealed.

Because probable cause, if later challenged in court, must be established by police testimony in warrantless arrests or searches, it is important that the police officer observe keenly and take careful notes of the facts and circumstances establishing that probable cause existed at the time he or she acted. For example, if an officer arrests a person seen coming out of a building at midnight, the officer must be able to articulate (if asked to do so later in court) what factors led him or her to make the arrest—such as the furtive behavior of the suspect, nervousness when being questioned, possession of what appeared to be stolen items, and prior criminal record.

Establishing Probable Cause by What Is Found after an Illegal Act

If no probable cause existed at the time the officer took action, the fact that probable cause is later established does not make the act legal; the evidence obtained cannot be used in court. For example, suppose an officer arrests a suspicious looking person, and a body search reveals that the person had several vials of cocaine in his pocket. The evidence obtained cannot be used in court because there was no probable cause to make the arrest.

When officers seek to obtain a warrant from a magistrate, it is important that the affidavit establishes probable cause. This is because what is not included in the affidavit cannot be used to determine probable cause even if the officer knew about that information at the time the affidavit was submitted. For example, suppose Officer P states in the affidavit that her information came from an informant. If this is insufficient to establish probable cause, the fact that Officer P had a second informant who added more information cannot save the warrant from being invalid if that fact is not included in the affidavit (*Whiteley v. Warden,* 401 U.S. 560 [1971]). In short, what is not in the affidavit does not count toward establishing probable cause. Probable cause is never established by what turns up after the initial illegal act.

Whiteley v. Warden (1971)

Suspicion alone (a lower degree of certainty than probable cause) is never sufficient for an arrest. However, what starts off as mere suspicion can develop into probable cause sufficient to make an arrest. For example, suppose a police officer asks questions of a motorist who failed to stop at a stop sign. The officer suspects that the driver may be drunk. If the initial inquiries show that the driver is, in fact, drunk, then the officer may make a valid arrest. Also, any evidence obtained as a result of that arrest is admissible in court.

An officer may have probable cause to arrest without having personally observed the commission of the crime. For example, suppose that, while out on patrol, an officer is told by a motorist that a robbery is taking place in a store down the block. The officer proceeds to the store and sees a man running toward a car with goods in his hands. The man sees the police car, drops the items, gets into the car, and tries to drive away. In this case, probable cause is present, and so an arrest would be valid.

United States v. Ventresca (1965)

The Supreme Court recognizes that affidavits or complaints are often prepared hastily in the midst of a criminal investigation. Therefore, the policy is to interpret the allegations in a commonsense rather than an overly technical manner and to consider the affidavit sufficient in close cases (*United States v. Ventresca,* 380 U.S. 102 [1965]).

What Can Be Used to Establish Probable Cause

In establishing probable cause, the officer may use any trustworthy information even if the rules of evidence prohibit its admission during the trial. For example, hearsay information and prior criminal record (both inadmissible in a trial) may be taken into consideration when determining probable cause. In cases of hearsay information, trustworthiness depends on the reliability of the source and the information given. Reliance on prior criminal record requires other types of evidence. The key point is that, in determining whether probable cause exists, the magistrate may consider any evidence, regardless of source.

Because probable cause is based on a variety and totality of circumstances, police officers must report accurately and exhaustively the facts that led them to believe that probable cause existed. As one publication notes: Probable cause can be obtained from police radio bulletins, tips from "good citizen" informers who have happened by chance to see criminal activity, reports from victims, anonymous tips, and tips from "habitual" informers who mingle with people in the underworld and who themselves may be criminals. Probable cause can be based on various combinations of these sources.[2] When in doubt, it is better to include too much rather than too little information, provided the information is true.

How Probable Cause Is Established

Probable cause can be established in three ways: through (1) the officer's own knowledge of particular facts and circumstances, (2) information given by a reliable third person (informant), and (3) information plus corroboration. All three means rely upon the officer to establish probable cause. If the officer seeks the issuance of an arrest or a search and seizure warrant from a magistrate or judge, probable cause is established through an affidavit (although some states allow what is in writing to be supplemented by oral testimony). If the officer acts without a warrant, probable cause is established by oral testimony in court during the trial. It is therefore important for the officer to be able to state clearly, whether in an affidavit or in court later, why he or she felt that probable cause was present. In some cases, in addition to the evidence contained in the affidavit, the police officer presents oral evidence to the judge. Courts are divided on whether such oral evidence should be considered in determining probable cause; some courts consider it, whereas others do not.

In one case, the Court ruled that a suspect's reputation for criminal activity may be considered by the magistrate issuing the warrant when determining probable cause (*United States v. Harris,* 403 U.S. 573 [1971]). In that case, the officer's affidavit submitted to the magistrate to support a request for a search warrant stated that the suspect "had a reputation with me for over four years as being a trafficker of non-tax-paid distilled spirits, and over this period I have received numerous information from all types of persons as to his activities." The affidavit further stated that another officer had located illicit whiskey in an abandoned house under the suspect's control and that an informant had purchased illegal whiskey from the suspect. Although a suspect's reputation for criminal activity can never by itself be sufficient to establish probable cause, reputation combined with factual statements about the suspect's activity may be considered by the magistrate issuing the warrant.

The next sections look further at the three ways in which probable cause can be established.

United States v. Harris **(1971)**

An Officer's Own Knowledge of Facts and Circumstances
The officer's own knowledge means that he or she has personally obtained the information, using any of the five senses. These are the sense of sight (Officer P sees X stab Y), hearing (Officer P hears a shotgun blast), smell (Officer P smells marijuana while in an apartment), touch (Officer P frisks a suspect and touches something she knows is a gun), and taste (Officer P tastes something alcoholic). This contrasts with knowledge obtained from another person. Factors that a police officer may take into account in establishing belief that probable cause exists include, but are not limited to, the following:

- The prior criminal record of the suspect
- The suspect's flight from the scene of the crime when approached by the officer
- Highly suspicious conduct on the part of the suspect
- Admissions by the suspect
- The presence of incriminating evidence
- The unusual hour
- The resemblance of the suspect to the description of the perpetrator
- Failure to answer questions satisfactorily
- Physical clues, such as footprints or fingerprints, linked to a particular person
- The suspect's presence in a high-crime area
- The suspect's reputation of criminal activity

This list is not exhaustive, and courts have taken other factors into account.

It is hard to say to what extent some or any of the preceding factors contribute to establishing probable cause. That would depend on the type of event, the strength of the relationship, and the intensity of the suspicion. One factor may be sufficient to establish probable cause in some instances; in others, several factors may be required. In *United States v. Cortez,* 449 U.S. 411 (1981), the Court said this about the determination of what constitutes probable cause:

> The process does not deal with hard certainty, but with probabilities. Long before the law of probabilities was articulated as such, practical people formulated certain common-sense conclusions about human behavior; jurors as factfinders are permitted to do the same—and so are law enforcement officers. Finally, the evidence thus collected must be seen and weighed not in terms of library analysis by scholars, but as understood by those versed in the field of law enforcement.

This statement illustrates how difficult it is to set highly specific rules about what can or cannot be taken into account in determining probable cause. One thing is certain, however: the more facts are included, the higher is the likelihood that probable cause will be established.

Information Given by an Informant This section looks at how the Court evaluates information given by informants, both those engaged in criminal activity and those who are not. The Court evaluates both the quality of the information and the credibility of the informant. The major decisions reflecting the Court's evolving views on the subject are discussed. The section also examines the role the informant's identity plays in determining the value of his or her information in establishing probable cause.

Aguilar v. Texas (1964)

Information given by an informant engaged in criminal activity In *Aguilar v. Texas,* 378 U.S. 108 (1964), the Court established a two-pronged test for determining probable cause on the basis of information obtained from an informant engaged in criminal activity (who therefore has low credibility with the court):

- *Prong 1: Reliability of the informant.* The affidavit must describe the underlying circumstances from which a neutral and detached magistrate can find that the informant is reliable. For example, "Affiant [a person who makes or subscribes to an affidavit] received information this morning from a trustworthy informant who has supplied information to the police during the past five years and whose information has proved reliable, resulting in numerous drug convictions."
- *Prong 2: Reliability of the informant's information.* The affidavit must describe the underlying circumstances from which the magistrate can find that the informant's information is reliable and not the result of mere rumor or suspicion. For example,

"My informant told me that he personally saw Henry Banks, a former convict, sell heroin worth $500 to a buyer named Skippy Smith, at ten o'clock last night in Banks's apartment located at 1300 Shady Lane, Apt. 10, and that Banks has been selling and continues to sell drugs from this location."

Spinelli v. United States (1969)

The *Aguilar* test was reiterated five years later in *Spinelli v. United States,* 393 U.S. 410 (1969). In *Spinelli,* the defendant was convicted in federal court of interstate travel in aid of racketeering. The evidence used against Spinelli was obtained by use of a search warrant issued by a magistrate authorizing the search of Spinelli's apartment. The warrant was issued based on an affidavit from an FBI agent that stated four things:

- That the FBI had kept track of Spinelli's movements on five days during the month of August 1965. On four of those five occasions, Spinelli was seen crossing one of two bridges leading from Illinois into St. Louis, Missouri, between 11 A.M. and 12:25 P.M.
- That an FBI check with the telephone company revealed that an apartment house near a parking lot that Spinelli frequented had two telephones listed under the name of Grace P. Hagen.
- That Spinelli was known by federal law enforcement agents and local police "as a bookmaker, an associate of bookmakers, a gambler, and an associate of gamblers."
- That the FBI "has been informed by a confidential informant that William Spinelli is operating a handbook and accepting wagers and disseminating wagering information by means of the telephones" listed under the name of Grace P. Hagen.

Upon conviction, Spinelli appealed, saying that the information in the affidavit did not establish probable cause sufficient for the issuance of a search warrant. The Court agreed and reversed the conviction, on the following grounds:

- Allegations 1 and 2 in the affidavit reflect only innocent-seeming activity and data: "Spinelli's travels to and from the apartment building and his entry into a particular apartment on one occasion could hardly be taken as bespeaking gambling activity; and there is nothing unusual about an apartment containing two separate telephones."
- Allegation 3 is "but a bald and unilluminating assertion of suspicion that is entitled to no weight in appraising the magistrate's decision."
- Allegation 4 must be measured against the two-pronged *Aguilar* test.

The Court then concluded that the reliability of the informant was not established; further, the affidavit did not prove the reliability of the informant's information.

The *Spinelli* case illustrates the types of allegations that are not sufficient to establish probable cause. It also restates the two-pronged *Aguilar* test and concludes that neither prong was satisfied by the affidavit. (Read more about *Spinelli* in the Case Brief.) However, the *Aguilar* and *Spinelli* decisions have now been modified by *Illinois v. Gates*.

■ *The Old Interpretation of* Aguilar. Court decisions interpreted the two prongs in *Aguilar* as separate and independent of each other. This meant that the reliability of each—informant and information—had to stand on its own and be established separately before probable cause could be established. For example, the fact that an informant is absolutely reliable (prong 1) cannot make up for the lack of a description of how the informant obtained his or her information (prong 2).

■ *The New Interpretation of* Aguilar: Illinois v. Gates. The "separate and independent" interpretation of the two prongs in *Aguilar* was overruled by the Supreme Court in *Illinois v. Gates,* 462 U.S. 213 (1983). In *Gates,* the Court abandoned the requirement of two independent tests as being too rigid, holding instead that the two prongs should be treated merely as relevant considerations in the totality of circumstances. Therefore, the **totality of circumstances** has replaced "separate and independent" as the standard for probable cause in the *Aguilar* test. The Court wrote:

Illinois v. Gates
(1983)

[W]e conclude that it is wiser to abandon the "two-pronged test" established by our decisions in *Aguilar* and *Spinelli.* In its place we reaffirm the totality of the circumstances analysis that traditionally has informed probable cause determinations.

The task of the issuing magistrate is simply to make a practical, common-sense decision whether, given all the circumstances set forth in the affidavit before him, including the "veracity" and "basis of knowledge" of persons supplying hearsay information, there is a fair probability that contraband or evidence of a crime will be found in a particular place. And the duty of a reviewing court is simply to ensure that the magistrate had a "substantial basis for concluding" that probable cause existed.

The new test, therefore, is this: If a neutral and detached magistrate determines that, based on an informant's information and all other available facts, there is probable cause to believe that an arrest or a search is justified, then the warrant may be issued.

Under the *Gates* ruling, if an informer has been very reliable in the past, then his or her tip may say little about how he or she obtained the information. Conversely, if the informant gives a lot of detail and says that he or she personally observed the event, then doubts about the informant's reliability may be overlooked. Corroboration by the police of the informant's story and/or all other available facts may be taken into account in determining probable cause based on the "totality of circumstances."

CASE BRIEF: The Leading Case on the Sufficiency of Allegations for Probable Cause

Spinelli v. United States, 393 U.S. 410 (1969)

Facts: Spinelli was convicted by a federal court of interstate travel in aid of racketeering. The evidence used against him was obtained with a search warrant issued by a magistrate, authorizing the search of his apartment. The warrant was issued on the basis of an affidavit from an FBI agent that stated the following:

1. That the FBI had kept track of Spinelli's movements on five days during the month of August 1965. On four of those five occasions, Spinelli was seen crossing one of two bridges leading from Illinois into St. Louis, Missouri, between 11 A.M. and 12:15 P.M.
2. That an FBI check with the telephone company revealed that an apartment house near a parking lot that Spinelli frequented had two telephones listed under the name of Grace P. Hagen.
3. That Spinelli was known to the affiant and to federal law enforcement agents and local police "as a bookmaker, an associate of bookmakers, a gambler, and an associate of gamblers."
4. That the FBI "has been informed by a confidential reliable informant that William Spinelli is operating a handbook and accepting wagers and disseminating wagering information by means of the telephones" listed under the name of Grace P. Hagen.

Issue: *Did the above affidavit contain probable cause sufficient for the issuance of a search warrant? No.*

Supreme Court Decision: Allegations 1 and 2 in the affidavit reflect only innocent-seeming activity and data: "Spinelli's travels to and from the apartment building and his entry into a particular apartment on one occasion could hardly be taken as bespeaking gambling activity; and there is nothing unusual about an apartment containing two separate telephones." Allegation 3 is "but a bald and unilluminating assertion of suspicion that is entitled to no weight in appraising the magistrate's decision." Allegation 4 must be measured against the two-pronged *Aguilar* test. Here, the reliability of the informant was not established; neither did the affidavit prove the reliability of the informant's information. The affidavit therefore failed to establish probable cause, so the conviction was reversed and remanded.

Case Significance: The *Spinelli* case illustrates the types of allegations that are insufficient to establish probable cause. It restates the two-pronged *Aguilar* test for probable cause if the information comes from an informant. However, note that the *Aguilar* test, though still valid, has been modified by *Illinois v. Gates*.

Excerpts from the Decision: We conclude, then, that in the present case the informant's tip—even when corroborated to the extent indicated—was not sufficient to provide the basis for a finding of probable cause. This is not to say that the tip was so insubstantial that it could not properly have counted in the magistrate's determination. Rather, it needed some further support. When we look to the other parts of the application, however, we find nothing alleged which would permit the suspicions engendered by the informant's report to ripen into a judgment that a crime was probably being committed. As we have already seen, the allegations detailing the FBI's surveillance of Spinelli and its investigation of the telephone company records contain no suggestion of criminal conduct when taken by themselves—and they are not endowed with an aura of suspicion by virtue of the informer's tip. Nor do we find that the FBI's reports take on a sinister color when read in light of common knowledge that bookmaking is often carried on over the telephone and from premises ostensibly used by others for perfectly normal purposes. Such an argument would carry weight in a situation in which the premises contain an unusual number of telephones or abnormal activity is observed, but it does not fit this case where neither of these factors is present. All that remains to be considered is the flat statement that Spinelli was "known" to the FBI and others as a gambler. But just as a simple assertion of police suspicion is not itself a sufficient basis for a magistrate's finding of probable cause, we do not believe it may be used to give additional weight to allegations that would otherwise be insufficient.

The affidavit, then, falls short of the standards set forth in Aguilar, Draper, and our other decisions that give content to the notion of probable cause. [7] In holding as we have done, we do not retreat from the established propositions that only the probability, and not a prima facie showing, of criminal activity is the standard of probable cause; that affidavits of probable cause are tested by much less rigorous standards than those governing the admissibility of evidence at trial that in judging probable cause issuing magistrates are not to be confined by niggardly limitations or by restrictions on the use of their common sense; and that their determination of probable cause should be paid great deference by reviewing courts. But we cannot sustain this warrant without diluting important safeguards that assure that the judgment of a disinterested judicial officer will interpose itself between the police and the citizenry.

The judgment of the Court of Appeals is reversed and the case is remanded to that court for further proceedings consistent with this opinion.

It is so ordered.

Information given by an informant not engaged in criminal activity The preceding discussion focused on informants who are themselves engaged in criminal activity and who therefore suffer from low credibility. If the information comes from noncriminal sources, the courts tend to look more favorably on the informant's reliability.

The importance of the identity of the informant The Constitution does not require an officer to reveal the identity of an informant either to the magistrate when seeking the issuance of a warrant or during the trial. As long as the magistrate is convinced that the police officer is truthfully describing what the informant told him or her, the informant need not be produced nor his or her identity revealed. For example, based on an informant's tip, police arrested a suspect without a warrant and searched him in conjunction with the arrest. Heroin was found on his person. During the trial, the police officer refused to reveal the name of the informant, claiming that the informant was reliable because the information he had given in the past had led to arrests. After being convicted, the defendant appealed. The Court held that a warrantless arrest, search, and seizure may be valid even if the police officer does not reveal the identity of the informant, because other evidence at the trial proved that the officer did rely on credible information supplied by a reliable informant. The Court added that the issue in this case was whether probable cause existed, not the defendant's guilt or innocence (*McCray v. Illinois,* 386 U.S. 300 [1967]).

McCray v. Illinois (1967)

An exception to the preceding rule is that, when the informant's identity is material to the issue of guilt or innocence, identity must be revealed. If the state refuses to reveal the identity of the informant, the case must be dismissed. Under what circumstances the informant's identity is material to the issue of guilt or innocence is a matter to be determined by the judge. In *McCray,* the Court said that the determination of whether the informant's name should be revealed "rests entirely with the judge who hears the motion to suppress to decide whether he needs such disclosure as to the informant in order to decide whether the officer is a believable witness." If the judge decides that the informant's name should be disclosed because the information is "material" (although nobody knows what that really means) to the issue of guilt or innocence, then the police must either drop the case to preserve the informant's anonymity or disclose the name and thereby blow his or her cover. An alternative to disclosing the informant's name in court is to hold an *in camera* (private) hearing, producing the informant only before the judge so he or she can interview the informant in private.

- *Information given by an ordinary citizen.* Most courts have ruled that the ordinary citizen who is either a victim of a crime or an eyewitness to a crime is a reliable informant, even though his or her reliability has not been established by previous incidents. For example, suppose a woman tells an officer that she has personally witnessed a particular individual selling narcotics in the adjoining apartment, gives a detailed description of the alleged seller, and describes the way sales are made. There is probable cause to obtain a warrant or, in exigent (meaning *emergency*) circumstances, to make a warrantless arrest.
- *Information given by another police officer.* Information given by a police officer is considered reliable by the courts. In one case, the Court noted, "Observations of fellow officers of the government engaged in a common investigation are plainly a reliable basis for a warrant applied for by one of their number" (*United States v. Ventresca,* 380 U.S. 102 [1965]). Sometimes the police officer makes an affidavit in response to statements made by other police officers, as in cases of inside information from a detective or orders from a superior. The Court has implied that under these circumstances the arrest or search is valid only if the officer who passed on the information acted with probable cause.
- *"Stale" information.* In search and seizure cases, problems may arise concerning whether the information provided has become "stale" after a period of time. The problem occurs in search and seizure cases because in these cases the issue is always whether evidence of a crime may be found at that time in a certain place. In one case,

the Court held that there was no probable cause to search for illegal sale of alcohol in a hotel where the affidavit alleged that a purchase of beer had occurred more than three weeks earlier (*Sgro v. United States*, 287 U.S. 206 [1932]).

Sgro v. United States (1932)

A more recent case involved an informant's claim that he had witnessed a drug sale at the suspect's residence approximately five months earlier and had observed a shoe box containing a large amount of cash that belonged to the suspect. The Court said that this was stale information that could not be used to establish probable cause (*United States v. Leon*, 468 U.S. 897 [1984]). However, the Court has not specified how much time may elapse between the informant's observation and the issuing of a warrant, stating instead that the issue "must be determined by the circumstances of each case."

United States v. Leon (1984)

Information plus Corroboration

If probable cause cannot be established by using information provided by the informant alone (despite the now more liberal *Gates* test for determining probable cause), the police officer can remedy the deficiency by conducting his or her own corroborative investigation. Together, the two may establish probable cause even if the informant's information or the corroborative findings alone would not have been sufficient. For example, suppose an informant tells a police officer that she heard that X is selling drugs and that the sales usually are made at night in the apartment of X's girlfriend. That information alone would not establish probable cause. However, if the officer, acting on the information, places the apartment under surveillance, sees people going in and out, and is actually told by a buyer that he has just purchased drugs from X inside the apartment, there is a strong basis for probable cause either to arrest X without a warrant (if exigent circumstances exist) or to obtain a warrant from a magistrate.

A leading case on information plus corroboration is *Draper v. United States*, 358 U.S. 307 (1959). In that case, a narcotics agent received information from an informant that the petitioner had gone to Chicago to bring 3 ounces of heroin back to Denver by train. The informant also gave a detailed description of Draper. Given this information, police officers set up surveillance of trains coming from Chicago on the mornings of September 8 and 9, the dates the informant had indicated. On seeing a man who fit the informant's description, the police moved in and made the arrest. Heroin and a syringe were seized in a *search incident to the arrest* (meaning a search that takes place during or right after the arrest). During trial, Draper sought exclusion of the evidence, claiming that the information given to the police failed to establish probable cause. Ultimately, the Supreme Court disagreed, saying that information received from an informant that is corroborated by an officer may be sufficient to provide probable cause for an arrest, even though such information was hearsay and would not otherwise have been admissible in a criminal trial.

Probable Cause and Motor Vehicle Passengers

In *Maryland v. Pringle,* 540 U.S. 366 (2003), the Court decided an important issue police officers face daily: Can the police arrest the passenger of a motor vehicle if they have probable cause to arrest the driver? In this case, a police officer stopped a car for speeding. The officer searched the car and seized $763 from the glove compartment and cocaine from behind the back-seat armrest. The three occupants denied ownership of the drugs and money. Pringle, who was the passenger on the front seat, was later convicted of drug possession with intent to distribute and was given ten years in prison without the possibility of parole. He appealed, saying that "the mere finding of cocaine in the back armrest," when he was "a front-seat passenger in a car being driven by its owner, was insufficient to establish probable cause for an arrest for drug possession."

The Court disagreed, holding instead that the officer had probable cause to arrest Pringle because it was an

> entirely reasonable inference from [the particular facts in this case] that any or all three of the occupants had knowledge of, and exercised dominion and control over, the cocaine. Thus a reasonable officer could conclude that there was probable cause to believe Pringle committed the crime of possession of cocaine, either solely or jointly.

Pringle had asserted that this was a case of "guilt by association," and cited *Ybarra v. Illinois* (444 U.S. 85 [1979]), in which the Court held that a search of a bartender for possession of a controlled substance, based on a warrant, "did not permit body searches of all the tavern's patrons and that the police could not pat down the patrons for weapons, absent individualized suspicion." The Court rejected this analogy, saying that Pringle and the other passengers were "in a relatively small automobile, not a public tavern," and that in this case "it was reasonable for the officer to infer a common enterprise among the three men."

It is important to note that *Pringle* does not automatically authorize the arrest of all car passengers if probable cause exists that a crime (such as drugs being found, as in the *Pringle* case) has been committed in the car. Instead, the test is "whether or not there is probable cause to believe that the passengers committed the crime solely or jointly." In the *Pringle* case, such inference was reasonable from the facts of that particular case. Under other circumstances, the inference might not be reasonable. Ultimately, whether the inference is reasonable or unreasonable is for the courts to decide on a case-by-case basis.

Reasonable Suspicion

Another important term in law enforcement is *reasonable suspicion*, a level of proof required by the courts in stop and frisk cases. A **level of proof** is the degree of certainty required by the law for an act to be legal. As a level of proof, reasonable

Table 3.1 Levels of Proof

Level of Proof	Degree of Certainty	Type of Proceeding
Absolute certainty	100%	Not required in any legal proceeding
Guilt beyond a reasonable doubt	↑	Convict an accused; prove every element of a criminal act
Clear and convincing evidence		Denial of bail in some states and insanity defense in some states
Probable cause*		Issuance of warrant; search, seizure, and arrest without warrant filing of an indictment
Preponderance of the evidence*		Winning a civil case; affirmative criminal defense
Reasonable suspicion		Stop and frisk by police
Suspicion		Start a police or grand jury investigation
Reasonable doubt		Acquit an accused
Hunch		Not sufficient in any legal proceeding
No information	0%	Not sufficient in any legal proceeding

*Probable cause and preponderance of the evidence have the same level of certainty—more than 50%. This means that anything above 50% will suffice. The difference is that "probable cause" is used in criminal proceedings, whereas "preponderance of the evidence" is usually used in civil proceedings, although aspects of a criminal proceeding use this term as well.

suspicion ranks below probable cause but above suspicion in its degree of certainty. (See Table 3.1 for more rankings of levels of proof.) This section looks at the definition of reasonable suspicion and how the "totality of circumstances" affects reasonable suspicion.

Reasonable Suspicion Defined

Black's Law Dictionary defines **reasonable suspicion** as that "quantum of knowledge sufficient to induce an ordinarily prudent and cautious man under similar circumstances to believe criminal activity is at hand. It must be based on specific and articulable facts, which, taken together with rational inferences from those facts, reasonably warrant intrusion."[3]

Alabama v. White (1990)

The Court has not clearly defined reasonable suspicion. However, in *Alabama v. White* (496 U.S. 325 [1990]), the Court said: Reasonable suspicion is a less demanding standard than probable cause not only in the sense that reasonable suspicion can be established with information that is different in quantity or content than that required to establish probable cause, but also in the sense that reasonable suspicion can arise from information that is less reliable than that required to show probable cause. The Case Brief gives more insight into *Alabama v. White*, which is the leading case on reasonable suspicion.

CASE BRIEF: The Leading Case on Reasonable Suspicion
Alabama v. White, 496 U.S. 325 (1990)

Facts: Police responded to an anonymous telephone call that conveyed the following information: White would be leaving her apartment at a particular time in a brown Plymouth station wagon with the right taillight lens broken; she was in the process of going to Dobey's Motel; and she would be in possession of about an ounce of cocaine hidden inside a brown attaché case. The police saw White leave her apartment without an attaché case, but she got into a car matching the description given in the telephone call. When the car reached the area where the motel was located, a patrol unit stopped the car and told White she was suspected of carrying cocaine. After obtaining her permission to search the car, the police found the brown attaché case. Upon request, White provided the combination to the lock; the officers found marijuana and arrested her. At the station, the officers also found cocaine in her purse. White was charged with and convicted of possession of marijuana and cocaine. She appealed her conviction, saying that the police did not have reasonable suspicion required under *Terry v. Ohio*, 392 U.S. 1 (1968), to make a valid stop and that the evidence obtained therefore should be suppressed.

Issue: *Did the anonymous tip, corroborated by independent police work, constitute reasonable suspicion to justify a stop? Yes.*

Supreme Court Decision: The stop made by the police was based on reasonable suspicion, and so the evidence obtained was admissible in court.

Case Significance: This case categorically states that reasonable suspicion is not as demanding a standard as probable cause and that it can be established with information that is different in quality and quantity from that required for probable cause. The information

here from the anonymous telephone call would likely not, in and of itself, have established reasonable suspicion. The Court said that "although it is a close question, the totality of the circumstances demonstrates that significant aspects of the informant's story were sufficiently corroborated by the police to furnish reasonable suspicion." What established reasonable suspicion in this case was therefore a combination of an anonymous telephone tip and corroboration by the police.

Excerpts from the Decision: Reasonable suspicion is a less demanding standard than probable cause not only in the sense that reasonable suspicion can be established with information that is different in quantity or content than that required to establish probable cause, but also in the sense that reasonable suspicion can arise from information that is less reliable than that required to show probable cause. *Adams v. Williams* demonstrates as much. We there assumed that the unverified tip from the known informant might not have been reliable enough to establish probable cause, but nevertheless found it sufficiently reliable to justify a *Terry* stop. Reasonable suspicion, like probable cause, is dependent upon both the content of information possessed by police and its degree of reliability. Both factors—quantity and quality—are considered in the "totality of the circumstances—the whole picture," that must be taken into account when evaluating whether there is reasonable suspicion. Thus, if a tip has a relatively low degree of reliability, more information will be required to establish the requisite quantum of suspicion than would be required if the tip were more reliable. The Gates Court applied its totality-of-the-circumstances approach in this manner, taking into account the facts known to the officers from personal observation, and giving the anonymous tip the weight it deserved in light of its indicia of reliability as established through independent police work. The same approach applies in the reasonable-suspicion context, the only difference being the level of suspicion that must be established. Contrary to the court below, we conclude that when the officers stopped respondent, the anonymous tip had been sufficiently corroborated to furnish reasonable suspicion that respondent was engaged in criminal activity and that the investigative stop therefore did not violate the Fourth Amendment.

The Court's opinion in Gates gave credit to the proposition that because an informant is shown to be right about some things, he is probably right about other facts that he has alleged, including the claim that the object of the tip is engaged in criminal activity. Thus, it is not unreasonable to conclude in this case that the independent corroboration by the police of significant aspects of the informer's predictions imparted some degree of reliability to the other allegations made by the caller.

We think it also important that, as in Gates, "the anonymous [tip] contained a range of details relating not just to easily obtained facts and conditions existing at the time of the tip, but to future actions of third parties ordinarily not easily predicted." The fact that the officers found a car precisely matching the caller's description in front of the 235 building

is an example of the former. Anyone could have "predicted" that fact because it was a condition presumably existing at the time of the call. What was important was the caller's ability to predict respondent's future behavior, because it demonstrated inside information— a special familiarity with respondent's affairs. The general public would have had no way of knowing that respondent would shortly leave the building, get in the described car, and drive the most direct route to Dobey's Motel. Because only a small number of people are generally privy to an individual's itinerary, it is reasonable for police to believe that a person with access to such information is likely to also have access to reliable information about that individual's illegal activities. See ibid. When significant aspects of the caller's predictions were verified, there was reason to believe not only that the caller was honest but also that he was well informed, at least well enough to justify the stop.

Although it is a close case, we conclude that under the totality of the circumstances the anonymous tip, as corroborated, exhibited sufficient indicia of reliability to justify the investigatory stop of respondent's car. We therefore reverse the judgment of the Court of Criminal Appeals of Alabama and remand the case for further proceedings not inconsistent with this opinion.

So ordered.

The Totality of Circumstances

United States v. Arvizu (2002)

In *United States v. Arvizu* (534 U.S. 266 [2002]), the Court said that "in making reasonable suspicion determinations, reviewing courts must look at the totality of the circumstances in each case to see whether the detaining officer has a particularized and objective basis for suspecting wrongdoing." In this case, the U.S. Border Patrol installed sensors in several border areas in Arizona. The sensors detected a vehicle; the officers followed for several miles, and then stopped the vehicle.

The stop was based on the following observations: the roads taken by the vehicle were remote and not well suited for the vehicle type, the time the vehicle was on the road coincided with a shift change for roving patrols in the area, the vehicle slowed dramatically upon first observing the officer, the driver of the vehicle would not look at the officer when passing, the children in the vehicle seemed to have their feet propped up on some cargo, the children waved mechanically at the officer as if being instructed, and the vehicle made turns that would allow it to completely avoid the checkpoint.

After the stop and having obtained a valid consent from Arvizu, the officer searched the vehicle and found drugs. Arvizu later claimed that the search was illegal because there was no reasonable suspicion for the stop, because each of the indicators noted was an innocent activity and therefore "carried little or no weight in the reasonable-suspicion calculus." The Court disagreed, saying that "in making reasonable-suspicion determinations, reviewing courts must look at the 'totality of the circumstances' of each case to see whether the detaining officer has a 'particularized and objective basis' for suspecting legal wrongdoing." The Court added that "this process allows officers to draw on their own experiences and specialized training to make inferences from and deductions about the cumulative information available." The Court then concluded that, although each of the factors used by the officer in this case is "susceptible to innocent explanation," taken together, they constituted a sufficient and objective basis for legally stopping the vehicle.

Probable Cause and Reasonable Suspicion Compared

Probable Cause	Reasonable Suspicion
Legal definition: Stated by the Court in *Brinegar v. United States,* 338 U.S. 160 (1949)	No good legal definition given by the Court
Practical definition: "More likely than not"	Practical definition: "Less certain than probable cause, but more than mere suspicion"

Sufficient for arrest	Sufficient for stop and frisk, but not for arrest
After arrest, officer may search arrested person and immediate vicinity	After valid stop, officer can frisk suspect if there is fear for officer's safety.
Sufficient for issuance of warrant	Not sufficient for issuance of warrant

Clearly, as noted in this chapter, probable cause and reasonable suspicion are "fluid" concepts that cannot be defined with precision. It is, however, important to remember the following:

- Probable cause requires a higher degree of certainty than reasonable suspicion.
- Both terms are subjective; what is probable cause or reasonable suspicion to one officer, judge, or juror may not be to another.
- If information such as a tip has a low degree of reliability (quality), more information (quantity) will be required to establish probable cause or reasonable suspicion than if the information were more reliable.
- Both terms are additive, meaning that the more facts an officer can articulate, the greater is the likelihood that probable cause or reasonable suspicion will be established.

Totality of circumstances must be considered when evaluating whether probable cause or reasonable suspicion or probable cause exists.

Appealing a Finding of Probable Cause or Reasonable Suspicion

The finding of probable cause is initially made by a police officer (in arrests or property searches without a warrant) and by a judge or magistrate in arrests or searches with a warrant. Reasonable suspicion is always initially determined by the officer in stop and frisk cases. However, these determinations are not binding; they can always be, and often are, challenged during trial. Should the challenge be made, usually in a defendant's motion to suppress the evidence obtained, the trial court then determines whether probable cause or reasonable suspicion did, in fact, exist.

As stated repeatedly in the chapter, the trial court's determination of probable cause or reasonable suspicion is not final and can be reviewed on appeal. In one case, the defendants had pleaded guilty to possession of cocaine with intent to distribute, but they reserved the right to appeal the federal district court's denial of their motion to suppress the evidence of cocaine found in their car. The court had ruled that the officer had reasonable suspicion to stop and question the petitioners as they entered their car, as well as probable cause to remove one of the car's panels, which concealed two kilos of cocaine.

The issue raised on appeal was whether a trial court's findings of reasonable suspicion and probable cause are final or whether they can be reviewed by an appellate court on appeal.

Ornelas et al. v. United States (1996)

In *Ornelas et al. v. United States,* 517 U.S. 690 (1996), the Supreme Court held that the ultimate questions of reasonable suspicion to stop and presence of probable cause to make a warrantless arrest "should be reviewed *de novo*" (meaning anew, afresh, or a second time) on appeal. The Court stressed that "we have never, when reviewing a probable-cause or reasonable-suspicion determination ourselves, expressly deferred to the trial court's determination." It added that "independent review is therefore necessary if appellate courts are to maintain control of and to clarify the legal principles." The Court cautioned, however, that "a reviewing court should take care both to review findings of historical fact only for clear error and to give due weight to inferences drawn from those facts by resident judges and local law enforcement officers." In sum, while trial court findings of probable cause and reasonable suspicion are reviewable on appeal, such reviews must be based on clear error and give due weight to whatever inferences and conclusions may have been drawn by the trial judge and law enforcement officers.

Summary

1. Probable Cause
   - *Legal definition:* Probable cause exists when "the facts and circumstances within the officers' knowledge and of which they had reasonably trustworthy information are sufficient in themselves to warrant a man of reasonable caution in the belief that an offense has been or is being committed."
   - *Practical definition:* Probable cause exists when it is *more likely than not* (more than 50 percent certainty) that the suspect committed an offense or that the items sought can be found in a certain place.
   - In the absence of probable cause, the act is illegal, and the evidence obtained must be excluded by the court.
   - Probable cause cannot be established by what is found after an illegal search or arrest.
   - *Probable cause is established in three ways:* Officer's own knowledge, information given by an informant, or information plus corroboration.
   - *Obtaining a warrant offers two clear advantages:* Probable cause is presumed present, and it is a good defense in civil cases for damages.

   - *Probable cause can be compared to other levels of proof:* Probable cause is lower than clear and convincing evidence, but it is higher than reasonable suspicion.

2. Reasonable Suspicion
   - *Legal definition:* "That quantum of knowledge sufficient to induce an ordinarily prudent and cautious man under similar circumstances to believe criminal activity is at hand."
   - *Practical definition:* It is lower in certainty than probable cause but higher than mere suspicion.
   - Determination of reasonable suspicion must be based on the totality of the circumstances, taking into account an officer's knowledge and experience.
   - It is required during stop and frisk cases but not sufficient for arrest.
   - Reasonable suspicion is initially determined by the officer but reviewable by a magistrate, trial judge, and appellate court judge.
   - *Reasonable suspicion can be compared to other levels of proof:* Reasonable suspicion is lower than probable cause but higher than mere suspicion.

Review Questions and Hypothetical Cases

1. What is the U.S. Supreme Court's definition of *probable cause*? For practical purposes, when does probable cause exist?

2. The Court says that probable cause is to be determined by using the standard of an "objectively reasonable police officer." What does that mean? Give your own example of an incident where an "objectively reasonable police officer" would have concluded that he or she had probable cause to make an arrest.

3. What are the advantages of obtaining a warrant in an arrest and in search and seizure cases?

4. What are the three general ways in which probable cause can be established? Discuss each.

5. How has the case of *Illinois v. Gates* changed the interpretation of the two-pronged test established earlier in *Aguilar v. Texas*?

6. What did the U.S. Supreme Court say in *Spinelli v. United States*? Was there probable cause in that case or not? Justify your answer.

7. Define *reasonable suspicion*. For what purpose can it be used in law enforcement?

8. "Reasonable suspicion determinations must be based on the totality of the circumstances." Explain what that means.

9. "A police officer's determination of probable cause or reasonable suspicion is final." Is that statement true or false? Discuss.

10. Officer P, a university police officer, received information that a student in a campus dormitory was selling drugs. That information was conveyed to Officer P by an anonymous caller to the officer's cell phone. The officer knew the student-suspect and had similar suspicions. Officer P immediately went to the dormitory and stopped the student as he was getting out of the building. He arrested him, searched his pockets, and found drugs. Was what the officer did valid? Justify your answer.

11. Officer Z was told by a criminal informant that the informant went out drinking with X last night and that X told him he had cocaine in his (X's) dormitory room. Acting on this information, Officer Z went to a magistrate and asked for a warrant to search X's dormitory room. You are the magistrate. Will you issue the warrant? Why or why not?

12. While on patrol, Officer M was told by a neighbor of P that P was selling drugs. Asked how he knew this, the neighbor-informant said that the last few evenings he saw people come in and out of that house and that "those people are seedy and suspicious, and always look like they are high on drugs, particularly after they come out of P's house." The neighbor said further that he was in the driveway of the house one evening last week and smelled marijuana coming from P's house. The informant added that P moved into the house about a year ago, did not have children, seemed to have no work and yet appeared to live well; that P and his wife refused to associate with anybody in the neighborhood; and that "they are simply weird." You are a judge from whom Officer M asks for the issuance of a warrant based on this information from a neighbor-citizen. Will you issue the warrant? Justify your response.

13. Officer A was told by an informant that the informant had suspicions that C, in the apartment next door, was selling drugs from her (C's) apartment. During the next three nights, Officer A surveilled C's apartment and saw people of all kinds going in and out. Officer A stopped one of them who, upon being stopped, threw away what she had in her hand. That turned out to be crack cocaine. After retrieving the crack cocaine, Officer A entered the apartment without a warrant and found more cocaine on the living room table. Officer A seized the drugs. Was there anything invalid about what Officer A did? State your reasons.

Key Terms

Go to the Criminal Procedure 7e website for flash cards that will help you master the definitions of these terms.

level of proof, 90

man of reasonable
    caution, 76

probable cause, 75

reasonable suspicion,
    91

"totality of circumstances" test
    (on information given by
    an informant), 85

Holdings of Key Cases

See Appendix C for information on how to find cases in this chapter on FindLaw.com.

(*Note:* U.S. Supreme Court cases are easily accessible through the Internet. Go to google.com or yahoo.com, and then enter the case title (as in *Miranda v. Arizona*). Or, go to *http://www.findlaw.com/casecode/supreme.html*, and then click on Supreme Court Decisions "by year." Click the year the case was decided. You will then see court decisions alphabetically arranged. Note, however, that these means of Internet access may change.)

Aguilar v. Texas, **378 U.S. 108 (1964)** The Supreme Court established a two-pronged test for determining probable cause on the basis of information obtained from an informant: (1) reliability of the informant and (2) reliability of the informant's information. Both conditions of the test must be satisfied before probable cause can be established on information obtained from an informant. (*Note:* The independent, two-pronged *Aguilar* test was replaced in 1983 by the "totality of circumstances" test in the *Illinois v. Gates* decision.)

Alabama v. White, **496 U.S. 325 (1990)** Reasonable suspicion is a less demanding standard than probable cause. It can be established with information different in quantity or content from that required to establish probable cause. It may also be established with the help of an anonymous telephone tip.

Brinegar v. United States, **338 U.S. 160 (1949)** Probable cause is more than bare suspicion; it exists when the facts and circumstances within the officers' knowledge and of which they had reasonably trustworthy information are sufficient in themselves to justify "a man of reasonable caution" in the belief that an offense has been or is being committed.

Draper v. United States, **358 U.S. 307 (1959)** Information received from an informant that is corroborated by an officer may be sufficient to provide probable cause for an arrest even though the information was hearsay and would not otherwise have been admissible in a criminal trial.

Illinois v. Gates, **462 U.S. 213 (1983)** A warrant may be issued on the basis of affidavits that are entirely hearsay (such as when a police officer swears to facts reported to him or her by the crime victim, witnesses, or police informants). However, the affidavit must show by a *totality of the circumstances* that there is a fair probability that contraband or evidence of a crime will be found in a particular place.

Maryland v. Pringle, **540 U.S. 366 (2003)** The police officer had probable cause to arrest the front passenger of a car from where baggies of cocaine were recovered between the back-seat armrest and the back seat. From the facts of the case, it was an "entirely reasonable inference that any or all of the car's occupants had knowledge of, and exercised dominion and control over, the cocaine."

McCray v. Illinois, **386 U.S. 300 (1967)** A warrantless arrest, search, and seizure may be valid even when the police officer does not reveal the identity of the informant, if other evidence at the trial proves that the officer did rely on credible information supplied by a reliable informant. The issue in this case was whether probable cause existed, not the defendant's guilt or innocence.

Michigan v. Summers, **452 U.S. 692 (1981)** The general rule is that every arrest, as well as every seizure having the essential attribute of a formal arrest, is unreasonable unless supported by probable cause.

Ornelas et al. v. United States, **517 U.S. 690 (1996)** An appellate court that reviews the legality of police conduct undertaken without a warrant should conduct a *de novo* (new or fresh) review of the trial's ultimate questions of reasonable suspicion and probable cause and not simply accept the trial court's decision that reasonable suspicion or probable cause did exist.

Sgro v. United States, **287 U.S. 206 (1932)** There was no probable cause to search for illegal alcohol sales in a hotel where the affidavit alleged that a purchase of beer had taken place more than three weeks earlier. The grounds for probable cause had become "stale."

Spinelli v. United States, **393 U.S. 410 (1969)** "Innocent-seeming activity and data" and a "bald and unilluminating assertion of suspicion" in an affidavit are not to be given weight in a magistrate's determination of probable cause. An officer may use credible hearsay to establish probable cause, but an affidavit based on an informant's tip must satisfy the two-pronged *Aguilar* test.

United States v. Arvizu, **534 U.S. 266 (2002)** "In making reasonable-suspicion determinations, reviewing courts must look at the totality of the circumstances of each case to see whether the detaining officer has a particularized and objective basis for suspecting legal wrongdoing."

United States v. Harris, **403 U.S. 573 (1971)** A suspect's reputation for criminal activity may be considered by the magistrate issuing the warrant when establishing probable cause.

United States v. Leon, **468 U.S. 897 (1984)** Five-month-old information from an informant is "stale" and cannot be used to establish probable cause. In this case, an informant supplied information that he had witnessed a sale of drugs at the suspect's residence approximately five months earlier and had at that time observed a shoe box containing a large amount of cash that belonged to the suspect.

United States v. Ortiz, **422 U.S. 891 (1975)** In determining probable cause, "officers are entitled to draw reasonable inferences from . . . facts in light of their knowledge of the area and their prior experience with aliens and smugglers."

United States v. Ventresca, **380 U.S. 102 (1965)** The Supreme Court recognizes that affidavits or complaints are often prepared hastily in the midst of a criminal investigation. Therefore, the policy is to interpret the allegations in a commonsense rather than in an overly technical manner and to uphold the sufficiency of the affidavit in close cases.

Whiteley v. Warden, **401 U.S. 560 (1971)** What is not in the affidavit does not count toward establishing probable cause.

 You Be the Judge . . .

In the United States Court of Appeals for the Ninth Circuit

In Lake Forrest, California, Deputy Sheriff Perez responded to a 911 call from a resident in the local Extended Stay America: the caller said that there were sounds of a woman being beaten in the next room. When he arrived, Deputy Perez met the caller in the lobby, and she showed him the room from which she had heard the noises of what she thought was domestic violence. Deputy Perez knocked on the door and heard a male voice say, "Honey, I think somebody is here."

The male, Brooks, came to the door, and Deputy Perez told him a complaint about a domestic disturbance had been called in, to which Brooks responded, "I knew you were coming. She was very loud." The Deputy noticed the room was a mess and asked if there was a female in the room, and

Brooks said that there was a woman in the bathroom, probably taking a shower. Deputy Perez asked to speak with the woman, and Brooks turned toward the bathroom. Deputy Perez stepped into the room without asking, then heard a woman crying from the bathroom and told Brooks to sit down to tell him what happened. Brooks claimed there had been a verbal argument, and the woman, Bengis, came out of the bathroom, and stated several times that she had not been hurt and needed no assistance.

Deputy Perez asked Brooks for ID, and Brooks said he had none with him, and showed him Bengis's driver's license. Perez asked Brooks if there was anything illegal in the room, and Brooks said there was some marijuana in the dresser. Brooks gave Deputy Perez permission to search for the marijuana, and he found Brooks's driver's license. Brooks then admitted he had absconded from parole in Oregon.

Deputy Perez testified that based on his training and experience, victims of domestic violence often initially deny the incident and are hesitant to accept assistance.

How will you decide this legal issue? Did Deputy Perez have probable cause to believe that a crime had taken place at the time he remained in the room to ask Brooks about any contraband (illegal items) in the room?

The Court's decision The U.S. Court of Appeals for the Ninth Circuit decided that Deputy Perez's decision to remain in the room "for a few minutes" was based upon probable cause that a crime had occurred. The 911 call, taken with the presence of Bengis crying in the room, was enough to justify the officer's remaining for a few minutes questioning to satisfy himself that the situation was as Bengis initially claimed. It was perfectly reasonable for Deputy Perez to be incredulous of Bengis's initial denials. *U.S. v. Brooks*, 367 F.3d 1128 (9th Cir., 2004).

In the United States Court of Appeals for the Sixth Circuit

In Detroit, Michigan, on October 1, 2001, ATF Agent Hoffman sought a search warrant for Chapman's residence in eastern Detroit. Agent Hoffman was responding to a tip from a confidential informant (the "CI"). Agent Hoffman put the following information in his affidavit to establish probable cause:

- On 9/25/2001, the CI claimed to have seen Chapman with an assault rifle at his residence nine months earlier.

- On 9/25/2001, the CI claimed to have seen Chapman one month earlier dealing drugs elsewhere in the city, while armed with a pistol.

- The CI had provided accurate information to the ATF previously, which resulted in the seizure of handguns and drugs.

- Chapman had been previously incarcerated six times for weapons and drug offenses.

- Agent Hoffman found duct-tape packaging in Chapman's curbside trash that Hoffman knew to be commonly used to package narcotics.

- A canine officer's dog indicated the presence of drugs in a file cabinet containing the duct-tape packaging.

The federal magistrate judge issued a search warrant based only upon this affidavit for Chapman's residence. ATF agents went to serve the search warrant at Chapman's residence. They found Chapman outside his residence and $25,000, cocaine, heroin, two pistols, and an assault rifle in his bedroom. After being read his *Miranda* rights, Chapman admitted these items were his.

How will you decide this legal issue? Did the magistrate judge have probable cause to issue the search warrant based on the information in the affidavit?

The Court's decision The U.S. Court of Appeals for the Sixth Circuit decided that there was not enough in the affidavit to establish probable cause. The information on the weapon actually being in the residence was too old ("stale") for something as portable as a weapon. The information pertaining to the dog was too vague: there was no information that the canine officer's dog was trained to detect drugs, or whether there were any other substances that the canine was trained to alert to, or whether there was anything else that had been in the file cabinet that could have left residue that the canine could have alerted to. (In spite of the Court of Appeals' finding that the search warrant was invalid, the Court denied suppression of the evidence, since the ATF agents were relying on a search warrant that appeared valid. See "good faith exception" to the exclusionary rule in Chapter 4.) *U.S. v. Chapman*, 112 Fed. Appx. 469 (2004).

Recommended Readings

Patrick V. Banks. Note. *Fourth and Fourteenth Amendments—search and seizure—police officers with probable cause to search a vehicle may inspect a passenger's belongings found in the vehicle that are capable of concealing the object of search* Wyoming vs. Hougton, *119 S.Ct. 1297 (1999).* 10 Seton Hall Constitutional Law Journal 2: 543, 575 (2000).

Daniel D. Blinka et. al. *Search and seizure-search incident to arrest—probable cause for arrest.* 78 Wisconsin Lawyer 6: 37–38 (June 2005).

Frank R. Cooper. *The un-balanced Fourth Amendment: A cultural study of the drug war, racial profiling and* Arvizu. Villanova Law Review 852, 895 (2002).

Gebriel M. Helmer. Note. *Strip search and the felony detainee: A case for reasonable suspicion.* 81 Boston University Law Review 1: 239, 288 (2001).

Debra M. Nelson. Note. Illinois v. Wardlow: *A single factor totality.* Utah Law Review 2: 509, 541 (2001).

Patrick Yatchak. Note. *Breaching the peace: The trivialization of the Fourth Amendment reasonableness standard in the wake of* Atwater v. City of Lago Vista, *121 S.Ct. 1536 (2001).* 25 Hamline Law Review 2: 329–372 (2002).

Marvin Zalman. *Fleeing from the Fourth Amendment.* 36 Criminal Law Bulletin 129 (2000).

Notes

1. Kermit L. Hall (ed.), *The Oxford Companion to the Supreme Court of the United States* (New York: Oxford University Press, 1992), pp. 681–682.
2. John G. Miles, Jr., David B. Richardson, and Anthony E. Scudellari, *The Law Officer's Pocket Manual* (Washington, D.C.: Bureau of National Affairs, 1988–89), 6:4.
3. Henry C. Black, *Black's Law Dictionary,* 6th ed., abridged (St. Paul, MN: West, 1991), p. 875.

Chapter **4** The Exclusionary Rule

What You Will Learn

- The purpose of the exclusionary rule is to deter police misconduct.

- The exclusionary rule is judge-made and can be eliminated by the courts.

- *Mapp v. Ohio* extended the exclusionary rule to state criminal proceedings.

- Illegally seized evidence and the fruit of the poisonous tree are both excludable.

- There are four general exceptions to the exclusionary rule.

- There are five types of proceedings to which the rule does not apply.

- There are arguments for and against the exclusionary rule.

- There are alternatives to the exclusionary rule, none of which is popular in the United States.

CASE BRIEFS

Mapp v. Ohio (1961)
Arizona v. Evans (1995)

The Top 5 Important Cases in the Exclusionary Rule

Silverthorne Lumber Co. v. United States **(1920):** Once the primary evidence (the "tree") is shown to have been unlawfully obtained, any secondary evidence (the "fruit") derived from it is also inadmissible. This case enunciated the fruit of the poisonous tree doctrine.

Elkins v. United States **(1960):** The Fourth Amendment prohibits the use of illegally obtained evidence in federal prosecutions, whether the evidence is obtained by federal or state officers. This case did away with the silver platter doctrine.

Mapp v. Ohio **(1961):** The exclusionary rule, which prohibits the use of evidence obtained as a result of unreasonable search and seizure, is applicable to state criminal proceedings.

Massachusetts v. Sheppard **(1984):** Evidence obtained by an illegal search is admissible in court when the officer conducting the search acted in objective reasonable reliance on a search warrant that is subsequently declared to be invalid.

United States v. Leon **(1984):** The Fourth Amendment's exclusionary rule should not be applied to bar the prosecution from using evidence that has been obtained by officers acting in reasonable reliance on a search warrant that is issued by a detached and neutral magistrate but that is ultimately found to be invalid because it lacked probable cause.

Introduction

The exclusionary rule is a controversial rule in criminal evidence that has generated debate among criminal justice professionals at all levels. No other rule of evidence has had as much impact on criminal cases. The rule is applied by the courts and has a direct effect on day-to-day law enforcement. It continues to undergo modification and refinement in

Supreme Court decisions. Every law enforcement officer should be thoroughly familiar with the exclusionary rule, because the success or failure of criminal prosecutions sometimes depends on it.

The Exclusionary Rule

This section looks at the definition of the exclusionary rule, its purpose, the role of judges in forming the rule, and how the rule developed in federal and in state courts.

The Exclusionary Rule Defined

The **exclusionary rule** provides that any evidence obtained by the government in violation of the Fourth Amendment guarantee against unreasonable search and seizure is not admissible in a criminal prosecution to prove guilt. U.S. Supreme Court decisions strongly suggest that the exclusionary rule applies only to Fourth Amendment search and seizure cases. But what happens if the constitutional right violated is a Fifth, Sixth, or Fourteenth Amendment right? For example, suppose X is charged with an offense and retains a lawyer to represent her. Nonetheless, the police interrogate X in the absence of her lawyer—a violation of her Sixth Amendment right to counsel. Or suppose X is interrogated by the police while in custody without having been given the *Miranda* warnings—a violation of her Fifth Amendment right to protection against self-incrimination. In both instances, the evidence obtained is inadmissible, but will it be suppressed under the exclusionary rule?

The Court has repeatedly stated that only the fruits, including any evidence obtained, of a violation of the Fourth Amendment guarantee of protection against unreasonable search and seizure will be suppressed under the exclusionary rule. In *United States v. Leon*, 468 U.S. 897 (1984), the Court said that the exclusionary rule is a "judicially created remedy designed to safeguard *Fourth Amendment* rights." Therefore, not every violation of a constitutional right comes under the exclusionary rule.

Evidence obtained in violation of any of the other constitutional rights is also excludable in a criminal trial—but not under the exclusionary rule. For example, suppose a confession is obtained without giving the suspect his or her *Miranda* warnings. *Miranda* is primarily a Fifth Amendment right to protection against self-incrimination, so it is the suspect's Fifth Amendment rights that are violated in this example. The evidence is excludable anyway, usually as a due process violation under the Fifth or Fourteenth Amendment. In *United States v. Patane* (542 U.S. 630 [2004]), involving an alleged violation of the *Miranda* warnings, the Court said that "the Self-Incrimination clause contains its own exclusionary rule," thus adding strength to the argument that the exclusionary rule does not apply to Fifth Amendment violations.

United States v. Leon (1984)

See Appendix C for information on how to find cases in this chapter on FindLaw.com.

United States v. Patane (2004)

United States v. Caceres (1979)

The exclusionary rule does not apply, however, if the violation is merely of a department policy rather than of a constitutional right (*United States v. Caceres,* 440 U.S. 741 [1979]). For example, suppose police department policy prohibits home searches without written consent. If an officer obtains evidence in the course of a home search without written consent, the exclusionary rule does not apply, because written consent is not required under the Constitution for the search to be valid. The evidence is admissible unless it is excludable under state statute or court decisions.

If the evidence was erroneously admitted by the judge during the trial, the defendant's conviction is overturned if appealed unless the error is proved by the prosecutor to be harmless. Appellate court judges determine what is a harmless error on a case-by-case basis from the facts and record of the case.

The Purpose of the Rule

United States v. Janis (1976)

The Court has stated in a number of cases that the primary purpose of the exclusionary rule is to *deter police misconduct,* adding in *United States v. Janis* (428 U.S. 433 [1976]) that where "the exclusionary rule does not result in appreciable deterrence, then, clearly, its use . . . is unwarranted." The assumption is that, if the evidence obtained illegally is not admitted in court, police misconduct in search and seizure cases will cease or be minimized. The rule now applies to federal and state cases. This means that evidence illegally seized by state or federal officers cannot be used in any state or federal prosecution. In the words of one writer: The exclusionary rule is the primary means by which the Constitution's prohibition of unreasonable searches and seizures is currently enforced; thus it is seen by some as the primary protection of personal privacy and security against police arbitrariness and brutality. It is also the basis for judges' decisions to exclude reliable incriminating evidence from the trials of persons accused of crimes, and it is thus considered by others to be little more than a misguided loophole through which criminals are allowed to escape justice.[1]

HIGHLIGHT

The Court's Justification for the Exclusionary Rule

"The effect of the Fourth Amendment is to put the courts of the United States and Federal officials, in the exercise of their power and authority, under limitations and restraints as to the exercise of such power and authority, and to forever secure the people, their persons, houses, papers, and effects, against unreasonable searches and seizures under the guise of law. This protection reaches all alike. . . . The tendency of those who execute the criminal laws of the country to obtain conviction by means of unlawful seizures and enforced confessions, the latter obtained after subjecting accused persons to unwarranted practices destructive of rights secured by the Federal Constitution, should find no sanction in the judgments of the courts, which are charged at all times with the support of the Constitution, and to which people of all conditions have a right to appeal for maintenance of such fundamental rights."

SOURCE: *Weeks v. United States,* 232 U.S. 383 (1914).

A Judge-Made Rule

Is the exclusionary rule a constitutional or a judge-made rule? If the rule is mandated by the Constitution, then the Supreme Court cannot eliminate it, and neither can Congress change it. If it is judge-made, however, the Court may eliminate it at any time, or, arguably, it can be modified by Congress. Some writers maintain that this rule of evidence is judge-made—that it cannot be found in the Constitution; instead, it has been established by case law. Its proponents disagree, claiming that the rule is of constitutional origin and therefore beyond the reach of Congress, even if Congress

Mapp v. Ohio (1961)

should want to limit it. The proponents point to a statement of the Court, in *Mapp v. Ohio,* 367 U.S. 643 (1961), that "the exclusionary rule is an essential part of both the Fourth and Fourteenth Amendments." However, the Court has more recently ruled in favor of the concept that the exclusionary rule is a judge-made rule of evidence. In *Arizona v. Evans,* 514 U.S. 1 (1995), the Court stated, "The exclu-

Arizona v. Evans (1995)

sionary rule operates as a judicially created remedy designed to safeguard against future violations of Fourth Amendment rights through the rule's general deterrent effect."

Historical Development

This section looks at how the exclusionary rule developed in both the federal and state courts.

In Federal Courts The exclusionary rule is of U.S. origin. In the words of one observer, "The exclusionary rule is the creation of the Supreme Court of the United States. It was unknown to the English law our ancestors brought with them to America and unknown to the generations that adopted the Fourth Amendment as part of the Constitution."[2]

The first exclusionary rule case involving searches and seizures was decided by the Court in 1886 when it held that the forced disclosure of papers amounting to evidence of a crime violated the constitutional right of the suspect to protection against unreasonable search and seizure, so such items were inadmissible in court

Boyd v. United States (1886)

proceedings (*Boyd v. United States,* 116 U.S. 616 [1886]). It is worth noting that two years before *Boyd,* the Court, in *Hopt v. The Territory of Utah* (110 U.S. 574 [1884]), addressed the issue of the exclusion of a confession in a murder case. The *Hopt* case, however, involved a confession and was not a search and seizure case to which the exclusionary rule traditionally applies. It was not until 1914 that evidence illegally obtained by federal officers held to be excluded in all federal criminal prosecutions (*Weeks v. United States,* 232 U.S. 383 [1914]). In the *Weeks*

Weeks v. United States (1914)

case, the Court stated:

> The efforts of the courts and their officials to bring the guilty to punishment, praiseworthy as they are, are not to be aided by the sacrifice of those great principles established by years of endeavor and suffering which have resulted in their embodiment in the fundamental law of the land. . . . To sanction such

proceedings would be to affirm by judicial decision a manifest neglect, if not an open defiance, of the prohibitions of the Constitution, intended for the protection of the people against such unauthorized action.

From 1914 to 1960, federal courts admitted evidence of a federal crime if the evidence had been illegally obtained by state officers, as long as it had not been obtained by or in connivance with federal officers. This dubious practice was known as the **silver platter doctrine**, a procedure that permitted federal courts to admit evidence illegally seized by state law enforcement officers and handed over to federal officers for use in federal cases. Under this doctrine, such evidence was admissible because the illegal act was not committed by federal officers. In 1960, the Court put an end to this questionable practice by holding that the Fourth Amendment prohibited the use of illegally obtained evidence in federal prosecutions, whether obtained by federal or by state officers, thereby laying to rest the silver platter doctrine (*Elkins v. United States,* 364 U.S. 206 [1960]).

Elkins v. United States (1960)

In State Courts

In 1949, the Court held that state courts were not constitutionally required to exclude illegally obtained evidence, so the exclusionary rule did not apply to state prosecutions (*Wolf v. Colorado,* 338 U.S. 25 [1949]). In 1952, the Court modified that position somewhat by ruling that, although the exclusionary rule did not apply to the states, some searches were so "shocking" as to require exclusion of the evidence seized under the Due Process Clause. However, these were limited to cases involving coercion, violence, or brutality (*Rochin v. California,* 342 U.S. 165 [1952]). (Evidence obtained in violation of the constitutional right to due process is clearly inadmissible at present because it violates a constitutional right, but not necessarily under the exclusionary rule since the rule is limited to Fourth Amendment violations. The right to due process comes under the Fifth or Fourteenth Amendment. Moreover, due process violations at present are also actionable under federal law and can lead to police civil liability.) Finally, in *Mapp v. Ohio* (1961), the Court overruled the *Wolf* decision and held that the Fourth Amendment required state courts to exclude evidence obtained by unlawful searches and seizures.

Wolf v. Colorado (1949)

Rochin v. California (1952)

HIGHLIGHT

The Origin of the Exclusionary Rule

"Under the exclusionary rule, evidence obtained in violation of the Fourth Amendment cannot be used in a criminal trial against the victim of the illegal search and seizure. The Constitution does not require this remedy; it is a doctrine of judicial design. Excluded evidence is oftentimes quite reliable and the 'most probative information bearing on the guilt or innocence of the defendant.' Nevertheless, the rule's prohibition applies to such direct evidence, as well as to the 'fruit of the poisonous tree'—secondary evidence derived from the illegally seized evidence itself."

SOURCE: *United States v. Houltin,* 566 F.2d 1027 (5th Cir. 1978).

The Exclusionary Rule Applied to State Criminal Prosecutions: *Mapp v. Ohio*

In *Mapp v. Ohio,* 467 U.S. 643 (1961), the defendant was convicted of knowingly possessing certain lewd and lascivious books, pictures, and photographs, in violation of Ohio law. Three Cleveland police officers went to Mapp's residence, knocked on the door, and demanded entrance. However, after telephoning her attorney, Mapp refused to admit them without a search warrant. The officers again sought entrance three hours later when at least four additional officers had arrived on the scene. When Mapp did not come to the door immediately, the police forced their way in. Meanwhile, Mapp's attorney arrived, but the officers would not permit him to see his client or to enter the house. Mapp demanded to see the search warrant, which the officers by then claimed to have. When one of the officers held up a paper and claimed it was a warrant, Mapp grabbed the "warrant" and placed it in her bosom. A struggle ensued in which the officers handcuffed Mapp because, they claimed, she was belligerent.

In handcuffs, Mapp was forced into her bedroom, where the officers searched a dresser, a chest of drawers, a closet, and some suitcases. They also looked into a photo album and through personal papers belonging to Mapp. The search spread to include a child's bedroom, the living room, the kitchen, a dinette, and the basement of the building and a trunk found in it. The obscene materials, for possession of which Mapp was ultimately convicted, were discovered in the course of that widespread search. At the trial, no search warrant was produced by the prosecution, nor was the absence of a warrant explained. The seized materials were admitted into evidence by the trial court, and the defendant was convicted. On appeal, the Court excluded the evidence, holding that the exclusionary rule prohibiting the use of evidence in federal courts if illegally obtained was now applicable to state criminal proceedings.

Mapp is significant because, since 1961, the exclusionary rule has been applied to federal and state criminal prosecutions (read the Case Brief to learn more about *Mapp*). Before *Mapp,* the use of the exclusionary rule was left to the discretion of the states; some used it, whereas others did not. It is perhaps the second most important law enforcement case ever to be decided by the Court (the first was *Miranda v. Arizona,* which is discussed in Chapter 11).

What caused the Court to change its mind on the exclusionary rule, which, twelve years earlier in *Wolf v. Colorado* (338 U.S. 25 [1949]), it had ruled was not applicable in state prosecutions? In *Mapp,* the Court said that the *Wolf* case had been decided on factual grounds, implying that factual circumstances rather than philosophical considerations guided the Court's decision. The Court then noted that, when *Wolf* was decided, almost two-thirds of the states were opposed to the exclusionary rule. However, since then more than half of those states, by either legislation or judicial decision, had adopted the *Weeks* rule excluding illegally obtained evidence in their own criminal prosecutions.

The Court further noted that *Wolf* was partially based on the assumption that "other means of protection" against officer misconduct made the exclusionary rule unnecessary. The Court considered that a mistake, finding instead that the experience of California and other states had established that "such other remedies have been worthless and futile." The Court therefore decided to abandon what it deemed the "obvious futility of relegating the Fourth Amendment to the protection of other remedies." Clearly, the Court realized the need to apply the exclusionary rule to all criminal prosecutions to protect Fourth Amendment rights.

 CASE BRIEF: The Leading Case on the Extension of the Exclusionary Rule to the States

Mapp v. Ohio, 367 U.S. 643 (1961)

Facts: Mapp was convicted of possession of lewd and lascivious books, pictures, and photographs in violation of Ohio law. Three Cleveland police officers went to Mapp's residence pursuant to information that a person who was wanted in connection with a recent bombing was hiding out in her home. The officers knocked on the door and demanded entrance, but Mapp, telephoning her attorney, refused to admit them without a warrant. The officers again sought entrance three hours later, after the arrival of more police officers. When Mapp did not respond, the officers broke the door open. Mapp's attorney arrived but was denied access to his client. Mapp demanded to see the search warrant the police claimed they had. When one of the officers held up a paper and claimed it was the warrant, Mapp grabbed the paper and placed it in her bosom. A struggle ensued, and the paper was recovered after Mapp was handcuffed for being belligerent. A search of the house turned up a trunk that contained obscene materials. The materials were admitted into evidence at the trial, and Mapp was convicted of possession of obscene materials.

Issue: *Is evidence obtained in violation of the Fourth Amendment guarantee against unreasonable search and seizure admissible in state court? No.*

Supreme Court Decision: The exclusionary rule that prohibits the use of evidence obtained as a result of unreasonable search and seizure is applicable to state criminal proceedings.

Case Significance: The *Mapp* case is significant because the Court held that the exclusionary rule was thenceforth to be applied nationally, thus forbidding both state and federal courts from admitting evidence obtained illegally in violation of constitutional protection against unreasonable search and seizure. The facts in the *Mapp* case are given here, as detailed in the Court decision, to show why it was relatively "easy" for the Court to decide to exclude the evidence. In the minds of the Court justices, the facts in *Mapp* illustrate what can happen if police conduct is not restricted. *Mapp* was therefore an ideal case for the Court to use in settling an issue that had to be addressed: whether the exclusionary rule should now be applicable to state criminal proceedings. The facts in *Mapp* made it easier for the Court to answer that question in the affirmative.

Excerpts from the Decision: [O]ur holding that the exclusionary rule is an essential part of both the Fourth and Fourteenth Amendments is not only the logical dictate of prior cases, but it also makes very good sense. There is no war between the Constitution and common sense. Presently, a federal prosecutor may make no use of evidence illegally seized, but a State's attorney across the street may, although he supposedly is operating under the enforceable prohibitions of the same Amendment. Thus the State, by admitting evidence unlawfully seized, serves to encourage disobedience to the Federal

Constitution which it is bound to uphold. Moreover, as was said in *Elkins,* "[t]he very essence of a healthy federalism depends upon the avoidance of needless conflict between state and federal courts." Such a conflict, hereafter needless, arose this very Term, in *Wilson v. Schnettler,* 365 U.S. 381 (1961), in which, and in spite of the promise made by *Rea,* we gave full recognition to our practice in this regard by refusing to restrain a federal officer from testifying in a state court as to evidence unconstitutionally seized by him in the performance of his duties. Yet the double standard recognized until today hardly put such a thesis into practice. In non-exclusionary States, federal officers, being human, were by it invited to and did, as our cases indicate, step across the street to the State's attorney with their unconstitutionally seized evidence. Prosecution on the basis of that evidence was then had in a state court in utter disregard of the enforceable Fourth Amendment. If the fruits of an unconstitutional search had been inadmissible in both state and federal courts, this inducement to evasion would have been sooner eliminated. There would be no need to reconcile such cases as *Rea* and *Schnettler,* each pointing up the hazardous uncertainties of our heretofore ambivalent approach.

Federal-state cooperation in the solution of crime under constitutional standards will be promoted, if only by recognition of their now mutual obligation to respect the same fundamental criteria in their approaches. "However much in a particular case insistence upon such rules may appear as a technicality that inures to the benefit of a guilty person, the history of the criminal law proves that tolerance of short-cut methods in law enforcement impairs its enduring effectiveness." Denying shortcuts to only one of two cooperating law enforcement agencies tends naturally to breed legitimate suspicion of "working arrangements" whose results are equally tainted.

There are those who say, as did Justice (then Judge) Cardozo, that under our constitutional exclusionary doctrine "[t]he criminal is to go free because the constable has blundered." In some cases this will undoubtedly be the result. But, as was said in *Elkins,* "there is another consideration—the imperative of judicial integrity." The criminal goes free, if he must, but it is the law that sets him free. Nothing can destroy a government more quickly than its failure to observe its own laws, or worse, its disregard of the charter of its own existence. As Mr. Justice Brandeis, dissenting, said in *Olmstead v. United States,* "Our Government is the potent, the omnipresent teacher. For good or for ill, it teaches the whole people by its example. . . . If the Government becomes a lawbreaker, it breeds contempt for law; it invites every man to become a law unto himself; it invites anarchy." Nor can it lightly be assumed that, as a practical matter, adoption of the exclusionary rule fetters law enforcement. Only last year this Court expressly considered that contention and found that "pragmatic evidence of a sort" to the contrary was not wanting. The Court noted that

> The federal courts themselves have operated under the exclusionary rule of *Weeks* for almost half a century [367 U.S. 643, 660]; yet it has not been suggested either that the Federal Bureau of Investigation has thereby been rendered ineffective, or that the administration of criminal justice in the federal courts has thereby been disrupted. Moreover, the experience of the states is impressive. . . . The movement towards the rule of exclusion has been halting but seemingly inexorable. Id., at 218–219.

The ignoble shortcut to conviction left open to the State tends to destroy the entire system of constitutional restraints on which the liberties of the people rest. Having once recognized that the right to privacy embodied in the Fourth Amendment is enforceable against the States, and that the right to be secure against rude invasions of privacy by state officers is, therefore, constitutional in origin, we can no longer permit that right to remain an empty promise. Because it is enforceable in the same manner and to like effect as other basic rights secured by the Due Process Clause, we can no longer permit it to be revocable at the whim of any police officer who, in the name of law enforcement itself, chooses to suspend its enjoyment. Our decision, founded on reason and truth, gives to the individual no more than that which the Constitution guarantees him, to the police officer no less than that to which honest law enforcement is entitled, and, to the courts, that judicial integrity so necessary in the true administration of justice.

The judgment of the Supreme Court of Ohio is reversed and the cause remanded for further proceedings not inconsistent with this opinion.

Procedures for Invoking the Exclusionary Rule

The exclusionary rule may be invoked by the defendant at just about any stage of the criminal justice proceeding and even while the defendant is serving a sentence after a conviction. This almost perpetual availability points to the importance of the exclusionary rule as a vehicle to remedy violations of the Fourth Amendment right. Indeed, opportunities to invoke the exclusionary rule in a criminal case are virtually unending—from the trial up to habeas corpus proceedings.

In Pretrial Motions and Motions during the Trial

In both federal and state courts, the basic procedure for excluding evidence on a claim of illegal search and seizure is a *pretrial motion to suppress* the evidence. If this fails, the motion can be filed again during the trial when the evidence is introduced. The burden of proof in a motion to suppress the evidence depends on whether the search or seizure in question was made with or without a warrant. If the search or seizure was pursuant to a warrant, there is a presumption of validity. The burden is therefore on the accused to show that the warrant was issued without probable cause. This is a heavy burden for the accused to bear, because it usually takes clear and convincing evidence (a higher degree of certainty than probable cause) to prove that probable cause did not, in fact, exist.

In contrast, if the search was made without a warrant, the prosecution has the burden of establishing probable cause or, in its absence, of proving that the search was an exception to the warrant requirement. To establish probable cause, the police officer usually must testify during the hearing on the defendant's motion to suppress.

On Appeal

If the evidence is admitted by the trial judge, the trial proceeds, and the prosecution uses the evidence. If the accused is convicted, the defense may appeal to the appellate court the allegedly erroneous decision to admit the evidence. If the trial judge decides to exclude the evidence, most jurisdictions allow the prosecution to appeal that decision immediately; otherwise, the effect of the allegedly wrongful decision might be the acquittal of the defendant. If the defendant is acquitted, there can be no appeal at all, which would thus deprive the prosecution of any opportunity to challenge the judge's decision to suppress. The appeal by the prosecutor, however, will likely cause a delay in the trial if it takes a long time for the appellate court to resolve the issue. The prosecutor might decide not to appeal the exclusion if she feels there is sufficient other evidence to convict.

If a motion to exclude was made in a timely manner, it is an error for the court to receive evidence obtained by an illegal search or seizure. On appeal, such mistakes automatically lead to the reversal of any conviction, unless the admission of the evidence is found by the appellate court to be a harmless error. To prove **harmless error**, the prosecution must show beyond a reasonable doubt that the evidence erroneously admitted did not contribute to the conviction. To establish harmless error, it is not enough for the prosecution to show that there was other evidence sufficient to support the verdict. Rather, it must show that there is no reasonable possibility that a different result would have been reached without the tainted evidence (*Chapman v. California,* 386 U.S. 18 [1967]).

Chapman v. California (1967)

In Habeas Corpus Proceedings

If the motion to exclude the evidence fails during appeal, the defendant must then serve the sentence imposed. The defendant may still invoke the exclusionary rule at this late stage through a *habeas corpus proceeding* (a proceeding that seeks the defendant's release from jail or prison because his or her constitutional rights were allegedly violated before or during trial). Suppose, for example, X is convicted of murder based on evidence illegally seized by the police. X's repeated motions to exclude were denied during pretrial and at trial. X was convicted and is now serving time in prison. While serving time, X obtains reliable and compelling evidence, not available to him during trial, that the police illegally seized the gun used in the murder. The time to appeal the conviction is past, but X may file a habeas corpus case asking the court to set him free because his constitutional rights were violated and therefore his imprisonment is unconstitutional. Strict limitations set by federal law limit what prisoners can do in habeas cases, but exceptions are made if a defendant can establish a strong case for the violation of a constitutional right and such evidence was not or could not be available to him or her during trial.

"Standing" and the Exclusion of Illegally Seized Evidence

Standing is a legal concept that generally determines whether a person can legally file a lawsuit or submit a petition. It therefore determines whether a person can be a proper party in a case and can seek certain remedies. The general rule on standing is that the exclusionary rule may be used only by the person whose Fourth

Amendment rights have been violated, meaning the person whose reasonable expectation of privacy was breached by the police. In *Minnesota v. Carter,* 525 U.S. 83 (1998), the Court said:

Minnesota v. Carter (1998)

> "The Fourth Amendment protects people, not places." But the extent to which the Fourth Amendment protects people may depend upon where those people are. We have held that "capacity to claim the protection of the Fourth Amendment depends . . . upon whether the person who claims the protection of the Amendment has a legitimate expectation of privacy in the invaded place."

Not everybody who was at the scene of the violation by the police can use the rule. The Court has held that an overnight guest, while the owner of the residence was away, has legal grounds to cite the exclusionary rule (*Minnesota v. Olson,* 495 U.S. 91 [1990]) because that guest has a reasonable expectation of privacy. In another case, however, the Court decided that defendants who were on a short-term visit and who, together with the lessee, "used the apartment for a business purpose—to package drugs," had no legitimate expectation of privacy in the apartment. Therefore, the action by a police officer in looking in an apartment window through a gap in the closed blinds and observing the defendants and the apartment's lessee bagging cocaine did not violate the defendants' legitimate expectation of privacy (*Minnesota v. Carter,* 525 U.S. 83 [1998]).

Minnesota v. Olson (1990)

Why did an overnight guest in *Olson* have standing, whereas defendants on a short-term visit and who used the apartment, together with the lessee, for a business purpose—to package drugs—in *Carter* did not? The Court reasoned that in *Carter,* the "purely commercial nature of the transaction . . . , the relatively short period of time on the premises, and the lack of any previous connection between respondents and the householder, all lead us to conclude that respondents' situation is closer to that of one simply permitted on the premises," and not that of an overnight guest, and therefore had no reasonable expectation of privacy.

Determining What Is Inadmissible

Illegally seized evidence and fruit of the poisonous tree are both inadmissible at trial.

Illegally Seized Evidence

Illegally seized evidence includes contraband, fruits of the crime (for example, stolen goods), instruments of the crime (such as burglary tools), or "mere evidence" (shoes, a shirt, or similar items connecting a person to the crime), which, if seized illegally, may not be admitted at a trial to show the defendant's guilt.

Fruit of the Poisonous Tree

The **"fruit of the poisonous tree" doctrine** states that once the primary evidence (the "tree") is shown to have been unlawfully obtained, any secondary or

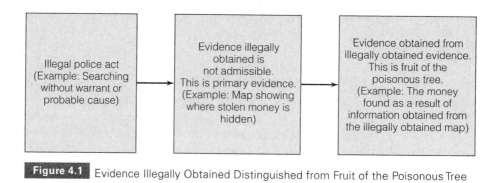

Figure 4.1 Evidence Illegally Obtained Distinguished from Fruit of the Poisonous Tree

Silverthorne Lumber Co. v. United States (1920)

derivative evidence (the "fruit") derived from it is also inadmissible (*Silverthorne Lumber Co. v. United States,* 251 U.S. 385 [1920]). This rule is based on the principle that evidence illegally obtained should not be used to gain other evidence, because the original illegally obtained evidence "taints" all evidence subsequently obtained. The tainted secondary evidence (some courts prefer to call it "derivative evidence" or "secondary evidence") can take various forms (see Figure 4.1):

■ *Example 1.* The police conduct an illegal search of a house and find a map that shows the location of the stolen goods. Using the map, the police recover the goods in an abandoned warehouse. Both the map and the goods are inadmissible as evidence but for different reasons. The map is not admissible because it is illegally seized evidence; the goods (physical evidence) are not admissible either because they are fruit of the poisonous tree.

■ *Example 2.* Police officers make an illegal search of D's house and find heroin. They confront D with the evidence, and she confesses to possession of an illicit drug. D's confession is the fruit of the illegal search (verbal evidence) and must be excluded.

■ *Example 3.* The police enter a suspect's house without probable cause or consent and discover the suspect's diary, an entry of which contains the details of a murder and the location of the murder weapon. The police go to the location and find the weapon. The diary is not admissible as evidence in court because it is illegally seized evidence; the murder weapon is not admissible because it is fruit of the poisonous tree.

In sum, these two types of inadmissible evidence may be distinguished as follows: Illegally seized evidence is obtained as a direct result of the illegal act (the search), whereas the fruit of the poisonous tree is the indirect result of the same illegal act. The fruit of the poisonous tree is thus at least once removed from the illegally seized evidence, but it is equally inadmissible.

Exceptions to the Exclusionary Rule

Court decisions have identified situations in which the evidence obtained is admissible in court even though something may have been wrong with either the conduct of the police or the court that issued the warrant. These exceptions fall into four categories: good faith, inevitable discovery, purged taint, and independent source. It must be noted, however, that some states have rules that exclude these types of evidence. Those more narrow rules prevail because they, in essence, give more rights to the accused than the Constitution allows.

The Good Faith Exceptions

Over the years, the Court has carved out several **"good faith" exceptions** to the exclusionary rule. This means that evidence obtained by the police is admissible in court even if there was an error or mistake, as long as the error or mistake was not committed by the police, or, if committed by the police, the error or mistake was honest and reasonable. It must be emphasized that not all claims of good faith result in the evidence being admissible. What is needed instead is an honest and "objectively reasonable belief" by the officer (as determined by the trial judge or jury) that the act was valid.

Thus far the Court has identified five instances, based on actual cases, that constitute exceptions under good faith:

- When the error was committed by the judge or magistrate, not by the police
- When the error was committed by a court employee
- When the police erroneously, but reasonably and honestly, believed that the information they gave to the magistrate when obtaining the warrant was accurate
- When the police reasonably believed the person who gave authority to enter the premises had the authority
- When the police action was based on a law that was later declared unconstitutional

When the Error Was Committed by the Judge or Magistrate, Not by the Police: The *Sheppard* and *Leon* Cases

Massachusetts v. Sheppard (1984)

The first significant good faith exception to the exclusionary rule applies when the error was committed by the judge or magistrate and not by the police. The Court held in *Massachusetts v. Sheppard*, 468 U.S. 981 (1984), that evidence obtained by the police acting in good faith on a search warrant that was issued by a neutral and detached magistrate, but that is ultimately found to be invalid, may be admitted and used at the trial.

In the *Sheppard* case, a police detective executed an affidavit for an arrest and search warrant authorizing the search of Sheppard's residence. The affidavit stated that the police wanted to search for certain described items, including clothing of the victim and a blunt instrument that might have been used on the victim. The affidavit was reviewed and approved by the district attorney. Because it was a Sunday, the local court was closed, and the police had a difficult time finding a warrant application form. The detective finally found a warrant form previously used in another district in the Boston area to search for controlled substances. After making some changes to the form, the detective presented it and the affidavit to the judge at his residence, informing him that the warrant form might need further revisions.

The judge concluded that the affidavit established probable cause to search the residence and told the detective that the necessary changes in the warrant form would be made. The judge made some changes, but he did not change the substantive portion, which continued to authorize a search for controlled substances, nor did he alter the form to incorporate the affidavit. The judge then signed the warrant and returned it and the affidavit to the detective, informing him that the warrant was of sufficient authority in form and content to authorize the search.

The ensuing search of Sheppard's residence was limited to the items listed in the affidavit, and several incriminating pieces of evidence were discovered. The defendant was convicted of first-degree murder in a trial at which the evidence obtained under the warrant was used. On appeal, the Court ruled that the evidence obtained was admissible in court because the officer conducting the search had acted in good faith, relying on a search warrant that had been issued by a magistrate but that was subsequently declared to be invalid.

In a companion case decided that same day, *United States v. Leon*, 468 U.S. 897 (1984), the Court made the same decision on a different set of facts. Acting on information from a confidential informant, officers of the Burbank, California, police department had initiated a drug-trafficking investigation that involved surveillance of Leon's activities. On the basis of an affidavit summarizing the officer's observations, the police prepared an application for a warrant to search three residences and Leon's automobiles for an extensive list of items. The application was reviewed by several deputy district attorneys, and a state court judge issued a warrant that was apparently valid. When Leon was later indicted for federal drug offenses, he filed motions to suppress the evidence seized. The trial court excluded the evidence on the grounds that no probable cause had existed for issuing the warrant, because the reliability of the informant had not been established and the information obtained from the informant was stale. This decision was affirmed by the court of appeals.

The government then took the case to the Supreme Court solely on the issue of whether a good faith exception to the exclusionary rule should be recognized. The Court ruled that the Fourth Amendment's exclusionary rule should not be applied to bar the use of evidence in the prosecution's case that has been obtained by officers acting in reasonable reliance on a search warrant issued by a detached and neutral magistrate but ultimately found to be invalid because probable cause was lacking.

The *Sheppard* and *Leon* cases are arguably the most important cases decided on the exclusionary rule since *Mapp v. Ohio*. They represent a significant, although narrow, exception to the exclusionary rule and thus a breakthrough that police proponents have long advocated. In these cases, the Court said that there were objectively reasonable grounds for the police's mistaken belief that the warrants authorized the searches. The officers took every step that could reasonably have been taken to ensure that the warrants were valid. The difference between these two cases is that in *Sheppard* the issue was the improper use of a form (a technical error) by the judge, whereas in *Leon* it was the use of a questionable informant and stale information by the judge to determine probable cause. The cases are similar, however, in that the mistakes were made by the judges, not the police. When the warrants were given to the officers, it was reasonable for them to conclude that each authorized a valid search.

In the *Sheppard* case, the Court noted: An error of constitutional dimension may have been committed with respect to issuing the warrant in this case, but it was the judge, not the police officer, who made the crucial mistake. Suppressing evidence because the judge failed to make all the necessary clerical corrections despite his assurance that such changes would be made will not serve the deterrent function that the exclusionary rule was designed to achieve.

And in the *Leon* case, the Court concluded: The exclusionary rule is designed to deter police misconduct rather than to punish the errors of judges and magistrates. Admitting evidence obtained pursuant to a warrant while at the same time declaring that the warrant was somehow defective will not reduce judicial officers' professional incentives to comply with the Fourth Amendment, encourage them to repeat their mistakes, or lead to the granting of all colorable warrant requests.

In sum, the Court reasoned that the evidence was admissible because the judge, and not the police, erred; therefore, the exclusionary rule did not apply, because it is designed to control the conduct of the police, not of judges. However, at least one state supreme court (Pennsylvania) has ruled that evidence seized with a deficient search warrant cannot be used in state court based on the provisions of the state constitution, even if the police acted in good faith when obtaining the warrant. Therefore, what the exclusionary rule allows as an exception may be negated by state case law or provisions of the state constitution.

When the Error Was Committed by a Court Employee: *Arizona v. Evans* The

most recent good faith exception to the exclusionary rule was decided by a divided Court in *Arizona v. Evans*, 514 U.S. 1 (1995). In that case, Evans was arrested by the Phoenix, Arizona, police during a routine traffic stop when a patrol car computer indicated that there was an outstanding misdemeanor warrant for his arrest. A subsequent search of Evans's car revealed a bag of marijuana. He was charged with possession of marijuana. Evans moved to suppress the evidence under the exclusionary rule, saying that the marijuana was illegally obtained because the misdemeanor warrant, which was the basis of the stop, was dismissed seventeen days before the arrest but was not entered in the computer due to court employee error. This claim was, in fact, true. Evans was convicted and appealed, claiming that the evidence obtained should have been held inadmissible under the exclusionary rule. The Court rejected Evans's claim and admitted the evidence, saying:

The exclusionary rule does not require suppression of evidence seized in violation of the Fourth Amendment where the erroneous information resulted from clerical errors of court employees. The exclusionary rule is a judicially created remedy designed to safeguard against future violations of Fourth Amendment rights through its deterrent effect. . . . The exclusionary rule was historically designed as a means of deterring police misconduct, not mistakes by court employees.

In admitting the evidence, the Court stressed the following: (1) The exclusionary rule historically has been designed to deter police misconduct, not to deter mistakes committed by court employees; (2) Evans in this case offered no evidence that court employees are inclined to ignore or subvert the Fourth Amendment or that lawlessness by court employees required the extreme Court action of exclusion of the evidence; and (3) there was no basis to believe that the application of the exclusionary rule would have a significant effect on the behavior of court employees responsible for informing the police that the warrant had been dismissed. (Read the Case Brief to learn more about *Arizona v. Evans*.)

When the Police Erred but Honestly and Reasonably Believed that the Information They Gave to the Magistrate when Obtaining the Warrant Was Accurate: *Maryland v. Garrison*

Maryland v. Garrison (1987)

In *Maryland v. Garrison,* 480 U.S. 79 (1987), police officers obtained a warrant to search "the premises known as 2036 Park Avenue, third-floor apartment" for drugs and drug paraphernalia that allegedly belonged to a person named McWebb. The police honestly believed that there was only one apartment at the location. In fact, however, there were two apartments on the third floor, one belonging to McWebb and the other one belonging to Garrison. Before the officers became aware that they were in Garrison's apartment instead of McWebb's, they discovered contraband that led to Garrison's conviction for violating provisions of Maryland's Controlled Substance Act. Garrison appealed his conviction, claiming that the evidence obtained by police was inadmissible based on the exclusionary rule. The Court disagreed, stating that "the validity of a warrant must be judged in light of the information available to officers when the warrant is sought." The Court added: Plainly, if the officers had known, or even if they should have known, that there were two separate dwelling units on the third floor . . . they would have been obligated to exclude respondent's apartment from the scope of the requested warrant. But we must judge the constitutionality of their conduct in light of the information available to them at the time they acted. . . . The validity of the warrant must be assessed on the basis of the information that the officers disclosed, or had a duty to discover and to disclose, to the issuing magistrate.

In the *Garrison* case, the officers had a warrant when they searched the apartment. The issue in that case, therefore, was whether the warrant itself was valid in light of the erroneous information given by the police that helped them obtain the warrant. A slightly different situation is a scenario in which the police have a valid warrant but act outside the scope of the warrant. In such cases, the good faith exception does not apply because although the warrant was valid, the extent of the search

CASE BRIEF: The Leading Case on the Good Faith Exception to the Exclusionary Rule

Arizona v. Evans, 514 U.S. 1 (1995)

Facts: Officers saw Evans going the wrong way on a one-way street in front of the police station. Evans was stopped, and officers determined that his driver's license had been suspended. When Evans's name was entered into a computer data terminal, it indicated that there was an outstanding misdemeanor warrant for his arrest. While being handcuffed, Evans dropped a hand-rolled cigarette that turned out to be marijuana. A search of Evans's car revealed more marijuana under the passenger's seat. At trial, Evans moved to suppress the evidence as the fruit of an unlawful arrest because the arrest warrant for the misdemeanor had been quashed seventeen days prior to his arrest but had not been entered into the computer due to clerical error of a court employee. This was, in fact, true. The motion was denied, and Evans was convicted.

Issue: *Does the exclusionary rule require suppression of the evidence of marijuana obtained from Evans? No.*

Supreme Court Decision: The exclusionary rule does not require suppression of evidence seized in violation of the Fourth Amendment where the erroneous information resulted from clerical errors of court employees.

Case Significance: This case adds another exception to the exclusionary rule: when the error is committed by court employees instead of by the police. The exclusionary rule was fashioned to deter police misconduct, so the Court has refused to apply it to cases where the misconduct was not by the police. Previous cases have held that if the error is committed by the magistrate (as in *Massachusetts v. Sheppard* and *United States v. Leon*) or by the legislature (as in *Illinois v. Krull*), the exclusionary rule

does not apply. The theme in these cases is that, if the error is not committed by the police, then the exclusionary rule should not apply because it was meant to control the behavior of the police. *Evans* is therefore consistent with the Court's holding in previous cases, and the ruling came as no surprise. The unanswered question is whether other errors by any public officer other than the police would be an exception to the exclusionary rule and therefore make the evidence admissible. The dissent in *Evans* argued that the Fourth Amendment prohibition against unreasonable searches and seizures applies to the conduct of all government officers, not just that of the police. The majority in *Evans* disagreed, preferring to focus on the original purpose of the exclusionary rule—which is to control police conduct.

Excerpts from the Decision: In *Leon,* we applied these principles to the context of a police search in which the officers had acted in objectively reasonable reliance on a search warrant, issued by a neutral and detached magistrate, that later was determined to be invalid. On the basis of three factors, we determined that there was no sound reason to apply the exclusionary rule as a means of deterring misconduct on the part of judicial officers who are responsible for issuing warrants. First, we noted that the exclusionary rule was historically designed "to deter police misconduct rather than to punish the errors of judges and magistrates." Second, there was "no evidence suggesting that judges and magistrates are inclined to ignore or subvert the Fourth Amendment or that lawlessness among these actors requires the application of the extreme sanction of exclusion." Third, and of greatest importance, there was no basis for believing that exclusion of evidence seized pursuant to a warrant would have a significant deterrent effect on the issuing judge or magistrate.

Applying the reasoning of Leon to the facts of this case, we conclude that the decision of the Arizona Supreme Court must be reversed. The Arizona Supreme Court determined that it could not "support the distinction drawn . . . between clerical errors committed by law enforcement personnel and similar mistakes by court employees," and that "even assuming . . . that responsibility for the error rested with the justice court, it does not follow that the exclusionary rule should be inapplicable to these facts." Ibid.

Finally, and most important, there is no basis for believing that application of the exclusionary rule in these circumstances will have a significant effect on court employees responsible for informing the police that a warrant has been quashed. Because court clerks are not adjuncts to the law enforcement team engaged in the often competitive enterprise of ferreting out crime, they have no stake in the outcome of particular criminal prosecutions. The threat of exclusion of evidence could not be expected to deter such individuals from failing to inform police officials that a warrant had been quashed.

If it were indeed a court clerk who was responsible for the erroneous entry on the police computer, application of the exclusionary rule also could not be expected to alter the behavior of the arresting officer. As the trial court in this case stated: "I think the police officer [was] bound to arrest. I think he would [have been] derelict in his duty if he failed to arrest." ("Excluding the evidence can in no way affect [the officer's] future conduct unless it is to make him less willing to do his duty."

The judgment of the Supreme Court of Arizona is therefore reversed, and the case is remanded to that court for proceedings not inconsistent with this opinion. It is so ordered.

was invalid. For example, the police have a valid warrant to seize a 42-inch flat panel plasma TV set, but while searching the police open cabinet drawers and find drugs. The good faith exception does not apply because the police clearly acted outside the scope of the warrant (it is unreasonable to search cabinet drawers to look for a 42-inch TV set); therefore, the drugs are not admissible as evidence.

When the Police Reasonably Believe that the Person Who Gave Authority to Enter the Premises Had Authority to Give Consent: *Illinois v. Rodriguez* A

Illinois v. Rodriguez (1990)

good faith exception has been fashioned by the Court under the "apparent authority" principle. In *Illinois v. Rodriguez*, 497 U.S. 117 (1990), the suspect, Rodriguez, was arrested in his apartment and charged with possession of illegal drugs that the police said were in plain view when they entered his apartment. The police gained entry into Rodriguez's apartment with the assistance of a woman named Fischer, who told police that the apartment was "ours" and that she had clothes and furniture there. She unlocked the door with her key and gave the officers permission to enter. In reality, Fischer had moved out of the apartment and therefore no longer had any common authority over it. The Court held that the consent given by Fischer was valid because the police reasonably and honestly believed, given the circumstances, that she had authority to give consent, thus resorting to the apparent authority principle as one of the exceptions to the exclusionary rule.

When the Police Action Was Based on a Law that Was Later Declared

Illinois v. Krull
(1987)

Unconstitutional: In *Illinois v. Krull,* 480 U.S. 340 (1987), police officers entered the wrecking yard belonging to Krull without a warrant and found evidence of stolen vehicles. Such warrantless entry was authorized by state statute. The next day, however, a federal court declared the statute unconstitutional, saying that it permitted police officers too much discretion and therefore violated the Fourth Amendment. On appeal, the Court did not dispute the constitutionality of the statute, saying instead that the evidence obtained was admissible under the good faith exception to the exclusionary rule. The Court concluded that suppression is inappropriate when the fault is not with the police, but—as in this case—with the legislature.

Some legal scholars believe that the good faith exceptions to the exclusionary rule, as enunciated in the preceding cases, "will hasten the ultimate demise of the exclusionary rule and weaken its application." Others believe that these decisions should be interpreted and applied very narrowly—only to cases in which the police are not at fault or, if the mistake is by the police, when the mistake is honest and the officer's belief in the legality of the act is reasonable. Despite all these rulings, there has been no indiscriminate application of the good faith exception to the exclusionary rule. The more reasonable view appears to be that the good faith exception has been and will continue to be applied cautiously by the Court. The belief by some law enforcement officers that courts will automatically admit evidence obtained illegally as long as the officer believes in good faith that what he or she did was legal is unsupported by case law.

The Inevitable Discovery Exception

The **"inevitable discovery" exception** says that evidence is admissible if the police can prove that they would inevitably have discovered it anyway by lawful means, regardless of their illegal action. The exception usually applies to instances when the evidence obtained is a weapon or a body. For example, while the police were taking a suspect back to Des Moines from Davenport, Iowa, where he surrendered, they induced him to tell them the location of the body of the girl they believed he had murdered by appealing to the suspect (whom the police addressed as "Reverend"), saying that it would be nice to give the deceased a Christian burial. The police did not directly question the suspect but instead asked him to "think it over." The suspect led the police to the body of the murdered girl. Before the departure from Davenport, the suspect's lawyer had repeatedly requested that no questioning take place during that drive. While conceding that the police violated the defendant's right to counsel by encouraging him to discuss the location of the body, the Court nevertheless admitted the evidence on the grounds that the police would have discovered it anyway. At the time that the police were being led by the suspect to the body, the searchers

Nix v. Williams
(1984)

were approaching the actual location, so the body would inevitably have been found (*Nix v. Williams,* 467 U.S. 431 [1984]).

An article in the *FBI Law Enforcement Bulletin* issues the following caution about the inevitable discovery exception: "Under the inevitable discovery doctrine, it is not sufficient to allege that the evidence *could* have been found in a lawful fashion if some hypothetical events had occurred. It must be shown that the evidence inevitably *would* have been discovered." The writer adds that "the inevitable discovery exception ensures that the exclusionary rule does not go beyond that limited goal of deterring illegal police conduct by allowing into evidence those items that the police would have discovered legally anyway."[3] The inevitable discovery claim by the police is strengthened if the department has a policy about such searches that, if followed, would have led to the inevitable discovery of what was seized—as long as the policy is constitutional.

The Purged Taint Exception

The **"purged taint" exception** applies when the defendant's subsequent voluntary act dissipates the taint of the initial illegality. A defendant's intervening act of free will is sufficient to break the causal chain between the tainted evidence and the illegal police conduct, so the evidence becomes admissible. For example, in one case, the police broke into a suspect's house illegally and obtained a confession from him, but the suspect refused to sign it. The suspect was released on his own recognizance. A few days later, he went back to the police station and signed the confession. The Court said that the suspect's act manifested free will and therefore purged the tainted evidence of illegality (*Wong Sun v. United States*, 371 U.S. 471 [1963]).

Wong Sun v. United States (1963)

In a subsequent case, the Court clarified what it meant by the "purged taint" exception it created in *Wong Sun*, in effect saying it is not that simple. In *Brown v. Illinois* (422 U.S. 590 [1975]), the police arrested suspect Brown without probable cause and without a warrant. After receiving the *Miranda* warnings, he made two incriminating statements while in custody. During the trial, he moved to suppress the statements, but the motions were rejected by the trial court and Brown was convicted. The Illinois Supreme Court later held that although the arrest was unlawful, the "statements were admissible on the ground that the giving of the *Miranda* warnings served to break the causal connection between the illegal arrest and the giving of the statements, and petitioner's act in making the statements was 'sufficiently an act of free will to purge the primary taint of the unlawful invasion.'" On appeal, the U.S. Supreme Court disagreed and held the statement inadmissible, saying that, circumstances in the case considered, the confession had not been purged of the taint of the illegal arrest without probable cause.

Brown v. Illinois (1975)

To break the causal connection between an illegal arrest and a confession that is the fruit of the illegal arrest, the intervening event must be meaningful. For example, in another case, after an unlawful arrest, a suspect confessed to the commission of a robbery. Even though the suspect received three sets of *Miranda* warnings and met briefly at the police station with friends prior to the confession, the Court said that these events were not meaningful and that the evidence obtained was therefore not admissible during the trial (*Taylor v. Alabama*, 457 U.S. 687 [1982]).

Taylor v. Alabama (1982)

Key to understanding the purged taint exception to the exclusionary rule is whether the defendant's subsequent voluntary act dissipated or negated the initial illegal act of the police. This is a subjective determination made by the court on a case-by-case basis and does not lend itself to specific rules. For example, in the *Wong Sun* case, the Court held that the suspect's subsequent act of going back to the police station and signing the confession sufficed to rid the confession of its initial illegality. But what if Wong Sun had come back an hour or a few hours later, instead of a few days later? Or, suppose it had been one day instead of a few days later—would his act have been considered one of free will sufficient to break the illegality?

By contrast, the Court held in the *Taylor* case that the intervening event (Taylor having been given three sets of *Miranda* warnings and meeting briefly with friends at the police station) after the unlawful arrest and confession was not meaningful enough to purge the taint of the initial illegal act of the police. What if the meeting with friends had lasted for hours or days instead of just briefly? Would the purged taint exception have applied? In sum, whether the initial taint has been sufficiently purged is a subjective judgment that may differ from one judge to another and does not have a bright-line rule or easy answers.

The Independent Source Exception

The **"independent source" exception** holds that evidence obtained is admissible if the police can prove that it was obtained from an independent source not connected with the illegal search or seizure (*United States v. Crews,* 445 U.S. 463 [1980]). In the *Crews* case, the Court said that the initial illegality (illegal detention of the suspect) could not deprive the prosecutors of the opportunity to prove the defendant's guilt through the introduction of evidence wholly untainted by police misconduct.

For example, in another case, a fourteen-year-old girl was found in the defendant's apartment during an illegal search. The girl's testimony that the defendant had had carnal knowledge of her was admissible because she was an independent source that predated the search of the apartment. Prior to the search, the girl's parents had reported her missing, and a police informant had already located her in the defendant's apartment (*State v. O'Bremski,* 423 P.2d 530 [1967]).

United States v. Crews (1980)

State v. O'Bremski (1967)

There are differences between the independent source and the purged taint exceptions. Under the independent source exception, the evidence was obtained from a source not connected with the illegal search or seizure. Thus, although the evidence might be viewed as suspect, it is admissible, because no illegality was involved (as when evidence was legally obtained before the police committed an illegal act). By contrast, under the purged taint exception, the evidence was obtained as a result of an illegal act, but the defendant's subsequent voluntary act removes the taint of the initial illegal act (as in the *Wong Sun* case, in which the suspect went back to the police station and voluntarily signed the confession). The subsequent voluntary act, in effect, purges the evidence of its initial illegality.

Proceedings to which the Rule Does Not Apply

The exclusionary rule is not applicable in all Fourth Amendment proceedings. Private searches, grand jury investigations, sentencing, violations of agency rules only, noncriminal proceedings, and parole revocation hearings all fall outside of the reach of the exclusionary rule. This section looks at each of these exceptions.

In Private Searches

The Fourth Amendment's prohibition against unreasonable searches and seizures applies only to the actions of governmental officials, so prosecutors may use evidence illegally obtained by private individuals (by methods such as illegal wiretap or trespass) as long as the police did not encourage or participate in the illegal private search. In one case, the Court said that the Fourth Amendment's "origin and history clearly show that it was intended as a restraint upon the activities of sovereign authority, and was not intended to be a limitation upon other than governmental agencies" (*Burdeau v. McDowell*, 256 U.S. 465 [1921]).

Burdeau v. McDowell (1921)

In Grand Jury Investigations

A person being questioned by the grand jury cannot refuse to answer questions on the grounds that the questions are based on illegally obtained evidence (such as information from an illegal wiretap). The reason is that the application of the exclusionary rule in such proceedings would unduly interfere with the grand jury's investigative function (*United States v. Calandra*, 414 U.S. 338 [1974]).

United States v. Calandra (1974)

In Sentencing

Some lower courts have likewise permitted the trial judge to consider illegally obtained evidence in fixing sentences after conviction, even when the same evidence had been excluded during the trial because it was illegally obtained. During sentencing, they reason, a trial judge should consider any reliable evidence. The fact that it was obtained illegally does not necessarily affect its reliability. The evidence is not admissible, however, if state law prohibits its admission.

In Violations of Agency Rules Only

The evidence is admissible if the search violates an agency rule but not the Constitution. Such violations do not offend fundamental fairness under the Constitution. For example, suppose police department rules provide that a person suspected of driving while intoxicated who refuses to take a blood-alcohol test must be informed that the refusal may be used as evidence against him or her in court. Failure by the police to give this warning does not exclude the evidence (*South Dakota v. Neville,* 459 U.S. 553 [1983]). An exception is made if state law provides that such evidence is not admissible.

South Dakota v. Neville (1983)

In Noncriminal Proceedings

The exclusionary rule applies only to criminal proceedings, not to proceedings such as civil or administrative hearings. Illegally obtained evidence may be admissible against another party in a civil tax proceeding or in a deportation hearing. It may also be admissible in administrative proceedings, as when an employee is being disciplined. For example, illegally obtained evidence may be admissible in cases in which a police officer is being investigated by the internal affairs division for violation of departmental rules.

However, court decisions have established that even in administrative cases there are instances when illegally obtained evidence may not be admitted. One is if state law or agency policy prohibits the admission of such evidence. Another is if the evidence was obtained in bad faith, as when evidence against a police officer under investigation is obtained illegally and for the purpose of establishing grounds for disciplinary action.

In Parole Revocation Hearings

Pennsylvania Board of Probation and Parole v. Scott (1998)

In *Pennsylvania Board of Probation and Parole v. Scott* (524 U.S. 357 [1998]), the Court held that the exclusionary rule does not apply in state parole revocation proceedings. In *Scott,* parole officers conducted what was later considered an invalid search because of the absence of reasonable suspicion to believe that a parole violation had, in fact, occurred. The Court held that the exclusionary rule does not apply to parole revocation proceedings primarily because the rule does not apply "to proceedings other than criminal trials" and because application of the rule "would both hinder the functioning of state parole systems and alter the traditionally flexible, administrative nature of parole revocation proceedings." Although *Scott* involved parole revocation, there is good reason to believe that the exclusionary rule does not apply to probation revocation proceedings either, given the similar goals and functions of parole and probation.

Arguments in Support of the Exclusionary Rule

Proponents make the following arguments in support of the exclusionary rule:[4]

1. It deters violations of constitutional rights by police and prosecutors. A number of studies and testimonies by police officers support this contention.
2. It manifests society's refusal to convict lawbreakers by relying on official lawlessness—a clear demonstration of our commitment to the rule of law that states that no person, not even a law enforcement official, is above the law.
3. It results in the freeing of the guilty in a relatively small proportion of cases. A 1978 study by the General Accounting Office found that, of 2,804 cases in which defendants were likely to file a motion to suppress evidence, exclusion succeeded in only 1.3 percent. Moreover, the same study reported that, of the cases presented to federal prosecutors for prosecution, only 0.4 percent were declined by the prosecutors because of Fourth Amendment search and seizure problems.[5] In 1983, another study found that "only between 0.6 and 2.35 percent of all felony arrests are 'lost' at any stage in the arrest disposition process (including trials and appeals) because of the operation of the exclusionary rule."[6]
4. It has led to more professionalism among the police and increased attention to training programs. Fear that evidence will be excluded has forced the police to develop greater expertise in their work.
5. It preserves the integrity of the judicial system, because the admission of illegally seized evidence would make the court a party to violations of constitutional rights.
6. It prevents the government, whose agents have violated the Constitution, from profiting from its wrongdoing. Somebody has to pay for the mistake—better it be the government than the suspect who has already been wronged.
7. It protects the constitutional right to privacy.

Arguments against the Exclusionary Rule

Opponents, including justices of the Supreme Court, have argued strongly in opposition to the exclusionary rule. Among their arguments are the following:

1. In the words of Justice Benjamin Cardozo, "The criminal goes free because the constable has blundered." It is wrong to make society pay for an officer's mistake—punish the officer, not society.
2. It excludes the most credible, probative kinds of evidence—fingerprints, guns, narcotics, dead bodies—and thereby impedes the truth-finding function of the courts.[7]

3. It discourages internal disciplinary efforts by law enforcement agencies. If police are disciplined when the evidence will be excluded anyway, they suffer a double setback.

4. It encourages police to perjure themselves in an effort to get the evidence admitted.

5. Particularly in major cases, the police might feel that the end justifies the means: It is better to lie than to let a presumably guilty person go free.

6. It diminishes respect for the judicial process and generates disrespect for the law and the administration of justice.[8]

7. There is no proof that the exclusionary rule deters police misconduct. In the words of Chief Justice Warren Burger, "There is no empirical evidence to support the claim that the rule actually deters illegal conduct of law enforcement officials."

8. Only the United States uses the exclusionary rule; other countries do not.

9. It has no effect on those large areas of police activity that do not result in criminal prosecutions. If the police make an arrest or search without any thought of subsequent prosecution (such as when they simply want to remove a person from the streets overnight or when they confiscate contraband to eliminate the supply), they do not have to worry about the exclusionary rule, because it takes effect only if the case goes to trial and the evidence is used.

10. The rule is not based on the Constitution; it is only an invention of the Court.[9]

11. It does not punish the individual police officer whose illegal conduct led to the exclusion of the evidence.

12. Justice Scalia says, "It has been 'universally rejected' by other countries."

HIGHLIGHT

The Exclusionary Rule Is Not Used in Other Countries

"The Court-pronounced exclusionary rule . . . is distinctly American. When we adopted that rule in *Mapp v. Ohio,* 367 U.S. 643 (1961), it was 'unique to American Jurisprudence.' Since then, a categorical exclusionary rule has been 'universally rejected' by other countries, including those with rules prohibiting illegal searches and police misconduct, despite the fact that none of those countries 'appears to have any alternative form of discipline for police that is effective in preventing search violations.' England, for example, rarely excludes evidence found during an illegal search or seizure and has only recently begun excluding evidence from illegally obtained confessions. Canada rarely excludes evidence and will only do so if admission will 'bring the administration of justice into disrepute.' The European Court of Human Rights has held that introduction of illegally seized evidence does not violate the 'fair trial' requirement in Article 6, Section 1 of the European Convention on Human Rights."

SOURCE: Dissenting opinion by Justice Antonin Scalia in *Roper v. Simmons,* 543 U.S. 551 (2005).

Alternatives to the Exclusionary Rule

The continuing debate about the exclusionary rule has produced several proposals to admit the evidence obtained and then to deal with the wrongdoing of the police. Among the proposals are the following:

- *An independent review board in the executive branch.* This proposal envisions a review board composed of nonpolice personnel to review allegations of violations of constitutional rights by the police. The problem with this alternative is that police oppose it because it singles them out among public officials for differential treatment. Moreover, they view outsiders as unlikely to be able to understand the difficulties and dangers inherent in police work.

- *A civil tort action against the government.* This would mean filing an action seeking damages from the government for acts by its officers. It poses real difficulty for the plaintiff, who would have to shoulder the financial cost of the litigation. Most defendants do not have the resources to finance a civil case, particularly after a criminal trial. However, low damages awards against police officers usually discourage the filing of civil tort actions except in egregious cases.

- *A hearing separate from the main criminal trial but before the same judge or jury.* The purpose of the hearing is to determine if, in fact, the officer behaved illegally in obtaining the evidence used during the trial and, if so, to impose the necessary sanctions on the officer. Although this is the least expensive and most expedient alternative, its effectiveness is questionable. If the violation is slight, the judge or jury will not look with favor on what may be considered an unnecessary extension of the original trial. Furthermore, if the criminal trial ends in a conviction, the chances of the officer being punished for what he or she did become remote.

- *Adoption of an expanded good faith exception.* The final report of the Attorney General's Task Force on Violent Crime in the late 1980s proposed a good faith exception different from and broader than that allowed by the Court in the *Sheppard* and *Leon* cases. The proposed good faith exception covers all cases in which the police would claim and can prove that they acted in good faith (not just when the magistrate issues an invalid warrant). It is based on two conditions: (1) The officer must allege that he or she had probable cause for the action in question, and (2) the officer's apparent belief that he or she was acting legally must be a reasonable one. These are questions of fact that would be determined by the judge or jury. Opponents fear that this proposal would lead to more violations of rights using good faith as a convenient excuse. Good faith is a vague concept that is best determined on a case-by-case basis; it may therefore vary from one judge or jury to another. It is also maintained that this exception discourages training and rewards lack of knowledge. (The theory is that the more untrained and uninformed the police officer, the greater the claim to good faith his or her ignorance would permit.)

■ *Adoption of the British system.* Under the British system, the illegally obtained evidence is admitted in court, but the erring officer is subject to internal departmental sanctions. The problem is that this system is not effective even in England, where the police system is highly centralized and generally has attained a higher level of professionalism. Internal discipline by peers has been and is a problem in U.S. policing; the public will most likely view this as an ineffective means of control.

The Future of the Exclusionary Rule: It Is Here to Stay

The debate on the exclusionary rule continues in some quarters, although the intensity has receded. Proponents and opponents of the exclusionary rule range across a continuum, from the purists to the accommodationists. Proponents want the rule to remain intact and to be applied strictly, the way it was applied in the two decades after *Mapp v. Ohio.* Any concession is interpreted as widening the door that will eventually lead to the doctrine's demise. Others are not so unbending, agreeing instead to "logical" and "reasonable" exceptions. Some opponents are not satisfied with such victories as the *Sheppard, Leon,* and other cases involving the good faith exception. They want to scrap the rule completely and admit the evidence without reservation or subsequent sanctions. Still others feel that the exclusionary rule should be modified, but there is no consensus about what that modification should be.

What, then, of the future? The controversy surrounding the exclusionary rule has abated, but the debate will not completely fade away. In view of the several exceptions carved out in Court decisions (as discussed in this chapter), the exclusionary rule is no longer as controversial as it once was, nor is it as much a controlling force in law enforcement as when it first emerged. In the words of one observer: "The exclusionary rule today is a shadow of that envisioned in *Weeks.* Ironically, the 'deterrence rationale' has been invoked to permit so many uses of unconstitutionally seized evidence that the rule's efficacy as a deterrent may well be diminished. Certainly, unconstitutionally seized evidence can often be used to the government's advantage."[10]

During his time on the Supreme Court, Chief Justice Burger called for the rule's abolition, calling it "conceptually sterile and practically ineffective." Other justices have publicly expressed dissatisfaction with the rule and want it to be abolished or modified. They have made some inroads, but chances of complete abolition appear remote. To paraphrase Mark Twain, reports concerning the demise of the exclusionary rule are greatly exaggerated.

Summary

- The exclusionary rule states that evidence obtained by the police in violation of the Fourth Amendment right against unreasonable searches and seizures is not admissible in court.

- The purpose of the exclusionary rule is to deter police misconduct.

- It is a judge-made rule designed to protect the Fourth Amendment right against unreasonable searches and seizures.

- It excludes two kinds of evidence: those illegally seized and "fruit of the poisonous tree."

- *Mapp v. Ohio* (1961) applied the exclusionary rule to state criminal cases.

- There are four general exceptions to the exclusionary rule: good faith, inevitable discovery, purged taint, and independent source.

- Despite continuing debate, the exclusionary rule is here to stay.

Review Questions and Hypothetical Cases

1. What is the exclusionary rule? Does it apply only to violations of Fourth Amendment rights or to violations of any constitutional right in the Bill of Rights (the first ten amendments to the Constitution)?

2. The purpose of the exclusionary rule is to deter police misconduct. Critics, however, say the exclusionary rule has failed to achieve that purpose. Do you agree? Why?

3. Is the exclusionary rule a constitutional or a judge-made rule? Can it be modified by the U.S. Congress through legislation?

4. What is the silver platter doctrine? Is it in use today?

5. "*Mapp v. Ohio* is the most significant case decided by the Court on the exclusionary rule." Is this statement true or false? Defend your answer.

6. Distinguish between illegally seized evidence and the "fruit of the poisonous tree." Give examples.

7. "The exclusionary rule does not apply if the police seize evidence illegally but in good faith." Is this statement true or false? Explain your answer.

8. What does *Arizona v. Evans* say? Is this case important?

9. Name at least four types of proceedings to which the exclusionary rule does not apply. Discuss each.

10. What is the inevitable discovery exception to the exclusionary rule? Give an illustration.

11. What is the purged taint exception to the exclusionary rule? Why is it difficult to apply?

12. "A trial court judge admits evidence during trial that, on appeal, was held not to be admissible. The conviction of the accused is automatically reversed." Is this statement true or false? Support your answer.

13. Officer P searched the house of Citizen Q based on a warrant. He found five pounds of cocaine. P then asked Q if there were other drugs in his residence. Q replied, "I might as well tell you—I have other drugs in my car in the garage." Officer P then went to the garage, searched the car, and found a pound of heroin and three illegal weapons. P seized all these. All seized evidence were later introduced in Q's trial. Questions: (a) What is admissible in court? All, some, or none of the evidence? and (b) If any evidence is to be excluded, is the exclusion based on "evidence illegally seized" or "fruit of the poisonous tree"? Give reasons for your answer.

14. Officer X was sent by a radio dispatcher one day to Apartment B in a dilapidated building at 44 Magnolia Avenue because the dispatcher received an urgent 911 call from there that said somebody was being harmed. Officer X went there and heard somebody moaning and groaning inside. Officer X identified himself,

demanded to be admitted, was admitted, and saw illegal drugs all over the place. Officer X seized the illegal drugs. It turned out later that Officer X, in fact, went to the wrong apartment. The 911 call came from Apartment D, at the same street address, but the dispatcher misheard the call and thought the 911 call came from Apartment B. You are the judge during the trial. Will you admit or exclude the drugs seized? State your reasons.

15. B and C, who for years were live-in lovers, had a big fight one night. C hastily moved out of the apartment they shared. A week later, C went to the police and told them that B, the boyfriend, was dealing drugs from his apartment. C said she no longer lived there but had a key to the apartment, she had gone back there a couple of times, and that she and B were in the process of reconciling—none of which was true. C led the police to the apartment and opened it with her key. The police saw marijuana, amphetamines, and other illegal drugs in various places in the apartment. They seized all those and introduced them later in court as evidence against B. You are the judge. Will you admit or exclude the evidence? Support your decision.

Key Terms

Go to the Criminal Procedure 7e website for flash cards that will help you master the definitions of these terms.

exclusionary rule, 104
fruit of the poisonous tree doctrine, 113
good faith exceptions, 115

harmless error rule, 112
independent source exception, 123
inevitable discovery exception, 121

purged taint exception, 122
silver platter doctrine, 107
standing, 112

Holdings of Key Cases

See Appendix C for information on how to find cases in this chapter on FindLaw.com.

(*Note:* U.S. Supreme Court cases are easily accessible through the Internet. Use google.com or yahoo.com, and then type in the case title (as in *Miranda v. Arizona*). Or, go to *http://www.findlaw .com/casecode/supreme.html*, and then click on Supreme Court Decisions "by year." Click the year the case was decided. You will then see court decisions alphabetically arranged. Note, however, that these means of Internet access may change.)

Arizona v. Evans, **514 U.S. 1 (1995)** The exclusionary rule does not require suppression of evidence seized in violation of the Fourth Amendment where the erroneous information resulted from clerical errors of court employees.

Boyd v. United States, **116 U.S. 616 (1886)** The forced disclosure of papers amounting to evidence of a crime violated the constitutional right of the suspect to protection against unreasonable search and seizure, so the papers were inadmissible in court proceedings.

Brown v. Illinois, **422 U.S. 590 (1975)** The defendant's statement did not come under the "purged taint" exception of the exclusionary rule and was therefore inadmissible. The Court said that "the question whether a confession is the product of a free will under *Wong Sun* must be answered on the facts of each case."

Burdeau v. McDowell, **256 U.S. 465 (1921)** The Fourth Amendment's origin and history clearly show that it was intended as a restraint upon the activities of sovereign authority, not a limitation upon other, nongovernmental agencies.

Chapman v. California, **386 U.S. 18 (1967)** In attempting to demonstrate mere "harmless error," it is not enough for the prosecution simply to show that there was other evidence sufficient to support the verdict. Rather, it must show that there was no reasonable possibility that a different result would have been reached without the tainted evidence.

***Elkins v. United States*, 364 U.S. 206 (1960)** The Fourth Amendment prohibits the use of illegally obtained evidence in federal prosecutions, whether the evidence is obtained by federal or state officers. This case did away with the silver platter doctrine.

***Illinois v. Krull*, 480 U.S. 340 (1987)** Evidence obtained by the police in accordance with a state law that is later declared unconstitutional is admissible in court as part of the good faith exception to the exclusionary rule.

***Illinois v. Rodriguez*, 497 U.S. 117 (1990)** Consent given by somebody whom the police reasonably and honestly believed had authority to give consent is valid.

***Mapp v. Ohio*, 367 U.S. 643 (1961)** The exclusionary rule, which prohibits the use of evidence obtained as a result of unreasonable search and seizure, is applicable to state criminal proceedings.

***Maryland v. Garrison*, 480 U.S. 79 (1987)** The validity of a warrant must be judged in light of the information available to the officers at the time they obtained the warrant. A warrant that is overbroad in describing the place to be searched is valid based on a reasonable but mistaken belief at the time the warrant was issued.

***Massachusetts v. Sheppard*, 468 U.S. 981 (1984)** Evidence obtained by search is admissible in court when the officer conducting the search acted in objectively reasonable reliance on a search warrant that is subsequently declared to be invalid.

***Minnesota v. Carter*, 525 U.S. 83 (1998)** Defendants who were on a short-term visit and who, together with the lessee, used the apartment for a business purpose—to package drugs—had no legitimate expectation of privacy in the apartment.

***Minnesota v. Olson*, 495 U.S. 91 (1990)** Someone who is an overnight guest while the owner of the residence is away has standing to raise the exclusionary rule.

***Nix v. Williams*, 467 U.S. 431 (1984)** Evidence discovered because of a violation of the Sixth Amendment is admissible if the evidence would have been discovered anyway by lawful means. The prosecution must show "inevitable discovery" by a preponderance of evidence and need not prove absence of bad faith by the law enforcement officer responsible for the violation of the Sixth Amendment.

***Pennsylvania Board of Probation and Parole v. Scott*, 524 U.S. 357 (1998)** Evidence illegally obtained in violation of parolees' Fourth Amendment rights does not have to be excluded from a parole revocation hearing.

***Rochin v. California*, 342 U.S. 165 (1952)** Even before the exclusionary rule was applied to the states, the Court held that some searches were so "shocking" as to require exclusion of the evidence seized. These cases were limited to acts of coercion, violence, or brutality.

***Silverthorne Lumber Co. v. United States*, 251 U.S. 385 (1920)** Once the primary evidence (the "tree") is shown to have been unlawfully obtained, any secondary evidence (the "fruit") derived from it is also inadmissible. This case enunciated the fruit of the poisonous tree doctrine.

***South Dakota v. Neville*, 459 U.S. 553 (1983)** Evidence obtained is admissible if the search does not violate the Constitution but only violates an agency rule.

***State v. O'Bremski*, 423 P.2d 530 (1968)** Evidence obtained in an illegal search is admissible when testimony from an independent source predates the search (*http://laws.findlaw.com/us/423/530.html*).

***Taylor v. Alabama*, 457 U.S. 687 (1982)** To break the causal connection between an illegal arrest and a confession that is the fruit of the illegal arrest, and therefore make the evidence admissible, the intervening event must be meaningful.

***United States v. Caceres*, 440 U.S. 741 (1979)** The exclusionary rule does not apply if the violation involves administrative policy and not a constitutional right.

***United States v. Calandra*, 414 U.S. 338 (1974)** A person being questioned by the grand jury cannot refuse to answer questions on the grounds that the questions are based on illegally obtained evidence.

***United States v. Crews,* 445 U.S. 463 (1980)** Illegally obtained evidence is admissible if the police can prove that it was obtained from an independent source not connected to the illegal search or seizure.

***United States v. Houltin,* 566 F.2d 1027 (5th Cir. 1978)** Under the exclusionary rule, evidence obtained in violation of the Fourth Amendment cannot be used in a criminal trial against the victim of the illegal search or seizure. The Constitution does not require this remedy; it is a doctrine of judicial design.

***United States v. Janis,* 428 U.S. 433 (1976)** The primary purpose of the exclusionary rule is to deter police misconduct. Where the exclusionary rule does not result in appreciable deterrence, its use is unwarranted.

***United States v. Leon,* 468 U.S. 897 (1984)** The Fourth Amendment's exclusionary rule should not be applied to bar the prosecution from using evidence that has been obtained by officers acting in reasonable reliance on a search warrant that is issued by a detached and neutral magistrate but that is ultimately found to be invalid because it lacked probable cause.

***United States v. Patane,* 542 U.S. 630 (2004)** The Fifth Amendment self-incrimination clause of the constitution contains its own exclusionary rule.

***Weeks v. United States,* 232 U.S. 383 (1914)** Evidence illegally obtained by federal officers is inadmissible in federal criminal prosecutions.

***Wolf v. Colorado,* 338 U.S. 25 (1949)** State courts were not constitutionally required to exclude illegally obtained evidence, so the exclusionary rule did not apply to the states. This decision was overturned in 1961 in *Mapp v. Ohio.*

***Wong Sun v. United States,* 371 U.S. 471 (1963)** A defendant's intervening act of free will is sufficient to break the causal chain between tainted evidence and illegal police conduct; thus, the evidence otherwise illegally obtained becomes admissible.

 ## You Be the Judge . . .

In the United States Court of Appeals for the Eighth Circuit

In Palo Alto County, Iowa, Sheriff's Deputy Suhr responded to a confidential informant's tip: the CI said there was a chemical smell and many people coming and going from Hessman's house. Deputy Suhr put the house under surveillance, quietly watching until a neighbor called two months later and also reported a chemical smell. When they discretely drove past the Hessman house, Deputy Suhr and Deputy Zweifel smelled a strong chemical smell. They began clandestine surveillance, which revealed a lot of "short-term traffic" at the Hessman house, which from his experience was associated with drug trafficking. Among the visitors to the house was a character Deputy Suhr knew to be involved in drugs.

The Deputies believed from their training and experience that there was a methamphetamine lab operating in Hessman's house. Deputy Suhr returned to his office to put all this information in an application for a search warrant. When he was done with his application, it was 11:00 P.M., and he paged the magistrate to apply for the warrant. The magistrate was out of town, staying at a hotel in Des Moines, about a 3-hour drive, but through a series of calls and faxes back and forth to the magistrate's hotel Deputy Suhr got his search warrant signed and faxed back to him at 1:00 A.M. Deputy Suhr had not signed the application, had not been put under oath to testify to its contents, nor had he been asked by the magistrate to do so.

At 3:20 A.M., Deputy Suhr moved in with several other officers to execute the search warrant, and they found a functioning "meth" lab in Hessman's house. Hessman was arrested and read his *Miranda* rights. He voluntarily made many incriminating statements while he was being "booked." Although the magistrate issued the warrant at 1:00 A.M., Deputy Suhr did not sign the application nor was he put under oath until several hours after all the following occurred: the warrant was executed, the meth lab was seized, Hessman was arrested, and Hessman made his statements in custody. The search warrant was illegal, even though Deputy Suhr was apparently trying to do things properly.

How will you decide this legal issue? Should all the evidence seized or taken as a result of the illegal search warrant be excluded as "fruit of the poisonous tree"?

The Court's decision The U.S. Court of Appeals for the Eighth Circuit decided that the evidence did not need to be suppressed, relying on the "good faith exception" to the exclusionary rule. Deputy Suhr relied in good faith on a warrant that was valid on its face. Even though the mistake of not signing the warrant was Deputy Suhr's, it was not done with any improper intent, and the final mistake was the magistrate's. Just as an officer is expected to rely on a magistrate's decision not to issue a warrant, an officer is entitled to reasonably rely on the magistrate's issuing of a warrant. *U.S. v. Hessman*, 8th Cir. No. 03–2464 (6/1/2004).

In the United States Court of Appeals for the Eighth Circuit

In rural Polk County, Arkansas, the Sheriff's Office and the State Police responded to a desperate 911 call: the caller said that R. L. Salter and his son R. J. were involved in a shooting at their home, and one of them had been shot in the head. When they arrived, the officers found the Salter family home to be a virtual fortress, with 14-inch thick concrete walls and oblong gun turrets. Officers found the father, R. L., outside, with a minor head wound. They could hear R. J. yelling from inside the house. They found that the son, R. J. Salter, was in an 8-foot-square gun room. R. J. pointed an AK-47 and an AR-15-type rifle at the officers when they tried to talk to him, so they quickly slammed the door. This was the start of a five-hour standoff between R. J. and the police.

During the standoff, officers saw an AK-47 and several AR-15-type rifles in the gun room. The police also spotted pipe bombs and blocks of C-4, a military explosive. The father, R. L., told an officer that there were illegal weapons inside the house, which R. J. was afraid would be seized by the police, and that R. J. had enough ammonium nitrate to level the entire house. When R. J. threw items the police believed to be explosives to the floor, R. L. stated, "We all don't need to die here" and pleaded with his son to calm down.

As soon as the standoff ended, the police took R. L. into custody as well, and immediately read him his rights. He said he wanted to exercise his right to remain silent. After this, *knowing that R. L. had invoked his right to remain silent,* Captain Fletcher of the State Police began questioning R. L. about any weapons or explosives in his home (his castle?) that might injure his officers as they searched. R. L. briefly told Fletcher what types of weapons and explosives were in the house.

Fletcher told a judge what R. L. had told him, and other officers prepared a 29-page affidavit when requesting a search warrant, which contained all the above facts that the officers had observed.

How will you decide this legal issue? Should a search warrant be issued for weapons and explosives, even though R. L.'s statements to Fletcher were taken in an illegal interrogation?

The Court's decision The U.S. Court of Appeals for the Eighth Circuit decided that yes, a search warrant was proper. All of R. L.'s statements to Captain Fletcher were "tainted" by the illegal nature of the questioning, but the police already had more than enough for a search warrant for weapons and explosives, from their observations and R. L.'s statements during the standoff. *U.S. v. Salter*, 358 F.3d 1080 (8th Cir., 2004).

Recommended Readings

Ed Cape. *Incompetent police station advice and the exclusion of evidence.* The Criminal Law Review 471–484 (2002).

Donald Dripps. *The case for the contingent exclusionary rule.* The American Criminal Law Review 1, 46 (2001).

Raymond Hayes. Note. *Balancing victim's rights and probative value with the Fourth Amendment right to security in the exclusion of unlawfully seized evidence.* 18 New York Law School Journal of Human Rights 271–303 (2002).

Stephen Saxby. *Bugging evidence admissible says district court.* 18 Computer Law and Society Report 222–223 (2002).

Symposium on the fortieth anniversary of Mapp v. Ohio *(81 S.Ct. 1684 [1961]).* Case Western Reserve Law Review 371–487 (2001).

Holly K. Vance. *Protestors have Fourth Amendment rights, too: In Graves v. City of Coeur d' Alene, the Ninth Circuit clouds clearly established law governing searches.* 79 Washington Law Review 2: 753–774 (May 2004).

Notes

1. Bradford P. Wilson, "Exclusionary Rule," *Crime File Study Guide* (Rockville, MD: National Institute of Justice, n.d.), p. 1.

2. Ibid.

3. *FBI Law Enforcement Bulletin,* September 1997, pp. 29, 32.

4. For an excellent discussion of the arguments for and against the exclusionary rule, see Yale Kamisar, Stephen H. Sach, Malcolm R. Wilkey, and Frank G. Carrington, "Symposium on the Exclusionary Rule," 1 *Criminal Justice Ethics,* pp. 4ff (1982). Some arguments for and against the exclusionary rule in these lists are taken from that source.

5. *Houston Chronicle,* July 8, 1979, sec. 4, p. 2.

6. A study by Thomas Davies, as cited in *The Oxford Companion to the Supreme Court of the United States,* ed. Kermit L. Hall (New York: Oxford University Press, 1992), p. 266.

7. Supra note 4, p. 118.

8. Steven Schlesinger, "Criminal Procedure in the Courtroom," in *Crime and Public Policy,* ed. James Q. Wilson (San Francisco: ICS Press, 1983), p. 195.

9. Supra note 1, p. 1.

10. Supra note 6, p. 266.

Chapter 5

Stop and Frisk and Stationhouse Detention

What You Will Learn

- Stop and frisk is usually spoken of as a single action but is better understood as two separate acts—the stop and the frisk.

- A stop and a frisk need reasonable suspicion for either to be valid.

- *Terry v. Ohio* is the leading case in stop and frisk and one of the most important cases in criminal procedure.

- In some cases, unprovoked flight justifies a stop.

- Stops based on hearsay information, an anonymous tip, or a flyer from another jurisdiction are valid.

- Stops based on race alone are not valid, but lower courts disagree on whether race can be taken as one factor in determining reasonable suspicion for a stop.

- Persons stopped by the police cannot be forced to answer questions but can be forced to identify themselves if this is authorized by state law.

- A frisk does not automatically follow a valid stop; it is justified only if an officer has reasonable suspicion that a threat to his or her safety exists.

- A frisk that goes beyond a mere pat-down for weapons is illegal.

- Stationhouse detentions are intimidating and should be considered the equivalent of arrest.

CASE BRIEFS
_____

Terry v. Ohio (1968)
Hiibel v. Sixth Judicial District Court of Nevada (2004)

Introduction

In this chapter, we deal with stop and frisk and stationhouse detention as forms of intrusion upon a person's freedom. In these cases, no arrest can be made, because probable cause has not been established. However, what begins as a stop and frisk can quickly turn into an arrest if subsequent developments lead the police to conclude that probable cause has been established. Stops, frisks, and stationhouse detentions come under the Fourth Amendment but are not subject to the same constitutional limitations as arrests, searches, or seizures and follow different rules. Stationhouse detentions are more intimidating than stops and frisks and, although less intrusive, are best considered arrests from a legal perspective. To play it safe, stationhouse detentions should be treated by the police as subject to the same rules as an arrest (discussed in Chapter 6).

Stop and Frisk

This section studies the issue and origin of stop and frisk law; *Terry v. Ohio,* the leading case on the law; the guidelines officers must follow to make a legally valid stop and frisk; and the role of reasonable suspicion in valid stop and frisk cases.

Issue and Origin

One legal issue in policing is whether a police officer may stop a person in a public place (or in an automobile), question the person about his or her identity and activities at the time, and frisk the person for dangerous (and perhaps illegally possessed) weapons. A *stop* and a *frisk* are forms of searches and seizures and therefore come under the Fourth Amendment. But because they are less intrusive than an arrest, searches, or seizures, all the police need to conduct them is *reasonable suspicion* rather than *probable cause.*

Several states have passed **stop and frisk** laws that allow an officer, based on reasonable suspicion rather than on probable cause, to stop a person in a public place, ask questions to determine if the person has committed or is about to commit an offense, and frisk the person for weapons if the officer has reasonable concern for his or her own personal safety. Other states and some federal courts have upheld such practices in judicial decisions even without statutory authorization.

Underlying both statutory and judicial approval of stop and frisk is the notion that this practice does not constitute an arrest (although it comes under the Fourth Amendment) and therefore can be justified on less than probable cause.

The Leading Case in Stop and Frisk: *Terry v. Ohio*

***Terry v. Ohio* (1968)**

See Appendix C for information on how to find cases in this chapter on FindLaw.com.

One of the most important cases in law enforcement, and the landmark case that declared stop and frisk constitutional, is *Terry v. Ohio,* 392 U.S. 1 (1968). On October 31, 1963, a police detective observed two men on a street in downtown Cleveland at about 2:30 P.M. It appeared to the detective that the two men were "casing" a store. Each walked up and down, peering into the store window, and then both returned to the corner to confer. At one point, a third person joined them but left quickly. The detective observed the two men rejoin the third man a couple of blocks away. The detective then approached them, told them who he was, and asked for some identification. Receiving a mumbled response, the detective frisked the three men. Terry and one of the other men were both carrying handguns. They were tried and convicted of carrying concealed weapons.

On appeal, the Supreme Court held that the police have the authority to detain a person briefly for questioning even without probable cause to believe that the person has committed a crime. Such an investigatory stop does not constitute an arrest and is permissible when prompted by both the observation of unusual conduct that would lead to a reasonable suspicion that criminal activity is about to take place and the ability to point to specific and articulable facts to justify that suspicion. After the stop, the officer may frisk the person if the officer reasonably suspects personal danger to himself or herself or to other persons. (Read the Case Brief to learn more details about this case.)

The last paragraph of the majority opinion in *Terry v. Ohio* sets the foundation and rules for stop and frisk:

> We . . . hold today that where a police officer observes unusual conduct which leads him reasonably to conclude in light of his experience that criminal activity may be afoot and that the person with whom he is dealing may be armed and presently dangerous, where in the course of investigating this behavior he identifies himself as a policeman and makes reasonable inquiries, and where nothing in the initial stages of the encounter serves to dispel his reasonable fear for his own or others' safety, he is entitled for the protection of himself and others in the area to conduct a carefully limited search of the outer clothing of such persons in an attempt to discover weapons which might be used to assault him. Such a search is a reasonable search under the Fourth Amendment, and any weapons seized may properly be introduced in evidence against the person from whom they are taken.

The Guidelines

Terry v. Ohio set the following guidelines, in sequence, to determine whether a stop and frisk is valid.

The Stop

- *Circumstances.* The police officer must observe unusual conduct that leads him or her reasonably to conclude, in the light of his or her experience that (1) criminal activity is about to take place or that criminal activity has just taken place and that (2) the person with whom he or she is dealing may be armed and presently dangerous.
- *Initial police action.* In the course of investigating such behavior, the officer must (1) identify himself or herself as a police officer and (2) make reasonable inquiries.

The Frisk If the two foregoing requirements are satisfied, the officer, for his or her own protection and that of others in the area, may conduct a carefully limited search (pat-down) of the outer clothing of the person in an attempt to discover weapons that might be used to assault him or her. The guidelines given in *Terry v. Ohio* are usually translated into instructions in police manuals as the steps officers are to follow in stop and frisk cases. These are

1. Observe.
2. Approach and identify.
3. Ask questions.

CASE BRIEF: The Leading Case on Stop and Frisk
Terry v. Ohio, 392 U.S. 1 (1968)

Facts: Police detective McFadden observed two men on a street in downtown Cleveland at approximately 2:30 P.M. on October 31, 1963. It appeared to McFadden that the two men (one of whom was the petitioner Terry) were "casing" a store. Each walked up and down, peering into the store window, and then both returned to the corner to confer. At one point, a third man joined them but left quickly. After McFadden observed the two rejoining the same third man a couple of blocks away, he approached them, told them who he was, and asked them for identification. Receiving a mumbled response, the officer frisked all three men. Terry and one of the other men were carrying handguns. Both were tried and convicted of carrying concealed weapons. They appealed.

Issue: *Is stop and frisk valid under the Fourth Amendment? Yes.*

Supreme Court Decision: The police have the authority to detain a person briefly for questioning even without probable cause to believe that the person has committed a crime. Such an investigatory stop does not constitute an arrest and is permissible when prompted by both the observation of unusual conduct leading to a reasonable suspicion that criminal activity may be afoot and the ability to point to specific and articulable facts to justify that suspicion. Subsequently, an officer may frisk a person if the officer reasonably suspects that he or she is in danger.

Case Significance: The *Terry* case made clear that the practice of stop and frisk is valid. Prior to *Terry*, police departments regularly used stop and frisk either by law or by judicial authorization. But its validity was doubtful because the practice is based on rea-

sonable suspicion instead of probable cause, which is necessary in arrest and search cases. The Court held that stop and frisk is constitutionally permissible despite the lack of probable cause for either a full arrest or a full search and despite the fact that a brief detention not amounting to a full arrest is a seizure, requiring some degree of protection under the Fourth Amendment.

Excerpts from the Decision: The Fourth Amendment provides that "the right of the people to be secure in their persons, houses, papers, and effects, against unreasonable searches and seizures, shall not be violated." This inestimable right of personal security belongs as much to the citizen on the streets of our cities as to the homeowner closeted in his study to dispose of his secret affairs. . . . We have recently held that "the Fourth Amendment protects people, not places," *Katz v. United States*, 389 U.S. 347, 351 (1967), and wherever an individual may harbor a reasonable "expectation of privacy," id., at 361 (Mr. Justice Harlan, concurring), he is entitled to be free from unreasonable governmental intrusion. Of course, the specific content and incidents of this right must be shaped by the context in which it is asserted. For "what the Constitution forbids is not all searches and seizures, but unreasonable searches and seizures." *Elkins v. United States*, 364 U.S. 206, 222 (1960). Unquestionably, petitioner was entitled to the protection of the Fourth Amendment as he walked down the street in Cleveland. . . . The question is whether in all the circumstances of this on-the-street encounter, his right to personal security was violated by an unreasonable search and seizure.

If the answers do not dispel the officers' concern for safety, they then follow this procedure:

1. Conduct a pat-down of the outer clothing.
2. If a weapon is felt, confiscate it and arrest the suspect (optional).
3. Conduct a full body search after the arrest (optional).

If, in the course of a frisk under these circumstances, the officer finds a dangerous weapon, he or she may seize it, and the weapon may be introduced into evidence against the party from whom it was taken.

An example taken from the *Law Officer's Pocket Manual* goes like this: An officer observes two men loitering outside a bank in broad daylight. The men confer several times in front of the bank, looking through the bank's windows. Each wears a topcoat although it is a warm day. One of the suspects goes to a car parked directly across from the bank and sits behind the wheel. As the bank guard leaves the bank, the second suspect starts to head into the bank. The officer can then stop the suspect, identify himself or herself, ask for an explanation of the suspect's conduct, and then frisk the suspect if the answers do not alleviate the officer's suspicions. There is reason, based on the officer's experience, to believe that criminal activity is about to take place, that the suspects are likely to be armed, and that they pose a threat to public safety.[1]

The Need for Reasonable Suspicion

For the stop and frisk to be valid, there must be reasonable suspicion to stop *and* reasonable suspicion to frisk. The term **reasonable suspicion** has not been defined with precision by the Court. In one case, however, the Court said, "Reasonable suspicion is a less demanding standard than probable cause not only in the sense that reasonable suspicion can be established with information that is different in quantity or content from that required to establish probable cause, but also in the sense that reasonable suspicion can arise from information that is less reliable than that required to show probable cause" (*Alabama v. White,* 496 U.S. 325 [1990]). On a scale of certainty, reasonable suspicion ranks lower than probable cause but higher than mere suspicion. Note, however, that reasonable suspicion is what the Constitution requires. States, by legislation, may require a higher degree of certainty, like probable cause, even in stop and frisk cases.

Alabama v. White (1990)

To justify a stop, *reasonable suspicion must be anchored in specific objective facts and logical conclusions based on the officer's experience.* Such general considerations as the high-crime nature of the area are no substitute for specific facts about the suspect or the suspect's conduct.[2] Reasonable suspicion cannot be based on a mere hunch (which has zero percent certainty) or even a suspicion (which may have 10 percent certainty). Specific, objective facts are needed. In *United States v. Arvizu* (534 U.S. 266 [2002]), the Court held that "in making reasonable suspicion determinations, reviewing courts must look at the totality of the circumstances in each case to see whether the detaining officer has particularized an objective basis for suspecting wrongdoing."

United States v. Arvizu (2002)

In *Arvizu,* the defendant argued on appeal that most of the ten factors relied upon by the border patrol agent to establish reasonable suspicion were not in themselves illegal. The Court rejected that argument, saying that the totality of the circumstances, not individual factors, was the test for reasonable suspicion. The Court then added that "this process allows officers to draw on their own experiences and specialized training to make inferences from and deductions about the cumulative information available." In an earlier case, the Court held that an appellate court that reviews, on appeal, the legality of police actions taken without a warrant should conduct a *de novo* (new) review of the trial court's finding on the ultimate issues of reasonable suspicion and probable cause and not simply rely on the trial court's findings (*Ornelas et al. v. United States,* 517 U.S. 690 [1996]).

Ornelas et al. v. United States (1996)

Stop and Frisk: Two Separate Acts, Not One Continuous Act

Although the term *stop and frisk* is often spoken as though one continuous act were involved, it is actually two separate acts, each having its own requirements for legality. They are best understood if discussed separately.

The Stop

A **stop** is justified only if the police officer has reasonable suspicion, in light of his or her experience, that criminal activity is about to take place or has taken place. A stop for anything else (such as to search for evidence) is illegal. For example, one officer stopped a suspect on the grounds that (1) the suspect was walking in an area that had a high incidence of drug traffic, (2) he "looked suspicious," and (3) he had not been seen in that area previously by the officer. The Court held that these circumstances, although amounting to vague suspicion, did not meet the "reasonable suspicion based on objective facts" test, so the stop was unconstitutional (*Brown v. Texas,* 443 U.S. 47 [1979]).

Brown v. Texas (1979)

Note, however, that what starts as a stop may turn into a valid arrest if probable cause is suddenly established. For example, suppose that, while on patrol late one night in a neighborhood notorious for burglary, Officer P sees a person emerge from an alley carrying something bulky. Officer P asks him to stop, whereupon the person drops the object and takes off running. Officer P would have probable cause to arrest that person because of the combination of circumstances.

The next sections examine several issues related to what constitutes a legally valid stop.

When Is a Stop a Seizure under the Fourth Amendment? *United States v. Mendenhall*

The Fourth Amendment forbids unreasonable searches and seizures. Not all contacts with the police, however, constitute a seizure. For example, the mere asking of questions by the police does not constitute a seizure. The important question is, When is contact with the police a "stop" that constitutes a seizure under Fourth Amendment protection and therefore requires reasonable suspicion, and when is it a "stop" that does not constitute a seizure under the Fourth Amendment? The Court has answered this question, saying, "We conclude that a person has been 'seized' within the meaning of the Fourth Amendment only if, in view of all of the circumstances surrounding the incident, a reasonable person would have believed that he was not free to leave" (*United States v. Mendenhall*, 446 U.S. 544 [1980]).

United States v. Mendenhall (1980)

Here, three phrases stand out: (1) "in view of all of the circumstances," (2) "a reasonable person," and (3) "free to leave." In *Mendenhall*, federal officers approached a suspect as she was walking through an airport concourse. They identified themselves and asked to see her identification and airline ticket, which she produced and the officers inspected. She later alleged that what the officers did amounted to a seizure (a stop) that was illegal unless supported by reasonable suspicion. On appeal, the Court disagreed, saying that what happened in this case did not constitute a seizure.

It cited several circumstances in this case, including these:

- The incident took place in a public concourse.
- The agents wore no uniforms and displayed no weapons.
- They did not summon the suspect to their presence but instead approached her and identified themselves as federal agents.
- They requested, but did not demand to see, her ticket.

Merely approaching the suspect, asking her if she would show them her ticket, and then asking a few questions did not constitute a seizure under the Fourth Amendment.

In the same case, the Court gave examples of conduct by the police that might indicate a seizure, even if the person did not attempt to leave. These included the display of a weapon, some physical touching by the officer, or the use of language or tone of voice indicating that compliance with the officer's request might be compelled. The Court then noted, "In the absence of some such evidence, other inoffensive contact between a member of the public and the police cannot, as a matter of law, amount to a seizure of that person." In sum, circumstances determine whether contact with the police constitutes a seizure.

Does Unprovoked Flight upon Seeing the Police Constitute Reasonable Suspicion?

Illinois v. Wardlow
(2000)

The Court has held that unprovoked flight upon observing police officers may constitute reasonable suspicion sufficient to justify a stop (*Illinois v. Wardlow,* 528 U.S. 119 [2000]). In *Wardlow,* the respondent had fled upon seeing a caravan of police motor vehicles as the vehicles converged in an area in Chicago known for heavy narcotics trafficking. A police officer stopped him and then conducted a frisk for weapons because in the officer's experience weapons were involved in that area of narcotics transactions. The officer found a handgun and arrested Wardlow.

On appeal of his conviction for use of an unlawful weapon by a felon, Wardlow maintained that the stop was invalid because his unprovoked flight upon seeing the police did not in itself constitute reasonable suspicion. The Court disagreed, holding that the action by the officer was valid because the flight in itself constituted reasonable suspicion and therefore justified the stop. (The frisk itself was not an issue in the case, the assumption being that the subsequent frisk was valid.) The Court said that this case, "involving a brief encounter between a citizen and a police officer on a public street, is governed by *Terry,* under which an officer who has a reasonable, articulable suspicion that criminal activity is afoot may conduct a brief investigatory stop." The unprovoked flight in *Wardlow* took place in an area of heavy narcotics trafficking.

Would the Court have decided differently had the vicinity been in an affluent suburb or in any other place not known for drug trafficking? The Court decision is unclear on this issue. Instead, the Court said: "Headlong flight—wherever it occurs—is the consummate act of evasion: it is not necessarily indicative of wrongdoing, but it is certainly suggestive of such." The Court then added that "the determination of reasonable suspicion must be based on commonsense judgments and inferences about human behavior." Responding to the argument by Wardlow that the flight from the police was in itself an innocent act, the Court said: "This fact is undoubtedly true, but does not establish a violation of the Fourth Amendment. Even in *Terry,* the conduct justifying the stop was ambiguous and susceptible of an innocent explanation." Thus the Court placed great emphasis on the unprovoked flight itself but then also mentioned the locale, saying: "In this case, moreover, it was not merely respondent's presence in an area of heavy narcotics trafficking that aroused the officers' suspicion but his unprovoked flight upon noticing the police." Given this language and the Court's lack of a categorical statement, lower courts will likely render conflicting decisions on the issue of whether or not unprovoked flight alone, in the absence of other circumstances, constitutes reasonable suspicion. That issue may have to be clarified later by the Court.

Are Stops Based on Hearsay Information Valid?

An investigative stop based on secondhand or hearsay information is valid. For example, in one case a police officer on patrol in a high-crime area received a tip from a person known to the officer that a suspect was carrying narcotics and had a gun. The officer approached the suspect's parked automobile and ordered him to step out. When the suspect

HIGHLIGHT

Reasonable Suspicion as a Standard in Policing

"Reasonable suspicion is a less demanding standard than probable cause not only in the sense that reasonable suspicion can be established with information that is different in quantity or content than that required to establish probable cause, but also in the sense that reasonable suspicion can arise from information that is less

reliable than that required to show probable cause. . . . Reasonable suspicion, like probable cause, is dependent upon both the content of information possessed by police and its degree of reliability. Both factors—quantity and quality— are considered in the 'totality of the circumstances—the whole picture.'"

Source: *Alabama v. White*, 496 U.S. 325 (1990).

responded by rolling down his window, the officer reached into the car and removed a loaded pistol from the suspect's waistband. The suspect was then arrested, and a subsequent search of the car led to the recovery of additional weapons and a substantial quantity of heroin. The Court rejected the defense's contention that a stop and frisk cannot be based on secondhand information, saying that the information from the known informant "carried enough indicia of reliability to justify" the forcible stop of the suspect (*Adams v. Williams*, 407 U.S. 143 [1972]).

Adams v. Williams **(1972)**

Is a Stop Based on an Anonymous Tip Valid?

The preceding case involved information obtained by the police from a known informant. But what if the tip is anonymous? The Court has ruled that an anonymous tip, corroborated by independent police work, may provide reasonable suspicion to make an investigatory stop if it carries sufficient indicia of reliability (*Alabama v. White*, 496 U.S. 325 [1990]). In this case, the police received an anonymous telephone tip that a certain White would leave a certain apartment at 3:00 P.M. in a brown Plymouth station wagon with a broken taillight, that she would be going to Dobey's Motel, and that she would have cocaine in a brown attaché case. The police immediately proceeded to the apartment building, where they saw a vehicle matching the anonymous caller's description. They then observed White leaving the building and driving the vehicle. The police followed her to Dobey's Motel, where she consented to a search of her vehicle, which revealed marijuana. White was then arrested; a subsequent search found cocaine in her purse. She was tried and convicted.

On appeal, she sought suppression of the evidence, alleging that the search was illegal because the stop was not based on reasonable suspicion. The Court disagreed, saying that "standing alone, the tip here is completely lacking in the necessary indicia of reliability, since it provides virtually nothing from which one might conclude that the caller is honest or his information reliable and gave no indication of the basis for his predictions regarding White's criminal activities." However, "although it is a close question, the totality of the circumstances demonstrates that significant aspects of the informant's story were sufficiently corroborated by the police to furnish reasonable suspicion."

In a subsequent case, however, the Court held that an anonymous tip lacking indicia of reliability does not justify a stop and frisk (*Florida v. J. L.*, 529 U.S. 266 [1999]). In this case, the police responded to an anonymous tip that a young black male, wearing a plaid shirt and carrying a gun, was standing with two companions at a bus stop. The officers went to the place, conducted a frisk, and found a gun in the pocket of suspect's pants. The defendant was convicted and appealed his conviction, saying that the search was illegal. In a unanimous decision, the Court excluded the gun from evidence, holding that an anonymous tip that a person is carrying a gun is not enough to justify a stop and frisk. More information is needed to establish reasonable suspicion.

In distinguishing this case from *Alabama v. White* (496 U.S. 325 [1990]), the Court said:

> Here the officers' suspicion that J. L. was carrying a weapon arose not from their own observations but solely from a call made from an unknown location by an unknown caller. The tip lacked sufficient indicia of reliability to provide reasonable suspicion to make a *Terry* stop: It provided no predictive information and therefore left the police without means to test the informant's knowledge or credibility.

Note that in this case the state of Florida and the federal government wanted *Terry* to be modified to create a "firearm exception" to the reasonable suspicion requirement. Under this exception, a tip alleging that the suspect had an illegal gun would have justified a stop and frisk even if reasonable suspicion did not exist. The Court refused to adopt this exception.

Is Information Based on a Flyer from Another Jurisdiction Sufficient for a Stop?

United States v. Hensley (1985)

The Court has decided that the police may stop a suspect on the basis of reasonable suspicion that the person is wanted for investigation in another jurisdiction (*United States v. Hensley*, 469 U.S. 221 [1985]). In this case, Hensley was wanted for questioning in connection with an armed robbery in St. Bernard, Ohio. The police circulated a "wanted" flyer to neighboring police departments. The police in nearby Covington, Kentucky, saw Hensley's car a week later and, knowing that he was wanted for questioning, stopped him and discovered firearms in the car. He was later convicted in federal court of illegal possession of firearms. He appealed the conviction, claiming that the stop was illegal because there was no probable cause, so the evidence obtained should have been excluded.

In a unanimous opinion, the Court held that the police may act without a warrant to stop and briefly detain a person they know is wanted for investigation by a police department in another city. If the police have a reasonable suspicion, grounded in specific and articulable facts, that a person they encounter was involved in or is wanted for questioning in connection with a completed felony, then a "*Terry*-type" stop is permissible. Any evidence legally obtained as a result of that stop is admissible in court.

In the *Hensley* case, the Court publicly recognized the need among law enforcement agencies for rapid communication and cooperation, saying:

> In an era when criminal suspects are increasingly mobile and increasingly likely to flee across jurisdictional boundaries, this rule is a matter of common sense: it minimizes the volume of information concerning suspects that must be transmitted to other jurisdictions and enables police in one jurisdiction to act promptly in reliance on information from another jurisdiction.

Are Stops Based on a Drug Courier Profile Alone Valid?

May a person who fits a **drug courier profile**—identifiers developed by law enforcement agencies indicating the types of individuals who are likely to transport drugs—be stopped by the police? The Court has said that profiles are helpful in identifying people who are likely to commit crimes, but a drug courier profile alone does not justify a *Terry*-type stop. The facts, taken in totality, must amount to a reasonable suspicion (*United States v. Sokolow*, 490 U.S. 1 [1989]).

United States v. Sokolow (1989)

The emphasis is on *totality of circumstances*. In this case, Sokolow purchased two round-trip tickets for a flight from Honolulu to Miami. The facts surrounding that purchase, known to Drug Enforcement Administration (DEA) agents, were as follows: (1) Sokolow paid $2,100 for two round-trip tickets from a roll of $20 bills; (2) he traveled under an assumed name that did not match his listed telephone number; (3) his original destination was Miami, a place known for illicit drugs; (4) he stayed in Miami for only forty-eight hours, although the flight from Honolulu to Miami and back took twenty hours; (5) he appeared nervous during his trip; and (6) he had luggage, but none was checked.

Because of these facts, which fit a drug courier profile developed by the DEA, Sokolow and his companion were stopped and taken to the DEA office at the airport, where their luggage was sniffed by a trained dog. Cocaine was found, and Sokolow was convicted of possession with intent to distribute. On appeal, the Supreme Court said that there was nothing wrong with the use of a drug courier profile in this case because the facts, taken together, amounted to reasonable suspicion that criminal conduct was taking place. The Court noted that whether the facts in this case fit a profile was less significant than the fact that, taken together, they established a reasonable suspicion that justified a stop; therefore, the stop was valid.

Sokolow indicates that, although a drug courier profile is helpful, the totality of circumstances is more important in establishing reasonable suspicion. The Court noted that the activities of Sokolow, taken in isolation and individually, were consistent with innocent travel, but taken together they amounted to reasonable suspicion. There is nothing wrong with using drug courier profiles for a stop if the facts in a particular case, taken together, amount to reasonable suspicion. But the practice of using drug courier profiles alone to stop people, whether they are in airports or motor vehicles, is unconstitutional, according to the Court.

Are Stops Based on a Racial Profile Alone Valid?

Stops based on racial profiles have generated intense controversy. **Racial profiling** occurs when the police or any government law enforcement agent stops a person on the basis of the person's ethnic identity. The process is known in some places as stopping a person for DWB (driving while black) or DWH (driving while Hispanic). In airports it is known as FWA (flying while Arab). A 1999 report by the state attorney general in New York notes that "blacks and Hispanics are much more likely than whites to be stopped and frisked by New York City police officers, often without legal reason." The same report states that "blacks were stopped six times more often than whites, while Hispanics were stopped four times more often."[3]

Are Stops Based on Race Alone Valid?

Are stops based on racial profiles alone valid? The Court has not directly addressed this issue, but it is safe to say that stopping a motorist based on race alone is unconstitutional, because it violates the Equal Protection Clause. The more difficult question is whether race can be taken as one factor in the "totality of circumstances" when determining reasonable suspicion for a stop. Again, the issue has not been addressed by the Court, but courts of appeals appear to differ.

The U.S. Court of Appeals for the Second Circuit has held that "police officers in Oneonta, New York, did not violate the Constitution when they tried to stop every black man in town in 1992 after a woman said she had been robbed in her home by a young black man." The court questioned the police's tactics but ruled that they did not constitute discriminatory racial profiling, because the officers were

Brown v. Oneonta (2nd Cir. 1999)

trying to find a suspect in a specific crime based on a description (*Brown v. Oneonta*, 195 F.3d 111 [2nd Cir. 1999]). In an earlier case, the Sixth U.S. Circuit Court of Appeals held that race is a permissible factor to justify reasonable suspicion during airport interdiction, based on facts known to the officer (*United States v. Travis*, 62 F.3d 170 [6th Cir. 1995]).

United States v. Travis (6th Cir. 1995)

By contrast, in a more recent case, the Ninth U.S. Circuit Court of Appeals ruled that "in most circumstances, law enforcement officials cannot rely on ethnic appearance as a factor in deciding whether to stop someone suspected of a crime," adding that "because of the growth in the Hispanic population in the region (the San Diego, California, area), ethnicity was an irrelevant criterion for law officers to stop a person, unless there was other very specific information identifying the suspect."[4] The case involved three Mexicans who were stopped

---

HIGHLIGHT

Are Stops Based on Race Alone Valid?

The Court has not addressed this issue directly, but it is safe to say that stopping a motorist based on race alone is unconstitutional, because it violates the Equal Protection Clause of the Fourteenth Amendment, which prohibits discrimination. The more difficult question is whether race can be taken as one factor in the "totality of circumstances" when determining reasonable suspicion for a stop. Again, this issue has not been addressed by the Courts, but courts of appeals appear to differ.

---

near San Diego by border patrol officers, based on a tip. The suspects were found to have bags of marijuana, a handgun, and ammunition. They were convicted and deported but later challenged their conviction, saying it was illegal because the border patrol had cited five factors in the decision to stop the suspects, "including a U-turn just before reaching an immigration checkpoint, other suspicious behavior and their Hispanic appearance." The court held that the stop was valid because of the presence of other factors but firmly rejected ethnic appearance as an acceptable criterion.

Racial profiling is banned by state law or police agency policy in many states. It is also banned in federal law enforcement, except for possible terrorism and other national security suspects. The practice of stopping a person for DWB (driving while black) or DWH (driving while Hispanic) occurs more often in stops involving motor vehicles and is discussed more extensively in Chapter 8, Motor Vehicle Stops, Searches, and Inventories.

Can Suspects Who Are Stopped Be Forced to Answer Questions? A suspect who is stopped cannot be forced by the officer to reply to questions. In one case, the Court implied that, although the police have a right to approach any person and ask questions, the person asked does not have any obligation to respond (*Florida v. Royer,* 460 U.S. 491 [1983]). Such a refusal, however, may give the officer sufficient justification to frisk because it may fail to dispel suspicions of danger. Such a refusal may also be taken to help establish reasonable suspicion or probable cause, provided other circumstances are present.

Florida v. Royer
(1983)

Can a Person Who Is Stopped Be Forced to Identify Oneself? Some places have ordinances providing that "it shall be unlawful for any person at a public place to refuse to identify himself by name and address at the request of a uniformed police officer, if the surrounding circumstances are such as to indicate to a reasonable man that the public safety requires such identification."[5] Are these ordinances or laws valid? The Court recently answered this question, saying that the Fourth Amendment allows officers, pursuant to a stop and frisk, to require a person to provide his or her name, and that the person may be arrested for refusing to comply, but only under certain circumstances (*Hiibel v. Sixth Judicial District Court of Nevada,* 542 U.S. 177 [2004]).

*Hiibel v. Sixth
Judicial District
Court of Nevada*
(2004)

In *Hiibel,* an officer asked a suspect if he had any identification. The man, apparently intoxicated, refused and began taunting the officer by putting his hands behind his back and daring the officer to arrest him. The officer arrested the suspect based on Nevada law that authorizes such arrests. The suspect later challenged the Nevada law as violative of his Fourth Amendment right against unreasonable searches and seizures and his Fifth Amendment right against self-incrimination. The Court rejected both challenges, saying that such laws in themselves are not unconstitutional as long as they are not vague or overly broad. (Read the Case Brief to learn more about the *Hiibel* case.)

CASE BRIEF: Leading Case on Whether the Police Can Arrest a Person Who Refuses to Give His or Her Name

Hiibel v. Sixth Judicial District Court of Nevada, et al. 542 U.S. 177 (2004)

Facts: The Humbolt County Sheriff's Office received a telephone call. The caller reported seeing a man assault a woman in a red and silver GMC truck on Grass Valley Road. When an officer arrived at the scene, he found a truck matching the description parked on the side of the road where the caller had described it. The officer observed skid marks in the gravel behind the vehicle, indicating a sudden stop. The officer also observed a man standing by the truck and a woman sitting inside. The officer approached the man and explained that he was investigating the report of an assault. The man appeared intoxicated. The officer asked if he had any identification, but the man refused to answer. After repeated requests and refusals to identify himself, the man began to taunt the officer by putting his hands behind his back and telling the officer to arrest him. After warning the man that he would be arrested if he refused to comply, the officer placed Hiibel under arrest pursuant to a Nevada law allowing officers to detain a person suspected of committing a crime to ascertain his or her identity. Nevada law states that "any person so detained shall identify himself, but may not be compelled to answer any other inquiry of any peace officer."

Issue: *Can a person be arrested for refusal to identify himself or herself to a police officer? Yes, but only under certain circumstances.*

Supreme Court Decision: Requiring a suspect to disclose his or her name in the course of a stop and frisk does not violate the Fourth or the Fifth Amendment.

Case Significance: This case is significant because it resolves an important issue in law enforcement: whether or not the "stop and identify" laws that many jurisdictions have are constitutional. An earlier California law that required a suspect to furnish an officer "credible and reliable" identification when asked to identify himself or herself was declared unconstitutional because of vagueness or overbreadth. What was at issue in this case was whether the Nevada "stop and identify" law, which is well worded, is constitutional. The Nevada law (Nev. Rev. Stat.[NRS] Section 199.280 (2003) provides as follows:

1. Any peace officer may detain any person whom the officer encounters under circumstances which reasonably indicate that the person has committed, is committing or is about to commit a crime.

    . . .

3. The officer may detain the person pursuant to this section only to ascertain his identity and the suspicious circumstances surrounding his presence abroad. Any person so detained shall identify himself, but may not be compelled to answer any other inquiry of any peace officer.

Hiibel claimed the law in itself violated his Fourth and Fifth Amendment rights, not simply because it was vague or overly broad (which would violate his Fourteenth Amendment right to due process). The Court rejected these claims, saying that the "Nevada statute is consistent with Fourth Amendment prohibitions against unreasonable searches and seizures because it properly balances the intrusion on the individual's interest against the promotion of legitimate government interest." The alleged violation of the Fifth Amendment right against self-incrimination was also rejected by the Court, saying that the "Fifth

Amendment prohibits only compelled testimony that is incriminating, and protects only against disclosures that the witness reasonably believes could be used in a criminal prosecution or could lead to other evidence that might be so used." In this case, "Hiibel's refusal to disclose was not based on any articulated real and appreciable fear that his name would be used to incriminate him, or that it would furnish evidence needed to prosecute him." He refused to identify himself "because he thought his name was none of the officer's business," and not because he feared subsequent prosecution; therefore, the Fifth Amendment right against self-incrimination could not be successfully invoked.

Excerpts from the Decision: The Nevada statute is consistent with Fourth Amendment prohibitions against unreasonable searches and seizures because it properly balances the intrusion on the individual's interests against the promotion of legitimate government interest. Hiibel's contention that his conviction violates the Fifth Amendment's prohibition on self-incrimination fails because disclosure of his name and identity presented no reasonable danger of incrimination. The Fifth Amendment prohibits only compelled testimony that is incriminating, and protects only against disclosures that the witness reasonably believes could be used in a criminal prosecution or could lead to other evidence that might be so reasonably used. In this case, [Hiibel's] refusal to disclose his name was not based on any articulated real and appreciable fear that his name would be used to incriminate him, or that "it would furnish a link in the chain of evidence needed to prosecute" him [internal citations omitted].

What Are the Reasonable Scope and Duration of a Stop?
An investigatory stop must be temporary and not last any longer than necessary under the circumstances to achieve its purpose. Officers cannot detain a person for as much time as is convenient. This has been decided by the Court in a number of cases.

In one case, the Court held that a ninety-minute detention of an air traveler's luggage was excessive. In that case, the suspect's luggage was detained long enough to enable a trained dog to sniff for marijuana. The Court decided that the initial seizure was justified under *Terry v. Ohio* but added that the ninety-minute delay exceeded the permissible limits of an investigative stop: "Although we decline to adopt any outside time limitation for a permissible Terry stop, we have never approved a seizure of the person for the prolonged ninety-minute period involved here and cannot do so on the facts presented by this case" (*United States v. Place,* 462 U.S. 696 [1983]).

United States v. Place (1983)

In another case, the Court held that the removal of a detainee without his consent from the public area in an airport to the police room in the airport converted the stop to an arrest. In this case, airport narcotics police stopped the suspect because he fit the drug courier profile. When the agents asked for and examined his ticket and driver's license, they discovered that he was traveling under an assumed name. They then identified themselves as narcotics agents and told him that he was suspected of being a drug courier. Without his consent, they took him to a separate police room about forty feet away from the main concourse. One officer sat with him in the room while another officer retrieved his luggage from the airline and brought it back to the room. The agents then asked the suspect if he would consent to a search of the suitcases. The suspect took out a key and unlocked one of the bags, which contained drugs.

The Court concluded that, although the initial stop and questioning were valid, the subsequent conduct of the officers was "more intrusive than necessary" to carry out the limited investigation permitted under stop and frisk; therefore, it constituted an arrest. Because the police were interested mainly in gaining consent to search the suspect's luggage, there was no need to isolate him to gain that consent (*Florida v. Royer*, 460 U.S. 491 [1983]).

In a third case, a certain Luckett was stopped for jaywalking. He was detained for longer than was necessary to write out a ticket because the police wanted to radio headquarters on an unsubstantiated hunch that there was a warrant for Luckett's arrest. The court of appeals held that the duration of the stop was unreasonable and that it turned the stop into an arrest. Because there was no basis at that time for an arrest, the detention was therefore unlawful (*United States v. Luckett*, 484 F.2d 89 [1973]).

United States v. Luckett (1973)

United States v. Sharpe (1985)

In a fourth case, *United States v. Sharpe* (470 U.S. 675 [1985]), the Court found it reasonable for the police to detain a truck driver for twenty minutes. The driver was suspected of carrying marijuana in a truck camper. The length of the stop was due in part to the fact that the driver attempted to evade the stop, causing the two officers pursuing him to become separated. The officer who performed the stop therefore had to wait fifteen minutes for his more experienced partner to arrive before making the search. Marijuana was found in the camper, and the driver was arrested. The Supreme Court held that, to determine whether a detention is reasonable in length, the court must look at the purpose to be served by the stop and the time reasonably needed to carry it out. It added that courts should refrain from second-guessing police officers' choices, especially when the police are acting in a swiftly developing situation, as in this case. This case indicates that the reasonableness of a stop must take into account not just the length of time involved but the needs of law enforcement as well.

In sum, it is difficult to state categorically how much time is sufficient for a valid stop. What we do know is that the Court uses this test: whether the stop is longer than necessary under the circumstances to achieve its purpose. If it is, the contact ceases to be a stop and becomes an arrest, which is invalid unless based on probable cause. This is determined by courts on a case-by-case basis, taking into account the circumstances surrounding the case.

Are Airport Stops and Searches Valid? Airplane passengers have for decades been subjected to stops and searches at airports. These have had few legal challenges, and those challenges have been rejected based on a variety of reasons. Stops and searches are presumably made with the consent of the passengers, who want to ensure their own safe air travel. A passenger who refuses is not allowed to board; hence, a self-enforcing process is involved. The procedure is also easily justified based on a compelling state interest, which is ensuring passengers safe travel. It is difficult to overcome the presumption that airport stops and searches result in passenger safety. These searches are also easily justified based on "special needs" rather than as a law enforcement activity. The Court has held in a number of cases that the Fourth Amendment does not apply rigidly to cases involving special needs. It may also be argued that airport searches are a form of administrative search with lower Fourth Amendment protection.

Some cases have addressed specific issues related to airport searches. In *9th Cir. v. United Airlines, Inc.* (No. 01–55319 [9th Cir. 2002]), the Ninth U.S. Circuit Court of Appeals held that airport security guards may conduct a random check of a traveler's carry-on bag, even if the bag has passed through an X-ray scan at an airport without arousing suspicion that it contained weapons or explosives.

Torbet v. United Airlines, Inc. **(9th Cir. 2002)**

United States v. Pulido-Baquerizo (9th Cir. 1986)

In *United States v. Pulido-Baquerizo* (800 F.2d 899 [9th Cir. 1986]), the Ninth Circuit also held that airline passengers who put their bags on an X-ray machine's conveyor belt at a secured boarding area implied consent to a visual inspection and limited hand search of the bag if the X-ray scan is inconclusive about whether there are dangerous items in the bag. In effect, this decision says that consent to search by putting the bag on an X-ray machine also constitutes consent to search further.

Since the events of 9/11, airport stops and searches have become more intense and intrusive. There are allegations of racial profiling and suspicions that some passengers are being singled out for FWA (flying while Arab). Even if proved to be true, legal challenges to this type of racial profiling may prove difficult because of serious and valid security concerns. As long as terrorism fears continue to be a part of air travel, courts will likely allow practices that are not blatantly violative of constitutional rights.

What Degree of Intrusiveness Is Permissible? The investigative method used must be the least intrusive and the most reasonably available to verify or dispel the officer's suspicion. Anything more intrusive makes the act invalid. Therefore, the greater the degree of police control over a detainee, the greater the likelihood that reviewing courts will impose the higher standard of probable cause. In the absence of some justification, the display of weapons by the police when making an investigative stop might turn a stop into an arrest. But the display of weapons in itself does not automatically convert a stop into an arrest.

Lower courts tend to look at the display of weapons on a case-by-case basis to determine if the stop has been converted into an arrest because of such a display of force. The Supreme Court has not clarified what amount of force, if any, can be used by the police in stop and frisk cases.

The Frisk

A **frisk** should follow a stop only if there is nothing in the initial stages of the encounter that would dispel fears based on reasonable suspicion about the safety of the police officer or of others. A frisk has only one purpose: the protection of the officer or of others. In *Terry,* the Court said:

> When an officer is justified in believing that the individual whose suspicious behavior he is investigating at close range is armed and presently dangerous to the officer or to others, it would appear to be clearly unreasonable to deny the officer the power to take necessary measures to determine whether the person is in fact carrying a weapon and to neutralize the threat of physical harm.

A frisk should take place after a stop only if justified by concerns of safety for the officer and for others, not as an automatic consequence of a valid stop. For example, suppose X is stopped by a police officer late one night in a dimly lighted street on reasonable suspicion that X is about to commit an offense. The officer asks X questions to which X gives evasive answers, appearing uneasy and nervous. The officer may go ahead and frisk, because nothing in the initial encounter has dispelled his reasonable concern for his or others' safety.

By contrast, suppose that after the stop and initial questioning, the officer becomes convinced that X in fact resides in one of the nearby apartments and that he is returning home from a trip to a nearby store to buy cigarettes. Then, the officer has no justification to go ahead and frisk.

The Court has stated that the *totality of circumstances* (meaning the whole picture) must be taken into account when determining the legality of a frisk. The detaining officers must have a specific, objective basis for suspecting the stopped person of criminal activity (*United States v. Cortez,* 449 U.S. 411 [1981]).

United States v.
Cortez (1981)

The legal requirement that an officer must have reasonable suspicion that his or her safety may be in jeopardy before frisking someone applies only to a frisk, not to a stop. This means that an officer does not need to have reasonable suspicion that a person is armed and dangerous before stopping a person. All the officer needs for a valid stop is reasonable suspicion that criminal activity is about to take place or has taken place.

This section looks at some of the other issues surrounding legally valid frisks.

What Is the Extent of the Frisk? A frisk must be limited initially to a pat-down of a person's outer clothing, and only an object that feels like a weapon may properly be seized. The object may turn out not to be a weapon, but if it feels like one, the frisk is justified. Conversely, if the object does not feel like a weapon, it cannot be seized. For example, suppose that, after a valid stop based on reasonable suspicion, a police officer has a reasonable fear that the suspect may be armed. She then frisks the suspect and in the process feels something soft that cannot possibly be considered a weapon. She cannot legitimately seize the object in question. If seized, the object is not admissible as evidence in court, regardless of how incriminating it might be.

United States v.
Robinson (1973)

Confusion has arisen over the extent a frisk can take after a stop because of the decision in *United States v. Robinson* (414 U.S. 218 [1973]). In the *Robinson* case, the Supreme Court held that a body search after an authorized arrest for driving without a permit is valid even when the officer admits that there was no possible danger to himself or herself and therefore no reason to look for a weapon. However, *Robinson* involved an arrest, not a stop and frisk, so arrest laws applied. Once the stop and frisk turns into an arrest based on probable cause, then the *Robinson* decision applies, and a body search may then be conducted. However, a frisk alone does not justify a body search, because its sole purpose is to protect the officer or others.

Use of force beyond a pat-down for weapons is likely to convert the contact into an arrest instead of a frisk. In *United States v. Robinson* (949 F.2d 851 [6th Cir. 1991]), the Court of Appeals for the Sixth Circuit said: "When actions by the police exceed the bounds permitted by reasonable suspicion, the seizure becomes an arrest and must be supported by probable cause."

United States v. Robinson (6th Cir. 1991)

Minnesota v. Dickerson (1993)

What Can an Officer Do and Not Do during a Frisk? *Minnesota v. Dickerson* (508 U.S. 366 [1993]) clarified the limits of what the police can or cannot do in the course of a frisk. Police officers in Minnesota, noticing a suspect's evasive actions when approached, coupled with the fact that he had just left a building known for cocaine traffic, decided to investigate further. They ordered the suspect to submit to a frisk. The frisk revealed no weapons, but the officer conducting it testified later that he "felt a small lump in suspect's jacket pocket." Upon examining the lump with his fingers, the officer concluded it was crack cocaine. He then reached into the suspect's pocket and retrieved what indeed turned out to be a small bag of cocaine. The suspect was convicted of possession of a controlled substance.

On appeal, Dickerson contended that the evidence should have been suppressed, because its seizure was illegal in that it went beyond a pat-down search. The Supreme Court held that objects that police detect in the course of a valid protective frisk under *Terry v. Ohio* may be seized without a warrant, but only if the officer's sense of touch ("plain feel") makes it *immediately apparent* that the object, although non-threatening, is contraband, so that probable cause is present. In this case, however, the officer went beyond the lawful scope of *Terry* when, having concluded that the object he felt inside the suspect's jacket was not a dangerous weapon, he proceeded to "squeeze, slide, and manipulate it" in an effort to determine if it was contraband. Given the circumstances under which the evidence was obtained, the Court considered the evidence inadmissible.

HIGHLIGHT

The Limits of a Frisk

"Although the officer was lawfully in a position to feel the lump in respondent's pocket, because *Terry* entitled him to place his hands upon respondent's jacket, the court below determined that the incriminating character of the object was not immediately apparent to him. Rather, the officer determined that the item was contraband only after conducting a further search, one not authorized by *Terry* or by any other exceptions to the warrant requirement. Because this further search of respondent's pocket was constitutionally invalid, the seizure of the cocaine that followed is likewise unconstitutional."

SOURCE: *Minnesota v. Dickerson*, 508 U.S. 366 (1993).

Dickerson is significant because it clarifies what an officer may validly confiscate in the course of a frisk and under what circumstances. The Court held that what the officer did in this case was illegal because, even though he felt no danger to his person during the frisk, he went ahead anyway and conducted a further search, saying, "I examined it with my fingers and it slid and it felt to be a lump of crack cocaine in cellophane," which he then confiscated. Officers during a frisk have only one justification for confiscating anything: they felt something that might reasonably be considered a weapon.

A valid frisk can turn in an instant into a valid search if, in the course of the frisk, the officer has probable cause to think that the object is seizable. For example, suppose Officer F frisks a suspect because she has reasonable grounds to believe that the suspect is carrying a weapon. While frisking, she feels something under the suspect's clothing, and although it does not feel like a weapon, the reasonable conclusion is that it is contraband—based on her experience as an officer in that area. Officer F may seize the item based on probable cause. In this case, the seizable nature of the object must be "immediately apparent" to the officer for the seizure to be valid. The Court in *Dickerson* said:

> Although the officer was lawfully in a position to feel the lump in respondent's pocket, because *Terry* entitled him to place his hands upon respondent's jacket, the court below determined that *the incriminating character of the object was not immediately apparent to him. Rather, the officer determined that the item was contraband only after conducting a further search,* one not authorized by *Terry* or by any other exception to the warrant requirement. [emphasis added]

What Constitutes Plain Touch? *Minnesota v. Dickerson* is considered in many quarters to officially recognize the use of the **plain touch** (also known as "plain feel") **doctrine** in law enforcement. For a long time, the Supreme Court has recognized the more popular "plain view" doctrine (discussed in Chapter 9), which holds that items in plain view are subject to seizure by officers because they are not protected by the Fourth Amendment. Although using the sense of touch has long been accepted by the courts as a way of establishing probable cause, the *Dickerson* case reiterated the Supreme Court's recognition of this "variant" of the plain view doctrine. The plain touch doctrine states that "if the officer, while staying within the narrow limits of a frisk for weapons, feels what he has probable cause to believe is a weapon, contraband or evidence, the officer may expand the search or seize the object."[6]

In *Minnesota v. Dickerson,* the search would probably have been considered valid if the officer had testified that, although what he touched did not feel like a weapon, it was immediately apparent to him, given his experience and the totality of circumstances, that the object was contraband.

Are "Fishing Expeditions" for Evidence Allowed? The frisk cannot be used as a **fishing expedition** to see if some type of usable evidence can be found on the suspect. Its only purpose is to protect the police officer and others in the area from

HIGHLIGHT

The Plain Touch Doctrine

Although using the sense of touch has long been accepted by the courts as a way of establishing probable cause, the *Dickerson* case reiterated the Supreme Court's recognition of this variant of the plain view doctrine. The plain touch doctrine states that "if the officer, while staying within the narrow limits of a frisk for weapons, feels what he has probable cause to believe is a weapon, contraband or evidence, the office may expand the search or seize the object." It differs from plain view in that what is used to determine probable cause is the sense of touch.

SOURCE: *Minnesota v. Dickerson*, 508 U.S. 366 (1993).

possible harm. A frisk for any other reason is illegal and leads to the exclusion of any evidence obtained, regardless of how incriminating the evidence may be.

Because the sole purpose of a frisk is police protection, anything felt in the course of the frisk that does not feel like a weapon cannot legally be seized. For example, suppose Officer X frisks a person because she suspects, after a valid stop, that the person is dangerous. In the course of the pat-down, Officer X feels a soft object in the person's pocket that she thinks might be cocaine. If confiscated based on that suspicion alone, the evidence is not admissible in court, because Officer X did not think that what she felt was a weapon, nor did she have probable cause to conduct a search. Suppose, however, that in the course of that frisk Officer X also comes across something that feels like a weapon. That weapon can be confiscated and the suspect arrested and then searched. If the cocaine is found in his pocket in the course of that search, that evidence is admissible because the frisk, which led to the arrest and subsequent search, is valid.

Is Consent to Frisk Based on Submission to Police Authority Valid?

Consent to frisk based on submission to police authority is not voluntary and intelligent and is therefore invalid. As in all search and seizure cases, consent must be obtained without coercion or intimidation. For example, suppose Officer P, after a valid stop but without fearing for his life, tells a suspect in an authoritative tone that he would like to conduct a frisk—to which the suspect accedes. Such a frisk is not valid because consent, if at all given, was likely an act of submission to police authority and therefore not voluntary or intelligent. Validity would depend on how that alleged consent was obtained.

Can an Officer Frisk after a Stop without Asking Questions?

In *Terry v. Ohio,* the Court stated:

> Where in the course of investigating this behavior he identifies himself as a policeman and makes *reasonable inquiries*, and where nothing in the initial stages of the encounter serves to dispel his reasonable fear for his own or others' safety, he is entitled for the protection of himself and others in the area to conduct a carefully limited search of the outer clothing of such persons in an attempt to discover weapons which might be used to assault him. [emphasis added]

■ Table 5.1 The Distinctions between Stop and Frisk and Arrest

	Stop and Frisk	Arrest
Degree of certainty needed	Reasonable suspicion	Probable cause
Extent of intrusion	Pat-down for weapons	Full body search
Purpose	Stop: To prevent criminal activity Frisk: To ensure the safety of officers and others	To take the person into custody or to determine if a crime has taken place
Warrant	Not needed	Required, unless arrest falls under one of the exceptions
Duration	No longer than necessary to achieve the purpose	In custody until legally released
Force allowed	Stop: None Frisk: Pat-down	Reasonable

This can be interpreted to mean that *reasonable inquiries* are required before a frisk. There may be instances, however, when a frisk is justified without the officer having to ask questions right after the stop. This is likely to occur in cases where the officer has reasonable suspicion, even before questions are asked, that the person stopped poses a danger to him or her or to others. The Court in *Terry* said that a frisk is justified if a "reasonably prudent man in the circumstances would be warranted in the belief that his safety or that of others was in danger." The only possible exception is if state law requires the officer to make reasonable inquiries before conducting a frisk.

Does a Frisk Include Things Carried by the Suspect?

Assume that X has been stopped and subsequently frisked. Is the frisk limited to patting down X for a weapon, or can luggage carried by X also be frisked? The Court has not directly addressed this issue, but there are reasons to believe that frisks of belongings (backpacks and other containers from which weapons may be easily retrieved and which are in the immediate possession of the suspect) are likely justifiable. The burden, however, is on the officer to establish that the extended frisk was necessary for officer safety, meaning that the belonging was located such that it constituted an immediate danger to the officer. Like other forms of searches, the frisk cannot be used as a fishing expedition for evidence.

The Distinctions between Stop and Frisk and Arrest

The concepts of stop and frisk and arrest can be confusing. Both involve a restriction of an individual's freedom by the police, and both can lead to a similar result—the individual's being charged with a crime. The distinctions between these two concepts need to be clearly understood; they are summarized in Table 5.1.

Other Applications of Stop and Frisk

Stop and frisk law has been applied to cases involving motor vehicles, weapons in a car, and residences. This section looks at what Court decisions have said about each of these applications.

Application to Motor Vehicles

Motorists are subject to stop and frisk under the same circumstances as pedestrians. This means that motorists can be stopped only if there is reasonable or articulable suspicion of possible involvement in an unlawful activity and may be frisked only if there is fear for the officer's safety. After a vehicle is stopped, a police officer may automatically order the driver to step out of the car even if the officer has no reasonable suspicion that the driver poses a threat to the officer's safety (*Pennsylvania v. Mimms*, 434 U.S. 106 [1977]).

Pennsylvania v. Mimms (1977)

In *Pennsylvania v. Mimms*, two police officers while on routine patrol observed Mimms driving an automobile with an expired license plate. The officers stopped the vehicle for the purpose of issuing a traffic summons. One of the officers approached and asked Mimms to step out of the car and produce his owner's card and operator license. When Mimms stepped out, the officers noticed a large bulge under his sports jacket. Fearing that it might be a weapon, one officer frisked Mimms and discovered in his waistband a .38-caliber revolver loaded with five rounds of ammunition. Mimms sought to exclude the evidence during trial, claiming that it was obtained illegally because he was asked to step out for no justifiable reason.

On appeal, the Court rejected Mimms's contention, saying that, once a police officer has lawfully stopped a vehicle for a traffic violation, he or she may order the driver to get out even without suspecting any other criminal activity or threat to the officer's safety. Such an intrusion upon the driver is minimal. After the driver has stepped out, if the officer then reasonably believes that the driver may be armed and dangerous, the officer may conduct a frisk. Note, however, that, although the authority of an officer to ask a driver to step out of the car is automatic after a valid stop, a frisk after the driver gets out of the car is not automatic. It can be undertaken only if there is reasonable suspicion of a threat to the officer's safety.

HIGHLIGHT

Stop and Frisk of Motorists

"Motorists are subject to stop and frisk under the same circumstances as pedestrians. Moreover, a police officer may order the driver to step out of the car after a routine stop for issuance of a

traffic ticket, even if the officer has no reasonable suspicion that the driver poses a threat to officer safety."

SOURCE: *Pennsylvania v. Mimms*, 434 U.S. 106 (1977).

After a valid stop, an officer may look around the vehicle and confiscate seizable items in plain view under the plain view doctrine. Items that are not in plain view cannot be seized without probable cause. A search of the car may also be conducted after a valid consent. (Vehicle stops and searches are discussed more extensively in Chapter 8.)

Application to Weapons in a Car

The police may also conduct a brief search of the vehicle after a stop if the officer has a reasonable suspicion that the motorist is dangerous and that there might be a weapon in the vehicle to which the motorist may have quick access.[7] If an officer has reasonable suspicion that a motorist who has been stopped is dangerous and may be able to gain control of a weapon in the vehicle, the officer may conduct a brief search of the passenger compartment even if the motorist is no longer inside the car. Such a search should be limited, however, to areas in the passenger compartment where a weapon might be found or hidden.

Application to Residences

Maryland v. Buie
(1990)

The Court has authorized the police practice of limited "protective sweeps" without a warrant while officers are conducting an in-house arrest of a suspect (*Maryland v. Buie,* 494 U.S. 325 [1990]). This practice allows officers to go to other rooms in the house when making an arrest. Some observers consider this practice similar to the "frisk of a house." In *Buie,* the Court held that protective sweeps are allowed if the following are present: (1) "a reasonable belief based on specific and articulable facts that the area to be swept harbors an individual posing a danger to those on the arrest scene; (2) that it extend only to a "cursory inspection of those spaces where a person may be found"; and (3) that the sweep lasts "no longer than it takes to complete the arrest and depart the premises." In sum, the requirements for the protective sweep of a house during arrest are similar to the requirements for the frisk of a person after a valid stop.

Stationhouse Detention

Like stop and frisk, **stationhouse detention** is a lesser limitation of freedom than arrest but a greater one than the on-the-street detention in a stop and frisk. It is used in many jurisdictions for obtaining fingerprints or photographs, ordering police lineups, administering polygraph examinations, and securing other identification or nontestimonial evidence.

This section looks at whether stationhouse detention can be used to obtain fingerprinting and for interrogations.

For Fingerprinting

Davis v. Mississippi (1969)

In *Davis v. Mississippi* (394 U.S. 721 [1969]), a rape case involving twenty-five youths who were detained for questioning and fingerprinting when the only leads were a general description and a set of fingerprints, the Supreme Court excluded the evidence obtained from the fingerprints. But the Court also implied that detention for fingerprinting might be permissible even without probable cause to arrest. However, the Court made it clear that "narrowly circumscribed procedures" were required, including at least some objective basis for suspecting the person of a crime, a legitimate investigatory purpose for the detention (such as fingerprinting), detention at a time not inconvenient for the subject, and a court order stating that adequate evidence existed to justify the detention.

Hayes v. Florida (1985)

In *Hayes v. Florida* (470 U.S. 811 [1985]), however, the Court held that mere reasonable suspicion alone does not permit the police to detain a suspect at the police station to obtain fingerprints. Therefore, when the police transported a suspect to the stationhouse for fingerprinting without his consent, probable cause, or prior judicial authorization, the detention violated the Fourth Amendment. Said the Court:

> Our view continues to be that the line is crossed when the police, without probable cause or a warrant, forcibly remove a person from his home or other place in which he is entitled to be and transport him to the police station, where he is detained, although briefly, for investigative purposes. We adhere to the view that such seizures, at least where not under judicial supervision, are sufficiently like arrests to invoke the traditional rule that arrests may constitutionally be made only on probable cause.

Note, however, that in the *Hayes* case, the suspect was transported without his consent to a stationhouse for fingerprinting. Therefore, in cases where consent is obtained, probable cause should not be necessary. The problem is that courts consider the confines of a stationhouse as generally intimidating; therefore, voluntary and intelligent consent may later be a problem if the absence of probable cause is challenged. Should the officer rely on consent, it is best to make it clear to the suspect that he or she is not under arrest, that he or she can leave at any time, and that the fingerprinting is purely voluntary. Moreover, the suspect's signature on a waiver form, duly witnessed, strengthens the officer's claim of voluntary and intelligent consent.

In the same case, however, the Court said that field detention (as opposed to stationhouse detention) for purposes of fingerprinting a suspect does not require probable cause as long as (1) there is reasonable suspicion that the suspect has committed a criminal act, (2) there is reasonable belief that the fingerprinting will either negate or establish the suspect's guilt, and (3) the procedure is promptly effected.

For Interrogation

Dunaway v. New York (1979)

The Court has held that probable cause is necessary for a stationhouse detention accompanied by interrogation (as opposed to just fingerprinting) even if no expressed arrest is made. In *Dunaway v. New York* (442 U.S. 200 [1979]), the defendant was asked to come to police headquarters, where he received his *Miranda* warnings, was questioned, and ultimately confessed. There was no probable cause to arrest him, but there was some reason for the police to suspect him in connection with the crime being investigated. The Court held that the defendant was in fact arrested and not simply stopped on the street, so probable cause was required to take him to the police station. Because probable cause was lacking, the confession obtained could not be admissible in court. The Court added that the detention of Dunaway in this case was indistinguishable from a traditional arrest because he was not questioned briefly where he was found but instead was transported to a police station and would have been physically restrained if he had refused to accompany the officers or had tried to escape from their custody.

Summary

- A stop is a police practice whereby a person is stopped in public and questioned.

- A frisk is a pat-down for weapons.

- Although often spoken of as a single action, stop and frisk are best understood as two separate acts; each must be based on reasonable suspicion.

- Stop and frisk are authorized by law or court decision.

- The purpose of a stop is to prevent criminal activity or to respond if criminal activity has just taken place.

- A frisk has one purpose—to protect officers. A frisk for any other purpose is illegal.

- Reasonable suspicion is less than probable cause but more than mere suspicion; it must be based on specific, objective facts.

- There are two limitations on a stop: (1) it must be temporary and no longer than necessary to achieve its purpose; and (2) it must be the least intrusive action available to the officer.

- There are two limitations on a frisk: (1) officers cannot squeeze, slide, or manipulate during a pat-down; and (2) it cannot be used as a fishing expedition for evidence.

- Motor vehicles can be stopped only if there is reasonable suspicion of possible involvement in an unlawful activity by its occupants; they may be frisked only if there is fear for the officer's safety.

- Stationhouse detention for fingerprinting or interrogation should be considered an arrest and subject to Fourth Amendment protection.

Review Questions and Hypothetical Cases

1. "An officer who makes a valid stop can, because of that valid stop, conduct a valid frisk." Is that statement true or false? Discuss your answer.

2. *Terry v. Ohio* is an important case in law enforcement. What did the Court say, and why is that case important?

3. Distinguish between stop and frisk and an arrest.

4. What does *Minnesota v. Dickerson* say about the scope and extent of what an officer can do during a frisk? That case also gives support to the "plain touch" doctrine. What does that doctrine say?

5. "A police officer who validly stops a motor vehicle can automatically ask the driver to get out of the vehicle and then frisk the driver." Is that statement true or false? Justify your answer.

6. Assume you are a resident of Denver, Colorado. One midnight, after a birthday celebration in one of the downtown bars, you fled after being followed by a police car in the Denver downtown area. Based on that fact alone, the police chased and immediately caught up with you. From your reading of *Illinois v. Wardlaw*, was the stop valid? Defend your answer.

7. X, a student, was stopped by the police, based on reasonable suspicion, after midnight in the suburbs of Los Angeles and detained for one hour. Is his detention valid? Give reasons for your answer.

8. Y was stopped by the police at early dawn one night in a Miami, Florida, suburb because he looked suspicious, was wearing heavy clothing although it was a warm night, looked lost in the neighborhood, and acted nervous upon seeing the police. Is the stop valid? Analyze each of these factors and determine if, in and of themselves, they justify the stop. Would your answer be different or the same if all of these circumstances were taken together? Explain.

9. Assume you are a rookie university police officer who has been on the job for a couple of weeks. While patrolling the campus one evening, you see a man emerge out of a dark alley near one of the dormitories. The man appears shabby and unkempt. You tell the man to stop and ask him questions. The man is nervous and incoherent in his answers, but says he is a janitor in the building and has just gotten off from work. You frisk him and recover bundles of crack cocaine from his pockets. Is this evidence admissible in court under stop and frisk? Explain why.

10. Officer P invited Y, a suspect in a robbery case, to come to the police station "to answer a few questions." Suspect Y willingly accepted. Y was kept at the station for four hours and was later fingerprinted. Were Y's fingerprints legally obtained by the police? Support your answer.

Key Terms

Go to the Criminal Procedure 7e website for flash cards that will help you master the definitions of these terms.

drug courier profile, 147
fishing expedition, 156
frisk, 153

plain touch doctrine, 156
racial profiling, 147
reasonable suspicion, 141

stationhouse detention, 160
stop, 142
stop and frisk, 138

Holdings of Key Cases

See Appendix C for information on how to find cases in this chapter on FindLaw.com.

***Adams v. Williams*, 407 U.S. 143 (1972)** The Fourth Amendment does not require a police officer who lacks the precise level of information necessary for probable cause to arrest simply to shrug his or her shoulders and allow a crime to occur or a criminal to escape. A brief stop of a suspicious individual, to determine his or her identity or to maintain the status quo momentarily while obtaining more information, may be most reasonable in light of the facts known to the officer at the time. The basis for a stop and frisk need not be the officer's personal observations; the information may be given by a reliable informant.

***Alabama v. White*, 496 U.S. 325 (1990)** Reasonable suspicion is a less demanding standard than probable cause, not only because it can be established with information different in quantity or content from that required to establish probable cause but also because reasonable suspicion can arise from information that is less reliable than that required to show probable cause.

Brown v. Oneonta, **195 F.3d 111 (2nd Cir. 1999)** The tactics used by the police in stopping every black man in town were questionable, but they did not constitute discriminatory racial profiling, because the officers were trying to find a suspect in a specific crime based on a description.

Brown v. Texas, **443 U.S. 47 (1979)** The following circumstances, although amounting to vague suspicion, did not meet the test for unreasonable suspicion based on objective facts, so the stop was unconstitutional: (1) the suspect was walking in an area that had a high incidence of drug traffic, (2) the suspect "looked suspicious," and (3) the suspect had not been seen in that area previously by the officer.

Davis v. Mississippi, **394 U.S. 721 (1969)** Implies that under certain limited circumstances a suspect may be fingerprinted even without probable cause to arrest.

Dunaway v. New York, **442 U.S. 200 (1979)** Probable cause is necessary for stationhouse detention of a suspect when accompanied by an interrogation (as opposed to just fingerprinting), even if no formal arrest is made.

Florida v. J. L., **529 U.S. 266 (1999)** "An anonymous tip that a person is carrying a gun is not, without more information, sufficient to justify a police officer's stop and frisk of that person."

Florida v. Royer, **460 U.S. 491 (1983)** Although the initial stopping and questioning of a suspect who fell within the drug courier profile was valid, the subsequent conduct of the police was more intrusive than necessary to carry out the limited investigation permitted under stop and frisk.

Hayes v. Florida, **470 U.S. 811 (1985)** Mere reasonable suspicion alone does not permit the police to detain a suspect at the police station to obtain fingerprints.

Hiibel v. Sixth Judicial District of the Court of Nevada, **542 U.S. 177 (2004)** The Fourth Amendment allows officers, pursuant to a stop and frisk, to require a person to provide his or her name. The person may be arrested for refusing to comply.

Illinois v. Wardlow, **528 U.S. 119 (2000)** Presence in a high-crime area, combined with unprovoked flight upon observing police officers, gives officers sufficient grounds to investigate further to determine if criminal activity is about to take place.

Maryland v. Buie, **494 U.S. 325 (1990)** The Fourth Amendment permits a properly limited protective sweep in conjunction with an in-home arrest when the searching officer possesses a reasonable belief based on specific and articulable facts that the area to be swept harbors an individual posing a danger to those on the arrest scene.

Minnesota v. Dickerson, **508 U.S. 366 (1993)** A frisk that goes beyond that allowed in *Terry v. Ohio* in stop and frisk cases is not valid. In this case, the search went beyond the pat-down search allowed by *Terry* because the officer "squeezed, slid, and otherwise manipulated the packet's content" before knowing it was cocaine.

Ornelas et al. v. United States, **517 U.S. 690 (1996)** An appellate court that is asked to review the legality of police conduct that taken without a warrant should conduct a de novo (new) review of the trial court's finding on the ultimate issues of reasonable suspicion and probable cause and not simply rely on the trial court's findings.

Pennsylvania v. Mimms, **434 U.S. 106 (1977)** A police officer may order the driver of a vehicle to step out of the vehicle after a routine stop even if the officer has no reasonable suspicion that the driver poses a threat to the officer's safety.

Terry v. Ohio, **392 U.S. 1 (1968)** The police have the authority to stop a person even without probable cause as long as there is reasonable suspicion to believe that the person has committed a crime or is about to commit a crime. The person may be frisked if there is reasonable suspicion that the person may jeopardize the officer's safety.

Torbet v. United Airlines, Inc. **(No. 01–55319 [9th Cir. 2002])** Airport security guards may conduct a random check of a traveler's carry-on bag even if the bag has passed through an X-ray scan at the airport without arousing suspicion that it contained weapons or explosives.

United States v. Arvizu, **534 U.S. 266 (2002)** "In making reasonable suspicion determinations, reviewing courts must look at the totality of the circumstances of each case to see whether the detaining officer has a particularized and objective basis for suspecting legal wrongdoing."

***United States v. Cortez,* 449 U.S. 411 (1981)**
The totality of circumstances must be taken into account when determining the legality of a frisk.

***United States v. Hensley,* 469 U.S. 221 (1985)**
The police may act without a warrant to stop and briefly detain a person they know is wanted for investigation by a police department in another jurisdiction. If the police have a reasonable suspicion, grounded in specific and articulable facts, that a person they encounter was involved in or is wanted for questioning in connection with a completed felony, then they can make a "*Terry*-type" stop to investigate that suspicion. Any evidence legally obtained as a result of that stop is admissible in court.

***United States v. Luckett,* 484 F.2d 89 (1973)**
Detaining a person (who was stopped for jaywalking) for longer than was necessary to write out a ticket—because the police wanted to radio headquarters on a completely unsubstantiated hunch that there was a warrant for his arrest—constitutes detention of unreasonable length. The detention had therefore turned into an arrest.

***United States v. Mendenhall,* 446 U.S. 544 (1980)** "A person has been seized within the meaning of the Fourth Amendment only if, in view of all the circumstances surrounding the incident, a reasonable person would have believed that he was not free to leave."

***United States v. Place,* 462 U.S. 696 (1983)** The detention of an air traveler's luggage for ninety minutes so a trained dog could sniff it for marijuana constituted an excessive investigative stop.

***United States v. Pulido-Baquerizo,* F.2d 899 (9th Cir. 1986)** Consent to search by putting the bag on an X-ray machine also constitutes consent to search further.

***United States v. Robinson,* 414 U.S. 218 (1973)**
A body search, after an authorized arrest for driving without a permit, is valid even when the officer admits that there was no possible danger to himself or herself and therefore no reason to search for a weapon.

***United States v. Robinson,* 949 F.2d 851 (6th Cir. 1991)** "When actions by the police exceed the bounds permitted by reasonable suspicion, the seizure becomes an arrest and must be supported by probable cause."

***United States v. Sharpe,* 470 U.S. 675 (1985)**
The twenty-minute detention of a truck driver who was suspected of carrying marijuana in a truck camper was reasonable because the truck driver had attempted to evade the stop, causing the two officers pursuing him to become separated.

***United States v. Sokolow,* 490 U.S. 1 (1989)**
Taken together, the circumstances in this case (which included the use of a drug courier profile) established a reasonable suspicion that the suspect was transporting illegal drugs, so the investigative stop without a warrant was valid under the Fourth Amendment. Although the use of a drug courier profile was helpful, the totality of the circumstances was more important in establishing reasonable suspicion.

***United States v. Travis,* 62 F.3d 170 (6th Cir. 1995)** Race is a permissible factor to justify reasonable suspicion during airport interdictions, based on facts known to the officer.

 You Be the Judge . . .

In the United States Court of Appeals for the First Circuit

In Hookset, New Hampshire, three officers from the Hookset PD responded at 5:15 A.M. to an ominous 911 call: the caller said that there was a drug deal that had gone bad in the Kozy 7 Motel

and that there was a dead body in room 10. The dispatcher told the officers there was a possible shooting. When they arrived, the officers, Sergeant (Sgt) Chamberlain and Officers Pinardi and

Sherrill, went straight toward room 10 and noticed it was the only room lit in the motel.

The officers placed themselves on either side of the door in case of a shootout. They saw movement in the room, announced themselves, and knocked on the door. Beaudoin answered, opening the door only wide enough for his face to be seen. He was told to step outside the room so the officers could speak with him, which he did, leaving the door partially open.

When Beaudoin stepped outside, Sgt Chamberlain asked him if he had any weapons on him. When Beaudoin said he had a knife in his back pocket, Sgt Chamberlain said he would retrieve the knife and put Beaudoin against the wall to frisk him. In Beaudoin's pocket, Sgt Chamberlain felt an object that felt like a knife and two cylindrical objects that he could not identify. He pulled a knife and two glass tubes containing "crack" cocaine from Beaudoin's pocket and placed him under arrest.

How will you decide this legal issue? Were the police justified in telling Beaudoin to step out of his motel room?

The Court's decision The U.S. Court of Appeals for the First Circuit decided that Sgt Chamberlain and his officers were justified in asking Beaudoin to step out of his room. There was enough evidence of some wrongdoing, with the 911 call about drug dealing and a killing, corroborated by the presence of some individuals in the room to amount to a reasonable articulable suspicion. This would justify a *Terry* "stop-and-frisk" were Beaudoin on the street, and it justifies his being asked to step out of the doorway of his room here. The officers could not see Beaudoin's hands, could not see if he were alone, and could not effectively frisk him in the doorway. *U.S. v. Beaudoin,* 362 F.3d 60 (1st Cir. 2004).

In the United States Court of Appeals for the Ninth Circuit

On the far Western end of Coronado, a peninsula jutting down into the Pacific Ocean west of San Diego and a few miles north of the Mexican border, Officer James of the Coronado PD was performing surveillance as a member of a joint task force, whose mission was to stop smuggling from Mexico into southern California. Officer James spotted something with his high-powered binoculars: a boat heading north at high speed, hugging the shoreline. He did not see it in Mexican waters, but it was headed in the direction that it would have had it come from Mexico. Officer James relayed the information to other task force members in accordance to the standard procedures of the task force for all boats spotted near the border. Officer Sena of the U.S. Coast Guard stopped the boat, which was driven by Bennett, at the mouth of San Diego Harbor. He noticed that Bennett's paperwork did not match the actual numbers on the boat and learned that Bennett had an outstanding state arrest warrant.

Officer Sena told Bennett to proceed to the police dock, where boarding would continue. The police there confirmed there was an arrest warrant for Bennett and took him into custody. En route, Officer Sena had noticed that Bennett's boat was

riding very low in the water, and there was space on the boat for which task force officers could not account. They continued to search the boat for many hours, and after drilling holes did not solve the space mystery. They held the boat overnight and hauled it to a Coast Guard facility to have it X-rayed. The X rays indicated the presence of over 1,500 pounds of marijuana in sealed compartments in the boat.

How will you decide this legal issue? Was the task force justified in stopping and searching Bennett's boat?

The Court's decision The U.S. Court of Appeals for the Ninth Circuit decided that the task force was justified in conducting a border search of Bennett's boat. The government has broad authority to conduct border searches at the border or at the "functional equivalent" of the border, such as the first harbor. A border search may be conducted when the government is "reasonably certain" that a vessel has crossed the border. Spotting a boat heading north from the direction of Mexico, hugging the coastline, establishes this reasonable certainty that a border crossing occurred. Border searches of vehicles require no showing of suspicion, unless they are either destructive or extended. Destructive or extended searches require reasonable suspicion. Even if the search of Bennett's boat was considered extended or the drilling considered destructive, the evidence supports reasonable suspicion: the discrepancy in the boat's papers, the boat's riding low, and the unaccountable space in the boat clearly establish a reasonable suspicion that there was some criminal activity afoot. *U.S. v. Bennett,* 363 F.3d 947 (9th Cir. 2004).

Recommended Readings

Bennett L. Gershman. *Use of race in "stop-and-frisk"; stereotypical beliefs linger, but how far can the police go.* 72 Journal (New York State Bar Association) 42, 45 (2000).

Fred E. Inbau. *Stop and frisk: The power and obligation of the police.* 89 Journal of Criminal Law and Criminology 1445, 1448 (1999).

Christo Lassiter. *The stop and frisk of criminal street gang members.* National Black Law Journal 1–58 (1995).

Matthew Lippman. *Stop and frisk: The triumph of law enforcement over private rights.* 24 Criminal Law Bulletin 24–27 (1988).

Michael C. Murphy and Michael R. Wilds. *X-rated x-ray invades privacy rights.* 12 Criminal Justice Policy Review 4:333–343 (2001).

Darnell Weeden. *It is not right under the Constitution to stop and frisk minority people because they don't look right.* University of Arkansas at Little Rock Law Review 829–844 (1999).

Notes

1. John G. Miles, Jr., David B. Richardson, and Anthony E. Scudellari, *The Law Officer's Pocket Manual* (Washington, D.C.: Bureau of National Affairs, 1988–89), 4:1–2.
2. Ibid.
3. "Report: NYC Cops Search Blacks More," *New York Times,* December 1, 1999, p. 1.
4. *Houston Chronicle,* April 13, 2000, p. 10A.
5. John M. Scheb and John M. Scheb, II, *Criminal Procedure,* 3rd ed. (Belmont, CA: Wadsworth, 2002), p. 105.
6. Steven L. Emanuel and Steven Knowles, *Emanuel Law Outlines: Constitutional Procedure* (Larchmont, NY: Emanuel, 1998), p. 129.
7. Supra note 1, at 4.3.

Chapter 6

Arrests, Use of Force, and Responses to Terrorism

What You Will Learn

- There are different types of seizure under the Fourth Amendment, and an arrest is but one type.

- The more intrusive the seizure, the greater is the protection given by the courts.

- Whether a person has been seized or not is determined by the standard of a reasonable person under the same circumstances, not by the perception of a suspect or the police.

- An arrest has four elements.

- There are specific requirements for arrests with a warrant and without a warrant.

- The common law rules for felony arrests, misdemeanor arrests, and citizen's arrests differ, but they are usually replaced by state law.

- There are rules for what an officer can and cannot do after an arrest.

- Officers must follow certain procedures after making an arrest.

The Top 5 Important Cases in Arrests, Use of Force, and Responses to Terrorism

Payton v. New York, **445 U.S. 573 (1980)** In the absence of exigent circumstances or consent, the police may not enter a private home to make a routine warrantless arrest.

Tennessee v. Garner, **411 U.S. 1 (1985)** It is constitutionally reasonable for a police officer to use deadly force when the officer has probable cause to believe that the suspect poses a threat of serious physical harm, either to the officer or to others.

Florida v. Bostick, **501 U.S. 429 (1991)** The appropriate test to use to determine if the act of the officers in this case was valid was whether, taking into account all of the circumstances surrounding the encounter (in a bus), a reasonable person would feel free to decline the officers' requests for consent to search the bag or otherwise terminate the encounter.

Wilson v. Arkansas, **514 U.S. 927 (1995)** The knock-and-announce rule is part of the Fourth Amendment's requirement that searches and seizures be reasonable, but that rule is not rigid and is subject to exceptions based on law enforcement interests.

Atwater v. City of Lago Vista, **532 U.S. 318 (2001)** An arrest for an offense not punishable with jail or prison time (in this case the maximum penalty set by law was a $50 fine) is constitutional.

Introduction

The Fourth Amendment to the U.S. Constitution provides that "the right of the people to be secure in their persons . . . against unreasonable . . . seizures, shall not be violated." Arrest constitutes a "seizure" of a person, so the restrictions of the Fourth Amendment apply. Police officers must be well informed about the law of arrest, because successful prosecution usually depends upon the legality of the arrest. If the arrest is legal, then searches of the arrestee and the area within his or her control are also legal; conversely, if the arrest is illegal, any evidence obtained thereafter is not admissible in court.

The validity of an arrest is determined primarily by federal constitutional standards, particularly the requirement of probable cause. An arrest, with or without a warrant, cannot be valid unless there is probable cause—as determined by federal constitutional standards. In seizures of persons (as distinguished from searches and seizures of things), probable cause "exists if the facts and circumstances known to the officer warrant a prudent man in believing that the offense has been committed" and that the person being arrested committed it.

State laws that are inconsistent with federal standards are invalid and unconstitutional, but state statutes may give more rights to a suspect than are required by the Fourth Amendment. For example, traffic offenders may be constitutionally arrested if there is probable cause, but state law may prohibit the police from making an arrest and provide instead for the issuance of a citation for the offender to appear in court at a specified time and date.

The Broad Picture: Seizures of Persons

What happens when persons, rather than things, are seized? This section addresses what the Fourth Amendment says about the seizure of persons, arrest as a form of seizure, the cases reflecting the top ten degrees of intrusive searches and seizures of persons, and the question of whose perception determines whether a person has been seized.

Seizure and the Fourth Amendment

When analyzing seizure cases under the Fourth Amendment, the first question should be whether a seizure under the Fourth Amendment has occurred. If no such seizure has occurred, then the provisions of the Fourth Amendment do not apply, because those provisions apply only to "unreasonable searches and seizures." If a seizure did in fact occur, the question becomes, What kind of seizure was it, and what kind of protection is given by the courts in that type of seizure?

Some contacts with the police are not considered seizures under the Fourth Amendment, because the degree of intrusiveness is minimal. For example, the following contacts do not enjoy the protection of the Constitution because they are not deemed seizures:

- The police asking questions of people on the street to gather general information
- The police asking a driver to get out of a car after being stopped (*Pennsylvania v. Mimms,* 434 U.S. 106 [1977])
- The police boarding a bus and asking questions that a person is free to refuse to answer (*Florida v. Bostick,* 501 U.S. 429 [1991])
- The police riding alongside a person "to see where he was going" (*Michigan v. Chesternut,* 486 U.S. 657 [1988]) and asking questions of witnesses to a crime

Arrest: Just One Form of Seizure

Seizures of persons are usually associated with arrest, *but arrest is only one form of seizure*—although one of the most intrusive. There are other intrusions into a person's freedom that do not constitute arrest but nonetheless come under the protection of the Fourth Amendment. For example, stop and frisk, border searches, and roadblocks are seizures that come under the Fourth Amendment, but the constitutional requirements for these types of police actions differ from those for an arrest because they are lesser forms of intrusion. The term *seizure* under the Fourth Amendment is therefore broader than the term *arrest*. Every arrest is a seizure, but not every seizure is an arrest.

Brower v. Inyo County (1989)

See Appendix C for information on how to find cases in this chapter on FindLaw.com.

In *Brower v. Inyo County* (489 U.S. 593 [1989]), the Court said that seizure "requires an intentional acquisition of physical control," adding that a seizure for purposes of the Fourth Amendment "does not occur whenever there is a governmentally caused termination of an individual's freedom of movement . . . but *only when there is governmental termination of freedom of movement through means intentionally applied*" (emphasis added).

The Top Ten Degrees of Intrusiveness in Searches and Seizures of Persons

This "top ten" list, with apologies to CBS's David Letterman, is presented to illustrate the degrees of intrusiveness in search and seizure cases. As gathered from Court decisions, the intrusiveness of searches and seizures of persons under the Fourth Amendment can be ranked as follows (with 10 being the most intrusive and 1 the least intrusive):

Winston v. Lee (1985)

10. *(Most intrusive)* Surgery to remove a bullet from a suspect's chest (*Winston v. Lee*, 470 U.S. 753 [1985])
9. Anal and cavity searches (*Kennedy v. Los Angeles Police Department*, 887 F.2d 920 [9th Cir. 1989])
8. Arrest (*United States v. Santana*, 427 U.S. 38 [1975])
7. Removal of blood in a hospital (*Schmerber v. California*, 384 U.S. 457 [1966])
6. Stationhouse detention (*Hayes v. Florida*, 470 U.S. 811 [1985])
5. Stop and frisk (*Terry v. Ohio*, 392 U.S. 1 [1968])
4. Searches of a passenger's belongings in motor vehicles (*Wyoming v. Houghton*, 526 U.S. 295 [1999])
3. Immigration and border searches (*Au Yi Lau v. United States Immigration and Naturalization Service*, 445 F.2d 217 [9th Cir. 1971])
2. Vehicle stops in general (*Carroll v. United States*, 267 U.S. 132 [1925])

United States v. Martinez-Fuerte (1976)

1. *(Least intrusive)* Roadblocks to control the flow of illegal aliens (*United States v. Martinez-Fuerte*, 428 U.S. 543 [1976])

This "top ten" list is merely illustrative and admittedly subjective. Individual perceptions differ about which is more intrusive. Its significance, however, lies in that it shows how, over the years, Court decisions have established a sliding scale of intrusion as well as a sliding scale of constitutional protection. *The more severe the intrusion, the greater is the protection given by the courts.* For example, in *Winston v. Lee* (470 U.S. 753, 1985), the Court held that a surgery (number 10 on the list) under general anesthetic to remove a bullet from a suspect's chest for use as evidence cannot be undertaken *even with probable cause and a judicial order* (the highest possible form of protection in Fourth Amendment cases) unless there are compelling reasons. This is because such a procedure is highly intrusive and violates the Fourth Amendment. In contrast, roadblocks to control the flow of illegal aliens (number 1 on the list) do not need much protection under the Fourth Amendment, because they are not highly intrusive and there is a strong governmental interest involved (*United States v. Martinez-Fuerte*, 428 U.S. 543 [1976]).

The Appropriate Test for Determining Seizure

Whose perception determines whether a person has in fact been arrested? This question is important because the perception of the police may be different from that of a suspect. For example, arrest may not be in an officer's mind when detaining a suspect, but the suspect may feel that he or she is under arrest. Whose perception determines whether a person has been seized—that of the police or that of the person detained? The answer is neither. In a leading case, the Supreme Court held that the appropriate test to determine if a seizure has occurred is whether a reasonable person, viewing the particular police conduct as a whole and within the setting of all the surrounding circumstances, would have concluded that the police had in some way restrained a person's liberty so that he or she was not free to leave (*Michigan v. Chesternut*, 486 U.S. 567 [1988]). In sum, it is the perception of a *reasonable person based on a totality of circumstances.*

Michigan v. Chesternut **(1988)**

The Court in *Chesternut* said that there can be no single clear, hard-and-fast rule applicable to all investigatory pursuits. In that case, after observing the approach of a police car, Chesternut began to run. Officers followed him "to see where he was going." As the officers drove alongside Chesternut, they observed him pull a number of packets from his pocket and throw them down. The officers stopped and seized the packets, concluding that they might be contraband. Chesternut was arrested, and a subsequent search revealed more narcotics.

Chesternut was charged with felony narcotics possession and convicted. On appeal, he sought exclusion of the evidence, alleging that the officers' investigatory pursuit "to see where he was going" constituted a seizure under the Fourth Amendment. The Supreme Court rejected this contention, noting that Chesternut was not seized before he discarded the drug packets and that the activity of the officers in following him to see where he was going did not violate the Fourth Amendment. Therefore, the evidence was admissible.

Florida v. Bostick **(1991)**

In another case, *Florida v. Bostick* (501 U.S. 429 [1991]), without any suspicion and with the intention of catching drug smugglers, two uniformed law enforcement officers boarded a bus in Fort Lauderdale, Florida, that was en route from Miami to Atlanta. The officers approached Bostick and asked to see some identification and his bus ticket. The officers also asked Bostick for consent to search his bag and told him he could refuse consent. Bostick consented to the search of his bag, and cocaine was found. In court, he sought to suppress the evidence, alleging it was improperly seized. On appeal, the Supreme Court held that the evidence was admissible. The Florida Supreme Court had adopted an inflexible rule stating that the officers' practice of "working the buses" was per se unconstitutional.

The U.S. Supreme Court rejected the Florida rule, holding that the result of such a rule was that the police in Florida (as elsewhere) could approach persons at random in most places, ask them questions, and seek consent to search, but they could not engage in the same behavior on a bus. Rather, the Court said, "[T]he appropriate test is whether, taking into account all of the circumstances surrounding the encounter, a reasonable passenger would feel free to decline the officers' requests or otherwise terminate the encounter." This was reemphasized by the Court in a later decision when it said that a seizure by the police of the person within the meaning of the Fourth and Fourteenth Amendments occurs only when "taking into account all of the circumstances surrounding the encounter, the police conduct would have communicated to a reasonable person that he was not at liberty to ignore the police presence and go about his business" (*Kaupp v. Texas,* 583 U.S. 626 [2003]).

Kaupp v. Texas (2003)

Who decides what is a "reasonable person" under this standard? The answer: the jury or judge that tries the case. The standard they use is subjective and can vary from one jury or judge to another. In *United States v. Mendenhall* (446 U.S. 544 [1980]), the Court took the circumstances into consideration: "the threatening presence of several officers, the display of a weapon by an officer, some physical touching of the person or the citizen, or the use of language or tone of voice indicating that compliance with the officer's request might be compelled."

United States v. Mendenhall (1980)

Arrest Defined

An **arrest** is defined as the taking of a person into custody against his or her will for the purpose of criminal prosecution or interrogation (*Dunaway v. New York,* 442 U.S. 200 [1979]). It occurs "only when there is governmental termination of freedom of movement through means intentionally applied" (*Brower v. County of Inyo,* 486 U.S. 593 [1989]). An arrest deprives a person of liberty by legal authority. Mere words alone do not normally constitute an arrest; there must be some kind of restraint. A person's liberty must be restricted by law enforcement officers to the extent that the person is not free to leave on his or her own volition. It does not matter whether the act is termed an "arrest" or a mere "stop" or "detention" under state law. The "totality of circumstances" determines whether an arrest has taken place or not.

Dunaway v. New York (1979)

This section looks at which actions constitute arrest and how long a person can be detained before it becomes an arrest.

Forced Detention and Arrest

When a person is taken into custody against his or her will for purposes of criminal prosecution or interrogation, it is an arrest under the Fourth Amendment, regardless of what state law says. For example, suppose state law provides that a police officer may "detain" a suspect for four hours in the police station for questioning without having "arrested" that person. If the suspect is, in fact, detained in the police station against his or her will, that person has been "arrested" under the Constitution and is therefore entitled to any rights given to suspects who have been arrested.

Conversely, no arrest or seizure occurs when an officer simply approaches a person in a public place and asks if he or she is willing to answer questions—as long as the person is not involuntarily detained. A voluntary encounter between the police and a member of the public is not an arrest or a seizure. For example, there is no seizure if an officer approaches a person who is not suspected of anything and, without show of force or intimidation, asks questions of the person—who may or may not respond voluntarily.

The Length of Detention and Arrest

An important question is, How long can the suspect be detained, and how intrusive must the investigation be before the stop becomes an arrest requiring probable cause? The answer depends on the reasonableness of the detention and the intrusion. The detention must not be longer than that required by the circumstances, and it must take place by the "least intrusive means," meaning that it must not be more than that needed to verify or dispel the officer's suspicions. In the words of the Court in *United States v. Sharpe* (470 U.S. 675

United States v. Sharpe (1985)

[1985]): "In assessing whether a detention is too long to be justified as an investigative stop, we consider it appropriate to examine whether the police diligently pursued a means of investigation that was likely to confirm or dispel their suspicions quickly, during which time it was necessary to detain the defendant." Detention for a longer period of time than is necessary converts a stop into an arrest.

In sum, *a person has been arrested if, under the totality of circumstances, a reasonable person would not have felt free to leave.* This rule applies to seizures of persons in general, such as in stop and frisk, and not just in arrest cases.

The Elements of an Arrest

Four essential elements must be present for an arrest to take place: seizure and detention, intention to arrest, arrest authority, and the understanding of the individual that he or she is being arrested.

Seizure and Detention

This first element of an arrest may be either actual or constructive. **Actual seizure** is accomplished by taking the person into custody with the use of hands or firearms (denoting use of force without touching the individual) or by merely touching the individual without the use of force. In contrast, **constructive seizure** is accomplished without any physical touching, grabbing, holding, or use of force. It occurs when the individual peacefully submits to the officer's will and control.

Mere words alone do not constitute an arrest. The fact that a police officer tells a person, "You are under arrest," is not sufficient. The required restraint must be accompanied by actual seizure or peaceful submission to the officer's will and control. Furthermore, mere authority to arrest alone does not constitute an arrest. There must be either an actual or a constructive seizure. When neither takes place, no arrest takes place.

California v. Hodari
(1991)

The case of *California v. Hodari* (499 U.S. 621 [1991] illustrates the element of seizure and detention in an arrest situation. In that case, two police officers were patrolling a high-crime area of Oakland, California, late one night. They saw four or five youths huddled around a small red car parked at the curb. When the youths saw the police car approaching, they fled. Officer Pertoso, who was wearing a jacket with the word "POLICE" embossed on its front, left the car to give chase. Pertoso did not follow one of the youths, who turned out to be Hodari, directly; instead, he took another route that brought them face to face on a parallel street. Hodari was looking behind himself as he ran and did not turn to see Officer Pertoso until they were right in front of each other—whereupon Hodari tossed away a small rock. The officer tackled Hodari and recovered the rock, which turned out to be crack cocaine.

The issue brought to the Supreme Court on appeal was whether Hodari had been seized within the meaning of the Fourth Amendment, thus necessitating a warrant, when he dropped the crack cocaine. The Court said no and admitted the evidence, saying:

> To constitute a seizure of the person . . . there must be either the application of physical force, however slight, or where that is absent, submission to the officer's "show of authority" to restrain the subject's liberty. No physical force was applied in this case, since Hodari was untouched by [Officer] Pertoso before he dropped the drugs. Moreover, assuming that Pertoso's pursuit constituted a "show of authority" enjoining Hodari to halt, Hodari did not comply with that injunction and therefore was not seized until he was tackled. Thus, the cocaine abandoned while he was running was not the fruit of a seizure . . . and his motion to exclude evidence of it was properly denied.

To summarize, there was no seizure because no physical force (actual seizure) had been applied prior to the suspect's tossing away the crack cocaine, nor had the suspect voluntarily submitted to the authority of the officer (constructive seizure).

The Intention to Arrest

The second element is intention to arrest. In the words of one police manual, "You have made an arrest as soon as you indicate by words or action your intention to take the person to the police station or before a judicial officer, or otherwise to take him into custody."[1] In this case, the intention to arrest is clear because it is either expressed or clearly implied in the officer's action.

Without the requisite intent, there is no arrest even if a person is temporarily stopped or inconvenienced. For example, no arrest is occurring when an officer pulls over a motorist to issue a ticket, asks a motorist to step out of his or her car, stops a motorist to check his or her driver's license, or stops a person to warn of possible danger. In these cases, there may be a temporary deprivation of liberty or a certain amount of inconvenience, but there is no intent by the police officer to take the person into custody; therefore, there is no arrest.

The requirement of intention to arrest is hard to prove because it exists in the mind of the police officer. There are cases, however, in which actions clearly indicated that the officer intended to take the person into custody, even though intent to arrest was later denied by the officer. For example, when an officer places handcuffs on a suspect, the intent to arrest likely exists even if the officer denies such intent.

When it is not clear from the officer's act whether there was an intent to arrest, the Supreme Court has said that "a policeman's unarticulated plan has no bearing on the question whether a suspect was 'in custody' at a particular time" (*Berkemer v. McCarty*, 468 U.S. 420 [1984]). The test is the interpretation of a reasonable person, regardless of what the officer had or did not have in mind. Example: Officer P invites a suspect to the police station for interrogation about a murder. The officer does not inform the suspect that she is free to leave; neither does the officer allow the suspect, upon her request, to leave prior to the end of the interrogation. The officer later testifies that he had no intention to arrest the suspect and that he merely wanted to "ask a few questions." Under the Fourth Amendment, however, that suspect had been arrested because a reasonable person under the same circumstances would likely conclude that an arrest had been made.

Berkemer v. McCarty (1984)

Arrest Authority

The third element of arrest, authority to restrain, distinguishes arrest from deprivations of liberty (such as kidnapping or illegal detention) by private individuals. When there is proper authorization, the arrest is valid; conversely, when proper authorization is lacking, the arrest is invalid. Invalid arrest can arise in the following cases: (1) when the police officer mistakenly thinks he or she has authority to arrest and (2) when the officer knows that he or she is not authorized to make the arrest but does so anyway. Whether a police officer has arrest authority when off duty varies from state to state. Some states authorize police officers (by law, court decision, or agency policy) to make an arrest any time they witness a criminal act. In these states, the officer is, in effect, on duty twenty-four hours a day seven days a week for purposes of making an arrest whether in uniform or not. Other states authorize police officers to make an arrest only when they are on duty.

Understanding by the Arrestee

The fourth element of an arrest, the understanding that he or she is being arrested, may be conveyed to the arrestee through words or actions. In most cases, the police officer says, "You are under arrest," thereby conveying intention through words. Similarly, some actions strongly imply that a person is being taken into custody even though the police officer makes no statement. Examples of actions that strongly imply arrest include a suspected burglar being subdued by police and taken to a squad car and a person being handcuffed to be taken to the police station even though no words are spoken. The element of understanding is not required for an arrest in the following instances: (1) When the suspect is drunk or under the influence of drugs and does not understand what is going on, (2) when the suspect is insane, and (3) when the suspect is unconscious.

Arrests with a Warrant

Black's Law Dictionary defines an **arrest warrant** as "a writ or precept issued by a magistrate, justice, or other competent authority, addressed to a sheriff, constable, or other officer, requiring him to arrest the body of a person therein named, and bring him before the magistrate or court to answer, or to be examined, concerning some offense which he is charged with having committed."[2] Warrant forms vary from state to state and even from one city or municipality to another, but they typically include the following: which court is issuing it, the name of the person to be arrested (unless it is a "John Doe warrant"—[see "The Contents of a Warrant" for explanation]), the offense charged and some specifics of the offense, an order for the officer to bring the arrested person before the issuing court, the date the warrant was issued, and the judge's or magistrate's signature. (See Figure 6.1 for an example of a warrant.)

This section looks at when a warrant is needed, what happens when one is issued, the contents of a warrant, what happens when a warrant is served, the time of day arrests can be made, the possession and expiration of a warrant, and legal authorizations other than a warrant.

When a Warrant Is Needed

Most arrests are made without a warrant. Nonetheless, there are specific instances when a warrant is needed.

WARRANT FOR ARREST

(FOR USE IN ANY COURT IN EITHER MISDEMEANOR OR FELONY CASES)

STATE OF MISSOURI,

County of } ss.

IN THE   COURT WITHIN AND FOR SAID COUNTY

THE STATE OF MISSOURI TO ANY PEACE OFFICER IN THE STATE OF MISSOURI:

You are hereby commanded to arrest
who is charged with

alleged to have been committed within the jurisdiction of this court and in violation of the laws of the State of Missouri, and to bring him forthwith before this court to be here dealt with in accordance with law; and you, the officer serving this warrant, shall forthwith make return hereof to this court.

WITNESS THE HONORABLE   , Judge of
the said court and the seal thereof, issued in the county and state aforesaid on this   day of   , 20

                                                        Judge/Clerk of said Court

RETURN:
     Served the within warrant in my County of
and in the State of Missouri on this   day of   , 20
by arresting the within named   and producing him before the said court on the
day of   , 20

Figure 6.1 Warrant for Arrest

Source: State of Missouri warrant form

1. *If the crime is not committed in the officer's presence.* When crimes are not committed in the presence of an officer, the crime victim reports the crime to the police and then the police investigate.

   - Example A: Report by a victim of a robbery
   - Example B: Report by a victim of a sexual assault
   - Example C: Report by a wife of her husband's murder

   After investigation, the police present an affidavit to the judge or magistrate and ask for an arrest warrant to be issued. If probable cause exists, the warrant is issued and then served by the police. This sequence, however, is subject to exceptions, particularly in cases where exigent [emergency] circumstances exist that make it necessary for the police to take prompt action to prevent the escape of the suspect.

2. *If the suspect is in a private residence and there is no reason for an immediate arrest.* The police may not enter a private home to make a routine warrantless arrest (*Payton v. New York*, 445 U.S. 573 [1980]). In this case, after two days of intensive investigation, detectives assembled evidence sufficient to establish probable cause to believe that Payton had murdered the manager of a gas station. They went to Payton's apartment to arrest him without a warrant. The warrantless entry and arrest was authorized by New York law. They knocked on the metal door, and when there was no response, they summoned emergency assistance and then used crowbars to open the door and enter the apartment. No one was there, but in plain view was a .30-caliber shell casing that was seized and later admitted into evidence at Payton's murder trial.

Payton v. New York (1980)

Payton was convicted; he appealed, alleging that the Fourth Amendment requires police officers to obtain a warrant if making a felony arrest in a private residence when there is time to obtain a warrant. The Supreme Court agreed, saying that a warrant is needed in these types of cases (routine arrests in the absence of consent) and that state laws, such as that of New York, authorizing warrantless arrests in routine felony cases, are unconstitutional. (See the Case Brief for more details on this case.)

3. *In home entries for minor offenses.* In the case of a minor offense, a warrantless entry into a home to make an arrest is seldom justified. For example, suppose an officer suspects a person of driving while intoxicated, a nonjailable offense in the particular state. The officer goes to the suspect's home to make an arrest before the alcohol can dissipate from the suspect's body. The officer cannot enter the home without a warrant or consent. Given the state's relatively tolerant view of this offense, an interest in preserving the evidence cannot overcome the strong presumption against the warrantless invasion of homes.[3] Thus, in determining whether there are exigent circumstances, a court must consider the seriousness of the offense (*Welsh v. Wisconsin*, 466 U.S. 740 [1984]). However, home entry in felony or misdemeanor cases is justified if there is valid consent or if state law or state court decisions allow it.

Welsh v. Wisconsin (1984)

The Issuance of a Warrant

To secure the issuance of a warrant, a complaint (by the offended party or by the police officer) must be filed before a magistrate, showing probable cause for arrest of the accused. It must set forth facts showing that an offense has

CASE BRIEF: The Leading Case on Home Arrests
Payton v. New York, 445 U.S. 573 (1980)

Facts: After two days of intensive investigation, New York detectives had assembled evidence sufficient to establish probable cause to believe that Payton had murdered the manager of a gas station. Early the following day, six officers went to Payton's apartment in the Bronx intending to arrest him. They had not obtained a warrant. Although light and music emanated from the apartment, there was no response to their knock on the metal door. They summoned emergency assistance and, about thirty minutes later, used crowbars to break open the door and enter the apartment. No one was there. In plain view was a .30-caliber shell casing that was seized and later admitted into evidence at Payton's murder trial. Payton was convicted, and he appealed.

Issue: *Does the Fourth Amendment prohibit the police from making a nonconsensual entry into a suspect's home to make a routine felony arrest without a warrant? Yes.*

Supreme Court Decision: In the absence of consent, the police may not enter a suspect's home to make a routine felony arrest without a warrant.

Case Significance: The *Payton* case settled the issue of whether the police can enter a suspect's home and make a warrantless arrest in a routine felony case, meaning cases in which there is time to obtain a warrant. The practice was authorized by the state of New York and twenty-three other states at the time *Payton* was decided. These authorizations are now unconstitutional, and officers must obtain a warrant before entering a suspect's home to make a routine felony arrest.

Excerpts from the Decision: It is thus perfectly clear that the evil the Amendment was designed to prevent was broader than the abuse of a general warrant. Unreasonable searches or seizures conducted without any warrant at all are condemned by the plain language of the first clause of the Amendment. Almost a century ago, the Court stated in resounding terms that the principles reflected in the Amendment "reached farther than the concrete form" of the specific cases that gave it birth, and "apply to all invasions on the part of the government and its employees of the sanctity of a man's home and the privacies of life." Without pausing to consider whether that broad language may require some qualification, it is sufficient to note that the warrantless arrest of a person is a species of seizure required by the Amendment to be reasonable. Indeed, as MR. JUSTICE POWELL noted in his concurrence in *United States v. Watson*, the arrest of a person is "quintessentially a seizure."

The simple language of the Amendment applies equally to seizures of persons and to seizures of property. Our analysis in this case may therefore properly commence with rules that have been well established in Fourth Amendment litigation involving tangible items. As the Court reiterated just a few years ago, the "physical entry of the home is the chief evil against which the wording of the Fourth Amendment is directed." And we have long adhered to the view that the warrant procedure minimizes the danger of needless intrusions of that sort.

It is a "basic principle of Fourth Amendment law" that searches and seizures inside a home without a warrant are presumptively unreasonable. Yet it is also well settled that objects such as weapons or contraband found in a public place may be seized by the police without a warrant. The seizure of property in plain view involves no invasion of privacy and is presumptively reasonable, assuming that there is probable cause to associate the property with criminal activity.

"The poorest man may in his cottage bid defiance to all the forces of the Crown. It may be frail—its roof may shake—the wind may blow through it—the storm may enter—the rain may enter—but the King of England cannot enter—all his force dares not cross the threshold of the ruined tenement."

SOURCE: Statement by Lord Chatham to the House of Commons in 1763, as quoted in John C. Hall, "Entering Premises to Arrest: The Threshold Question," *FBI Law Enforcement* Bulletin, September 1994, p. 27.

been committed and that the accused is responsible for it. If it appears to the magistrate from the complaint and accompanying documents or testimony that probable cause exists for the charges made against the accused, the magistrate issues an arrest warrant.

In most states, the issuance of arrest warrants is strictly a judicial function and must therefore be performed by a judge or judicial officer. The issuing party must also be "neutral and detached." However, some states hold that, because the requirement of probable cause is designed to be applied by laypeople (as when a police officer arrests a suspect without a warrant upon probable cause), a nonjudicial officer such as a court clerk may properly issue warrants if empowered to do so by statute and if otherwise "neutral and detached." For example, the Court has decided that a municipal court clerk can issue an arrest warrant for municipal ordinance violations as long as such an issuance is authorized by state law (*Shadwick v. City of Tampa*, 407 U.S. 345 [1972]).

Shadwick v. City of Tampa (1972)

The term **neutral and detached magistrate** means that the issuing officer is not unalterably aligned with the police or prosecutor's position in the case. Several cases illustrate its meaning.

- *Example 1.* A magistrate who receives a fee when issuing a warrant but not when denying one is not neutral and detached (*Connally v. Georgia*, 429 U.S. 245 [1977]).

Connally v. Georgia (1977)

- *Example 2.* A magistrate who participates in the search to determine its scope lacks the requisite neutrality and detachment (*Lo-Ji Sales, Inc., v. New York*, 442 U.S. 319 [1979]).

Lo-Ji Sales, Inc., v. New York (1979)

- *Example 3.* A state's chief investigator and prosecutor (state attorney general) is not neutral and detached, so any warrant issued by him or her is invalid (*Coolidge v. New Hampshire*, 403 U.S. 443 [1971]).

Coolidge v. New Hampshire (1971)

The warrant requirement assumes that the complaint or affidavit has been reviewed by a magistrate before it is issued. Therefore, presigned warrants, which are used in some jurisdictions, are of doubtful validity. Nonetheless, they continue to be used, primarily because their use has not been challenged in court.

The Contents of a Warrant

The warrant must describe the offense charged and contain the name of the accused or, if that is unknown, some description by which he or she can be identified with reasonable certainty. Thus, a **"John Doe" warrant**—one in which only the name John Doe appears because the real name of the suspect is not known to the police—is valid only if it contains a description of the accused by which he or she can be identified with reasonable certainty. A John Doe warrant without such a description is invalid, for it could be used by the police to arrest almost anyone and therefore lends itself to abuse. Some jurisdictions allow the issuance of a John Doe based on DNA identification even though the name of the suspect has not been ascertained. This practice enables the prosecutor to prevent the statute of limitations from running out on an offense. John Doe warrants based on DNA identification are not susceptible to abuse because the nature of the evidence precludes a broad and arbitrary sweep of suspects.

The Service of a Warrant

An arrest warrant is directed to, and may be executed by, any peace officer in the jurisdiction. In some states, a properly designated private citizen can also serve a warrant. The rules for serving warrants within and outside of a state differ.

1. *Service within a state.* Inside the state of issuance, a warrant issued in one county or judicial district may be served by peace officers of any other county or district in which the accused is found. Some states, such as Texas and California, have statutes giving local peace officers statewide power of arrest—thereby allowing the peace officers of the county or district where the warrant was issued to make the arrest anywhere in the state. Even if statewide power of arrest is given, it is better, whenever possible, to inform local police agencies of activity within their jurisdiction as a matter of courtesy and to avoid jurisdictional misunderstanding.

2. *Service outside the state.* A warrant generally does not carry any authority beyond the territorial limits of the state in which it is issued. For example, an arrest cannot be made in Illinois on the basis of a warrant issued in Wisconsin. There are exceptions, perhaps the most important of which is the **hot pursuit** exception (or fresh pursuit), which authorizes peace officers from one state who enter another state in hot pursuit to arrest the suspect for a felony committed in the first state. Most states have adopted a uniform act authorizing hot pursuit service of a warrant. Another exception occurs when an in-state officer makes an arrest based on a "hit," which refers to a finding that a warrant has been issued for a person in another state and is known by the in-state officer through a national computer search.

The Time of the Arrest

In general, felony arrests may be made at any time, day or night, but misdemeanor arrests are usually made during daylight hours. In some states, an arrest for any crime—felony or misdemeanor—can be made at any hour of the day or night.

The Possession and Expiration of a Warrant

The arresting officer does not need to have the arrest warrant in his or her possession at the time of the arrest as long as it is shown to the accused after the arrest if so requested. An arrest warrant should be executed without unreasonable delay. But unlike a search warrant, which must be served within a limited period of time, an arrest warrant does not expire until it is executed or withdrawn.

Legal Authorization Other than an Arrest Warrant

The use of an arrest warrant is one way in which a person is taken into custody or held accountable by the courts. Other ways are

- *Citation.* A **citation** is a writ from a court ordering a person to appear in court at a specified time. Statutes in many states authorize the use of a citation for less serious offenses, such as traffic violations. A citation means the offender does not have to be taken into custody for that offense at that time. In the event of the person's failure to appear at the time and date indicated, however, a warrant of arrest may be issued.
- *Bench warrant.* A **bench warrant** is a writ "from the bench" used to arrest and bring nonappearing defendants before the court.
- *Capias.* This is the general name for several types of writ that require an officer, for various causes, to take a defendant into custody. A **capias** is more generic than a bench warrant in that it is used to bring a person before the court for a variety of reasons, some of which are not necessarily related to a criminal case (as in cases of protecting a witness or a hearing judgment). It may also be issued when a defendant skips bail or is indicted by a grand jury if the defendant is not already in custody. In contrast, a bench warrant is more specific; it is usually issued to effect an arrest when a person has been found in contempt, when an indictment has been handed down, or when a witness disobeys a subpoena.

Arrests without a Warrant

Although arrest warrants are preferred by the courts and desirable for purposes of protecting police from liability lawsuits, they are, in fact, seldom used in police work. About 95 percent of all arrests are made without a warrant. Police officers have a general power to arrest without a warrant when (1) felonies or misdemeanors are committed in their presence, (2) crimes are committed in public places, (3) emergency circumstances exist, or (4) there is danger to the arresting officer. This section looks at each of these.

Felonies Committed in the Presence of Officers

The authority to arrest for felonies committed in the presence of officers is generally based on old common law principles, which have since been enacted into law in various states. For example, suppose, while on patrol, an officer sees a robbery being committed. She can make the arrest without a warrant. The term *in the presence* of a police officer refers to knowledge gained firsthand by the officer as a result of using any of his or her five senses—sight, hearing, smell, touch, or taste. Therefore, the police may make a warrantless arrest if probable cause is established by any of these means:

- *Sight.* The officer sees X stab Y or S breaking into a residence.
- *Hearing.* The officer hears a shot or a cry for help from inside an apartment.
- *Smell.* The officer smells gasoline, gunpowder, gas fumes, or marijuana.
- *Touch.* The officer examines doors or windows in the dark or touches a car muffler or engine to determine if it has just been used.
- *Taste.* Officer tastes a white substance to identify it as sugar, salt, or something else. This is probably the least used of the five senses. Some officers instead are equipped with packets that can be used to field test suspicious substances.

Misdemeanors Committed in the Presence of Officers

The rule in most states is that misdemeanors committed in the presence of officers also give the police authority to make an arrest. Under the old common law, however, the police could not make an arrest if the misdemeanor was merely reported to them by a third party. In states that still observe this rule, the officer must obtain an arrest warrant or have the complaining party file a complaint, which can lead to the issuance of a warrant or summons. However, this "in police presence" common law rule is now subject to so many exceptions specified by state laws that arrests even for misdemeanors not committed in the presence of police officers have virtually become the general rule.

Given common law rules and variations through legislation among states, the general guideline is whether an officer may arrest for misdemeanors that are not committed in the officer's presence (but where the police may have probable cause because of other evidence) is governed by state law or agency policy.

Crimes Committed in Public Places

The police are not required to obtain an arrest warrant before arresting a person in a public place, even if there was time and opportunity to do so, as long as the police are duly authorized to do so by statute (*United States v. Watson*, 423 U.S. 411 [1976]). This applies in both felonies and misdemeanors. In the *Watson* case, the Court noted that such authorization is given by federal law and "in almost all of the States in the form of express statutory authorization." The warrantless arrest is valid because a public place has minimum protection under the Fourth Amendment or under the right to privacy.

When Exigent (Emergency) Circumstances Are Present

The term **exigent circumstances** has many meanings, as the following examples illustrate.

- *Example 1: Possibility of disappearance.* An officer is told by a reliable informant that he has just bought cocaine from a stranger in Apartment 141 at the corner of Main and Commerce and that the seller was getting ready to leave. Given the possibility of the suspect's disappearance, the officer can make the arrest without a warrant.
- *Example 2: Hot pursuit.* In cases of hot pursuit, when a suspect enters his or her own or another person's dwelling, an officer can make the arrest without a warrant. In one case, police officers, acting without a search or arrest warrant, entered a house to arrest an armed-robbery suspect who had been seen entering the place just minutes before. The Supreme Court upheld the warrantless entry and search as reasonable because to delay the entry would have allowed the suspect time to escape (*Warden v. Hayden*, 387 U.S. 294 [1967]).

The term *hot pursuit* denotes some kind of chase, but it need not be extended. The fact that the pursuit ended almost as soon as it began does not render it any less a hot pursuit sufficient to justify an entry without warrant into a suspect's house. The following factors are relevant in a fleeing-suspect case: "(1) the gravity of the offense committed, (2) the belief that the suspect was armed, and (3) the likelihood that the suspect would escape in the absence of swift police action" (*United States v. Williams*, 612 F.2d 735 [3rd Cir. 1979]).

In sum, exigent circumstances are those emergency circumstances that make obtaining a warrant impractical, useless, dangerous, or unnecessary, and that justify warrantless arrests or entries into homes or premises.

When There Is Danger to the Arresting Officer

In *Warden v. Hayden*, 387 U.S. 294 (1967), the Court said, "The Fourth Amendment does not require officers to delay in the course of an investigation if to do so would gravely endanger their lives or the lives of others. Speed . . . was essential." This safety consideration has been extended by lower courts to include the safety of informants and the public.

Be aware, however, that these rules on arrests without a warrant are generally based on common law and court decisions. They can be, and often are, superseded by laws enacted by state legislatures that either limit or expand the power of the officer to make an arrest without a warrant. These state laws govern the conduct of the police in that particular jurisdiction—unless they are declared unconstitutional by the courts.

What the Police May Do after an Arrest

Arrest is a significant part of the criminal justice process—for both the suspect and the police officer. For the suspect, the arrest signifies the start of a deprivation of freedom that can last (if the suspect is convicted) until the sentence term has been served. For the police, it sets in motion certain procedures that must be followed for the arrestee to be processed properly. It is important that the officer fully understands what he or she can do, particularly immediately after an arrest is made, or else the whole process can be subject to legal challenge.

Some of the things an officer may do after an arrest, according to court decisions, include (1) search the arrestee, (2) search the area of immediate control, (3) search the vehicle the arrestee was riding in, (4) search the passenger compartment, (5) handcuff the arrestee, (6) monitor the person's movements, and (7) search the arrestee at the place of detention.

Search the Arrestee

United States v. Robinson (1973)

After an arrest, the police may automatically search the arrested person regardless of the offense for which the person has been placed under arrest (*United States v. Robinson,* 414 U.S. 218 [1973]). In *Robinson,* the Court said that a "custodial arrest of a suspect based on probable cause is a reasonable intrusion under the Fourth Amendment; that intrusion being lawful, a search incident to the arrest requires no additional justification."

The "full body search" rule applies to all kinds of arrests—whether the suspect is arrested for a brutal murder or for shoplifting. The rule is designed to protect the police and prevent the destruction of evidence. Authorization to body search, however, does not authorize strip or body-cavity searches, which are more intrusive.

Search the Area of Immediate Control

Chimel v. California (1969)

Once a lawful arrest has been made, the police may search the area within the suspect's immediate control (sometimes known in police lingo as the "grabbable" area), meaning the area within which the suspect may grab a weapon or destroy evidence (*Chimel v. California,* 395 U.S. 752 [1969]). What is the "area within immediate control"? The Court has not set clear limits.

In *Chimel,* the Court defined the allowable area of search as follows:

> When an arrest is made, it is reasonable for the arresting officer to search the person arrested in order to remove any weapons that the latter might seek to use in order to resist arrest or effect his escape. . . . In addition, it is entirely reasonable

for the arresting officer to search for and seize any evidence on the arrestee's person in order to prevent its concealment or destruction. And the area into which an arrestee might reach in order to grab a weapon or evidentiary items must, of course, be governed by a like rule.

The most limited (and most accurate) interpretation of that phrase is that the search is limited to the person's wingspan—meaning the area covered by the spread of the suspect's arms and hands.

Some lower courts tend to be liberal in defining the area into which there is some possibility that an arrested person might reach for a weapon. In one case, an accused was sitting on a bed at the time of her arrest; the area underneath her bed was deemed to be within her reach. In another case, the fact that the arrestee was handcuffed (and his reach thereby limited) did not mean that the officers could not go ahead and search the area of immediate control. In a third case, the search of a kitchen shelf six feet away from the arrestee was considered by the court as a search incident to an arrest, although an officer stood between the female arrestee (who was being arrested for forgery) and the shelf while the arrest was being made.[4]

The Court has held that a search incident to arrest is valid only if it is "substantially contemporaneous with the arrest and is confined to the immediate vicinity of the arrest." The Court added that "if a search of a house is to be upheld as incident to an arrest, that arrest must take place inside the house, not somewhere outside—whether two blocks away, twenty feet away, or on the sidewalk near the front steps" (*Vale v. Louisiana*, 399 U.S. 30 [1970]).[5] If the search goes beyond the area of immediate control, the officer must obtain a search warrant.

Vale v. Louisiana (1970)

However, some courts have permitted the police to search areas in a residence that are beyond a defendant's reach even without a warrant if (1) there is some type of emergency requiring immediate action that cannot await the preparation of a search warrant (such as possible destruction of evidence) and (2) the search is focused on a predetermined target (such as narcotics in a particular dresser drawer), rather than being a general exploratory search.

Search the Motor Vehicle Even If the Initial Contact and Arrest of the Driver Took Place Outside the Vehicle

Thornton v. United States (2004)

In *Thornton v. United States* (541 U.S. 615 [2004]), the Court held that officers may search a vehicle after a lawful arrest even if the suspect was not in the vehicle when arrested, thus expanding the concept of the "area of immediate control" in motor vehicles. In this case, an officer pulled over to get behind the suspect so that he could check his license plate. The check revealed the tags were not registered to the vehicle the suspect was driving. Before the officer could pull him over, Thornton went into a parking lot, parked, and got out of his vehicle. When Thornton left his vehicle, the officer stopped him and asked about the tags. Thornton acted nervous and suspicious. The officer asked him if he had illegal narcotics or weapons on him or his vehicle. The suspect said no but consented to a frisk. When the officer felt a bulge in Thornton's pocket, he then admitted he had drugs. He reached into his pocket and retrieved two bags, one containing marijuana and the other containing crack cocaine. The officer went to the car, searched it, and found a handgun under the driver's seat.

Thornton appealed his federal drug and firearms conviction, claiming that the search of the car as a contemporaneous incident of his arrest was illegal because he was not in the car at the time of the arrest. The Court rejected Thornton's claim saying that the police are authorized to search the vehicle even if the initial contact and the arrest did not take place while the suspect was still in the car.

Search the Passenger Compartment of a Motor Vehicle

In arrests involving automobiles, the Court has held that, when the police have made a lawful custodial arrest of the occupant of a car, they may, incident to that arrest, search the car's entire passenger compartment (front and back seats) and open any containers found therein. This includes "closed or open glove compartments, consoles, or other receptacles located anywhere within the passenger compartment, as well as luggage, boxes, bags, clothing, and the like" (*New York v. Belton*, 453 U.S. 454 [1981]). The only limitation is that such containers must reasonably contain something that might pose a danger to the officer or hold evidence in support of the offense for which the suspect has been arrested. However, the Court has also said that "our holding encompasses only the interior of the passenger compartment and does not encompass the trunk." Neither does it authorize the opening of a locked glove compartment.

New York v. Belton (1981)

Use Handcuffs Subject to Departmental Policy

The use of handcuffs in arrests is either governed by departmental rules or left to the discretion of the police. The Supreme Court has not addressed the use of handcuffs by police, and there are no authoritative lower court decisions on the issue. As a general rule, however, handcuffs are required or recommended by police departments in felony offenses but not in misdemeanor cases unless there is potential personal danger to the police. If there is a stated policy (or, if not, on grounds of discretion), it is unlikely that a police officer will be held liable for using handcuffs in the process of making an arrest.

Monitor the Movement of the Arrestee

The police may accompany an arrested person into his or her residence after a lawful arrest if they allow the arrestee to go there before being transported to the police station. For example, suppose X is arrested by virtue of an arrest warrant. After the arrest, X asks permission to go to his apartment to inform his wife and pick up some things he will need in jail. The officer may allow X to do that, but the movements of the arrestee can be monitored. In one case, the Supreme Court said, "It is not unreasonable under the Fourth Amendment for a police officer, as a matter of routine, to monitor the movements of an arrested person, as his judgment dictates, following an arrest. The officer's need to ensure his own safety—as well as the integrity of the arrest—is compelling" (*Washington v. Chrisman*, 455 U.S. 1 [1982]). The Court held that the officer is allowed to remain with the arrestee at all times after the arrest.

Search the Arrestee at the Place of Detention

Once brought to the place of detention (usually either a jail or a police lockup), the arrestee may be subjected to a complete search of his or her person if this was not done during the arrest. This procedure is valid even in the absence of probable cause to search. The justification for the search of an arrestee's person on arrival at the station is that it is simply an inventory incidental to being booked in jail.

The inventory, which is a search under the Fourth Amendment, has these legitimate objectives: (1) to protect the arrestee's property while he or she is in jail, (2) to protect the police from groundless claims that they have not adequately safeguarded the defendant's property, (3) to safeguard the detention facility by preventing the introduction of weapons or contraband, and (4) to ascertain or verify the identity of the person arrested.[6] Such searches may include the individual's wallet or other personal property. This rule that a routine inventory search is lawful applies only when the prisoner is to be jailed. If the suspect is brought in merely to be booked and then released, some other reasons will have to be used to justify a warrantless search by the officers.

What the Police Cannot Do during an Arrest

There are many actions the police cannot take during an arrest, including (1) enter a third-party resident, except in emergencies; (2) strip or body-cavity search an arrestee without reasonable suspicion; (3) conduct a warrantless sweep; (4) or invite the media to ride along. This section looks at each of these issues.

Enter Third-Party Residences, Except in Exigent Circumstances

In the absence of exigent circumstances, police officers executing an arrest warrant may not search for the person named in the warrant in the home of a third party without first obtaining a separate search warrant to enter the home. For example, in *Steagald v. United States* (451 U.S. 204 [1981]), federal agents learned from an informant that a federal fugitive could probably be found at a certain address. They procured a warrant for his arrest, but the warrant did not mention the address. Armed with the arrest warrant, the agents went to the address, which was the residence of a third party. The Court held that the arrest warrant could not be used as a legal authority to enter the home of a person other than the person named in the warrant.

In *Minnesota v. Olson* (495 U.S. 91 [1990]), the Court said that a warrantless, nonconsensual entry of a residence to arrest an overnight guest was not justified by exigent circumstances and therefore violated the Fourth Amendment. In that case, the police suspected a certain Olson of being the driver of a getaway car used in a robbery and murder. The police arrested the suspected murderer and recovered the murder weapon. They then surrounded the home of two women with whom they believed Olson had been staying. Without seeking permission and with weapons drawn, they entered the home and found Olson hiding in a closet. They arrested him, and he implicated himself in the crime. On appeal, Olson sought to exclude his statement, saying that there were no exigent circumstances to justify the warrantless entry. The Court agreed, saying that Olson's status as an overnight guest was in itself sufficient to show that he had an expectation of privacy in the home, which society was prepared to recognize as reasonable. The Court further said that there were no exigent circumstances justifying the warrantless entry, so the statement could not be admitted in court.

Strip or Cavity Search an Arrestee Unless Justified by Reasonable Suspicion

Kennedy v. Los Angeles Police Department (9th Cir. 1989)

Although a full body search after an arrest is allowed, a departmental policy that orders body-cavity searches in all felony arrests has been declared unconstitutional by at least one federal circuit court of appeals (*Kennedy v. Los Angeles Police Department,* 887 F.2d 920 [9th Cir. 1989]). The policy challenged in that case required the Los Angeles police to conduct a body-cavity search in all felony arrests but limited that form of strip search in misdemeanor cases to narcotics arrests and arrestees suspected of concealing weapons. The policy was justified by the department as necessary for "safety, security, and the proper administration of the jail system." The Ninth U.S. Circuit Court of Appeals held such searches in felony and misdemeanor arrests to be unconstitutional, saying that they are allowed only if the police have "reasonable suspicion that the individual arrested may be likely to conceal a weapon, drugs, or other contraband prior to conducting a body cavity search." The reason for the "reasonable suspicion" requirement, as opposed to automatic authorization for a full body search in arrests, is that "strip searches involving the visual exploration of body cavities [are] dehumanizing and humiliating." Unlike ordinary body searches, therefore, strip and body-cavity searches are not allowed after arrest unless "reasonable suspicion" justifies the search.

Conduct a Warrantless Protective Sweep Unless Justified

Maryland v. Buie (1990)

The practice of warrantless protective sweeps (where the police look at rooms or places in the house other than where the arrest is taking place) has been authorized by the Court in *Maryland v. Buie* (494 U.S. 325 [1990]) as long as the sweep is justified. In that case, police officers obtained and executed arrest warrants for Buie and an accomplice in connection with an armed robbery. On reaching Buie's house, the officers went through the first and second floors. One of the officers watched the basement so that no one would surprise the other officers. This officer shouted into the basement and ordered anyone there to come out. A voice asked who was there. The officer ordered the person to come out three more times before that person, Buie, emerged from the basement and was placed under arrest. Another officer then entered the basement to see if anyone else was there. Once in the basement, the officer noticed in plain view a red running suit similar to the one worn by one of the suspects in the robbery. The running suit was admitted into evidence at Buie's trial over his objection, and he was convicted of robbery with the use of a deadly weapon.

Buie challenged the legality of the protective sweep (which led to the discovery of the evidence) on appeal. The Court rejected Buie's challenge, saying that "[t]he Fourth Amendment permits a properly limited **protective sweep** in conjunction with an in-home arrest *when the searching officer possesses a reasonable belief based on specific and articulable facts that the area to be swept harbors an individual posing a danger to those on the arrest scene*" (emphasis added). This means that protective sweeps when making arrests are not always valid; a search is valid only if the searching officer can justify it "based on specific and articulable facts that the area to be swept harbors an individual posing a danger to those on the arrest scene." In the absence of such justification, the protective sweep is invalid.

Invite the Media to "Ride Along"

Wilson v. Layne (1999)

The Court has held that the practice of "media ride-alongs" violates a suspect's Fourth Amendment rights and is therefore unconstitutional (*Wilson v. Layne*, 526 U.S. 603 [1999]). In this case, federal marshals and local sheriff's deputies invited a newspaper reporter and a photographer to accompany them while executing a warrant to arrest the petitioners' son in their home. The early-morning entry led to a confrontation with the petitioners. A protective sweep revealed that the son was not in the house. The reporters (who did not participate in executing the warrant) photographed the incident, but their newspaper never published the photographs.

The Wilsons sued, claiming a violation of their Fourth Amendment rights. The Court agreed that their constitutional rights were violated but did not award monetary damages, because of the "good faith" defense, saying that the right violated at the time of the media ride-along was not yet "clearly established." Balancing the petitioners' right to privacy and the officers' objectives for a media ride-along, the Court said, "Surely the possibility of good public relations for the police is simply not enough, standing alone, to justify the ride-along into a private home. And even the need for accurate reporting on police issues in general bears no direct relation to the constitutional justification for the police intrusion into a home in order to execute a felony arrest warrant."

The Announcement Requirement

The Constitution requires that in most situations, the police must announce their purpose before breaking into a dwelling. There are exceptions to this. This section looks at the general rule and the exceptions.

The General Rule: Knock and Announce Required

Federal and many state statutes require that an officer making an arrest or executing a search warrant announce his or her purpose and authority before breaking into a dwelling. The idea is to enable voluntary compliance by the suspect and avoid violence. Breaking into the premises without first complying with the announcement requirement may or may not invalidate the entry and any resulting search, depending on the law or court decisions in the state. Some states invalidate the entry and resulting search; others do not. The Court has addressed the issue of whether the "knock and announce" rule is required by the Constitution. The Court said that the Constitution does require an announcement but not in all cases.

Wilson v. Arkansas **(1995)**

In *Wilson v. Arkansas* (514 U.S. 927 [1995]), police officers obtained an arrest warrant for the suspect and a search warrant for her home. At Wilson's residence, the officers identified themselves as they entered the home through an unlocked door and stated that they had a warrant. They did not, however, knock and announce, because Arkansas law did not require this. The police seized various drugs, a gun, and some ammunition. Tried and convicted of violating state drug laws, Wilson moved to suppress the evidence, saying that knock and announce was required by the Fourth Amendment in all cases.

In a unanimous opinion, the Court ruled that the "knock and announce common law principle is part of the Fourth Amendment's requirement that searches and seizures be reasonable." It quickly added, however, that this did not mean that every entry should be preceded by an announcement, recognizing that "the common law principle of announcement was never stated as an inflexible rule requiring announcement under all circumstances."

More significantly, the Court said that "[t]he Fourth Amendment's flexible requirement of reasonableness should not be read to mandate a rigid rule of announcement that ignores countervailing law enforcement interests." In essence, the Court held that, although knock and announce is part of the requirement of reasonableness in searches and seizures, it is not a rigid rule and is subject to exceptions based on law enforcement interests. Such "reasonableness" need only be based on reasonable suspicion, not on probable cause.

HIGHLIGHT

Is Knock and Announce Required?

"Given the long-standing common-law endorsement of the practice of announcement, we have little doubt that the framers of the Fourth Amendment thought that the method of an officer's entry into a dwelling was among the factors to be considered in accessing the reasonableness of a search or seizure.

"This is not to say, of course, that every entry must be preceded by an announcement.

The Fourth Amendment's flexible requirement of reasonableness should not be read to mandate a rigid rule of announcement that ignores countervailing law enforcement interests: The common-law principle of announcement was never stated as an inflexible rule requiring announcement under all circumstances."

SOURCE: *Wilson v. Arkansas*, 57 Crl 2122 (1995), at 2124.

The Exceptions and Other Rules

The Court in *Wilson* did not enumerate the legally acceptable exceptions to the knock-and-announce rule. Instead, the Court stated that

> for now, we leave to the lower courts the task of determining the circumstances under which an unannounced entry is reasonable under the Fourth Amendment. We simply hold that although a search or seizure of a dwelling might be constitutionally defective if police officers enter without prior announcement, law enforcement interests may also establish the reasonableness of an announced entry.

There are cases where, because of *exigent circumstances,* an announcement is not required or necessary because of officer safety or third-person safety or to preserve evidence. The usual instances are

- When announcing presents a strong threat of violence or danger to the officers—for example, when the police are serving a warrant on a fugitive who is armed and dangerous.
- When there is danger that contraband or other property sought might be destroyed. Some states permit a magistrate to issue so-called no-knock searches, particularly in drug cases. They authorize entry without announcement because otherwise the evidence might be destroyed.
- When officers reasonably believe that persons within the premises are in imminent peril of bodily harm, as when the police hear a scream for help from inside a residence.
- When people within are reasonably believed to be engaged in the process of destroying evidence or escaping because they are aware of the presence of the police.
- When the person to be arrested is in the process of committing the crime.

Be aware, however, that some states require officers to knock and announce without exception. In these states, the above exceptions do not apply.

Even though the Court has allowed exceptions, it has determined that blanket exceptions in drug-dealing cases are unconstitutional. Also, the same standards apply even if entry by the police results in property damage. The next sections look at these two issues.

Blanket Exceptions Unconstitutional Exceptions to the announcement requirement are governed by law, court decisions, and agency regulations and so vary from state to state. The Court has ruled, however, that blanket exceptions (exceptions that apply to a certain type of case regardless of circumstances) are not allowed in drug-dealing cases even by judicial authorization (*Richards v. Wisconsin,* 520 U.S. 385 [1997]).

Richards v. Wisconsin (1997)

In *Richards v. Wisconsin*, a judge in Wisconsin created a rule that did away with the knock-and-announce requirement in all warrants to search for evidence involving drug deals. The justification for the rule was that drug-dealing cases frequently involved threats of physical violence or possible destruction of evidence anyway, so there was no need to knock and announce. The Supreme Court disagreed, saying that the Fourth Amendment does not allow a bright-line exception to the knock-and-announce requirement in cases involving felony drug dealing. They added that even in these cases, exceptions to the requirement must be made case by case based on the reasonableness requirement. The Court did not say whether any type of blanket exception would be allowed at all. It is safe to say, however, that if the Court is disinclined to allow a blanket exception in drug-dealing cases, it is hard to imagine what types of cases might justify a blanket exception.

The Knock-and-Announce Requirement and Property Damage by the Police

United States v. Ramirez (1998)

In *United States v. Ramirez* (523 U.S. 65 [1998]), the Court held that the knock-and-announce rule does not set a higher standard for unannounced entries even if they result in property damage. In this case, federal agents had a warrant authorizing unannounced entry to search the defendant's home for a fugitive, a certain Shelby, an escaped prisoner who had a prior record of violence and who, according to an informant, was in Ramirez's home. The agents set up a portable loudspeaker system and announced that they had a search warrant. Simultaneously, they broke a single window in the garage to discourage occupants from rushing to the garage where, the informant said, weapons were kept.

Ramirez later admitted that he had fired a weapon because he thought his house was being burglarized, that he had a gun, and that he was a convicted felon but not the person sought by the agents. Indicted on charges of being a felon in possession of firearms, he sought to exclude the evidence, claiming that there were insufficient exigent circumstances to justify the agents' destruction of his property when executing the warrant.

The Court disagreed, saying that the Fourth Amendment does not hold law enforcement officers to a higher standard when the no-knock entry results in property destruction. That standard, set in *Wilson v. Arkansas* (514 U.S. 927 [1995]), is that a no-knock entry is justifiable if officers have reasonable suspicion that obeying the rule would be dangerous or futile or would hamper an effective investigation. That standard was met in this case.

Other Arrest Issues

Other arrest issues include (1) whether the police can temporarily detain a suspect while obtaining warrant; (2) whether they can place a person under arrest for traffic violations and other petty offenses; (3) whether they can arrest people for offenses that are not punishable by jail or prison; and (4) whether citizens can make valid arrests.

Detaining a Suspect While Obtaining a Warrant

The Court has held that, under exigent circumstances and where there is a need to preserve evidence until a warrant can be obtained, the police may temporarily restrain a suspect's movements without violating his or her Fourth Amendment right (*Illinois v. McArthur*, 531 U.S. 326 [2001]).

Illinois v. McArthur (2001)

In *Illinois v. McArthur*, a woman asked police officers to accompany her to the trailer where she lived with her husband, McArthur, while she removed her belongings. The woman went inside where McArthur was, while the officers waited outside. When the woman came out, she told the officers that McArthur had drugs in the trailer. This established probable cause. The officers knocked and asked permission to search the trailer, which McArthur denied. One officer then left to obtain a warrant. When McArthur stepped onto his porch, the officer prevented him from reentering his trailer. McArthur did reenter the trailer on three occasions, but the officer stood in the doorway and observed him. When the other officer returned with a warrant, they searched the trailer and found drugs and drug paraphernalia.

On appeal, the Court ruled that, under exigent circumstances and where there is a need to preserve evidence until the police obtain a warrant, they may temporarily restrain a suspect without violating the Fourth Amendment. The minimal nature of the intrusion and the law enforcement interest involved justified the brief seizure.

Arrests for Traffic Violations or Petty Offenses

Most states classify offenses as either felonies or misdemeanors. Other states have additional categories such as traffic offenses and petty offenses. City or municipal ordinances may create additional offenses. Penalties vary, as do permissible police actions after detention. In some states, an arrest is required in some traffic offenses; in others, an arrest is left to the officer's discretion. Other jurisdictions do not authorize any arrest at all; issuing citations is the only allowable procedure. (See Figure 6.2 for an example of traffic citation.)

Arrests for Offenses Not Punishable by Prison or Jail Time

For a long time it was not clear whether the police could constitutionally arrest an offender for minor offenses not punishable by prison or jail time. Arrest for minor and nonjailable offenses is currently authorized in all fifty states and the District of Columbia. The issue was settled by the Court, however, in the case of *Atwater v. City of Lago Vista*, 532 U.S. 318 (2001), in which the Court said that such arrests are constitutional.

Atwater v. City of Lago Vista (2001)

In that case, Atwater, who was driving her children home from school, was arrested by a police officer for not wearing a seat belt. The offense was punishable under Texas law by a fine of not more than $50. Atwater pleaded no contest and paid the $50 fine but later challenged the law as violative of her Fourth Amendment right against unreasonable searches and seizures, saying it was not authorized under common law. On appeal, the Court held that "the Fourth Amendment does not forbid

MISSOURI UNIFORM COMPLAINT AND SUMMONS

ABSTRACT OF COURT RECORD

ORI NO. MO0510000
JOHNSON CO. SHERIFF'S DEPT.
STATE OF MISSOURI
IN THE CIRCUIT COURT OF JOHNSON
JOHNSON COUNTY ASSOC. CIRCUIT DIV.

No. 851402263

THE UNDERSIGNED POLICE OFFICER STATES THAT:			
on or about (DATE)	upon/at or near (LOCATION/LOG PT.)	at (TIME)	☐ AM ☐ PM

WITHIN COUNTY AND STATE AFORESAID

Name (LAST, FIRST, MIDDLE)

Street Address

City	State	Zip Code

Date of Birth	Age	Race	Sex	Height	Weight

Driver's License No.   ☐ OP   ☐ CH State
                              ☐ MC QUAL

Dept. of Revenue use only — Do not write in this space.

Disobeyed Signal (when light turned red)	☐ Past Middle of Intersection ☐ Middle of Intersection	☐ Not Reached Intersection
Disobeyed Stop Sign	☐ Stopped Wrong Place	☐ Walk Speed ☐ Faster
Improper Turn ☐ Left ☐ Right ☐ "U"	☐ No Signal ☐ Into Wrong Lane ☐ Cut Corner	☐ From Wrong Lane ☐ Prohibited
☐ Improper Passing ☐ Improper Lane Use	☐ At Intersection ☐ Between Traf. ☐ Cut In ☐ On Right ☐ On Hill ☐ Wrong Side of Pavement	☐ Lane Straddling ☐ Wrong Lane ☐ On Curve

DID UNLAWFULLY	V E H I C L E	Year	Make	Model	Style	Color
☐ OPERATE ☐ PARK		Number			State	Year

AND THEN AND THERE COMMITTED THE FOLLOWING OFFENSE.

Describe Violation

Driving _____ MPH when limited to _____ MPH | Detection Method
☐ STA RADAR
☐ MOV RADAR
☐ WATCH (AIR)   ☐ PACE
☐ WATCH (GRND)   ☐ OTHER

In violation of ☐ RSMO ☐ ORD	Missouri Charge Code	☐ IN ACCIDENT ☐ DWI/BAC

THE ABOVE COMPLAINT IS TRUE AS I VERILY BELIEVE.

Officer	Badge No.

SWORN TO BEFORE ME THIS DATE.

Name & Title	Date

I promise to dispose of the charges of which I am accused through court appearance or prepayment of fine and court costs.	Court Date	Court Time	☐ AM ☐ PM

Street Address
COUNTY COURTHOUSE

Signature	City
X	WARRENSBURG, MO 64093

ON INFORMATION UNDERSIGNED PROSECUTOR COMPLAINS AND INFORMS COURT THAT ABOVE FACTS ARE TRUE AS HE VERILY BELIEVES.

Prosecutor's Signature	Date

FORM 37.1162A   G. A. THOMPSON, P. O. BOX 64681, DALLAS, TEXAS 75206   FORM MO17-5R

Figure 6.2 Missouri Uniform Complaint and Summons

Source: Official form for the state of Missouri

a warrantless arrest for a minor criminal offense, such as a misdemeanor seatbelt violation, punishable only by a fine." It reasoned that "there is no historical evidence that the framers or proponents of the Fourth Amendment . . . were at all concerned about warrantless arrests by local constables and other peace officers." The Court then went on to say: "We simply cannot conclude that the Fourth Amendment, as originally understood, forbade peace officers to arrest without warrant for misdemeanor not amounting to or involving breach of the peace." (Read the Case Brief to learn more about the *Atwater* case.)

CASE BRIEF: The Leading Case on Whether the Police Can Arrest Suspects on Nonjailable Offenses

Atwater v. City of Lago Vista, 532 U.S. 318 (2001)

Facts: A Texas law requires all front-seat passengers to wear a seat belt, a crime punishable by a fine of not more than $50. Texas law also expressly authorizes a police officer to arrest without a warrant if a person is found in violation of the law, although the police may issue a citation in lieu of arrest. Atwater was driving a vehicle with her two young children in the front seat; none was wearing a seat belt. An officer observed the violation and stopped Atwater—telling her as he approached the vehicle that she was going to jail. Following the release of Atwater's children to a neighbor, the officer handcuffed Atwater, placed her in his police car, and took her to the police station, where she was made to remove her shoes, jewelry, and eyeglasses and empty her pockets. Officers later took her mug shot and placed her in a cell for about an hour. She was then taken before a magistrate and released on bond. She later pleaded no contest and paid a $50 fine. She subsequently brought suit alleging a violation of her Fourth Amendment right against unreasonable searches and seizures.

Issue: *Does the Fourth Amendment forbid a warrantless arrest for a minor criminal offense punishable only by a fine? No.*

Supreme Court Decision: "The Fourth Amendment does not forbid a warrantless

arrest for a minor criminal offense, such as a misdemeanor seat belt violation, punishable only by a fine."

Case Significance: This case settles an issue of concern to the police: whether the police can arrest persons who violate laws or ordinances that are not punishable with jail or prison time. At present, all 50 states and the District of Columbia have laws authorizing such warrantless arrests. Atwater maintained that no such arrests were authorized under common law and that the history and intent of the framers of the Constitution did not allow such arrests.

The Court disagreed, saying that it was unclear whether or not such arrests were authorized under common law or that the framers of the Fourth Amendment were at all concerned about warrantless arrests by local constables and other peace officers. The Court then said that "[w]e simply cannot conclude that the Fourth Amendment, as originally understood, forbade peace officers to arrest without warrant for misdemeanors not amounting to or involving breach of the peace." Given these, the Court held that warrantless arrests for nonjailable offenses are constitutional.

Excerpts from the Decision: The Court rejects Atwater's request to mint a new rule of constitutional law forbidding custodial arrest,

---

even upon probable cause, when conviction could not ultimately carry any jail time and the government can show no compelling need for immediate detention. She reasons that, when historical practice fails to speak conclusively to a Fourth Amendment claim, courts must strike a current balance between individual and societal interests by subjecting particular contemporary circumstances to traditional standards of reasonableness. Atwater might well prevail under a rule derived exclusively to address the uncontested facts of her case, since her claim to live free of pointless indignity and confinement clearly outweighs anything the City can raise against it specific to her. However, the Court has traditionally recognized that a responsible Fourth Amendment balance is not well served by standards requiring sensitive, case-by-case determinations of government need, lest every discretionary judgment in the field be converted into an occasion for constitutional review. Complications arise the moment consideration is given the possible applications of the several criteria Atwater proposes for drawing a line between minor crimes with limited arrest authority and others not so restricted. The assertion that these difficulties could be alleviated simply by requiring police in doubt not to arrest is unavailing because, first, such a tie breaker would in practice amount to a constitutionally inappropriate least-restrictive-alternative limitation, and, second, whatever guidance the tie breaker might give would come at the price of a systematic disincentive to arrest in situations where even

Atwater concedes arresting would serve an important societal interest. That warrantless misdemeanor arrests do not demand the constitutional attention Atwater seeks is indicated by a number of factors, including that the law has never jelled the way Atwater would have it; that anyone arrested without formal process is entitled to a magistrate's review of probable cause within 48 hours; that many jurisdictions have chosen to impose more restrictive safeguards through statutes limiting warrantless arrests for minor offenses; that it is in the police's interest to limit such arrests, which carry costs too great to incur without good reason; and that, under current doctrine, the preference for categorical treatment of Fourth Amendment claims gives way to individualized review when a defendant makes a colorable argument that an arrest, with or without a warrant, was conducted in an extraordinary manner, unusually harmful to his privacy or physical interests. The upshot of all these influences, combined with the good sense (and, failing that, the political accountability) of most local lawmakers and peace officers, is a dearth of horribles demanding redress. Thus, the probable cause standard applies to all arrests, without the need to balance the interests and circumstances involved in particular situations. An officer may arrest an individual without violating the Fourth Amendment if there is probable cause to believe that the offender has committed even a very minor criminal offense in the officer's presence.

The Validity of a Citizen's Arrest

Common law authorizes a **citizen's arrest**—an arrest made by a citizen without a warrant. Such arrests are limited under common law, however, to situations where the following conditions are present: (1) a felony (or a misdemeanor involving a breach of the peace) has been committed, and (2) the citizen has probable cause to believe that the person arrested committed the crime. This common law rule has been modified by legislation in many states. One problem with the common law authorization of citizen's arrests (in states where they are used) is that the definition of "breach of the peace" varies from one state to another and is usually unclear.

The citizen who makes a citizen's arrest runs two risks: (1) that the crime committed is not a felony, and (2) if it is a misdemeanor, that it does not constitute a breach of the peace. If the arrest turns out to be illegal, the citizen is exposed to civil liability under state tort law for false imprisonment. In general, the person making a citizen's arrest is allowed to use as much reasonable force as is available to police officers when making a similar arrest.

Some states provide by law that police officers, when making an arrest, may enlist the aid of citizens and that citizens are obliged to respond. This is not a citizen's arrest situation but instead an arrest in aid of the police. Arrests by police officers with probable cause outside their territorial jurisdiction are valid, but they are in the category of citizen's arrests and are therefore subject to the above limitations.

The Disposition of Prisoners after Arrest

For minor offenses, police usually have the discretion to arrest or not to arrest. The more serious the offense, the less discretion the officer has to release the suspect. If an officer makes an arrest, he or she fills out an arrest report and submits it, and it is kept on file in the department. (See Figure 6.3 for an example of an arrest report form.) After a suspect has been arrested, the police must follow constitutionally prescribed procedures (often incorporated into departmental policy) for keeping that person in detention.

An important and often-asked question is whether a person who has been arrested is entitled to a telephone call after the arrest. Although the Supreme Court has not addressed this issue, it is safe to say that an arrestee has no *constitutional* right to a telephone call. Such a right, however, may be given by state law or agency policy. When the call is to be made (whether immediately after the arrest or days later, before booking or after booking) varies by jurisdiction. It must be added, however, that an arrestee is constitutionally entitled to call an attorney and that right, if requested by the suspect, must be granted prior to questioning. Failure to allow the suspect to exercise this right results in the exclusion of whatever evidence may be obtained during questioning.

The remainder of this section looks at what happens after a person is arrested, including booking, first appearance, and bail.

Booking

As discussed in Chapter 2, *booking* involves making an entry in the police blotter or arrest book, indicating the suspect's name, the time of arrest, and the offense involved. If the offense is serious, the suspect may also be photographed and fingerprinted. If the offense is minor, the suspect may be released based on "stationhouse

STATE OF VERMONT
ARREST / CUSTODY REPORT

		CAUTION
		Y	N

|＿|＿|＿|＿|＿|＿|＿|＿|＿|＿|
AGENCY COMPLAINT NO.

DATE OF ARREST

| MO | DAY | YR |

ARRESTING AGENCY ＿＿＿＿＿＿＿＿＿＿＿＿

IDENTIFICATION:

| LAST NAME | FIRST NAME | MIDDLE NAME | DOB | AGE | SEX | RACE* | ETHNIC* |

| STREET | | | EMPLOYED | UNEMPLOYED | STUDENT | REFUSED TO ANSWER |

PLACE OF BIRTH (CITY/STATE)

CITY/TOWN

EMPLOYER/SCHOOL

| STATE | ZIP CODE | SOC. SEC. NO. | ID NUMBER |

ADDRESS

| ALIAS | LAST NAME | FIRST NAME | MIDDLE NAME |

SCARS/MARKS

1	2	3	4	5	6
SING	MAR	SEP	DIV	WID	COHAB

MARITAL STATUS

| HEIGHT | WEIGHT lb. |

1	2	3	4	5	6	7
BLA	BRO	BLD	RED	GREY	BALD	WHI

HAIR COLOR

1	2	3	4
BRO	BLU	HAZ	OTH

EYE COLOR   SPECIFY

D.M.V. INFORMATION:

D.M.V. CASE NO. ＿＿＿＿＿＿

| INJURY | FATAL | PROP. DAMAGE | | REFUSED | NO | YES | RESULT | % |
| OPERATOR LICENSE NO. | STATE | EXPIRATION DATE | ACCIDENT | | | | TEST | |

| REGISTRATION NO. | STATE | EXPIRATION DATE | VEHICLE MAKE | TYPE | YEAR |

ARREST DATA:

| TIME | PLACE | GRID/COUNTY-TOWN | OFFENSE GRID |

V.S.A.

| OFFENSE | TITLE | SECTION | SUB-SECTION | OFFENSE DATE |

| FINGERPRINTS | PHOTOGRAPH |
| Y | N | Y | N |

| RELEASED TO GUARDIAN | ARRAIGNED | CITED | LODGED | BAIL |

| OFFENSE CODE | ATTACH TO A/C-3 | IMMEDIATE DISPOSITION | COMMENTS |

COMPANION CASE NO.

ARRESTING OFFICER SIGNATURE   ID. NO.

FINGERPRINT OFFICER

PHOTOGRAPH OFFICER   APPROVING OFFICER SIGNATURE   ID. NO.

OFFENSE: (STATE'S ATTORNEY USE)

DOCKET # ＿＿＿＿＿＿

V.S.A.

COUNT: ＿＿ OF ＿＿

| CHARGED | TITLE | SECTION | SUB-SECTION |

| NO PROSECUTION | DIVERSION | FORWARDED TO COURT | RETURNED | COMMENT: ＿＿＿＿＿＿ |

*RACE CODE: W-WHITE, B-BLACK, I-INDIAN, A-ASIAN, U-UNKNOWN

*ETHNIC CODE: 1-HISPANIC, 2-NON HISPANIC   **A/C - 1 AGENCY**

VT 453
7/83

Figure 6.3 Arrest Report

Source: Official form of the state of Vermont

bail," which involves posting cash and promising to appear in court for a hearing at a specified date. If the offense is serious, the arrestee will be kept in jail or a *holding facility* (a temporary facility usually maintained by the police department instead of by the county) until bail, as set by the magistrate, is posted.

In the process of booking, the officer may, in accordance with departmental procedures, carry out (without a warrant) an inventory of the arrestee's personal property. However, such an inventory may not be used as a fishing expedition for evidence. Although containers may be opened for the purpose of listing their contents, private documents found in the course of the inventory may not be read. If the officer feels that further search is needed beyond that allowed in the booking procedure, a search warrant must be obtained.

The First Appearance before a Magistrate

Statutes or court rules in most states require that an arrested person be brought before a magistrate without unnecessary delay. What does that mean? Although there is no fixed meaning, the Court has stated that the detention of a suspect for forty-eight hours (excluding weekends, holidays, and other "nonjudicial" days) is presumed to be reasonable. If the time for a probable cause hearing is longer than that, the burden of proof shifts to the police to prove reasonableness. Conversely, if the time for a probable cause hearing is shorter than forty-eight hours, there may still be unreasonable delay, but the burden of proof shifts to the suspect (*County of Riverside v. McLaughlin,* 59 U.S. 4413 [1991]).

County of Riverside v. McLaughlin (1991)

In *McLaughlin,* a suspect brought a lawsuit challenging the process of determining probable cause for warrantless arrests in Riverside County, California. The county's policy was to combine probable cause determinations with arraignment proceedings. This policy was similar to the provisions of the California Penal Code, which states that arraignments must be conducted without unnecessary delay and within two days (forty-eight hours) of arrest, excluding weekends and holidays. The U.S. District Court issued an injunction requiring the county to provide a probable cause hearing within thirty-six hours for all persons arrested without a warrant.

The issue on appeal was whether the Fourth Amendment requires a judicial determination of probable cause immediately after completing the administrative steps incident to arrest within thirty-six hours after the arrest, as the lower court had ordered. The Supreme Court said no, adding that if a probable cause determination is combined with arraignment, it is presumptively reasonable for the arrest-to-hearing period to last up to forty-eight hours. If more time than that elapses, the government bears the burden of showing that the delay is reasonable. Conversely, if the release is made before forty-eight hours after arrest, the burden of showing unreasonable delay shifts to the person arrested.

In a subsequent case, the Court held that *McLaughlin* does not apply retroactively, saying that "were *McLaughlin* to be applied retroactively, untold numbers of prisoners would be set free because they were not brought before a magistrate within forty-eight hours" (*Powell v. Nevada,* 511 U.S. 79 [1992]).

Powell v. Nevada (1992)

The purposes of the initial appearance vary from place to place, but usually they are

- To warn the suspect of his or her rights, including being given the *Miranda* warnings
- To determine if there is probable cause to process the suspect further through the system or, if not, to set the suspect free
- If the suspect is to be further processed, to set bail for release, except if the offense is nonbailable

In many places, the magistrate before whom the arrestee is brought is required to give the *Miranda* warnings during the initial appearance. If the suspect is questioned by the police while under arrest prior to this time, however, the *Miranda* warnings must be given by the officer; otherwise, the confession or admission obtained is not admissible in court to prove the suspect's guilt. In arrests with a warrant, the likelihood that the suspect will be asked questions by the police prior to the initial appearance is less, because the officer only has to execute the warrant and deliver the suspect to the magistrate. Questions do not need to be asked. In warrantless arrests, the officer is more likely to have asked questions before the arrest was made because this may be how the officer established probable cause.

Bail

Many cases, particularly nonserious offenses, end at the initial appearance stage through a guilty plea, a negotiated plea, or outright release without charges being filed. If the case is not disposed of at this time, however, the arrestee is sent back to jail, or allowed to post a bail bond in an amount determined by the magistrate, or released on his or her own recognizance (ROR). In some cases, bail may be denied, particularly with serious offenses when evidence of guilt is strong.

When the charge is merely a misdemeanor, most courts use bail schedules. The arrestee can post bail with the police or clerk of court in an amount designated in the schedule without having to see the magistrate. If there is enough evidence to justify charging the accused with a felony, and if the offense is bailable and no bail has been set, the magistrate will fix the amount. The amount of bail in misdemeanor or felony cases is usually determined in light of the facts then known to the magistrate. These include the nature and seriousness of the crime, the previous criminal record of the accused, and the likelihood of flight from the state. Bail is not an absolute right—it may be denied in capital punishment cases in which evidence of guilt is strong.

The setting of bail by the magistrate, if the case gets this far, usually ends police involvement in an arrest. Although bail generally is set by the courts, some jurisdictions allow the police to accept bail for minor offenses; the amount has been predetermined by the magistrate. From then on, the processing of the case is in the hands of the prosecutor and the judge, except that the officer probably will be called to testify during trial.

The Use of Force during an Arrest

This section addresses the issues surrounding the use of force during an arrest, including the factors that govern the use of force by police, the difference between nondeadly and deadly force, and the rules surrounding their use.

The Factors Governing Police Use of Force

The use of force, nondeadly or deadly, is governed by (1) the Constitution of the United States, particularly the due process and "cruel and unusual punishment" provisions; (2) state law, usually the Penal Code or Code of Criminal Procedure, which defines when an officer may or may not legally use force; (3) judicial decision, if any, specifying what type of force can be used and when; and, (4) most important, departmental or agency rules or guidelines.

Officers must be very familiar with all of these sources but particularly with their police department's rules on the use of force. Departmental rules are often more limiting than state law and are binding on the officer, regardless of what state law allows. For example, suppose the law of the State of Illinois provides that deadly force may be used to prevent the escape of a jail inmate. In contrast, assume that the policy of the Chicago Police Department limits the use of deadly force only to cases of self-defense by the police and therefore precludes the use of deadly force to prevent jail escapes. The departmental policy is binding on Chicago police officers. Violation of departmental policy makes the act punishable even if the use of force is authorized by the state law.

In contrast, assume that departmental policy allows the officer to use deadly force to prevent escapes, but state law prohibits it. In this case, state law prevails over departmental policy. The general rule on use of force is that the more limiting rule binds the police officer and renders the more liberal policy nonbinding.

Nondeadly and Deadly Force Distinguished

The law on the use of force during an arrest can be confusing unless viewed in a proper legal framework. That framework is this: there are two kinds of force in police work—nondeadly force and deadly force. **Nondeadly force** is force that, when used, is not likely to result in serious bodily injury or death. In contrast, **deadly force** is force that, when used, poses a high risk of death or serious injury to its human target, regardless of whether or not death, serious injury, or any harm actually occurs. Examples are firearms, knives, daggers, and lead pipes. Nightsticks and chokeholds are considered by some courts to be deadly force, but much depends on how they are used. It is important to know that these two types of force in policing are governed by very different rules for purposes of legal liabilities.

The Rule on the Use of Nondeadly Force

The rule is that *nondeadly force* may be used as long as it is reasonable force. **Reasonable force** is force that a prudent and cautious person would use if exposed to similar circumstances. Moreover, it is limited to the amount of force necessary to accomplish lawful results. Anything beyond that is unreasonable force. For example, the police arrest a suspect who kicks, uses fists, and refuses to be handcuffed. The police may use as much force as is necessary to bring that person under control. However, suppose that after subduing the arrestee, the police administer a few blows. Such force is unreasonable, because it is unnecessary to accomplish the lawful purpose of placing the suspect under control. That force becomes punitive.

The problem, however, is that the term *reasonable force* is subjective, meaning it depends on the circumstances in each case and the perception of the judge or jury that tries the case. The officer must be able to remember the circumstances that led to the use of a certain amount of force and hope that the judge or jury would consider it reasonable. Most states allow the use of nondeadly force in specific circumstances, such as to overcome an offender's resistance to a lawful arrest, to prevent escape, to retake a suspect after escape, to protect people and property from harm, and to protect the officer from bodily injury.

HIGHLIGHT

The Use of Taser Stun Guns in Law Enforcement

Tasers are electric stun guns that "shoot barbs that deliver 50,000 volts of electricity to the body and incapacitate the target they hit." They can be fired effectively up to 25 feet. They are not as deadly as a gun but can cause death. The *New York Times* reports that, as of October 19, 2005, 140 people had died from police use of Taser electric guns. The same article reports that 7,000 police departments throughout the country now use them and that their popularity peaked in 2003 and 2004.

Should Tasers be used in policing? Many police departments say it is an acceptable alternative to firearms, which are more lethal. True, they have caused death, but more deaths would have resulted if real guns had been used. Those who oppose their use argue that they are also lethal and might encourage police use of them in cases where such use might be unnecessary.

The Police Executive Research Forum (PERF), an influential police research and policy organiza-

tion, recently recommended new restrictions on the use of Tasers. After an eighteen-month study and consultation with major police departments, the group suggested that "officers be allowed to use the stun guns only on people who are aggressively resisting arrest, not just refusing to follow orders." The group further recommends that "officers pause and evaluate suspects after shocking them once, instead of repeatedly shocking someone without a break" and that "anyone who is shocked should receive follow-up medical treatment, either at the scene or at a hospital."

PERF believes that Tasers have a place in police work, saying: "Electric weapons like Tasers should remain in use, because they give officers a way to handle difficult or potentially violent suspects without resorting to deadly force," but that they should be used with caution. As a result of this recommendation, shares in Taser International (the company that makes these weapons) fell by 80% in 2005.

SOURCES: This Highlight is based on news items from the *New York Times*, October 19, 2005, p. A13, and the *Huntsville Item*, October 31, 2005, p. 4A.

The opposite of reasonable force is unreasonable force. Unfortunately, that contrast does not give the police a clear idea of what is allowed or prohibited, particularly in situations when there is no time to think. Given this, it is best to think of the opposite of reasonable force as **punitive force**, meaning force that is used to punish rather than to accomplish lawful results. This distinction is more instructive because an officer, even in highly emotional situations, generally knows whether the force he or she is using is necessary to control the situation or is being used to punish the person arrested.

The Rule on the Use of Deadly Force

The rule on the use of deadly force is more specific, narrow, and precise than that of nondeadly force, but it varies in felony and nonfelony cases.

Tennessee v. Garner **(1985)**

The Use of Deadly Force in Felony Cases
Tennessee v. Garner (411 U.S. 1.1 [1985]) sets the following guideline on the use of deadly force to arrest a suspect: It is constitutionally reasonable for a police officer to use deadly force when the officer has probable cause to believe that the suspect poses a threat of serious physical harm, either to the officer or to others.

The Court in *Garner* concluded that the use of deadly force in that case to prevent the escape of an apparently unarmed suspected felon was constitutionally unreasonable. It emphasized that "where the suspect poses no immediate threat to the officer and no threat to others, the harm resulting from failing to apprehend him does not justify the use of deadly force," adding that "a police officer may not seize an unarmed non-dangerous suspect by shooting him dead." The *Garner* decision rendered unconstitutional the then-existing "fleeing felon" statutes in nearly half of the states, insofar as those statutes allowed the use by the police of deadly force to prevent the escape of a fleeing felon regardless of the circumstances. "Fleeing Felon" statutes are constitutional only if they comport with the requirements set in *Garner*.

Tennessee v. Garner was not a criminal prosecution case; the officer who killed the suspect was not being prosecuted for murder or homicide. Instead, it was a civil case, in which the plaintiffs sought monetary damages from the department and the state of Tennessee for Garner's death. Nonetheless, *Garner* is the only case decided by the Court thus far that sets guidelines for the use of deadly force by the police. The implications of *Garner* are still being addressed by lower courts; these cases may eventually find their way to the U.S. Supreme Court.

The Use of Deadly Force in Misdemeanor Cases
In misdemeanor cases, the safest rule for the officer to follow is: Never use deadly force in misdemeanor cases, except if absolutely necessary for self-defense or the defense of the life of a third person. The use of deadly force in other circumstances in misdemeanor cases exposes the officer to possible criminal and civil liabilities. It raises questions of disproportionality, because the classification by the penal code of the offense as a

misdemeanor signifies that the state does not consider the act so serious as to warrant a more severe penalty. Possible death might be too serious of a punishment to prevent the escape of a nonserious offender.

Responses to Terrorism

The tragic and traumatic events of September 11, 2001, have left a deep and lasting effect on American immigration, law enforcement, and security laws. Responses to terrorism and national security are primarily the responsibility of the federal government, but law enforcement personnel on the state and local levels are also involved in the national government's efforts to prevent terrorist attacks and preserve national security. One observer notes that "American law enforcement has a long tradition of reactive patrol, that is, responding to crimes and calls for assistance."[7] The writer adds: "The problem of terrorism brings the need for preemptive, offensive policing to a new level. If law enforcement simply responds, it will have little impact on the prevention of terrorism. . . . If state and local agencies shift to offensive thinking and action . . . police contact with potential terrorists will increase."[8] As the problem of terrorism continues, local and state law enforcement agencies have become more involved in the effort to prevent it and in collaborating with national law enforcement agencies to ensure that the possibility of future attacks is minimized, if not completely prevented.

Even before the events of 9/11, the United States had legislation in place aimed at punishing and blunting the effects of terrorism. Among the earliest laws is the Foreign Intelligence Surveillance Act (FISA), passed in 1978, which authorized wiretaps in the interest of foreign intelligence. A later and more significant law is the Antiterrorism and Effective Death Penalty Act (AEDPA) of 1996, passed as a response to the Oklahoma bombing and the 1993 bombing of the World Trade Center in New York. The AEDPA, among others, authorizes the Secretary of State to identify and label an organization as terrorist if it meets certain criteria. It also seeks to abort financial contributions to terrorist organizations and makes it difficult for a criminal alien to apply for a waiver of deportation.

Two other major laws have been passed by the Congress of the United States since 9/11—the USA Patriot Act and the law creating the Department of Homeland Security. This section looks at their impact as well as the issues raised by the INS special registration for men of selected foreign countries, legal issues arising from terrorism, and what the future of laws designed to fight terrorism may hold.

The USA Patriot Act of 2001

Six weeks after 9/11, Congress passed a 342-page law proposed by the Bush Administration just eight days after the destruction of the World Trade Center buildings. This comprehensive law has a lengthy title and is officially known as the "Uniting and Strengthening America by Providing Appropriate Tools Required to Intercept and Obstruct Terrorism Act of 2001." It is, however, more popularly known as the **USA Patriot Act**. The law has more than 1,000 anti-terrorism measures that are subdivided into ten titles. It made sweeping changes to existing U.S. statutes in the form of amendments to the following laws:[9]

Title III of the Wiretap Statute
Electronic Communications Privacy Act
Computer Fraud and Abuse Act
Foreign Intelligence Surveillance Act
Family Education Rights and Privacy Act
Pen Register and Trap and Trace Statute
Money Laundering Act
Immigration and Nationality Act
Money Laundering Control Act
Bank Secrecy Act
Right to Financial Privacy Act
Fair Credit Reporting Act

Among its significant provisions are that it

- Gives federal law enforcement and intelligence officers greater authority (at least temporarily) to gather and share evidence, particularly with respect to wire and electronic communications;
- Creates new federal crimes, increases the penalties for existing federal crimes, and adjusts existing federal criminal procedure, particularly with respect to acts of terrorism;
- Modifies immigration law, increasing the ability of federal authorities to prevent foreign terrorists from entering the U.S., to detain foreign terrorist suspects, to deport foreign terrorists, and to mitigate the adverse immigration consequences for the foreign victims of September 11; and
- Authorizes appropriations to enhance the capacity of immigration, law enforcement, and intelligence agencies to more effectively respond to the threats of terrorism.[10]

Among other things, the law "gives police unprecedented authority to search, seize, detain or eavesdrop in their pursuit of possible terrorists." More specifically, the law (1) expands the FBI's wiretapping and electronic surveillance authority; (2) allows the FBI nationwide jurisdiction to obtain search warrants; (3) expands the FBI's authority in electronic surveillance, including the expansion of devices to include e-mail and the Internet; and (4) allows FBI agents to use roving wiretaps to monitor any telephone used by a terrorism suspect, rather than getting separate authorizations for each phone a suspect uses.[11]

The USA Patriot Act of 2006

Many provisions of the USA Patriot Act of 2001 expired on December 31, 2005. Before the expiration date, Congress extended the act to February 3, 2006, then extended it again to March 10, 2006. After intense negotiations and a series of compromises with Congress, President George W. Bush signed the new USA Patriot Act on March 9, 2006. Some provisions of the original law had become highly controversial, particularly the provisions on access to library information and those that were interpreted by the government as allowing domestic eavesdropping (more popularly known as the "sneak and peek" provision) without a warrant.

The USA Patriot Act of 2006 contains new provisions; among them, it

- Gives recipients of National Security Letters . . . the right to challenge them in court;
- Gives recipients of court-approved subpoenas for information in terrorist investigations the right to challenge a requirement that they refrain from telling anyone; and
- Cracks down on port security by imposing tough punishments on crew members who try to stop or mislead law enforcement officials investigating their ships.[12]

Some of the provisions have been renewed, including the following:

- Lending libraries are exempt from being subject to national security letters requesting information, even if they offer Internet access,
- Those receiving a national security letter do not have to tell the FBI if they contact a lawyer.
- The FBI must notify the court and justify surveillance of the new location within ten days after starting surveillance of a target at a new place, such as a home, business, or Internet café.
- The attorney general must report to Congress annually on the use of national security letters.
- The attorney general and the director of national intelligence must report on the protection of innocent parties whose private data are found in an inquiry.[13]

The USA Patriot Act is one of the most controversial laws ever passed by the United States Congress. It has the potential to modify current Court decisions on the Fourth Amendment, particularly those involving foreigners, nonresidents, and enemy combatants. Despite the 2006 modifications and changes to the original law, challenges to the USA Patriot Act will continue in forthcoming years because some groups believe provisions of the law give too much power to the government at the expense of Fourth Amendment rights and the right to privacy.

The Law Creating the Department of Homeland Security

The **Department of Homeland Security** was created by law in 2002, as another response to the events of September 11, 2001. Its general purpose is to "mobilize and organize our nation to secure the homeland from terrorist attacks."[14] Organizationally, the law brings together twenty-two federal agencies with widely varying histories and missions, like the Coast Guard, the Secret Service, the federal security guards in airports, and the Customs Service. As of late 2005, it had

180,000 employees.[15] It aims to "improve security along and within the nation's borders, strengthen the ability of federal, state and local authorities to respond to an attack, better focus research into nuclear, chemical and biological threats, and more rigorously assess intelligence about terrorists."[16] Its specific goals are

- *Awareness:* Identify and understand threats, assess vulnerabilities, determine potential impacts, and disseminate timely information to our homeland security partners and the American public.
- *Prevention:* Detect, deter, and mitigate threats to our homeland.
- *Protection:* Safeguard our people and their freedoms, critical infrastructure, property, and the economy of our nation from acts of terrorism, natural disasters, or other emergencies.
- *Response:* Lead, manage, and coordinate the national response to acts of terrorism, natural disaster, or other emergencies.
- *Recovery:* Lead national, state, local, and private sector efforts to restore services and rebuild communities after acts of terrorism, natural disasters, or other emergencies.
- *Service:* Service the public effectively by facilitating lawful trade, travel, and immigration.
- *Organizational excellence:* Value our most important resource, our people. Create a culture that promotes a common identity, innovation, mutual respect, accountability, and teamwork to achieve efficiencies, effectiveness, and operational synergies.[17]

The top priority of the Department of Homeland Security is to "prevent further terrorist attacks within the United States." But the department also plays the leading role in mitigating the aftermath of natural disasters and coordinating efforts to alleviate their impact. Thus, the DHS played a big role, with mixed results, in coordinating the government's response to the hurricane disasters in 2005.

The INS Special Registration Program for Foreigners

The Special Registration Program, designed by the Immigration and Naturalization Service in response to the September 11, 2001, attacks, required 24,200 men, ages 16 and older, from twenty countries to visit local Immigration and Naturalization Services offices in December 2002 to be photographed and fingerprinted and to show certain documents. Hundreds who had either overstayed or could not provide adequate evidence of their immigration status were detained in temporary lockups and local jails.

Moreover, some 3,000 visitors from Iraq, Iran, Libya, the Sudan, and Syria were also required to register by December 16, 2002. Another 7,200 men from Afghanistan, Algeria, Bahrain, Eritrea, Lebanon, Morocco, North Korea, Oman, Quatar, Somalia, Tunisia, the United Arab Emirates, and Yemen had to register by January 10, 2003. These measures have understandably raised allegations of unfair and selective enforcement from nationalities involved, noting that "all the detainees are from Muslim states."[18] The government, however, justifies these measures, saying that "the countries selected for the program are known to house al-Qaeda or other terrorist groups and were chosen based strictly on national security concerns." The program is part of the National Security Entry–Exit Registration System, initiated by the Immigration and Naturalization Service to track millions of foreigners in the United States on temporary visas.[19]

Legal Issues Arising from Responses to Terrorism

The broad sweep of the various laws, administrative rules, practices, and regulations aimed at curtailing terrorism has predictably spawned legal challenges that are finding their way into American courts. Among the practices that are controversial and have generated legal challenges are[20]

- Treating terror suspects that are also American citizens as enemy combatants or as common criminals
- Conducting closed-door immigration deportation hearings for terror suspects
- Keeping secret the names of people swept up in the anti-terrorism dragnet

- Locking away U.S. citizens in military prisons and blocking their access to lawyers or federal courts after designating them as "enemy combatants"
- Blocking access to courts or lawyers for Afghan battlefield detainees held at the U.S. Navy base in Guantanamo Bay, Cuba
- Holding in detention visa holders in an effort to track down potential terrorists[21]
- Focusing selectively on nationals from certain countries for closer immigration scrutiny.

On June 28, 2004, the U.S. Supreme Court decided three cases involving terrorism and its aftermath. In the first case, *Hamdi v. Rumsfeld* (542 U.S. 507 [2004]), the Court held that due process requires that where a U.S. citizen is detained for allegedly fighting against the United States in Afghanistan as an enemy combatant, that person should be given a meaningful opportunity to contest the factual basis for his detention before a neutral decision maker. In this case, Yaser Esam Hamdi is an American citizen of Saudi descent. After his case was decided by the Court, he was released and sent to Saudi Arabia.

Rasul v. Bush (2004)

In a second case, *Rasul v. Bush* (542 U.S. 466 [2004]), the Court held that courts in the United States have the power to hear cases challenging the legality of the detention of foreign nationals captured abroad in connection with the fighting in Afghanistan and their detention in Guantanamo Bay, in Cuba.

Rumsfeld v. Padilla (2004)

In a third case, *Rumsfeld v. Padilla* (542 U.S. 426 [2004]), the Court held that it lacked jurisdiction in a habeas petition filed by a detainee, an American citizen, because the U.S. secretary of state, against whom the petition was brought, was not the immediate custodian of the detainee and therefore was not the person against whom the habeas should be filed. In this case, Jose Padilla, an American citizen, was held in a Navy detention center in South Carolina as an enemy combatant.

In late November 2005, he was finally indicted by a federal grand jury after being held in isolation for three years by the Armed Forces, without being charged, because he was classified as an enemy combatant. After being charged, Padilla was moved from the custody of the Armed Forces to the Department of Justice.

On April 3, 2006, the U.S. Supreme Court "let stand a lower court's decision that said the president could order a U.S. citizen who was arrested in this country for suspected ties to terrorism to be held indefinitely without charges and trial."[21] The Court, by a vote of 6–3, turned down an appeal by Padilla, who was held without charges for $3^{1}/_{2}$ years as an enemy combatant. That case had, in fact, become academic because Padilla's case was earlier moved to the federal court, where he was charged with conspiracy. These conspiracy charges are yet to be tried.[22]

Aside from Hamdi and Padilla, one other American has been classified as an enemy combatant in connection with the war against terrorism: John Walker Lindh of California. The case of John Walker Lindh, the original so-called American Taliban, would have raised similar issues, but his plea bargain prevented legal issues from reaching higher courts. He is currently serving a 20-year sentence for fighting with the Taliban in Afghanistan. As of September 2004, the federal

Hamdi v. Rumsfeld (2004)

HIGHLIGHT

An Important Case on Trials Involving Terrorism

On March 28, 2006, the United States Supreme Court heard oral arguments in the case of *Hamdan v. Rumsfeld* (No. 05–184). The main issue is whether U.S. military tribunals can try cases involving alleged "enemy combatants" who face charges in connection with 9/11. The defendant alleges that a military tribunal has no jurisdiction to try him as an alleged enemy combatant and that he should be tried in the regular courts. The government counters that "the President has the constitutional, congressional, and statutory authority to create military commissions to use them in the ongoing conflict with al Qaeda."

The defendant is Salim Ahmed Hamdan, an alleged former aide to and driver of Osama bin Laden. Hamdan, a citizen of Yemen, is charged with conspiracy to commit terrorism. He was arrested by the U.S. military in Afghanistan in 2001 and then sent to Guantanamo for detention. The government alleges that Hamdan "delivered weapons to al-Qaeda members and was aware that bin Laden and his associates had been involved in attacking the United States."

Hamdan was later labeled by President Bush as an "enemy combatant" who could be tried by a military commission instead of in a civilian criminal court. Lawyers for the government maintain that a congressional resolution (the Detainee Treatment Act, passed by Congress in December 2006) authorizes the president to "use all necessary and appropriate force" against those involved in the 9/11 attacks. They further maintain that the authority to try Hamdan by a military commission stems from the "Congress' authorization of the use of military force within days of the attack and includes decisions on how those captured by the U.S. forces are tried." They also cite parts of the Uniform Code of Military Justice and the powers inherent in the presidency. Lawyers for Hamdan counter that the congressional resolution "does not cover military tribunals, and that the tribunals violate the military's Uniform Code and international rules for treatment of prisoners." They argue that the U.S. Supreme Court "has never before recognized the legitimacy of a mission except to the extent it has been specifically authorized by Congress."

A lot is at stake for Hamdan, because defendants in trials by a military commission do not have the same rights as those tried in the regular criminal courts. For example, in trials before a military commission, a defendant does not have the right to be present in all proceedings; nor is the defendant entitled to see all the evidence. The military prosecutor "sets the rules, and the evidence used is not subject to the same procedural safeguards as in civilian or courts-martial proceedings."

The case probably will be decided by the U.S. Supreme Court before July 2007, when the 2006–07 term ends.

Source: Linda Greenhouse, "Detainee Case Will Pose Delicate Question for Court," *New York Times*, March 27, 2006, p. A12; Joan Biskupic, "Court Scrutinizes Military Tribunals Plan for Detainees," *USA Today*, March 28, 2006, p. 6A.

government claimed it had charged over 350 individuals with acts related to terrorism and had convicted or secured guilty pleas from over 185 individuals.[23]

Prospects

The United States has passed laws and crafted administrative regulations as the country's immediate responses to the terror of September 11, 2001. They are comprehensive, complex, and controversial. More laws and administrative regulations will be issued as the country experiences further terrorist threats or attacks and as the war in Iraq and the violence in Afghanistan continue. Predictably, these responses have raised and will continue to raise constitutional and legal concerns that the courts will have to resolve. Judicial decisions thus far have been mixed, indicating that, although the courts are willing to give the government more power in the name of national security, upper limits must be drawn. More cases probably will find their way to the U.S. Supreme Court, which has the task of setting the balance between national security and constitutional rights, particularly of non-U.S. citizens and enemy combatants. Given the current composition of the Court and the compelling need for national security, if not survival, it will not be a surprise if the government prevails in most of its forthcoming 9/11 legal battles.

Summary

- The term *seizure* is broader than the term *arrest*. All arrests are seizures, but not all seizures amount to an arrest.

- Some contacts with the police are so minimally intrusive they are not considered seizures.

- Neither the perception of the person detained nor of the officer determines whether a seizure has taken place. Instead, the trial judge or jury determines whether a "reasonable person under the same circumstances" would consider the situation a seizure.

- Arrests have four elements: seizure and detention, intention to arrest, arrest authority, and understanding by the arrestee.

- There are two types of arrests: with a warrant and without a warrant. Each is governed by a different set of legal rules.

- After an arrest, the police may search the arrestee and the area of immediate control.

- The general rule is that the police must "knock and announce" before making an arrest. This rule, however, is subject to many exceptions.

- The rules for police use of deadly force and nondeadly force differ.

- In general, punitive force must never be used.

- In response to the events of 9/11, the United States has passed several laws to ensure national security, the most significant of which are the USA Patriot Act and the law creating the Department of Homeland Security.

Review Questions and Hypothetical Cases

1. Are the terms *seizure* and *arrest* similar or different? Justify your answer and give examples.

2. Identify the four elements of an arrest, and then give an example of each element.

3. "A police officer may make an arrest anytime he or she sees a crime being committed." True or false? Explain.

4. What are *exigent circumstances*? Give examples in police work of exigent circumstances. Is it important for police officers to know about exigent circumstances? Why or why not?

5. What is meant by the "area of immediate control" where the police can search after an arrest?

6. Assume you are an officer who has just arrested a suspect 20 yards away from her car. Can you search her car? Is it an "area of immediate control"? Justify your answer.

7. "A citizen is empowered to make an arrest any time he or she sees a crime being committed." True or false? Discuss your answer.

8. Assume you are a campus police officer. You see a student park a motor vehicle with expired license plates and without a campus sticker. Can you arrest the student?

9. State the rules on police use of nondeadly and deadly force.

10. What are the basic provisions of the USA Patriot Act and the law creating the Department of Homeland Security?

11. Assume you are a police officer and have a warrant to arrest a parolee (who is on parole for robbery) for parole violation and possession of pornographic materials. You are now at the parolee's apartment. Should you knock and announce before making an arrest? Defend your answer.

12. Assume you are a university police officer. X, a student, has just parked his car in a university parking lot. X gets out of the car. You look at X and immediately realize he is wanted in a recently issued campus poster for sexual assault. X is 30 yards away from his car. You arrest X, place handcuffs on him, and then search his car. During the search you recover a pound of marijuana and burglary tools in the car's passenger compartment. Are the marijuana and the burglary tools admissible in court? Explain your answer.

13. Y was stopped by a patrol officer one night and questioned for 20 minutes. In court during the trial, Y said he felt he was under arrest. The officer denied this, saying this was farthest from his mind; he merely wanted to ask Y questions to determine if he was a resident of the neighborhood. Was Y arrested or not? Justify your answer using the standard of a "reasonable person under the same circumstances."

Key Terms

Go to the Criminal Procedure 7e website for flash cards that will help you master the definitions of these terms.

actual seizure, 176
arrest, 174
arrest warrant, 178
bench warrant, 184
capias, 184
citation, 184
citizen's arrest, 199
constructive seizure, 176

deadly force, 204
Department of
    Homeland Security, 209
exigent circumstances, 186
hot pursuit exception
    (to the warrant
    rule), 183
John Doe warrant, 183

neutral and detached
    magistrate, 182
nondeadly force, 204
protective sweep, 192
punitive force, 206
reasonable force, 205
USA Patriot Act, 208

Holdings of Key Cases

See Appendix C for information on how to find cases in this chapter on FindLaw.com.

Atwater v. City of Lago Vista, **532 U.S. 318 (2001)**
An arrest for an offense not punishable with jail or prison time (in this case the maximum penalty set by law was a $50 fine) is constitutional.

Berkemer v. McCarty, **468 U.S. 420 (1984)** A police officer's unarticulated plan has no bearing on the question of whether a suspect was "in custody" at a particular time; the only relevant inquiry is how a reasonable person in the suspect's position would have understood the situation. Also, the roadside questioning of a motorist pursuant to a routine traffic stop (not an arrest) is not custodial interrogation and therefore does not require the *Miranda* warnings.

Brower v. Inyo County, 486 U.S. 593 (1989)
A seizure occurs only when there is governmental termination of freedom of movement through means intentionally applied.

California v. Hodari, 499 U.S. 621 (1991) To constitute a seizure of a person, there must be either the application of physical force, however slight, or else submission to the officer's show of authority to restrain the person's liberty.

Chimel v. California, 395 U.S. 752 (1969) After making an arrest, the police may search the area of the arrestee's immediate control to discover and seize any evidence in his or her possession and to prevent its concealment or destruction.

Connally v. Georgia, 429 U.S. 245 (1977) A magistrate who receives a fee when issuing a warrant but not when denying one is not neutral and detached; therefore, any warrant issued by him or her is invalid.

Coolidge v. New Hampshire, 403 U.S. 443 (1971) The state's chief investigator and prosecutor (state attorney general) is not neutral and detached; therefore, any warrant issued by him or her is invalid.

County of Riverside v. McLaughlin, 59 U.S. 4413 (1991) If probable cause determination is combined with the arraignment, it is presumptively reasonable for the arrest-to-hearing period to last up to forty-eight hours. If more time than that elapses, the government bears the burden of showing that the delay is reasonable. Conversely, if the release is made less than forty-eight hours after arrest, the burden of showing unreasonable delay shifts to the arrestee.

Dunaway v. New York, 442 U.S. 200 (1979) An *arrest* is defined as the taking of a person into custody against his or her will for the purpose of criminal prosecution or interrogation.

Florida v. Bostick, 501 U.S. 429 (1991) The appropriate test to determine if the act of the officers in this case was valid was whether, taking into account all the circumstances surrounding the encounter (in a bus), a reasonable person would feel free to decline the officers' requests for consent to search the bag or otherwise terminate the encounter.

Hamdi v. Rumsfeld, 542 U.S. 507 (2004) Due process requires that a U.S. citizen who is detained for allegedly fighting against the United States in Afghanistan as an enemy combatant must be given a meaningful opportunity to contest the factual basis for his detention before a neutral decision maker.

Illinois v. McArthur, 531 U.S. 326 (2001) Under exigent circumstances and where there is a need to preserve evidence until a warrant can be obtained, the police may temporarily restrain a suspect's movements without violating his or her Fourth Amendment right.

Kaupp v. Texas, 538 U.S. 626 (2003) Seizure by the police of the person within the meaning of the Fourth and Fourteenth Amendments occurs only when "taking into account all of the circumstances surrounding the encounter, a reasonable passenger would feel free to decline the officers' request or otherwise terminate the encounter."

Kennedy v. Los Angeles Police Department, 887 F.2d 920 [9th Cir. 1989]) A departmental policy that orders body-cavity searches in all felony arrests is unconstitutional. There must be reasonable suspicion, prior to conducting a body-cavity search, that the arrestee may be likely to conceal a weapon, drugs, or other contraband.

Lo-Ji Sales, Inc., v. New York, 442 U.S. 319 (1979) A magistrate who participates in a search to determine its scope lacks the requisite neutrality and detachment.

Maryland v. Buie, 494 U.S. 325 (1990) "The Fourth Amendment permits a properly limited protective sweep in conjunction with an in-home arrest when the searching officer possesses a reasonable belief based on specific and articulable facts that the area to be swept harbors an individual posing a danger to those on the arrest scene."

Michigan v. Chesternut, 486 U.S. 567 (1988) The appropriate test to determine if a seizure has occurred is "whether a reasonable man, viewing the particular police conduct as a whole and within the setting of all the surrounding circumstances, would have concluded that the police had in some way restrained his liberty so that he was not free to leave."

Minnesota v. Olson, 495 U.S. 91 (1990) A warrantless nonconsensual entry by the police into a residence to arrest an overnight guest is not justified by exigent circumstances and therefore violates the Fourth Amendment.

New York v. Belton, 453 U.S. 454 (1981) The police may examine the contents of any container found in the passenger compartment of a car, as long as it may reasonably be thought to contain something that might pose a danger to the officer or hold evidence in support of the offense for which the suspect has been arrested.

Payton v. New York, 445 U.S. 573 (1980) In the absence of exigent circumstances or consent, the police may not enter a private home to make a routine warrantless arrest.

Powell v. Nevada, 511 U.S. 79 (1992) The decision in *County of Riverside v. McLaughlin,* 59 U.S. 4413 (1991), saying that the detention of a suspect for forty-eight hours is presumed to be reasonable is not retroactive.

Rasul v. Bush, 542 U.S. 466 (2004) Courts in the United States have the power to hear cases challenging the legality of the detention of foreign nationals captured abroad in connection with the fighting in Afghanistan and their detention in Guantanamo Bay.

Richards v. Wisconsin, 520 U.S. 385 (1997) The blanket exception to the knock-and-announce rule in drug-dealing cases is unconstitutional. Exceptions must be determined on a case-by-case basis.

Rumsfeld v. Padilla, 542 U.S. 426 (2004) The Court lacked jurisdiction in a habeas petition filed by a detainee, an American citizen, because the U.S. secretary of state, against whom the petition was brought, was not the immediate custodian of the detainee.

Shadwick v. City of Tampa, 407 U.S. 345 (1972) A municipal court clerk can issue an arrest warrant for municipal ordinance violations as long as this is authorized by state law.

Steagald v. United States, 451 U.S. 204 (1981) An arrest warrant cannot be used as a legal authority to enter the home of a person other than the person named in the arrest warrant. If the person to be arrested is in the home of another person, a search warrant must be obtained to enter that home to make an arrest. The only exception is when exigent circumstances exist; they justify a warrantless entry.

Tennessee v. Garner, 411 U.S. 1 (1985) It is constitutionally reasonable for a police officer to use deadly force when the officer has probable cause to believe that the suspect poses a threat or serious physical harm, either to the officer or to others.

Thornton v. United States, 541 U.S. 615 (2004) Officers may search a vehicle as an area of immediate control after a lawful arrest even if the initial contact and arrest of the suspect took place outside the vehicle.

United States v. Martinez-Fuerte, 428 U.S. 543 (1976) Roadblocks to control the flow of illegal aliens do not need much protection under the Fourth Amendment, because they are not highly intrusive and there is a strong governmental interest involved.

United States v. Mendenhall, 446 U.S. 544 (1980) When determining whether a person has been arrested, the court takes into account the totality of the surrounding circumstances, including such considerations as "the threatening presence of several officers, the display of a weapon by an officer, some physical touching of the person or the citizen, or the use of language or tone of voice indicating that compliance with the officer's request might be compelled."

United States v. Ramirez, 523 U.S. 65 (1998) The knock-and-announce rule does not set a higher standard for unannounced entries even if that entry involves property damage.

United States v. Robinson, 414 U.S. 218 (1973) After making an arrest, the police may make a warrantless search of the arrestee.

United States v. Sharpe, 470 U.S. 675 (1985) In assessing whether a detention is too long to be justified as an investigative stop, the Court considers it appropriate to examine whether the police diligently pursued a means of investigation that was likely to confirm or dispel their suspicions quickly, during which time it was necessary to detain the defendant.

United States v. Watson, 423 U.S. 411 (1976) Law enforcement officers may find it wise to seek arrest warrants when practical to do so, and their judgments about probable cause may be more readily accepted when backed by a warrant issued by a magistrate. Also, the police are not required to obtain an arrest warrant before arresting a person in a public place, even if there was time and opportunity to do so.

Vale v. Louisiana, 399 U.S. 30 (1970) A search incidental to an arrest is valid only if it is "substantially contemporaneous with the arrest and is confined to the immediate vicinity of the arrest." Also, "if a search of a house is to be upheld as incident to an arrest, that arrest must take place inside the house, not somewhere outside—whether two blocks away, twenty feet away, or on the sidewalk near the front steps."

Warden v. Hayden, 387 U.S. 294 (1967) Warrantless entries and searches are reasonable if delaying them would allow the suspect time to escape. Also, the Fourth Amendment does not require officers to delay an arrest if doing so would endanger their lives or the lives of others.

Washington v. Chrisman, 455 U.S. 1 (1982) It is not unreasonable under the Fourth Amendment for a police officer, as a matter of routine, to monitor the movements of an arrestee following an arrest as his or her judgment dictates. The officer's need to ensure his or her own safety, as well as the integrity of the arrest, is compelling.

Welsh v. Wisconsin, 466 U.S. 740 (1984) In determining whether exigent circumstances exist to justify a home entry without a warrant, the seriousness of the offense must be considered. In the case of a minor offense, a warrantless entry into a home will rarely be justified.

Wilson v. Arkansas, 514 U.S. 927 (1995) The knock-and-announce rule is part of the Fourth Amendment's requirement that searches and seizures be reasonable, but that rule is not rigid and is subject to exceptions based on law enforcement interests.

Wilson v. Layne, 526 U.S. 603 (1999) The practice of "media ride-alongs" violates a suspect's Fourth Amendment rights and is therefore unconstitutional.

Winston v. Lee, 470 U.S. 753 (1985) Certain types of seizures (in this case the removal of a bullet lodged in the chest of the suspect) are so intrusive that they are prohibited by the Fourth Amendment even with probable cause and prior judicial authorization unless justified by compelling reasons.

 You Be the Judge . . .

In the United States Court of Appeals for the Second Circuit

In Rochester, New York, on May 17, 2000, Monroe County Sheriff's Deputy Rojos and three other officers were sent to serve an arrest warrant on Alejandro at his apartment, for conspiracy to distribute cocaine and heroin. When they arrived, the officers listened for activity at the door to the apartment. Hearing nothing, they knocked. Eventually, after knocking three times, Rojos heard someone moving around inside the apartment, but no one answered the door. Rojos continued knocking for another 3 to 5 minutes without answer. Rojos called out that they were from Rochester Gas & Electric Company, and they were looking for a gas leak. Alejandro opened the door to find the four uniformed officers with weapons drawn, who then identified themselves and placed him under arrest.

How will you decide this legal issue? Was the deputy's use of a ruse to serve an arrest warrant, without identifying himself as a law enforcement officer improper? Did it violate the "knock and announce" requirement?

The Court's decision The U.S. Court of Appeals for the Second Circuit decided that there was nothing improper about the use of the ruse here. The use of a ruse only avoided the necessity of breaking down the door. The "knock and announce" rule would have required the officers to announce their purpose before breaking in, but it is inapplicable here because there was no force involved in the arrest. *U.S. v. Alejandro,* 100 Fed. Appx. 846 (2nd Cir. 2004).

In the United States Court of Appeals for the Eleventh Circuit

In Coweta County, Georgia Sheriff's Deputy Reynolds stopped a tractor trailer traveling on I-85 for a tag light that was not lit. Deputy Reynolds approached the cab, and found the truck to be driven by Draper. Draper alleged that Deputy Reynolds was rude when asking him to get out of the cab.

Deputy Reynolds told Draper to come with him to the back of the truck, in front of his car. As soon as he reached that area, Deputy Reynolds unholstered his Taser, a gun which shoots out two darts attached to electric wires, delivering an incapacitating shock to the subject. Draper yelled at Deputy Reynolds for having blinded him with his flashlight while in the truck's cab. Deputy Reynolds calmly asked for Draper's driver's license, but Draper continued to yell about Reynolds's previous use of his flashlight.

Draper paced, made animated gestures, shouted and appeared very excited. Deputy Reynolds repeatedly asked Draper to calm down, to stop yelling, and to produce his log book, bill of lading and insurance. Draper did not comply, but paced back and forth, screaming at Deputy Reynolds that Reynolds was harassing him. After the fourth time

Deputy Reynolds asked for these documents and Draper again paced back towards him, Deputy Reynolds unceremoniously discharged his Taser into Draper. Draper dropped to the ground, and Deputy Reynolds's backup handcuffed him. Draper was arrested for obstruction of an officer.

Draper sued Deputy Reynolds for false arrest and using excessive force in the arrest.

How will you decide this legal issue? Did Deputy Reynolds use excessive force arresting Draper?

The Court's decision The U.S. Court of Appeals for the Eleventh Circuit decided that Deputy Reynolds used reasonable force in arresting Draper. The "totality of the circumstances" involved in this arrest make Deputy Reynolds's use of a Taser prior to any verbal arrest command reasonable. Specifically, Draper had repeatedly refused to obey Deputy Reynolds, so Deputy Reynolds had no reason to believe he would suddenly become compliant. *Draper v. Reynolds,* 369 F.3d 1270 (11th Cir. 2004).

Recommended Readings

Jennifer Cook. Note. *Discretionary warrantless searches and seizures and the Fourth Amendment: A need for clearer guidelines.* South Carolina Law Review 641–659 (2002).

John J. Donahue III and Steven D. Levitt. *The impact of race on policing and arrests.* 44 Journal of Law and Economics 367, 394 (2001).

Sarah Oliver. Note. Atwater v. City of Lago Vista: *The disappearing Fourth Amendment and its impact on racial profiling.* Whittier Law Review 335–355 (2002).

Jennifer Reichert. *After a traffic stop, police can make unrelated arrests, New York high court says.* 38 Trial 79, 81 (2002).

Lisa Ruddy. Note. *From seat belts to handcuffs: May police arrest for minor traffic violations?* 10 American Journal of Gender, Social Policy, and the Law 479–519 (2002).

Melanie Schoenfield. Note. *Constitutional amnesia: Judicial validation of probable cause for arresting the wrong person on a facially valid warrant.* 79 Washington University Law Quarterly 1227–1257 (2001).

Notes

1. John G. Miles, Jr., David B. Richardson, and Anthony E. Scudellari, *The Law Officer's Pocket Manual* (Washington, D.C.: Bureau of National Affairs, 1988–89), 6:1.
2. Henry C. Black, *Black's Law Dictionary*, 4th ed. (St. Paul, MN: West, 1968), p. 1756.
3. Supra note 1, 6:11–12.
4. Steven L. Emanuel and Steven Knowles, *Emanuel Law Outlines* (Larchmont, NY: Emanuel, 1989–90), p. 59.
5. Ibid., p. 62.
6. Wayne R. LaFave and Jerold H. Israel, *Criminal Procedure* (St. Paul, MN: West, 1985), p. 147.
7. Jonathan R. White, *Terrorism and Homeland Security*, 5th ed. (Thomson/Wadsworth, 2006), p. 279.
8. Ibid.
9. Electronic Privacy Information Center, The USA PATRIOT Act, *http://www.epic.org/privacy/terrorism/usapatriot*.
10. Charles Doyle, CRS Report for Congress, Terrorism: Section by Section Analysis of the USA Patriot Act, updated December 10, 2001, Congressional Research Service, The Library of Congress.
11. *Huntsville Item*, October 27, 2001, p. 8A.
12. "Provisions of the USA Patriot Act," *Guardian Unlimited*, March 7, 2006, p. 1.
13. "Bush Signs Renewal of Patriot Act into Law," *USA Today*, March 10, 2006, p. 6A.
14. Homeland Security: DHS Organization, *http://www.dhs.gov/dhspublic/interapp/editorial/editorial_0413.xml*.
15. Ibid.
16. Ibid.
17. Homeland Security: DHS Organization, *http://www.dhs.gov/dhspublic/interapp/editorial/editorial_0413.xml*.
18. USA: Special Registration Process Must Be Reviewed, Amnesty International USA, *http://www.amnestyusa.org/regions/americas/document.do?id=80256AB9000584F680256CAA0049B4A3*.
19. *Houston Chronicle*, January 1, 2002, p. 15A; *New York Times*, December 20, 2002, p. A18.
20. *Houston Chronicle*, October 26, 2002, p. 14A.
21. "Supreme Court Rebuffs Appeal by Terror Suspect Padilla," *USA Today*, April 4, 2006, p. 2A.
22. Ibid.
23. The White House: Three Years of Progress in the War on Terror—Fact Sheet, *http://www.whitehouse.gov/news/releases/2004/09/20040911.html*.

Chapter 7

Searches and Seizures of Things and Electronic Surveillance

What You Will Learn

- The constitutional right to privacy is often invoked in search and seizure cases in addition to the Fourth Amendment right against unreasonable searches and seizures.

- The phrase "reasonable expectation of privacy" is important in search and seizure cases.

- Four categories of things are subject to searches and seizures.

- Four things are required to issue a search warrant.

- Searches have specified rules limiting their scope, duration, and procedures.

- Warrantless searches and seizures are legal in many instances.

- Electronic surveillance is governed primarily by three federal laws, supplemented by state laws.

The Top 5 Important Cases in Searches and Seizures and Electronic Surveillance

***Schmerber v. California* (1966)** The police may, without a search warrant and by force if necessary, take a blood sample from a person arrested for drunk driving, as long as the setting and procedures are reasonable (as when the blood is drawn by a doctor in a hospital).

***Katz v. United States* (1967)** The prohibition against unreasonable search and seizure is not limited to homes, office buildings, or other enclosed places. It applies even in public places where a person has a "reasonable expectation of privacy." The Fourth Amendment protects people, not places.

***Chimel v. California* (1969)** Once a lawful arrest has been made, the police may search any area within the suspect's area of immediate control, meaning the area from which the suspect may grab a weapon or destroy evidence.

***New York v. Belton* (1981)** When the police have made a lawful custodial arrest of the occupant of a car, they may, incident to that arrest, search the car's entire passenger compartment (front and back seats) and open any containers found in the compartment.

***Wilson v. Arkansas* (1995)** Although "knock and announce" is part of the requirement of reasonableness in searches and seizures, it is not a rigid rule and is subject to exceptions based on law enforcement interests. These exceptions are determined by state law.

Introduction

This chapter primarily discusses searches and seizures of *things*—as distinguished from seizures of persons, which are arrests. It does not deal with searches of motor vehicles, which are discussed in Chapter 8. Both searches and seizures of things and searches and seizures of persons are primarily governed by the Fourth Amendment of the U.S. Constitution, which states:

> The right of the people to be secure in their persons, houses, papers, and effects, against unreasonable searches and seizures, shall not be violated, and no Warrants shall issue, but upon probable cause, supported by Oath or affirmation, and particularly describing the place to be searched, and the persons or things to be seized.

It also involves, however, the right to privacy. Many cases involving the Fourth Amendment also raise claims of possible violation of the right to privacy. This is because searches and seizures often require entry into homes or residences or searches of a person's belongings; hence, a person's privacy is inevitably involved. For example, suppose the police illegally enter a couple's home to search for drugs without probable cause. In the process of the search, they enter the couple's bedroom, conduct an extensive search, and recover drugs and pornographic materials. During the trial, the evidence seized probably will be excluded based on violations of the Fourth Amendment and the right to privacy.

The law on searches and seizures of things is understood best if two basic concepts are clear:

1. There are two types of search and seizure: with a warrant and without a warrant; each is governed by its own rules.
2. The term *search and seizure* is sometimes misunderstood as a single and continuous act. It is, in fact, two separate acts, each with its own meaning. Both are under the Fourth Amendment and subject to the probable cause requirement. After defining them, however, the discussion in this chapter considers search and seizure together because Fourth Amendment cases do not often make clear distinctions between the two acts. Moreover, in police work, one usually follows the other or is often the result of it. This means that a search can result in a seizure, and seizure is often the result of a search.

Searches and Seizures and the Right to Privacy

This section looks at two issues: whether the right to privacy is guaranteed in the Constitution and the meaning of the words "a reasonable expectation of privacy."

The Right to Privacy: A Constitutional Right?

The right to privacy is a constitutional right, but it is not specifically mentioned in the Constitution—unlike the prohibition against unreasonable searches and seizures, which is specified in the Fourth Amendment. Instead, it is a "penumbra" (shadow) right that is derived from other rights specifically mentioned in the Constitution.

Griswold v. Connecticut (1965)

See Appendix C for information on how to find cases in this chapter on FindLaw.com.

In a 1965 seminal decision, the Court said that "specific guarantees in the Bill of Rights have penumbras, formed by emanations from those guarantees that help give them life and substance" (*Griswold v. Connecticut*, 381 U.S. 479 [1965]). The Court added that "various guarantees create zones of privacy." These are the First Amendment freedom of association; the Third Amendment prohibition against the quartering of soldiers "in any house"; the Fourth Amendment affirmation of the "right of the people to be secure in their persons, houses, papers, and effects, against unreasonable searches and seizures"; the Fifth Amendment prohibition against self-incrimination; and the Ninth Amendment provision that the "enumeration in the Constitution, of certain rights, shall not be construed to deny or disparage others retained by the people."

Despite not being mentioned in the Constitution, the right to privacy is well-established by Court decisions and is one of the most active and often-litigated rights in an age of sophisticated electronic technology. The great protection given by the Court to the right to privacy is reflected in these words in *Griswold*: "We deal with a right of privacy (referring in the *Griswold* case to the right of the Planned Parenthood League of Connecticut to give "information, instruction, and medical advice to married persons") older than the Bill of Rights—older than our political parties, older than our school system."

The more popular meaning of the **right to privacy** is "the right to be let alone by other people" (*Katz v. United States*, 389 U.S. 347 [1967]). That includes being "let alone" by the government and its law enforcement agents.

Katz v. United States (1967)

The Meaning of "Reasonable Expectation of Privacy"

Privacy is a broad term that encompasses a myriad of situations. The question is, When does privacy enjoy constitutional protection and when does it not? The Court's response is, Privacy enjoys constitutional protection when there is a *reasonable expectation of privacy*. In a concurring opinion in *Katz v. United States* (389 U.S. 347 [1967]), Justice Harlan specified two requirements for a **reasonable expectation of privacy** to exist: (1) the person must have exhibited an actual expectation of privacy, and (2) the expectation must be one that society is prepared to recognize as reasonable.

These are the same requirements used by courts in today's decisions. Justice Harlan added:

> Thus a man's home is, for most purposes, a place where he expects privacy, but objects, activities, or statements that he exposes to the "plain view" of outsiders are not "protected" because no intention to keep them to himself has been exhibited. On the other hand, conversations in the open would not be protected against being overheard, for the expectation of privacy under the circumstances would be unreasonable.

To use a more current example, does a person who talks on a cell phone have a reasonable expectation of privacy? Applying the two tests, a person who talks on his or her cell phone loudly and in public does not exhibit an actual expectation of

Two Legal Requirements for "Reasonable Expectation of Privacy"
in Search and Seizure Cases

1. The "person must have exhibited an actual expectation of privacy."

2. The expectation "must be one that society is prepared to recognize as reasonable."

privacy and, even if he does, society probably is not prepared to recognize this expectation as reasonable. By contrast, couples who are in bed in their own home have a reasonable expectation of privacy, which society is prepared to accept as reasonable. What society is prepared to recognize as reasonable evolves over time, particularly as technology and morals change. But the phrase *reasonable expectation of privacy* will always be a question of fact that is ultimately determined in an actual case by a judge or jury, based on surrounding circumstances.

Definitions and General Rule

This section defines searches and seizures, examines the general rules limiting each, and identifies things that are subject to searches and seizures.

Search Defined

A **search** of things is defined as the exploration or examination of an individual's house, premises, or person to discover things that may be used by the government for evidence in a criminal prosecution. A search is not limited to homes, offices, buildings, or other enclosed places; rather, it can occur in any place where a person has a reasonable expectation of privacy, even if the place is in a public area, meaning a place to which anyone has access (*Katz v. United States,* 389 U.S. 347 [1967]). For example, in one case, police installed a peephole in the ceiling of a public restroom to observe what occurred in the stalls. Officers observed two people engaging in illegal sexual acts in one of the stalls. What the officers did without a warrant was illegal, because the two people involved had a reasonable expectation of privacy—they could reasonably expect that their acts would not be observed by others, even though the restroom was in a public place. The evidence obtained was not admissible in court.

Seizure Defined

A **seizure** of things or items is defined as the exercise of dominion or control by the government over a person or thing because of a violation of law. The distinction between a search and a seizure can be summarized as follows: *Search* is looking, whereas *seizure* is taking. In one case, the Supreme Court said that "a seizure occurs when there is some meaningful interference with an individual's possessory interests in the property seized" (*Maryland v. Macon,* 472 U.S. 463 [1985]). If the search succeeds, it can lead to a seizure.

The General Rule for Searches and Seizures

The general rule is that searches and seizures can be made only with a warrant. Therefore, warrantless searches and seizures are exceptions to the general rule. According to the Court, the most basic constitutional rule is that searches conducted outside the judicial process, without prior approval by a judge or a magistrate, are per se unreasonable under the Fourth Amendment—subject only to a few specifically established and well-delineated exceptions (*Katz v. United States,* 389 U.S. 347 [1967]).

In reality, most searches and seizures are made without a warrant. Nonetheless, police officers must always be aware of the general rule so that they make warrantless searches only if justified under one of the exceptions. In the words of the Court: The point of the Fourth Amendment, which often is not grasped by zealous officers, is not that it denies law enforcement the support of the usual inferences that reasonable people draw from evidence. Its protection consists in requiring that those inferences be drawn by a neutral and detached magistrate instead of being judged by the officer engaged in the often competitive enterprise of ferreting out crime (*Johnson v. United States,* 333 U.S. 10 [1948]).

Johnson v. United States (1948)

Things Subject to Search and Seizure

Generally, four types of things can be searched and seized:

- *Contraband,* such as drugs, counterfeit money, and gambling paraphernalia. With limited exceptions these items are illegal for anybody to possess.
- *Fruits of the crime,* such as stolen goods and forged checks.
- *Instrumentalities of the crime,* such as weapons and burglary tools.
- *"Mere evidence" of the crime,* such as a suspect's clothing containing bloodstains of the victim, or a suspect's mask, shoes, or wig—provided there is probable cause to believe that the item is related to criminal activity.

These are merely general categories of things officers may search and seize. In many states, the law (usually the code of criminal procedure or the penal code) enumerates in detail the items subject to search and seizure. Whatever the listing, an item listed by state law is likely to fall into one of the four categories listed here.

Search and Seizure with a Warrant

A **search warrant** is a written order, issued by a magistrate, directing a peace officer to search for property connected with a crime and bring it before the court. In nearly all states, the police officer seeking a search warrant must state the facts that establish probable cause in a written and signed affidavit. The general rule is that a search or seizure is valid under the Fourth Amendment only if made with a warrant. Searches without a warrant may be valid, but they are the exception rather than the rule.

This section looks at several issues related to search warrants, including the requirements for issuing them; the procedure for serving them; the knock-and-announce rule; the scope of search and seizure; the time allotted to conduct a search; and the procedure after the search. Last, the section compares search and arrest warrants.

Requirements

There are four basic requirements for the valid issuance of a search warrant: (1) a statement of probable cause, (2) a supporting oath or affirmation, (3) a description of the place to be searched and the things to be seized, and (4) the signature of a magistrate.

Probable Cause The conditions required to establish probable cause are discussed more extensively in Chapter 3. For our purposes here, it is sufficient to restate the definition of probable cause used in Chapter 3. **Probable cause** is defined as more than bare suspicion; "it exists when the facts and circumstances within the officers' knowledge and of which they have reasonably trustworthy information are sufficient in themselves to warrant a person of reasonable caution in the belief that an offense has been or is being committed."

This definition is the same for arrests and in searches and seizures of things. The difference is that in arrests the focus is on (1) whether a crime has been committed and (2) whether the person to be arrested committed the crime. By contrast, in searches and seizures of things and items, the issue of probable cause focuses on (1) whether the property to be seized is connected with criminal activity and (2) whether it can be found in the place to be searched.

A Supporting Oath or Affirmation A search warrant is issued based on a sworn affidavit, establishing grounds for the warrant, presented to the magistrate (see Figure 7.1). The magistrate issues the warrant only if he or she is satisfied, based on the affidavit, that probable cause for a warrant exists. The contents of the affidavit must be sufficient to allow an independent evaluation of probable cause by the magistrate. To enable the magistrate to make an independent evaluation, the affidavit must contain more than mere conclusions by the police officer. It must allege facts showing that seizable evidence will be found in the place to be searched. The affidavit may be filed by the police officer or the offended or injured party. A warrant may be issued on the basis of affidavits containing only hearsay, as long as there is probable cause.

Supporting oaths and affirmations can be based on oral statements. Anticipatory warrants can be issued based on the expectation of the imminent arrival of contraband. However, supporting oaths must be based on recent information that

THE STATE OF TEXAS
COUNTY OF _____

THE UNDERSIGNED AFFIANT, BEING A PEACE OFFICER UNDER THE LAWS OF TEXAS AND BEING DULY SWORN, ON OATH MAKES THE FOLLOWING STATEMENTS AND ACCUSATIONS.

1. THERE IS IN _____ COUNTY, TEXAS A SUSPECTED PLACE DESCRIBED AND LOCATED AS FOLLOWS:

2. SAID SUSPECTED PLACE IS IN CHARGE OF AND CONTROLLED BY EACH OF THE FOLLOWING NAMED PARTIES (HEREAFTER CALLED "SUSPECTED PARTY" WHETHER ONE OR MORE) TO WIT:

3. IT IS THE BELIEF OF AFFIANT, AND AFFIANT HEREBY CHARGES AND ACCUSES THAT SAID SUSPECTED PARTY HAS POSSESSION OF AND IS CONCEALING AT SAID SUSPECTED PLACE IN VIOLATION OF THE LAWS OF TEXAS THE FOLLOWING DESCRIBED PERSONAL PROPERTY, TO WIT:

4. AFFIANT HAS PROBABLE CAUSE FOR THE SAID BELIEF BY REASON OF THE FOLLOWING FACTS, TO WIT:

WHEREFORE, AFFIANT ASKS FOR ISSUANCE OF A WARRANT THAT WILL AUTHORIZE THE SEARCH OF SAID SUSPECTED PLACE FOR SAID PERSONAL PROPERTY AND SEIZE THE SAME AND TO ARREST EACH SAID SUSPECTED PARTY, AND TO TAKE CUSTODY OF ALL SEIZED PROPERTY AND SAFEKEEP SUCH PROPERTY AS PROVIDED BY STATUTE.

_____
AFFIANT

SUBSCRIBED AND SWORN TO BEFORE ME BY SAID AFFIANT ON THIS THE _____ DAY OF _____, A.D., 20_____.

_____
MAGISTRATE

Figure 7.1 Affidavit for a Search Warrant

Source: Official form of the state of Texas

helps establish probable cause before a warrant can be issued. We turn to each of these issues next.

Warrants based on oral statements There is no constitutional requirement that a warrant application must be in writing. In some jurisdictions, a warrant may be issued based on an oral statement either in person or by telephone. The oral statement is usually recorded and becomes the basis for a probable cause determination. If probable cause is found, the judge or magistrate then "causes an original warrant to be prepared and orally authorizes the officer to prepare a duplicate warrant for use in execution." This procedure has been held valid and in compliance with the "Oath or affirmation" of the Constitution.[1]

Anticipatory search warrant An **anticipatory search warrant** is a warrant obtained based on probable cause and on an expectation that seizable items will be found at a certain place at a certain time. An article in the *FBI Law Enforcement Bulletin* characterizes the warrant in this manner: "Where officers have probable cause to believe that evidence or contraband will arrive at a certain location within a reasonable period of time, they do not need to wait until delivery before requesting a warrant. Instead, officers may present this probable cause to a magistrate before the arrival of that evidence, and the magistrate can issue an anticipatory search warrant based on probable cause that the evidence will be found at the location to be searched at the time the warrant is executed."[2]

United States v. Grubbs (2006)

In a 2006 case, *United States v. Grubbs,* 547 U.S.____(2006), the Court decided that "anticipatory" search warrants are valid. In this case, a judge issued an anticipatory search warrant for the suspect Grubb's house based on a federal officer's affidavit, which explained that "the warrant would not be executed until a parcel containing a videotape of child pornography—which Grubbs had ordered from an undercover postal inspector—was received at, and physically taken into, the residence." Grubbs was seized by the officers after the package was delivered. During his trial for receiving child pornography, Grubbs moved to suppress the evidence.

On appeal, the Court rejected his arguments and said that "anticipatory warrants are not categorically unconstitutional under the Fourth Amendment's provision" as long as there is probable cause. The Court added that "when an anticipatory warrant is issued, the fact that the contraband is not presently at the place described is immaterial, so long as there is probable cause to believe it will be there when the warrant is executed."

A judge or magistrate is not required to issue an anticipatory warrant, so it is a matter of judicial discretion. But if the judge or magistrate decides to issue it, the warrant is valid.

United States v. Ricciardelli (1st Cir. 1993)

In an earlier case, the U.S. Court of Appeals for the First Circuit said that in issuing an anticipatory warrant, the conditions set by the magistrate must be "explicit, clear, and narrowly drawn so as to avoid misunderstanding or manipulation by government agents." The court said that the issuing judge must narrow the discretion of government agents in two ways: (1) the event that triggered the warrant must be ascertainable and preordained, and (2) the item sought (in this case, contraband) must be on a sure and irreversible course to its destination (*United States v. Ricciardelli,* 998 F.2d 8 [1st Cir. 1993]).

United States v. Leon (1984)

A need for fresh information To be valid, the warrant must be based on fresh information. If the information is "stale," the warrant lacks probable cause and is invalid (*United States v. Leon,* 468 U.S. 897 [1984]). In the *Leon* case, the information contained in the affidavit was given by the police officer to the magistrate in September 1981. It was based partially on information the officer had obtained from a confidential informant in August 1981. The Court ruled that "to the extent that the affidavit set forth facts demonstrating the basis of the informant's knowledge of criminal activity, the information included was fatally stale."

The reason for the "fresh information" rule is that conditions change fast, and an item found in one place at one time may not be there when the warrant is issued and executed. The Court has not specified exactly how much time must elapse before an information becomes stale. It is safe to say, however, that "the longer the delay, the greater the chance that the information will be 'stale.'"[3]

A Description of the Place to Be Searched and Persons or Things to Be Seized
The affidavit must identify both the place that will be searched and the things that will be seized. This section addresses each of these requirements.

The place to be searched
The warrant must remove any doubt or uncertainty about which premises are to be searched. For example, if the premise is an apartment in a multiple-dwelling building, the warrant must specify which apartment is to be searched. The address of the apartment building is not sufficient. An exact address prevents confusion and avoids intrusions on the privacy of innocent people.

In one case, however, the Court held that the validity of a warrant must be judged in light of the "information available to the officers at the time they obtained the warrant" (*Maryland v. Garrison,* 480 U.S. 79 [1987]). In this case, police officers obtained a warrant to search "the premises known as 2036 Park Avenue, third-floor apartment" for drugs and drug paraphernalia that supposedly belonged to a person named McWebb. The police reasonably believed there was only one apartment at that location. In fact, there were two apartments on the third floor, one belonging to McWebb and the other belonging to Garrison. Before the officers became aware that they were in Garrison's apartment instead of McWebb's, they searched the apartment and discovered drugs that provided the basis for Garrison's subsequent conviction.

Garrison sought exclusion of the evidence, saying that the search warrant was so unnecessarily broad that it allowed the search of the wrong apartment. The Supreme Court admitted the evidence, saying that the validity of a warrant must be judged in light of the information available to the officers when the warrant is sought: There was a reasonable effort on the part of the officers to ascertain and identify the place that was the target of the search; nonetheless, a mistake took place.

Garrison should not be interpreted as validating all search warrants where there is a mistake made in the description of the place to be searched. The test of the validity of search warrants that are "ambiguous in scope" appears to be "whether the officers' failure to realize the overbreadth of the warrant was objectively understandable and reasonable." Therefore, a warrant that is overly broad in describing the place to be searched is not in violation of the Fourth Amendment *if it was based on a reasonable but mistaken belief* at the time the warrant was issued.

Art. 18.02. Ground for issuance.

A search warrant may be issued to search for and seize:

    (1) property acquired by theft or in any other manner which makes its acquisition a penal offense;

    (2) property specially designed, made, or adapted for or commonly used in the commission of an offense;

    (3) arms and munitions kept or prepared for the purposes of insurrection or riot;

    (4) weapons prohibited by the Penal Code;

    (5) gambling devices or equipment, altered gambling equipment, or gambling paraphernalia;

    (6) obscene materials kept or prepared for commercial distribution or exhibition, subject to the additional rules set forth by law;

    (7) drugs kept, prepared, or manufactured in violation of the laws of this state;

    (8) any property the possession of which is prohibited by law;

    (9) implements or instruments used in the commission of a crime;

    (10) property or items, except the personal writings by the accused, constituting evidence of an offense or constituting evidence tending to show that a particular person committed an offense;

    (11) persons; or

    (12) contraband subject to forfeiture under Chapter 59 of this code.

Figure 7.2 State Code Enumerating Items Police Can Search and Seize

Source: Texas Code of Criminal Procedure, 2005–2006

Relying on *Maryland v. Garrison,* the Fourth Circuit Court of Appeals has said that the execution of a warrant for a different apartment from that named in the warrant was valid because there were only two apartments on the floor, one of which was vacant. Moreover, the correct apartment was readily ascertainable, and the mistake (which in this case was a reliance on utility company information) was reasonable and made in good faith (*United States v. Owens,* 848 F.2d 462 [4th Cir. 1988]).

United States v. Owens (4th Cir. 1988)

Things to be seized Things to be seized must also be described in detail sufficient to narrow the discretion officers can exercise over what may be seized (see Figure 7.2). For example, the warrant cannot simply provide for the seizure of "stolen goods," because this language is too general and can lead to a fishing expedition. An acceptable identification would be "a 25-inch Zenith television set." Contraband, however, does not have to be described with as much particularity, because it is in itself seizable. So the words *cocaine* or *heroin* would suffice, as would *gambling paraphernalia.*

In *Groh v. Ramirez et al.* (540 U.S. 551 [2004]), the Court held that a search warrant that does not comply with the requirement that the warrant particularly describe the person or things to be seized is unconstitutional. In that case, Groh, an agent of the Bureau of Alcohol, Tobacco, and Firearms (ATF), prepared an application for a search warrant based on information that weapons and explosives were located on Ramirez's farm. The application was supported by a detailed affidavit listing the items to be seized and describing the basis for the agent's belief that the items were concealed on the property. Groh presented these documents, along with a warrant form he also completed, to a magistrate. The magistrate signed the warrant form. Although the application and affidavit described the contraband to be discovered, the form only indicated that the place to be searched was Ramirez's home. It did not incorporate any reference to the itemized list contained in the warrant application or affidavit. The day after the magistrate signed the warrant, officers searched Ramirez's home but found no illegal weapons or explosives. Groh left a copy of the warrant at the home but did not leave a copy of the warrant application. The following day, in response to a request from Ramirez's attorney, Groh faxed a copy of the application. No charges were filed against Ramirez, but Ramirez later filed suit for damages, claiming his Fourth Amendment rights were violated by the nonspecific warrant.

The Court agreed with Ramirez, saying that a search and seizure warrant that does not contain a particular description of the things to be seized is unconstitutional even if the application for the warrant contains such descriptions. The Court rejected Groh's argument that the searched was based on a particular description because it was in the supporting documents. The Court, however, refused to address two other issues involved in the case: (1) whether the warrant would have been valid if it had mentioned that the application clearly listed the items to be seized but that the list was not available during the search and (2) whether orally describing the items to the defendant during the search complies with the specificity requirement.

The Signature of a Magistrate

As in the cases of arrest warrants, search warrants must be issued only by a "neutral and detached" magistrate. The Court has said, "Inferences must be drawn by a neutral and detached magistrate instead of being judged by the officer engaged in the often competitive enterprise of ferreting out crime" (*Johnson v. United States,* 333 U.S. 10 [1948]). Several examples should help illuminate this requirement.

- *Example 1.* A magistrate who receives a fee when issuing a warrant but not when denying one is not neutral and detached (*Connally v. Georgia,* 429 U.S. 245 [1977]).
- *Example 2.* A magistrate who participates in the search to determine its scope lacks the requisite neutrality and detachment (*Lo-Ji Sales, Inc., v. New York,* 442 U.S. 319 [1979]).
- *Example 3.* The state's chief investigator and prosecutor (state attorney general) is not neutral and detached, so any warrant issued by him or her is invalid (*Coolidge v. New Hampshire,* 403 U.S. 443 [1971]).

SEARCH WARRANT

State of Iowa

County of _____

Criminal Case No. _____

To any peace officer of the state:

Proof having been this day made before me as provided by law that (here, with reasonable certainty and in accordance with the information and other proof obtained by the magistrate, designate the property, its location, the person in possession thereof, and the unlawful use or purpose to which it has been, or is being employed or held) and being satisfied that the foregoing recital relative to said property is probably true, now, therefore, you are commanded to make immediate search of (here state whether the search is of the person of a named person or of said premises, or of another designated thing) and if said property or any part thereof be found, you are commanded to bring said property forthwith before me at my office.

Dated at _____ this _____ day of _____, 20___ .

_____

(official title)

Acts 1976 (66 G.A.) ch. 1245, ch. 2, forms app. form 1, effective Jan. 1, 1978; amended by Acts 1977 (67 G.A.) ch.153, §92.

Figure 7.3   Search Warrant for the State of Iowa

Source: Official form of the state of Iowa

The Procedure for Serving a Warrant

The search warrant is directed to a law enforcement officer and must state the grounds for issuance and the names of those who gave affidavits in support of it. The execution of a warrant is specified in detail by state law, usually in the state's code of criminal procedure (see Figure 7.3). Failure to execute the warrant in accordance with state or local law generally results in exclusion of the evidence during trial. The warrant usually directs that it be served during the daytime, but if the affidavits are positive that the property is on the person or in the place to be searched, the warrant may direct that it be served at any time. Some states, by law, authorize night searches. The warrant must designate the judge or magistrate to whom the warrant is to be returned. It also must be executed and delivered within a specified number of days from the date of issuance. Some states specify ten days; others allow less time. If the warrant is not served during that time, it expires and can no longer be served.

Note that search warrants differ in this respect from arrest warrants, which are usually valid until served. The officer executing the search warrant must either (1) give a copy of the warrant and a receipt for any seized property to the person from whom it is taken or (2) leave a copy and receipt on the premises. A written inventory must be made, and the officer's report, accompanied by the inventory, must be submitted promptly.

The Announcement Requirement

The rule for announcements in searches and seizures is the same as for arrests (discussed in Chapter 6). Federal and many state statutes require that an officer making an arrest or executing a search warrant announce his or her purpose and authority before breaking into a dwelling. The goal is to allow voluntary compliance and avoid violence. Breaking into the premises without first complying with the announcement requirement may or may not invalidate the entry and any resulting search, depending on the law or court decisions in that state. Some states invalidate the entry and resulting search; others do not.

Wilson v. Arkansas (1995)

In *Wilson v. Arkansas* (514 U.S. 927 [1995]), the Court ruled that the "knock and announce common law principle is part of the Fourth Amendment's requirement that searches and seizures be reasonable." It added, however, that this did not mean that every entry should be preceded by an announcement. The current rule is that, although knock and announce is part of the requirement of reasonableness in searches and seizures, it is not a rigid rule and is subject to exceptions based on law enforcement interests. **No-knock searches**, searches without an announcement, may be authorized by state statute, particularly for drug cases.

Richards v. Wisconsin (1997)

United States v. Ramirez (1998)

Exceptions to the announcement requirement are usually determined by state law, state court decisions, and agency regulations. They therefore vary from state to state. The Court has ruled, however, that a blanket exception (issued by a judge) to the Fourth Amendment's knock-and-announce rule in felony drug-dealing cases is not allowed (*Richards v. Wisconsin*, 520 U.S. 385 [1997]). This means that exceptions to the announcement requirement must be determined on a case-by-case basis. In *United States v. Ramirez* (523 U.S. 65 [1998]), the Court held that the knock-and-announce rule does not set a higher standard for unannounced entries even if that entry involves property damage.

United States v. Banks (2003)

The knock-and-announce rule gives notice to occupants of the place that an officer is at the door with a warrant and wants admission or entry. After making the announcement, the officer must give occupants reasonable time to respond. In *United States v. Banks* (540 U.S. 31 [2003]), the Court held that after knocking and announcing their presence and intention to search, 15 to 20 seconds is sufficient time for officers to wait before forcing entry into a home to execute a search warrant for drugs. In that case, federal officers obtained and executed a search warrant based on information that Banks was selling cocaine from his apartment. Upon reaching the apartment, the officers announced "police search warrant" and knocked on the door loud enough to be heard by the other officers at the back door. Banks was in the shower and later testified that he did not hear the officers until they broke down the door. The search produced weapons, crack cocaine, and other evidence of drug dealing. Banks moved to suppress the evidence, arguing that the officers waited an unreasonably short time before forcing entry.

The Court rejected his allegation, saying that "the facts known to the police are what count in judging a reasonable waiting time, and there is no indication they knew Banks was in the shower and thus unaware of an impending search." The Court relied on a "totality of circumstances" analysis, in effect saying that whether the time to wait before any forcible entry was reasonable depends on an analysis of all surrounding circumstances. In this case, the Court concluded that the defendant could easily have disposed of the drugs within that short time.

The Scope of Search and Seizure

The scope and manner of the search must be reasonable based on the object of the search. A wise legal maxim for officers to remember is this: *It is unreasonable for a police officer to look for an elephant in a matchbox.* For example, suppose a search warrant is issued for the recovery of a stolen 25-inch Zenith TV set. In looking for the TV set, the officer cannot open lockers and drawers—unless, of course, the locker or drawer is big enough to contain the TV set. But, if the search warrant is for the confiscation of heroin, then the officer is justified in opening lockers and drawers in the course of the search. It therefore follows that the smaller the item sought, the more extensive the scope of allowable search.

Michigan v. Summers (1981)

While the search is being conducted, the police may detain persons who are on the premises to search them (*Michigan v. Summers*, 452 U.S. 692 [1981]). However, these people must have been named in the warrant. For example, a search warrant for a bar and the bartender does not authorize body searches of all bar patrons (*Ybarra v. Illinois*, 444 U.S. 85 [1979]). Searches of property belonging to persons not suspected of a crime are permissible as long as probable cause exists to suspect that evidence of someone's guilt or other items subject to seizure will be found. For example, in one case, several police officers were hurt at a political demonstration. The police could not identify their attackers, but they knew that a newspaper staff photographer had taken photographs of the demonstration. The police were able to obtain a warrant to search the newspaper's offices because probable cause existed that evidence of someone's guilt would be found (*Zurcher v. Stanford Daily*, 436 U.S. 547 [1978]).

Ybarra v. Illinois (1979)

Zurcher v. Stanford Daily (1978)

The Time Allowed for a Search

The search cannot last indefinitely, with or without a warrant. Once the item mentioned in the warrant is recovered, the search must cease. Continued search without justification becomes a fishing expedition for evidence and is illegal. An illegal search is never made legal by what is subsequently found. For example, suppose the police go to an apartment to execute a search for a shotgun allegedly used in a murder. After the shotgun is recovered, the police continue to search for other evidence in connection with the murder. They open a bedroom closet and find a pair of bloodied jeans worn by the suspect during the murder. The bloodied jeans, if seized and used in evidence, will not be admissible, because they were illegally obtained. Note, however, that items in plain view in the course of executing the warrant can be seized by the police because plain view items are not protected by the Fourth Amendment.

The Procedure after the Search

City of West Covina v. Perkins et al. (1999)

After the search, the usual police practice is to give the occupant a list of the things or items that have been seized. If nobody is on the premises, the list must be left "at the scene in a prominent place."[4] In *City of West Covina v. Perkins et al.* (525 U.S. 234 [1999]), the Court held that the police are not required by the Constitution to provide the owner of the seized property with a notice of remedies specified by state law for the property's return and the information necessary to use those procedures. The Court stressed the need for some type of notice, saying that "individualized notice that officers have taken property is necessary in a case such as this one because the owner has no other reasonable means of ascertaining who is responsible for his loss." But the Court concluded that the other requirements specified by California state law, such as detailed notice of the state procedures for the return of the seized property and the information necessary to use those procedures, are not required by the Due Process Clause of the Constitution.

Comparison of Search Warrants and Arrest Warrants

Search warrants and arrest warrants have the following similarities:

- Probable cause is needed to issue a search warrant or an arrest warrant.
- The definition of probable cause is the same for both.
- Probable cause in both is ultimately determined by a judge, not by the officer.
- In both, officers need to "knock and announce," subject to state law exceptions.
- Items in plain view may be seized when executing a search warrant or an arrest warrant.

They have the following differences:

Search Warrant	Arrest Warrant
The officer looks for items to be used as evidence.	The officer seeks to arrest a suspect for detention.
If not served, a search warrant usually expires after a period of time specified by law.	An arrest warrant does not expire, unless recalled by the court that issued it.
Some jurisdictions limit the execution of the warrant to reasonable hours during the day.	It may be executed at any time, unless exceptions are specified by law.

Search and Seizure without a Warrant

In searches and seizures without a warrant, the burden is on the police to prove in court that probable cause existed at the time of the warrantless search or seizure. It is therefore essential for law enforcement officers to be thoroughly familiar with the law on warrantless searches and seizures. Generally, there are seven exceptions to the rule that searches and seizures must be made with a warrant and with probable cause:

- The "searches incident to lawful arrest" exception
- The "searches with consent" exception
- The "special needs beyond law enforcement" exception
- The "exigent circumstances" exception
- The "administrative searches and inspections" exception
- The "stop and frisk" exception
- The "motor vehicles" exception

The first five exceptions are discussed in this chapter. The stop and frisk exception is discussed in Chapter 5, and the motor vehicles exception is discussed in Chapter 6.

The Searches Incident to Lawful Arrest Exception

The search incident to lawful arrest exception is widely used in policing. It is invoked almost every time an officer makes an arrest, with or without a warrant. There are three justifications for warrantless searches incident to arrest: (1) to ensure officer safety, (2) to prevent escape, and (3) to prevent concealment or destruction of evidence. The authorization to search incident to arrest is always available to the officer after an arrest, even if there is no probable cause to believe it is necessary to ensure officer safety, to prevent escape, or to prevent concealment or destruction of evidence. These searches take two forms: body search and search of the area within the person's immediate control. To be legal, searches must be contemporaneous with the arrest.

The Body Search of an Arrested Person As discussed in Chapter 6 on arrest, a body search is valid in any situation in which a full-custody arrest of a person occurs. There is no requirement that the officers fear for their safety or believe that they will find evidence of a crime before the body search can be made (*United States v. Robinson*, 414 U.S. 218 [1973]). But while a full body search is allowed, anal or cavity searches are prohibited unless justified by circumstances surrounding the search. For example, a police department policy that authorizes automatic anal and cavity searches after every arrest will likely be declared unconstitutional. This issue has not been decided by the U.S. Supreme Court, but lower courts have held that such searches, in the absence of compelling reason to support them, are too intrusive. Conversely, however, a policy that allows anal and cavity searches if there is reasonable suspicion—for example, if an officer has information from a reliable informant that the arrestee may be hiding contraband in these places—probably will be upheld.

United States v. Robinson (1973)

Even in a jail or a prison setting, anal and cavity searches are not allowed unless justified—for example, after home furlough or a contact visit. In addition to a body search after a lawful arrest, other types of body searches may be conducted by police officers. The general rule is that exterior intrusions on a person's body (such as swabbing, inspecting hands, taking hair samples, and retrieving evidence from the mouth) do not normally require a search warrant. In one case, a court held that the clipping by an officer of a few strands of hair from the appellant's head was so minor an imposition that the appellant suffered no true humiliation or affront to his dignity, so no search warrant was required to justify the officer's act (*United States v. D'Amico*, 408 F.2d 331 [2nd Cir. 1969]).

United States v. D'Amico (2nd Cir. 1969)

Interior intrusions on a person's body (such as blood tests, stomach pumping, and surgery) are permitted by the Fourth Amendment only if they are conducted pursuant to a warrant or if exigent circumstances exist and there is a clear indication that the desired evidence will be found.[5] For example, in *Breithaupt v. Abram* (352 U.S. 432 [1957]), the Court ruled that a blood test performed by a skilled technician is not conduct that shocks the conscience, nor is this method of obtaining evidence offensive to a sense of justice. However, in *Rochin v. California* (342 U.S. 165 [1952]), the Court held that the police restraint of a suspect while a heroin capsule was removed from his stomach by a stomach pump shocks the conscience and therefore violates the suspect's right to due process.

Breithaupt v. Abram (1957)

Rochin v. California (1952)

The Area within a Person's Immediate Control: *Chimel v. California* In addition to performing a body search, the officer may also search the area within the person's immediate control. The leading case on this issue is *Chimel v. California* (395 U.S. 752 [1969]), which was also discussed in Chapter 6 on arrests. In *Chimel,* the Court said:

Chimel v. California (1969)

> When an arrest is made, it is reasonable for the arresting officer to search the person arrested in order to remove any weapons that the latter might seek to use in order to resist arrest or effect his escape. . . . In addition, it is entirely reasonable for the arresting officer to search for and seize any evidence on the arrestee's person in order to prevent its concealment or destruction.

The **Chimel rule** holds that a warrantless search incident to arrest is valid if limited to the **area of immediate control**, meaning the area from which the person might be able to obtain a weapon or destroy evidence. Some departments refer to this as the "grabbable area." The most limited, and arguably the most accurate, interpretation of that phrase is that the area is limited to the arrested person's *wingspan*—the area covered by the spread of the person's arms and hands. Officer protection and prevention of the destruction of evidence are the justifications for the rule. (Read the *Chimel* Case Brief to learn more about the case.)

Nonetheless, courts allow officers to search the area of immediate control even after the arrested person has been handcuffed and therefore no longer poses a threat to the safety of the officer or the preservation of the evidence. In motor vehicle searches, the Court has held that, when the police have made a lawful custodial arrest of the occupant of a car, they may search not only his or her wingspan but also the car's entire passenger compartment (front and back seats), and they may open any containers found in the compartment (*New York v. Belton*, 453 U.S. 454 [1981]).

New York v. Belton (1981)

In *Thornton v. United States* (541 U.S. 615 [2004]), the Court extended the *Belton* holding beyond the front or back seats of vehicles, saying that "there is simply no basis to conclude that the span of the area generally within the arrestee's immediate control is determined by whether the arrestee exited the vehicle at the officer's direction, or whether the officer initiated contact with him while he was in the car." Thus the Court admitted into evidence a firearm found under the driver's seat even though the initial contact with the suspect and the arrest took place outside the motor vehicle after the suspect had parked it.

Thornton v. United States (2004)

The Requirement that the Warrantless Search Be Contemporaneous To be **contemporaneous**, the search must occur at the same time as, or very close in time and place to, the arrest. A search is illegal if conducted long after the arrest. In one case, the police arrested several smugglers and seized the footlocker in which they believed marijuana was being transported. One hour after the arrest, after the suspects were in jail, the officers opened and searched the footlocker without a warrant. The Court invalidated the search, saying that it was "remote in time and place from the arrest" (*United States v. Chadwick*, 433 U.S. 1 [1977]).

United States v. Chadwick (1977)

However, the custodial search may be deemed "incident to arrest" even when carried out later than the time of arrest, if there was a valid reason for the delay. For example, in *United States v. Edwards* (415 U.S. 800 [1974]), a suspect was arrested and jailed late at night, but a clothing search for evidence was not conducted until the following morning. The Court said that the delayed search was justified because substitute clothing was not available for the suspect's use at the time of the booking.

United States v. Edwards (1974)

The Searches with Consent Exception

This is perhaps the most common exception to the warrant requirement rule. It basically states that, if the object of the request gives proper consent, the consent is valid, and anything illegal found and confiscated during the search may be

CASE BRIEF: The Leading Case on a Search Incident to an Arrest

Chimel v. California, 395 U.S. 752 (1969)

Facts: Chimel was suspected of having robbed a coin shop. Armed with an arrest warrant (but not a search warrant), police officers went to Chimel's house and were admitted by his wife. Chimel was not at home but was immediately arrested when he arrived. The police asked Chimel if they could "look around." Chimel denied the request, but the officers searched the entire house anyway and discovered some stolen coins. At the trial, the coins were introduced as evidence over Chimel's objection. Chimel was convicted of robbery.

Issue: *In the course of making a lawful arrest, may officers search the immediate area where the person was arrested without a search warrant? Yes.*

Supreme Court Decision: After making an arrest, the police may search the area within the person's immediate control. The purpose of such a search is to discover and remove weapons and to prevent the destruction of evidence.

Case Significance: *Chimel* categorically states that the police may search the area in the arrestee's "immediate control" when making a valid arrest, whether the arrest takes place with or without a warrant. That area of "immediate control" is defined by the Court as "the area from within which he might gain possession of a weapon or destructible evidence." *Chimel* therefore authoritatively settled an issue over

which lower courts had given inconsistent and diverse rulings. The current rule is that the police may search without a warrant after a lawful arrest, but the extent of that search is limited to the area of the arrestee's "immediate control." The safest, and most limited, interpretation of the term "area of immediate control" is a person's wingspan, within which it might be possible to grab a weapon or destroy evidence. Some lower courts have given a more liberal interpretation to include such areas as the whole room in which the person is arrested. This interpretation appears to go beyond what the Court had in mind in *Chimel.*

Excerpt from the Decision: When an arrest is made, it is reasonable for the arresting officer to search the person arrested in order to remove any weapons that the latter might seek to use in order to resist arrest or effect his escape. Otherwise, the officer's safety might well be endangered, and the arrest itself frustrated. In addition, it is entirely reasonable for the arresting officer to search for and seize any evidence on the arrestee's person in order to prevent its concealment or destruction. And the area into which an arrestee might reach in order to grab a weapon or evidentiary items must, of course, be governed by a like rule. . . . There is ample justification, therefore, for a search of the arrestee's person and the area within his immediate control.

introduced as evidence in court. There are limits to that search, however. The three most important limits are discussed here: consent must be voluntary, the search must stay within the boundaries consented to, and the person must have the authority to consent.

Voluntary Consent Required Warrantless searches with consent are valid, but the consent must be *voluntary* (although not necessarily spoken), meaning it was not obtained by the use of force, duress, or coercion. Voluntariness is determined by looking at the totality of circumstances. For example, consent given only after the officer demands entry cannot be deemed free and voluntary. "Open the door" will most likely be interpreted by the courts as giving the occupant no choice and therefore making the consent involuntary. The better practice is for the officer to "request" rather than "demand." Requests such as "Would you mind if I come in and look around?" are more likely to result in voluntary consent than "I am going to look around."

Florida v. Bostick (1991)

In *Florida v. Bostick* (501 U.S. 429 [1991]), two officers, with badges and insignia, boarded a bus. They explained their presence as being "on the lookout for illegal drugs." Without any articulable suspicion, they approached Bostick, a passenger, and asked to see some identification and inspect his bus ticket. The officers asked the suspect for consent to search his bag and told him he had the right to refuse consent. Bostick gave consent. On appeal of his conviction, the Court held that the consent was valid.

United States v. Drayton (2002)

In *United States v. Drayton* (536 U.S. 194 [2002]), the Court went further and said that the Fourth Amendment permits police officers to approach bus passengers, ask questions, and request their consent to search, provided that a reasonable person would understand that he or she is free to refuse. There is no requirement in the Fourth Amendment for officers to advise persons of their right to refuse to cooperate.

Mere silence or failure to object to a search does not necessarily mean the person is giving consent. The consent must be clear. For example, a shrug of the shoulder may signify indifference or resignation rather than consent, but multiple nods strongly imply consent. In *United States v. Shaibu* (920 F.2d 1423 [9th Cir. 1990]),

United States v. Shaibu (9th Cir. 1990)

the Ninth Circuit Court of Appeals said that there was no valid consent where the resident opened his door, stepped into the hallway, listened to the officers identify themselves and explain the purpose of their visit, and then retreated wordlessly back into the apartment without closing the door. The government in this case failed to meet its heavy burden of proving consent merely by showing that the defendant left his door open.

There is also no valid consent if permission is given as a result of police misrepresentation or deception, such as saying, "We have a warrant," when none exists

Bumper v. North Carolina (1968)

(*Bumper v. North Carolina*, 391 U.S. 543 [1968]). Lower courts are divided on the issue of whether consent is valid if the officer does not have a warrant but threatens to obtain one.[6] The issue has not been resolved by the Supreme Court.

Consent to enter does not necessarily mean consent to search. For example, consent to enter for the purpose of asking questions does not mean consent to search. However, any seizable item in plain view after valid entry may be properly seized because items in plain view are not protected by the Fourth Amendment.

To be valid, the consent to search does not have to be in writing. Oral consent is sufficient. Many police departments, however, suggest or require that the officer obtain consent in writing. This is a good policy because the voluntariness of the consent often becomes an issue of whose word the judge or jury believes. A written consent tilts the scale of voluntariness in favor of the officer, particularly if the consent is signed by witnesses. There are instances, however, when a written consent may be impractical or difficult to obtain. The evidence obtained will nonetheless be admissible as long as voluntariness is established by the police. There is no need for the police to prove in court that the person giving consent knew that he or she actually had a right to refuse consent. The Court has held that ignorance of such a right is only one of the factors to be considered in determining whether the consent given was voluntary (*Schneckloth v. Bustamonte*, 412 U.S. 218 [1973]).[7]

Schneckloth v. Bustamonte (1973)

Search Must Stay within Allowable Scope The scope of allowable search depends on the type of consent given. For example, the statement "You may look around" does not authorize the opening of closets, drawers, trunks, and boxes. The consent to search a garage does not imply consent to search an adjoining house, and vice versa. Conversely, consent for police to search a vehicle does extend to closed containers found inside the vehicle, as long as it is objectively reasonable for the police to believe that the scope of the suspect's consent permitted them to open that container (*Florida v. Jimeno*, 500 U.S. 248 [1991]).

Florida v. Jimeno (1991)

However, in *State v. Wells* (539 So.2d 464 [Sup. Ct. Fla. 1989]), the Florida state supreme court held that consent to search a car does not authorize police officers to pry open a locked briefcase found in the car's trunk. In *United States v. Osage*, 235 F.3d 518 [10th Cir. 2000], the suspect gave police officers permission to search his bags. The officers found four cans labeled "tamales in gravy," which the officers opened with the use of a tool. The can yielded narcotics. The Federal Court of Appeals for the Tenth Circuit held that the consent to search given by the suspect did not include consent to destroy the container being searched. The court concluded that "the opening of a sealed can, thereby rendering it useless and incapable of performing its designated function, is more like breaking open a locked briefcase than opening the folds of a paper bag."

State v. Wells (Sup. Ct. Fla. 1989)

United States v. Osage (10th Cir. 2000)

In general, consent to search does not include consent to open a locked (as opposed to closed) container unless the key is voluntarily given to the police. Consent may be revoked even in the course of a search, by the person who gave the consent or by anybody else who possesses authority to do so. However, any evidence obtained before revocation is admissible.

Authority to Give Consent Required Table 7.1 summarizes who can and cannot give valid consent to a search.

The Special Needs beyond Law Enforcement Exception

The Supreme Court has carved out, comparatively recently, a series of exceptions to the warrant requirement, collectively known as the **"special needs beyond law enforcement" exception**. What these situations have in common is that they are not police searches (although sometimes the police are asked to help) but instead

Table 7.1 Who Has the Authority to Give Consent?

Who	Authority?	Explanation
Wife or husband	Yes	A wife or a husband can give effective consent to search the family home. Exception: In *Georgia v. Randolph* (No. 04-1067 [2006]), the Court held that "a physically present co-occupant's stated refusal to permit entry renders warrantless entry and search unreasonable and invalid as to him." In this case, the defendant's estranged wife gave police permission to search their residence for items of drug use after the defendant, who was also present, had unequivocally refused to give consent to the search. The Court ruled that, under the circumstances, the search was unreasonable and invalid.
Parent of a child	Yes	Courts tend to rule that parents may give consent to search the rooms of their minor children who are living with them but not if the minor child is paying room and board. In *Colbert v. Commonwealth* (2001 WL 174809 [Ky. 2001]), the Kentucky state court held that a parent may consent to the search of a child's room in the parent's home even over the child's objection. In (*State v. Kinderman* (271 Minn. 405 [1965]), the Minnesota state supreme court held valid a father's consent to the search of his son's room even though the son was 22. The court reasoned that "[i]f a man's house is still his castle in which his rights are superior to the state, those rights should also be superior to the rights of the children who live in his house. "We cannot agree that a child, whether he be dependent or emancipated, has that same constitutional right of privacy in the family home which he might in a rented hotel room."
Child of a parent	No	In most states, a child cannot validly give consent to a search of his or her parents' home. This is because consent given by a child is not likely to be considered intelligent or voluntary. For example, suppose the police knock at an apartment door, a ten-year-old boy opens the door, and the officers ask if his parents are in. When told that the parents are out, the officers ask if they can "look around." The boy willingly consents, and they find drugs on the kitchen table. The consent is invalid, the search illegal, and the evidence is inadmissible in court. Whether adult offspring who live with their parents can give consent to search their parents' home has not been clearly addressed by the courts.
Former girlfriend	Yes, if she has apparent authority	The Supreme Court has held that the warrantless entry of private premises by police officers is valid if based on the **"apparent authority" principle**. This applies when police obtained the consent of a third party whom they, at the time of entry, reasonably believed to possess common authority over the premise but who, in fact, did not have such authority (*Illinois v. Rodriguez*, 497 U.S. 177 [1990]). In *Illinois v. Rodriguez*, Rodriguez was arrested in his apartment and charged with possession of illegal

Georgia v. Randolph (2006)

Colbert v. Commonwealth (Ky. 2001)

State v. Kinderman (Minn. 1965)

Illinois v. Rodriguez (1990)

(Continued)

Who	Authority?	Explanation
		drugs that the police said were in plain view on entry. The police gained entry to Rodriguez's apartment with the assistance of a certain Fischer, who represented that the apartment was "ours" and that she had clothes and furniture there. She unlocked the door with her key and gave the officers permission to enter. In reality, Fischer had moved out of the apartment and therefore no longer had any common authority over the apartment. The Court nonetheless held the consent given by Fischer to be valid because the police reasonably believed, given the circumstances, that she had the authority to give consent.
Roommate	Yes, but . . .	A roommate may give valid consent to search the room. However, that consent cannot extend to areas in which another roommate has a reasonable expectation of privacy, because only he or she uses it. For example, suppose X gives consent for the police to search the studio apartment X and Y occupy. That consent is valid with respect to all areas that both X and Y use, such as the bathroom or study table. The consent is not valid for the search of Y's closet, to which only Y has access. If Y lives in another room (as in a multiroom apartment), X cannot give consent to search the room used only by Y.
Landlord	No	A landlord cannot give valid consent to search property that he or she has rented to another person (*Stoner v. California*, 376 U.S. 483 [1964]).
Lessor	No	Generally, a lessor (the person who leased out the property) cannot give valid consent to search the premises of a property leased to another person (*United States v. Impink*, 728 F.2d 1228 [9th Cir. 1985]).
Apartment manager	Yes	The consent of an apartment manager to the warrantless search of apartment building common areas (such as public hallways and lobbies) is valid as long as the landlord has joint access to or control over those areas (*United States v. Kelly*, 551 F.2d 760 [8th Cir. 1977]).
Driver of a vehicle	Yes	The consent given by the driver of a vehicle for the search of the vehicle, including the trunk, glove compartment, and other areas, is valid even if the driver is not the owner of the vehicle (*United States v. Morales*, 861 F.2d 396 [3rd Cir. 1988]).
Hotel clerk	No	A hotel clerk cannot give consent to the search of a guest's room (*Stoner v. California*, 376 U.S. 483 [1964]).
College and university administrators	No	Most lower courts hold that college administrators (such as dormitory managers) cannot give consent for the police to search a student's dormitory room. The fact that some resident or dormitory managers may enter a student's room for certain purposes (such as health and safety issues) does not mean that they can give consent for the police to enter a student's room for purposes related to criminal prosecution (*Piazzola v. Watkins*, 442 F.2d 284 [5th Cir. 1971]). This issue, however, has not been authoritatively settled by the Supreme Court.

Stoner v. California (1964)

United States v. Impink (9th Cir. 1985)

United States v. Kelly (8th Cir. 1977)

United States v. Morales (3rd Cir. 1988)

Piazzola v. Watkins (5th Cir. 1971)

High school administrators	Yes	Most lower courts hold that high school administrators, under proper circumstances, may give consent for the police to search a student's locker. This is because high school students are considered wards of the school. Therefore, the authority given to high school administrators is greater than that afforded to their college counterparts.	
Business employer	No	If the property is under the exclusive use and control of the employee, the employer cannot give valid consent to search (*United States v. Block*, 188 F.2d 1019 [D.C. Cir. 1951]). For example, a department store supervisor cannot give consent to search an employee's desk if only the employee is using it; similarly, a college dean or department head cannot give consent for the police to search a desk assigned to a faculty member for his or her exclusive use.	
Business employee	No	Unless specifically authorized, a business employee cannot consent to the search of his or her employer's business premises. Although the employee may have access to the property, he or she does not own it.	

United States v. Block (D.C. Cir. 1951)

involve searches conducted by other public agencies that perform tasks related to law enforcement. Examples are school searches, searches of probationers and parolees, and airport searches. The Court has repeatedly held that these types of searches may be made *without a warrant* and on *less than probable cause*. This section looks at each of the examples.

New Jersey v. T.L.O. (1985)

Public School Searches In *New Jersey v. T.L.O.* (469 U.S. 325 [1985]), the Court resolved an issue that had long bothered public school students, teachers, and administrators. Voting 6 to 3, the Court said that public school teachers and administrators *do not need a warrant or probable cause* to search a student they believe is violating the law or school rules. What is needed are *reasonable grounds* (lower than probable cause) for suspecting that the search will turn up evidence that the student has violated or is violating either the law or the rules of the school.

In this case, a teacher at a New Jersey high school discovered a student and her companion smoking cigarettes in a school lavatory in violation of the school rule. She took them to the principal's office, where they met with the assistant vice principal. When the student denied that she had been smoking, the assistant vice principal demanded to see her purse. On opening the purse, he found a pack of cigarettes and also noticed a package of cigarette-rolling papers, which are commonly associated with the use of marijuana. He then searched the purse thoroughly and found marijuana, a pipe, plastic bags, a fairly substantial amount of money, and other items that implicated her in marijuana dealing.

She moved to suppress the evidence in juvenile court, alleging that the search was illegal for lack of probable cause and a warrant. The Supreme Court rejected her allegation, saying that the Fourth Amendment prohibition against unreasonable searches and seizures applies to searches conducted by public school officials, but the school's legitimate need to maintain a positive learning environment requires some easing of the Fourth Amendment restrictions. Therefore, public school officials do not need a warrant or probable cause to conduct a search. All they need are *reasonable grounds* to suspect that the search will turn up evidence that the student has violated or is violating either the law or the rules of the school.

The *T.L.O.* ruling applies only to public school teachers and administrators. It does not apply to police officers, who are bound by the probable cause and warrant requirements even in school searches. The only possible exception is if the officers perform the search at the request of school authorities. The *T.L.O.* ruling does not apply to college or university students, either. Unlike high school or elementary school students, for whom teachers and administrators serve **in loco parentis** (in place of parents), college students are considered adults and therefore entitled to undiminished constitutional rights.

Searches of Probationers' and Parolees' Homes In probation cases, the Court has held that a state law or agency rule permitting probation officers to search probationers' homes without a warrant and based on reasonable grounds (lower than probable cause) is a reasonable response to the "special needs" of the probation system and is therefore constitutional (*Griffin v. Wisconsin,* 483 U.S. 868 [1987]). The Court added that the supervision of probationers is a "special need" of the state that justifies a departure from the usual warrant and probable cause requirements.

Griffin v. Wisconsin (1987)

Although the *Griffin* case involved probationers, there is little doubt that the same principle applies to warrantless searches of parolees' homes. The Court has also ruled that evidence obtained by parole officers during an illegal search and seizure need not be excluded in a parole revocation proceeding (*Pennsylvania Board of Probation and Parole v. Scott,* 524 U.S. 357 [1998]).

Pennsylvania Board of Probation and Parole v. Scott (1998)

In a more recent case, the Court held that a warrantless search by an officer of a probationer's apartment, supported by reasonable suspicion and authorized by the judge as a condition of probation, is valid under the Fourth Amendment under the special needs exception (*United States v. Knights,* 534 U.S. 112 [2001]). This case must not be interpreted to mean, however, that police officers can now search the homes of probationers or parolees without probable cause. In the *Knights* case, the condition of probation imposed by the judge authorized the police to conduct such a search based on less than probable cause. Without that authorization, the search probably would have been invalid.

United States v. Knights (2001)

Some states allow warrantless searches of probationers' homes by probation officers based on *suspicion,* an even lower degree of certainty than reasonable grounds. Although the Supreme Court has not ruled on this issue, lower courts have upheld the practice based on the twin concepts of probationers' *diminished constitutional rights* and *special needs.*

Airport Searches A search of air travelers is permissible for the purpose of discovering weapons, preventing hijackings, and safeguarding against in-flight bombings through checked-in luggage. Airport searches have become more necessary and strict as a result of the sad events of September 11, 2001. Since then, major changes have been made in airport searches. The responsibility for such searches has been transferred to the federal government, and there is a much more intrusive search of persons and a more thorough search of carry-ons and baggage.

Searchers do not need probable cause, reasonable suspicion, or even mere suspicion. Searches can be and are done routinely. The search is an administrative measure based on urgent and proven safety needs. Even before 9/11, however, airport searches had gained strong support from the courts. In *United States v. Davis* (482 F.2d 893 [9th Cir. 1973]), the court said, "The need to prevent airline hijacking is unquestionably grave and urgent. . . . A pre-boarding screening of all passengers and carry-on articles sufficient in scope to detect the presence of weapons or explosives is reasonably necessary to meet the need."

United States v. Davis (9th Cir. 1973)

If an electronic search is performed using a magnetometer and the reading indicates the possible presence of a weapon, a frisk or pat-down of the traveler's clothing is then justified. Evidence discovered is admissible in court. A person who refuses to submit to the limited search may be excluded from entry to the boarding area.

The Fourth Amendment issues in searches and seizures at airports are many, among them: the pre-boarding request for identification, the search of a passenger's luggage pursuant to a hijacker profile, the search of a passenger's checked-in baggage, the search of the person, and the arrests of persons in some cases.[8] Although Fourth Amendment issues have been an ongoing source of dispute, a great majority of search and seizure challenges filed by airplane passengers have been rejected by the courts.[9] One court of appeals judge justified airport searches in this way:

> When the risk is the jeopardy to hundreds of human lives and millions of dollars of property inherent in the pirating or blowing up of a large airplane, that danger alone meets the test of reasonableness, so long as the search is conducted in good faith for the purpose of preventing hijacking or like damage and with reasonable scope and the passenger has been given advance notice of his liability to such a search so that he can avoid it by choosing not to travel by air. (*United States v. Bell*, 464 F.2d 667 [1972])

United States v. Bell (1972)

United States v. Hartwell (E.D.Pa. 2003)

In *United States v. Hartwell* (296 F.Supp. 2d 596 [E.D.Pa. 2003]), a court held that "a prospective airline passenger impliedly consents to a search when placing handheld luggage on an X-ray belt and walking through a magnetometer, and once this procedure begins, the passenger may not later revoke that consent."

The use of police dogs to sniff containers and luggage to detect contraband at airports does not constitute a search. No warrant or probable cause is needed as long as the container or luggage is located in a public place. In *United States v. Sullivan* (625 F.2d 9 [4th Cir. 1980]), the court said, "It cannot be considered a search within the protection of the Fourth Amendment for a dog to sniff bags handled by an airline. There can be no reasonable expectation of privacy when any passenger's bags may be subjected to close scrutiny for the protection of public safety."[10]

United States v. Sullivan (4th Cir. 1980)

To summarize, the concept of special needs is a fast-developing area of the law on searches and seizures that will occupy the attention of the Court in future years. This exception, however, is of no immediate concern in policing because the searches are conducted by administrative officials, not by the police. There are instances, however, when the police are asked by administrative and other public officials (as in school searches, searches in juvenile detention centers, and searches by probation officers) to help. Whether it is an administrative search (and therefore falls under special needs) or a law enforcement search is usually determined by whether administrative officials asked the police to help, or the administrative officials are being used by the police to search things and places they otherwise cannot search or seize because of the absence of probable cause.

The Exigent (Emergency) Circumstances Exception

The **exigent circumstances** exception is a general catchall category that encompasses a number of diverse situations. What they have in common is some kind of an emergency that makes obtaining a search warrant impractical, useless, dangerous, or unnecessary. Among these situations are the danger of physical harm to the officer or destruction of evidence, searches in hot pursuit, danger to a third person, and driving while intoxicated.

Danger of Physical Harm to the Officer or Destruction of Evidence The Court has implied that a warrantless search may be justified if there are reasonable grounds to believe that delaying the search until the warrant is obtained would endanger the physical safety of the officer or would allow the destruction or removal of the evidence (*Vale v. Louisiana*, 399 U.S. 30 [1970]). However, in *Vale*, the Supreme Court did not allow a warrantless search when there was *merely a possibility* that the evidence would be destroyed. Thus, *Vale* has a narrow interpretation: The threat of danger or destruction must be real or imminent.

Three years later, in *Cupp v. Murphy* (412 U.S. 291 [1973]), the Court held that the taking of fingernail scrapings without consent or formal arrest does not violate the Fourth Amendment protection against unreasonable search and seizure if the evidence is likely to disappear before a warrant can be obtained.

The Court has ruled, however, that the fact that the place searched was the scene of a serious crime (in this case the murder of an undercover officer) did not in itself justify a warrantless search in the absence of any "indication that the evidence would be lost, destroyed, or removed during the time required to obtain a search warrant and there [was] no suggestion that a warrant could not easily and conveniently have been obtained" (*Mincey v. Arizona*, 437 U.S. 385 [1978]).

In *Mincey*, an undercover police officer was shot and killed in the process of making a narcotics raid on Mincey's apartment. Shortly thereafter, homicide detectives arrived at the scene of the crime and conducted "an exhaustive four-day warrantless search of the apartment which included the opening of dresser drawers, the ripping up of carpets, and the seizure of 200 to 300 objects." At trial, Mincey sought to

Vale v. Louisiana (1970)

Cupp v. Murphy (1973)

Mincey v. Arizona (1978)

suppress the evidence obtained, saying that the warrantless search was invalid. The government justified the warrantless search based on the "murder scene" exception to the warrant requirement created by the Arizona Supreme Court in previous cases. The Court disagreed, saying that the warrantless search in this case could not be justified based on "the ground that a possible homicide inevitably presents an emergency situation, especially since there was no emergency threatening life or limb." The "seriousness of the offense . . . did not itself create exigent circumstances of the kind that under the Fourth Amendment justify a warrantless search, where there is no indication that evidence would be lost, destroyed, or removed during the time required to obtain a search warrant and there is no suggestion that a warrant could not easily and conveniently have been obtained."

In sum, the Court said that a warrant must be obtained in crime scene investigations, regardless of the seriousness of the offense. The only exception to this rule is if obtaining a warrant would mean that the evidence would be lost, destroyed, or removed during the time required to obtain a warrant.

Flippo v. West Virginia (1999)

In *Flippo v. West Virginia* (528 U.S. 11 [1999]), the Court reaffirmed its decision in *Mincey* when it said that there is no crime scene exception to the search warrant requirement, adding that "a warrantless search by the police is invalid unless it falls within one of the narrow and well-delineated exceptions to the warrant requirement." In this case, Flippo's conviction was influenced by photographs removed by the police from a briefcase they found at the scene and opened without a warrant. The photographs, admitted at trial, suggested that Flippo was having a homosexual affair with a member of his church and that this provided a motive for him to kill his wife. The Court rejected this "murder scene" exception to the warrant requirement used by the prosecution, saying that this exception was squarely in conflict with *Mincey*.

Searches in "Hot Pursuit" (or "Fresh Pursuit") of Dangerous Suspects

The police may enter a house without a warrant to search for a dangerous suspect who is being pursued and whom they have reason to believe is on the premises. For example, in one case, the police pursued a robbery suspect to a house (which later turned out to be his own). The suspect's wife opened the door to the police, who asked and received permission to search for a "burglar." The police looked for weapons that might have been concealed and found incriminating clothing in a washing machine. The clothing was confiscated and introduced as evidence during the trial. The Court held that the warrantless search was justified by hot pursuit (regardless of the validity of the suspect's wife's consent). Because the police were informed that an armed robbery had taken place and that the suspect had entered a certain house less than five minutes before they got there, they acted reasonably when they entered the house and began to search for a man of the description they had obtained and for weapons that he had allegedly used in the robbery (*Warden v. Hayden*, 387 U.S. 294 [1967]).

Warden v. Hayden (1967)

Danger to a Third Person

An officer may enter a dwelling without a warrant in response to screams for help. In *Warden v. Hayden* (387 U.S. 294 [1967]), the

Court said, "The Fourth Amendment does not require police officers to delay in the course of an investigation if to do so would gravely endanger their lives or the lives of others."

Driving While Intoxicated (DWI) The police may, without a search warrant and by force, if necessary, take a blood sample from a person arrested for drunk driving, as long as the setting and procedures are reasonable (as when the blood is drawn by a doctor in a hospital). Exigent circumstances exist because alcohol in the suspect's bloodstream might disappear in the time required to obtain a warrant (*Schmerber v. California*, 384 U.S. 757 [1966]).

Schmerber v. California (1966)

However, in *Welch v. Wisconsin* (466 U.S. 740 [1984]), the Court placed limits on what the police can do in simple DWI cases. The Court held that the Fourth Amendment prohibits the police from making a warrantless nighttime entry into a suspect's house to arrest him or her for drunk driving if the offense is a misdemeanor for which state law does not allow any jail sentence. The fact that the police had an interest in preserving the evidence (because the suspect's blood-alcohol level might diminish while the police procured a warrant) was ruled insufficient to create the required exigent circumstance.

Welch v. Wisconsin (1984)

In *Welsh,* the defendant had run his car off the road and abandoned it. By the time police officers arrived at the scene and learned from a witness that the defendant was either inebriated or very ill, the defendant had gone home and fallen asleep. The officers checked the vehicle's registration and learned that the defendant lived close by. Without obtaining a warrant, they went to the suspect's home and arrested him. The Wisconsin Supreme Court held that the officers' actions were justified by exigent circumstances.

The U.S. Supreme Court reversed that decision, saying that "an important factor to be considered when determining whether any exigency exists is the gravity of the underlying offense for which the arrest is being made. . . . Application of the exigent circumstances exception in the context of a home entry should rarely be sanctioned when there is probable cause to believe that only a minor offense has been committed." Implicit in this is the assumption that, had the offense been serious (such as if the driver had seriously injured somebody before running off the road and abandoning his car), the warrantless search of his home would have been allowed. The Court concluded that in this case there was no immediate pursuit of the defendant from the scene, nor was there any need to protect either the public or the defendant inasmuch as he had abandoned the vehicle and was at home sleeping. Only the need to preserve the evidence remained, and that was not enough, given the type of offense involved and the state's treatment of it as a civil matter, to justify the warrantless intrusion.

The Administrative Searches and Inspections Exception

Administrative searches are searches conducted by government investigators to determine whether there are violations of government rules and regulations. These searches are usually authorized by local ordinances or regulations of administrative agencies and are generally conducted by agents or investigators of these agencies rather than by the police. In some jurisdictions, the warrant issued is known as an *administrative* instead of a *judicial* warrant. In a case involving a prosecution for arson, the Court provided the following distinctions between the need for administrative warrants and a criminal search warrant and what these warrants require (*Michigan v. Clifford*, 464 U.S. 287 [1984]):

Michigan v. Clifford (1984)

If the primary object is to determine the cause and origin of a recent fire, an administrative warrant will suffice. To obtain such a warrant, fire officials need show only that a fire of undetermined origin has occurred on the premises, that the scope of the proposed search is reasonable and will not intrude unnecessarily on the fire victim's privacy, and that the search will be executed at a reasonable and convenient time.

If the primary object of the search is to gather evidence of criminal activity, a criminal search warrant may be obtained only on a showing of probable cause to believe that relevant evidence will be found in the place to be searched. If evidence of criminal activity is discovered during the course of a valid administrative search, it may be seized under the "plain view" doctrine. This evidence may then be used to establish probable cause to obtain a criminal search warrant. Fire officials may not, however, rely on this evidence to expand the scope of their administrative search without first making a successful showing of probable cause to an independent judicial officer.

Next, we discuss the different types of administrative searches and then compare administrative and law enforcement searches.

Types of Administrative Searches Court decisions have identified three types of administrative searches and inspections. These are entering private residences for code violations, entering commercial buildings for inspection purposes, and searching closely regulated businesses.

Entering private residence for code violations—consent or warrant needed The Court has held that health, safety, or other types of inspectors cannot enter private premises without the owner's consent or a search warrant (*Camara v. Municipal Court*, 387 U.S. 523 [1967]). In *Camara v. Municipal Court*, defendant Camara was charged with violating the San Francisco Housing Code for refusing building inspectors a warrantless inspection of a building he leased and used as a residence, allegedly in violation of the city's occupancy rules. Subsequently charged in a criminal case with refusal to permit a warrantless inspection of his residence, Camara claimed that the city ordinance authorizing such warrantless inspections was unconstitutional and a violation of the Fourth Amendment. On appeal, the Court agreed, saying, "It is surely anomalous to say that the individual and his private property are fully protected by the Fourth Amendment only when the individual is suspected of criminal behavior."

Camara v. Municipal Court (1967)

Note that, although a warrant is required, as one source states: "[T]he inspector does not have to demonstrate probable cause to believe that a violation of an ordinance within his domain will be discovered in the premises to be searched." Instead, the inspector must simply demonstrate that "reasonable legislative or administrative standards for conducting an area inspection are satisfied with respect to a particular dwelling." Thus the inspector does not have to show that the dwelling probably contains code violations but simply that it belongs to a class of structures (for example, multifamily apartment buildings or commercial buildings not inspected in the previous year) designated administratively or legislatively for inspection.[11]

Entering commercial buildings for inspection purposes—consent or warrant needed

See v. City of Seattle (1967)

The rule also applies to commercial structures that are not used as private residences. In *See v. City of Seattle* (387 U.S. 541 [1967]), the defendant See was convicted for refusing to permit an agent of the Seattle Fire Department to enter and inspect his locked commercial warehouse without a warrant and without probable cause to believe that a violation of any municipal ordinance had taken place. Such inspection was conducted routinely as part of a periodic citywide canvass to ensure compliance with Seattle's fire code.

On appeal, the Court held that "administrative entry, without consent, upon the portions of commercial premises which are not open to the public may only be compelled through prosecution or physical force within the framework of a warrant procedure." It added that "the basic component of a reasonable search under the Fourth Amendment—that it not be enforced without a suitable warrant procedure—is applicable in this context, as in others, to business as well as to residential premises." As in the case of entries into a private residence for code violations, probable cause is not required. All that is needed is for the inspector to show that the place being inspected belongs to a class of structures that is mandated by administrative rules or ordinances to be inspected.

Searches of closely regulated businesses—no need for consent or warrant

In contrast to the other two types of administrative searches, the Court has decided in a number of cases that searches of highly regulated businesses or industries do not need a warrant or probable cause. The justification for this "no need for warrant or probable cause" rule is the urgent public interest involved in the search. Another justification is the implied consent given for the government to search without a warrant when these businesses applied for a government license to get into this type of highly regulated business.

United States v. Biswell (1972)

In *United States v. Biswell* (406 U.S. 311 [1972]), the Court held that the warrantless inspection of a weapons dealer by a federal agent was valid, saying that the dealer had chosen to engage in a business that was inherently subject to heavy federal licensing regulation and that such regulation could be enforced only by the government's making unannounced and frequent visits. In *New York v. Burger* (482 U.S. 691 [1987]), the Court upheld the warrantless inspection of an automobile junkyard, saying that the warrantless inspection was valid because the business was "closely regulated" by the government and there was substantial government interest involved in preventing car theft. The same holds true for liquor businesses

New York v. Burger (1987)

(*Colonnade Catering Corporation v. United States,* 397 U.S. 72 [1970]) and strip-mining (*Donovan v. Dewey,* 452 U.S. 594 [1981]).

Comparison of Administrative Searches and Law Enforcement Searches

The following list compares administrative and law enforcement searches.

Administrative Searches	Law Enforcement Searches
Done by administrative agents or investigators, not by the police	Done by law enforcement personnel
Purpose is enforcement of administrative regulations	Purpose is enforcement of criminal laws
Consent or warrant is needed except for highly regulated businesses	Consent or warrant is always needed
Probable cause is not needed; must show that the place being inspected is subject to administrative rules or ordinances	Probable cause is always needed unless there is consent

Specific Search and Seizure Issues

This section examines several issues that are specific to search and seizure. They include (1) the search and seizure of students; (2) squeezing luggage on a bus; (3) temporarily restraining a suspect; (4) searches and seizures by private persons; (5) searches by off-duty officers; (6) the use of dogs to detect drugs; and (7) surgery to remove a bullet from a suspect.

Searches and Seizures of Students

The Court has decided a few cases involving searches and seizures of students. In one of the earlier cases involving high school students, the Court held that "reasonable grounds" are all that public high school officials need for a valid search of students; they do not need probable cause or a warrant (*New Jersey v. T.L.O.,* 469 U.S. 325 [1985]). *New Jersey v. T.L.O.* (discussed on pp. 245–246) involved a 14-year-old high school

student who violated school rules by smoking a cigarette in the school lavatory and whose purse was later extensively searched by the high school vice principal, yielding drug paraphernalia and other incriminating evidence of drug sale. Delinquency charges were brought against the student in juvenile court. She moved to suppress the evidence seized by the vice principal, alleging the search was illegal because there was no warrant or probable cause. The Court disagreed, saying that for high school searches to be valid, all that public school officials need are "reasonable grounds," to suspect that the search will produce evidence that the student has violated or is violating either the law or the rules of the school. The Court based its decision on two grounds: (1) the need to maintain an environment in which learning can take place, and (2) high school administrators are considered acting in the place of parents under the principle of in loco parentis because they are dealing with young students.

Does this ruling apply to college students? This was not addressed by the Court, but it probably would not because most college students are adults and therefore the in loco parentis principle does not apply. Besides, the need to maintain an environment in which learning can take place is less compelling in a college setting. Lower court decisions have held that college students, regardless of age, are considered adults. It can be assumed, however, that the ruling applies to public elementary school students because the need to "maintain an environment in which learning can take place" applies with greater force in elementary schools because of the age of the students. Whether it applies to private high school and elementary schools has not been decided by the Court.

The other high-profile Court decisions involving high school students have to do with drug testing, which is a form of search and seizure under the Fourth Amendment. In *Vernonia School District v. Acton* (515 U.S. 646 [1995]), the Court held that drug testing student athletes did not require individualized suspicion and that random drug testing was constitutional. In that case, the Vernonia School District discovered, after an official investigation, that some of their high school athletes had participated in illicit drug use. The school authorities then adopted a policy that authorized random urinalysis drug testing of its student athletes. James Acton was denied participation in the football program when he and his parents refused to consent to drug testing.

Vernonia School District v. Acton (1995)

On appeal, the Court held that the drug testing policy was valid, saying that the constitutionality of a search is determined by "balancing the intrusion on the individual's Fourth Amendment interests against the promotion of legitimate governmental interests." Finding that the privacy interests involved when collecting urine samples are "negligible," the Court concluded that high school athletes are under state supervision when they are in school and are subject to greater control than free adults.

Seven years later, the Court extended this holding in *Board of Education of Independent School District No. 92 of Pottawatomie County et al. v. Earls,* 536 U.S. 822 [2002]), another case involving middle and high school students. The Court held that the random urinalysis testing policy that applied to all middle and high school students participating in any extracurricular activity, not just athletics, was constitutional. The Court stressed that the random drug testing was "a reasonable means of furthering the School District's important interest in preventing and deterring drug use among its schoolchildren and does not violate the Fourth Amendment." Whether or not this decision applies to college students has not been decided by the Court.

Board of Education of Independent School District No. 92 of Pottawatomie County et al. v. Earls (2002)

Squeezing Luggage in a Bus

A traveler's luggage is an "effect" and is under the protection of the Fourth Amendment. Therefore, officers may not physically manipulate (such as squeeze) the luggage to inspect it without a warrant or probable cause. In *Bond v. United States* (529 U.S. 334 [2000]), Bond was riding on a Greyhound bus when a border patrol agent boarded the bus to check the immigration status of passengers.

Bond v. United States (2000)

The agent went to the back of the bus. On the way back to the front, he squeezed a canvas bag above Bond's seat and felt that it contained a "brick-like" object. Bond admitted owning the bag and agreed to allow the agent to open it. The agent found methamphetamine. Bond later appealed his conviction, saying that the search by the officer violated his constitutional right.

The Court based its decision on the following: First, Bond had an expectation of privacy. He sought to preserve that privacy "by using an opaque bag and placing it directly above his seat." Second, that expectation of privacy is "one that society is prepared to recognize as reasonable." The Court concluded that "although there is expectation that the luggage will be handled by other passengers or bus employees, there is no expectation that the luggage will be physically manipulated in an exploratory manner," which was what the police did. The Court further said that "a physically invasive inspection is more intrusive than a visual inspection; therefore the law enforcement officer's physical manipulation of the luggage violated the Fourth Amendment."

The Temporary Restraint of a Suspect

Under exigent circumstances, and where there is a need to preserve evidence until a warrant can be obtained, the police may temporarily restrain a person's movements without violating his or her Fourth Amendment rights. In *Illinois v. McArthur* (531 U.S. 326 [2001]), a woman asked police officers to accompany her to the trailer where she lived with her husband, McArthur, while she removed her belongings. The woman went inside where her husband was, while the officer remained outside. When the woman emerged, she told one of the officers that McArthur had drugs in the trailer. The officers knocked on the door and asked permission to search the trailer, but McArthur denied permission. One officer then left to obtain a warrant. When the husband stepped onto his porch, the officer prevented him from reentering his trailer unaccompanied. McArthur reentered the trailer on three occasions, but the officer stood in the doorway and observed him. The other officer returned with a warrant, and the officers searched the trailer and found drugs and paraphernalia. Convicted, McArthur appealed, saying his Fourth Amendment right was violated.

Illinois v. McArthur
(2001)

The Court held there was no violation, saying that "we have found no case in which this Court has held unlawful a temporary seizure that was supported by probable cause and was designed to prevent the loss of evidence while the police diligently obtained a warrant in a reasonable period of time."

In another case, *Muehler v. Mena* (544 U.S._____[2005]), the Court held that detaining occupants of the premises in handcuffs and for a certain period of time while executing a search does not necessarily violate the Fourth Amendment prohibition against unreasonable searches and seizures.

Muehler v. Mena
(2005)

Searches and Seizures by Private Persons

Searches and seizures by private persons do not come under Fourth Amendment protection, because the constitutional amendments apply only to acts of government agencies and officers. This is true even if the act by private persons is illegal.

Evidence obtained by private persons is admissible in court as long as they acted purely on their own and the police did not encourage or participate in the private search and seizure. For example, suppose X breaks into his neighbor's house because he suspects the neighbor of having stolen his TV set. X recovers the set and now brings a case of robbery against his neighbor. The TV set is admissible in evidence because the Fourth Amendment protection against unreasonable searches and seizures applies only to acts of government officers, not to private persons. However, X may be liable for breaking into and entering his neighbor's house in a separate criminal case.

Note also that the evidence is not admissible if a police officer participated in, ordered, or encouraged X to make the search. If a government official helps in a search or seizure by a private citizen, then the Fourth Amendment protections apply.[12] It is immaterial whether the government officer proposed the idea or merely joined in while the search was in progress. If he or she was involved in any way before the object of the search was completely accomplished, the law says the officer participated in it; the evidence secured is therefore inadmissible.

Searches by Off-Duty Officers

A search by an off-duty officer is usually considered a government search. Many jurisdictions consider police officers to be law enforcement officers twenty-four hours a day. If this were not the rule, it would be convenient for police officers to conduct searches while off-duty and therefore subvert the Fourth Amendment. Although this issue has not been litigated in court, the rule probably will be the same even in jurisdictions where police officers are considered on duty at all times.

The Use of Police Dogs for Detection of Drugs

There is no "search" within the meaning of the Fourth Amendment if the police use narcotics detection dogs to smell closed containers for drugs, as long as the police are on the premises legally. There is therefore no need for a search warrant or for probable cause to conduct dog sniffs (*United States v. Place*, 462 U.S. 696 [1983]).

United States v. Place (1983)

Justifications for this judicial rule include the following: (1) the use of dogs does not involve any physical intrusion, (2) the intrusion upon an individual's privacy is inoffensive, (3) the intrusion is restricted because the dog is discriminate, (4) the intrusion is not aimed at persons but rather at an inanimate object, and (5) the use of dogs is not the same as using a sophisticated electronic device.[13] In *Illinois v. Caballes* (543 U.S. _____ [2005]), the Court held that a dog sniff conducted during a lawful traffic stop that reveals no information other than the location of an illegal substance that no individual has any right to possess does not violate the Fourth Amendment.

Illinois v. Caballes (2005)

Surgery to Remove a Bullet from a Suspect

In *Winston v. Lee* (470 U.S. 753 [1985]), the Court held that a proposed surgery to remove a bullet from a suspect's chest for use as evidence would involve such

Winston v. Lee (1985)

severe intrusion on his interest in privacy and security that it would violate the Fourth Amendment and could not be allowed unless the government demonstrated a compelling need for it. The surgery could not be constitutionally undertaken, even though probable cause existed and the suspect was provided with all relevant procedural safeguards, because the government failed to establish the compelling need for such surgery.

Schmerber v. California (1966)

This decision is significant because in an earlier case, *Schmerber v. California* (384 U.S. 757 [1966]), the Court held that a state may, over the suspect's objections, have a physician extract blood if he or she is suspected of drunken driving, without violating his or her Fourth Amendment right not to be subjected to unreasonable searches and seizures. However, according to the *Schmerber* decision, the holding that the Constitution does not forbid a state's minor intrusions into an individual's body under stringently limited conditions in no way indicates that it permits more substantial intrusions or intrusions under other conditions.

In the *Lee* case, the state of Virginia sought to compel Lee, a suspect in an attempted armed robbery who had allegedly been wounded by gunfire in that attempt, to undergo a surgical procedure under a general anesthetic for removal of the bullet lodged in his chest. Prosecutors alleged that the bullet would provide evidence of the suspect's guilt or innocence. The suspect opposed the surgery. The Court concluded that the procedure was an example of the "more substantial intrusion" cautioned against in the *Schmerber* case and held that to permit the procedure to take place would violate the suspect's right to be secure in his person as guaranteed by the Fourth Amendment.

The Court did not say that evidence retrievals of this nature could never be undertaken simply because they were per se intrusive. Instead, it used a balancing test, stating that "the medical risks of the operation, although apparently not extremely severe, are a subject of considerable dispute." But the Court also said that, "although the bullet may turn out to be useful . . . in prosecuting respondent, the Commonwealth [of Virginia] failed to demonstrate a compelling need for it."

Issues in Searches and Seizures and Technology

Changing technology is creating new issues in search and seizure laws. This section examines how these changes have been interpreted by constitutional law. We will look at evolving concepts in electronic surveillance and the federal laws that govern this technology; searches and seizures of computers; and the treatment of electronic devices that do not intercept communication.

Evolving Concepts in Electronic Surveillance

Electronic surveillance is the use of electronic devices to monitor a person's activities or whereabouts. It is a type of search and seizure and can take various forms, such as wiretapping or bugging. This form of surveillance is regulated strictly by the

U.S. Constitution, federal law, and state statutes. The Fourth Amendment prohibition against unreasonable searches and seizures protects a person's conversation from unreasonable intrusion. Federal and state laws further limit what the police can do. This section examines both the old and the new concepts of what is a constitutional use of electronic surveillance.

The Old Concept–Constitutional If There Is No Trespass: *Olmstead v. United States*

Olmstead v. United States (1928)

The first major case in electronic surveillance was *Olmstead v. United States* (277 U.S. 438 [1928]). *Olmstead* involved a bootlegging operation against which evidence was gathered through the use of wiretaps on telephone conversations. The Court held that wiretapping did not violate the Fourth Amendment unless there was "some trespass into a constitutionally protected area." Under this concept, evidence obtained through a bugging device placed against a wall to overhear conversation in an adjoining office was admissible because there was no actual trespass.

The Court said, "The Amendment does not forbid what was done here. There was no searching. There was no seizure. The evidence was secured by the use of the sense of hearing and that only. There was no entry of the houses or offices of the defendants." This **old concept of electronic surveillance** prevailed from 1928 to 1967.

In 1934, Congress passed the Federal Communications Act, which provided that "no person not being authorized by the sender shall intercept any communication and divulge or publish the existence, contents, substance, purport, effect or meaning of such intercepted communication to any person." In 1937, in *Nardone v. United States* (302 U.S. 379 [1937]), the Court interpreted this provision as forbidding federal agents, as well as other persons, from intercepting and disclosing telephone messages by the use of wiretaps. However, in 1942, in *Goldstein v. United States* (316 U.S. 114 [1942]), the Court held that wiretap evidence could be used against persons other than those whose conversations had been overheard and whose Fourth Amendment rights were therefore violated. That same year, the Court also held that the use of a "bug" (an electronic listening device that is not a wiretap on telephone lines) was not in violation of the Federal Communications Act, because the act applied only to actual interference with communication wires and telephone lines.

Nardone v. United States (1937)

Goldstein v. United States (1942)

In 1961, the Court took a tougher view on electronic surveillance in the case of *Silverman v. United States* (365 U.S. 505 [1961]). In *Silverman,* the Court held that driving a "spike mike" into a building wall to allow police to overhear conversations within the building without a warrant violated the Fourth Amendment. The fact that the device, although tiny, actually penetrated the building wall was sufficient to constitute physical intrusion in violation of the Fourth Amendment. In 1964, in *Clinton v. Virginia* (377 U.S. 158 [1964]), the Court further decided that evidence the police obtained by attaching an electronic device to the exterior wall of a building was illegally obtained. These decisions eroded the impact of the *Olmstead* decision.

Silverman v. United States (1961)

Clinton v. Virginia (1964)

***Olmstead v. United States* (1928)** Wiretapping does not violate the Fourth Amendment unless there is "some trespass into a constitutionally protected area."

***Nardone v. United States* (1937)** The Federal Communications Act forbids federal agents, as well as other persons, from interpreting and disclosing telephone messages through wiretaps.

***Goldstein v. United States* (1942)** Wiretap evidence can be used against persons other than those whose conversations were overheard and whose Fourth Amendment rights were therefore violated.

***Silberman v. United States* (1961)** Driving a "spike mike" into a building wall to allow police to overhear conversations within the building without a warrant violated the Fourth Amendment.

***Clinton v. Virginia* (1964)** Evidence the police obtained by attaching an electronic device to the exterior wall of a building was illegally obtained.

***Katz v. United States* (1967)** The prohibition against unreasonable search and seizure is not limited to homes, office buildings, or other enclosed spaces. It applies even in public places where a person has a "reasonable expectation of privacy." The Court expressly overruled *Olmstead v. United States* (1928).

The New Concept—Unconstitutional If It Violates a Reasonable Expectation of Privacy: *Katz v. United States*

The old concept of "some trespass into a constitutionally protected area" was abandoned by the Court in 1967 in *Katz v. United States* (389 U.S. 347 [1967]). (Read the *Katz v. United States* Case Brief to learn more about this case.) Under the **new concept of electronic surveillance** enunciated in *Katz,* a search occurs whenever there is police activity that violates a "reasonable expectation of privacy." Such activity includes any form of electronic surveillance, with or without actual physical trespass or wiretap.

In the *Katz* case, the police attached an electronic listening device to the outside of a public telephone booth that the defendant was using. Although there was no tapping of the line, the Court held that the listening device violated the defendant's reasonable expectation that his conversations, held in a public telephone booth, were private. The Court said that what Katz "sought to exclude when he entered the booth was not the intruding eye—it was the uninvited ear." He did not shed his right to do so simply because he made his calls from a place where he might be seen. Thus, the key phrase in determining intrusion is "reasonable expectation of privacy."

Aside from popularizing and giving substance to the phrase "reasonable expectation of privacy" (the current standard used in Fourth Amendment cases), the *Katz* case is also significant because it makes the Fourth Amendment protection "portable," meaning that its protections accompany the individual wherever he or she goes. In the words of the Court, the Fourth Amendment "protects people, not places." This concept is key to understanding the full extent of the protection afforded by the Fourth Amendment against any and all unreasonable searches and seizures, not just in electronic surveillance cases. A person enjoys the protection of the Fourth Amendment not only at home but also in a public place as long as there is a reasonable expectation of privacy by that person and that expectation is acceptable to the public.

Facts: Katz was convicted in federal court of transmitting wagering information by telephone across state lines. Evidence of Katz's end of the conversation, overheard by FBI agents who had attached an electronic listening and recording device to the outside of the telephone booth from which the calls were made, was introduced at the trial. Katz sought to suppress the evidence, but the trial court admitted it. The court of appeals affirmed the conviction, finding that there was no Fourth Amendment violation, because there was "no physical entrance into the area occupied" by Katz.

Issue: *Is a public telephone booth a constitutionally protected area such that obtaining evidence by attaching an electronic listening/recording device to the top of it violates the user's right to privacy? Yes.*

Supreme Court Decision: Any form of electronic surveillance, including wiretapping, that violates a reasonable expectation of privacy constitutes a search. No actual physical trespass is required.

Case Significance: The *Katz* decision expressly overruled the decision thirty-nine years earlier in *Olmstead v. United States,* 277 U.S. 438 (1928), which found that wiretapping did not violate the Fourth Amendment unless there was some trespass into a "constitutionally protected area." In *Katz,* the Court said that the Fourth Amendment's coverage does not depend on the presence or absence of a physical intrusion into a given enclosure. The current test is that a search exists and therefore comes under the Fourth Amendment protection whenever there is a reasonable expectation of privacy. The concept that the Constitution "protects people rather than places" is

significant, because it makes the protection of the Fourth Amendment "portable"—carried by persons wherever they go, as long as their behavior and circumstances are such that they are entitled to a reasonable expectation of privacy.

Excerpts from the Decision: The petitioner has phrased those questions as follows:

> A. Whether a public telephone booth is a constitutionally protected area so that evidence obtained by attaching an electronic listening recording device to the top of such a booth is obtained in violation of the right to privacy of the user of the booth. [389 U.S. 347, 350]
>
> B. Whether physical penetration of a constitutionally protected area is necessary before a search and seizure can be said to be violative of the Fourth Amendment to the United States Constitution.

We decline to adopt this formulation of the issues. In the first place, the correct solution of Fourth Amendment problems is not necessarily promoted by incantation of the phrase "constitutionally protected area." Secondly, the Fourth Amendment cannot be translated into a general constitutional "right to privacy." That Amendment protects individual privacy against certain kinds of governmental intrusion, but its protections go further, and often have nothing to do with privacy at all. . . . Other provisions of the Constitution protect personal privacy from other forms of governmental invasion. . . . But the protection of a person's general right to privacy—his right to be let alone by other people . . . —is, like the [389 U.S. 347, 351] protection of his property and of his very life, left largely to the law of the individual States.

Three Federal Laws Governing Electronic Surveillance

Electronic surveillance is governed primarily by federal laws, often supplemented by state laws. In case of a conflict, however, federal laws prevail. The U.S. Congress has passed a number of laws on electronic surveillance and is considering more, particularly after the sad events of 9/11. Three laws, however, deserve mention because they are the most significant pieces of legislation on electronic surveillance: (1) Title III of the Omnibus Crime Control and Safe Streets Act of 1968, (2) the Electronic Communications and Privacy Act of 1986 (ECPA), and (3) the Communications Assistance for Law Enforcement Act of 1994 (CALEA). Following is a brief discussion of each.

Title III of the Omnibus Crime Control and Safe Streets Act of 1968
The use of wiretaps, electronic surveillance, and bugging devices is largely governed by the provisions of **Title III of the Omnibus Crime Control and Safe Streets Act of 1968** and subsequent federal laws amending or supplementing it. This law is long and complex. Its main provision may, however, be summarized as follows: Law enforcement officers nationwide, federal and state, cannot tap or intercept wire communications or use electronic devices to intercept private conversations, except in these two situations:

- *If a court order has authorized the wiretap.* The state, however, must have passed a law authorizing the issuance of a court order; without such a law, courts are not authorized to issue a judicial order.
- *If consent is given by one of the parties.* But such consent is not valid if state law prohibits this type of recording even with the consent of one of the parties.

This section looks at these two exceptions, how state laws are affected by Title III, and the effect of *Berger v. New York* on surveillance laws.

Court orders authorizing the wiretap
If the legislature, federal or state, has passed a law authorizing the issuance of a court order, a judge may then issue such an order as long as the following four conditions are present:

- There is probable cause to believe that a specific individual has committed one of the crimes enumerated under the act.
- There is probable cause to believe that the interception will furnish evidence of the crime.
- Normal investigative procedures have been tried and have failed or reasonably appear likely to fail or to be dangerous.
- There is probable cause to believe that the facilities or the place from which or where the interception is to be made are used in connection with the offense or are linked to the individual under suspicion.

Once law enforcement officials have obtained judicial authorization to intercept wire or oral communications, they do not have to obtain another judicial

The main provisions of Title III of the Omnibus Crime Control and Safe Streets Act of 1968 may be summarized as follows: Law enforcement officers, federal and state, cannot tap or intercept wire communications or use electronic devices to intercept conversations except in two situations:

1. *A court order has authorized the wiretap.* The state, however, must have

passed a law authorizing the issuance of a court order; without such a law, courts are not authorized to issue a judicial order.

2. *Consent has been given by one of the parties.* The exception is the prohibition of this type of recording by state law even with the consent of one of the parties.

---

authorization to enable them to enter the premises to install the listening device. Such authorization comes with the court order.

Consent by one of the parties Consent is one of the exceptions to the court order requirements under Title III, and it has also been exempted from the warrant requirement by several court decisions. However, some states expressly prohibit by law, on pain of civil consequences or criminal prosecution, electronic eavesdropping or wiretapping even if consent is given by one of the parties.[14] Such statutes take precedence over any consent given by one of the parties and must therefore be followed.

An example is Linda Tripp's taping of her conversations with Monica Lewinsky during the Clinton-Lewinsky affair. Tripp's recordings constituted crucial evidence in the impeachment proceedings against then-President Clinton in 1999. Later, however, Tripp was indicted in Maryland on charges of illegal wiretapping, based on a "rarely used Maryland law that makes it a crime to record telephone conversations without the consent of all parties."[15] Maryland law requires that the person doing the recording knew that it was illegal without the other person's consent and yet went ahead and did it anyway.

United States v. White (1971)

However, in *United States v. White* (401 U.S. 745 [1971]), the Court concluded that the Constitution does not prohibit a government agent from using an electronic device to record a telephone conversation between two parties if one party to the conversation consents. The Court has also ruled that the Fourth Amendment does not protect persons from supposed friends who turn out to be police informants. Thus, a person assumes the risk that whatever he or she says to others may be reported by them to the police; there is no police "search" in such cases. It follows that, if the supposed friend allows the police to listen in on a telephone conversation with the suspect, there is no violation of the suspect's Fourth Amendment rights. The evidence obtained is admissible because of the consent

On Lee v. United States (1952)

given by one party to the conversation (*On Lee v. United States,* 343 U.S. 747 [1952]).

Title III and state laws As noted, under Title III of the Omnibus Crime Control and Safe Streets Act of 1968, an electronic surveillance is illegal even if authorized by a state or a local judge if there is no law passed by the state legislature authorizing the judge to issue the order. Twenty-eight states, including such big states as California, Illinois, Pennsylvania, Michigan, and Ohio, have not passed laws authorizing such surveillance.[16] It is therefore important that police officers ascertain whether electronic surveillance is specifically authorized in their state and, if so, what procedures they must follow. Without an enabling state statute, a police officer faces possible federal criminal prosecution for unauthorized electronic surveillance, punishable by a maximum of five years of imprisonment and/or a $10,000 fine. Moreover, evidence obtained in violation of this federal law is not admissible in any federal or state proceeding.

States may pass laws *further limiting, but not broadening,* the restrictions imposed by Title III. For example, although Title III allows the use of evidence obtained with the consent of one party to the conversation, a state statute may prohibit such use without the consent of both parties. In states having that prohibition, the evidence is not admissible in state court for criminal prosecution.

***Title III and* Berger v. New York** If the language of a state law authorizing eavesdropping is too broad in scope, it intrudes into a constitutionally protected area and therefore violates the Fourth Amendment. An example of such a statute was a New York law that the Supreme Court declared unconstitutional because it was too broad and did not contain sufficient safeguards against unwarranted intrusions on constitutional rights (*Berger v. New York,* 388 U.S. 41 [1967]).

Berger v. New York (1967)

The 1967 *Berger v. New York* decision is significant because it specifies six requirements for a warrant authorizing any form of electronic surveillance to be valid:

1. The warrant must describe with *particularity* the conversations that are to be overheard.
2. There must be a showing of *probable cause* to believe that a specific crime has been or is being committed.
3. The wiretap must be for a *limited period,* although extensions may be obtained upon adequate showing.
4. The *suspects* whose conversations are to be overheard *must be named* in the judicial order.
5. A *return must be made to the court,* showing what conversations were intercepted.
6. The wiretapping *must terminate* when the desired information has been obtained.

The 1967 *Berger* case was decided one year before the enactment of Title III of the Omnibus Crime Control and Safe Streets Act. Title III enacted into law these six requirements, along with the other provisions discussed here. *Berger* is important because it says that overly broad eavesdropping statutes are unconstitutional, and it also defines what state statutes must include to be valid.

The Electronic Communications and Privacy Act of 1986 (ECPA) Title III of the Omnibus Crime Control and Safe Streets Act of 1968 continues to be the main federal law on electronic surveillance. In 1986, however, the U.S. Congress passed the Electronic Communications and Privacy Act (ECPA), which amends and supplements the provisions of Title III. A series of law-oriented articles in the FBI Law Enforcement Bulletin discusses the main provisions of that law.[17] According to the author, Robert Fiatal, the **ECPA** contains three provisions that relate to federal, state, and local law enforcement work:

1. It amends the law of nonconsensual interception of wire communications [wiretaps] and oral communications by a concealed microphone or electronic device [bugs].
2. It sets forth specific procedures for obtaining authorization to use pen registers [telephone decoders], which record the numbers dialed from a telephone, and trap-and-trace devices, which ascertain the origin of a telephone call.
3. It prescribes the procedure law enforcement officers must follow to obtain stored communications and records relating to communications services, such as telephone toll records and unlisted telephone subscriber information.[18]

The aims of the ECPA are twofold: to safeguard private electronic communications—such as in-transit and stored electronic mail, computing services, and voice mail—from unauthorized government access and to ban Internet and other electronic communication service providers from divulging the contents of those communications without the consent of the customer who originated the communication.[19] The ECPA sets forth some rules to protect privacy relative to the use of cellular telephones, radio paging, customer records, and satellite communication.

It also includes rules on workplace privacy in public or private employment. Under this law, "an employer cannot monitor employee telephone calls or electronic mail when employees have a reasonable expectation of privacy." It adds, however, that an employer is allowed to eavesdrop "if employees are notified in advance or if the employer has reason to believe the company's interests are in jeopardy."[20]

ECPA provisions, particularly those enhancing the power of government to wiretap under various conditions, have become a focus of debate about individual privacy issues and the right of the government to uphold national security. Overall, it gives the government more power than in the past to conduct electronic surveillance in various law enforcement and security situations.

The Communications Assistance for Law Enforcement Act of 1994 (CALEA) Recognizing the importance of and growing concern about cell phones, the U.S. Congress passed the Communications Assistance for Law Enforcement Act of 1994. **CALEA** was enacted to keep up with further advances in telecommunications technology. It has provisions relating to three primary techniques of lawfully authorized electronic surveillance devices: pen registers, trap-and-trace devices, and content interceptions. It supplements and amends provisions of Title III of the Omnibus Crime Control and Safe Streets Act of 1968 and ECPA.

CALEA's stated purpose is "to make clear a telecommunications carrier's duty to cooperate in the interception of communications for law enforcement purposes, and for other purposes." Significantly, its provisions require the cell phone industry to design its systems to comply with new standards that would make it easier for the FBI to monitor calls. The act also left it to the Federal Communications Commission (FCC) to determine specific standards related to the FBI's authority to monitor more than just cell phone conversations.

After years of negotiations, the FCC, in August 1999, announced rules that expanded the power of law enforcement agents to keep track of conversations and locate suspects. Among other things, the 1999 regulations authorize government agents (1) to determine the general location of a cell phone user by identifying which cellular antenna the phone company used to transmit the beginning and end of any call under surveillance, (2) to identify all callers on a conference call and monitor such conversations even after the target of the inquiry is no longer part of the conversation, and (3) to determine whether suspects are making use of such cell phone features as call forwarding and call waiting.[21]

Do users of cellular telephones have a "reasonable expectation of privacy," thereby enjoying protection under the Fourth Amendment? Although the Supreme Court has not resolved this issue, lower courts have said no. The rationale is that cell phones—"unlike standard wire phones and sophisticated cellular devices—transmit radio signals between a handset and a base unit that occasionally can be intercepted by other cordless telephones or even by short-wave radio sets."[22] In the words of one observer, "Those who seek privacy protection for their conversations on cordless telephones should remember that the airwaves are public." Despite the public nature of cell phone conversations, federal and local agents at present can monitor those calls only with a warrant.

In summary, Title III of the Omnibus Crime Control and Safe Streets Act of 1968, the ECPA (1986), and the CALEA (1994) are currently the three main laws governing electronic surveillance by law enforcement personnel. However, each year, Congress introduces laws seeking to meet the challenges of technological advances. Some state legislatures have also passed laws to supplement (but not to limit) federal laws. Electronic surveillance laws, however, are difficult to keep up with because they are detailed and complex due to the nature of the field they regulate. The discussions here merely represent the tip of the iceberg. The good news is that we now have laws to guide law enforcement personnel as they track crimes involving the use of electronic technology; the bad news is that these laws always lag behind technological changes, which criminals can instantly use, and they are too complex.

The Three Major Federal Laws on Electronic Surveillance

- *Title III of the Omnibus Crime Control and Safe Streets Act of 1968* forbids law enforcement officers from tapping or intercepting wire communications or using electronic devices to intercept private conversations, except if (1) there is a court order authorizing the wiretap and (2) consent is given by one of the parties.

- *The Electronic Communications and Privacy Act of 1986 (ECPA)* (1) amends the law of nonconsensual interception of wire communications and oral communications by a concealed microphone or electronic device, (2) specifies procedures for obtaining authorization to use pen registers, and (3) prescribes the procedure law enforcement officers must follow to obtain stored communications and records relating to communications services.

- *The Communications Assistance for Law Enforcement Act of 1994* governs the use of cellular telephones through regulations passed by the Federal Communications Commission. Regulations allow government agents to (1) determine the general location of a cell phone user by identifying which cellular antenna was used by the phone company to transmit the beginning and end of any call under surveillance, (2) identify all callers on a conference call and monitor such conversations even after the target of the inquiry is no longer part of the conversation, and (3) determine if suspects are making use of such cell phone features as call forwarding and call waiting.

Searches and Seizures of Computers

Searches and seizures of computers and gadgets associated with it (laptops, palm pilots, cellular phones that receive and print electronic messages) have increasingly become problems in policing because they are used by criminals more frequently. The good news is that the police now use computers to solve crimes; the bad news is that criminals also use computers to commit crimes. Two issues arise in computer searches: Are these searches constitutional or Fourth Amendment violations? and What procedures must law enforcement use to preserve the evidence seized? Computer search and seizure is still a young and developing area of law, and so decided cases and legal guidance are limited. This will doubtless change in the immediate future because legal issues are starting to reach the courts and are also being addressed through legislation that authorizes or limits what the police can do. But for now, the legal picture on computer searches is far from clear. In this section, we examine the legal requirements for searches and seizures of computers.

Legal Requirements In general, searches and seizures of computers have the same legal requirements as any other type of seizures, meaning there must be a warrant based on probable cause. One of the few available manuals on computer searches, titled *Computer Searches*, states that there are two requirements to issue a warrant to search a computer: (1) "probable cause to believe the data to be seized exists, is evidence of a crime, and is presently located at the place to be searched," and (2) "a reasonably detailed description of the place to be searched and the data to be seized."[23]

This same publication explains that probable cause based on direct evidence exists when officers have received reliable, firsthand knowledge that the suspect is now storing incriminating data on a certain computer or removable storage device. Such information may come from a reliable police informant, a citizen informant, or an undercover officer. In any event, it must be shown that the information is based on personal knowledge, not rumor, speculation, or some other dubious source.

Probable cause in computer searches Probable cause is likely established if the suspect is in possession of incriminating data, if the data are stored on a computer, and if the computer is likely to be found in the place to be searched.[24] The requirement for a description of the place to be searched is similar to that required for other types of warrants; the warrant must "contain a reasonably detailed description of the home or office that will be searched." Describing the hardware or software to be searched also needs particularity.

Computer Searches adds: "If the warrant is based on firsthand knowledge that the incriminating data [are] stored in a computer or removable storage device, this requirement can be satisfied rather easily because the source of the information will usually have seen the type of equipment on which the data [were] stored." If the data are stored in a removable storage device, such as a disk, the search becomes more difficult because the disk could be located anywhere near the computer or just about anywhere in the house. Lower court decisions have "developed a rule that the description of the hardware need only be as specific as is reasonably possible." In *United States v. Santarelli* (778 F.2d 609 [11th Cir. 1985]), the U.S. Court of Appeals for the Eleventh Circuit said:

United States v. Santarelli (11th Cir. 1985)

> There are circumstances in which the law enforcement officer applying for a warrant cannot give an exact description of the materials to be seized even though he has probable cause to believe that such materials exist and that they are being used in the commission of a crime. In these situations, we have upheld warrants when the description is as specific as the circumstances and the nature of the activity under investigation permit.

The same exceptions to the warrant requirement also apply to searches of computers. This means that police officers may search computers without a warrant if they have a valid consent, if exigent circumstances are present (as long as there is probable cause), in searches incident to a lawful arrest, and if items are in plain view. The scope of the search resulting from consent is covered by the same general rules concerning reasonable searches and seizures. In short, it is reasonableness.

Computers and reasonable expectation of privacy How is "reasonable expectation of privacy" determined for computers? A Justice Department publication says:

> To determine whether an individual has a reasonable expectation of privacy in information stored in a computer, it helps to treat the computer like a closed container such as a briefcase or file cabinet. The Fourth Amendment generally

prohibits law enforcement from accessing and viewing information stored in a computer without a warrant if it would be prohibited from opening a closed container and examining its contents in the same situation.[25]

There is no reasonable expectation of privacy, however, in the following cases: (1) when a person has made such information openly available, (2) when the contents of stolen computers are involved, (3) when the control of the computer has been given to a third party, and (4) when the owner loses control of the file.[26]

Electronic Devices that Do Not Intercept Communication

Some electronic devices gather information (such as a suspect's location) but do not necessarily intercept communication. These devices do not come under Title III coverage, nor are they governed strictly by the concept of a reasonable expectation of privacy under the Fourth Amendment. Pen registers and beepers are two examples. The constitutionality of the use of cameras to monitor traffic and other offenders has not been addressed by the Court.

Pen Registers The Fourth Amendment does not require that the police obtain judicial authorization before using **pen registers**, which record the numbers dialed from a particular telephone. In *Smith v. Maryland* (442 U.S. 735 [1979]), the Court held that not every use of an electronic device to gather information is governed by the Constitution. Pen registers gather information but do not necessarily intercept communication, so they do not come under Fourth Amendment protection.

Smith v. Maryland (1979)

The Court gave two reasons for this decision. First, it is doubtful that telephone users in general have any expectation of privacy regarding the numbers they dial, because they typically know that the telephone company has facilities for recording all phone numbers dialed and in fact records them routinely for various legitimate business and billing purposes. Second, even if the petitioner did harbor some subjective expectation of privacy, this expectation is not one that society is prepared to recognize as reasonable. When the petitioner voluntarily conveyed numerical information to the phone company and "exposed" that information to its equipment in the normal course of business, he assumed the risk that the company would reveal the information to the police.

United States v. New York Telephone Company (1977)

The Court has held that the police may obtain a court order to require the telephone company to assist in installing the pen register (*United States v. New York Telephone Company,* 434 U.S. 159 [1977]). Note, however, that ECPA (discussed earlier) requires law enforcement agencies to obtain a court order (instead of a wiretap order) and specifies the procedure to be followed for obtaining that order.

In sum, the Fourth Amendment does not require the police to obtain judicial authorization before using pen registers, but federal law requires it and sets the procedure for obtaining it.

Electronic Beepers The use of a beeper to keep track of a person traveling on public roads does not constitute a search, because a person has no reasonable expectation of privacy when traveling on a public thoroughfare (*United States v. Knotts,* 460 U.S. 276 [1983]). In a subsequent case that same year, the Court said that the warrantless monitoring of a beeper (which was installed by the police in an ether can and later delivered to the defendants), after the device had been unwittingly taken into a private residence, violated the Fourth Amendment rights of the residents and others. Nonetheless, the Court concluded that the evidence obtained could not be excluded, because there was ample probable cause, aside from the information that had been obtained as a result of the beeper, to justify the issuance of a warrant.

United States v. Knotts (1983)

In sum, beepers can be used legally to monitor the movements of a suspect in a public place but not in a private residence (*United States v. Karo,* 468 U.S. 705 [1984]).

United States v. Karo (1984)

Cameras to Monitor Traffic and Other Offenders Many cities in the United States today use automatic red-light ticketing technology for law enforcement. This technology involves photographing vehicle drivers (such as those beating traffic red lights or not paying toll fees) in some instances, and in others photographing only the license plate of the offending vehicle and then mailing tickets to violators.

This form of law enforcement surveillance has reportedly spread to nontraffic situations. As one news item put it: "Go for dinner or a drink in Tampa's most popular entertainment district, and cameras mounted above the congested streets may scan your face for a match against a photo database of runaways and felons." It adds, "If the cameras find a probable match, you could be explaining yourself to a police officer within minutes." More and more places across the country are experimenting with these technological tools for law enforcement purposes.[27]

The constitutionality of these forms of surveillance has not been addressed by the Court, but cases probably will reach the lower courts soon. The issue probably will be a possible violation of the right to privacy rather than a Fourth Amendment violation, although that will also likely be raised. How the Court will eventually decide the issue is hard to tell.

Kyllo v. United States (2001)

The case of *Kyllo v. United States* (533 U.S. 27 [2001]) holds that using a technological device to explore details of a home that would previously have been unknowable without physical intrusion is a form of search and is presumptively unreasonable without a warrant. *Kyllo,* however, involves exploring the details of a home, although from a public place; it does not address the use of a camera or similar device in a *public place* that does not involve any home intrusion. Unless declared otherwise by the courts, law enforcement use of cameras to monitor traffic and other offenders is presumed constitutional. This practice, however, may be prohibited by state law.

Summary

- The Fourth Amendment and the right to privacy are the two constitutional rights limiting the powers of the police in search and seizure cases.

- A "reasonable expectation of privacy" exists when these two requirements are present: (1) the person must have exhibited an actual expectation of privacy, and (2) the expectation must be one that society is prepared to recognize as reasonable.

- There are two kinds of seizures: with a warrant (the rule) and without a warrant (the exception).

- Some types of searches do not need a warrant. These are searches incident to lawful arrest, searches with consent, searches involving special needs beyond law enforcement, exigent circumstances, and administrative searches and inspections.

- Reasonableness governs the scope of a search. For practical purposes, it is best for officers to remember this rule: Do not search for an elephant in a matchbox.

- A search of an arrestee's body after an arrest is valid.

- When making an arrest, the police may search the area of immediate control.

- Searches by off-duty officers are Fourth Amendment searches.

- Electronic surveillance is governed primarily by three complex federal laws: Title III of the Omnibus Crime Control and Safe Streets Act of 1968 (the main law), the Electronic Communications and Privacy Act of 1986 (ECPA), and the Communications Assistance for Law Enforcement Act (CALEA).

- Searches and seizures of computers and related devices are governed by the Fourth Amendment, but case law and statutes are still evolving.

Review Questions and Hypothetical Cases

1. Assume you are talking on your cell phone with your parents while you are in the hallway of a university building in between classes. You are telling them confidential things you do not want anybody else to hear. Do you have a reasonable expectation of privacy? Justify your answer.

2. What are the requirements of a valid search warrant? Discuss each.

3. What four categories of items are subject to search and seizure?

4. "Police officers executing a search warrant must knock and announce before entry; otherwise the search is invalid." Is this true or false? Justify your answer.

5. Distinguish between administrative and law enforcement searches.

6. What does the phrase *area of immediate control* mean?

7. What is the "special needs beyond law enforcement" exception to the warrant and probable cause requirements? What is its common element? Give examples.

8. What is the "exigent circumstances" exception to the warrant requirement? Give examples.

9. What is the rule concerning searches of students by public school teachers and administrators? Does the same rule apply to school searches by police? Explain.

10. Explain what is meant by this statement: "The scope and manner of a search must be reasonable."

11. Officers X and Y were executing a search warrant for a shotgun allegedly used in a murder. They knocked at the house of the suspect and waited a full minute. When there was no response, they busted in and conducted a search but did not find the shotgun.

They were later sued for unlawful entry. Was it? Justify your answer.

12. C, a crack dealer, was shot by the police during a police raid of a crack house. The bullet hit C in the leg and stayed there. Assume you are a judge. The officers come to you seeking a warrant for the removal by surgery in a hospital of the bullet lodged in C's leg. Using the case of *Winston v. Lee* as an authority, will you issue the warrant? Why or why not?

13. John, a student, had a bad fight with his girlfriend, Gail. They agreed to split up. Prior to that, Gail was living with John in the apartment and had a key to the apartment. When John left for class, Gail immediately went to the police and reported that John was selling drugs in his apartment. Gail said she was John's girlfriend and was living in the apartment. Without obtaining a warrant, the police went to the apartment and asked Gail to open it. She did and the police found heroin. Was the seizure valid? State your reasons.

Key Terms

Go to the Criminal Procedure 7e website for flash cards that will help you master the definitions of these terms.

administrative searches, 250
anticipatory search warrant, 229
apparent authority principle, 243
area of immediate control, 239
CALEA, 265
Chimel rule, 239
contemporaneous search, 239
ECPA, 264
electronic surveillance, 257
exigent circumstances, 248

in loco parentis, 246
new concept of electronic surveillance, 259
no-knock searches, 234
old concept of electronic surveillance, 258
pen registers, 268
probable cause, 227
reasonable expectation of privacy, 224

right to privacy, 224
search, 225
search warrant, 226
seizure, 225
special needs beyond law enforcement exception, 242
Title III of the Omnibus Crime Control and Safe Streets Act of 1968, 261

Holdings of Key Cases

See Appendix C for information on how to find cases in this chapter on FindLaw.com.

Berger v. United States, **388 U.S. 41 (1967)** An electronic eavesdropping law that is too broad is unconstitutional.

Board of Education of Independent School District No. 92 of Pottawatomie County et al. v. Earls, **536 U.S. 822 (2002)** Random drug testing policy that applied to all middle and high school students participating in any extracurricular activity, not just athletics, was constitutional.

Bond v. United States, **529 U.S. 334 (2000)** A traveler's luggage in a bus is protected by the Fourth Amendment; officers may not physically manipulate (such as squeeze) the luggage to inspect it without a warrant or probable cause.

Breithaupt v. Abram, **352 U.S. 432 (1957)** A blood test performed by a skilled technician is not conduct that shocks the conscience, nor does this method of obtaining evidence offend a sense of justice.

Bumper v. North Carolina, **391 U.S. 543 (1968)** There is no valid consent to a search if permission is given as a result of police misrepresentation or deception.

Camara v. Municipal Court, **387 U.S. 523 (1967)** Health, safety, or other types of inspectors cannot enter private premises without the owner's consent or a search warrant.

Chimel v. California, 395 U.S. 752 (1969) Once a lawful arrest has been made, the police may search any area within the suspect's "immediate control," meaning the area from which the suspect may grab a weapon or destroy evidence.

City of West Covina v. Perkins et al., 525 U.S. 234 (1999) The police do not have to provide the owner of the seized property with notice of remedies specified by state law for the property's return and the information necessary to use those procedures.

Clinton v. Virginia, 377 U.S. 158 (1964) Evidence obtained by the police using an electronic device attached to the exterior wall of a building was illegally obtained.

Colbert v. Commonwealth, 2001 WL 174809 (Ky. 2001) This Kentucky state court held that a parent may consent to the search of a child's room in the parent's home even over the child's objection.

Colonnade Catering Corporation v. United States, 397 U.S. 72 (1970) The warrantless inspection of liquor businesses is valid.

Connally v. Georgia, 429 U.S. 245 (1977) A magistrate who receives a fee when issuing a warrant but not when denying one is not neutral and detached.

Coolidge v. New Hampshire, 403 U.S. 443 (1971) A state's chief investigator and prosecutor (state attorney general) is not neutral and detached, so any warrant issued by him or her is invalid.

Cupp v. Murphy, 412 U.S. 291 (1973) Without a warrant, the police may make a seizure of evidence that is likely to disappear before a warrant can be obtained.

Donovan v. Dewey, 452 U.S. 594 (1981) The warrantless inspection of strip-mining businesses is valid.

Flippo v. West Virginia, 528 U.S. 11 (1999) There is no crime scene exception to the search warrant requirement.

Florida v. Bostick, 501 U.S. 429 (1991) Consent is valid if officers ask for consent to search a bag and inform the person that he or she has a right to refuse consent.

Florida v. Jimeno, 500 U.S. 248 (1991) Consent for police to search a vehicle extends to closed containers found inside the vehicle, as long as it is objectively reasonable for the police to believe that the scope of the suspect's consent permitted them to open that container.

Georgia v. Randolph, No. 04–1067 (2006) A physically present co-occupant's [husband] stated refusal to permit entry into a home occupied by him and his estranged wife renders a warrantless entry and search unreasonable and invalid "as to him" despite the wife's consent to the search.

Goldstein v. United States, 316 U.S. 114 (1942) Wiretap evidence can be used against persons other than those whose conversations were overheard and whose Fourth Amendment rights were therefore violated.

Griffin v. Wisconsin, 483 U.S. 868 (1987) A state law or agency rule permitting probation officers to search probationers' homes without a warrant based on reasonable grounds rather than probable cause is a reasonable response to the special needs of the probation system and is therefore constitutional.

Griswold v. Connecticut, 381 U.S. 479 (1965) "Specific guarantees in the Bill of Rights have penumbras, formed by emanations from those guarantees that help give them life and substance."

Groh v. Ramirez, 540 U.S. 551 (2004) A search warrant that does not comply with the requirement that the warrant particularly describe the person or things to be seized is unconstitutional.

Illinois v. Caballes, 543 U.S. _____ (2005) A dog sniff conducted during a lawful traffic stop that reveals no information other than the location of an illegal substance that no individual has any right to possess does not violate the Fourth Amendment.

Illinois v. McArthur, 531 U.S. 326 (2001) Under emergency circumstances, and where there is a need to preserve evidence until the police can obtain a warrant, they may temporarily restrain a person's movements without violating his or her Fourth Amendment rights.

Illinois v. Rodriguez, 497 U.S. 117 (1990) The warrantless entry into private premises by police officers is valid if based on the consent of a third party whom the police, at the time of entry, reasonably believed to possess common authority over the premises, but who in fact did not have such authority.

Johnson v. United States, 333 U.S. 10 (1948)
Inferences leading to the issuance of a search warrant must be drawn by a neutral and detached magistrate, not by the officer engaged in the often competitive enterprise of ferreting out crime.

Katz v. United States, 389 U.S. 347 (1967) The prohibition against unreasonable search and seizure is not limited to homes, offices, buildings, or other enclosed places. It applies even in public places where a person has a "reasonable and justifiable expectation of privacy." The Fourth Amendment protects people, not places.

Kyllo v. United States, 533 U.S. 27 (2001) A technological device to explore details of a home that would previously have been unknowable without physical intrusion is a form of search and is presumptively unreasonable without a warrant.

Lo-Ji Sales, Inc., v. New York, 442 U.S. 319 (1979) A magistrate who participates in a search to determine its scope lacks the requisite neutrality and detachment.

Maryland v. Garrison, 480 U.S. 79 (1987) The validity of a warrant must be judged in light of the information available to the officers at the time they obtained the warrant. A warrant that is overbroad in describing the place to be searched is valid if based on a reasonable but mistaken belief at the time the warrant was issued.

Maryland v. Macon, 472 U.S. 463 (1985) Seizure occurs when there is some meaningful interference with an individual's possessory interest in the property seized.

Michigan v. Clifford, 464 U.S. 687 (1984) Administrative warrants and criminal search warrants are different; one difference is that administrative warrants do not require probable cause, the criminal search warrants do.

Michigan v. Summers, 452 U.S. 692 (1981) While a search is being conducted, the police may detain persons found on the premises that are to be searched.

Mincey v. Arizona, 437 U.S. 385 (1978) The fact that a place searched was the scene of a serious crime did not in itself justify a warrantless search in the absence of any "indication that the evidence would be lost, destroyed, or removed during the time required to obtain a search warrant and there is no suggestion that a warrant could not easily and conveniently have been obtained."

Muehler v. Mena, 544 U.S. _____ (2005) Detaining occupants of the premises in handcuffs and for a certain period of time while executing a search does not necessarily violate the Fourth Amendment prohibition against unreasonable searches and seizures.

Nardone v. United States, 302 U.S. 379 (1937) The Federal Communications Act forbids the Court as well as other persons from interpreting and disclosing telephone messages through wiretaps.

New Jersey v. T.L.O., 469 U.S. 325 (1985) Public school teachers and administrators do not need a warrant or probable cause before searching a student. What they need are merely reasonable grounds for suspecting that the search will turn up evidence that the student has violated or is violating either the law or the rules of the school.

New York v. Belton, 453 U.S. 454 (1981) When the police have made a lawful custodial arrest of the occupant of a car, they may, incident to that arrest, search the car's entire passenger compartment (front and back seats) and open any containers found in the compartment.

New York v. Burger, 482 U.S. 691 (1987) The warrantless inspection of an automobile junkyard is valid because the business is "closely regulated" by the government, and there is a substantial government interest involved in preventing car theft.

Olmstead v. United States, 277 U.S. 438 (1928) Wiretapping does not violate the Fourth Amendment unless there is "some trespass into a constitutionally protected area." This decision was overruled by the Court in a later case.

On Lee v. United States, 343 U.S. 747 (1952) There is no violation of a suspect's Fourth Amendment rights if his or her supposed friend allows the police to listen in on a telephone conversation; the evidence thereby obtained is admissible in court.

Pennsylvania Board of Probation and Parole v. Scott, **524 U.S. 357 (1998)** Evidence illegally obtained in violation of parolees' Fourth Amendment rights does not have to be excluded from a parole revocation hearing.

Piazzola v. Watkins, **442 F.2d 284 (5th Cir. 1971)** A university regulation allowing inspection of rooms does not authorize university authorities to give consent to police officers to enter dormitory rooms to search for evidence.

Richards v. Wisconsin, **520 U.S. 385 (1997)** A blanket exception (issued by a judge) to the knock-and-announce rule in felony drug-dealing cases is not allowed.

Rochin v. California, **342 U.S. 165 (1952)** Police restraining a suspect while a heroin capsule was removed from his stomach by a stomach pump shocks the conscience and therefore violates the suspect's right to due process.

Schmerber v. California, **384 U.S. 757 (1966)** The police may, without a search warrant and by force if necessary, take a blood sample from a person arrested for drunk driving, as long as the setting and procedures are reasonable (as when the blood is drawn by a doctor in a hospital).

Schneckloth v. Bustamonte, **412 U.S. 218 (1973)** There is no need for an officer to prove in court that the person giving consent knew, when the consent was given, that he or she had a right to refuse consent.

See v. City of Seattle, **387 U.S. 541 (1967)** Administrative entry without consent into the portions of commercial premises that are not open to the public may be compelled through prosecution or physical force only within the framework of a warrant procedure (*http://laws.findlaw.com/us/387/541.html*).

Silverman v. United States, **365 U.S. 505 (1961)** Driving a "spike mike" into a building wall to allow police to overhear conversations within the building without a warrant violated the Fourth Amendment.

Smith v. Maryland, **442 U.S. 735 (1979)** Not every use of an electronic device to gather information is governed by the Constitution.

State v. Kinderman, **271 Minn. 405 (1965)** A father's consent to the search of his son's room even though the son was 22 years old is valid.

State v. Wells, **539 So.2d 464 (Sup. Ct. Fla. 1989)** Consent to search a car does not authorize police officers to pry open a locked briefcase found in the car's trunk.

Stoner v. California, **376 U.S. 483 (1964)** A landlord cannot give valid consent to search property that he or she has rented to another person, nor can a hotel clerk give valid consent to the search of a guest's room.

Thornton v. United States, **541 U.S. 615 (2004)** Officers may search the passenger compartment of a vehicle after a lawful arrest even if the suspect was not in the vehicle when arrested.

United States v. Banks, **540 U.S. 31 (2003)** After knocking and announcing their presence and intention to search, 15 to 20 seconds is sufficient time for officers to wait before forcing entry into a home to execute a search warrant for drugs.

United States v. Bell, **464 F.2d 667 (1972)** "When the risk is the jeopardy to hundreds of human lives and millions of dollars of property inherent in the pirating or blowing up of a large airplane, that danger alone meets the test of reasonableness, so long as the search is conducted in good faith for the purpose of preventing hijacking or like damage and with reasonable scope and the passenger has been given advance notice of his liability to such a search so that he can avoid it by choosing not to travel by air."

United States v. Biswell, **406 U.S. 311 (1972)** The warrantless inspection of a weapons dealer by a federal agent is valid because the dealer had chosen to engage in a business that is inherently subject to heavy federal licensing regulation, and such regulation could be enforced only by the government's making unannounced and frequent visits.

United States v. Block, **188 F.2d 1019 (D.C. Cir. 1951)** An employer cannot give valid consent to a search if the property is under the exclusive use and control of the employee.

United States v. Chadwick, **433 U.S. 1 (1977)** A search that is remote in time and place from the arrest is not contemporaneous and is therefore invalid. In this case, the officers opened and searched a footlocker without a warrant one hour after the arrest.

United States v. D'Amico, 408 F.2d 331 (2nd Cir. 1969) The clipping by an officer of a few strands of hair from a suspect's head is so minor an imposition that the suspect suffered no true humiliation or affront to his dignity, so a search warrant was not required to justify the officer's act.

United States v. Davis, 482 F.2d 893 (9th Cir. 1973) A preboarding screening of all passengers and carry-on articles, sufficient in scope to detect the presence of weapons or explosives, is reasonable to meet the administrative needs (of discovering weapons and preventing hijacking) that justify it.

United States v. Edwards, 415 U.S. 800 (1974) A clothing search of a suspect arrested and jailed late at night that was not conducted until the following morning was justified because substitute clothing was not available for the suspect's use at the time of booking.

United States v. Grubbs, 547 U.S._____(2006) Anticipatory search warrants are valid as long as there is probable cause at the time the warrant is issued.

United States v. Impink, 728 F.2d 1228 (9th Cir. 1984) In general, a lessor cannot validly consent to the search of leased premises.

United States v. Karo, 468 U.S. 705 (1984) The warrantless monitoring of a beeper after the device has been unwittingly taken into a private residence violates the Fourth Amendment rights of the residents and others.

United States v. Kelly, 551 F.2d 760 (8th Cir. 1977) Consent of an apartment manager to the warrantless search of an apartment building's common areas, over which the landlord has joint access or control, is valid.

United States v. Knights, 534 U.S. 112 (2001) A warrantless search by a police officer of a probationer's apartment supported by reasonable suspicion and authorized by a condition of probation is valid under the Fourth Amendment.

United States v. Knotts, 460 U.S. 276 (1983) The use of a beeper to monitor the whereabouts of a person traveling in a car on public highways does not turn the surveillance into a search. Such monitoring falls under the plain view

doctrine and therefore does not require a warrant.

United States v. Leon, 468 U.S. 897 (1984) Evidence obtained by the police based on a search warrant that is later found to be without probable cause (stale information and failure to establish credibility of an informant) is admissible in court because the mistake was committed by a magistrate, not by the police.

United States v. Morales, 861 F.2d 396 (3rd Cir. 1988) The driver of a vehicle has the authority to consent to the search of a vehicle, including the trunk, glove compartment, and other areas.

United States v. New York Telephone Company, 434 U.S. 159 (1977) The police may obtain a court order to require the telephone company to assist in installing a pen register device.

United States v. Osage, 235 F.3d 518 (10th Cir. 2000) Consent to search does not include consent to destroy the container being searched.

United States v. Owens, 848 F.2d 462 (4th Cir. 1988) The execution of a warrant for an apartment different from the one named in the warrant was valid because there were only two apartments on the floor, one of which was vacant. Moreover, the correct apartment was not readily ascertainable, and the mistake was made in good faith.

United States v. Place, 462 U.S. 696 (1983) There is no search within the meaning of the Fourth Amendment if the police use narcotics detection dogs to smell closed containers for drugs, as long as the police are on the premises legally. There is no need for a search warrant or for probable cause to conduct dog sniffs.

United States v. Ramirez, 523 U.S. 65 (1998) The knock-and-announce rule does not set a higher standard for unannounced entries, even if that entry involves property damage.

United States v. Ricciardelli, 998 F.2d 8 (1st Cir. 1993) In anticipatory warrants, the issuing judge must be sure that the discretion of government agents is narrowed in two ways: (1) that the event that triggered the warrant is ascertainable and preordained, and (2) the item sought must be on a sure and irreversible course to its destination.

United States v. Robinson, 414 U.S. 218 (1973) The police may conduct a body search of the arrestee after a full custodial arrest even if the officers do not fear for their safety or believe that they will find evidence of the crime.

United States v. Santarelli, **778 F.2d 609 (11th Cir. 1985)** There are situations when warrants have been upheld despite the absence of the exact description of the materials to be seized if the description is as specific as the circumstances and the nature of the activity under investigation permit.

United States v. Shaibu, **920 F.2d 1423 (9th Cir. 1990)** There is no valid consent when a resident opens his door, steps into the hallway, listens to the officers identify themselves and explain the purpose of their visit, and then retreats wordlessly back into the apartment without closing the door. The government in this case failed to meet its heavy burden of proving consent by merely showing that the defendant left his door open.

United States v. Sullivan, **625 F.2d 9 (4th Cir. 1980)** It is not a search within the protection of the Fourth Amendment for a dog to sniff bags handled by an airline. There can be no reasonable expectation of privacy when any passenger's bags may be subjected to close scrutiny for the protection of public safety.

Vale v. Louisiana, **399 U.S. 30 (1970)** A warrantless search may be justified if there are reasonable grounds to believe that delaying the search until the warrant is obtained would endanger the physical safety of the officer or would allow the destruction or removal of the evidence.

Vernonia School District v. Acton, **515 U.S. 646 (1995)** Drug testing high school student athletes did not require individualized suspicion, and random drug testing is constitutional.

Warden v. Hayden, **387 U.S. 294 (1967)** The police may make a warrantless search and seizure when they are in "hot pursuit" of a dangerous suspect. The scope of such a search may be as extensive as is reasonably necessary to prevent the suspect from resisting or escaping.

Welsh v. Wisconsin, **466 U.S. 740 (1984)** The Fourth Amendment prohibits the police from making a warrantless nighttime entry into a suspect's house to arrest him or her for drunken driving if the offense is a misdemeanor for which state law does not allow any jail sentence.

Wilson v. Arkansas, **514 U.S. 927 (1995)** Although knock and announce is part of the requirement of reasonableness in searches and seizures, it is not a rigid rule and is subject to exceptions based on law enforcement interests.

Winston v. Lee, **470 U.S. 753 (1985)** Surgery to remove a bullet from a suspect for use as evidence would involve such severe intrusion into the suspect's privacy and security that it would violate the Fourth Amendment; it can be allowed only if the state establishes a compelling need.

Ybarra v. Illinois, **444 U.S. 85 (1979)** A search warrant for a bar and its bartender does not authorize body searches of all bar patrons.

Zurcher v. Stanford Daily, **436 U.S. 547 (1978)** Searches of property belonging to persons not suspected of a crime are permissible as long as probable cause exists to believe that evidence of someone's guilt or other items subject to seizure will be found.

 ## You Be the Judge . . .

In the United States Court of Appeals for the Fifth Circuit

In East Baton Rouge, Louisiana, Sheriff's Deputies responded to a confidential informant's telephone tip: the tipster said Gould, a known felon with a reputation for violence, intended to kill two local judges and to destroy telephone company equipment. The informant had some credibility, because he was known to be Gould's employee. They responded the same day they received the tip. They did not go to a magistrate for either an arrest or search warrant, because they wanted to investigate further by confronting Gould at his home and asking him some questions.

When they arrived at Gould's trailer, the deputies were met at the door by Cabral, another resident of the trailer. Cabral told them Gould was asleep in his bedroom and invited them in to talk to Gould. Cabral pointed out Gould's bedroom to the deputies. They cautiously approached the open door of the room, but they did not see Gould in the bedroom. Concerned he was hiding, they looked under the bed and in both bedroom closets for him. Gould was not to be found, but when they opened one closet door they saw it contained three rifles. (Firearms are illegal for a convicted felon to possess.)

The deputies rushed outside to search for Gould. They found Gould hiding in the woods outside his trailer and asked him about the rifles. He said he was holding them for a female friend of his. The deputies placed Gould under arrest for possession of a firearm as a convicted felon. He then signed a consent to search form, giving the deputies permission to search for the rifles, which they promptly seized.

How will you decide this legal issue? Could the deputies, without probable cause or warrants, legally conduct a "protective sweep" of Gould's room before they arrested him?

The Court's decision The U.S. Court of Appeals for the Fifth Circuit, sitting en banc, decided that the "protective sweep" was legal. In doing this, the Court overturned the trial court and a panel of the Court of Appeals. The officers had a reasonable articulable suspicion that the area swept held someone dangerous to those on the scene. They had reason to believe Gould was dangerous and that he had just been in his bedroom. The sweep was not a full search, but a cursory inspection of the places that a person could hide in Gould's room (under the bed and in the closets). The sweep lasted no longer than necessary to check if Gould was there. *U.S. v. Gould,* 326 F.3d 651 (5th Cir. 4/12/2004).

In the United States Court of Appeals for the Second Circuit

In the Bronx, New York, eight law enforcement agents, from the U.S. Secret Service, the U.S. Postal Inspection Service, and the N.Y.P.D., converged on the apartment of a person they had determined was making fraudulent purchases of computer parts with a stolen credit card. Though there had been time to apply for either a search or an arrest warrant, neither had been sought by any of the law enforcement involved. They decided to conduct a controlled delivery of the computer parts, arresting whoever claimed to be the fraudulent addressee.

Postal Inspector Esannason, dressed as a mail carrier, delivered the computer parts to the apartment where they were to be shipped, to a "Robert Heskey." Isiofia answered the door, and claimed he was "Heskey" and signed for the packages from Inspector Esannason, who gave the signal for the other agents to make the arrest. As two other agents approached, Isiofia backed into his apartment where they arrested and cuffed him. Special Agents McGee and Guida made a two-minute protective sweep of the apartment without their guns drawn. By this time there were seven officers in the apartment, and Isiofia was handcuffed to a chair. Special Agent McGee asked Isiofia his name, but had difficulty understanding him and had to get an identification card from Isiofia's briefcase.

The officers then completed the paperwork for the arrest while Isiofia remained there handcuffed in his apartment. Isiofia was yelled at by the agents, and threatened with deportment. While filling out this paperwork officers asked Isiofia a great deal of personal information, on everything from bank accounts, residences, and social security number to his relatives, children, and employment. Agents then asked for Isiofia's permission to search his computer, his home, and his car, which he granted by signing blank permission to search forms. The searches turned up fifteen social security cards and numerous other fraudulently obtained or created documents.

How will you decide this legal issue? Was the permission to search voluntarily given?

The Court's decision The U.S. Court of Appeals for the Second Circuit decided that these searches were not voluntary. Looking at the totality of the circumstances, there was too much coercion: Isiofia had at least some problem with the language, he was handcuffed, he was not informed of the charges against him nor the evidence sought by the government. The number of officers in the apartment, the length of their stay, and the tenor of their questioning all taken together make Isiofia's consent invalid. *U.S. v. Isiofia,* 370 F.3d 226 (2nd Cir. 2004).

In the Supreme Court of Montana

In Clancy, Montana, Sheriff's Deputy Gleich responded to a disturbing dispatch call. Stone ran a zoo in Clancy, called the Stone Cave Reptile/Amphibian Ranch Hatchery and Hospital, from his home. Stone had previously hired two local boys to help him care for his animals after school. Stone had "laid off" the two, claiming he could not afford to pay them, but had just hired them back. One of the boys had just returned to help with the animals after school when he was greeted by an appalling sight: animals were without food and water, some were dead, and some rabbits were feeding on the bodies of the dead rabbits in their cages. Upset, the boy called his father who rushed home from work. The father, saw that the situation was as morbid as his boy had described, and called the police.

No one from outside the property could have seen the macabre scene because Stone had high fences surrounding his property, posted with plenty of "No Trespassing" signs. The dispatch asked the boy's father to have him meet Deputy Gleich at the property, to show him where the animals were.

When Deputy Gleich arrived, he found Stone was not at home, but could see the starving animals as the boy had described them, including dogs, guinea pigs, and the cannibalistic rabbits.

On surveying the scene, Deputy Gleich immediately requested that his dispatcher send a veterinarian to assist the animals. Deputy Gleich met other officers at the property, and they went around wherever the boy showed them the cages to cut the locks on the cages so that the vet could get to the starving animals.

Stone, who was also on probation, was present during none of these activities. He was ultimately charged with several counts of felony animal cruelty.

How will you decide this legal issue? Should Deputy Gleich's entry onto the property without warrant or permission be justified by exigent circumstances, based on the danger and distress to the animals?

The Court's decision The Supreme Court for the State of Montana decided that the entry onto the property was justified by exigent circumstances. Exigent circumstances require that some person is in danger, or that some evidence is being destroyed or removed. Neither of those cases applies here. No person was in danger, and the animals were going nowhere. The court, however, extended the legal doctrine of exigent circumstances to cover the peril of the animals. *State v. Stone,* 321 Mont 489 (2004).

Recommended Readings

Andrea G. Bough. Note. *Searches and seizures in schools: Should reasonable suspicion or probable cause apply to school resource/liaison officers?* UMKC Law Review 453–563 (1999).

Brian H. Chun. *The unclearly established rule against unreasonable searches and seizures.* 90 Journal of Law and Criminology 799–825 (2000).

Jennifer I. Cook. Note. *Discretionary warrantless searches and seizures and the Fourth Amendment: A need for clearer guidelines.* South Carolina Law Review 410, 440 (2001).

Craig S. Lerner. *The reasonableness of probable cause* [Zacarias Moussaoui's laptop: "the search that wasn't"]. 81 Texas Law Review 951–1029 (2003).

Tracey Maclin. *"Voluntary" interviews and airport searches of Middle Eastern men: The Fourth Amendment in a time of terror.* 73 Mississippi Law Journal 471–524 (2003).

Daniel L. Rotenberg. *On searches and seizures.* Creighton Law Review 323–346 (1995).

Notes

1. Wayne R. LaFave, Jerold H. Israel, and Nancy J. King, *Criminal Procedure,* 4th ed. (St. Paul, MN: Thomson/West, 2004), p. 161.
2. A. L. Dipietro, "Anticipatory Search Warrants," *FBI Law Enforcement Bulletin,* July 1990, p. 27.
3. John G. Miles, Jr., David B. Richardson, and Anthony E. Scudellari, *The Law Officer's Pocket Manual* (Washington, D.C.: Bureau of National Affairs, 1988–89), 9:27.
4. Lloyd L. Weinreb and James D. Whaley, *The Field Guide to Law Enforcement: 1999 Edition* (New York: Foundation Press, 1999), p. 24.
5. Michele G. Hermann, *Search and Seizure Checklists,* 3rd ed. (New York: Clark Boardman, 1983), pp. 192–193.
6. Steven L. Emanuel and Steven Knowles, *Emanuel Law Outlines: Criminal Procedure* (Larchmont, NY: Emanuel, 1995), p. 95.
7. Ibid., p. 101.
8. 125 ALR [American Law Reports] 5th 281ff.
9. Ibid.
10. Supra note 6, p. 166.
11. Supra note 7, p. 137.
12. Supra note 7, p. 204.
13. "Constitutional Limitations on the Use of Canines to Detect Evidence of Crime," *Fordham Law Review* 973 (1976), p. 44.
14. Supra note 3, 10:4–6.
15. *Houston Chronicle,* July 31, 1999, p. A6.
16. Steven L. Emanuel and Steven Knowles, *Emanuel Law Outlines: Criminal Procedure* (Larchmont, NY: Emanuel, 1998–99), p. 172.
17. Robert A. Fiatal, "The Electronic Communications (and) Privacy Act: Addressing Today's Technology" (Part I), *FBI Law Enforcement Bulletin,* February 1988, pp. 25–30; Robert A. Fiatal, "The Electronic Communications (and) Privacy Act: Addressing Today's Technology" (Part II), *FBI Law Enforcement Bulletin,* March 1988, pp. 26–30; Robert A. Fiatal, "The Electronic Communications (and) Privacy Act: Addressing Today's Technology" (Part III), *FBI Law Enforcement Bulletin,* April 1988, pp. 24–30.
18. Ibid., Part I, p. 25.
19. "Electronic Communication Privacy Act (ECPA)," *http://www.stanford.edu/group/privacyproject/legalEcpa.html.*
20. Ibid.
21. *Time Magazine,* February 12, 2000, p. 8.
22. Ibid.
23. *Computer Searches,* by the District Attorney's Office in Alameda County, California, *http://www.acgov.org/da/pov/documents/web.htm.*
24. Ibid.
25. *Searching and Seizing Computers and Obtaining Electronic Evidence in Criminal Investigations.* Computer Crimes and Intellectual Property Section, Criminal Division U.S. Department of Justice, July 2002.
26. Ibid.
27. *Houston Chronicle,* September 22, 1996, p. A15.

Chapter **8**

Motor Vehicle Stops, Searches, and Inventories

What You Will Learn

- Vehicle stops and searches are governed by different rules and should be treated separately.

- An officer can legally do many things after a vehicle stop.

- Racial profiling is unconstitutional, but some legal issues are unresolved.

- *Carroll v. United States* (1925) was the first major case involving motor vehicles, but it was a search—and not a stop—case.

- Warrantless searches of motor vehicles are valid, but probable cause is required.

- The power of the police to search a vehicle based on probable cause is extensive.

- Inventory searches of vehicles are valid but must follow departmental rules.

Introduction

Vehicle Stops

Vehicle Searches

Vehicle Inventory Searches

The Importance of State Laws and Departmental Policies

CASE BRIEFS

Carroll v. United States (1925)
United States v. Ross (1982)

Introduction

Stops and searches of motor vehicles are an important and highly visible part of routine police patrol work. They will continue to require the attention of the courts in the coming years as the number of motor vehicles on the road grows and vehicle gadgets become more sophisticated. Questions about what the police can and cannot do in motor vehicle cases are

---

The Top 5 Important Cases in Vehicle Stops, Searches, and Inventories

***Carroll v. United States* (1925)** The search of an automobile does not require a warrant because the vehicle can be moved quickly out of the locality or jurisdiction in which the warrant must be sought.

***New York v. Belton* (1981)** Once a driver has been arrested, the police may conduct a warrantless search of the passenger compartment of the automobile. The police may examine the contents of any container found within the passenger compartment as long as they may reasonably believe it might contain something that could pose a danger to the officer or hold evidence of the offense for which the suspect has been arrested.

***United States v. Ross* (1982)** If the police legitimately stop a car and have probable cause to believe that it contains contraband, they can conduct a warrantless search of the car. Every part of the vehicle in which the contraband might be stored may be inspected, including the trunk and all receptacles and packages that could possibly contain the object of the search.

***Whren v. United States* (1996)** The temporary detention of a motorist that is supported by probable cause that the motorist has committed a traffic violation is valid even if the actual motivation of the law enforcement officer is to determine if the motorist has drugs.

***Atwater v. City of Lago Vista* (2001)** The Fourth Amendment allows a warrantless arrest for a minor criminal offense that is punishable only by a fine, such as a misdemeanor seat belt violation.

■ Table 8.1 Summary of the Rules for Vehicle Stops, Searches, and Inventories

	Need a Warrant?	Need Probable Cause?
To stop a vehicle	No	No, but need reasonable or articulable suspicion of involvement in criminal activity
To search a vehicle	No	Yes
To inventory a vehicle	No	No, but must be guided by department policy

addressed by the Court each year, and this trend will continue as the case law on motor vehicles becomes more extensive and refined. It is important that the police be familiar with the laws on motor vehicle stops and searches because a large percentage of arrests and searches are either made in or related to motor vehicles, and a lot of day-to-day police work involves motor vehicles.

The law on vehicle stops and searches is best understood if discussed under three general headings: vehicle stops, vehicle searches, and vehicle inventories. Each is governed by different Fourth Amendment and other legal rules, so we will discuss them separately.

Carroll v. United States (1925)

See Appendix C for information on how to find cases in this chapter on FindLaw.com.

Carroll v. United States (267 U.S. 132 [1925]), decided in 1925, is arguably the most important case involving motor vehicles ever to be decided by the Court. It is, however, a *vehicle search* rather than a *vehicle stop* case and is therefore discussed in this chapter under vehicle searches. We begin with a discussion on vehicle stops, which often precede vehicle searches.

Table 8.1 summarizes the rules for vehicle stops, searches, and inventories—the three types of vehicle searches and seizures discussed in this chapter. The rest of the chapter simply expands on this table. Understanding the rest of the chapter is easier if you understand and learn this table.

Vehicle Stops

Delaware v. Prouse (1979)

A form of seizure occurs every time a motor vehicle is stopped, so the Fourth Amendment prohibition against unreasonable searches and seizures applies. In *Delaware v. Prouse* (440 U.S. 648 [1979]), the Court said, "The Fourth and Fourteenth Amendments are implicated in this case because stopping an automobile and detaining its occupants constitute a 'seizure' within the meaning of those Amendments, even though the purpose of the stop is limited and the resulting detention quite brief." A **stop** is the brief detention of a person when the police officer has reasonable suspicion, in light of his or her experience, that criminal activity is about to take place. The courts have long held that motor vehicles, because of their mobility, should be governed by a different set of Fourth Amendment rules. This was emphasized by the Court in

Illinois v. Lidster (2004)

Illinois v. Lidster (540 U.S. 419[2004]) when it stated that the "Fourth Amendment does not treat a motorist's car as his castle."

In this section, we will examine the rules that govern vehicle stops. The most basic rule is that law enforcement officers must have reasonable suspicion that the occupants are involved in criminal activity before effecting a stop. Other rules include (1) roadblocks are an exception to the reasonable suspicion rule; (2) officers are limited in what they can do after making a stop; (3) traffic stops that are only pretexts for vehicle searches are valid; (4) vehicle stops based solely on racial profiling are not valid; (5) consensual searches do not require that detainees be advised that they are free to leave; (6) arresting occupants for nonjailable offenses is valid; and (7) passengers can be arrested during a stop. We will look at each of these rules and the cases that led to them.

The General Rule for Stops: Reasonable Suspicion of Criminal Activity Required

Although a vehicle stop is a form of seizure, the motorist is not fully protected by the Fourth Amendment. Because the vehicle stop is less intrusive, neither a warrant nor probable cause is required. Nonetheless, *some type of justification is necessary for a valid stop;* a stop by a police officer for no reason or without any justification is illegal. In *United States v. Cortez* (449 U.S. 411 [1981]), the Court ruled that there must be at least a reasonable suspicion to justify an investigatory stop of a motor vehicle in connection with possible involvement in criminal activity.

In *Cortez,* the Court stated:

> Based upon that whole picture, the detaining officers must have a particularized and objective basis for suspecting the particular person stopped of criminal activity. . . . First, the assessment must be based upon all of the circumstances. The analysis proceeds with various objective observations, information from police reports, if such are available, and consideration of the modes or patterns of operation and certain kinds of lawbreakers. . . . The second element contained in the idea that an assessment of the whole picture must yield a particularized suspicion is the concept that the process just described must raise a suspicion that the particular individual being stopped is engaged in wrongdoing.

A lower court has also said, "The police do not have an unrestricted right to stop people, either pedestrians or drivers. The 'good faith' of the police is not enough, nor is an inarticulate hunch. They must have an articulable suspicion of wrongdoing, done or in prospect" (*United States v. Montgomery,* 561 F.2d 875 [1977]).[1]

These cases hold that the warrantless exception in motor vehicle stop cases does not give the police unlimited authority to stop vehicles. Some justification is necessary, but it does not have to be probable cause. Some courts say *reasonable suspicion* is needed; other courts use the term *articulable suspicion.* Whatever term a jurisdiction uses, the level of certainty necessary for the police to be able to stop a vehicle is about the same—lower than probable cause but higher than mere suspicion. It is the same level of certainty needed in stop and frisk cases (discussed in Chapter 5).

In *United States v. Arvizu* (534 U.S. 266 [2001]), the Court held that a reasonable suspicion determination in automobile stop cases is based on the totality

United States v. Cortez (1981)

United States v. Montgomery (1977)

United States v. Arvizu (2001)

of the circumstances rather than each act viewed separately. In this case, the U.S. Border Patrol operated a checkpoint in an isolated area in Arizona. Some roads circumvented this checkpoint and were routinely used by smugglers to avoid detection. Because of this, sensors were placed along those roads to detect vehicular traffic.

An officer responded when the sensor was activated. He followed the suspect vehicle for several miles and observed several suspicious behaviors, including the following: the time the vehicle was on the road coincided with a shift change for roving patrols in the area; the roads the vehicle took were remote and not well suited for the vehicle type; the vehicle slowed dramatically upon first observing the officer; the driver of the vehicle would not look at the officer when passing; the children in the vehicle seemed to have their feet propped up on some cargo; the children waived mechanically at the officers as if being instructed; and the vehicle made turns that would allow it to completely avoid the checkpoint. Based on these observations, the officer stopped the vehicle. After obtaining consent from Arvizu, the officer searched the vehicle and found drugs. Convicted of drug possession, Arvizu appealed, claiming that none of these factors, taken individually, constituted reasonable suspicion.

The Court disagreed, saying that "in making reasonable suspicion determinations, reviewing courts must look at the totality of the circumstances of each case to see whether the detaining officer has a particularized and objective basis for suspecting legal wrongdoing." This case is significant in vehicle stop cases because (1) it makes it easier for officers to establish reasonable suspicion because they can rely on a number of factors that individually may not constitute reasonable suspicion, and (2) the Court said that, in determining reasonable suspicion, the process "allows officers to draw on their own experiences and specialized training to make inferences from and deductions about the cumulative information available."

Roadblocks: An Exception to the "Reasonable Suspicion" Requirement

Roadblocks are an exception to the rule that vehicle stops must be justified by suspicion of the occupant's involvement in criminal activity. Roadblocks are used by police for a variety of purposes, so there is always some kind of justification for the action. The difference is that the justification is general rather than specific to the individual being stopped. Five types of roadblocks are discussed here, four of which have been upheld as constitutional by the courts even without individualized suspicion of criminal activity. These are

- Roadblocks to combat drunk driving (constitutional)
- Roadblocks to control the flow of illegal aliens (constitutional)
- Roadblocks to check for a driver's license and vehicle registration (constitutional)
- Roadblocks to obtain specific information motorist (constitutional)
- Roadblocks for general law enforcement purposes (unconstitutional)

Michigan Department of State Police v. Sitz (1990)

Roadblocks to Control Drunk Driving In *Michigan Department of State Police v. Sitz* (496 U.S. 444 [1990]), the Court held that **sobriety checkpoints**, a form of roadblock in which the police stop every vehicle for the purpose of controlling drunk driving, do not violate the Fourth Amendment protection against unreasonable searches and seizures and are therefore constitutional.

In the *Sitz* case, the Michigan State Police Department established a highway checkpoint program. Pursuant to established guidelines, checkpoints were to be set up at selected sites along state roads. All vehicles passing through the checkpoint were to be stopped and their drivers checked for signs of intoxication. If officers suspected the driver was intoxicated, they were to pull the vehicle to the side of the road and conduct further tests; all other drivers would be permitted to resume their journeys. During the only operation of the checkpoint, which lasted about an hour and fifteen minutes, they checked 126 vehicles, with an average delay of twenty-five seconds. Officers arrested two individuals for DWI, including Sitz. He challenged these guidelines and the Michigan sobriety checkpoint practice in the courts as violating the Fourth Amendment.

The Supreme Court rejected the challenge, saying that sobriety checkpoints are a form of seizure, but one that is reasonable because the "measure of intrusion on motorists stopped briefly at sobriety checkpoints is slight." The *Sitz* case is significant, because for a long time lower courts had given conflicting decisions about the constitutionality of sobriety checkpoints. Courts in twenty-one states had upheld them, whereas courts in twelve states had declared them unconstitutional. However, by a 6-to-3 vote, the Supreme Court ruled that the police may establish highway checkpoints in an effort to catch drunk drivers.

It is important to note that the *Sitz* case does not allow the police to make random stops; it authorizes well-conceived and carefully structured sobriety checkpoints, such as Michigan's, that leave virtually no discretion to the officers operating the checkpoint. This eliminates the danger of arbitrariness.

In *Sitz,* the Court adopted the balancing test applied in *Delaware v. Prouse* (440 U.S. 647 [1979]), which focused on three factors to determine the constitutionality of what the police do in these cases: (1) the gravity of the public concerns served by the seizure, (2) the degree to which the seizure advances the public interest, and (3) the severity of the interference with individual liberty. Although sobriety checkpoints are constitutional, they may be prohibited by departmental policy or state law.

Roadblocks to Control the Flow of Illegal Aliens

Stops in the form of roadblocks for brief questioning, routinely conducted at permanent checkpoints, are consistent with the Fourth Amendment, so it is not necessary to obtain a warrant before setting up a checkpoint (*United States v. Martinez-Fuerte,* 428 U.S. 543 [1976]).

United States v. Martinez-Fuerte (1976) involved a "fixed checkpoint" set up not at the border but in the interior, where all vehicles were stopped. After the stop, certain motorists were referred to a "secondary inspection area" where they could be questioned and their vehicles searched if it seemed justified. The Court permitted such "suspicionless" stops in the interest of controlling the flow of illegal aliens.

Stops to Check a Driver's License and Vehicle Registration

Establishing a roadblock to check driver's licenses and vehicle registrations is legitimate. In the process, if the officers see evidence of other crimes, they are not required to close their eyes; they have the right to take reasonable investigative steps (*United States v. Prichard,*

645 F.2d 854 [1981]). However, police officers may not stop a single vehicle for the sole purpose of checking the driver's license and vehicle registration. To do that, the officers must reasonably believe that the motorist has violated a traffic law. Mere suspicion is not enough (*Delaware v. Prouse,* 440 U.S. 648 [1979]).

Roadblocks to Obtain Information from Motorists about a Hit-and-Run Accident

The Court held in *Illinois v. Lidster* (540 U.S. 419 [2004]) that police checkpoints set up to obtain information from motorists about a hit-and-run accident are valid under the Fourth Amendment.

In *Lidster,* the police in Lombard, Illinois, set up a highway checkpoint to obtain information from motorists about a hit-and-run accident. The checkpoint was set up at about the same time of night and at the same location as the hit-and-run accident that had happened about one week earlier. Police officers stopped every vehicle for 10–15 seconds, asked the occupants if they had seen anything related to the accident, and handed them a flyer asking for their assistance. As Robert Lidster approached the checkpoint, his van swerved, almost hitting an officer. The officer smelled alcohol on Lidster's breath, so he directed him to a side street where another officer administered a sobriety test, which Lidster failed. They arrested him. Lidster was later convicted in state court of driving under the influence of alcohol. He appealed, saying that the police checkpoint violated his Fourth Amendment right.

The Court rejected his challenge, saying that the checkpoint stop was constitutional, citing three reasons: (1) "the relevant public concern was grave," (2) "the stop advanced this grave public concern to a significant degree," and (3) "more importantly, the stops interfered only minimally with liberty of the sort the Fourth Amendment seeks to protect."

Roadblocks to Detect Evidence of Criminal Wrongdoing Although vehicle roadblocks or checkpoints are constitutional for some purposes, they are unconstitutional if used to detect evidence of ordinary criminal wrongdoing (*Indianapolis v. Edmond*, 531 U.S. 32 [2000]).

Indianapolis v. Edmond (2000)

In *Indianapolis v. Edmond* (2000), Indianapolis, Indiana, police set up a program of vehicle checkpoints to detect illegal drugs. The roadblocks were operated during daylight hours and clearly marked by signs. The locations of the roadblock were planned well in advance, and a predetermined number of vehicles were to be stopped. After the stop, an officer required the driver to produce a driver's license and registration. Only if the officer developed particularized suspicion of illegality was the driver detained. The total time of the stop averaged less than five minutes. Edmond and others were stopped at the checkpoints. They later brought suit, claiming the stops violated the Fourth Amendment because they lacked individualized reasonable suspicion.

On appeal, the Court agreed, saying that the roadblocks they had approved in prior cases were for purposes of controlling drunk driving, controlling the flow of illegal aliens, and checking driver's licenses and vehicle registrations. The difference between those cases and *Edmond* was that in *Edmond* the purpose was to detect criminal wrongdoing, in particular the flow of drugs. The Court acknowledged that the drug problem is severe, but it does not justify setting up roadblocks. The Court concluded by saying: "We have never approved a checkpoint program whose primary purpose was to detect evidence of ordinary criminal wrongdoing. Rather, our checkpoint cases have recognized only limited exceptions to the general rule that a seizure must be accompanied by some measure of individualized suspicion."

In summary, these cases on roadblocks as an exception to the need for reasonable suspicion in motor vehicle cases say this: Properly designed roadblocks for specific purposes are valid, but roadblocks for general crime control are unconstitutional. If the purpose is crime control (such as to detect drugs), there must be individualized suspicion before a police officer can stop motor vehicles.

What an Officer May Do after a Vehicle Stop

Stopping the vehicle is not an end in itself; it is only a means to determine whether a criminal activity has occurred or is about to occur. What follows after a stop is important for both the officer's protection and the admissibility of any seized evidence. There are many things an officer may do after a valid stop. Our discussion is classified into what the officer can do based on the following considerations: (1) general law enforcement authority, (2) reasonable suspicion, (3) probable cause, and (4) consent.

Based on General Law Enforcement Authority

In general, police officers may do the following after a valid stop of a vehicle (but subject to limitations set by state law or departmental policy): order the driver and passengers out of the car; ask to see the driver's license; question the vehicle's occupants; examine the vehicle's VIN; and confiscate illegal items in plain view.

Order the driver to get out of the vehicle Once a vehicle is lawfully stopped for a traffic violation, the officer may order the driver to get out, even without suspecting criminal activity. If the officer then reasonably believes that the driver may be armed and dangerous, he or she may conduct a limited protective frisk for a weapon that might endanger his or her personal safety (*Pennsylvania v. Mimms,* 434 U.S. 106 [1977]).

Pennsylvania v. Mimms **(1977)**

For example, suppose X is stopped by the police for running a red light. X may be asked to get out of the car. If, after X complies, the officer reasonably believes that X may be armed and dangerous, then X may be frisked. If an illegal weapon is found during the frisk, then X may be arrested. Conversely, if the officer does not believe that the driver may be armed and dangerous, all the officer can do is ask the driver to get out of the car. If there is no belief that the driver is armed and dangerous, a subsequent frisk is illegal even if the initial traffic stop was legal.

Order passengers to get out of the vehicle The Court has long held that the driver of a car may be automatically required to get out of a car after a valid stop—whether or not the officer is concerned about personal safety. What was uncertain was whether that rule extended to vehicle passengers. But in *Maryland v. Wilson,* 519 U.S. 408 [1997]), the Court ruled that police officers may order passengers to get out of motor vehicles during traffic stops.

Maryland v. Wilson **(1997)**

HIGHLIGHT

Summary of U.S. Supreme Court Cases on the Constitutionality of Roadblocks

United States v. Martinez-Fuerte (1976) Stops for brief questioning that are routinely conducted at permanent checkpoints are constitutional.

Delaware v. Prouse (1979) Roadblocks may be set up for inspection purposes, provided the officer stops every car passing the checkpoint or has an articulable, neutral principle (such as stopping every fifth car) for justifying the stop.

Michigan Department of State Police v. Sitz (1990) Sobriety checkpoints in which the police stop every vehicle are constitutional.

Indianapolis v. Edmund (2000) Roadblocks to detect evidence of ordinary criminal wrongdoing are unconstitutional.

Illinois v. Lidster (2004) Police checkpoints set up to obtain information from motorists about a hit-and-run accident are constitutional.

HIGHLIGHT

Asking the Driver to Get Out of the Car

"We think this additional intrusion [referring to the officer's order for the driver to get out of the car] can only be described as de minimis. The driver is being asked to expose to view very little more of this person than is already exposed. The police have already lawfully decided that the driver shall be briefly detained; the only question is whether he shall spend that period sitting in the driver's seat of his car or standing along side of it. Not only is the insistence of the police on the latter choice not a 'serious intrusion upon the sanctity of the person,' but it hardly rises to the level of 'petty indignity.' . . . What is at most a mere inconvenience cannot prevail when balanced against legitimate concerns for the officer's safety."

SOURCE: *Pennsylvania v. Mimms*, 434 U.S. 106 (1977).

In *Wilson,* a state trooper stopped a motor vehicle clocked at 65 miles per hour where the posted limit was 55 miles per hour. During the pursuit, the trooper noticed three occupants in the car. As the trooper approached what turned out to be a rented car, the driver got out and met him halfway. He produced a valid driver's license but was trembling and appeared extremely nervous. The trooper also noticed that one of the passengers, Wilson, was sweating and appeared extremely nervous. The trooper ordered Wilson out of the car. As Wilson got out, crack cocaine fell to the ground. Arrested and charged with possession of cocaine, Wilson argued during his trial that ordering him out of the car constituted an unreasonable seizure.

The trial court and the state court of appeals agreed, but the Supreme Court reversed the decision, holding that the "danger to an officer from a traffic stop is likely to be greater when there are passengers in addition to the driver in the stopped car." It added that the government's "legitimate and weighty interest in protecting officers prevails against the minimal infringement on the liberties of both the car driver and the passengers." This decision provides a bright-line rule saying that an officer making a traffic stop may also order passengers to get out of the car pending completion of the stop.

Ask the driver to produce documents required by state law An officer has the authority, after a valid stop, to ask the driver to show a driver's license and other documents that state laws require. A number of states require that the driver produce the vehicle registration and proof of insurance in addition to a driver's license. The justification for this authorization is that operating a motor vehicle on public highways is a privilege rather than a right. Practically all states consider the refusal to produce the required documents a criminal offense, and the driver can be punished accordingly.[2]

Question the driver and passengers Once a valid stop has been made, the officer may question the driver and passengers without giving the *Miranda* warnings. The Court has said that the roadside questioning of a motorist pursuant to a routine traffic stop (provided it is not an arrest) does not constitute custodial interrogation and therefore does not require the *Miranda* warnings (*Berkemer v. McCarty*, 468 U.S. 420 [1984]). But, although the officer may ask questions, the driver and passengers have a constitutional right not to respond. Such a refusal to respond, however, may be taken into consideration by the officer in determining whether there is probable cause to arrest or search.[3]

Berkemer v. McCarty (1984)

Locate and examine the vehicle identification number Federal rules require that vehicles sold in the United States have a vehicle identification number (VIN). The VIN must be displayed on the dashboard of recently manufactured cars so that it can be read from outside the car through the windshield.[4] The Court has decided that motorists have no reasonable expectation of privacy with respect to the VIN located on the vehicle's dashboard, even if objects on the dashboard prevent the VIN from being observed from outside the car (*New York v. Class*, 475 U.S. 106 [1986]).

New York v. Class (1986)

In *New York v. Class* (1986), two New York City police officers stopped a motor vehicle for traffic violations. One of the officers looked for the vehicle identification number (VIN). Not finding it on the doorjamb, he reached into the car's interior to move some papers that were obscuring the area of the dashboard where he believed the VIN was located. While doing that, the officer saw a gun protruding from underneath the driver's seat and seized it. The driver, Benigno Class, was arrested and later convicted of criminal possession of a weapon. On appeal, he sought exclusion of the gun, claiming the search was illegal. The Court disagreed, saying that since the "VIN is placed in plain view, respondent had no reasonable expectation of privacy."

Seize items in plain view After a valid stop, the officer may seize illegal items *in plain view*. The seizure then establishes probable cause, which justifies an arrest. For example, suppose officers lawfully stop a car to issue the driver a citation for running a red light. While writing out the citation, the officers see contraband in the passenger compartment. The officers may then seize the contraband and place the driver under arrest. They may then search the driver and the vehicle.

Based on Reasonable Suspicion

Based on reasonable suspicion (a lower degree of certainty than probable cause, but higher than mere suspicion), the officer may do the following: require drunk-driving suspects to take a Breathalyzer™ test and search the passenger compartment for weapons if they have a reasonable suspicion of a threat to their safety.

Require drunk-driving suspects to take a Breathalyzer test All fifty states require drivers suspected of drunk driving to take Breathalyzer tests. Refusal to take the test, or test failure because the alcohol level is beyond that allowed by law, leads to suspension of the person's driver's license. An interesting issue is whether a driver who fails a Breathalyzer test may also be criminally charged with drunk driving.

Some argue that this constitutes two prosecutions for the same offense; others maintain that there is no double jeopardy, because license suspensions are administrative, not criminal, proceedings. Lower courts are divided. Trial courts in eighteen states have ruled that these two proceedings arising from the same act constitute double jeopardy; the highest courts of five states (New Mexico, Maine, Hawaii, Vermont, and Louisiana) have held otherwise. But the U.S. Supreme Court has not ruled on the issue, so uncertainty remains.[5]

Search the passenger compartment for weapons if there is reasonable suspicion of a threat to officer safety If the officer has reasonable suspicion that the motorist he or she has stopped is dangerous and may be able to gain control of a weapon in the car, the officer may conduct a brief search of the passenger compartment even if the motorist is no longer inside the car (*Michigan v. Long*, 463 U.S. 1032 [1983]). This search should be limited to areas in the passenger compartment where a weapon might be found or hidden. The authorization for a brief search for a weapon is an extension of stop and frisk rather than of an arrest. In contrast, a routine stop to issue a traffic ticket (not a stop and frisk situation) does not authorize the police to search the vehicle's passenger compartment.[6]

Michigan v. Long (1983)

Based on Probable Cause

If probable cause is present, after making a valid stop, the officer may search the vehicle, search the passengers' belongings, and make arrests.

Search the vehicle As long as the vehicle stop is based on reasonable suspicion, what officers observe may quickly evolve into probable cause to believe that the car contains the fruits and instrumentalities of crime or contraband, thereby establishing a justification for a full warrantless search of the vehicle.

In *Colorado v. Bannister*, 449 U.S. 1 (1980), the police stopped Bannister's automobile to issue him a speeding ticket. While writing out the citation, the officer made two observations: (1) Bannister and his companion fit a broadcast description of persons involved in the theft of auto parts, and (2) there were wrenches and other materials in the back seat that could have been used for that crime. The Court held that what the officer observed established probable cause to justify a warrantless search because, had a magistrate been present while Bannister's car was stopped, the police could have obtained a warrant on the information the officer possessed. The warrantless search was therefore proper under the automobile exception.

Colorado v. Bannister (1980)

Probable cause to search must exist prior to the search of the car; otherwise, the search is illegal. For example: Officer P stops a car because it is weaving erratically on the road. Immediately after stopping the car, Officer P sees open liquor containers in the front and back seats, which are prohibited. There is now probable cause to search the car further for more evidence. If drugs are found in the course of the search, the evidence is admissible in court. By contrast, Officer Q stops a car because of an illegal right turn. Inside are five teenagers who say they are coming home from a basketball game at a local park. Assume that Officer Q has no probable cause, based on her observations, to believe an offense has been or is being committed. Nonetheless, Officer Q searches the car on the assumption that teenagers who look like and are of the age of the occupants are more likely to drink and use drugs. If she finds drugs, the evidence will not be admissible in court, because Officer Q had no probable cause and was on a virtual "fishing expedition" when she searched the car. The officer may, however, look around the car (under the plain view rule) but cannot search it.

Wyoming v. Houghton (1999)

Search passengers' belongings The Court's decision in *Wyoming v. Houghton* (526 U.S. 295 [1999]) settled another important issue concerning what officers can do after a vehicle stop. The Court has ruled that police officers who have probable cause to search a car may inspect passengers' belongings found in the car if they are capable of concealing the object of the search.

In *Wyoming v. Houghton* (1999), a Wyoming Highway Patrol officer stopped a motor vehicle in which Houghton was riding. While questioning the driver for a traffic violation, the officer noticed a hypodermic needle in the driver's shirt pocket. When the driver admitted using the needle to inject drugs, the passengers were ordered out of the car. The officer then searched the passenger compartment of the vehicle. On the back seat, he found a purse that Houghton claimed was hers. After finding methamphetamines and drug paraphernalia in the purse, he arrested Houghton. She appealed her felony conviction for possession of drugs, claiming that the search of a passenger's personal belongings inside an automobile is a violation of Fourth Amendment rights.

The Court disagreed, saying that police officers who have probable cause to search a car may also inspect passengers' belongings found in the car if they are capable of concealing the object of the search. The Court cited two justifications for the search: (1) the passenger's reduced expectation of privacy and (2) "the governmental interest in effective law enforcement [which] would be appreciably impaired without the ability to search the passenger's belongings, because an automobile's ready mobility creates the risk that evidence or contraband will be permanently lost while a warrant is obtained." But although they may search passengers' belongings, officers may not conduct body searches of passengers (*United States v. Di Re*, 332 U.S. 581 [1948]). The only time a body search is allowed is when the passenger has been arrested.

United States v. Di Re (1948)

Make an arrest A stop may immediately turn into an arrest *if probable cause is established*. For example, suppose an officer stops a vehicle for speeding and orders the driver to get out of the car. The officer senses danger to himself, frisks the driver, and finds an illegal weapon. The officer may then arrest the driver and search the whole car. He may also conduct a full body search of the arrested driver.

Based on Consent Even if there is no probable cause or reasonable suspicion, the officer may search the car if valid consent is given. The Court has said that an officer, after validly stopping a car, may ask the person in control of the vehicle for permission to search (*Schneckloth v. Bustamonte*, 412 U.S. 218 [1973]). Such consent must be intelligent and voluntary, although it does not have to be in writing. In *United States v. Benitez* (899 F.2d 995 [10th Cir. 1990]), the U.S. Court of Appeals for the Tenth Circuit held that the consent given in vehicle searches does not have to be verbal as long as it is intelligent and voluntary. The burden is on the officer to prove, if challenged, that the consent was valid. The Court has also ruled, in *Florida v. Bostick* (501 U.S. 429 [1991]), that there is no requirement under the Fourth Amendment for the officer to inform the person that he or she has the right to refuse consent for it to be valid. It suffices if a reasonable person under the same circumstances would understand that he or she is free to refuse.

Schneckloth v. Bustamonte (1973)

United States v. Benitez (10th Cir. 1990)

Florida v. Bostick (1991)

Traffic Stops as Pretexts for Vehicle Searches

The Court has held that the temporary detention of a motorist based on probable cause to believe that he or she has violated traffic laws is valid, even if a reasonable officer would not have stopped the motorist in the absence of some other law enforcement objective—in this case, *Whren v. United States* (517 U.S. 806 [1996]), determining whether the occupants of the vehicle had drugs.

Whren v. United States (1996)

In *Whren* (1996), plainclothes vice officers were patrolling a high-drug area in an unmarked car when they saw a vehicle with youthful occupants waiting at an intersection. The vehicle remained at the intersection for what appeared to be an unusually long time. The officers made a U-turn and headed toward the vehicle, whereupon it suddenly made a right turn without signaling and took off at an unreasonable speed. The officers overtook the vehicle when it stopped at a red light. One of the officers approached the vehicle and observed two large plastic bags of what appeared to be crack cocaine in Whren's hands. At trial, the defendant sought to suppress the evidence, saying that, based on departmental policy, the plainclothes officers would not normally have dealt with this type of civil traffic violation; therefore, it was merely a **pretextual stop**—a stop used as a pretext to search the vehicle—in this case, to determine whether the occupants had drugs.

A majority of the Court ruled that the temporary detention of the vehicle based on probable cause to believe that traffic laws had been broken did not violate the Fourth Amendment even if the officers would not have stopped the motorist without some additional law enforcement objective. The Court in effect ruled that whether ordinarily the police officers "would have" (subjective test) made the stop is not the test for validity; instead, the test is whether the officers "could have" made the stop. The fact that they "could have" made a valid stop because there was a traffic violation made the stop valid even though the actual purpose of the stop was to look for drugs. In sum, the real purpose of the stop of a motor vehicle does not make the subsequent search invalid if there was, in fact, a valid reason for the stop.

An added factor made the traffic stop in *Whren* highly questionable. Police regulations in that jurisdiction permitted plainclothes officers (who made the arrest in this case) in unmarked cars to stop vehicles and enforce traffic laws "only in the case of a violation that is so grave as to pose an immediate threat to the safety of others." Such was not the case, and so the plainclothes officers did not follow departmental policy. This did not make any difference to the Court, however. The Court noted, "We cannot accept that the search and seizure protections of the Fourth Amendment are so variable . . . and can be made to turn upon such trivialities." The Court concluded that the fact that local law enforcement practices did not allow such stops was not significant because, if Fourth Amendment issues were decided based on departmental policy, it would make the Fourth Amendment protections vary from place to place.

Note, however, that although pretextual stops are constitutional, they may be invalidated by state courts based on state law or the state constitution. For example, in *State of Washington v. Ladson* (No. 65801–3 [1999]), a case decided three years after *Whren,* the Supreme Court of the state of Washington held that there is no pretextual stop exception to the warrant requirement under the state's constitution. Therefore, pretextual stops in the state of Washington are not valid.

State of Washington v. Ladson (1999)

Vehicle Stops Based on Racial Profiles Alone

A current and highly controversial issue in law enforcement is the practice in some agencies of stopping motorists, particularly in drug-corridor highways and streets, based on **racial profiles**. (This topic is also discussed in Chapter 5 under Stop and Frisk.) The U.S. Department of Justice defines *racial profiling* as any police-initiated action that relies on race, ethnicity, or the national origin of an individual instead of on individual acts or behavior. In some places and among some groups, the perception is pervasive that law enforcement departments disproportionately stop drivers belonging to minority groups, usually blacks and Hispanics. Media reports of this practice have increased dramatically. As the *Houston Chronicle* puts it: "The practice has become so common that black Americans have coined a name for it: Driving while black (DWB)." The same source states that, "by some estimates, about 72 percent of people pulled over in traffic stops are black, even though they represent only 15 percent of the population, according to the NAACP."[7]

A study of state documents in New Jersey revealed that "at least 8 out of every 10 automobile searches carried out by state troopers on the New Jersey Turnpike over most of the last decade were conducted on vehicles driven by blacks and Hispanics."[8] Major studies conducted since the controversy started have concluded that some law enforcement agencies, consciously or unconsciously, do in fact practice racial profiling.

Is racial profiling valid? Although the Court has not directly addressed this issue, it is safe to say, based on previous Court decisions involving race, that stopping a motorist based on race alone is clearly unconstitutional because it violates the Equal Protection Clause. The more difficult question, however, is whether race can legally be taken into consideration at all when looking at the "totality of circumstances," a phrase the Court often uses in reasonable suspicion or probable cause cases. In short, if race is merely a contributing factor instead of being the sole factor, is its use constitutional? In *United States v. Sokolow* (490 U.S. 1 [1989]), the Court said that stops cannot be based on drug courier profiles alone; instead, the facts, taken in totality, must amount to reasonable suspicion that can justify a stop. Although *Sokolow* did not involve race, it would apply even more strongly if the stop had been made solely on the basis of race. Court decisions allowing certain types of discrimination have always prohibited discrimination based on race because race is a highly protected category both under the Constitution and in various federal and state laws.

United States v. Sokolow (1989)

In the *Whren* case, discussed under pretextual stops, the Court said that, although pretextual vehicle stops are constitutional, racially motivated law enforcement could be challenged under the Equal Protection Clause (meaning based on discriminatory treatment) of the Fourteenth Amendment but not under the Due Process Clause (meaning based on absence of fundamental fairness). Therefore, based on *Whren,* if a motorist is stopped because of a valid reason (such as running a stop sign), the stop is valid even if the officer would not have stopped the vehicle if the driver had not been Hispanic. The Court said, however, that if something like this situation arose, it could be challenged under the Equal Protection Clause. The Court did not indicate how it would probably rule on such a case. Saying it can be challenged under the Fourteenth Amendment is different from categorically saying it is unconstitutional.

Easley v. Cromartie (2001)

In *Easley v. Cromartie* (532 U.S. 1076 [2001]), the Court held that using race as a factor in political redistricting is constitutional. In that case, the Court upheld a long-disputed North Carolina congressional district against the allegation that the district, which was 47% black, was a product of an unconstitutional racial gerrymander. It must be pointed out, however, that political redistricting based on race usually benefits racial minority groups, whereas racial profiling does not benefit racial minorities at all.

United States v. Travis (6th Cir. 1995)

Among lower courts, the Court of Appeals for the Sixth Circuit held that race is a permissible factor to justify reasonable suspicion during airport interdiction, based on facts known to the officer (*United States v. Travis,* 62 F.3d 170 [6th Cir. 1995]). In a 1999 case, a panel in the U.S. Court of Appeals for the Ninth Circuit voted 2 to 1 that "border patrol agents can consider ethnicity when making traffic stops."[9] That case involved "two Hispanic men who allegedly turned their cars around to avoid a checkpoint" fifty miles inside the United States, and it was a border patrol rather than a "DWB" case. Immigration and territorial border cases have traditionally been treated less strictly by the courts—with more authority given to government officers who deal with border patrol and immigration cases. Other cases have been decided on the federal district court and state court levels with varying results.

The U.S. Congress, state legislatures, and local legislative agencies have passed laws, and others are currently pending, seeking authorization to gather data that would prove racial profiling in law enforcement.[10] Lawsuits have been filed seeking damage awards for violations of constitutional rights and a discontinuance of the practice. Awareness abounds among certain racial groups that the practice exists; the question is how pervasive it is and how the victim can prove racial profiling in court in the absence of systemic data. One report states that racial minorities, "particularly African Americans, long have complained that they are routinely detained, frisked and even handcuffed by police for no apparent cause." The same report notes, however, that "police chiefs across the country have countered that racial profiling is essentially a myth, and they bridle at the suggestion that cops are motivated by racism."[11]

Given the controversy this issue has generated, legal challenges to racial profiling will doubtless continue in criminal prosecutions and legal liability cases. It will not be surprising if the Court decides the issue squarely in the near future, or if more legislatures and police agencies flatly prohibit the practice as constitutionally and morally wrong. Some legislatures and law enforcement agencies have already done that. For now, however, and from a purely legal perspective, stops based on racial profiles need a more definitive ruling from the courts.

Consensual Searches and the Freedom to Leave

Ohio v. Robinette (1996)

The Court has held that a police officer does not need to inform the defendant first that he or she is free to go for a consent to search to be valid (*Ohio v. Robinette,* 519 U.S. 33 [1996]). In *Ohio v. Robinette* (1996), an Ohio deputy sheriff stopped the defendant for speeding, gave him a verbal warning, returned his driver's license, and then asked whether he was carrying contraband, drugs, or weapons in his car. The defendant replied "no" but consented to a search of the car. The search revealed a small amount of marijuana and a controlled substance. At trial, Robinette argued that the consent given was invalid because, even in cases of lawful detention, the suspect must first be informed by the officer that he or she is "legally free to go" before consent to search can validly be given.

The Court disagreed, saying that "the Fourth Amendment does not require that a lawfully seized defendant be advised that he is 'free to go' before his consent to search will be recognized as voluntary." Again, however, the evidence obtained may not be admissible if state law requires that such information be given before consent to search is sought.

Arrest for a Minor (Nonjailable) Traffic Offense

Atwater v. City of Lago Vista (2001)

The Court has held that the Fourth Amendment does not forbid a warrantless arrest for a minor criminal offense punishable only by a fine, such as a misdemeanor seat belt violation (*Atwater v. City of Lago Vista,* 532 U.S. 318 [2001]). This case, *Atwater v. City of Lago Vista* (2001), settles an issue to which previously there was no definitive answer: How can a suspect be arrested without a warrant for an offense whose maximum penalty does not include serving time in jail or prison?

In *Atwater,* a Texas law required all front seat passengers to wear a seat belt; failure to do so was a crime punishable by a fine of not more than $50. Texas law also expressly authorized the police officer to arrest with a warrant if a person was found in violation of the law, although the police could issue a citation instead of making an arrest. The police observed Atwater driving a vehicle with her two young children in the front seat; none was wearing a seat belt. Arrested and later fined $50, she appealed her conviction, saying it was unconstitutional because, under common law, violators of nonjailable minor offenses could not be arrested.

The Court disagreed, saying that such laws are now present in all fifty states and that "there is no historical evidence that the framers or proponents of the Fourth Amendment . . . were at all concerned about warrantless arrests by local constables and other peace officers." The Court concluded by saying: "We simply cannot conclude that the Fourth Amendment . . . forbade peace officers to arrest without warrant for misdemeanors not amounting to or involving breach of the peace"; hence, arrests for nonjailable offenses are constitutional.

The Arrests of Passengers in a Vehicle

May the police arrest the passengers of a car in addition to the driver? The Court says yes—if there is probable cause to believe that a crime has been committed in a motor vehicle and it is not clear who committed it, and as long as there is reasonable inference from the circumstances that the person arrested could have committed it (*Maryland v. Pringle,* 540 U.S. 366 [2003]).

Maryland v. Pringle
(2003)

In *Pringle* (2003), the police stopped a car for speeding. Pringle was a passenger. When the driver opened the glove compartment to get the car registration, the officer saw a large amount of rolled-up money. After issuing the driver a warning, the officer asked for and received permission to search the vehicle. The officer found $753.00 and five plastic bags of cocaine. None of the three people in the car admitted ownership of the drugs and money, so the officer arrested all of them.

Was the arrest of the passengers valid? The Court said yes based on the circumstances of the case, saying the officer had probable cause to believe that the passengers could have committed the crime. The Court added this standard: "To determine whether an officer had probable cause to make an arrest, a court must examine the events leading up to the arrest" before making a decision. The presence of probable cause is determined by asking "whether . . . viewed from the standpoint of an objectively reasonable police officer," the facts amounted to probable cause. Given the circumstances of this case, the Court ruled, "it is an entirely reasonable inference from the facts here that any or all of the car occupants had knowledge of, and exercised dominion and control over, the cocaine . . . either solely or jointly."

Note that *Pringle* does not automatically authorize officers to arrest passengers in the car. Instead, the arrest of passengers must be based on probable cause that they are involved in the crime and not just the driver.

Vehicle Searches

A valid stop does not automatically give officers the authority to search the vehicle. A vehicle stop is *totally* different from a vehicle search, and each is governed by different rules. A stop does not need a warrant, but there must be reasonable suspicion that the vehicle is involved in some criminal activity for the stop to be valid. The rule for searches is different; in searches, probable cause must be present, whereas reasonable suspicion suffices for a vehicle stop.

In this section, we examine the main issues related to searches. These include (1) the earliest and seminal case decided by the Court on vehicle searches; (2) warrantless vehicle searches; (3) automatic searches during the issuing of traffic citations; (4) searches of passengers' compartments; (5) searches of trunks and closed packages in trunks; (6) searches of locked trunks or glove compartments; (7) dog sniffs after a traffic stop; (8) searches conducted significantly later than an arrest; (9) warrantless searches when there is time to obtain a warrant; (10) the objective reasonableness rule and the extent of car searches; (11) warrantless searches of containers in a car; (12) searches of vehicles found in public places; (13) searches of motor homes without a warrant; (14) the use of beepers to detect cars; (15) searches of vehicles in immigration borders; and (16) other car search issues.

The Earliest Case on Vehicle Searches and Warrants: *Carroll v. United States*

The rule is that *the search of an automobile does not require a warrant*. A vehicle search is therefore an exception to the warrant requirement of the Fourth Amendment. However, there are two requirements for warrantless vehicle searches: (1) probable cause must be present, and (2) the vehicle must be mobile, meaning capable of being driven away at any time. A vehicle that is up on blocks, missing an essential part, or being repaired and cannot be driven away, is not mobile.[12] A warrant is needed to search these immobilized vehicles.

The seminal case on automobile searches is *Carroll v. United States* (267 U.S. 132 [1925]). In that case, decided way back in 1925, Carroll and a certain Kiro were indicted and convicted for transporting "intoxicating spirituous liquor" (sixty-eight quarts of bonded whiskey and gin, in violation of the National Prohibition Act). They appealed their conviction, saying that it was wrong for the trial court to admit two of the sixty-eight bottles because they had been seized by law enforcement officers without a warrant. The officers countered that they had had probable cause to believe that the automobile contained bootleg liquor. They said that if they had taken the time to obtain a warrant, the car, which they had stopped on a highway, would have disappeared.

The Court agreed that the warrantless search of the automobile was reasonable, because it would have been gone if the officers had tried to obtain a warrant. After a discussion of various laws, the Court said:

We have made a somewhat extended reference to these statutes to show that the guaranty of freedom from unreasonable searches and seizures by the Fourth Amendment has been construed, practically since the beginning of the government, as recognizing a necessary difference between a search of a store, dwelling house, or other structure in respect of which a proper official warrant readily may be obtained and a search of a ship, motor boat, wagon, or automobile for contraband goods, *where it is not practicable to secure a warrant, because the vehicle can be quickly moved out of the locality or jurisdiction in which the warrant must be sought.* [emphasis added]

Although, in *Carroll,* the Court ruled that there is no need for a warrant to search vehicles "where it is not practicable to secure a warrant," subsequent court decisions have held that warrantless vehicle searches are constitutional even if there is time to obtain one.

The "automobile exception" to the warrant requirement is justified by five considerations (*Robbins v. California,* 453 U.S. 420 [1981]):

***Robbins v. California* (1981)**

- The mobility of motor vehicles often makes obtaining a judicial warrant impractical.
- A diminished expectation of privacy surrounds the automobile.
- A car is used for transportation, not as a residence or a repository of personal effects.
- The car's occupants and contents travel in plain view.
- Automobiles are necessarily highly regulated by the government.

Note that, although *Carroll* is acknowledged as the "mother" of all motor vehicle cases, it is primarily a vehicle *search* case, not a vehicle *stop* case. (Read the Case Brief to learn more about this case.)

CASE BRIEF: The Earliest Case on Vehicle Search
Carroll v. United States, 267 U.S. 132 (1925)

Facts: Officers observed the automobile of Carroll while on a regular patrol from Detroit to Grand Rapids. The same officers had been in contact with Carroll twice in the four months prior to this sighting. In September, the officers attempted to buy illegal liquor from Carroll, but he was alerted to their true identity and did not produce the contraband. In October, the officers recognized Carroll's automobile returning to Grand Rapids from Detroit (a city possessing an international boundary and that was known as a city from which illegal liquor was regularly imported). The officers gave chase but failed to apprehend Carroll. Carroll was later apprehended. He and his companion were ordered out of the car. No liquor was visible in the front seat of the automobile. Officers then opened the rumble seat and looked under the cushions, again finding no liquor. One of the officers then struck the "lazyback" of the seat, tore open the seat cushion, and discovered sixty-eight bottles of gin and whiskey. Carroll was arrested and convicted of transporting intoxicating liquor.

continued

Issue: *May officers search an automobile without a search warrant but with probable cause that it contains illegal contraband? Yes.*

Supreme Court Decision: The risk of the vehicle being moved from the jurisdiction, or the evidence being destroyed or carried off, justifies a warrantless search as long as the search is conducted with probable cause that the vehicle contains contraband.

Case Significance: The general rule is that searches may be conducted only if a warrant has been issued. There are several exceptions to this rule, however, with searches of automobiles one of them. This case, decided in 1925, created the so-called automobile exception to the warrant requirement by ruling that warrantless searches of motor vehicles are valid as long as there is probable cause to believe that there are seizable items in the vehicle. The justification for this exception is the mobile nature of the automobile.

Excerpts from the Decision: We have made a somewhat extended reference to these statutes to show that the guaranty of freedom from unreasonable searches and seizures by the Fourth Amendment has been construed, practically since the beginning of the government, as recognizing a necessary difference between a search of a store, dwelling house, or other structure in respect of which a proper official warrant readily may be obtained and a search of a ship, motor boat, wagon, or automobile for contraband goods, where it is not practicable to secure a warrant, because the vehicle can be quickly moved out of the locality or jurisdiction in which the warrant must be sought.

Having thus established that contraband goods concealed and illegally transported in an automobile or other vehicle may be searched for without a warrant, we come now to consider under what circumstances such search may be made. It would be intolerable and unreasonable if a prohibition agent were authorized to stop every automobile on the chance of finding liquor, and thus subject all persons lawfully using the highways to the inconvenience and indignity of such a search. Travelers may be so stopped in crossing an international boundary because of national self-protection reasonably requiring one entering the country to identify himself as entitled to come in, and his belongings as effects which may be lawfully brought in. But those lawfully within the country, entitled to use the public highways, have a right to free passage without interruption or search unless there is known to a competent official, authorized to search, probable cause for believing that their vehicles are carrying contraband or illegal merchandise.

Warrantless Vehicle Searches

As noted previously, warrantless searches of automobiles have been upheld as reasonable and therefore valid. However, the warrantless search *must be based on probable cause that seizable items are contained in the vehicle*. The absence of probable cause makes the search invalid; reasonable suspicion (such as that required in stops) is not enough. Probable cause should focus on whether the item to be searched for is subject to seizure and whether it may be found in the place where the search is being conducted. As in all other types of searches, reasonableness governs the scope of the search; a fishing expedition for evidence is not allowed.

DATE: _____

I, _____ , having been informed of my constitutional right not to have a search made of the automobile hereinafter mentioned without a search warrant and of my right to refuse such a search, hereby authorize _____ _____ and _____ , police officers of the Houston Police Department, to conduct a complete search of my automobile, which is a _____ located at _____ _____ .

These officers are authorized by me to take from my automobile any letters, papers, materials, or any other property which they may desire. This permission is being given by me to the above named officers voluntarily without threats or promises of any kind and is given with my full and free consent.

SIGNED: _____

WITNESSES:

_____

_____

Figure 8.1 Voluntary Consent for Search and Seizure of Automobile

Source: Official consent form of the Houston Police Department

Automatic Searches during the Issuance of Traffic Citations

Knowles v. Iowa (1998)

In *Knowles v. Iowa* (525 U.S. 113 [1998]), the Court held that a state law authorizing a search during the issuance of a traffic citation violates the Fourth Amendment unless there is consent (see Figure 8.1) or probable cause.

In the *Knowles* case, Knowles was stopped for speeding and issued a citation. The officer then conducted a full search of Knowles's car, where he found marijuana and drug paraphernalia. The state of Iowa had a law providing that the issuance of a citation instead of an arrest "does not affect the officer's authority to conduct an otherwise lawful search." This was interpreted by the Iowa Supreme Court to mean that officers could "conduct a full-blown search of an automobile and driver in those cases where police elect not to make a custodial arrest and instead issue a citation—that is, a search incident to citation." Convicted of possession of drug paraphernalia, Knowles appealed, claiming that the search was unconstitutional.

The Court agreed, saying that such searches, even if authorized by state law, violate the Fourth Amendment. They can be done only if there is valid consent or probable cause, neither of which was present in this case.

The mere issuance of a citation does not justify a full-blown search. However, this decision does not include items in plain view, because such items are not protected by the Fourth Amendment. For example, suppose Officer X stops a pickup truck and issues a citation. Officer X cannot automatically conduct a full-blown search of the car, as she could if there was probable cause to arrest the driver or to search the car. But nothing prevents Officer X from looking in the car to see if there are seizable items. If there are, these can validly be seized under the plain view doctrine.

Searches of Passenger Compartments

Once a driver has been arrested, the police may conduct a warrantless search of the passenger compartment of the car. This means they may examine the contents of any container found within the passenger compartment, as long as it may reasonably be thought to contain something that might pose a danger to officers or to hold evidence related to the offense for which the suspect has been arrested.

New York v. Belton (1981)

In *New York v. Belton* (453 U.S. 454 [1981]), a New York state officer noticed an automobile traveling at an excessive rate of speed. The officer gave chase and ordered the car to pull over to the side of the road. The officer asked to see the driver's license; in the process, he smelled burned marijuana and saw on the floor of the car an envelope marked "Supergold." He placed the four occupants under arrest, picked up the envelope, and found marijuana. He then searched the passenger compartment and on the back seat found a black leather jacket belonging to Belton; in one of the pockets of the jacket he discovered cocaine. During the trial, Belton moved to suppress the cocaine, claiming it was not within the *area of his immediate control,* so its seizure was illegal. The Supreme Court rejected this contention, saying that the police may conduct a warrantless search of the passenger compartment of a car incident to a lawful arrest because that space is within the suspect's area of immediate control.

Belton is significant because it defines the extent of allowable search inside an automobile after a lawful arrest. Prior to *Belton,* there was confusion about whether the police could search parts of the automobile outside the driver's "wingspan." The Court expanded the area of allowable search to the whole compartment, including the back seat; it also authorized the opening of containers found in the passenger compartment that might contain the object sought. However, *Belton* did not authorize the search of the trunk or beneath the hood of the car.

Searches of the Passenger Compartment after a Lawful Arrest When the Suspect Was Not in the Vehicle When Arrested

Thornton v. United States (2004)

In *New York v. Belton,* the driver was in the car when arrested, and the search took place after the occupants were placed under arrest. Would the *Belton* holding apply in cases where the initial contact with the police and the arrest took place outside the motor vehicle? In *Thornton v. United States* (541 U.S. 615 [2004]), the Court said yes; *Belton* would nonetheless apply, thus expanding further the concept of "area of immediate control" in motor vehicles.

In *Thornton,* an officer became suspicious when Thornton slowed down to avoid driving next to the officer. The officer pulled over so that he could get behind Thornton and check his license plate. The check revealed the tags did not belong to the car Thornton was driving. Thornton pulled into a parking lot, parked, and got out of his vehicle. The officer stopped Thornton after he left the car and asked about the tags on the car. Thornton consented to a pat-down search. The officer felt a bulge in Thornton's pocket and asked him if he had illegal narcotics. Thornton then admitted he had drugs and retrieved two bags from his pocket, one containing marijuana and the other crack cocaine. The officer arrested Thornton, handcuffed him, and placed him in the back seat of the patrol car. The officer then searched Thornton's vehicle and retrieved a handgun under the driver's seat.

After being convicted for possession of drugs and firearm, Thornton sought exclusion of the evidence, saying it was illegally obtained because it was not in his "area of immediate control" because he was outside the vehicle when the arrest took place. The Court disagreed and said that the *Belton* principle of allowable search of the passenger compartment applied even if the arrest took place outside the vehicle.

Warrantless Searches of Trunks and Closed Packages Found in Trunks

United States v. Ross (1982)

If the police legitimately stop a car and have probable cause to believe that it contains contraband, they may conduct a warrantless search of the car. This search can be as thorough as a search authorized by a warrant issued by a magistrate. Therefore, every part of the vehicle in which the contraband might be stored may be inspected, including the trunk and all receptacles and packages (*United States v. Ross,* 456 U.S. 798 [1982]).

In *United States v. Ross* (1982), after effecting a valid stop and arrest for a narcotics sale, one of the officers opened the car's trunk and found a closed brown paper bag. Inside the bag were glassine bags containing white powder, which was later determined to be heroin. The officer then drove the car to police headquarters, where another warrantless search of the trunk revealed a zippered leather pouch containing cash. During the trial, the suspect argued that the police officers should not have opened either the paper bag or the leather pouch found in the trunk without first obtaining a warrant. The Supreme Court disagreed and allowed the evidence to be admitted.

The *Ross* case is important because it further defines the scope of police authority in searches of vehicles. In *Belton,* the Court specifically refused to address the issue of whether the police may open the trunk of a car in connection with a warrantless search incident to a valid arrest. Although based on slightly different facts, as it involved a warrantless search based on probable cause, *Ross* addressed that issue and authorized such action. But it went further, holding that any packages or luggage found in the trunk that could reasonably be thought to contain the items for which the officers have probable cause to search may also be opened without a warrant. *Ross* has therefore greatly expanded the scope of allowable warrantless car searches, focusing the search on the whole automobile as the possible source of evidence. Opening the brown paper bag and the pouch were legitimate by extension of police authority to conduct a warrantless search of the car. (Read the *Ross* Case Brief to learn more about this case.)

CASE BRIEF: The Leading Case on the Search of Car Trunks and Closed Packages in Trunks

United States v. Ross, 456 U.S. 798 (1982)

Facts: Police in Washington, D.C., received information from an informant that Ross was selling narcotics kept in the trunk of his car, which was parked at a specified location. The police drove to the location, spotted the person and car that matched the description given by the informant, and made a warrantless arrest. The officers opened the car's trunk and found a closed brown paper bag containing glassine bags of a substance that turned out to be heroin. The officers then drove the car to police headquarters, where another warrantless search of the trunk revealed a zippered leather pouch containing cash. Ross was charged with possession of heroin with intent to distribute. He sought to suppress the heroin and cash as evidence, alleging that both were obtained in violation of his constitutional rights because there were no exigent circumstances that would justify a warrantless search.

Issue: *After a valid arrest, may the police open the trunk of the car and containers found therein without a warrant and in the absence of exigent circumstances? Yes.*

Supreme Court Decision: When the police have probable cause to justify a warrantless search of a car, they may search the entire car and open the trunk and any packages or luggage found therein that could reasonably be thought to contain the items for which they have probable cause to search.

Case Significance: The *Ross* case is important in that it further defines the scope of police authority in vehicle searches. The Court's *Belton* decision had specifically refused to address the issue of whether the police could open the trunk of a car in connection with a search incident to a valid arrest. *Ross* addressed that issue and authorized such an action. But it went beyond that: Any packages or luggage found in the car that could reasonably be thought to contain the items for which there was probable cause to search could also be opened without a warrant. *Ross* has therefore greatly expanded the scope of allowable warrantless search, limited only by what is reasonable.

Excerpts from the Decision: As we have stated, the decision in *Carroll* was based on the Court's appraisal of practical considerations viewed in the perspective of history. It is therefore significant that the practical consequences of the *Carroll* decision would be largely nullified if the permissible scope of a warrantless search of an automobile did not include containers and packages found inside the vehicle. Contraband goods rarely are strewn across the trunk or floor of a car; because by their very nature such goods must be withheld from public view, they rarely can be placed in an automobile unless they are enclosed within some form of container. . . . The Court in *Carroll* held that "contraband goods concealed and illegally transported in an automobile or other vehicle may be searched for without a warrant." As we noted in *Henry v. United States,* the decision in *Carroll* "merely relaxed the requirements for a warrant on grounds of practicability." It neither broadened nor limited the scope of a lawful search based on probable cause.

A lawful search of fixed premises generally extends to the entire area in which the object of the search may be found and is not limited by the possibility that separate acts of entry or opening may be required to complete the search. Thus, a warrant that authorizes an officer to search a home for illegal weapons also provides authority to open closets, chests, drawers, and containers in which the weapon might be found. A warrant to open a footlocker to search for marihuana would also authorize the opening of packages found inside. A warrant to search a vehicle would support a search of every part of the vehicle that might contain the object of the search. When a legitimate search is under way, and when its purpose and its limits have been precisely defined, nice distinctions between closets, drawers, and containers, in the case of a home, or between glove compartments, upholstered seats, trunks, and wrapped packages, in the case of a vehicle, must give way to the interest in the prompt and efficient completion of the task at hand.

Searches of Locked Trunks or Glove Compartments

Whether the police may open a *locked* (as opposed to a closed) glove compartment or trunk was not addressed by the Court in *New York v. Belton* (453 U.S. 454 [1981]) or in any other case involving a warrantless arrest situation. In a footnote to *Belton,* the Court stated:

> "Container" here denotes any object capable of holding another object. It thus includes closed or open glove compartments, consoles, or other receptacles located anywhere within the passenger compartment, as well as luggage, boxes, bags, clothing, and the like. Our holding encompasses only the interior of the passenger compartment of an automobile and does not encompass the trunk.

At least one state supreme court has held, however, that consent to search a car does not authorize police officers to pry open a locked briefcase found in the car's trunk (*State v. Wells,* 539 So.2d 464 [Sup. Ct. Fla. 1989]).

State v. Wells (Sup. Ct. Fla. 1989)

In general, consent to search does not mean consent to open a locked container unless the key is given voluntarily to the police or the police lawfully obtain possession of the key. The search will most likely be valid, however, if the trunk is opened by pressing a release button inside the car. What is highly questionable is the forcible opening of locked glove compartments or car trunks. Such intrusions, if necessary, are best done with a warrant.

Dog Sniffs after a Traffic Stop

Illinois v. Caballes (2005)

In *Illinois v. Caballes* (543 U.S. _____ [2005]), the Court held that "a dog sniff conducted during a concededly lawful traffic stop that reveals no information other than the location of a substance that no individual has any right to possess does not violate the Fourth Amendment."

In this case, the driver was stopped for speeding. While one officer was issuing the warning ticket, another officer walked around the car with his narcotics-detection dog. The dog alerted the officers to the car's trunk. Upon searching the trunk, the officers found marijuana and arrested the driver. On appeal for drug possession, the driver alleged that the search was illegal because there was no probable cause to conduct the search. The Court rejected the claim and held that there was probable cause to search based on the dog's sniff. Because the sniff "revealed no information other than the location of a substance that no individual has any right to possess," the search was legal.

Searches that Are Not Contemporaneous

The cases previously discussed involved car searches conducted *contemporaneously*, meaning at the time of or immediately after the arrest. Sometimes, however, the officer may not be able to conduct a search contemporaneously. In these cases, the rule is that, if the police have probable cause to stop and search an automobile on the highway, they may take the automobile to the police station and search it there without warrant. The ruling in the *Ross* case was later used to justify the warrantless search of a container even though there was a significant delay between the time the police stopped the vehicle and the time they performed the search of the container.

United States v. Johns (1985)

In *United States v. Johns* (469 U.S. 478 [1985]), customs officers stopped two trucks suspected of carrying marijuana. Officers removed several sealed packages believed to contain marijuana and placed them in a government warehouse. Three days later, officers opened them without a warrant and found marijuana. The Court said that neither *Ross* nor any other case establishes a requirement that a vehicle search occur immediately as part of the vehicle inspection or soon thereafter; a three-day delay before making the search is permissible. The search still must be done within a reasonable time, but the burden of proving unreasonableness is on the defendant, not the police.

Warrantless Searches When There Is Time to Obtain a Warrant

Closely related to the issue of contemporaneous searches is whether the police may conduct a warrantless search even if there is time to obtain a warrant. The answer is yes. This is different from a contemporaneous search (where a warrant could not have been obtained) in that this type of search assumes that the police could have obtained a warrant because they had time to do so but did not. For example, suppose the police, having probable cause, stopped W's car on the highway and arrested her for robbery. There was probable cause to search the car, but the police instead towed the car to the police station and searched it there. During her trial, W objected to the introduction of seized evidence, saying that the search was illegal because the police had had time to obtain a warrant. The police already had the car at the police station, so no exigent circumstances existed. The Court said that the warrantless search was proper, because the police had probable cause to search when the vehicle was first stopped on the highway, and that probable cause justified a later search without a warrant (*Chambers v. Maroney*, 399 U.S. 42 [1970]).

Chambers v. Maroney (1970)

A subsequent case in 1984, *Florida v. Meyers* (466 U.S. 380 [1984]), reiterated this principle; that is, a vehicle may be searched under the automobile exception to the Fourth Amendment even if it has been immobilized and released to the custody of the police. And in *Maryland v. Dyson* (527 U.S. 465 [1999]), the Court reiterated the rule that, if the police have probable cause to search a car, they do not need a warrant even if there was ample opportunity to obtain one.

Florida v. Meyers (1984)

Maryland v. Dyson (1999)

The Extent of Car Searches and the Objective Reasonableness Rule

Florida v. Jimeno (1991)

The Court decided in *Florida v. Jimeno* (500 U.S. 248 [1991]) that valid consent justifies a warrantless search of a container in a car if it is objectively reasonable for the police to believe that the scope of the suspect's consent permitted them to open that container.

In *Florida v. Jimeno,* a Dade County police officer overheard Jimeno arranging what appeared to be a drug transaction over a public telephone. The officer followed Jimeno's car, observed him make an illegal right turn at a red light, and stopped him to issue a traffic citation. After informing Jimeno why he had been stopped, the officer told Jimeno he had reason to believe Jimeno was carrying narcotics in his car and asked permission to search. The officer explained that Jimeno did not have to grant permission, but Jimeno said he had nothing to hide and gave consent to the search, whereupon the officer found a kilogram of cocaine in a brown paper bag on the floor of the passenger compartment. Jimeno appealed his conviction, saying that his consent to search the vehicle did not extend to closed containers found inside the vehicle.

The Court disagreed, stating that a search is valid if it is objectively reasonable for the police to believe that the scope of the suspect's consent permits them to open a container. This case differs from *Ross,* in which the police had probable cause to search the car. Here, there was no probable cause, but there was consent to search. This ruling defines what officers can do in car searches where there may not be probable cause but where consent to search is given.

Warrantless Searches of Containers in a Car

California v.
Acevedo (1991)

The Court held in *California v. Acevedo* (500 U.S. 565 [1991]) that the police may search a *container* located in a car without a search warrant even though they lack probable cause to search the *car* as a whole and have probable cause to believe only that the container itself contains contraband or evidence.

In *Acevedo,* the police in Santa Ana, California, observed Acevedo leaving an apartment known to contain marijuana carrying a brown paper bag the size of marijuana packages the police had seen earlier. The police had probable cause to search the brown paper bag because a federal drug agent in Hawaii had phoned earlier and said that the bag contained marijuana. Acevedo placed the bag in his car's trunk and then drove away. The police stopped the car, opened the trunk and the bag, and found marijuana.

Acevedo pleaded guilty to possession of marijuana for sale but later appealed his conviction, saying that the marijuana should have been suppressed as evidence. He claimed that, even if the police had probable cause to believe the container itself contained contraband, they did not have probable cause to search the car.

The Supreme Court agreed to review the case to "reexamine the law applicable to a closed container in an automobile, a subject that has troubled courts and law enforcement officers since it was first considered in *Chadwick.*" The Court ultimately disagreed with the defendant, saying that probable cause to believe that a container in a car holds contraband or seizable evidence justifies a warrantless search of that container even in the absence of probable cause to search the car. The Court said, "We therefore interpret *Carroll* as providing one rule to govern all automobile searches. The police may search an automobile and the containers within it where they have probable cause to believe contraband or evidence is contained."

United States v.
Chadwick (1977)

Acevedo is significant because it reverses two earlier Court rulings on essentially the same issue. In a 1977 case, *United States v. Chadwick* (433 U.S. 1 [1977]), the Court held that the police could seize movable luggage or other closed containers from a car but could not open them without a warrant, because a person has a heightened privacy expectation for such containers even if they are in a car. That case involved the seizure by government agents in Boston of a 200-pound, padlocked footlocker that contained marijuana. Upon arrival by train from San Diego, the footlocker was placed in the trunk of Chadwick's car, whereupon it was seized

HIGHLIGHT

The Scope of Warrantless Car Searches

"We hold that the scope of the warrantless search authorized by that [automobile] exception is no broader and no narrower than a magistrate could legitimately authorize by warrant. If probable cause justifies the search of a lawfully stopped vehicle, it justifies the search of every part of the vehicle and its contents that may conceal the object of the search."

SOURCE: *United States v. Ross,* 456 U.S. 798 (1982).

by the agents and opened without a warrant. The Court declared the warrantless search of the footlocker unjustified.

Arkansas v. Sanders (1979)

Two years later, in *Arkansas v. Sanders* (442 U.S. 753 [1979]), the Court ruled unconstitutional the warrantless search of a suitcase located in a vehicle when there was probable cause to search only the suitcase but not the vehicle. In this case, the police had probable cause to believe that the suitcase contained marijuana. The police watched as the suspect placed the suitcase in the trunk of a taxi, which was then driven away. The police pursued the taxi for several blocks and then stopped it. They found the suitcase in the trunk, searched it, and found marijuana. Again, however, the Court refused to extend the warrantless search doctrine enunciated in *Carroll* to searches of personal luggage if the only justification for the search was that the luggage was located in an automobile that was lawfully stopped by the police.

The Court in *Acevedo* rejected *Chadwick* and *Sanders* and instead reiterated its ruling in the *Carroll* and *Ross* cases. In *Carroll*, the Court held that a warrantless search of an automobile was valid based on probable cause to believe that the vehicle contained evidence of a crime and in light of the vehicle's likely disappearance. In *Ross*, the Court allowed the warrantless search of a container found in a car where there was probable cause to search the car and as long as the opening of the container was reasonable—given the object of the search. *Acevedo* extended the *Carroll–Ross* line of cases in that it allows the warrantless search of a container as long as there is probable cause to believe that the container holds contraband, even if there is no probable cause to search the car itself. In essence, *Acevedo* (probable cause for the *container* but not for the car) is the opposite of *Ross* (probable cause for the *car* but not for the container), but the effect is the same—it expands the power of the police to conduct warrantless car searches.

Seizures of Vehicles Found in Public Places

Florida v. White (1999)

In a 1999 case, *Florida v. White* (526 U.S. 23 [1999]), the Court held that "the Fourth Amendment does not require the police to obtain a warrant before seizing an automobile from a public place if they have probable cause to believe it is forfeitable contraband."

In *Florida v. White,* officers had previously observed White using his car to deliver cocaine but did not arrest him at that time. However, they did arrest him several months later at his workplace on unrelated charges. During the arrest, the officers seized White's car without a warrant, claiming they were authorized to do so because the car was subject to forfeiture under the Florida Contraband Forfeiture Act. They searched the car and found two pieces of crack cocaine in the ashtray. Convicted of a state drug violation, White moved to suppress the evidence seized during that search, saying his Fourth Amendment rights had been violated.

On appeal, the Court disagreed, holding that the search and seizure was valid because the car itself constituted forfeitable contraband under state law and probable cause was present. The Court added that, "because the police seized respondent's vehicle from a public area—respondent's employer's parking lot—the warrantless seizure also did not involve any invasion of respondent's privacy."

Police Use of Cameras to Monitor Traffic and Other Offenders

Many cities in the United States use automatic red-light ticketing technology for law enforcement. In some cities, this involves photographing vehicle drivers (such as those beating traffic red lights or not paying toll fees) and in others photographing only the license plate of the offending vehicle and then mailing tickets to violators. This form of law enforcement surveillance has spread to nontraffic situations, such as restaurants or crowded streets. Your face may be scanned for a match against a photo database of runaways and felons. The constitutionality of this practice has not been decided by the Court; hence, the presumption is that it is constitutional. However, it may be prohibited by state law.

Searches of Motor Homes without a Warrant

The Court has held that motor homes are automobiles for purposes of the Fourth Amendment and are therefore subject to the automobile exception: They can be searched without a warrant. However, the application of this decision is limited to a motor home capable of being driven on the road and located in a place not regularly used for residential purposes. The Court decision in *California v. Carney* (471 U.S. 386 [1985]) specifically stated that the case does not resolve whether the automobile exception applies to a motor home "situated in a way or place that objectively indicates that it is being used as a residence."

California v. Carney (1985)

In the *Carney* case, federal narcotics agents had reason to believe that the defendant was exchanging marijuana for sex with a boy in a motor home parked on a public lot in downtown San Diego. The vehicle was outfitted to serve as a residence. The agents waited until the youth emerged and convinced him to return and ask the defendant to come out. When the defendant came out, an agent entered the motor home without a warrant and found marijuana lying on a table. During the trial, the defendant sought to suppress the evidence, saying that it was excludable because it was obtained without a warrant.

The Court disagreed, saying that the evidence was admissible. The Court added that the vehicle in question was readily mobile, that there was a reduced expectation of privacy stemming from its use as a licensed motor vehicle, and that it was situated as to suggest that it was being used as a vehicle, not a residence. The Court refused to distinguish motor homes from ordinary automobiles simply because motor homes are capable of functioning as dwellings, saying that motor homes lend themselves easily to use as instruments of illicit drug traffic and other illegal activity.

The Use of Beepers to Detect Cars

A person traveling in a car on a public road has *no reasonable expectation of privacy,* so visual surveillance by the police does not constitute a search. Moreover, the Fourth Amendment does not prohibit the police from supplementing their sensory faculties with technological aids to help the police identify the car's location (*United States v. Knotts,* 460 U.S. 276 [1983]).

United States v. Knotts (1983)

"[There is] . . . a necessary difference between a search of a store, dwelling house or other structure in respect of which a proper official warrant readily may be obtained, and a search of a ship, motorboat, wagon or automobile, for contraband goods, where it is not practicable to secure a warrant because the vehicle can quickly be moved out of the locality or jurisdiction in which the warrant must be sought."

SOURCE: *Carroll v. United States*, 267 U.S. 132 (1925).

The facts in *United States v. Knotts* (1983) are as follows: With the cooperation of a chemical supply company, state narcotics agents installed an electronic **beeper** in a container of chloroform. When a man the agents suspected of manufacturing controlled substances turned up at the chemical company to purchase chloroform, the bugged can was sold to him. The agents used both the beeper signal and visual means to follow the suspect to a house, where the container was placed in another car. The second car then proceeded into another state, where the agents lost both visual and beeper contact. However, the beeper signal was picked up again by a monitoring device aboard a helicopter. By this means, the agents learned that the container was located in or near a secluded cabin owned by Knotts. Armed with this and other information, the agents obtained a search warrant and discovered a secret drug laboratory.

The Court held the police act to be valid and the evidence admissible, saying that by using the public roadways the driver of the car voluntarily conveyed to anyone that he was traveling over particular roads and in a particular direction. Moreover, no expectation of privacy extended to the visual observation of the automobile arriving on private premises after leaving the public highway, nor to movements of objects such as the drum of chloroform outside the cabin in the "open fields." But the *Knotts* case did not address the question of monitoring in private places, nor did it examine the legality of the original installation and transfer of the beeper.

United States v. Karo (1984)

That issue was addressed in *United States v. Karo* (468 U.S. 705 [1984]), decided a year later. In *Karo*, government agents, upon learning that the defendants had ordered some cans of ether from a government informant to use in extracting cocaine, obtained a court order authorizing the installation and monitoring of a beeper in one of the cans. The agents installed the beeper with the informant's consent, and the can was subsequently delivered to the defendants. Over a period of months, the beeper enabled the agents to monitor the can's movements to a variety of locations, including several private residences and two commercial storage facilities. The agents obtained a search warrant for one of the homes. When the evidence obtained from that warrant was introduced in court, the defendant promptly objected.

The Supreme Court first explained that neither the initial installation of the beeper nor the container's subsequent transfer to defendant Karo infringed any constitutional right to privacy of the defendant, nor did they constitute a search or seizure under the Fourth Amendment. The monitoring of the beeper, however, was an entirely different matter. The Court said that the monitoring of a beeper in a private dwelling, a location not open to visual surveillance, violates the rights of individuals to privacy in their own homes. Although the monitoring here was less intrusive than a full search, it revealed facts that the government was interested in knowing and that it could not otherwise have obtained legally without a warrant. The Court determined that the use of the beeper violated Karo's Fourth Amendment right. Nevertheless, the evidence obtained was not suppressed, because there was ample evidence other than that obtained through use of the beeper to establish probable cause for the issuance of the warrant.

Karo is different from *Knotts* because in *Knotts,* the agents learned nothing from the beeper that they could not have visually observed, so there was no Fourth Amendment intrusion. Moreover, the monitoring in *Knotts* occurred in a public place, whereas the beeper in *Karo* intruded on the privacy of a home.

Immigration and Border Searches of Vehicles

The Fourth Amendment protection against unreasonable searches and seizures does not apply in immigration and border searches, particularly of motor vehicles. There is no need for reasonable suspicion nor probable cause for government agents to be able to stop, search, and seize. The scope of border searches is also much more extensive than in nonborder searches. In *United States v. Flores-Montano* (541 U.S. 149 [2004]), the Court held that the government's authority to conduct suspicionless inspections at the border includes the authority to remove, disassemble, and reassemble a vehicle's fuel tank.

United States v. Flores-Montano (2004)

In this case, Manuel Flores-Montano attempted to enter the United States at a port of entry in Southern California. Immigration officers asked Flores-Montano to leave his vehicle for secondary inspection. During the inspection, the officer noticed that the gas tank sounded solid, so he requested a mechanic's help in removing it. When the gas tank was removed, the inspector found 37 kilograms of marijuana. Flores-Montano later sought suppression of the evidence, claiming the inspector did not have any reasonable suspicion he was engaged in criminal activity and that reasonable suspicion was required under the Fourth Amendment to remove the gas tank.

The Court ruled that "the government's authority to conduct suspicionless inspections at the border includes the authority to remove, disassemble, and reassemble a vehicle's fuel tank," adding that "on many occasions, we have noted that the expectation of privacy is less at the border than it is in the interior." It is clear from this case that (1) there is no need for suspicion, reasonable suspicion, or probable cause for border inspectors to conduct a vehicle search, and (2) the extent of allowable search (removing the gas tank, disassembling, and then reassembling it) is much more extensive than in nonborder searches.

Other Valid Car Searches

Other circumstances that may justify warrantless car searches include the following:

- *Accident cases.* Sometimes, because of an accident or other circumstances, a car must remain in a location where it is vulnerable to intrusion by vandals. If the police have probable cause to believe that the vehicle contains a weapon or a similar device that would constitute a danger if it fell into the wrong hands, they may make a warrantless search for the particular item (*Cady v. Dombrowski,* 413 U.S. 433 [1973]).

Cady v. Dombrowski (1973)

- *Cases in which the vehicle itself has been the subject of crime.* An officer who has probable cause to believe that a car has been the subject of burglary, tampering, or theft may make a limited warrantless entry and investigation of those areas that are reasonably believed to contain evidence of ownership.
- *Cases in which the vehicle is believed abandoned.* A limited search of an automobile in an effort to ascertain ownership is allowable when the car has apparently been abandoned or when the arrested driver is possibly not the owner and does not otherwise resolve the matter of ownership.

Vehicle Inventory Searches

In this section, we examine warrantless vehicle inventory searches that take place immediately after an arrest and those of vehicles impounded by the police.

Warrantless Vehicle Inventory Searches Immediately after an Arrest

The Court decided two cases addressing the validity and scope of **vehicle inventory** searches, in which the police list the personal effects and properties they find in the vehicle, without a warrant immediately after an arrest.

Colorado v. Bertine (1987)

In the first case, *Colorado v. Bertine* (479 U.S. 367 [1987]), the Court held that warrantless inventory searches of the person and possessions of arrested individuals are permissible under the Fourth Amendment. Bertine was arrested for driving under the influence of alcohol. After he was taken into custody and before the arrival of a tow truck to impound his van, an officer inventoried the van in accordance with departmental procedures. During the inventory search, the officer opened a backpack and found controlled substances, drug paraphernalia, and money. Bertine challenged the admissibility of the evidence, saying that a warrant was needed to open the closed backpack. The Court rejected his challenge, saying that the police must be allowed to conduct warrantless inventory searches to secure an arrestee's property from loss or damage and to protect the police from false claims. Because closed containers may hold items that need to be secured, the police must be allowed to open them without a warrant.

The *Bertine* case specified two prerequisites for the valid inventory search of a motor vehicle: (1) the police must follow standardized procedures (to eliminate their uncontrolled discretion to determine the scope of the search), and (2) there must be no bad faith on the part of the police (the inventory search must not be used as an excuse for a warrantless search).

Florida v. Wells (1990)

In a subsequent case reiterating *Bertine, Florida v. Wells* (495 U.S. 1 [1990]), the Court ruled that a police department's "utter lack of any standard policy regarding the opening of closed containers encountered during inventory searches requires the suppression of contraband found in a locked suitcase removed from the trunk of an impounded vehicle and pried open by police after the driver's arrest on drunken driving charges."

In the *Wells* case, Wells gave the Florida Highway Patrol permission to open the trunk of his car following his arrest for DWI. An inventory search turned up two marijuana cigarette butts in an ashtray and a locked suitcase in the trunk. The officers opened the suitcase and found marijuana. Wells sought to reverse his conviction for drug possession on appeal, saying that the marijuana found in his locked suitcase should not have been admitted as evidence. The Court agreed to suppress the evidence, saying that, "absent any Highway Patrol policy with the opening of closed containers . . . the instant search was insufficiently regulated to satisfy the Fourth Amendment."

The message for the police from the *Bertine* and *Wells* cases is clear: A standardized policy is a must in cases where the police list the personal effects and properties found in the vehicle after impoundment. Such a policy, said the Court, "prevents individual police officers from having so much latitude that inventory searches are turned into a ruse for a general rummaging in order to discover incriminating evidence." It is also clear from the preceding cases that opening a closed container or a locked suitcase is allowed in a vehicle inventory search but only if specifically authorized by departmental policy. The absence of a departmental policy authorizing the opening of closed or locked containers means that such opening is prohibited. But if such a departmental policy is in place, officers may inspect the outside and inside of a vehicle in the process of taking an inventory, including the passenger compartment, the trunk, and any containers found in the vehicle—as long as such a search is conducted for legitimate reasons, not as a fishing expedition.

Warrantless Inventory Searches of Vehicles Impounded by Police

The police have authority for **vehicle impoundment** for various reasons, such as when the vehicle has been used for the commission of an offense or when it should be removed from the streets because it impedes traffic or threatens public safety. This type of search is distinguished from searches immediately after an arrest, where the vehicle is not necessarily impounded. When the police lawfully impound a vehicle, they may conduct a routine inventory search without warrant

"Our view that standardized criteria or established routine must regulate the opening of containers found during inventory searches is based on the principle that an inventory search must not be a ruse for a general rummaging in order to discover incriminating evidence. The policy or practice governing inventory searches should be designed to produce an inventory. The individual officer must not be allowed so much latitude that inventory searches are turned into a 'purposeful and general means of discovering evidence of a crime.'"

SOURCE: *Florida v. Wells,* 495 U.S. 1 (1990).

South Dakota v. Opperman (1976)

or probable cause to believe that the car contains seizable evidence. The leading case on impoundment searches is *South Dakota v. Opperman,* 428 U.S. 364 (1976).

In that case, the defendant's illegally parked car was taken to the city impound lot, where an officer, observing articles of personal property in the car, proceeded to inventory it. In the process, he found a bag of marijuana in the unlocked glove compartment. The Court concluded that, "in following standard police procedures, prevailing throughout the country and approved by the overwhelming majority of courts, the conduct of the police was not 'unreasonable' under the Fourth Amendment."

The ruling legitimizes car inventories, but the Court also made it clear in *Opperman* and other cases that inventory searches must be guided by departmental policy, so that the inventory becomes merely an administrative function by the police. Inventory searches conducted solely for the purposes of discovering evidence are illegal regardless of what is discovered in the course of the inventory. In the words of the Court, "Our view that standardized criteria or established routine must regulate the opening of containers is based on the principle that an inventory search must not be a ruse for a general rummaging in order to discover incriminating evidence" (*Florida v. Wells,* 495 U.S. 1 [1990]).

It is true that when vehicles are abandoned or illegally parked or when the owner is arrested, the courts permit them to be impounded and inventoried. But that rule should not apply when the driver has been arrested for a minor traffic violation, primarily because the police are expected to give the suspect a reasonable opportunity to post bail and obtain his or her prompt release. In *Dyke v. Taylor Implement Manufacturing Company* (391 U.S. 216 [1968]), a driver who had been arrested for reckless driving was at the courthouse to make bail when his vehicle was searched. The Court concluded that the search of the vehicle could not be deemed incident to impoundment, because the police seemed to have parked the car near the courthouse merely as a convenience to the owner, who, if he were soon to be released from custody, could then have driven it away.

Dyke v. Taylor Implement Manufacturing Company (1968)

Another issue in car impoundment is whether other alternatives to impoundment should be explored before placing the vehicle under police control (at least in cases in which the vehicle itself has not been involved in the crime). In their book *Emanuel Law Outlines,* Emanuel and Knowles note: "There is a growing body of authority that when the arrestee specifically requests that his car be lawfully parked in the vicinity of the arrest or that it be turned over to a friend, the police must honor his request. Indeed more and more courts are moving to the sound conclusion that the police must take the initiative with respect to apparent alternatives, such as permitting a licensed passenger to take custody of the car."[13]

The Importance of State Laws and Departmental Policies

The rules discussed in this chapter on motor vehicle searches are based primarily on U.S. Supreme Court decisions. They do not reflect state law or law agency regulations in specific police departments, which may vary greatly. State law and departmental policies may limit what the police can do. Where state law or departmental policy is more limiting than Court decisions, an officer must follow state law and departmental policy. They are binding on the police officer, regardless of what the Court held in the cases discussed in this chapter.

- *Example 1*. The Court has decided that, if the police have probable cause to stop and search an automobile on the highway, they may take it to the police station and search it there without a warrant— thus doing away with the contemporaneousness requirement. Assume, however, that, according to state law and departmental policy, once the car is brought to the police station and the driver detained, the police must obtain a warrant before conducting a search of the car. In this case, a warrant must be obtained; otherwise, the search is illegal and the evidence obtained inadmissible.
- *Example 2*. Despite what the Court has said, assume that state law or departmental policy prohibits officers from automatically ordering drivers or passengers to get out of the car or from making pretextual traffic stops. These limitations are binding on the police officer and must be followed despite what the Court in the *Mimms* and *Whren* cases in this chapter say police officers can do constitutionally. The more limiting policy governs police conduct.

Summary

The law on vehicle stops is:

- There is no need for a warrant or probable cause to legally stop a motor vehicle, but there must be reasonable suspicion of involvement in criminal activity.
- Reasonable suspicion is determined by the totality of circumstances.
- Roadblocks for specific purposes do not need reasonable suspicion, but roadblocks for

general law enforcement purposes are unconstitutional.

- After a valid stop, the officer may do the following:

  ✔ Order the driver and passengers to get out of the vehicle

  ✔ Ask the driver to produce a driver's license and other documents required by state law

✔ Ask questions of the driver and passengers

✔ Locate and examine the vehicle identification number (VIN)

✔ Require drunk-driving suspects to take a Breathalyzer test based on reasonable suspicion

✔ Search the passenger compartment for weapons if there is reasonable suspicion

✔ Search the vehicle if there is probable cause

✔ Search passengers' belongings if there is probable cause

✔ Make an arrest if there is probable cause

✔ Search the car if there is consent, even without probable cause

The law on vehicle searches is:

■ Warrantless vehicle searches are valid, but probable cause is required.

■ Searches of passengers' belongings are valid.

■ Searches of passenger compartments are valid.

■ Searches of trunks and closed packages found in trunks are valid.

■ There is no authoritative decision on whether searches of locked trunks or glove compartments are constitutional.

■ Searches of vehicles do not need to be made immediately after an arrest.

■ Warrantless vehicle searches are valid even if there was time to obtain a warrant.

■ The extent of car searches is governed by the objective reasonableness rule.

■ Searches of motor homes without a warrant are valid.

■ A warrant is sometimes needed for use of beepers to locate cars.

Review Questions and Hypothetical Cases

1. Compare and contrast the legal requirements for motor vehicle stops and searches. How are they similar? How are they different?

2. Why is a roadblock set up to catch drunk drivers constitutional whereas a road-block to catch lawbreakers is unconstitutional?

3. "Stops based on racial profiles are never valid." Is that statement true or false? Explain.

4. Assume you are stopped by the police for making an illegal turn. The penalty for that offense is a fine of $20, no jail time. Discuss whether or not you can be arrested by the police for that offense. What are the legal issues involved if you are arrested?

5. Assume that a police officer has made a valid arrest of a driver for possession of drugs. Discuss the extent of the officer's power to search as a result of that arrest.

6. "A police officer who makes a valid stop is authorized to ask the driver to get out of the car and then frisk the driver for officer protection." Is that statement true or false? Discuss.

7. *Carroll v. United States* is arguably the most important case ever to be decided on vehicle searches. What did that case say, and why is that case important?

8. Suspect S was arrested in a rest stop by a police officer for highway speeding. S was arrested by the officer about 30 yards from his car. The officer nonetheless searched the car and found illegal weapons. At trial, Suspect S sought to exclude the weapons saying they were not in the area of immediate control when seized. You are the judge. Will you admit or exclude the evidence? Justify your ruling.

9. While on patrol, P, a police officer, saw a vehicle, driven by D, that failed to heed a stop sign. Officer P saw many drivers do the same thing that day, but she did not bother to stop them because she considered them minor

traffic violations and a waste of her time. She stopped D's vehicle, however, because she had a hunch that D had drugs in the car. After the stop, Officer P had a dog sniff the car for drugs. The sniff led to the discovery of five pounds of marijuana in the passenger compartment of the car. Was the search valid? Defend your answer.

10. X, a highway patrol officer, stopped a vehicle on the freeway for speeding. Prior to issuing a ticket for speeding, X looked around the car and asked the driver to open the glove compartment. The driver voluntarily complied. Drugs were found in the glove compartment. X then arrested the driver and searched the whole car, including a briefcase marked "private" that was found in the trunk of the car. Was the search of the trunk valid? Justify your answer.

11. Officer Y was a Chicago detective who, after weeks of investigation, arrested a murder suspect in her home based on an arrest warrant. Immediately after the arrest, Officer Y searched the suspect's car, found in her driveway, for possible incriminating evidence. The search yielded drugs, which Officer Y confiscated. Was the warrantless search of the car in the suspect's driveway valid? Explain your answer.

12. Officer Z arrested a suspect on one of the city streets for robbery, based on a warrant. The driver and the car were brought to the police station where the driver was booked and detained because he could not post bail. The day after the arrest, Officer Z searched the vehicle without a warrant and found incriminating evidence that linked the suspect to the robbery. During trial, the suspect sought to exclude the evidence, saying it was obtained without a warrant and therefore the search was illegal. You are the judge. Will you admit or exclude the evidence? Justify your ruling.

Key Terms

Go to the Criminal Procedure 7e website for flash cards that will help you master the definitions of these terms.

beeper, 311
pretextual stops, 293
racial profile stops, 294

roadblock, 284
stop, 282
sobriety checkpoint, 285

vehicle impoundment, 314
vehicle inventory, 313

Holdings of Key Cases

See Appendix C for information on how to find cases in this chapter on FindLaw.com.

Arkansas v. Sanders, **442 U.S. 753 (1979)** The *Carroll* doctrine allowing warrantless searches of automobiles does not extend to warrantless searches of personal luggage merely because it was located in an automobile lawfully stopped by the police.

Atwater v. City of Lago Vista, **532 U.S. 318 (2000)** The Fourth Amendment does not forbid a warrantless arrest for a minor criminal offense that is punishable only by a fine, such as a misdemeanor seat belt violation.

Berkemer v. McCarty, **468 U.S. 420 (1984)** The roadside questioning of a motorist pursuant to a routine traffic stop is not custodial interrogation and therefore does not require the *Miranda* warnings.

Cady v. Dombrowski, **413 U.S. 433 (1973)** If, because of an accident or other circumstances, a car must remain in a location where it is vulnerable to intrusion by vandals, the police, if they have probable cause to believe that the vehicle contains a weapon or a similar device that would constitute a danger if it fell into the wrong hands, may make a warrantless search for the particular item.

California v. Acevedo, 500 U.S. 565 (1991) Probable cause to believe that a container in a car holds contraband or seizable evidence justifies a warrantless search of that container even if there is no probable cause to search the car.

California v. Carney, 471 U.S. 386 (1985) Motor homes are automobiles for purposes of the Fourth Amendment and are therefore subject to the automobile exception—meaning that they can be searched without a warrant.

Carroll v. United States, 267 U.S. 132 (1925) The search of an automobile does not require a warrant where it is not practicable to obtain one, because the vehicle can be quickly moved out of the locality or jurisdiction in which the warrant must be sought.

Chambers v. Maroney, 399 U.S. 42 (1970) For constitutional purposes, there is no difference between seizing and holding a car before presenting the probable cause issue to a magistrate and carrying out an immediate search without a warrant. Given probable cause to search, either course is reasonable under the Fourth Amendment.

Colorado v. Bannister, 449 U.S. 1 (1980) As long as the stopping of the vehicle was lawful, what officers observe can evolve into probable cause to believe that the car contains the fruits and instrumentalities of crime or contraband, thereby establishing a justification for a full warrantless search of the vehicle.

Colorado v. Bertine, 479 U.S. 367 (1987) Inventory searches without a warrant to search the person and possessions of arrested individuals are permissible under the Fourth Amendment.

Delaware v. Prouse, 440 U.S. 648 (1979) Stopping an automobile and detaining its occupants constitute a "seizure" within the meaning of the Fourth and Fourteenth Amendments, even if the purpose of the stop is limited and the resulting detention is quite brief. Roadblocks may be set up for inspection purposes, provided the officer stops every car passing the checkpoint or has an articulable, neutral principle (such as stopping every fifth car) for justifying the stop.

Dyke v. Taylor Implement Manufacturing Co., 391 U.S. 216 (1968) The search of the vehicle in this case could not be deemed incident to impoundment, because the police seemed to have parked the car near the courthouse merely as a convenience to the owner, who, if he were soon to be released from custody, could then have driven it away.

Easley v. Cromartie, 532 U.S. 1076 (2001) Using race as a factor in political redistricting is constitutional.

Florida v. Bostick, 501 U.S. 429 (1991) Consent is valid if officers ask for consent to search an item and inform the person that he or she has a right to refuse consent. However, there is no requirement under the Fourth Amendment that the officer inform the person that he or she has the right to refuse consent for it to be valid. It suffices if a reasonable person under the same circumstances would understand that he or she is free to refuse.

Florida v. Jimeno, 500 U.S. 248 (1991) Valid consent justifies a warrantless search of a container in a car if it is objectively reasonable for the police to believe that the scope of the suspect's consent permitted them to open that container.

Florida v. Meyers, 466 U.S. 380 (1984) A vehicle may be searched under the automobile exception to the Fourth Amendment even if it has been immobilized and released to the custody of the police.

Florida v. Wells, 495 U.S. 1 (1990) A police department's utter lack of any standard policy regarding the opening of closed containers encountered during inventory searches requires the suppression of contraband found in a locked suitcase removed from the trunk of an impounded vehicle and pried open by the police after the driver's arrest for drunk driving.

Florida v. White, 526 U.S. 23 (1999) The Fourth Amendment does not require the police to obtain a warrant before seizing an automobile from a public place if they have probable cause to believe it is forfeitable contraband.

Illinois v. Caballes, 543 U.S. _____ (2005) "A dog sniff conducted during a lawful traffic stop that reveals no information other than the location of a substance that no individual has any right to possess does not violate the Fourth Amendment."

***Illinois v. Lidster*, 540 U.S. 419 (2004)** Police checkpoints set up to obtain information from motorists about a hit-and-run accident are valid under the Fourth Amendment.

***Indianapolis v. Edmond*, 531 U.S. 32 (2000)** Highway checkpoints whose primary purpose is to detect evidence of ordinary criminal wrongdoing violate the Fourth Amendment.

***Knowles v. Iowa*, 525 U.S. 113 (1998)** State law that authorizes a search incident to the issuance of a traffic citation violates the Fourth Amendment unless there is consent or probable cause.

***Maryland v. Dyson*, 527 U.S. 465 (1999)** If the police have probable cause to search a car, they do not need a warrant even if there was ample opportunity to obtain one.

***Maryland v. Pringle*, 540 U.S. 366 (2003)** The police officer had probable cause to arrest the front passenger of a car from where baggies of cocaine were recovered between the back-seat armrest and the back seat. From the facts of the case, it was an "entirely reasonable inference that any or all of the car's occupants had knowledge of, and exercised dominion and control over, the cocaine."

***Maryland v. Wilson*, 519 U.S. 408 (1997)** Police officers may order passengers to get out of a motor vehicle during traffic stops.

***Michigan Department of State Police v. Sitz*, 496 U.S. 444 (1990)** Sobriety checkpoints in which the police stop every vehicle do not violate the Fourth Amendment protections against unreasonable searches and seizures and are therefore constitutional.

***Michigan v. Long*, 463 U.S. 1032 (1983)** If the officer has reasonable suspicion that the motorist who has been stopped is dangerous and may be able to gain control of a weapon in the car, the officer may conduct a brief search of the passenger compartment even if the motorist is no longer inside the car. Such a search should be limited to areas in the passenger compartment where a weapon might be found or hidden.

***New York v. Belton*, 453 U.S. 454 (1981)** Once a driver has been arrested, the police may conduct a warrantless search of the passenger compartment of the automobile. The police may examine the contents of any container found within the passenger compartment as long as it may reasonably be thought to contain something that might pose a danger to the officer or hold evidence of the offense for which the suspect has been arrested (*http://laws.findlaw.com/us/453/454.html*).

***New York v. Class*, 475 U.S. 106 (1986)** Motorists have no reasonable expectation of privacy with respect to the vehicle identification number (VIN) located on the car's dashboard even if objects on the dashboard prevent the VIN from being observed from outside the car (*http:/ /laws.findlaw.com/us/475/106.html*).

***Ohio v. Robinette*, 519 U.S. 33 (1996)** The Court reiterated its ruling in *Whren v. United States,* saying that the subjective motivation of a law enforcement officer in asking a lawfully stopped motorist to exit his or her vehicle does not affect the lawfulness of the detention. The Court also held that the officer does not need to inform the defendant first that he or she is free to go for a consent to search to be valid.

***Pennsylvania v. Mimms*, 434 U.S. 106 (1977)** Once a vehicle has been lawfully stopped for a traffic violation, the officer may order the driver to get out even without suspecting criminal activity. If the officer then reasonably believes that the driver may be armed and dangerous, the officer may conduct a limited protective frisk for a weapon that might endanger his or her personal safety.

***Robbins v. California*, 453 U.S. 420 (1981)** The automobile exception to the warrant requirement is justified by the following considerations: (1) the mobility of motor vehicles, (2) the diminished expectation of privacy, (3) the fact that the car is used for transportation, not as a residence or a repository of personal effects, (4) the fact that the car's occupants and contents travel in plain view, and (5) the necessarily high degree of regulation of automobiles by the government.

***Schneckloth v. Bustamonte*, 412 U.S. 218 (1973)** After validly stopping a car, an officer may ask the person in control of the car for permission to search.

South Dakota v. Opperman, 428 U.S. 364 (1976) When the police lawfully impound a vehicle, they may conduct a routine inventory search without a warrant or probable cause to believe that the car contains seizable evidence. This procedure is reasonable to protect the owner's property, to protect the police against a claim that the owner's property was stolen while the car was impounded, and to protect the police from potential danger.

State v. Wells, 539 So.2d 464 (Sup. Ct. Fla. 1989) Consent to search a car does not authorize police officers to pry open a locked briefcase found in the car's trunk.

Thornton v. United States, 541 U.S. 615 (2004) Officers may search the passenger compartment of a vehicle after a lawful arrest even if the initial contact and the arrest did not take place in the vehicle.

United States v. Arvizu, 534 U.S. 266 (2001) Reasonable suspicion in automobile stop cases is based on the totality of the circumstances rather than each act viewed separately.

United States v. Benitez, 899 F.2d 995 (10th Cir. 1990) The consent to search in motor vehicle searches does not have to be verbal.

United States v. Chadwick, 433 U.S. 1 (1977) The warrantless search of a footlocker that has been loaded into an automobile is invalid because the container does not come under the automobile exception even if it happens to have been removed from a car.

United States v. Cortez, 449 U.S. 411 (1981) There must be at least a reasonable suspicion to justify an investigatory stop of a motor vehicle.

United States v. Di Re, 332 U.S. 581 (1948) An officer may not conduct a body search of a passenger in a car.

United States v. Flores-Montano, 541 U.S. 149 (2004) The government's authority to conduct suspicionless inspections at the border includes the authority to remove, disassemble, and reassemble a vehicle's fuel tank.

United States v. Johns, 469 U.S. 478 (1985) The warrantless search of containers found in a car is valid even if there is a significant delay (three days in this case) between the time the police stop the vehicle and the time they perform the search.

United States v. Karo, 468 U.S. 705 (1984) The monitoring by a beeper in a private dwelling, a location not open to visual surveillance, violates the rights of individuals to privacy in their own homes. It therefore cannot be conducted without a warrant.

United States v. Knotts, 460 U.S. 276 (1983) The use by the police of a beeper to locate a car on a public road does not constitute a search, because there is no reasonable expectation of privacy. Moreover, the Fourth Amendment does not prohibit the police from supplementing their sensory faculties with technological aids to help them pinpoint a car's location.

United States v. Martinez-Fuerte, 428 U.S. 543 (1976) Stops for brief questioning that are routinely conducted at permanent checkpoints are consistent with the Fourth Amendment, so it is not necessary to obtain a warrant before setting up a checkpoint.

United States v. Montgomery, 561 F.2d 875 (1977) The police do not have an unrestricted right to stop people, either pedestrians or drivers. The "good faith" of the police is not enough, nor is an inarticulate hunch. They must have an articulable suspicion of wrongdoing, done or in prospect.

United States v. Prichard, 645 F.2d 854 (1981) Establishing a roadblock to check drivers' licenses and car registrations is legitimate. If, in the process of doing so, the officers see evidence of other crimes, they have the right to take reasonable investigative steps and are not required to close their eyes.

United States v. Ross, 456 U.S. 798 (1982) If the police legitimately stop a car and have probable cause to believe that it contains contraband, they can conduct a warrantless search of the car. The search can be as thorough as a search authorized by a warrant issued by a magistrate. Therefore, every part of the vehicle in which the contraband might be stored may be inspected, including the trunk and all receptacles and packages that could possibly contain the object of the search.

United States v. Sokolow, 490 U.S. 1 (1989) Stops cannot be based on drug courier profiles alone; the facts, taken in totality, must amount to reasonable suspicion that can justify a stop.

United States v. Travis, 62 F.3d 170 (6th Cir. 1995) The Court of Appeals for the Sixth Circuit held that race is a permissible factor to justify reasonable suspicion during airport interdictions, based on facts known to the officer.

Whren v. United States, 517 U.S. 806 (1996) The temporary detention of a motorist that is supported by probable cause to believe that the motorist has committed a traffic violation is valid even if the actual motivation of the law enforcement officer is to determine if the motorist has drugs.

Wyoming v. Houghton, 526 U.S. 295 (1999) Police officers with probable cause to search a car may inspect passengers' belongings found in the car that are capable of concealing the object of the search.

 # You Be the Judge . . .

In the Court of Appeals for the First District of Texas

In Harris County, Texas, Sheriff's Deputy Kelly was on patrol around midnight in late October of 1999. Deputy Kelly saw the van driven by Garza make an illegal left-hand turn, and he turned on the emergency lights of his patrol car to pull Garza over. Kelly pulled into a post office parking lot. Kelly determined that Garza was the only person in the van, and got Garza's driver's license. When he went back to his can to run Garza's license, he found out that there were two outstanding warrants for Garza's arrest and called for backup.

When Harris County Deputy Rooth and Sergeant Taylor arrived, Deputy Kelly placed Garza under arrest. As Kelly took Garza back to his car, Rooth and Taylor began inventorying the contents of Garza's van. Deputy Rooth spotted, in plain view, a baby formula can containing a small metal bowl, screen, spoon, and plastic bags, which he knew from experience were commonly used to sift and package cocaine. Sergeant Taylor, meanwhile, found what appeared to be a dirty diaper wrapped in a plastic bag, on top of a box of papers. He noticed no odor coming from the diaper, so he opened it and found over 28 grams of cocaine. Sergeant Taylor did complete the inventory paper work, and included it with his report. Deputy Rooth testified at the suppression hearing that they were not looking for contraband but simply conducting an inventory of Garza's property to safeguard it while his vehicle was impounded.

How will you decide this legal issue? Should the opening of a "dirty" diaper be allowed as an inventory search to safeguard Garza's property?

The Court's decision The Court of Appeals for the First District of Texas decided that the search was allowable as an inventory search. Deputy Rooth claimed the officers were not looking for contraband. The court was clear that it was giving great deference to the trial court's finding that the search was legitimate, without arguing the reasonableness of opening a "dirty" diaper per se. *Garza v. Texas*, Texas App. No. 01-00-625 (5/27/2004).

In the United States Court of Appeals for the Eighth Circuit

In Phelps County, Missouri, trickery was afoot. Martinez was driving a tractor-trailer East on Interstate 44. Just before the Sugar Tree Road exit, there were signs erected that stated "Drug Enforcement Checkpoint Ahead, One Fourth Mile" and "Drug Dogs in Use" in both English and Spanish. At that spot on the Interstate there was a sharp curve, such that Martinez could not see whether there was a checkpoint a quarter mile ahead on the Interstate or not. Martinez took the Sugar Tree Road exit, though. He rolled through the stop sign at the top of the exit ramp without stopping, turned left across the overpass over the Interstate and turned back onto the entrance ramp for the westbound lanes of traffic for I-44. There he was stopped by Sheriff Blanckenship and Deputy Rightnowar, who had been parked watching this exit ramp.

Deputy Rightnowar told Martinez that he had stopped him for running the stop sign, and asked him why he had turned around. Martinez said he was returning to the last exit to get something to eat. This made the deputy suspicious, because he knew there were no restaurants at the last exit. In fact, the last restaurant was three exits back. He noticed that Martinez was nervous and shaking uncontrollably. The deputy asked Martinez if he had anything in the truck, and Martinez said, "No." He asked Martinez if he could search the truck, and Martinez agreed, handing him the keys voluntarily.

Martinez had tried to deceive the officers here, but it was he who in fact had been deceived. There was no drug checkpoint: there were only the signs, a clever ruse designed by the Phelps County Sheriff's officer for drug interdiction. The idea was to panic any drug courier and cause them to commit a traffic infraction in their attempts to avoid the nonexistent checkpoint.

A drug dog arrived and alerted to the presence of narcotics in the trailer. The trailer was searched, and a duffle bag was found to contain 17 kilograms of cocaine.

How will you decide this legal issue? Should the use of a ruse, involving a fake checkpoint, be allowed?

The Court's decision The U.S. Court of Appeals for the Eighth Circuit decided that there was nothing impermissible about the stop in this case. The use of checkpoints that stop every vehicle or randomly selected vehicles is tightly controlled. Here, however, the officers were only stopping those committing traffic violations on the exit ramp. Even though their intent was to catch drug couriers, if an actual traffic violation occurred in their presence, then that was more than a sufficient basis for a stop. *U.S. v. Martinez,* 358 F.3d 1005 (8th Cir. 2004).

Recommended Readings

Patrick V. Banks. Note. *Fourth and Fourteenth Amendments—search and seizure—police officers with probable cause to search a vehicle may inspect a passenger's belongings found in the vehicle that are capable of concealing the object of search—* Wyoming vs. Houghton, *119 S.Ct. 1297 (1999).* 10 Seton Hall Constitutional Law Journal 543, 575 n. 2 (2000).

William J. Barry. *What's so special about trucks?* 20 Maine Bar Journal 110–114 (2005).

Daniel J. Hewitt. *Don't accept rides from strangers: The Supreme Court hastens the demise of passenger privacy in American automobiles.* 90 Journal of Criminal Law and Criminology 875, 915 (2000).

Wayne R. LaFave. *The "routine traffic stop" from start to finish: Too much "routine," not enough Fourth Amendment.* 102 Michigan Law Review 1843–1905 (2004).

Nicole C. Lally. Note. *Constitutional law—Fourth Amendment protection against unreasonable searches and seizures—Valid automobile search includes passenger's belongings.* Tennessee Law Review 455, 473 (2000).

Susan E. McPherson. Note. *Constitutional law—Fourth Amendment—warrantless arrest for misdemeanor traffic violation does not violate Fourth Amendment protection against unreasonable seizure.* Cumberland Law Review 265, 280 (2002).

Notes

1. Michele G. Hermann, *Search and Seizure Checklists,* 3rd ed. (New York: Clark Boardman, 1983), p. 78.
2. J. Gales Sauls, "Traffic Stops: Police Powers under the Fourth Amendment," *FBI Law Enforcement Bulletin,* September 1989, p. 29.
3. Ibid.
4. Tommy Sangchommpuphen, "Drunk Drivers Claim They Are Punished Twice," *Wall Street Journal,* June 21, 1995, p. B1.
5. Steven L. Emanuel and Steven Knowles, *Emanuel Law Outlines: Criminal Procedure* (Larchmont, NY: Emanuel, 1998–99), p. 100.
6. *Houston Chronicle,* May 2, 1999, p. A10.
7. *Houston Chronicle,* May 16, 1999, p. A17.
8. David Kocieniewski and Robert Hanley, "Racial Profiling Was the Routine, New Jersey Finds," *New York Times,* November 28, 2000.
9. Supra note 2, p. 30.
10. *Washington Post,* August 11, 1999, p. A13.
11. Lloyd L. Weinreb and James D. Whaley, *The Field Guide to Law Enforcement* (Westbury, NY: Foundation Press, 1999), p. 49.
12. Supra note 1, p. 78.
13. Steven L. Emanuel and Steven Knowles, *Emanuel Law Outlines* (Larchmont, NY: Emanuel, 1995–96), p. 86.

Chapter 9

Searches and Seizures Not Fully Protected by the Fourth Amendment: Plain View, Open Fields, Abandonment, and Border Searches

What You Will Learn

- The plain view doctrine has three requirements: officers must become aware of the items by seeing them, the officer must be in that specific location legally, and it must be immediately apparent that the item is subject to seizure.

- Inadvertence (accidental discovery) is no longer a requirement of plain view.

- The plain view doctrine allows evidence obtained without a warrant or probable cause to be used in court.

- Open fields do not come under the Fourth Amendment.

- Open fields begin where curtilage ends.

- Abandoned properties are not protected by the Fourth Amendment.

- Border searches at the point of entry do not come under the Fourth Amendment, but searches inside the border do.

The Top **5** Important Cases in Plain View, Open Fields, Abandonment, and Border Searches

United States v. Ramsey (1977)
"Searches made at the border pursuant to the longstanding right of the sovereign to protect itself by stopping and examining persons and property crossing into this country, are reasonable simply by virtue of the fact that they occur at the border."

Oliver v. United States (1984) A place that posts a "no trespassing" sign, has a locked gate (with a foot-path around it), and is located more than a mile from the owner's house has no reasonable expectation of privacy and is considered an open field, unprotected by the Fourth Amendment.

Boyd v. United States (1986) Curtilage is the area to which extends the inti-mate activity associated with the sanctity of a person's home and the privacies of life.

United States v. Dunn (1987) Whether an area is considered a part of the curtilage and therefore covered by the Fourth Amendment rests on four factors: (1) the proximity of the area to the home, (2) whether the area is in an enclosure surrounding the home, (3) the nature and uses of the area, and (4) the steps taken to con-ceal the area from public view.

Horton v. California (1990) The Fourth Amendment does not prohibit the warrantless seizure of evidence in plain view, even though the discovery of the evidence was not inadvertent.

Introduction

This chapter discusses four situations related to searches and seizures that do not enjoy full Fourth Amendment pro-tection. These are plain view, open fields, abandonment, and border searches. What these situations have in common is some form of "taking" by the government of something that belongs to or used to belong to somebody. The legal rules and requirements surrounding them differ, however, and so we will discuss them separately. All four situations involve some type of contact with or action by the police, but they concern the seizure of items or things—not of people. In these cases, ownership of the item seized cannot be established (in the case of plain view, open fields, or abandonment) or property interest is subordinate to a higher need for security (as in the case of border searches).

They therefore differ from contacts (discussed in Chapter 6), which are also unprotected by the Fourth Amendment. These are contacts, such as the police

- Asking questions of people they see or meet
- Asking a vehicle driver to get out of a car after stopping him
- Boarding a bus and asking questions that a person is free to refuse to answer
- Riding alongside a person "to see where he was going"

These contacts with the police involve people, not items, but are also unprotected by the Fourth Amendment because they are casual and only minimally intrusive.

The Plain View Doctrine

The plain view doctrine gives officers the right to seize items that are plainly within their view as long as they have the legal right to be in the position to see the items. This section discusses the application of this doctrine. We begin with the case that defined the plain view doctrine and then examine (1) the requirements of the doctrine; (2) situations in which it applies; (3) how it is used as a justification for admitting evidence into court; (4) the change in the Court's ruling on inadvertent viewing; (5) the application of plain view to open spaces, motor vehicles, and the use of mechanical devices; and end by (6) comparing plain view with open view, plain touch, and plain odor.

Plain View Defined

***Harris v. United States* (1968)**

See Appendix C for information on how to find cases in this chapter on FindLaw.com.

The **plain view doctrine** states that items that are within the sight of an officer who is legally in the place from which the view is made may properly be seized without a warrant—as long as such items are immediately recognizable as subject to seizure.

What the officer sees in plain view can be seized without having to worry about the Fourth Amendment. In the words of the Court, "It has long been settled that objects falling in the plain view of an officer who has a right to be in a position to have that view are subject to seizure and may be introduced in evidence" (*Harris v. United States*, 390 U.S. 234 [1968]).

In *Harris v. United States* (1968), a police officer searched an impounded automobile in connection with a robbery. While opening the door, the officer saw, in plain view, the automobile registration card belonging to the victim of the robbery. Harris was charged with robbery. At trial, he moved to suppress the automobile registration card, claiming it was obtained illegally because the officer had no warrant, although he had time to obtain one. On appeal, the Court admitted the evidence, saying that the automobile registration card was in plain view and therefore did not need a warrant to be seized.

Although generally considered an exception to the search warrant requirement, plain view is really not a search under Fourth Amendment, because there is no search by the police for that specific item. No warrant or probable cause is necessary; the officer simply seizes what is seen, not something that has been searched. Sighting the item is usually accidental and unexpected.

Requirements of the Plain View Doctrine

Three basic requirements of the plain view doctrine must be met for the evidence to be seized legally by the police: the officer must have gained awareness of the item solely by sighting it; the officer must be in that physical position legally; and it must be immediately apparent that it is a seizable item.

Awareness of the Item through Use of Sight
Awareness of the items must be gained solely through the officer's sight, not through the other senses—hearing, smelling, tasting, or touching. This means that the item must be *plainly visible* to the officer. For example, suppose that while executing a search warrant for a stolen typewriter an officer sees marijuana on the suspect's nightstand. The marijuana may be seized because the officer knows through the sense of sight that the item is illegal and therefore seizable. But if the officer merely suspects that there is marijuana in the apartment because of the smell, as might occur if it were hidden in a closet or drawer, its seizure in the course of a search cannot be justified under the plain view doctrine. Of course, it may be seized validly without a warrant if the officer can establish probable cause and the presence of exigent circumstances.

The Officer Must Be Legally in the Place from which the Item Is Seen
The officer must not have done anything illegal to get to the spot from which he or she sees the items in question. An officer comes to be in a place properly in a number of ways: (1) when serving a search warrant, (2) while in hot pursuit of a suspect, (3) having made entry through valid consent, and (4) when making a valid arrest with or without a warrant. For example, suppose that while executing a search warrant for a stolen TV set an officer sees gambling slips on a table. She may properly seize them, even though they were not included in the warrant, as long as her presence on the premises is legal. By contrast, a police officer who forces her way into

a house and then sees drugs on the table cannot validly seize the drugs, because she entered the house illegally. What the officer sees subsequent to entry can never cure the initial illegality.

The Item Must Be Immediately Apparent as Subject to Seizure

Recognition of the items in plain view must be immediate and not the result of further prying or examination. In other words, the items must be out in the open, and it must be immediately apparent that they are seizable. For example, suppose an officer sees something that she immediately recognizes as gambling paraphernalia. She may seize it under plain view. By contrast, suppose that after a valid entry the officer sees a typewriter she suspects is stolen. She calls the police station to ask for the serial number of a typewriter earlier reported stolen and, after verification of the number, seizes the typewriter. This seizure cannot be justified under the plain view doctrine, because the item was not immediately recognizable as subject to seizure. The evidence may be seized, but the seizure will have to be justified based on other legal grounds, such as consent or exigent circumstances.

Arizona v. Hicks
(1987)

The "immediately apparent" requirement must be based on *probable cause,* not on any lesser degree of certainty, such as reasonable suspicion (*Arizona v. Hicks,* 480 U.S. 321 [1987]). In *Arizona v. Hicks* (1987), a bullet fired through the floor of Hicks's apartment injured a man below, prompting the police to enter Hicks's apartment to search for the suspect, weapons, and other potential victims. An officer discovered three weapons and a stocking-cap mask. He also noticed several pieces of stereo equipment, which seemed out of place in the ill-appointed apartment. The officer therefore read and recorded the serial numbers of the equipment, moving some of the pieces in the process. A call to police headquarters confirmed that one of the pieces of equipment was stolen; a later check revealed that the other pieces were also stolen. Hicks was convicted of robbery.

On appeal, Hicks sought suppression of the evidence, saying that the plain view search was illegal. The Court agreed, noting that with plain view there must be probable cause to believe that the items being searched are, in fact, contraband or evidence of criminal activity. A lesser degree of certainty, such as reasonable suspicion, as in this case, would not suffice.

On the other hand, "certain knowledge"—a higher degree of certainty than probable cause—is not necessary. For example, in *Texas v. Brown* (460 U.S. 730 [1983]), an officer stopped a car at night to check the driver's license. He shone his flashlight into the car's interior and saw the driver holding an opaque green party balloon knotted about a half inch from the tip. The officer also saw white powder in the open glove compartment. In court, the officer testified that he had learned from experience that inflated, tied-off balloons often were used to transport narcotics. The Court concluded that the officer had probable cause to believe that the balloon contained narcotics, so the warrantless seizure was justified under plain view (*Texas v. Brown,* 460 U.S. 730 [1983]).

Texas v. Brown
(1983)

Situations in which the Plain View Doctrine Applies

In police work, there are many situations in which the plain view doctrine applies and the items seen may be seized without a warrant. Among these are the following:

- Making an arrest with or without a warrant
- In hot pursuit of a fleeing suspect
- Making a search incident to a valid arrest
- Out on patrol
- Making a car inventory search
- Conducting an investigation in a residence
- Making an entry into a home after obtaining valid consent

This list is illustrative, not comprehensive. In sum, the plain view doctrine applies to every aspect of police work as long as all three of the requirements of plain view are met.

Plain View: One of Many Justifications for Admission of Evidence in Court

The plain view doctrine is only one of many possible legal justifications for admitting evidence obtained by the police in court. It is used as a legal justification for seizure only if all three requirements are met. The absence of one of these elements means that the evidence is not admissible under plain view, but it may still be admissible under another legal doctrine. For example, suppose an officer arrests a suspect at home by authority of an arrest warrant. While there, the officer sees in the living room several TV sets that he suspects may be stolen. He telephones the police department to give the serial numbers and is informed that those sets have been reported stolen. At this stage, the officer has probable cause to seize the items.

The officer cannot seize them under plain view, because the items were not immediately recognizable as subject to seizure. Ordinarily, the officer would need a warrant to seize the sets, but warrantless seizures may be justified if the officer can establish exigent circumstances (such as that the sets would most likely be

HIGHLIGHT

Requirements of the Plain View Doctrine

All three of the following requirements must be met for the item to be seized legally; the absence of one means the plain view doctrine does not apply:

1. The awareness of the item must be through use of the sense of sight.

2. The officer must be legally in the place from which the item is seen.

3. It must be immediately apparent that the item is subject to seizure.

hauled away by the other occupants if the officer left the house). The TV sets are then admissible in court under the probable cause and exigent circumstances exception, but not under plain view.

Inadvertence No Longer Required: *Horton v. California*

For a long time, inadvertence was one of the plain view requirements. **Inadvertence** means that the officer must have no prior knowledge that the evidence was present in the place; the discovery must be purely accidental. In the words of one court, "The plain view doctrine is properly applied to situations in which a police officer is not searching for evidence against the accused but nevertheless inadvertently comes across an incriminating object" (*United States v. Sedillo,* 496 F.2d 151 [9th Cir. 1974]).

United States v. Sedillo (9th Cir. 1974)

In *Coolidge v. New Hampshire* (403 U.S. 443 [1971]), the Supreme Court said, "The . . . discovery of evidence in plain view must be inadvertent. . . . But where the discovery is anticipated, where the police know in advance the location of the evidence and intend to seize it, the situation is altogether different." However, the Court has abandoned the inadvertence requirement. In a 1990 case, *Horton v. California* (496 U.S. 128 [1990]), the Court stated, "The Fourth Amendment does not prohibit the warrantless seizure of evidence in plain view even though the discovery of the evidence was not inadvertent. Although inadvertence is a characteristic of most legitimate plain view seizures, it is not a necessary condition."

Coolidge v. New Hampshire (1971)

Horton v. California (1990)

In *Horton,* a police officer determined that there was probable cause to search Horton's home for the proceeds from a robbery and for weapons used in the robbery. The affidavit filed by the officer referred to police reports that described both the weapons and the proceeds, but for some reason the warrant issued by the magistrate only authorized a search for the proceeds. When the officer went to Horton's home to execute the warrant, he did not find the stolen property (proceeds), but he did see the weapons (an Uzi machine gun, a .38-caliber revolver, and two stun guns) in plain view and seized them. At trial, the officer testified that, while he was searching Horton's home for the proceeds, he was also interested in finding "other evidence" related to the robbery. Tried and convicted, Horton argued on appeal that the weapons should have been suppressed because their discovery was not inadvertent.

The Court disagreed, saying that, "although inadvertence is a characteristic of most legitimate plain view seizures, it is not a necessary condition." The Court expressly rejected the inadvertence requirement, noting that (1) evenhanded law enforcement is best achieved by the application of objective standards of conduct rather than by standards that depend on the officer's subjective state of mind, and (2) the suggestion that the inadvertence requirement is necessary to prevent the police from conducting a general search or from converting specific warrants into general warrants is not persuasive. In this case, "the scope of the search was not enlarged in the slightest by the omission of any reference to the weapons in the warrant." The Court held that the evidence was admissible.

The *Horton* decision means that most plain view cases will still be the result of inadvertence (meaning that the officer sees a seizable item that he or she did not expect to see), but in the process of serving a warrant, an officer may also seize an item he or she knew beforehand would be there even if the item is not listed in the warrant as one of those to be seized.

Authors Steven Emanuel and Steven Knowles interpret *Horton* this way:

- The "plain view" doctrine applies even where the police's discovery of a piece of evidence they want to seize is not inadvertent. Thus if the police know that they are likely to find, say, both the gun used in a robbery as well as the proceeds of the robbery, they may procure a warrant for the proceeds, and may then seize the gun if they happen upon it in plain view while they are searching for the proceeds.[1]

(Read the Case Brief to learn more about the *Horton* case.)

CASE BRIEF: The Leading Case on "Plain View" and Inadvertence
Horton v. California, 496 U.S. 128 (1990)

Facts: A police officer determined that there was probable cause to search the suspect Horton's home for the proceeds of a robbery and weapons used in the robbery. The affidavit filed by the officer referred to police reports that described both the weapons and the proceeds, but the warrant that was issued only authorized a search for the proceeds. When the officer went to Horton's home to execute the warrant, he did not find the stolen property (proceeds) but did find the weapons in plain view and seized them. At the trial, the officer testified that while he was searching Horton's home for the proceeds, he was also interested in finding other evidence related to the robbery. Tried and convicted, Horton argued on appeal that the weapons should have been suppressed during the trial because their discovery was not "inadvertent."

Issue: *Is inadvertence a necessary element of the plain view doctrine? No.*

Supreme Court Decision: "The Fourth Amendment does not prohibit the warrantless seizure of evidence in plain view even though the discovery of the evidence was not inadvertent.

Although inadvertence is a characteristic of most legitimate plain view seizures, it is not a necessary condition."

Case Significance: This case does away with the requirement that for plain view to apply, the discovery of the evidence must be purely accidental. The police officer in this case knew that the evidence was there. It was, in fact, described in the officer's affidavit, but for some reason the warrant issued by the magistrate only authorized a search for the proceeds. The Court said that the seizure was valid, nonetheless, because

1. "The items seized from petitioner's home were discovered during a lawful search authorized by a valid warrant."
2. "When they were discovered, it was immediately apparent to the officer that they constituted incriminating evidence."
3. "The officer had probable cause, not only to obtain a warrant to search for the stolen property, but also to believe that the weapons and handguns had

---

been used in the crime he was investigating."

4. "The search was authorized by the warrant."

Excerpts from the Decision: Justice Stewart [in *Coolidge v. New Hampshire,* 403 U.S. 443 (1979)] concluded that the inadvertence requirement was necessary to avoid a violation of the express constitutional requirement that a valid warrant must particularly describe the things to be seized. He explained: "The rationale of the exception to the warrant requirement, as just stated, is that a plain view seizure will not turn an initially valid (and therefore limited) search into a 'general' one, while the inconvenience of procuring a warrant to cover an inadvertent discovery is great. But where the discovery is anticipated, where the police know in advance the location of the evidence and intend to seize it, the situation is altogether different. The requirement of a warrant to seize imposes no inconvenience whatever, or at least none which is constitutionally cognizable in a legal system that regards warrantless searches as 'per se unreasonable' in the absence of 'exigent circumstances.'"

We find two flaws in this reasoning. First, evenhanded law enforcement is best achieved by the application of objective standards of conduct, rather than standards that depend upon the subject state of mind of the officer. The fact that an officer is interested in an item of evidence and fully expects to find it in the course of a search should not invalidate its seizure if the search is confined in area and duration by the terms of a warrant or a valid exception to the warrant requirement. If the officer has knowledge approaching certainty that the item will be found, we see no reason why he or she would deliberately omit a particular description of the items to be seized from the application of a search warrant. Specification of the additional item could only permit the officer to expand the scope of the search. On the other hand, if he or she has a valid warrant to search for one item and merely a suspicion concerning the second, whether or not it amounts to probable cause, we fail to see why that suspicion should immunize the second item from seizure if it is found during a lawful search for the first.

Second, the suggestion that the inadvertence requirement is necessary to prevent the police from conducting general searches, or from converting specific warrants into general warrants, is not persuasive because that interest is already served by the requirements that no warrant issue unless it "particularly describes the place to be searched and the persons or things to be seized," and that a warrantless search be circumscribed by the exigencies which justify its initiation.

Plain View and Open Spaces

Plain view usually applies when the officer is within an enclosed space (such as a house, an apartment, or an office)—hence, the concept used by some courts of a "prior valid intrusion into a constitutionally protected area." It also applies when the officer is out in the open, such as out on the street on patrol. In open spaces, however, a distinction must be made between *seeing* and *seizing*. For example, suppose that, while walking around an apartment complex, an officer sees illegal weapons through a window. This is also plain view. The difference between this scenario and one in which the officer is within the apartment itself is that here the officer cannot make an entry into the apartment to seize the items without a warrant unless he or she obtains consent or establishes exigent circumstances.

When the officer is in an enclosed space (such as a house or apartment), *seizing automatically follows seeing* as a matter of natural sequence. By contrast, when an entry is needed, seeing and seizing become two separate acts because of the need for a legal entry. In the absence of consent or exigent circumstances, the officer needs a warrant if he or she must make some form of entry before seizing the item. An exigent circumstance would exist, for example, if the officer could establish that the evidence would most likely no longer be available unless immediate action were taken. Without an exigent circumstance, the officer must obtain a warrant.

Plain view also applies to items seen from outside fences or enclosures. For example, suppose an officer on patrol sees pots of marijuana inside a fenced yard. This falls under plain view, but the officer needs a warrant to enter the fenced yard to seize the marijuana.

Plain View and Motor Vehicles

Plain view also applies to motor vehicles. For example, suppose that, while out on patrol, Officer Y observes a car parked on the street, looks at the front seat, and sees drugs and drug paraphernalia. This scenario falls under plain view. Whether Officer Y can seize these items without a warrant, however, is not clear, particularly if the vehicle is closed and locked. This is different from the usual plain view situation, in which seeing immediately leads to seizing, because no further entry is necessary. The Supreme Court has not addressed this issue. In view of this uncertainty, the better practice is for Officer Y to obtain a warrant to gain entry to the vehicle, unless entry could be made without using force (as when Officer Y obtains possession of the key), consent were given, or exigent circumstances were present that would justify immediate entry.

Plain View and the Use of Mechanical Devices

The use of mechanical devices by the police does not affect the applicability of the plain view doctrine. For example, the use of a flashlight by an officer to look into the inside of a car at night does not constitute a search under the Fourth Amendment. Evidence that would not have been discovered and seized without the use of a flashlight is nonetheless admissible in court (*Texas v. Brown*, 460 U.S. 730 [1983]). The same is true for the use of binoculars. In *United States v. Knotts* (460 U.S. 276 [1983]), the police use of a beeper to monitor the whereabouts of a person traveling in a car on public highways did not turn the surveillance into a search. Such monitoring on a public highway was considered by the Court to fall under the plain view doctrine.

United States v. Knotts (1983)

The officer does not need to be standing upright for plain view to apply. For example, in the *Brown* case, the police officer who legally stopped the automobile bent down so that he could see what was inside the car. The Court said that the fact that the officer got into an unusual position to see the contents of the vehicle did not prevent the plain view doctrine from applying.

Comparison between Plain View and Open View

Some lower courts distinguish between plain view and open view. They apply plain view to cases in which the officer has made a "prior valid intrusion into a constitutionally protected area" (meaning when the officer is inside an enclosed space, such as a house or an apartment) and apply the term **open view** to instances when the officer is out in open space (such as the street) but sees an item within an enclosed area (*State v. Stachler*, 570 P.2d 1323 [1977]). The Supreme Court, however, has not made this distinction, so the discussion of plain view in this text includes the concept of open view.

State v. Stachler (1977)

Comparison between Plain View and Plain Touch

As discussed in Chapter 3, probable cause is usually established through the use of the officer's five senses—sight, touch, smell, hearing, and taste. Plain view refers to the sense of sight, which is the most common way probable cause is established.

Does a similar doctrine apply to the sense of touch? Although not as well known or as extensively developed in case law as plain view, recent Court decisions have reaffirmed the existence of the **plain touch** (some call it "plain feel") **doctrine**. It holds that if an officer touches or feels something that is immediately identifiable as seizable, the object can be seized as long as such knowledge amounts to probable cause. The most recent Court case on plain touch is *Minnesota v. Dickerson* (508 U.S. 366 [1993]), discussed in Chapter 5 in the context of stop and frisk. The Court in *Dickerson* excluded the evidence obtained, because the officer went beyond what is allowable in a pat-down frisk when he proceeded to "squeeze, slide, and manipulate" the item he felt in the suspect's jacket and which he admitted was not a dangerous weapon.

Minnesota v. Dickerson (1993)

The Court, however, refused to go along with the Minnesota Supreme Court's rejection of the doctrine of plain touch, saying that "the very premise of *Terry* [*Terry v. Ohio*, 392 U.S. 1 (1968)], after all, is that officers will be able to detect the presence of weapons through the sense of touch," and further added: "We think this doctrine [referring to plain view] has an obvious application by analogy to cases in which an officer discovers contraband through the sense of touch during an otherwise lawful search." The Court then concluded that, "If a police officer lawfully pats down a suspect's outer clothing and feels an object whose contour or mass makes its identity immediately apparent, there has been no invasion of the suspect's privacy beyond that already authorized by the officer's search for weapons; if the object is contraband, its warrantless seizure would be justified by the same practical considerations that inhere in the plain-view context."

Terry v. Ohio (1968)

The Court in *Dickerson* would probably have held the evidence admissible if the officer had testified that during the pat-down he touched something that, although not a weapon, he knew from his background and experience and the totality of circumstances was contraband. That would have been a clear case of plain feel leading to probable cause.

Comparison between Plain View and Plain Odor

United States v. Johns (1985)

Emanuel and Knowles maintain that the plain view doctrine also applies to plain odor. In the **plain odor doctrine**, if an officer smells something that is immediately recognizable as seizable, that object can be seized as long as that knowledge amounts to probable cause. These writers cite the case of *United States v. Johns* (469 U.S. 478 [1985]), in which the Court said that "whether defendant ever had a privacy interest in the packages reeking of marijuana is debatable."[2]

This issue has not been directly addressed by the Court; most plain view cases involve the sense of sight and, more recently, the sense of touch. In the absence of any definitive pronouncement from the Court, it is better to limit the "plain" doctrine, for now, to the twin senses of sight and touch. Note, however, that the sense of smell is one of the senses that can establish probable cause. Plain odor, however, has simply not been clearly established thus far as a legal doctrine by Court decisions.

The Open Fields Doctrine

In this section, we define the open fields doctrine, identify areas not included in this doctrine, define and discuss curtilage, examine the significance of *Oliver v. United States* in expanding the open fields doctrine, look at the impact of the use of sense-enhancement technology and beepers on this doctrine, and then compare the open fields and plain view doctrines.

The Open Fields Doctrine Defined

Hester v. United States (1924)

The **open fields doctrine** states that items in open fields are not protected by the Fourth Amendment's guarantee against unreasonable searches and seizures, so they can properly be taken by an officer without a warrant or probable cause. The Fourth Amendment protects only "houses, papers, and effects" against unreasonable searches and seizures. Open fields do not come under "houses, papers, and effects," so the constitutional protection does not apply. In the words of Justice Oliver Wendell Holmes, "The special protection accorded by the Fourth Amendment to the people in their persons, houses, papers, and effects is not extended to the open fields" (*Hester v. United States,* 265 U.S. 57 [1924]).

Areas Not Included in Open Fields

Certain areas come under the protection of the Fourth Amendment and therefore cannot be classified as open fields. This includes houses.

Courts have interpreted the term *houses* under the Fourth Amendment broadly, applying it to homes (owned, rented, or leased), apartments, hotel or motel rooms, hospital rooms, and even sections not generally open to the public in places of business. *Black's Law Dictionary* defines a *house* as a "structure that serves as living quarters for one or more persons or families."[3] Under this definition, a homeless person can have a "house" that is protected against unreasonable searches and seizures as long as whatever shelter there is has a reasonable expectation of privacy.

Curtilage

Curtilage is "the area to which extends the intimate activity associated with the 'sanctity of a man's home, and the privacies of life'" (*Boyd v. United States,* 116 U.S. 616 [1886]). In general, "curtilage has been held to include all buildings in close proximity to a dwelling, which are continually used for carrying on domestic employment; or such place as is necessary and convenient to a dwelling and is habitually used for family purposes" (*United States v. Potts,* 297 F.2d 68 [6th Cir. 1961]). Curtilage is considered a part of the building and is therefore protected against unreasonable searches and seizures. Officers need a warrant and probable cause to seize items in the curtilage.

Boyd v. United States (1886)

United States v. Potts (6th Cir. 1961)

Curtilage may encompass a variety of places, including the following:

- *Residential yards.* Courts disagree on whether yards are part of the curtilage. If members of the public have access to the yard at any time, it is probably not curtilage. But if only members of the family have access to it, it may be part of the curtilage.
- *Fenced areas.* A fence around a house makes the immediate environs within that fence a part of the curtilage, because the owner clearly intended that area to be private and not open to the general public.
- *Apartment houses.* Areas of an apartment building that are used in common by all tenants are not considered part of any tenant's curtilage. However, if the apartment building is of limited size (such as a four-unit building), and each apartment has its own backyard or front yard that is not accessible to the general public, such areas would be part of the curtilage.
- *Barns and other outbuildings.* Outbuildings are usually considered part of the curtilage if they are used extensively by the family, are enclosed by a fence, or are close to the house. The farther such buildings are from the house, the less likely it is that they will be considered part of the curtilage.
- *Garages.* Garages are usually considered part of the curtilage unless they are far from the house and seldom used.

The relationship between houses, curtilage (both protected by the Fourth Amendment), and open fields can be illustrated as follows:

House Curtilage   Open Field

Protected by the   Not protected by the Fourth Amendment
Fourth Amendment

Open field begins where curtilage ends. Fourth Amendment protection applies only to the home and the curtilage, not to open fields.

Next, we will look at the case that defined the test to determine curtilage and the case that determined whether evidence gathered from aerial surveillance of curtilage was admissible.

The Test to Determine Curtilage: *United States v. Dunn*

United States v. Dunn (1987)

How is curtilage determined? The Court ruled in *United States v. Dunn* (480 U.S. 294 [1987]) that determining whether an area is considered a part of the curtilage and therefore covered by Fourth Amendment protections rests on four factors:

1. The proximity of the area to the home
2. Whether the area is in an enclosure surrounding the home
3. The nature and uses of the area
4. The steps taken to conceal the area from public view

The Court quickly added this caution, however:

> We do not suggest that combining these factors produces a finely tuned formula that, when mechanically applied, yields a "correct" answer to all extent-of-curtilage questions. Rather, these factors are useful analytical tools only to the degree that, in any given case, they bear upon the centrally relevant consideration—whether the area in question is so intimately tied to the home itself that it should be placed under the "umbrella" of Fourth Amendment protection.

Applying these factors in *Dunn,* the Court concluded that the barn in this case could not be considered part of the curtilage. In *Dunn,* after learning that a co-defendant had purchased large quantities of chemicals and equipment used in the manufacture of controlled substances, drug agents obtained a warrant to place an electronic tracking beeper in some of the equipment. The beeper ultimately led agents to Dunn's farm. The farm was encircled by a perimeter fence, with several interior fences of the type used to hold livestock. Without a warrant, officers entered the premises over the perimeter fence, interior fences, and a wooden fence that encircled a barn, approximately fifty yards from the respondent's home. En route to the barn, the officers crossed two barbwire fences and one wooden fence. Without entering the barn, the officers stood at a locked gate and shone a flashlight into the barn, where they observed what appeared to be a drug laboratory. Officers returned twice the following day to confirm the presence of the laboratory, each time without entering the barn. Based on information gained from these observations, officers obtained a search warrant and seized incriminating evidence from the barn.

Dunn was convicted of conspiracy to manufacture controlled substances. On appeal, he sought exclusion of the evidence, saying that (1) a barn located sixty yards from a house and fifty yards from a second fence surrounding the house is part of the curtilage and therefore could not be searched without a warrant, and (2) the officers committed trespass en route to the barn. The Court disagreed, saying that, judged in terms of the four tests (enumerated previously), this particular barn could not be considered a part of the curtilage, despite the presence of three fences.

The Court added that the concept of *physical trespass is no longer the test* that determines whether the Fourth Amendment applies. Instead, the test is *whether there exists a reasonable expectation of privacy* that deserves protection. In this case, despite the presence of fences, there was none. But the Court added that, although the barn itself was part of the open field, the inside of the barn was protected by the Fourth Amendment, and so a warrant was needed for a lawful entry.[4]

The good news about *Dunn* is that for the first time the Court laid out the tests lower courts should use to determine whether a barn, building, garage, or the like is part of the curtilage. The bad news is that these factors are difficult for trial courts to apply with precision. Given the existing tests, what is curtilage to one court may not be curtilage to another. Nonetheless, they are an improvement over the complete absence of a standard under which the lower courts decided cases prior to *Dunn*.

Aerial Surveillance of Curtilage: *California v. Ciraolo*

California v. Ciraolo (1986)

The fact that a space is part of a home's curtilage does not mean it is automatically entitled to constitutional protection against any and all intrusions. In *California v. Ciraolo* (476 U.S. 207 [1986]), the Court decided that the constitutional protection against unreasonable search and seizure is not violated by the naked-eye aerial observation by the police of a suspect's backyard, which admittedly is a part of the curtilage.

In this case, police in Santa Clara, California, received an anonymous phone tip that marijuana was being grown in Ciraolo's backyard. The backyard was shielded from public view by a six-foot outer fence and a ten-foot inner fence completely enclosing the yard. On the basis of the tip, officers trained in marijuana identification obtained a private airplane and flew over the suspect's house at an altitude of 1,000 feet. They readily identified the plants growing in the yard as marijuana. A search warrant was obtained on the basis of the naked-eye observation by one of the officers, supported by a photograph of the surrounding area taken from the airplane. Officers executed the warrant and seized the marijuana plants. In a motion to suppress the evidence, the defendant alleged that the warrantless aerial observation of the yard violated the Fourth Amendment.

The Court rejected Ciraolo's contention, saying that no Fourth Amendment right was violated. The Court admitted that he "took normal precautions to maintain his privacy" by erecting the fence, but added:

> The area is within the curtilage and does not itself bar all police observation. The Fourth Amendment protection of the home has never been extended to require law enforcement officers to shield their eyes when passing by a home on public thoroughfares. Nor does the mere fact that an individual has taken measures to restrict some views of his activities preclude an officer's observations from a public vantage point where he has a right to be and which renders the activities clearly visible. . . . The observations by Officers Shutz and Rodriguez in this case took place within public navigable airspace, in a physically nonintrusive manner; from this point they were able to observe plants readily discernible to the naked eye as marijuana. . . . On this record, we readily conclude that respondent's expectation that his garden was protected from such observation is unreasonable and is not an expectation that society is prepared to honor.

Florida v. Riley
(1989)

In the *Ciraolo* case, the private airplane flew over the suspect's house at an altitude of 1,000 feet to make the observations. Suppose the flight had been made by the police in a helicopter at a height of 400 feet. Would the evidence still have been admissible? In *Florida v. Riley* (488 U.S. 445 [1989]), the Court answered yes, saying that, as long as the police are flying at an altitude at which Federal Aviation Administration (FAA) regulations allow members of the public to fly (the FAA sets no minimum for helicopters), such aerial observation is valid because, in the absence of FAA prohibitions, the homeowner would have no reasonable expectation of privacy from such flights. Note, however, that these cases involved mere "looking" or "peering," but not entering, so the degree of intrusion was minimal.

Open Fields Despite a Locked Gate and a "No Trespassing" Sign: *Oliver v. United States*

Oliver v. United States (1984)

In a 1984 decision, *Oliver v. United States* (466 U.S. 170 [1984]), the Supreme Court gave the open fields doctrine a broader meaning. In that case, the Court said that it is legal for the police to enter and search unoccupied or underdeveloped

HIGHLIGHT

Open Fields

Definition. Items in open fields are not protected by the Fourth Amendment guarantee against unreasonable searches and seizures, so they can be seized by an officer without a warrant or probable cause.

Curtilage. "The area to which extends the intimate activity associated with the sanctity of a man's home, and the privacies of life."

Test to determine curtilage. If a person has a reasonable expectation of privacy in a place, it is part of the curtilage and is protected by the Fourth Amendment.

Applications. Aerial surveillance of curtilage is valid. Also, an area may be an open field despite the presence of a locked gate and a "no trespassing" sign.

areas outside the curtilage without either a warrant or probable cause, as long as the place comes under the category of "fields," even if the police had to pass a locked gate and a "no trespassing" sign. The field in this case was secluded and not visible from any point of public access. The Court defined the term *open fields* to include "any unoccupied or underdeveloped area outside the curtilage"—a definition sufficiently broad to include the heavily wooded area where the defendant's marijuana crop was discovered by the police.

The significance of *Oliver* is that it reaffirms the doctrine that the "reasonable expectation of privacy" standard in Fourth Amendment cases does not apply when the property involved is an open field. The Court stressed that steps taken to protect privacy—such as planting the marijuana on secluded land, erecting a locked gate (but with a footpath along one side), and posting "no trespassing" signs around the property—do not necessarily establish any reasonable expectation of privacy. The test, according to the Court, is not whether the individual chooses to conceal assertedly "private activity, but whether the government's intrusion infringes upon the personal and societal values protected by the Fourth Amendment." The fact that the government's intrusion upon an open field (as in this case) is a trespass according to common law does not make it a "search" in the constitutional sense, so the Fourth Amendment does not apply.

The *Oliver* case involved a warrantless observation of a marijuana patch located more than a mile from Oliver's house. The *Dunn* case involved the warrantless observation of a barn located just sixty yards from a house and fifty yards from a wooden fence that, in turn, was within a bigger perimeter fence. In both cases, the Court concluded that neither property could be considered a part of the curtilage and therefore became open field.

The *Dunn, Ciraolo,* and *Oliver* cases all tell us that the concept of curtilage has become restricted and that of open field has been significantly expanded by the Court, thus giving law enforcement officials greater leeway in search and seizure cases. The relationship among houses and buildings, curtilage, and open fields may generally be stated as follows: Houses and buildings are the most protected, then comes curtilage, and then come open fields. Houses, buildings, and curtilage are protected by the Fourth Amendment; open fields are not. (Read the Case Brief to learn more about the *Oliver* case.)

Open Fields and the Use of Sense-Enhancement Technology

Kyllo v. United States (2001)

In *Kyllo v. United States* (533 U.S. 27 [2001]), the Court held that using a technological device to explore the details of a home that would previously have been unknowable without physical intrusion is a search and is presumptively unreasonable without a warrant.

In *Kyllo,* officers suspected Kyllo of growing marijuana in his home. They used a thermal imaging device from across the street (therefore an open field) to examine the heat radiating from his house. The scan showed that the roof over the garage and a side wall of the house were relatively hot compared to the rest of his house and substantially hotter than neighboring homes. Based on this information, on utility bills,

Facts: Acting on reports that marijuana was grown on the petitioner's farm, but without a search warrant, probable cause, or exigent circumstances, police officers went to a farm to investigate. They drove past Oliver's house to a locked gate with a No Trespassing sign but with a footpath around one side. Officers followed the footpath around the gate and found a field of marijuana more than a mile from Oliver's house. He was charged with and convicted of manufacturing a controlled substance.

Issue: *Is a place that is posted with a No Trespassing sign, has a locked gate (with a footpath around it), and is located more than a mile from the owner's house considered an open field? Yes.*

Supreme Court Decision: A place where the property owner posts a No Trespassing sign and has a locked gate but with a footpath around it, located more than a mile from the house, has no reasonable expectation of privacy and is considered an open field. Therefore, it is legal for the police to enter that area without a warrant or probable cause, because it is unprotected by the Fourth Amendment.

Case Significance: This case makes clear that the reasonable expectation of privacy doctrine does not apply when the property involved is an open field. The Court defines what areas enjoy the protection extended by the reasonable expectation of privacy doctrine. The Court stressed that steps taken to protect privacy, such as planting marijuana on secluded land and erecting a locked gate (but with a footpath along one side) and posting No Trespassing signs around the property, do not establish any reasonable expectation of privacy, so the property comes under open fields. Therefore, the police could enter the property without a warrant or probable cause. The test to determine whether the property

comes under a reasonable expectation of privacy or is considered an open field is not whether the individual chooses to conceal assertedly "private activity," but whether the government's intrusion infringes upon the personal and societal values protected by the Fourth Amendment."

Excerpts from the Decision: No single factor determines whether an individual legitimately may claim under the Fourth Amendment that a place should be free of government intrusion not authorized by warrant. . . . In assessing the degree to which a search infringes upon individual privacy, the Court has given weight to such factors as the intention of the Framers of the Fourth Amendment . . . the uses to which the individual has put a location . . . and our societal understanding that certain areas deserve the most scrupulous protection from government invasion.

In this light, the rule of *Hester v. United States* [265 U.S. 57 (1924)] that we reaffirm today, may be understood as providing that an individual may not legitimately demand privacy for activities conducted out of doors in fields, except in the area immediately surrounding the home. . . . This rule is true to the conception of the right to privacy embodied in the Fourth Amendment. The Amendment reflects the recognition of the Founders that certain enclaves should be free from arbitrary government interference. For example, the Court since the enactment of the Fourth Amendment has stressed "the overriding respect for the sanctity of the home that has been embedded in our traditions since the origins of the republic."

We concluded, from the text of the Fourth Amendment and from the historical and contemporary understanding of its purposes, that an individual has no legitimate expectation that open fields will remain free from warrantless intrusion by government officers.

and on tips from informants, the officers obtained a search warrant for Kyllo's home. The search revealed more than 100 marijuana plants. Appealing his conviction, Kyllo argued that what the police did without a warrant constituted an illegal search of his home. The federal prosecutor argued that thermal imaging does not constitute a search because (1) it detects "only heat radiating from the external surface of the house" and therefore there was no entry, and (2) it did not detect private activities occurring in private areas because "everything that was detected was on the outside."

The Court disagreed, saying that the Fourth Amendment draws "a firm line at the entrance of the house." The Court said further:

> The very core of the Fourth Amendment stands the right of a man to retreat into his own home and there be free from unreasonable governmental intrusions. With few exceptions, the question whether a warrantless search of a home is reasonable and hence constitutional must be answered no. . . . We think that obtaining by sense-enhancement technology any information regarding the interior of the home that could not otherwise have been obtained without physical intrusion into a constitutionally protected area constitutes a search, at least where (as here) the technology in question is not in general public use. . . . On the basis of this criterion, the information obtained by the thermal images in this case was the product of a search.

The significance of *Kyllo* for the open fields doctrine is that the use of electronic devices from an open field may constitute a violation of the Fourth Amendment if such use obtains information that would not otherwise be obtainable from the open field alone. The use of thermal imaging in *Kyllo* was deemed by the Court as equivalent to physical intrusion into a home, although through the use of sense-enhancing technology. Nonetheless, this constitutes physical entry and is prohibited by the Fourth Amendment.

Open Fields and the Use of Electronic Beepers: The *Knotts* and *Karo* Cases

As discussed in Chapter 8 (Motor Vehicle Stops, Searches, and Inventories), two cases govern the use of beepers to detect motor vehicles. In *United States v. Knotts* (460 U.S. 276 [1983]), the Court held that a person traveling in a car on a public road has no reasonable expectation of privacy and so visual surveillance by the police through the use of a beeper does not constitute a search. The Court added that "the Fourth Amendment does not prohibit the police from supplementing their sensory faculties with technological aids to help the police identify the car's location." A year later, however, in *United States v. Karo* (468 U.S. 705 [1984]), the Court held that the monitoring of a beeper in a private dwelling, a location not open to visual surveillance, violates the rights of individuals to privacy in their own homes.

United States v. Karo (1984)

The difference between *Knotts* and *Karo* is that in *Knotts,* the agents learned nothing from the beeper that they could not have visually observed from a public place, so there was no Fourth Amendment violation. More important, however, the monitoring in *Knotts* occurred in a public place, whereas the use of the beeper in *Karo* involved an intrusion into the privacy of a person's home and therefore violated the Fourth Amendment.

Comparison between Open Fields and Plain View

Open fields and items in plain view are similar in that neither is protected by the Fourth Amendment; there is no need for a search warrant or probable cause to obtain the item. The differences between open fields and items in plain view before the law are summarized in the following list:

Open Fields	Plain View
Seizable item is not in a house, dwelling, or curtilage	Seizable item usually is in a house, dwelling, or curtilage
Items hidden from view may be seized	Only items not hidden from view may be seized
Awareness of the item may be through sense of sight, hearing, smell, touch, or taste	Awareness of item is limited to sense of sight
Open space	May be in an enclosed or open space

Abandonment

Items that are abandoned are not protected by the Fourth Amendment. This section defines abandonment and then looks at the factors that determine whether an item has been abandoned, when motor vehicles may be declared abandoned, how police actions affect abandonment issues, and concludes with a comparison between abandonment and the plain view doctrine.

Abandonment Defined

Abandonment is defined as the giving up of a thing or item absolutely, without limitation as to any particular person or purpose. Abandonment implies giving up possession, ownership, or any reasonable expectation of privacy. Abandoned property is not protected by the Fourth Amendment guarantee against unreasonable searches and seizures, so it may be seized without a warrant or probable cause. For example, if a car is left in a public parking lot for so long that it is reasonable to assume that the car has been abandoned, the police may seize the car without a warrant.

Abandoned property does not belong to anyone, because the owner has given it up—in some cases involuntarily (such as when items are thrown out of a house or car for fear of discovery by the police). Persons who find such property, including the police, may therefore keep it and introduce it as evidence in a criminal proceeding. For example, suppose the police approach a group of juveniles in an apartment complex parking lot to quiet them down because of complaints from nearby residents. One of the juveniles throws away an envelope, which is retrieved by the police and later ascertained to contain drugs. The recovery is legal, and the evidence is usable in court.

Factors that Determine When Items Are Considered Abandoned

Abandonment is frequently difficult to determine, but the two basic guidelines are (1) where the property is left and (2) the intent to abandon the property.

Where the Property Is Left
This section looks at whether property left in an open field, public place, or private premises is abandoned. It also considers the issue of whether trash should be considered abandoned.

Property left in an open field or public place
Property discarded or thrown away in an open field or public place is considered abandoned. For example, drugs discarded by a suspect at an airport restroom when she realizes she is under surveillance, or drugs thrown by the suspect from a speeding car when he realizes that the police are closing in, would be considered abandoned.

Property left on private premises
Property may sometimes be considered abandoned on private premises if circumstances indicate that the occupant has left the premises. For example, if a suspect pays his bill and checks out of a hotel room, items left behind that are of no apparent value but that the police can use as evidence—such as photographs or clippings—are considered abandoned property and may be seized by the police.

If the occupant has not left the premises, there is no abandonment. For example, suppose that, while "looking around" the house after receiving valid consent, the police see the occupant grab a package containing marijuana from the kitchen table and throw it into the bedroom. That package might be seized by the police, but not under the abandonment doctrine, because the property is still in the house and the occupant has not left the premises. However, the seizure might still be justified under probable cause and exigent circumstance.

California v. Greenwood (1988)

Is trash or garbage abandoned?
The Court decided in *California v. Greenwood* (486 U.S. 35 [1988]) that garbage left outside the curtilage of a home for regular collection is considered abandoned and therefore may be seized by the police without a warrant. In this case, the Court said that "having deposited their garbage in an area particularly suited for public inspection . . . [the owners] could have no reasonable expectation of privacy in the inculpatory items that they discarded" (here, items indicating narcotics use). There is no Fourth Amendment protection if trash is left in an area accessible to the public, so no warrant or probable cause is needed. By contrast, leaving trash in the curtilage of a home (not accessible to the public but where trash collectors are allowed to enter) or on one's own property would not be considered abandonment, so Fourth Amendment protections would apply.

This means that the police would need a warrant to enter the premises and retrieve that trash. May trash obtained by trash collectors be legally turned over to the police? Once trash is gathered by trash collectors, it loses its reasonable expectation of privacy even if obtained inside a curtilage. It may therefore be voluntarily turned over to the police by trash collectors. Problems may arise, however, if this is done at the request of the police. In these cases, trash collectors may be seen as acting as agents of the police and doing something the police cannot legally do. Court decisions have not addressed this issue authoritatively, so police officers are cautioned to seek advice from legal counsel before resorting to this course of action.

The Intent to Abandon the Property The intent to abandon is generally determined objectively—by what a person does. Throwing items away in a public place shows an intent to abandon; denial of ownership when questioned also constitutes abandonment. For example, suppose that, when questioned by the police, a suspect denies that the confiscated wallet belongs to him. If, in fact, the suspect owns that wallet, it may now be considered abandoned. Failure to claim something over a long period of time also indicates abandonment; the longer the period, the clearer the intent. But the prosecution must prove that there was, in fact, an intent to abandon the item.

Abandonment of Motor Vehicles

An article in the *FBI Law Enforcement Bulletin* sheds light on the issue of motor vehicle abandonment. The writer, John Gales Sauls, states that courts consider "somewhat different" factors in determining whether a vehicle has been abandoned. He identifies four key factors:[5]

1. "Flight from the vehicle by the person in an apparent effort to avoid apprehension by law enforcement." Quoting a lower court decision,

Sauls writes, "When Tate fled the scene of the murder, leaving the van unoccupied and unlocked, he abandoned his expectation of privacy in the van and its contents."

2. "Where, and for how long, a vehicle is left unattended." Sauls writes that "a person who leaves a car in a traveled lane of a busy highway should expect the police to remove the car with some promptness, the more difficult abandonment question is presented when a person parks a vehicle lawfully. Unless other factors are present, such as flight, abandonment is only found in such cases where the vehicle is parked on someone else's property either without authorization or for a period of time that exceeds the permission granted."

3. "The condition in which the vehicle is left unattended." Quoting a lower court decision, Sauls writes, "One who chooses to leave luggage in an unlocked, burned-out automobile at the side of a highway in the country can fairly be thought to have a much lower expectation of privacy."

4. "Denial, by a person who is present, of possession or ownership of the vehicle." Sauls gives the example of the case of three men who, when approached by customs agents after the three had loaded the contents of two boxes into the rear of a Chevrolet station wagon, denied any knowledge of the station wagon or its cargo (understandably, because the agents discovered 30 milligrams of cocaine in the car). The writer quotes the Court of Appeals for the Eleventh Circuit, which concluded that the defendant "effectively abandoned any Fourth Amendment rights he possessed in the station wagon and its contents."

Police Actions and Abandonment

The police activities that led to the abandonment must be legal, or else the evidence obtained is not admissible in court. For example, suppose the police, for no justifiable reason, decide to search a pedestrian one evening. Terrified, the pedestrian throws away what turns out to be a bag of cocaine. The cocaine cannot be used in evidence, because the abandonment was caused by illegal police conduct. Or suppose police officers stop a motor vehicle on the highway for no justifiable reason. Just before the vehicle stops, the driver throws away a pistol that is later ascertained to have been a weapon used in a robbery. The pistol is not admissible in evidence, because the abandonment was triggered by illegal police conduct.

Comparison between Abandonment and Plain View

Items that are abandoned and those that are in plain view are similar in that neither is protected by the Fourth Amendment; there is no need for a search warrant

Definition. The giving up of a thing or item absolutely, without limitation as to any particular person or purpose.

Factors determining when items are considered abandoned. (1) Property left in an open field or public place is abandoned; (2) for property left on private premises, it depends on whether the occupant has left the premises; (3) for trash or garbage, it depends on where it is left; and (4) intent to abandon is determined by what a person does.

Motor vehicles. Abandonment of motor vehicles is determined by four key factors: (1) flight from the vehicle, (2) where and for how long a vehicle is left unattended, (3) the condition in which the vehicle is left unattended, and (4) denial of possession or ownership of the vehicle.

or probable cause to obtain the items. Differences between the two are summarized in the following list:

Abandonment	Plain View
Owner or possessor has given up possession of item	Owner or possessor has not given up possession of item
Seized item may be legal or illegal	Seized item must be illegal
Discovery of item may be through the sense of sight, touch, hearing, smell, or taste	Discovery of item must be through the sense of sight

Border Searches

Fourth Amendment rules are applied differently in immigration and border searches. This section examines some of those differences. We will look at several issues including (1) whether the Fourth Amendment applies to aliens away from the border; (2) whether vehicles can be stopped at fixed checkpoints without probable cause or reasonable suspicion; (3) the legality of disassembling a vehicle's fuel tank during a suspicionless search at the border; (4) the forced temporary detention of aliens; suspected of being illegal; (5) factory surveys of aliens; (6) detention of alimentary canal smugglers; and (7) a summary of case law for stops and searches at the border.

Fourth Amendment Rules Applied Differently in Immigration and Border Searches

Full Fourth Amendment protections do not apply at immigration borders, particularly right at the point of entry. Searches may be conducted by immigration and border agents in the absence of probable cause, reasonable suspicion, or suspicion.

No amount of certainty is needed in border searches—whether the person searched is a noncitizen or a citizen. This is because of a compelling state interest involved in stopping illegal immigration and the flow of prohibited goods into the country.

United States v. Ramsey (1977)

In *United States v. Ramsey* (431 U.S. 606 [1977]), the Court held that "searches made at the border, pursuant to the long-standing right of the sovereign to protect itself by stopping and examining persons and property crossing into this country, are reasonable simply by virtue of the fact that they occur at the border." Authors Steven Emanuel and Steven Knowles note, however, that "where a search requires the subject to undress, and particularly where anal and vaginal cavities are examined, officials must make a stronger showing of reason to believe that the particular suspect in question is concealing smuggled objects."[6]

The rules for border stops and searches are governed by immigration laws and agency policies, subject to the minimum required by the Bill of Rights, particularly as they apply to citizens or valid residents. These rules are currently undergoing reexamination as a result of the events of 9/11 and will doubtless lead to further tightening of rules on stops, searches, and exclusions. They will be challenged in court, but government regulations will likely prevail as long as they do not violate minimum constitutional rights.

Roving Patrols Searching Vehicles Away from the Border

While searches at border crossings are not subject to Fourth Amendment protection, searches made once the person is inside the U.S. border (called extended border searches) are subject to different rules. For example, in *Almeida-Sanchez v.*

Almeida-Sanchez v. United States (1973)

United States (413 U.S. 266 [1973]), the Court held that the warrantless search of a Mexican citizen's car 25 air miles north of the Mexican border was unconstitutional. In that case, the border patrol conducted a warrantless search of the car of a Mexican citizen who was a holder of a valid work permit. The search yielded marijuana, which was used to convict the petitioner. He appealed, alleging that his constitutional rights were violated. The Court agreed, saying that the search was not a border search or the functional equivalent thereof and therefore needed probable cause or a warrant. Distance from the border makes a difference in the Fourth Amendment protection given.

Border patrol agents can detain and question the occupants of a car as long as they have reasonable suspicion. However, a roving patrol cannot detain persons for questioning in an area near the border solely because the occupants of the vehicle "looked Mexican" (*United States v. Brignoni-Ponce*, 422 U.S. 873 [1975]).

United States v. Brignoni-Ponce (1975)

In *United States v. Brignoni-Ponce* (1975), a roving border patrol stopped a vehicle on Interstate 5, south of San Clemente, California, and questioned the driver and his two passengers about their citizenship. The officers later admitted that the only reason they stopped the vehicle was because its three occupants appeared to be of Mexican descent. On interrogation, the officer learned that the passengers were illegal aliens. All three were arrested and the driver charged with knowingly transporting illegal immigrants. The driver later claimed that the testimonies of the two passengers against him were the fruit of an illegal seizure. The Court agreed, saying that stopping a motor vehicle inside the United States solely because the occupants "looked Mexican" was unconstitutional.

Stopping Vehicles at Fixed Checkpoints

United States v. Martinez-Fuerte (1976)

It is permissible for border officials to stop vehicles at reasonably located, fixed checkpoints (such as those set up in the interior) to question occupants of vehicles even without reasonable suspicion that the vehicles contain illegal aliens. Moreover, no warrant is needed before setting up a checkpoint for immigration purposes (*United States v. Martinez-Fuerte,* 428 U.S. 543 [1976]). Note, however, that stopping vehicles at fixed checkpoints and questioning occupants after the stop (which is constitutional) is different from roving border patrols stopping vehicles away from the border and questioning occupants without reasonable suspicion (which is unconstitutional). This is because the stopping and questioning at fixed checkpoints are not arbitrary, whereas stopping and questioning away from the border without reasonable suspicion can be arbitrary and open to abuse.

Disassembling the Gas Tank of a Motor Vehicle

United States v. Flores-Montano (2004)

In a 2004 border case, *United States v. Flores-Montano* (541 U.S. 149 [2004]), the Court held that "the government authority to conduct suspicionless inspections at the border includes the authority to remove, disassemble, and reassemble a vehicle's fuel tank." In that case, Flores-Montano attempted to enter the United States at a border crossing. A customs inspector examined the vehicle and asked him to leave it for secondary inspection. At the secondary station, another customs inspector tapped on the gas tank and noted it

HIGHLIGHT

The Extent of Government Power in Border Searches

"The Government's interest in preventing the entry of unwanted persons and effects is at its zenith at the international border. Time and again, we have stated that 'searches made at the border, pursuant to the long-standing right of the sovereign to protect itself by stopping and examining persons and property crossing into this country, are reasonable simply by virtue of the fact that they occur at the border.

"Respondent asserts two main arguments with respect to his Fourth Amendment

interests. First, he urges that he has a privacy interest in his fuel tank, and that the suspicionless disassembly of his tank is an invasion of his privacy. But on many occasions, we have noted that the expectation of privacy is less at the border than it is in the interior. . . . It is difficult to imagine how the search of a gas tank, which should be solely a repository for fuel, could be more of an invasion of privacy than the search of the automobile's passenger compartment."

SOURCE: *United States v. Flores-Montano,* 541 U.S. 149 (2004).

sounded solid. The inspector then asked a mechanic to help remove the gas tank. When the inspector opened an access plate underneath the putty, he found 37 kilograms of marijuana. Flores-Montano sought suppression of the evidence, claiming that the inspectors did not have reasonable suspicion he was engaged in criminal activity and that reasonable suspicion was required to remove a gas tank.

The Court disagreed and held the disassembly valid. It reasoned that "on many occasions, we have noted that the expectation of privacy is less at the border than it is in the interior," adding that "we have long recognized that automobiles seeking entry into this country may be searched." This case illustrates the extensive power of the government in border searches.

The Forced Temporary Detention of Aliens Believed to Be Illegal

The Court has held that, for the purpose of questioning, an immigration officer may detain against his or her will an individual reasonably believed to be an alien. The Court added:

> We hold that immigration officers, in accordance with the Congressional grant of authority found in Section 287(a)(1) of the Immigration and Naturalization Act, may make forcible detentions of a temporary nature for the purposes of interrogation under circumstances created by reasonable suspicion, not arising to the level of probable cause to arrest, that the individual so detained is illegally in this country. (*Au Yi Lau v. United States Immigration and Naturalization Service,* 445 F.2d 217, 223 [9th Cir.], cert. denied, 404 U.S. 864 [1971])

Au Yi Lau v. United States Immigration and Naturalization Service (1971)

The person searched does not need to be entering the country. Anyone found in a "border area" is subject to search on the basis of reasonable suspicion, including visitors, employees, and transportation workers. Moreover, the area in which a border search may be conducted is not limited to the actual point of territorial entry. It may also be conducted at any place that is the "functional equivalent" of the border, such as an established station or intersection near the border or the place where an airplane first lands. For example, O'Hare Airport in Illinois is the functional equivalent of a border for international flights landing there.

Factory Surveys of Aliens

Immigration officials sometimes conduct **factory surveys**, in which they pay surprise visits to factories and ask employees questions to determine if they are illegal aliens: "What is your nationality?" "Where were you born?" and so on. The Court has declared that this type of brief questioning does not constitute a Fourth Amendment "seizure," so no "particularized and objective basis" for suspecting the worker of being an illegal alien need be shown before conducting the survey (*Immigration and Naturalization Service v. Delgado,* 466 U.S. 210 [1984]).

Immigration and Naturalization Service v. Delgado (1984)

The Detention of Alimentary Canal Smugglers

United States v. Montoya de Hernandez (1985)

In a case involving the alimentary canal smuggling of narcotics across the nation's borders, *United States v. Montoya de Hernandez* (473 U.S. 531 [1985]), the Court held that reasonable suspicion (instead of probable cause) is sufficient to permit customs agents at the border to detain a traveler suspected of engaging in this offense. The Court also concluded that agents were justified in detaining a traveler (who was suspected of having swallowed balloons containing drugs) for twenty-seven hours before they found drugs in her rectum and arrested her. The Court emphasized that such detention was necessary because of "the hard-to-detect nature of alimentary canal smuggling and the fact that the detention occurred at the international border." The Court took into account the needs of law enforcement under those circumstances and concluded that what the customs agents did was reasonable. Had this not been an immigration and border seizure case, the Court would not have considered the length of time involved to be reasonable.

Summary of Case Law for Border Stops and Searches

Court decisions indicate that the Fourth Amendment does not apply at immigration borders or their equivalent, such as international airports, seaports, or other places of entry. Foreigners seeking entry for the first time into the United States have no Fourth Amendment rights whatsoever at the border. They can be stopped and asked questions without reasonable suspicion. Their vehicles and belongings can be searched extensively without probable cause.

Once foreigners are legally inside the United States, however, they are entitled to constitutional protection. The tragic events of 9/11 will likely intensify litigation aimed at defining the basic rights of foreigners and citizens at the border, particularly those suspected of involvement in terrorist activities. Advance technology and more detailed procedures are being used in border searches to detect illegal entries and the inflow of prohibited items. This area of law is fast changing through national legislation, court decisions, and administrative regulations. It will continue to change as the threat to national security persists. Stay tuned for further changes.

Summary

Plain View

- *Definition.* Items that are within the sight of an officer who is legally in a place from which the view is made, and who had no prior knowledge that the items were present, may properly be seized without a warrant—as long as the items are immediately recognizable as subject to seizure.

- *Three requirements.* (1) Awareness of the item must be through use of the sense of sight; (2) the officer must be legally in the place from which the item is seen; and (3) it must be immediately apparent that the item is subject to seizure.

- Inadvertence is no longer a plain view requirement.

- Plain view applies to open spaces and to motor vehicles.
- Plain view applies even if mechanical devices are used.

Open Fields

- *Definition.* Items in open fields are not protected by the Fourth Amendment guarantee against unreasonable searches and seizures, so they can be seized by an officer without a warrant or probable cause.
- *Curtilage.* "The area to which extends the intimate activity associated with the sanctity of a man's home, and the privacies of life."
- *Test to determine curtilage.* If a person has a reasonable expectation of privacy in a place, it is part of the curtilage and is protected by the Fourth Amendment.
- *Applications.* Aerial surveillance of curtilage is valid. An area may be an open field despite a locked gate and a "no trespassing" sign.

Abandonment

- *Definition.* The giving up of a thing or item absolutely, without limitation as to any particular person or purpose.

- *Factors determining when items are considered abandoned.* (1) Property left in an open field or public place is abandoned; (2) for property left on private premises, it depends on whether the occupant has left the premises; (3) for trash or garbage, it depends on where it is left; and (4) intent to abandon is determined by what a person does.
- *Motor vehicles.* Abandonment of motor vehicles is determined by four key factors: (1) flight from the vehicle, (2) where andfor how long a vehicle is left unattended, (3) the condition in which the vehicle is left unattended, and (4) denial of possession or ownership of the vehicle.

Border Searches

- Fourth Amendment protections do not apply at immigration borders, particularly at the point of entry, but once inside the border some protections are afforded.
- The suspicionless disassembling of a tank of a motor vehicle at the border is valid.
- Vehicles may be stopped at fixed checkpoints and their occupants questioned.
- The search of vehicles away from the border needs a warrant or probable cause.

Review Questions and Hypothetical Cases

1. What is the plain view doctrine? Discuss its basic requirements.

2. What is inadvertence? Is it currently a plain view requirement?

3. What is curtilage? How is curtilage determined?

4. In what ways are plain view and open fields similar? In what ways are they different?

5. "The use of electronic beepers in law enforcement is always valid." Is that statement true or false? Justify your answer.

6. Assume you are a police officer who sees a car in a parking lot that has been there and has not been moved or driven away for months. Do you think that car has been abandoned or not? Justify your answer based on court standards for abandonment.

7. Assume you are a police officer serving a search warrant for drugs. While inside the house, you see a flat-screen TV set in the suspect's living room you think is stolen. You call the police department and are able to ascertain that the TV set is in fact stolen. You seize the TV set. Is that TV set admissible in court under plain view? Is it admissible at all as evidence? Explain.

8. While on patrol, W, a police officer, sees what she is certain are marijuana plants inside the fence of one of the residences. She goes inside the fence and seizes the plants. Are the seized plants admissible in evidence during a criminal trial? Justify your answer.

9. While on patrol in a place with a lot of student apartment complexes, M, a sheriff's deputy, sees illegal drugs through the window of an apartment

building. He sees people inside the apartment and they also see him. He knocks at the door, but is refused entry. He forces entry anyway and seizes the drugs. Is the seizure valid? Why or why not?

10. Assume you are a border patrol agent assigned to a city located near the Arizona-Mexico border. One day, you see a truck loaded with people who, from your experience, look like they just arrived from the Mexican border located 20 miles away, and do not look like they are Americans. You stop the vehicle and begin asking questions. You could not get an answer because none of its occupants speaks English. You arrest the occupants in the vehicle. Was the arrest valid? Explain.

11. Officer Jones of the Police Department of Brazos University was informed by one of the dormitory resident assistants that Student X

had drugs in his room in a campus fraternity house. Acting on that information, Officer Jones knocked at X's door and asked if he could look around. Officer Jones was admitted by X. He immediately saw a suspicious bag on X's study table. Before Officer Jones could seize it, X ran to the table, grabbed the pound of marijuana, and threw it outside the window and into the campus street below. Officer Jones hurriedly went down and recovered the contraband. Assume you are the prosecuting attorney in the case against Student X. What is your best ground for admissibility of this evidence in a criminal prosecution—plain view, abandonment, open fields, or none of the above? Select one, give reasons for your choice, and state why you would not use the others.

Key Terms

Go to the Criminal Procedure 7e website for flash cards that will help you master the definitions of these terms.

Holdings of Key Cases

See Appendix C for information on how to find cases in this chapter on FindLaw.com.

Almeida-Sanchez v. United States, **413 U.S. 266 (1973)** The warrantless search of a Mexican citizen's car 25 air miles north of the Mexican border is unconstitutional.

Arizona v. Hicks, **480 U.S. 321 (1987)** The "immediately apparent" requirement of the plain view doctrine must be based on probable cause, not on any lesser degree of certainty such as reasonable suspicion.

Au Yi Lau v. United States Immigration and Naturalization Service, **445 F.2d 217 (9th Cir.), cert. denied, 404 U.S. 864 (1971)** An immigration officer may, for purposes of questioning, detain against his or her will an individual reasonably believed to be an alien.

Boyd v. United States, **116 U.S. 616 (1886)** Curtilage is the area to which extends the intimate activity associated with the sanctity of a man's home and the privacies of life.

California v. Ciraolo, **476 U.S. 207 (1986)** The constitutional protection against unreasonable search and seizure is not violated by the naked-eye aerial observation by the police of a suspect's backyard, which is admittedly a part of the curtilage.

California v. Greenwood, **486 U.S. 35 (1988)** Garbage left outside the curtilage of a home for regular collection is considered abandoned and therefore may be seized by the police without a warrant.

Coolidge v. New Hampshire, 403 U.S. 443 (1971) The discovery of evidence in plain view must be inadvertent. But where the discovery is anticipated, where the police know in advance the location of the evidence and intend to seize it, the situation is altogether different.

Florida v. Riley, 488 U.S. 445 (1989) Evidence obtained by the police in a helicopter flight at a 400-foot altitude is admissible because such flights are allowed by FAA regulations and so the homeowner would have no reasonable expectation of privacy from such flights.

Harris v. United States, 390 U.S. 234 (1968) Objects falling within the plain view of an officer who has a right to be in a position to have that view are subject to seizure and may be introduced in evidence.

Hester v. United States, 265 U.S. 57 (1924) The special protection accorded by the Fourth Amendment to people in their persons, houses, papers, and effects is not extended to open fields.

Horton v. California, 496 U.S. 128 (1990) The Fourth Amendment does not prohibit the warrantless seizure of evidence in plain view, even though the discovery of the evidence was not inadvertent.

Immigration and Naturalization Service v. Delgado, 466 U.S. 210 (1984) Factory surveys in which INS officials pay surprise visits to factories and ask employees questions to determine if they are in this country legally do not constitute a Fourth Amendment seizure, so no specific, objective basis for suspecting the worker of being an illegal alien need be shown.

Kyllo v. United States, 533 U.S. 27 (2001) The use of thermal imaging to explore the details of a home is presumptively unreasonable without a warrant.

Minnesota v. Dickerson, 508 U.S. 366 (1993) Although the evidence in this case was not admissible because the officer went beyond what is allowable in frisk cases, the Court said that officers may detect the presence of contraband through the sense of touch and confiscate it if probable cause exists.

Oliver v. United States, 466 U.S. 170 (1984) A place that is posted with a "no trespassing" sign, has a locked gate (with a footpath around it), and is located more than a mile from the owner's house has no reasonable expectation of privacy and is considered an open field, unprotected by the Fourth Amendment.

State v. Stachler, 570 P.2d 1323 (1977) The plain view doctrine can be applied to cases in which the officer has made "a prior valid intrusion into a constitutionally protected area" (meaning when the officer is inside an enclosed space, such as a house or an apartment); the term *open view* applies to instances when the officer is out in open space (such as on the streets) but sees an item within an enclosed area.

Texas v. Brown, 460 U.S. 730 (1983) Although items must be immediately recognizable as subject to seizure if they are to fall under the plain view doctrine, it is not necessary that there be certain knowledge that incriminating evidence is involved. Probable cause is sufficient to justify seizure. Also, the use of a flashlight by an officer to look into the inside of a car at night does not constitute a search under the Fourth Amendment.

United States v. Dunn, 480 U.S. 294 (1987) Whether an area is considered a part of the curtilage and therefore covered by the Fourth Amendment rests on four factors: (1) the proximity of the area to the home, (2) whether the area is in an enclosure surrounding the home, (3) the nature and uses of the area, and (4) the steps taken to conceal the area from public view.

United States v. Flores-Montano, 541 U.S. 149 (2004) "The government authority to conduct suspicionless inspections at the border includes the authority to remove, disassemble, and reassemble a vehicle's fuel tank."

United States v. Johns, 469 U.S. 478 (1985) The plain view doctrine might not be limited to plain sight; it might also include plain odor ("Whether defendant ever had a privacy interest in packages reeking of marijuana is debatable").

United States v. Karo, 468 U.S. 705 (1984) The warrantless monitoring of a beeper after the device has been unwittingly taken into a private residence violates the Fourth Amendment rights of the residents and others.

United States v. Knotts, 460 U.S. 276 (1983) The use of a beeper to monitor the whereabouts of a person traveling in a car on public highways does not turn the surveillance into a search. Such monitoring falls under the plain view doctrine and therefore does not require a warrant.

***United States v. Martinez-Fuerte*, 428 U.S. 543 (1976)** No warrant is needed before setting up a checkpoint for immigration purposes.

***United States v. Montoya de Hernandez*, 473 U.S. 531 (1985)** The detention for 27 hours of a suspect for alimentary canal drug smuggling was reasonable because of the hard-to-detect nature of that type of smuggling and the fact that the detention occurred at the international border where the Fourth Amendment balance of interests is weighted heavily in favor of the government.

***United States v. Potts*, 297 F.2d 68 (6th Cir. 1961)** In general, the term *curtilage* has been held to include all buildings that are in proximity to a dwelling and are continually used for carrying on domestic employment or places that are necessary and convenient to a dwelling and habitually used for family purposes.

***United States v. Ramsey*, 431 U.S. 606 (1977)** "Searches made at the border pursuant to the long-standing right of the sovereign to protect itself by stopping and examining persons and property crossing into this country, are reasonable simply by virtue of the fact that they occur at the border."

***United States v. Sedillo*, 496 F.2d 151 (9th Cir. 1974)** The plain view doctrine is properly applied to situations in which the police officer is not searching for evidence against the accused but nevertheless inadvertently comes across an incriminating object.

 ## You Be the Judge . . .

In the United States Court of Appeals for the Tenth Circuit

In Adair County, Oklahoma, the Sheriff's Department received an anonymous tip that Hatfield was growing marijuana behind his house. The Department dispatched Lieutenant McCullum and Deputy Sinclaire that afternoon to conduct a "knock and talk" interview. The purpose of the interview was to inform Hatfield of the tip and request his permission to search. Upon arriving, Deputy Sinclaire and Lieutenant McCullum parked behind Hatfield's pickup truck on a concrete pad by the side of his house. Deputy Sinclaire went to the door to talk to Hatfield, and Lieutenant McCullum walked to the front of Hatfield's truck, to provide his deputy with protection if anyone came around from the back of the house. McCullum was able to see structures in Hatfield's backyard where he believed marijuana could be growing. Hatfield denied the two permission to search without a warrant, and they retreated to a country road, off of Hatfield's property. The officers called in to their supervisor who told them to wait until he arrived.

The next officer to arrive, however, was Deputy Harold. He had worked as a marijuana spotter for the Oklahoma Bureau of Narcotics, so when he overheard the radio traffic he went directly to the scene to see if he could help. He learned of the tip and structures in Hatfield's backyard from Lieutenant McCullum, and started walking through a pasture that was next to Hatfield's backyard. From that pasture, Deputy Harold could see approximately 12 marijuana plants growing in a chicken coop and behind a shed in Hatfield's backyard. Meanwhile, Hatfield was walking in his backyard along the other side of the fence, screaming obscenities at Harold, and insisting that Harold was trespassing and must leave.

After seeing the plants, Deputy Harold told Hatfield to walk back down the road to where Lieutenant McCullum and Deputy Sinclaire were waiting, and he instructed them to arrest Hatfield for cultivation of marijuana.

Deputy Harold then obtained a search warrant for Hatfield's backyard based upon his own observations, and the Sheriff's Department seized the marijuana plants.

How will you decide this legal issue? Should Lieutenant McCullum's observations of the structures in Hatfield's backyard, made while "covering" Deputy Sinclaire, be suppressed? Should Deputy Harold's observations of Hatfield's yard made while trespassing in Hatfield's pasture be suppressed?

The Court's decision The U.S. Court of Appeals for the Tenth Circuit decided that there was nothing defective about the seizure of the marijuana. Hatfield's driveway was open to the public, and so he had no expectation of privacy for anything Lieutenant McCullum could see from this driveway. The Lieutenant's observations were not, therefore, a search. Deputy Harold observed Hatfield's backyard (the "curtilage" of his house) from the "open field" of the pasture. While Hatfield had an expectation of privacy in the curtilage of his house similar to that he enjoyed in his house proper, this expectation was sufficient to keep him free from intrusion into these areas, not from common observation of them from outside. Even though Deputy Harold had to trespass in the pasture, this does not constitute impermissible search, because Hatfield had no constitutionally recognized expectation of privacy from observation from an open field. *U.S. v. Hatfield,* 333 F.3d 1189 (10th Cir. 2003)

In the United States Court of Appeals for the Sixth Circuit

In Inkster, Michigan, Officers Snow and Shafer of the Inkster PD were patrolling Inkster Public Housing Authority property, by agreement between Inkster PD and the Authority. Part of this agreement was that Inkster PD officers were authorized to issue "Notice of Trespass" notices to nonresidents of the property. Martin had received such a Notice when he had been previously arrested on the Authority property. While patrolling in their car, Officers Snow and Shafer spotted Martin and another person who had received a Notice walking beside the road, and they pulled over.

Martin ran, ignoring the officers' commands to stop. Officer Schafer chased him on foot. While chasing Martin, Officer Schafer saw him throw away a revolver. Martin was eventually cornered with the assistance of other officers, who surrounded him. Schafer told Officer Snow where to look for the gun, and Snow retrieved it. Officer Schafer later identified the revolver that Snow had found as the one he saw Martin throw down.

The sidewalks upon which Martin was walking were open to the public, and thus were not Authority property. Because of this, Martin was not on Authority property, and not subject to being stopped for trespassing there by Officers Snow and Schafer.

How will you decide this legal issue? Snow and Schafer were not authorized to stop Martin on the public sidewalk; so, should the revolver be suppressed as the fruit of an illegal seizure?

The Court's decision The U.S. Court of Appeals for the Sixth Circuit decided that the revolver was abandoned. Because Martin had been neither seized by the police nor submitted to their authority when he threw away the gun, it is considered abandoned. If he had been in custody, then the gun would have been seized, and if the custody was illegal, then the seizure would have been illegal. *U.S. v. Martin,* 399 F.3d 750 (6th Cir. 2005)

Recommended Readings

Kate Martin. *Domestic intelligence and civil liberties.* SAIS Review XXIV:1 (Winter–Spring 2004).

Sharlene A. McEvoy. *Email and internet monitoring and the workplace: Do employees have a right of privacy?* 24 Communications and the Law 69–83 (2002).

Roger L. Michel. Note. *Criminal law: Electronic surveillance—general laws chapter 272, section 99*. Massachusetts Law Review 62, 66 (2001).

Sharon H. Rackow. Note. *How the USA Patriot Act will permit government infringement upon the privacy of Americans in the name of "intelligence"*

investigations. University of Pennsylvania Law Review 1651, 1696 (2002).

Donald Ressegule. Note. *Computer searches and seizure.* Cleveland State Law Review 185–214 (2000).

Notes

1. Steven L. Emanuel and Steven Knowles, *Emanuel Law Outlines: Criminal Procedure* (Larchmont, NY: Emanuel, 1998–99), p. 91.
2. Ibid., p. 23.
3. *Black's Law Dictionary,* 5th ed. (St. Paul, MN: West, 1979), p. 665.
4. Edward M. Hendrie, "Curtilage: The Expectation of Privacy in the Yard," *FBI Law Enforcement Bulletin,* April 1998, p. 25.
5. John Gales Sauls, "Search of Abandoned Property: Fourth Amendment Considerations," *FBI Law Enforcement Bulletin,* May 1994, pp. 29–31.
6. Supra note 1, p. 148.

10 Lineups and Other Means of Pretrial Identification

What You Will Learn

- The police use three procedures in pretrial identification: lineups, showups, and photographic identifications.

- Suspects usually invoke four constitutional rights during these proceedings: the right to counsel, the right to due process, the right to protection against unreasonable searches and seizures, and the right to protection against self-incrimination.

- The rights to counsel and to due process apply in lineups, showups, and photographic identification, but the rights to protection against unreasonable searches and seizures and self-incrimination do not.

- The U.S. Department of Justice has issued guidelines for use in lineups, showups, and photographic identifications, which seek to ensure fairness and reliability.

- There are other means of pretrial identification; among them are DNA testing, polygraph examination, Breathalyzer™ tests, hair samples, and brain fingerprinting.

The Top 5 Important Cases in Lineups and Other Means of Pretrial Identification

United States v. Wade (1967) A police lineup or other face-to-face confrontation after the accused has been formally charged with a crime is considered a "critical stage of the proceedings," so the accused has a right to have counsel present.

Gilbert v. California (1967) Police identification procedures that are "fraught with dangers of suggestion" are invalid because they violate the accused's right to due process.

Kirby v. Illinois (1972) There is no right to counsel at police lineups or identification procedures prior to the time the suspect is formally charged with a crime.

Neil v. Biggers (1972) Identification procedures must be fair. To determine whether the procedures were fair, courts must consider all the circumstances leading to the identification. Courts will find the procedure was unfair only when, in light of all such circumstances, it was so suggestive as to give rise to a real and substantial likelihood of irreparable identification.

Daubert v. Merrell Dow Pharmaceuticals, Inc. (1993) Federal courts now allow the admission of expert testimony pertaining to scientific, technical, or other specialized knowledge that will assist the judge or jury in understanding the evidence or in determining the fact in issue. The *Daubert* doctrine replaces the *Frye* doctrine (still used in most state courts) as the standard for admissibility of scientific evidence in federal courts.

Introduction

The police use a variety of procedures to verify that a suspect who has been taken into custody is, in fact, guilty of an offense. These identification procedures serve the dual functions of identifying suspects and providing evidence at trial. The police generally use three procedures for the immediate identification of suspects:

360

- A lineup, at which a victim of or witness to a crime is shown several possible suspects at the police station for identification
- A showup, at which only one suspect is shown to the witness or victim, usually at the scene of the crime and immediately following a quick arrest of the suspect
- Photographic identification, at which photographs of possible suspects are shown to the victim or witness

Four constitutional rights are often invoked by suspects during each of these pretrial identification stages:

- The right to counsel
- The right to due process
- The right against unreasonable searches and seizures
- The right against self-incrimination

In addition to eyewitness identifications, the police have other available tools for identifying suspects, most of which are more scientific and reliable. This chapter discusses some of them and some of the legal issues involved in their use. These are DNA testing, polygraph examination, Breathalyzer tests, hair samples, fingernail scrapings, and brainwave fingerprinting.

Lineups

Black's Law Dictionary defines a **lineup** as "a police identification procedure by which the suspect in a crime is exhibited, along with others with similar physical characteristics, before the victim or witness to determine if he can be identified as having committed the offense."[1] The same source says, "Lineup involves and requires lining up of a number of individuals from which one of those lined up may or may not be identified as committer of a crime, and there cannot be a one-man lineup" (see Figure 10.1).

The specifics of lineup procedures vary from one department to another, but a lineup always involves a victim or a witness at the police station trying to identify a suspect from a group of usually five or more individuals. Lineups are often conducted with one-way mirrors so that those in the lineup cannot see the person making the identification. Some departments photograph the lineup as a possible defense if its fairness is challenged later.

The Right to Counsel during Lineups

The right to counsel during lineups must be considered in terms of two stages: prior to the filing of a formal charge and after the filing of a formal charge.

No Right to Counsel Prior to a Formal Charge: *Kirby v. Illinois* A suspect in a lineup has no right to a lawyer if he or she has not been **formally charged with**

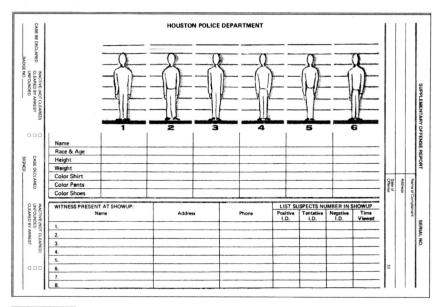

Figure 10.1 Lineup Form

Source: Houston Police Department form

Kirby v. Illinois (1972)

See Appendix C for information on how to find cases in this chapter on FindLaw.com.

Miranda v. Arizona (1966)

Coleman v. Alabama (1970)

an offense, meaning before an indictment, information, preliminary hearing, or arraignment (*Kirby v. Illinois,* 406 U.S. 682 [1972]).

In *Kirby v. Illinois* (1972), a robbery suspect was identified by the victim in a pretrial procedure at the police station. No lawyer was present in the room during the identification, nor was Kirby advised by the police of any right to the presence of counsel. Kirby later was convicted of robbery and appealed his conviction. The Court held that Kirby was not entitled to the presence and advice of a lawyer during a lineup or other face-to-face confrontation, *because he had not been formally charged with an offense.* This is known as the **Kirby rule**. (See the Case Brief to learn more about the *Kirby* case.) The identification process in which he participated was a matter of routine police investigation and thus was not considered a "critical stage of the prosecution." Only when the proceeding is considered a "critical stage of the prosecution" is a suspect entitled to the presence and advice of counsel.

The Court has not defined what "critical stage" means, except to say that counsel is needed in such other proceedings as custodial interrogations before or after charges have been filed (*Miranda v. Arizona,* 384 U.S. 436 [1966]) and in preliminary hearings to determine whether there is sufficient evidence to bring the case to a grand jury (*Coleman v. Alabama,* 399 U.S. 1 [1970]).

Most lower courts have held that taking the accused into custody under an arrest warrant is equivalent to filing a formal charge. But if the lineup is conducted after a warrantless arrest, formal charges have not yet been filed; the suspect therefore has no right to the presence of counsel. In these cases, though, officers must be careful not to violate the suspect's right to due process (discussed shortly).

CASE BRIEF: The Leading Case on the Right to Counsel during a Lineup before Formal Charges Are Filed

Kirby v. Illinois, 406 U.S. 682 (1972)

Facts: A man named Willie Shard reported to the Chicago police that the previous day, on a Chicago street, two men had robbed him of a wallet containing traveler's checks and a Social Security card. The following day, two police officers stopped Kirby and a companion named Bean. When asked for identification, Kirby produced a wallet that contained three traveler's checks and a Social Security card, all bearing the name of Willie Shard. Papers with Shard's name on them were also found in Bean's possession. The officers took Kirby and his companion to a police station. Only after arriving at the police station and checking the records there did the arresting officers learn of the Shard robbery. A patrol car was dispatched to Shard's place of employment, and it brought him to the police station. Immediately upon entering the room in the police station where Kirby and his companion were seated at a table, Shard positively identified them as the men who had robbed him two days earlier. No lawyer was present in the room, and neither Kirby nor his companion had asked for legal assistance or been advised by the police of any right to the presence of counsel. Kirby was convicted of robbery and appealed his conviction, alleging that his identification should have been excluded because it was extracted unconstitutionally.

Issue: *Was Kirby entitled to the presence and advice of a lawyer during this pretrial identification stage? No.*

Supreme Court Decision: There is no right to counsel at police lineups or identification procedures prior to the time the suspect is formally charged with the crime.

Case Significance: *Kirby* was decided five years after *United States v. Wade.* It clarified

an issue that was not directly resolved in *Wade:* whether the ruling in *Wade* applies to cases in which the lineup or pretrial identification takes place prior to the filing of a formal charge. The Court answered this question in the negative, saying that what happened in *Kirby* was a matter of routine police investigation; hence, it was not considered a "critical stage of the prosecution." The Court reasoned that a postindictment lineup is a critical stage, whereas a preindictment lineup is not. Some justices disagreed with this distinction, but the majority of the Court apparently felt that it was a good standard to use in determining when a suspect's right to counsel applies in pretrial identification procedure.

Excerpts from the Decision: The initiation of judicial criminal proceedings is far from a mere formalism. It is the starting point of our whole system of adversary criminal justice. For it is only then that the government has committed itself to prosecute, and only then that the adverse positions of government and defendant have solidified. It is then that a defendant finds himself faced with the prosecutorial forces of organized society, and immersed in the intricacies of substantive and procedural criminal law. It is this point, therefore, that marks the commencement of the "criminal prosecutions" to which alone the explicit guarantees of the Sixth Amendment are applicable.

In this case, we are asked to import into a routine police investigation an absolute constitutional guarantee historically and rationally applicable only after the onset of formal prosecutorial proceedings. We decline to do so. Less than a year after *Wade* and *Gilbert* were decided, the Court explained the rule of those decisions as follows: "The rationale of those cases was that an accused is entitled to counsel at any 'critical stage of the prosecution,' and that a post-indictment lineup is such a 'critical stage.'" We decline to depart from that rationale today by imposing a per se exclusionary rule upon testimony concerning an identification that took place long before the commencement of any prosecution whatever.

Some states require the presence of counsel for the suspect at all lineups whether before or after formal charges are filed. State law or local policy prevails. The stage at which formal charges are considered to have been filed varies from state to state and even from one court to another, so it is best to know the law in a particular jurisdiction.

Right to Counsel Applies after Formal Charge: *United States v. Wade*

United States v. Wade (1967)

In contrast, a lineup or other face-to-face confrontation after the accused has been formally charged with an offense is considered a critical stage of the proceedings; therefore, the accused has a right to have counsel present (*United States v. Wade*, 388 U.S. 218 [1967]). As with other rights, however, the right to counsel at this stage may be waived by the suspect.

In the *Wade* case, the suspect was arrested for bank robbery and later indicted. He was subsequently assigned a lawyer to represent him. Fifteen days after the lawyer was assigned, an FBI agent, without notice to Wade's lawyer, arranged to have two bank employees observe a lineup of Wade and five or six other prisoners in a courtroom of the local county courthouse. Each person in the lineup wore strips of tape like those allegedly worn by the robber during the bank robbery. On request, each said something like "Put the money in the bag," the words allegedly uttered by the robber. Wade was tried for the offense and convicted. He appealed, claiming that the bank employees' courtroom identifications were unconstitutional because the lineup violated his rights to protection against self-incrimination and to the assistance of counsel.

The Court rejected the first claim but upheld the second. The Court noted that there is a grave potential for prejudice, intentional or not, in the pretrial lineup, which might do damage at trial. Because the presence of counsel can often avert prejudice and ensure a meaningful confrontation at trial, the lineup is a "critical stage of the prosecution" at which the accused is as much entitled to the aid of counsel as at the trial itself.

Is the filing of a formal charge a logical dividing line by which to determine whether an accused should have a right to counsel in cases involving pretrial identification? The Supreme Court says yes. In the *Kirby* case, the Court said that "the initiation of judicial criminal proceedings is far from a mere formalism," adding that "it is . . . only then that the adverse positions of government and defendant have solidified. . . . [A] defendant finds himself faced with the prosecutorial forces of organized society and immersed in the intricacies of substantive and procedural criminal law."

Critics of the Court maintain that the boundary between "prior to" and "after" filing is artificial and that any identification made against the suspect at any stage is important in establishing guilt or innocence. The Court rejects this, saying the difference is significant enough to require the presence of counsel in one and not in the other. (See the Case Brief to learn more about the *Wade* case.)

Gilbert v. California (1967)

In a companion case to *Wade*, *Gilbert v. California* (388 U.S. 263 [1967]), the Court held that requiring a suspect to give a handwriting sample without a lawyer present does not violate the suspect's right to avoid compulsory self-incrimination or the right to counsel. In the *Gilbert* case, the lineup was conducted in an auditorium in which about a hundred witnesses to alleged offenses by the suspect were gathered. They made wholesale identification of the suspect in one another's presence. Aside from being legally deficient because of the absence of counsel, this procedure, the Court said, was "fraught with dangers of suggestion."

The two cases led to the rule defining at what point counsel must be allowed at lineups. We will look at this rule and examine the relationship between the right to counsel and the *Miranda* warnings, the role of the lawyer during lineups, and what happens when the counsel for the suspect fails to appear.

The **Wade-Gilbert** *rule* Together, the decisions in *United States v. Wade* and *Gilbert v. California* are known in legal circles as the **Wade-Gilbert** **rule**, as distinguished from the *Kirby* rule (taken from *Kirby v. Illinois*) discussed earlier. According to *Wade-Gilbert*, after being formally charged with a crime, a suspect in a lineup or other confrontation is entitled to have a lawyer present. Failure to provide a lawyer at a lineup after a formal charge has been filed against the suspect makes the evidence inadmissible. However, it does not automatically exclude the testimony of the witness if he or she can identify the accused in court without having to rely on the earlier lineup identification (*Gilbert v. California,* 388 U.S. 263 [1967]).

To determine that this in-court testimony is admissible, the judge must conclude that the testimony is "purged of the primary taint" caused at the lineup. For example, suppose the police require X, a suspect, to appear in a lineup without a lawyer after he has been indicted by a grand jury. The witness identifies X as the person who raped her. This identification is invalid because X was not assigned a lawyer. However, if it can be established in court that the victim would have identified X in court anyway without the lineup (if, for instance, it is established that she, in fact, saw X a couple of times before the lineup or had a good view of the suspect at the time of the crime), then the identification may be admissible because the judge may determine that it has been purged of the illegality associated with the lineup.

Although a suspect is entitled to a lawyer during a lineup after formal charges are filed, the suspect cannot refuse to participate in the lineup even if the lawyer advises against appearing. The lawyer is present primarily to observe the proceedings. If the suspect cannot afford a lawyer, the state must appoint one. A lawyer may be appointed temporarily just for the lineup to protect a suspect from possible prejudicial actions by the police. The assumption is that even a temporary counsel can adequately protect a suspect's right to due process.

CASE BRIEF: The Leading Case on the Right to Counsel
After Formal Charges Are Filed

United States v. Wade, 388 U.S. 218 (1967)

Facts: A man with a small piece of tape on each side of his face entered a bank, pointed a pistol at a cashier and the vice president of the bank, and forced them to fill a pillowcase with the bank's money. The man then drove away with an accomplice. An indictment was returned against Wade and others suspected of being involved in the robbery. Wade was arrested and counsel was appointed. Fifteen days later, without notice to his counsel, Wade was placed in a lineup to be viewed by the bank personnel. Both employees identified Wade as the robber, but in court they admitted seeing Wade in the custody of officials prior to the lineup. At trial, the bank personnel re-identified Wade as the robber and the prior lineup identifications were admitted as evidence. Wade was convicted of bank robbery.

Issue: *Should the courtroom identification of an accused be excluded as evidence because the accused was exhibited to the witness before trial at a postindictment lineup conducted for identification purposes and without notice to and in the absence of the accused's appointed lawyer? Yes.*

Supreme Court Decision: A police lineup or other "face-to-face" confrontation after the accused has been formally charged with a crime is considered a "critical stage of the proceedings"; therefore, the accused has the right to have counsel present. The absence of counsel during such proceedings renders the evidence obtained inadmissible.

Case Significance: The *Wade* case settled the issue of whether an accused has a right to counsel after the filing of a formal charge. The standard used by the Court was whether

identification was part of the "critical stage of the proceedings." The Court, however, did not say exactly what this phrase meant; hence, lower courts did not know where to draw the line. In a subsequent case, *Kirby v. Illinois* (see the Case Brief on page 363), the Court said that any pretrial identification prior to the filing of a formal charge was not part of a "critical stage of the proceedings," and therefore no counsel was required. The *Wade* case did not authoritatively state what is meant by "formal charge" either, so that phrase has also been subject to varying interpretations, depending on state law or practice.

Excerpts from the Decision: Since it appears that there is grave potential for prejudice, intentional or not, in the pretrial lineup, which may not be capable of reconstruction at trial, and since presence of counsel itself can often avert prejudice and assure a meaningful confrontation at trial, there can be little doubt that for Wade the post-indictment lineup was a critical stage of the prosecution at which he was "as much entitled to such aid [of counsel] . . . as at the trial itself." Thus both Wade and his counsel should have been notified of the impending lineup, and counsel's presence should have been a requisite to conduct of the lineup, absent an "intelligent waiver." No substantial countervailing policy considerations have been advanced against the requirement of the presence of counsel. Concern is expressed that the requirement will forestall prompt identifications and result in obstruction of the confrontations. As for the first, we note that in the two cases in which the right to counsel is today held to apply, counsel had already been appointed and no argument is made in either case that notice to counsel would have prejudicially delayed the confrontations. Moreover, we leave open the question whether the presence of substitute counsel might not suffice where notification and presence of the suspect's own counsel would result in prejudicial delay. And to refuse to recognize the right to counsel for fear that counsel will obstruct the course of justice is contrary to the basic assumptions upon which this Court has operated in Sixth Amendment cases. We rejected similar logic in *Miranda v. Arizona* concerning presence of counsel during custodial interrogation.

In our view counsel can hardly impede legitimate law enforcement; on the contrary, for the reasons expressed, law enforcement may be assisted by preventing the infiltration of taint in the prosecution's identification evidence. That result cannot help the guilty avoid conviction but can only help assure that the right man has been brought to justice.

The relationship between the right to counsel and the Miranda *warnings* Why is a suspect not entitled to a lawyer during a police lineup prior to the filing of formal charges and yet is entitled to the *Miranda* warnings (which state that the suspect has a right to a lawyer and that, if the suspect cannot afford a lawyer, the state will provide one) immediately upon arrest even if he or she is still out in the streets? The answer is that the *Miranda* warnings must be given any time a police officer *interrogates* a suspect who is in custody. This rule protects the suspect's right against self-incrimination. By contrast, lineups do not involve any form of interrogation, and therefore the danger of self-incrimination is merely physical, which is not protected by the Fifth Amendment, and not testimonial or communicative, to which the constitutional right applies.

The role of the lawyer during the lineup The main role of a lawyer is to *make sure the procedure is fair*. The lawyer's function is that of a "interested observer" who makes sure that things are done right and that the suspect's due process rights are not violated. Authors Lloyd Weinreb and James Whaley express it this way: "The role of the attorney at a lineup is that of a nonparticipant observer."[2] The Supreme Court, however, has not given any authoritative guidelines on the role of a lawyer during lineups. Most commentators believe the lawyer should, at the very least, observe the proceedings—including taking notes or making a recording—and be able to state any objection to the proceedings. Others have suggested that the lineup procedure should be treated as an adversarial proceeding in which the lawyer may question the witnesses, make objections, and have any reasonable recommendations respected by the police. Because no guidelines have been set by the Supreme Court, the officer should follow the practice in the local jurisdiction. Most jurisdictions follow the "observe the proceeding" rule for the lawyer and allow nothing beyond that.

Lawyers should be accorded all professional courtesies but must not be allowed to control the proceedings; nor should an attorney's disruptive presence be tolerated.

If the lawyer acts improperly, it is best to invite the judge or the district attorney to witness the proceedings. Counsel should not be allowed to question the witness before, during, or after the lineup, although, if an attorney asks to speak to his or her client prior to or after the lineup, he or she should be allowed to do so. If the suspect has an attorney (that is, after the suspect has been formally charged with the offense), the attorney must be notified of the lineup in advance.

If the main role of a lawyer during the lineup is as an observer (unless local practice provides otherwise), how does the suspect benefit from the lawyer's presence? One justice of the Court has answered thus: "Attuned to the possibilities of suggestive influences, a lawyer could see any unfairness at a lineup, question the witnesses about it at trial, and effectively reconstruct what had gone on for the benefit of the jury or trial judge" (*United States v. Ash*, 413 U.S. 300 [1973]).

United States v. Ash (1973)

When the lawyer fails to appear The officer has a number of options if the lawyer, after having been duly informed of the lineup, fails to show up:

- Ask the suspect if he or she is willing to waive the right to counsel; such a waiver is valid as long as it is voluntary and intelligent. The waiver is best obtained in writing.
- Postpone the lineup to another time when counsel can be present.
- Get a substitute counsel only for the lineup.
- If the preceding options are not feasible, conduct a "photo lineup": Those appearing are photographed or videotaped in one room, and the witness is kept isolated in a different room. The photograph or tape is then shown to the witness. The theory is that "because there is no constitutional right to have counsel present when a suspect's photograph is shown to witnesses for identification, the Sixth Amendment is not implicated."[3]

The Right to Due Process Applies

A suspect has a right to *due process* of law in a lineup. This means that the lineup must not be unfair; that is, *it must not be impermissibly suggestive*. In the words of the Court: "The influence of improper suggestion upon identifying witnesses probably accounts for more miscarriages of justice than any other single factor— perhaps it is responsible for more such errors than all other factors combined" (*United States v. Wade*, 388 U.S. 218 [1967]).[4]

In determining what is fair or unfair in identification procedures, courts generally consider all the circumstances leading up to the identification. Courts will find the procedure was unfair only when, in light of all such circumstances ("totality of circumstances"), the identification procedure is so *impermissibly suggestive* as to give rise to a real and substantial likelihood of irreparable misidentification (*Neil v. Biggers*, 409 U.S. 188 [1972]). When that point is reached is determined by the trial court, with some guidelines provided by the Supreme Court, as the cases discussed in this chapter show. Recall that, in *Gilbert v. California* (388 U.S. 363 [1967]), the

Neil v. Biggers (1972)

Court held that a lineup conducted in an auditorium where the defendant was identified by about a hundred witnesses violated the suspect's due process rights, because the procedure was "fraught with dangers of suggestion." Similarly, the use of force to compel the suspect to appear in a lineup may also make the proceeding so suggestive as to violate the suspect's due process rights.

Foster v. California (1969)

In *Foster v. California* (394 U.S. 440 [1969]), the Court found that a pretrial identification by a certain David, the only witness to the crime, violated due process. In the *Foster* case, the suspect was lined up with two other men several inches shorter. The suspect was close to 6 feet tall, whereas the two other men were short—"five feet five or six." Only the suspect wore a jacket similar to that of the robber. When the lineup produced no positive identification, the police used a one-man showup of the suspect. Because even the showup was inconclusive, the police later used a second lineup in which only the suspect was a repeater from the earlier lineup.

The Court said that the suspect's due process rights were violated, because under those conditions the identification of the suspect was inevitable. The Court said: "The suggestive elements in this identification procedure made it all but inevitable that David would identify petitioner whether or not he was in fact 'the man.' In effect, the police repeatedly said to the witness, 'This is the man.'"

Impermissibly suggestive identification procedures may include the following: (1) the suspect is Asian or African American, and there is only one person of that category in the lineup; (2) before the lineup, the police give hints to the witness about the physical characteristics of the suspect; (3) the suspect in the lineup is in jail clothes or wearing handcuffs; and (4) the police allow witnesses to talk to each other and share observations before the lineup takes place.

No Right against Unreasonable Searches and Seizures

Schmerber v. California (1966)

In *Schmerber v. California* (384 U.S. 757 [1966]), the defendant claimed a violation of the guarantee against unreasonable search and seizure during pretrial identification. At the request of a police officer, a sample of Schmerber's blood was taken by a doctor in a hospital for use as evidence in a drunk-driving case. The defendant raised the issue on appeal, claiming that the police should have obtained a warrant before extracting blood from him.

The Court rejected this claim, saying that the officer might reasonably have believed that he was confronted with an emergency in which the delay necessary to obtain a warrant, under the circumstances, would have led to the destruction of the evidence. The Court added, "Particularly in a case such as this, where time had to be taken to bring the accused to a hospital and to investigate the scene of the accident, there was no time to seek out a magistrate and secure a warrant. Given these special facts, we conclude that the attempt to secure evidence of blood-alcohol content in this case was an appropriate incident to petitioner's arrest."

Claims of unreasonable search and seizure in pretrial identification procedures are few and, when raised, do not succeed. They fail because they basically allege, as in *Schmerber,* that the police should have obtained a warrant before conducting the identification procedure.

Compelling a suspect to appear in a lineup or showup is a form of seizure, but it is usually easily justified under the numerous exceptions to the warrant rule, such as the exigent circumstances justification invoked by the police in *Schmerber.* Moreover, many lineups occur after a warrant has been issued or the suspect has been brought before a magistrate. In these cases, the search and seizure challenge becomes moot because of the issuance of a warrant.

No Right against Self-Incrimination

Suspects may think they cannot be required to appear in a lineup or showup because it forces them to incriminate themselves. That claim appears logical—indeed, it is incriminating to be fingered as the culprit in a lineup or to be identified in a showup. However, the Supreme Court has repeatedly rejected this claim. The rule is that a suspect may be required to appear in a police lineup before or after being charged with an offense. The reason is that the right against compulsory self-incrimination applies only to evidence that is testimonial or communicative, which occurs when a suspect is required to *"speak his guilt"*—or communicate orally. It does not extend to **physical self-incrimination**, which *involves the physical body or objects.*

Courts have decided that the government can force a suspect to do the following because they involve only the giving of physical, not testimonial, evidence:

- Appear in a police lineup before or after formal charge
- Give a blood sample, even unwillingly, as long as proper conditions are present; even if state law allows a suspect to refuse to take a blood-alcohol test, a refusal may be constitutionally introduced as evidence of guilt in court
- Submit to a photograph
- Give handwriting samples
- Submit to fingerprinting
- Repeat certain words or gestures or give voice exemplars (the voice here is used as an identifying physical characteristic, not as oral testimony).

The rule that the Fifth Amendment right not to incriminate oneself protects only against self-incrimination that is testimonial or communicative rather than real or physical was reiterated in *Schmerber v. California* (384 U.S. 757 [1966]). Following the *Schmerber* decision, the Court ruled in *United States v. Wade* (388 U.S. 218 [1967]) that appearance in a police lineup is a form of physical, not testimonial, self-incrimination and therefore is not protected by the Fifth Amendment. There is no self-incrimination even if the suspect is required to "speak up" for identification by repeating phrases such as "Put the money in the bag." This is because the purpose of having the suspect speak up is not to evaluate what is said, which would be testimonial, but to determine the level, tone, and quality of voice, which are physical properties.

It follows from the *Schmerber* ruling that a suspect does not have a constitutional right to refuse to appear or participate in a lineup. A suspect who is in the custody of the police may be required to appear in a lineup. However, the use of force to compel a suspect's appearance is inadvisable because it might constitute a violation of the suspect's right to due process. If the suspect is not in custody, appearance in a lineup may be compelled only by court order.[5] If a suspect refuses to appear despite a court order, he or she may be held in contempt of court and kept in jail. A suspect's refusal to cooperate in the identification procedure may also be commented on by the prosecution during the trial. Alternatively, if a suspect refuses to participate in a lineup, the police might be justified in arranging a showup, in which only the suspect is viewed by the witness.[6]

Showups

A **showup** is defined as a "one-to-one confrontation between a suspect and a witness to crime." It usually "occurs within a short time after the crime or under circumstances which would make a lineup impractical or impossible."[7] As in the case of lineups, the rights to counsel and to due process apply; the rights to protection against unreasonable searches and seizures and against self-incrimination do not.

The Right to Counsel during Showups

The right to counsel during showups must be considered in terms of two stages: prior to the filing of a formal charge and after the filing of a formal charge.

No Right to Counsel Prior to the Filing of a Formal Charge
In most cases, the police bring a suspect to the scene immediately after the commission of a crime, to be identified by the victim or other eyewitnesses. Because the suspect has not been charged with a crime, there is no right to counsel (*Kirby v. Illinois*, 406 U.S. 682 [1972]). For example, suppose that, minutes after a purse is snatched, a suspect fitting the description given by the victim is apprehended several blocks away and is brought back to the scene of the crime for identification by the victim. The suspect has no right to counsel even if he or she requests it. If the police question the suspect, however, they must give the *Miranda* warnings, because the situation has escalated beyond a police lineup, where no questions are asked, to a custodial interrogation, which then triggers *Miranda*.

Right to Counsel Applies after Formal Charge
The rule is different once the adversarial judicial criminal proceedings are initiated. In *Moore v. Illinois* (434 U.S. 220 [1977]), for example, a rape suspect appeared with a police officer in the courtroom for a preliminary hearing to determine whether his case should be sent to the grand jury and to set bail. After the suspect's appearance before the judge, the rape victim was asked by the prosecutor if she saw the perpetrator in the

Moore v. Illinois
(1977)

courtroom. She then pointed to the suspect. During the trial, this identification was admitted in court over the defendant's objections. But on appeal, the Supreme Court held that this violated the defendant's right to counsel; because the adversarial criminal proceedings had been initiated at that time, the defendant was entitled to a lawyer at that form of showup.

The Right to Due Process Applies

The leading case on the right to due process in showups is *Neil v. Biggers* (409 U.S. 188 [1972]). In this case, the rape victim could give no description of her attacker other than that he was a black man wearing an orange-colored shirt and that he had a high-pitched voice. The victim was assaulted in her dimly lighted kitchen and then forcibly taken out of the house and raped under a bright, full moon. The victim went through a number of photographs and was shown several lineups but could not make a positive identification. The police arrested the defendant seven months later on information supplied by an informant. The defendant was brought before the victim alone. The police showed the victim the defendant's orange-colored shirt and asked her if she could identify the defendant's voice (from an adjoining room). No other voices were provided for comparison.

The Court held that, though the confrontation procedure itself was suggestive, the totality of circumstances made the identification reliable. Among the factors considered by the Court was "the opportunity of the witness to view the criminal at the time of the crime, the witness's degree of attention, the accuracy of the witness's prior description of the criminal, the level of certainty demonstrated by the witness at the confrontation, and the length of time between the crime and the confrontation." Applying these factors, the Court concluded that the totality of circumstances showed that the identification was reliable, saying:

> The victim spent a considerable period of time with her assailant, up to half an hour. She was with him under adequate artificial light in her house and under a full moon outdoors, and at least twice, once in the house and later in the woods, faced him directly and intimately. She was no casual observer, but rather the victim of one of the most personally humiliating of all crimes. Her description to the police, which included the assailant's approximate age, height, weight, complexion, skin texture, build, and voice, might not have satisfied Proust, but was more than ordinarily thorough. She had "no doubt" that respondent was the person who raped her.

The courts take five factors into account when determining whether, in the totality of circumstances, the suspect's due process rights have been violated during a lineup (*Neil v. Biggers* (409 U.S. 188 [1972]):

- The witness's opportunity to view the criminal at the time of the crime
- The witness's degree of attention at that time
- The accuracy of any prior description given by the witness
- The level of certainty demonstrated by the witness at the identification
- The length of time between the crime and the identification

Although *Neil v. Biggers* is a photographic showup case, the test to determine the violation of a suspect's due process rights should be the same in lineups and photographic identifications because they are all forms of eyewitness identification. In sum, *Neil v. Biggers* is the leading case on eyewitness identification procedures and the right to due process. In every case, the question courts ask is: Was the procedure fair or was it unduly suggestive?

Stovall v. Denno
(1967)

In *Stovall v. Denno* (388 U.S. 293 [1967]), the Court ruled a showup in a hospital valid because the possible unfairness of the showup was justified by the urgent need to confront the suspect because the only living eyewitness, who was hospitalized, was in danger of dying. In this case, the defendant, Stovall, was convicted and sentenced to die for murdering a certain Dr. Behrendt. Stovall was arrested the day after the murder and, without having been given time to obtain a lawyer, was taken by police officers to the hospital to be viewed by Mrs. Behrendt, who had been seriously wounded by her husband's assailant. After observing Stovall and hearing him speak, when she was told to do so by an officer, Mrs. Behrendt identified him as the murderer of her husband. On appeal, Stovall claimed a violation of his right to due process.

The Court rejected his claim, quoting with approval the findings of the State Court of Appeals, which said:

> Here was the only person in the world who could possibly exonerate Stovall. Her words, and only her words, "He is not the man," could have resulted in freedom for Stovall. The hospital was not far distant from the courthouse and jail. No one knew how long Mrs. Behrendt might live. Faced with the responsibility of identifying the attacker, with the need for immediate action and with the knowledge that Mrs. Behrendt could not visit the jail, the police followed the only feasible procedure and took Stovall to the hospital room. Under these circumstances, the usual police station lineup, which Stovall now argues he should have had, was out of the question.

Showups, however, have been under legal siege lately because of their unreliability. In a 2005 decision, the Wisconsin State Supreme Court had these strong words about showups:

> We conclude that evidence obtained from an out-of-court showup is inherently suggestive and will not be admissible unless, based on the totality of circumstances, the procedure was necessary. . . . A lineup or photo array is generally fairer than a showup, because it distributes the probability of identification among the number of persons arrayed, thus reducing the risk of a misidentification. In a showup, however, the only option for the witness is to decide whether to identify the suspect.[8]

No Right against Unreasonable Searches and Seizures

As in the case of lineups, showups are not considered unreasonable searches and seizures, because the circumstances usually warrant them. They are usually conducted at the scene of the crime (as when the victim is taken to the scene to identify an alleged purse snatcher) and immediately following the quick arrest of the suspect. Showups are a form of intrusion, but they are usually justified under the exigent circumstances exception because of the absence of an opportunity to obtain a warrant. Moreover, the degree of intrusion is usually minimal and necessary under the circumstances.

No Right against Self-Incrimination

As in the case of lineups, showups do not violate the prohibition against self-incrimination because, although self-incriminatory, the self-incrimination involved is real or physical, not testimonial or communicative.

Photographic Identifications

Photographic identification (rogue's gallery) is a process in which a victim or witness is shown photographs of possible suspects in a one-on-one situation. Only the right to due process applies in this form of pretrial identification.

No Right to Counsel

There is no right to counsel when the prosecution seeks to identify the accused by displaying photographs to witnesses prior to trial (a process otherwise known as *mug shot identification*) (*United States v. Ash*, 413 U.S. 300 [1973]). This is true even if the suspect has already been formally charged with the crime.

In *United States v. Ash* (1973), the defendant was charged with five counts of bank robbery. In preparing for trial, the prosecutor decided to use a photographic display to determine whether the witnesses he planned to call would be able to make in-court identifications of the accused. Shortly before the trial, an FBI agent and the prosecutor showed five color photographs to the four witnesses who had tentatively identified the black-and-white photograph of Ash. Three of the witnesses selected the picture of Ash, but one was unable to make any selection.

This postindictment identification provided the basis for Ash's claim on appeal that he was denied the right to counsel at a "critical stage" of the prosecution. The Court disagreed, holding that photographic identification is not like a lineup, because the suspect is not present when the witnesses view the photographs. Because the main reason for lawyers' presence at lineups is to prevent suspects from being disadvantaged by their ignorance and failure to ascertain and object to biased conditions, there is no need for lawyers when the suspects are absent.

The Right to Due Process Applies

As in the case of lineups and showups, the right to due process applies, meaning that the photographic identification must not be unduly suggestive. In photographic identifications, a number of photographs must be shown to avoid charges of impermissible suggestion. In addition, there should be nothing in the photographs that focuses attention on a single person. For example, if the suspect is Hispanic, the photographs should feature several Hispanic individuals. To do otherwise would be fundamentally unfair to the suspect and would violate due process.

Simmons v. United States (1968)

In *Simmons v. United States* (390 U.S. 377 [1968]), witnesses identified a bank robbery suspect from six photos obtained from a relative a day after the crime. This was followed by an in-court identification of the suspect by the same five witnesses. The Court held that the photographic identification was not unnecessarily suggestive so as to create a "very substantial likelihood of irreparable misidentification." Among the factors the Court took into account were the seriousness of the crime, the need for immediate apprehension, and the fact that the risk of misidentification was small.

Manson v. Brathwaite (1977)

In another case, *Manson v. Brathwaite* (432 U.S. 98 [1977]), the Court held that the showing of a single photograph to a witness was unnecessary and suggestive, but the Court nonetheless admitted the identification based on the totality of circumstances.

In this case, Glover, an undercover state police officer, purchased heroin from a seller through the open doorway of an apartment while standing for two or three minutes within 2 feet of the seller in the hallway, which was illuminated by natural light. A few minutes later, Glover described the seller to another police officer as "a colored man, approximately five feet eleven inches tall, dark complexioned, black hair, short Afro style, and having high cheekbones, and of heavy build." The other officer, suspecting that the defendant was the seller, left a police photograph of the suspect in Glover's office, who viewed it two days later and identified the individual in the photograph as the seller. The photograph was introduced during the trial as the picture of the suspect, and an in-court identification was made.

On appeal, the Court agreed with the trial court that the examination of the single photograph was unnecessary and suggestive but ruled that the identification in court did not have to be excluded. The Court noted that "Glover, no casual observer but a trained police officer, had a sufficient opportunity to view the suspect,

HIGHLIGHT

Due Process and Photographic Identification

"We hold that each case must be considered on its own facts, and that convictions based on eye-witness identification at trial following a pre-trial identification by photograph will be set aside on that ground only if the photographic identification procedure was so impermissibly suggestive as to give rise to a very substantial likelihood of irreparable misidentification. This standard accords with our resolution of a similar issue in *Stovall v. Denno* (388 U.S. 293 [1967]), and with decisions of other courts on the question of identification by photograph."

SOURCE: *Simmons v. United States* (1968).

	Right to Counsel?	Right to Due Process?	Right against Unreasonable Search and Seizure?	Right against Self-Incrimination?
Lineups	Yes, if after a formal charge; no, if before a formal charge	Yes	No	No
Showups	Yes, if after a formal charge; no, if before a formal charge	Yes	No	No
Photographic Identification	No	Yes	No	No

accurately described him, positively identified respondent's photograph as that of the suspect, and made the photograph identification only two days after the crime." The photograph identification alone would have violated the defendant's due process right, but the totality of circumstances justified admission of the court identification.

This case reiterates previous Court decisions holding that the suggestiveness of the identification procedure is but one of the factors courts should take into account to determine whether a suspect's due process rights were violated. Much more important than a single factor is the totality of circumstances. The Court in *Brathwaite* also restated the main concern of the Court in identification cases, saying, "Reliability is the linchpin in determining the admissibility of identification testimony for confrontations."

No Right against Unreasonable Searches and Seizures

Photographic identification does not involve any unreasonable search and seizure because no search or seizure takes place, as long as the photographs are obtained legally. Showing photographs does not come under the Fourth Amendment, nor is it unduly intrusive.

No Right against Self-Incrimination

There is no self-incrimination when photographs are shown because, as in the case of lineups and showups, the self-incrimination involved is real or physical, not testimonial or communicative. Table 10.1 summarizes the rules for eyewitness identification and suspects' constitutional rights.

Problems with Eyewitness Identification

There are many perceived problems with eyewitness identification. Among them are charges that it is unreliable and that it lacks prescribed guidelines.

"Hopelessly Unreliable?"

All three forms of eyewitness identification—lineups, showups, and photographic identification—have raised serious concerns among law as well as criminal justice professionals because of their demonstrated unreliability in many cases. Eyewitness identification used to be considered the most damning piece of evidence against a suspect. Various studies show, however, that eyewitness identification is not always reliable and that other forms of circumstantial evidence (DNA or fingerprints, for example) are much more accurate in identifying suspects or proving guilt.

A U.S. Justice Department report notes that eyewitness testimony is far from infallible and that "even honest and well-meaning witnesses can make errors, such as identifying the wrong person or failing to identify the perpetrator of a crime."[9] A journal article written by noted authorities, John Turtle, R. C. L. Lindsay, and Gary Wells, and published in 2003, says that "there are approximately 100 documented cases in the U.S. in which a convicted person who has served time in prison has been exonerated by DNA evidence indicating that someone else committed the crime. It has been estimated that of those 100 cases, over 75% were primarily the result of mistaken eyewitness identification of the convicted suspect."[10]

Wisconsin v. Dubose (2005)

In a case decided in 2005, *Wisconsin v. Dubose* (205 WI 126 [2005]), the Wisconsin Supreme Court summarized the state of research on eyewitness testimony as follows:

> Over the last decade, there have been extensive studies on the issue of identification evidence, research that is now impossible for us to ignore. . . . These studies confirm that eyewitness testimony is often "hopelessly unreliable." The research strongly supports the conclusion that eyewitness misidentification is now the single greatest source of wrongful convictions in the United States, and responsible for more wrongful convictions than all other causes combined."[11]

No Prescribed Guidelines

Given current skepticism about the reliability of eyewitness evidence, the pressure is on for police departments and prosecutors to ensure that identification procedures are fair and reliable. Despite the frequent use of lineups for suspect identification, standards and guidelines vary from state to state and even within a state. A State of Virginia Crime Commission recently found that many law enforcement agencies within that state "have no written policies on lineup procedures, and . . . smaller departments often lack the resources needed to produce reliable lineups."[12] That study also says that "currently there is no law requiring Virginia police and sheriff's departments to have a written policy on conducting lineups."

In cases of photographic identification, studies show that "when witnesses are shown all six photos at once—rather than one at a time—a natural tendency kicks in to compare faces and judge which looks most like the one they remember. They make a relative judgment as opposed to a true recognition," according to experts.[13] Many states do not have prescribed legislative or administrative guidelines for police departments to follow and so practices vary from one department to another.

In sum, studies on eyewitness testimony show that its reliability is low and its procedures flawed. The evidence is strong that eyewitness testimony has led to numerous wrongful convictions, even in death penalty cases. Courts and legal scholars have expressed skepticism over its credibility; thus, law enforcement agencies across the nation are revising their procedures to ensure that procedures are fair and highly reliable based on the totality of circumstances and not simply on mere eyewitness identification.

Eyewitness Identification Guidelines from the U.S. Department of Justice

In April 2001, the National Institute of Justice of the U.S. Justice Department released a research report titled "Eyewitness Evidence: A Guide for Law Enforcement."[14] It is a major study initiated by then-Attorney General Janet Reno that involved a thirty-four-member working group of top criminal justice professionals in law enforcement, law, psychology, and other fields. Their recommendations are supported by social science research of the last twenty years, which "combines research and practical perspectives." The group's task was to identify the "best practices" in the field of eyewitness evidence and "relay this information to criminal justice professionals who can practically apply this knowledge."

The guidelines have not been enacted into law, and therefore their adoption by law enforcement agencies is optional. Nonetheless, this work constitutes the most recent, comprehensive, and authoritative effort by the U.S. Department of Justice, or any other law enforcement agency, to produce guidelines that ensure fair and legally defensible identification procedures. These guidelines are reproduced here because they are currently the most often used models in numerous jurisdictions that are establishing pretrial identification guidelines or revising them. The guidelines are for lineups, showups, and photographic identifications.

For Lineups

The report offered guidelines for composing and presenting lineups.

Composing
In composing a live lineup, the investigator should:

- Include only one suspect in each identification procedure.
- Select fillers who generally fit the witness's description of the perpetrator. When the description of the perpetrator provided by

the witness is limited or inadequate, or when the description of the perpetrator differs significantly from the appearance of the suspect, fillers should resemble the suspect in significant features.

- Consider placing suspects in different positions in each lineup, both across cases and with multiple witnesses in the same case. Position the suspect randomly unless, where local practice allows, the suspect or the suspect's attorney requests a particular position.
- Include a minimum of four fillers (nonsuspects) per identification procedure.
- When showing a new suspect, avoid reusing fillers in lineups shown to the same witness.
- Complete uniformity of features is not required. Avoid using fillers who so closely resemble the suspect that a person familiar with the suspect might find it difficult to distinguish the suspect from the fillers.
- Create a consistent appearance between the suspect and fillers with respect to any unique or unusual feature (for example, scars, tattoos) used to describe the perpetrator by artificially adding or concealing that feature.

Summary: The foregoing procedures will result in a photo or live lineup in which the suspect does not unduly stand out. An identification obtained through a lineup composed in this manner may have stronger evidentiary value than one obtained without these procedures.

Presenting In presenting a live lineup, the investigator should:

- Instruct the witness that he or she will be asked to view a group of individuals.
- Instruct the witness that it is just as important to clear innocent persons of suspicion as to identify guilty parties.
- Instruct the witness that individuals present in the lineup may not appear exactly as they did on the date of the incident, because features such as head and facial hair are subject to change.
- Instruct the witness that the person who committed the crime may or may not be present in the group of individuals.
- Assure the witness that, regardless of whether or not an identification is made, the police will continue to investigate the incident.
- Instruct the witness that procedure requires the investigator to ask the witness to state in his or her own words how certain he or she is of any identification.

Summary: Instructions provided to the witness prior to presentation of a lineup will likely improve the accuracy and reliability of any identification obtained from the witness and can facilitate the elimination of innocent parties from the investigation.

For Showups

When conducting a showup, the investigator should:

- Determine and document, prior to the showup, a description of the perpetrator.
- Consider transporting the witness to the location of the detained suspect to limit the legal impact of the suspect's detention.

When multiple witnesses are involved:

- Separate witnesses and instruct them to avoid discussing details of the incident with other witnesses.
- If a positive identification is obtained from one witness, consider using other identification procedures (for example, lineup or photo array) for remaining witnesses.
- Caution the witness that the person he or she is looking at may or may not be the perpetrator.
- Obtain and document a statement of certainty for both identifications and nonidentifications.

Summary: The use of a showup can provide investigative information at an early stage, but the inherent suggestiveness of a showup requires careful use of procedural safeguards.

For Photographic Identifications

In completing a photo lineup, the investigator should:

- Include only one suspect in each identification procedure.
- Select fillers who generally fit the witness's description of the perpetrator. When the description of the perpetrator provided by the witness is limited or inadequate, or when the description of the perpetrator differs significantly from the appearance of the suspect, fillers should resemble the suspect in significant features.
- If multiple photos of the suspect are reasonably available to the investigator, select a photo that resembles the suspect's description or appearance at the time of the incident.
- Include a minimum of five fillers (nonsuspects) per identification procedure.
- Complete uniformity of features is not required. Avoid using fillers who so closely resemble the suspect that a person familiar with the suspect might find it difficult to distinguish the suspect from the fillers.
- Create a consistent appearance between the suspect and filler with respect to any unique or unusual feature (for example, scars, tattoos) used to describe the perpetrator by artificially adding or concealing that feature.

- Consider placing suspects in different positions in each lineup both across cases and with multiple witnesses in the same case. Position the suspect randomly in the lineup.
- When showing a new suspect, avoid reusing fillers in lineups shown to the same witness.
- Ensure that no writings or information concerning previous arrest(s) will be visible to the witness.
- View the spread, once completed, to ensure that the suspect does not unduly stand out.
- Preserve the presentation order of the photo lineup. In addition, preserve the photos themselves in their original condition.

Other Means of Identifying Suspects

In addition to lineups, showups, and photographic arrays, the police often use other identification procedures such as DNA testing, polygraph examination, Breathalyzer tests, handwriting and hair samples, and brain fingerprinting. The admissibility of these forms of scientific evidence in court varies. Constitutional rights may also be involved in each procedure.

DNA Testing: Results Admissible into Evidence

DNA testing results are admissible into evidence. In this section, we look at the background of DNA testing, results and some of the legal issues testing has created, the reliability of testing, the need for a national database, and the future of DNA testing.

Background A comparatively new but powerful tool in suspect identification and crime solving is **DNA testing**, which matches the suspect's DNA with DNA (such as that found in the semen or blood) recovered from the scene of the crime. DNA is the short term for deoxyribonucleic acid, the chemical that carries a person's genetic information. Known in some circles as genetic fingerprinting, DNA may be recovered from a variety of sources, including semen, blood, hair, skin, sweat, and saliva. The *National Institute of Justice Journal* says, "Today's investigators can solve crimes using the DNA collected from the perspiration on a rapist's discarded baseball cap, the saliva on a stamp of a stalker's threatening letter, and the skin cells shed on a ligature of a strangled victim."[15]

If DNA testing is performed properly, the chances of the method producing a false match are several hundred thousand to one and sometimes several million to one.[16] In a 2005 article, the *New York Times* reported that "DNA can remove much of the guesswork for the police and prosecutors, and it can reach back to grab those who committed crimes decades ago or were charged but dodged conviction."[17] The same article stated that the "F.B.I., which maintains the national databank of DNA criminal case profiles, says that DNA has so far [November 2005] helped in the prosecution of 27,806 cases nationwide."

Although DNA research goes back to the 19th century, DNA testing first gained prominence in England in the mid-1980s. It quickly caught the fancy of the law enforcement community and prosecutors in the United States as an infallible means of suspect identification.[18] When first introduced in a U.S. court in 1987, DNA typing was billed as the "greatest advance in forensics since the discovery of fingerprints."[19] In *United States v. Jakobetz* (955 F.2d 786 [1992]), a federal court of appeals ruled that "the district court properly exercised its discretion in admitting the DNA profiling evidence proffered by the government in this case; we also conclude that courts facing a similar issue in the future can take judicial notice of the general theories and specific techniques involved in DNA profiling." In addition to affirming the trial court's admission of the evidence, *Jakobetz* featured a lengthy discussion of the science and technology of DNA testing and the reasons it is reliable. (See Figure 10.2 to learn more about how DNA testing works and where DNA can be found.)

United States v. Jakobetz (1992)

Results and Some Legal Issues

DNA testing has been useful for the police in identifying suspects, and it has also led to the exoneration of some defendants. The National Institute of Justice, upon orders of the attorney general, conducted a study to determine how often DNA had exonerated wrongfully convicted defendants. The report, released in 1996, stated that it identified "28 inmates for whom DNA analysis was exculpatory."[20] As of October 2002, DNA testing had freed ten wrongly convicted murderers from death row, exonerated 100 prisoners of lesser crimes, and helped clear thousands of cases.[21] The *New York Times* reported that from 1989 to November 2005, DNA testing had led to the exoneration of 163 people.

Aside from identifying criminals and helping free the innocent, DNA is also used to identify missing persons. For example, there were a lot of missing people and unidentified victims after the tragic events of September 11, 2001 in New York. DNA was used to identify missing persons.[22]

Although the admissibility of DNA testing results as evidence is settled, other legal questions have arisen. For example, in January 2002, a three-judge panel of the Fourth U.S. Circuit Court of Appeals ruled that convicted felons do not have a constitutional right to postconviction DNA testing, although such a test could have proved a felon's innocence.[23] At about that same time, the Texas Court of Criminal Appeals (the highest state court for criminal cases) ruled that a district judge did not have the authority to order DNA testing for an inmate whose case did not qualify under state law for state-paid testing.[24] A judge in Massachusetts "halted the gathering of blood samples for DNA profiling from thousands of prison inmates, probationers, and parolees after several sued the state, arguing that it was an illegal search and seizure performed without proper safeguards."[25]

Problems concerning the admissibility of DNA evidence continue to bother some courts. It came under heavy scrutiny and challenge during the celebrated O. J. Simpson criminal trial, a trial that did little to increase public confidence in the reliability of DNA testing and the way it is administered in some government

Identifying DNA Evidence

Since only a few cells can be sufficient to obtain useful DNA information to help your case, the list below identifies some common items of evidence that you may need to collect, the possible location of the DNA on the evidence, and the biological source containing the cells. Remember that just because you cannot see a stain does not mean there are not enough cells for DNA typing. Further, DNA does more than just identify the source of the sample; it can place a known individual at a crime scene, in a home, or in a room where the suspect claimed not to have been. It can refute a claim of self-defense and put a weapon in the suspect's hand. It can change a story from an alibi to one of consent. The more officers know how to use DNA, the more powerful a tool it becomes.

Evidence	Possible Location of DNA on the Evidence	Source of DNA
baseball bat or similar weapon	handle, end	sweat, skin, blood, tissue
hat, bandanna, or mask	inside	sweat, hair, dandruff
eyeglasses	nose or ear pieces, lens	sweat, skin
facial tissue, cotton swab	surface area	mucus, blood, sweat, semen, ear wax
dirty laundry	surface area	blood, sweat, semen
toothpick	tips	saliva
used cigarette	cigarette butt	saliva
stamp or envelope	licked area	saliva
tape or ligature	inside/outside surface	skin, sweat
bottle, can, or glass	sides, mouthpiece	saliva, sweat
used condom	inside/outside surface	semen, vaginal or rectal cells
blanket, pillow, sheet	surface area	sweat, hair, semen, urine, saliva
"through and through" bullet	outside surface	blood, tissue
bite mark	person's skin or clothing	saliva
fingernail, partial fingernail	scrapings	blood, sweat, tissue

Figure 10.2 Identifying DNA Evidence

Source: "What Every Law Enforcement Officer Should Know about DNA Evidence," National Institute of Justice, *http://www.ncjrs.org/nij/DNAbro/id.html*

HIGHLIGHT

The Impact of DNA Testing

"DNA has become a fixture in the U.S. justice system. It has sprung 10 wrongly convicted murderers from death row, exonerated 100 other convicts of lesser crimes, and helped prosecutors clear thousands of cases that might have gone unsolved. An FBI computer system that compares DNA from unsolved state and federal crimes with samples drawn from convicts has scored nearly 5,500 matches in the 10 years it has operated."

SOURCE: "DNA Testing Fails to Live Up to Potential," *USA Today*, October 7, 2002, p.1A.

laboratories. Despite that, DNA testing methods over the past decade have improved tremendously, prompting one former DNA-testing opponent to admit that the remaining scientific debate is purely academic and that the "DNA wars are over."[26]

Unassailable Scientific Reliability Considered by some to be the gold standard of criminal evidence, the consensus is that the scientific foundation of DNA testing is solid and unassailable. If competently interpreted, the test is reliable and the results are admissible in court. It is generally accepted that each person's DNA is unique except for the DNA of identical twins, and that the chances of similarity in DNA are infinitesimally small. There is no question that DNA technology is scientifically reliable. Under existing evidence rules on admissibility (the *Frye* doctrine or the *Daubert* doctrine, both discussed later in this chapter), DNA testing easily satisfies both standards.

The legal controversy, however, centers around the skill of technicians who conduct the tests and the validity of their interpretations. In April 1992, the chairman of a National Academy of Sciences panel looking into DNA testing recommended that laboratories analyzing DNA should be held to higher standards in the way the tests are performed and interpreted. Admitting that, when performed properly, DNA testing can be invaluable in solving crimes, the panel also called for adherence to very strict standards to ensure that the "technique is performed properly in crime laboratories and that its results are accurate." It further urged that scientists set the standards for admissibility. Judges and jurors should not be put in a position where, based on complex data, they have to decide whether a laboratory test result is reliable.[27]

DNA technology has made giant strides over the years. Just a few years ago, a DNA test required a sizable sample (such as a blood stain or semen) with high-quality DNA, and the test took several weeks. Today, as the *FBI Law Enforcement Bulletin* states, "FBI scientists can type DNA from the back of a postage stamp, the shaft of a hair, and the end of a cigarette in a matter of days."[28] DNA testing results constitute convincing evidence, but jurors are nonetheless free to disregard it, as they are any type of evidence. What DNA does is establish that the odds of a false match are astronomically high; what it cannot do, however, is "positively link a specific person with a particular evidence stain."[29] Stated differently, the evidence of guilt in the possession of the police is overwhelming, but to whom does it belong?

Toward a National DNA Database The federal government has opened a national DNA database aimed at significantly reducing the number of rapes and other crimes by identifying and catching repeat offenders earlier. As one source describes it, the "FBI's Combined DNA Index System (CODIS) is a national database into which law-enforcement officials around the country can upload DNA information about criminals." It adds that "states participating in the program (almost all have joined) can draw from the common DNA basket when investigating unsolved crimes. So far, more than 1.2 million profiles have been registered."[30] Although CODIS has critics worried about possible violations of civil liberties, one plus side for it is that it has already cleared numerous innocent convicts in the United States through DNA testing after their conviction.

Some states have expanded their state DNA database. Under a law passed in the state of New York, "Anyone convicted of a long list of felonies will have a DNA profile entered into a state database for use in solving crimes and aiding prosecutions. The law permits DNA to be collected either from a blood sample or by taking cells from the inside of the mouth with a cotton swab." New York already "collects fingerprints, and has begun taking blood samples from people convicted of sex crimes and a few other violent offenses."[31]

As of April 2006, all fifty states and the FBI had laws or other forms of authorization allowing the collection of DNA samples from convicted offenders. These samples form profiles that are compared against available DNA profiles of biological evidence. The DNA databases include information on the range of included offenses and of some characteristics of offenders, such as whether they are adults or juveniles. The data collected are extensive and a major help in solving crimes, but their use is controlled and limited. For example, criminal penalties are imposed for such acts as tampering with the samples or records, the improper entry of DNA samples into the database, improper access and use, and improper disclosure of DNA information.[32]

The constitutionality of forensic DNA databanks has been challenged in various state and federal courts based on the Fourth Amendment prohibition against unreasonable searches and seizures. Most courts, however, have upheld their constitutionality. For example, in 2004–2005, there were four DNA databank challenges in the U.S. Circuit Courts of Appeals alone. In all four cases, the courts held DNA databank statutes constitutional.[33] The U.S. Supreme Court has yet to rule on this issue, but a review of these challenges reveals that most U.S. Courts of Appeals and state courts have held DNA databanks constitutional against Fourth Amendment challenges.

The Future of DNA Testing DNA testing continues to be a welcome bonanza in law enforcement and will continue to be an effective tool in the war on crime. It has come a long way since the mid-1980s, when it first came to the attention of the police. Its cost continues to decrease; it now varies from $10,000 in complex homicide cases to $500 in a typical rape case. The federal government is looking at new programs to improve state and local crime laboratories and is making the national DNA matching system easier for police and prosecutors to use. The FBI has also begun to increase the capacity of DNA systems computers from the current 1.5 million DNA profiles to 50 million and to maintain all the system's records at a central website.[34]

The federal government, the states, and local agencies are spending a lot of money to improve their DNA testing capability. In September 2005, the U.S. Department of Justice "announced more than $84 million in DNA grants nationwide as part of President Bush's DNA Initiative."[35] That initiative, called "Advancing Justice through DNA Technology," consists of a "five-year $1 billion commitment to improve the nation's capacity to use DNA evidence by eliminating casework and convicted offender backlogs; funding research and development; improving crime lab capacity; providing training for all stakeholders in the criminal justice system; and conducting testing to identify the missing."[36] Awards worth $13.6 million were also given that same month to improve the administration of criminal justice forensic services.[37]

DNA testing is an effective instrument in the search for justice both for the state and for the wrongfully accused or convicted. Its potential for crime solving is far-reaching and still unfolding. As one expert notes, "The day is coming when, conceivably, a criminal would have to wrap himself in a plastic body bag to avoid leaving some trace of his DNA at a scene."[38] Future years will see the effectiveness of DNA testing enhanced and its use more common. That bodes well for the police and defendants in their common quest for evidence that truly serves the ends of justice.

Polygraph Examinations: Results Not Admissible

Most courts refuse to admit the results of polygraph (lie detector) tests in either civil or criminal proceedings unless admissibility is agreed to by both parties. The reliability of polygraphs is questionable, particularly when the test is administered by an unqualified operator. In the words of one observer, "Polygraphy is very different from other scientific evidence. It is in essence the opinion of the polygrapher. The underlying scientific basis for polygraphy has always been the subject of heated controversy."[39] Despite progress in technology, most courts still consider it "junk science."[40]

Aside from the problem of unqualified operators, many scholars feel that people who are adept at deception or who have convinced themselves that they are telling the truth can beat the polygraph. After interviewing polygraph experts from the CIA, FBI, and other agencies, a committee of the National Academy of Sciences concluded in October 2002 that "it is possible to fool a lie detector, especially if the subject is being screened for general criminal or spy activity and not for some specific act."[41] It then added that "polygraphs cannot be relied on for mass screening of federal employees, because they can falsely suggest an honest employee is lying and can be fooled by someone who is trained to do so."

Frye v. United States (D.C. Cir. 1923)

Polygraph results fail to conform to the ***Frye* doctrine** and are therefore inadmissible as evidence in court. This doctrine, enunciated in *Frye v. United States* (293 F. 1013 [D.C. Cir. 1923]), states that, before the results of scientific tests will be admissible as evidence in a trial, the procedures used must be sufficiently established to have gained general acceptance in the particular field to which they belong.[42] Although some states, by case law or statute, have abandoned the *Frye* doctrine in favor of more liberal rules, it is still the test used in most states.

By contrast, the Court has held that in federal cases the *Frye* doctrine has been replaced by the adoption of the Federal Rules of Evidence, Rule 702, which provides, in part:

A. Witness qualified as an expert by knowledge, skill, experience, training, or education, may testify thereto in the form of an opinion or otherwise, if:

1. the testimony is based upon sufficient facts or data,
2. the testimony is the product of reliable principles and methods, and
3. the witness has applied the principles and methods reliably to the facts of the case.

Daubert v. Merrell Dow Pharmaceuticals, Inc. (1993)

These rules embody the ***Daubert* doctrine**, which allows the admission in court of expert testimony pertaining to "scientific, technical, or other specialized knowledge" that will "assist the trier of fact to understand the evidence or to determine a fact in issue" (*Daubert v. Merrell Dow Pharmaceuticals, Inc.,* 509 U.S. 579 [1993]). It is a decidedly more liberal admissibility standard than the *Frye* test. In federal courts, the admissibility of polygraph results is now left to the discretion of the trial court judge. This is not true in most state courts, where strict rules prohibit the admission into evidence of polygraph results. Moreover, some states by law prohibit the polygraph examination of a complainant by the police for any offense.[43]

United States v. Scheffer (1998)

However, in *United States v. Scheffer* (523 U.S. 303 [1998]), the Court held that a prohibition against the admissibility in court of polygraph evidence in favor of a defendant does not violate his or her constitutional right to present a defense. In that case, the results of a polygraph examination of an airman indicated that there was no deception in his denial that he used drugs. He sought to introduce that evidence to help exonerate himself, but military rules of evidence prohibit the admission of polygraph evidence in court-martial proceedings. Convicted of using drugs, the airman appealed, claiming that excluding the exonerating polygraph evidence violated his constitutional right to present a defense.

The Court disagreed, holding that there was no violation of Scheffer's constitutional right. Significantly, the Court assessed the state of polygraph evidence reliability as follows: To this day, the scientific community remains extremely polarized about the reliability of polygraph techniques. Some studies have concluded that polygraph tests overall are accurate and reliable. Others have found that polygraph tests assess truthfulness significantly less accurately—that scientific field studies suggest the accuracy rate of the "control question technique" polygraph is "little better than could be obtained by the toss of a coin," that is, 50 percent. This lack of scientific consensus is reflected in the disagreement among state and federal courts concerning both the admissibility and reliability of polygraph evidence.

The Office of Technology Assessment has stated that "there is at present only limited scientific evidence for establishing the validity of polygraph testing." It also stated that its review of twenty-four relevant studies meeting minimal acceptable scientific criteria found that correct detections ranged from about 35 to 100 percent.[44] The mathematical chance of misidentification is highest when the polygraph is used for screening purposes. In the words of one writer: "Departmental policy should recognize that [the] polygraph is not a perfect investigative process and that polygraph results, both examiner opinions following chart evaluation and [even] confessions and admissions obtained from examinees, are subject to error. Therefore, results should be considered in the context of a complete investigation. They should not be relied upon to the exclusion of other evidence or used as the sole means of resolving questions of verity."[45]

Even if reliability were to be greatly enhanced in the near future, polygraphs might still find limited use in criminal proceedings because of objections based on self-incrimination. It can be argued, with some justification, that forcing a person to take a polygraph examination and using the results against the person would violate the right to protection against compulsory self-incrimination because the nature of the examination is testimonial or communicative instead of real or physical. Issues pertaining to the right to counsel and due process might also arise, but chances of their being upheld in court probably would be minimal.

Breathalyzer™ Tests: Results Admissible

All states and the District of Columbia have laws against drunk driving that make it a crime to drive with a blood alcohol concentration (BAC) at a prohibited level of 0.08 percent or above. There are various consequences for violations, including incarceration, forfeiture of vehicles that are driven while the driver is impaired by alcohol use, and license suspension. Forty-three states and Washington, D.C. also have laws against the possession by drivers or passengers of open containers of alcohol in the passenger compartment of a motor vehicle.[46] Most jurisdictions suspend the driver's license if the suspect refuses to submit to a Breathalyzer test.

A Comparison of the Frye *and the* Daubert *Doctrines for Admissibility in Court of Expert Scientific Testimony*

Similarities

Both doctrines are based on court rulings. The *Frye* doctrine was laid out by a federal Court of Appeals in 1923; the *Daubert* doctrine was enunciated by the U.S. Supreme Court in a federal case in 1993. Both have since been enacted into law for use in state (*Frye*) or federal (*Daubert*) courts.

Differences

Frye *Doctrine*	Daubert *Doctrine*
Allows the admission in court of expert scientific testimony if the procedures used are sufficiently established to have gained acceptance in the particular field to which they belong	Allows the admission in court of expert scientific testimony if it will assist the trier of fact to understand the evidence or to determine a fact in issue
Focus of the standard is acceptance by peers in that field	Focus of the standard is whether it will help the judge or jury determine and understand the facts in the case
A strict standard for admission of scientific evidence in court	A liberal standard for admission of scientific evidence in court
Used in most state courts	Used in federal courts and some state courts

The results of Breathalyzer tests have been challenged based on scientific inaccuracy caused by "improperly calibrated equipment or inadequately trained officers." They have also been challenged based on "the circumstances of the particular testing at issue, including the skill and experience of the tester and the quality of the particular equipment used."[47] In a 2003 case, a class action case was reportedly won in Iowa because the state failed to establish uniform instructions for operating the breath testing device used.[48] Some states have strict rules governing the procedure for use of and administering Breathalyzer tests, and adherence to these prescribed rules and procedures is mandatory. In another case, the Supreme Court of the state of Ohio ruled that "tests of breath, blood or urine for alcohol content must closely comply with state regulations designed to minimize errors."[49] The reliability of Breathalyzer tests has long been recognized in courts, but legal issues persist concerning the fairness of their administration and adherence to procedures prescribed by state law.

Handwriting Samples: Results Admissible

Courts have consistently ruled that obtaining handwriting samples for use in criminal prosecutions does not violate a suspect's right against self-incrimination under the Fifth Amendment. In *Gilbert v. California* (388 U.S. 263 [1967], discussed earlier under Lineups), the Court held that the admission of a handwriting sample did not violate the Fifth Amendment. In that case, the Court cited an earlier Court ruling in *Schmerber v. California* (284 U.S. 757 [1966]), which held that "the Fifth Amendment offers no protection against compulsion to submit to fingerprinting, photographing, or measurements, to write or to speak for identification to appear in court, to stand, to assume a stance, or to make a particular gesture." This is because the right against self-incrimination prohibits the admission of testimonial evidence but does not prohibit the incriminatory use of physical evidence. In a later case, *United States v. Mara* (410 U.S. 19 [1973]), the Court declared: "Handwriting, like speech, is repeatedly shown to the public and there is no more expectation of privacy in the physical characteristics of a person's script than there is in the tone of his voice."

United States v. Mara (1973)

In sum, obtaining a handwriting sample from a suspect is constitutional because handwriting is considered public. Consent for obtaining it is advisable but is not a requirement for its admissibility as evidence in court.

Hair Samples: Results Admissible

Hair samples are used with more frequency in criminal prosecutions to prove guilt. One advantage of using hair samples is that it keeps the information (such as drug use) for a long period of time. Court cases have arisen questioning the constitutionality of this use. In a 2004 case, *Coddington v. Evanko,* the U.S. Court of Appeals for the Third Circuit held that law enforcement officers may shave large amounts of hair from a suspect's head, neck, and shoulders, without a warrant, probable cause, or any basis for suspecting that the hair would provide evidence of crime."[50]

In *Coddington,* the Pennsylvania state trooper's hair was cut by his superiors because they had received confidential information of Coddington's cocaine use. They cut the hair from Coddington's "head, neck, and a small section in the area of his left shoulder blade." Additional hair was taken from Coddington while he was in the home of a retired state police trooper by the retired trooper's wife, a retired beautician. Test results from the hair samples did not show any evidence of cocaine use or use of any other illegal drugs. Coddington sued his superiors, claiming a violation of his constitutional rights against unreasonable searches and seizures and his right to privacy. His lawsuit was dismissed.

He appealed to the federal Third Circuit Court of Appeals, which upheld the dismissal, saying that "the fact that Coddington had very short hair on his head, requiring the police officers and the beautician to shave some of his hair to the skin in order to obtain a sufficient quantity for the drug test, does not alter the fact that the only hair that was taken was above the body surface and on public display, and that hair was taken in proper manner." This ruling followed a 1982 decision from the same court that held that "taking hair samples from visible parts of a suspect's body does not invade any reasonable expectation of privacy," and therefore does not amount to a Fourth Amendment search.[51]

Although held by courts as valid, one source recommends that "sample collection should be performed by a responsible authority respecting the legal, ethical and human rights of the person to be tested for drugs of abuse. Hair samples should be obtained in a non–drug-contaminated environment by an appropriately trained individual, not necessarily a physician. A sufficient amount of sample should be collected so that a repeat analysis or a confirmation analysis by another laboratory can be performed should it be needed."[52]

Brain Fingerprinting: Too Early to Tell

Brain fingerprinting is a new and controversial tool in solving crimes. The technique was invented by Lawrence Farwell, a Seattle-born neuroscientist trained at the University of Illinois. It is characterized as "a real-time psycho-physiological assessment of a subject's response to stimuli in the form of words or pictures presented on a computer monitor. As a forensic method, the test assesses the subject's knowledge of a crime scene or of the instrumentalities or fruits of a crime, and it can also be used to assess knowledge of the particulars of an alibi scene or sequence of events."

Although it does not claim to prove the suspect's guilt or innocence, brain fingerprinting testing supposedly provides "extremely strong scientific evidence that the record of the time of the crime stored in the suspect's brain does or does not contain the salient facts about the crime, and does or does not contain the salient facts about the alibi." It has generated national attention for possible use in crime detection, such as whether a person has been trained as a terrorist and other effects on a person's memory. At least one state court has ruled that brain fingerprinting testing is admissible in court.[53] This form of evidence, however, is still new and its admissibility will continue to be tested in court based on the *Frye* or the *Daubert* standard.

Summary

Lineups

- *Definition.* A police identification procedure in which the suspect in a crime is exhibited, along with others with similar physical characteristics, before the victim or witness to determine if the suspect committed the offense
- *The right to counsel.* Applies after a formal charge has been filed but not before
- *The role of a lawyer during a lineup.* To make sure the procedure is fair, but the lawyer must not be allowed to control the proceedings

- *The right to due process.* Applies and is violated if the identification procedure is impermissibly suggestive
- *The right to protection against unreasonable searches and seizures.* Does not apply
- *The right to protection against self-incrimination.* Does not apply, because the self-incrimination involved is physical, not testimonial

Showups

- *Definition.* One-to-one confrontation between a suspect and a witness to a crime

- *The right to counsel.* Applies after a formal charge has been filed but not before

- *The right to due process.* Applies and is violated if the identification procedure is impermissibly suggestive

- *The right to protection against unreasonable searches and seizures.* Does not apply

- *The right to protection against self-incrimination.* Does not apply, because the type of self-incrimination involved is physical, not testimonial

Photographic Identifications

- *Definition.* A process in which a victim or witness is shown photographs of possible suspects in a one-on-one situation

- *The right to counsel.* Does not apply

- *The right to due process.* Applies and is violated if the identification procedure is impermissibly suggestive

- *The right to protection against unreasonable searches and seizures.* Does not apply

- *The right to protection against self-incrimination.* Does not apply, because the type of self-incrimination involved is physical, not testimonial

Other Means of Pretrial Identification

- *DNA testing.* Results admissible
- *Polygraph examination.* Results not admissible
- *Breathalyzer tests.* Results admissible
- *Handwriting samples.* Results admissible
- *Hair samples.* Results admissible
- *Brain fingerprinting.* Too early to tell

Review Questions and Hypothetical Cases

1. What four constitutional rights are likely to be invoked by suspects during the pretrial identification stage? Briefly discuss how each applies to lineups, showups, and photographic displays.

2. "A suspect is entitled to a lawyer during a police lineup." Is that statement true or false? Explain your answer.

3. "A suspect's right to protection against self-incrimination is violated in a police lineup." Is that statement true or false? Justify your answer.

4. What can the police do if a suspect refuses to appear in a lineup?

5. "A suspect is entitled to counsel during a lineup." Is that statement true or false? Discuss your answer.

6. Some critics maintain that despite its frequent use in police work and in courts, eyewitness identification is actually "hopelessly unreliable." Do you agree or disagree? Support your answer.

7. What is DNA testing? Why are DNA test results admissible as evidence in court?

8. Identify and discuss some legal problems associated with DNA testing.

9. Distinguish between the *Frye* and the *Daubert* doctrines as tests of the admissibility in court of scientific evidence. If you were a defense lawyer, which test would you want the trial court to use, and why? If you were the prosecutor, would your answer be the same? Explain.

10. Discuss why the results of polygraph examinations are not admissible in most courts.

11. Suspect X was arrested by the police in downtown San Francisco. He was charged with robbery. He asked for a lawyer and was given a public defender. A week later, X was made to appear in a police lineup. He refused, saying that he would do so only if his lawyer was present during the lineup. He further objected to the lineup on the ground that it would violate his constitutional right to due process and protection against self-incrimination and that this constitutes a violation of his Fourth Amendment right against unreasonable searches and seizures. You are the judge in the

case. Will you uphold or reject X's allegations? Analyze each allegation and give reasons for your decision.

12. Assume you are a suspect and are made to appear in a police lineup. You are suspected of a sexual assault allegedly committed by "a Hispanic who was about five feet eight, wore jeans, and spoke with an accent." You are Hispanic, about five feet ten, and one of three Hispanics of similar height in the lineup. All three of you speak with an accent; all three of you are wearing jeans. You are identified by the victim after you were made to repeat the statement "I will kill you if you shout." Were your constitutional rights violated and, if so, what right? Support your answer.

Key Terms

Go to the Criminal Procedure 7e website for flash cards that will help you master the definitions of these terms.

brain fingerprinting, 391
Daubert doctrine, 387
DNA testing, 381
formally charged with an offense, 361

Frye doctrine, 387
Kirby rule, 362
lineup, 361
photographic identification (rogue's gallery), 374

physical self-incrimination, 370
showup, 371
Wade-Gilbert rule, 365

Holdings of Key Cases

See Appendix C for information on how to find cases in this chapter on FindLaw.com.

***Coleman v. Alabama*, 399 U.S. 1 (1970)** The term *critical stage* for purposes of the right to counsel includes preliminary hearings to determine whether there is sufficient evidence to bring the case to a grand jury.

***Daubert v. Merrell Dow Pharmaceuticals, Inc.*, 509 U.S. 579 (1993)** The *Frye* doctrine has been superseded in federal cases by the adoption of the Federal Rules of Evidence. In particular, those rules have a more liberal admissibility standard, permitting the admission of expert testimony pertaining to scientific, technical, or other specialized knowledge that will assist the trier of fact in understanding the evidence or determining a fact in issue.

***Foster v. California*, 394 U.S. 440 (1969)** The suspect's right to due process is violated during a lineup in which the circumstances are such that identification of the suspect by the witness is inevitable.

***Frye v. United States*, 293 F. 1013 (D.C. Cir. 1923)** Before the results of scientific tests will be admissible as evidence in a trial, the procedures used must be sufficiently established to have gained general acceptance in the particular field to which they belong.

***Gilbert v. California*, 388 U.S. 263 (1967)** Police identification procedures that are "fraught with dangers of suggestion" are invalid because they violate the accused's right to due process.

***Kirby v. Illinois*, 406 U.S. 682 (1972)** There is no right to counsel at police lineups or identification procedures prior to the time the suspect is formally charged with a crime.

***Manson v. Brathwaite*, 432 U.S. 98 (1977)** The suggestiveness of the identification procedure is but one factor courts will take into account to determine whether there was a violation of a suspect's due process right.

***Moore v. Illinois*, 434 U.S. 220 (1977)** A defendant is entitled to a lawyer at a showup during the preliminary hearing, because at that time the criminal proceedings are considered to have been initiated.

Neil v. Biggers, **409 U.S. 188 (1972)** Identification procedures must be fair. To determine whether the procedure was fair, courts consider all the circumstances leading up to the identification. Courts will find unfairness only when, in the light of all such circumstances, the identification procedure is so suggestive as to give rise to a real and substantial likelihood of irreparable misidentification. The courts will most likely take the following factors into account: (1) the witness's opportunity to view the criminal at the time of the crime, (2) the witness's degree of attention at that time, (3) the accuracy of any prior description given by the witness, (4) the level of certainty demonstrated by the witness at the identification, and (5) the length of time between the crime and the identification.

Schmerber v. California, **384 U.S. 757 (1966)** The removal of blood from a suspect without his or her consent to obtain evidence is not a violation of any constitutional rights, as long as the removal is done by medical personnel using accepted medical methods.

Simmons v. United States, **390 U.S. 377 (1968)** Under the circumstances of this case, the photographic identification was not [so] unnecessarily suggestive as to create a very substantial likelihood of irreparable misidentification.

Stovall v. Denno, **388 U.S. 293 (1967)** Holding the showup of a suspect in a hospital is valid when the only living eyewitness is in danger of dying.

United States v. Ash, **413 U.S. 300 (1973)** There is no right to counsel when the prosecution seeks to identify the accused by displaying photographs to witnesses prior to trial.

United States v. Jakobetz, **955 F.2d 786 (1992)** The trial court properly exercised its discretion in admitting the DNA profiling evidence, and trial courts facing a similar issue in the future can take judicial notice of the general theories and specific techniques involved in DNA profiling.

United States v. Mara, **410 U.S. 19 (1973)** "Handwriting, like speech, is repeatedly shown to the public and there is no more expectation of privacy in the physical characteristics of a person's script than there is in the tone of his voice."

United States v. Scheffer, **523 U.S. 303 (1998)** A prohibition against the admissibility in court of polygraph evidence in favor of a defendant does not violate his or her constitutional right to present a defense.

United States v. Wade, **388 U.S. 218 (1967)** A police lineup or other face-to-face confrontation after the accused has been formally charged with a crime is considered a "critical stage of the proceedings," so the accused has a right to have counsel present. The absence of counsel during such proceedings renders the evidence obtained inadmissible. Also, requiring the suspect to "speak up" for identification is not a violation of the safeguard against self-incrimination, because it is physical instead of testimonial self-incrimination.

Wisconsin v. Dubose, **205 WI 126 (No. 2003AP1690 [2005])** This case concludes, from a study of the extensive research on eyewitness identification, that eyewitness testimony is often "hopelessly unreliable."

 ## You Be the Judge . . .

In the United States Court of Appeals for the Sixth Circuit

In Detroit, Michigan, at about 4 A.M., four men were attempting to repossess a pickup truck purchased on credit by Cynthia Schumate. Schumate was five months pregnant with Howard's child. Hankinson was the driver of the tow truck, Chorney was riding in the passenger's seat, and Gapinski and Carter were riding in the back.

They backed up the driveway and into the yard to tow the Toyota pickup truck they were to repossess. Gapinski put the Toyota on the tow bar and was crawling onto the hood to check the Vehicle Identification Number through the windshield when a car alarm went off. A gunshot rang out.

Gapinski and Carter jumped back into the bed of the truck, while Hankinson pulled the truck abreast of the porch. A man with a rifle stood there with Schumate, to whom Hankinson showed the repossession paperwork. At this point the truck was about 3 feet from the people on the porch. The man with the rifle demanded "Put the truck down!" and Hankinson complied. The man with the rifle pointed it at Chorney, in the passenger's seat, who had just called the police and told him to put the phone down. The tow truck continued down the driveway without the repossessed truck, and the man on the porch fired four or five more shots, hitting Hankinson in the head.

Gapinski went to the hospital with his fatally injured brother Hankinson. Carter and Chorney meanwhile went to the police station when the police arrived. Carter and Chorney could not identify the shooter from a photo lineup in which Howard was placed in the first position.

Howard was charged with the shooting, however. There were two cancelled preliminary hearings where the three surviving witnesses (Carter, Chorney, and Gapinski) claim they never really saw Howard clearly, as they were seated behind him. They then each individually picked Howard out of a lineup.

How will you decide this legal issue? Was the lineup, conducted after Carter, Chorney, and Gapinski may have had an opportunity to observe Howard in court, too suggestive?

The Court's decision The U.S. Court of Appeals for the Sixth Circuit decided that the lineup was not too suggestive. It is not clear that the witnesses had a clear chance to observe Howard, and the lineups were conducted individually. There was nothing about the in-court lineup that demanded that the witnesses pick Howard. *Howard v. Bouchard,* 405 F.3d 459 (6th Cir. 2005).

In the United States Court of Appeals for the Fourth Circuit

In Greensboro, North Carolina, a man walked into the Fidelity Bank and requested change for a ten- and twenty-dollar bill from a teller. He then asked to change a money order, but because he did not have an account with Fidelity, the teller told him he would have to go to the post office to cash it. A co-teller, Chadwick, was giving the man directions to the nearest post office when he brandished a gun and demanded money and an ATM bag. Chadwick and the other teller complied with his demands. He threatened to shoot the tellers if they continued to look at him. He demanded that the tellers walk toward the back of the bank and left the bank with over $12,000.

Detective Landers of the Greensboro P.D. believed identification of the bank robber was a key issue for his investigation. Isom was a suspect, and he complicated the investigation by posing as a certain Young, whom he resembled. Isom presented to Detective Landers a driver's license he stole from Young as his own identification. Isom did in fact closely resemble Young. He also claimed that the black BMW parked outside his residence belonged to his girlfriend. When Detective Landers ran the registration, it came back to Young and Isom's girlfriend.

In investigating further, the detective found that Isom, posing as Young, had traded the black BMW in the day after they had spoken. Detective Landers made another appointment to talk to Isom, but he failed to show.

Isom was arrested on unrelated charges. It was when he was fingerprinted that Detective Lander learned his true identity. The detective then set up a photo lineup with six photographs. Isom's photo was in the first position, and he was the only one in the lineup with short hair. Isom was also one of two who were looking away from the camera. Even though Chadwick was robbed by Isom some four months earlier, she identified him out of the lineup.

How will you decide this legal issue? Was the lineup unduly suggestive, so as to be inadmissible as evidence for the jury?

The Court's decision The U.S. Court of Appeals for the Fourth Circuit decided that the lineup was not unduly suggestive. Even though the issue of identification is raised from time to time by defendants, such identifications are hardly ever found to be unduly suggestive. *U.S. v. Isom,* 138 Fed. Appx. 574 (4th Cir. 2005).

Recommended Readings

Angus J. Dodson. *DNA "line-ups" based on a reasonable suspicion standard.* University of Colorado Law Review 221, 254 (2000).

Michael J. Ligons. *Polygraph evidence: Where are we now?* Missouri Law Review 209, 227 (2000).

J. Wall. *DNA analysis: Current status in court.* Journal of International Biotechnology Law 1: 130–133 (2004).

Gary L. Wells, Mark Small, Steven Penrod, Roy S. Malpass, Soloman M. Fulero, and C.A.E. Brimacombe. *Eyewitness identification procedures: Recommendations for lineups and photospreads.* Law and Human Behavior 22 (6): 603–645 (1998).

Notes

1. Henry C. Black, *Black's Law Dictionary,* 6th ed., abridged (St. Paul, MN: West, 1991), p. 641.
2. Lloyd L. Weinreb and James D. Whaley, *The Field Guide to Law Enforcement* (Westbury, NY: Foundation Press, 1999), p. 67.
3. Larry Rissler, "The Role of Defense Counsel at Lineups, *FBI Law Enforcement Bulletin,* February 1980, p. 24.
4. Ibid., p. 23.
5. Supra note 2, p. 64.
6. W. LaFave and J. Israel, *Criminal Procedure* (St. Paul, MN: West, 1985), p. 325.
7. Supra note 1, p. 962.
8. *Wisconsin v. Dubose,* 205 WI 126 (No. 2003AP1690 [2005]).
9. *http://www.ncjrs.gov/txtfiles1/nij/178240.txt.*
10. John Turtle, R. C. L. Lindsay, and Gary L. Wells, "Best Practice Recommendations for Eyewitness Evidence Procedures: New Ideas for the Oldest Way to Solve a Case," *Canadian Journal of Police & Security Services* 1(1): March 2003, p. 3.
11. *Wisconsin v. Dubose,* 205 WI 126 (No. 2003AP1690 [2005]).
12. Dara McLeod, "Problems with Police Lineups," *Virginia Lawyers' Weekly, http://www.vachiefs.org/vacp/news/2005-02-8.html.*
13. "Police Lineup Methods Often Flawed, Experts Say," *Miami Herald,* August 4, 2005.
14. Available electronically at *http://www.ncjrs.gov/txtfiles1/nij/178240.txt.*
15. "DNA Commission Continues to Hear Testimony," *National Institute of Justice Journal,* October 1999, p. 32.
16. *Houston Chronicle,* August 8, 1992, p. A3.
17. "For '73 Rape Victim, DNA Also Revives Horror," *New York Times,* November 2, 2005, p. A1.
18. "*A Trial of High-Tech Detectives,*" *Time Magazine,* June 5, 1989, p. 63.
19. "Courtroom Genetics," *U.S. News & World Report,* January 27, 1992, pp. 60–61.
20. Christopher H. Asplen, "Forensic DNA Evidence: National Commission Explores Its Future," *National Institute of Justice Journal,* January 1999, p. 18.
21. *USA Today,* October 2002, p. 1A.
22. *Advancing Justice through DNA Technology,* published by the Office of the President of the United States, March 2003, p. iii.
23. "U.S. Appeals Court Reverses Ruling on DNA Testing," *Washington Post,* January 25, 2002, p. B01 19.
24. *Houston Chronicle,* September 12, 2002, p. 31A.
25. *New York Times,* February 19, 1998, p. 1.
26. *U.S. News & World Report,* November 7, 1994, p. 14.
27. *New York Times,* April 15, 1992, p. 1.
28. *FBI Law Enforcement Bulletin,* February 1998, p. 24.
29. Ibid.
30. "Privacy v. Security, Special Edition: Criminal Justice," *Time Magazine* (1), p. 4.
31. *New York Times,* August 16, 1999, p. 1.
32. Seth Axelrad, "Survey of State DNA Database Statutes," ASLME (American Society of Law, Medicine, and Ethics), *www.aslme.org/dna_04/grid/guide.pdf.*

33. *United States v. Kincade,* 379 F. 3d 813 (9th Cir. 2004); *United States v. Sczubelek,* 402 F. 3d 175 (3rd Cir. 2005); *Groceman v. U.S. Department of Justice,* 354 F. 3d 411 (5th Cir. 2004); *Green v. Berge,* 354 F.3d 675 (7th Cir. 2004).

34. *USA Today,* October 7, 2000, p. 2A 30.

35. "Department of Justice Announces $98 Million in Grants for President Bush's DNA Initiative and Other Crime-Solving Forensic Services," *http://www.ojp.usdoj.gov/newsroom/2005/NIJ05048.htm.*

36. Ibid.

37. Ibid.

38. Professor Walter F. Rowe, George Washington University, as quoted in the *Houston Chronicle,* September 12, 1999, p. 1.

39. U.S. Deputy Solicitor General Michael Dreeben, as quoted in the *Houston Chronicle,* November 4, 1997, p. A9 32.

40. *USA Today,* April 6, 1999, p. A11.

41. *Houston Chronicle,* October 9, 2002, p. 15A.

42. P. Lewis and K. Peoples, *The Supreme Court and the Criminal Process—Cases and Comments* (Philadelphia: Saunders, 1978), p. 496.

43. See, for example, Texas Code of Criminal Procedure, Article 15.051.

44. *Houston Chronicle,* November 23, 1985, sec. 3, p. 1.

45. R. Ferguson, "Polygraph Policy for Model Law Enforcement." *FBI Law Enforcement Bulletin,* July 1987, p. 7.

46. "Drinking and Driving Issues: DWI/DUI Laws of U.S. States," *http://www2.potsdam.edu/hansondj/DrivingIssues/1104284869.html.*

47. See DUI/Drunk Driving: Frequently Asked Questions about Drunk Driving/DUI, Marlow Law Offices, PLLC, *http://www.marlowelaw.net/CM/FSDP/PracticeCenter/Criminal-Law/Drunk-DrivingDUI.asp?focus=faq.*

48. "New Breath Test Challenged," Alcohol: In the News, *http://www2.potsdam.edu/hansondj/InThe News/DrinkingAndDriving/1070654115.html.*

49. "DUI Tests Must Now Be Accurate," Alcohol: In the News, *http://www2.potsdam.edu/hasondj/InTheNews/DrinkingAndDriving/1070544548.html.*

50. *Coddington v. Evanko,* 112 Fed. Approx. 835 (C.A. 3rd, 2004).

51. Ibid.

52. "Statement of the Society of Hair Testing Concerning the Examination of Drugs in Human Hair," *http://www.soht.org/html/Statements.html.*

53. "Brain Fingerprinting Testing Rules Admissible in Court," *http://www.brainwavescience.com/Ruled%20Admissable.php.*

Chapter 11

Confessions and Admissions: *Miranda v. Arizona*

What You Will Learn

- Before *Miranda,* voluntariness was the sole test for the admissibility of a confession or admission, but that standard was difficult for courts to apply.

- *Miranda v. Arizona* changed the rules on admissibility from voluntariness to the "three questions test."

- The *Miranda* warnings must be given whenever there is custodial interrogation by the police.

- "Custodial interrogation" is one phrase, but it is composed of two separate terms: custody and interrogation.

- There are many situations, based on Court decisions, when the *Miranda* warnings are not required.

- The "harmless error" rule applies to *Miranda* cases on appeal.

Introduction

The Fifth Amendment to the U.S. Constitution provides that "No person shall . . . be compelled in any criminal case to be a witness against himself, nor be deprived of life, liberty, or property, without due process of law." This right has been a source of controversy and has generated a host of litigated issues, some of which are still unresolved. The main question is, When are confessions and admissions admissible as evidence in a criminal trial, and when are they excludable? The answers are not simple, but this chapter's discussion should provide some insights. One case stands out over all other cases on the admissibility of confessions and admissions— *Miranda v. Arizona*. By the **Miranda rule**, evidence obtained

The Top 5 Important Cases on Confessions and Interrogations

***Miranda v. Arizona* (1966):** Law enforcement officers must give suspects the following warnings whenever there is a custodial interrogation:

1. You have a right to remain silent.
2. Anything you say can be used against you in a court of law.
3. You have a right to the presence of an attorney.
4. If you cannot afford an attorney, one will be appointed for you prior to questioning.
5. You may terminate this interview at any time.

***Edwards v. Arizona* (1981):** Once the suspect has invoked the right to remain silent, the suspect cannot be questioned again for the same offense unless he or she initiates further communication, exchanges, or conversations with the police.

***Berkemer v. McCarty* (1984):** A person subjected to custodial interrogation must be given the *Miranda* warnings regardless of the nature or severity of the offense. Exception: The roadside questioning of a motorist detained pursuant to a routine traffic stop does not constitute a custodial interrogation, so there is no need to give the *Miranda* warnings.

***Arizona v. Fulminante* (1991):** The harmless error rule is applicable to cases on appeal involving confessions.

***Dickerson v. United States* (2000):** *Miranda v. Arizona* governs the admissibility in federal and state courts of confessions and admissions given during a custodial interrogation by the police. The *Miranda* warnings are a constitutional rule; therefore, any law passed by Congress that seeks to overturn *Miranda* is unconstitutional.

by the police during custodial interrogations of a suspect cannot be used in court during trial unless the suspect was first informed of the right not to incriminate himself or herself and unless that right is waived intelligently and voluntarily.

The terms *confession* and *admission* are often used as though they are interchangeable, but they are not. In criminal justice, a **confession** means that a person says he or she committed the act; an **admission** means that the person owns up to something related to the act but may not have committed it. A confession is more incriminating than an admission. Here are examples: Confession: "Yes, I shot him." Admission: "Yes, I was there, but I did not shoot him. Somebody else did."

Before *Miranda*: Only Voluntary Confessions Were Admissible

Before the *Miranda* decision, the only test for whether a confession was admissible into court was whether it was voluntary. But what was a *voluntary* confession? This section examines that issue and looks at cases on confessions that were decided before *Miranda*.

Voluntary Confessions

Before the *Miranda* decision, the Supreme Court decided the admissibility of confessions and admissions on a case-by-case basis. The sole test was whether the confession was voluntary or involuntary. Voluntariness was determined by the courts based on whether the suspect's will was "broken" or "overborne" by the police during interrogation. This approach, however, did not provide much guidance to the lower courts because the Supreme Court had failed to set any definitive guidelines by which the admissibility of confessions could be determined. In general, the Court held that confessions obtained by force or coercion could not be used in court; conversely, confessions were admissible if they were voluntary. *Voluntariness* was the standard used, but the meaning of that word was imprecise and changed over the years.

Originally, only confessions or statements obtained by physical force (such as beating, whipping, or maiming) were considered inadmissible. Later, courts recognized that coercion could be mental as well as physical. Even then, the hard question remained, At what point did physical or mental (psychological) coercion become so excessive as to render the confession involuntary? Clearly, physical torture was prohibited, but what about a push, a shove, a slap, or a mere threat? As for mental coercion, suppose the police did not physically abuse the suspect but simply detained him "until he talked"? Was this coercion? If so, how long must the detention last before the confession could be considered coerced? A few hours? A day? A week?

U.S. Supreme Court Cases before *Miranda v. Arizona*

The following cases, all decided prior to *Miranda*, give a glimpse into the evolution of the Court's rulings and illustrate the difficulty the Court faced in prescribing a viable criterion for the admissibility of confessions or statements before the *Miranda* decision. Each case was decided on the old voluntariness standard and under circumstances that could hardly be replicated in other cases. This led to confusing and conflicting decisions in the lower courts, a confusion that was largely cleared by the *Miranda* decision.

Brown v. Mississippi, 297 U.S. 278 (1936): Coercion and Brutality—Confession Not Valid

A deputy sheriff, accompanied by other persons, took one of the suspects to a murder scene, where he was questioned about the crime. Brown denied his guilt and was hanged by a rope from the limb of a tree for a period of time. He was then let down, after which he again denied his guilt. He was next tied to the tree and whipped, but he still refused to confess and was allowed to go home. Later Brown was seized again and whipped until he confessed.

The Court reversed the conviction and held that the confession was a product of utter coercion and brutality and thus violated the Fourteenth Amendment right to due process. (At that time, the Fifth Amendment protection against compulsory self-incrimination had not been applied to state prosecutions, so the Court had to use the Due Process Clause of the Fourteenth Amendment to reverse the conviction.)

Chambers v. Florida, 309 U.S. 227 (1940): Coercion—Confession Not Valid

Four youths were convicted of murder primarily on the basis of their confessions. No physical coercion was used by the police, but pressure was exerted through prolonged questioning while the defendants were held in jail without contact with the outside world. The Court reversed the convictions on the grounds that the confessions had been coerced and that the defendants had therefore been deprived of their Fourteenth Amendment right to due process.

Spano v. New York, 360 U.S. 315 (1959): Deception—Confession Not Valid

The defendant was suspected of murder in New York. About ten days after the murder, Spano telephoned a close friend who was a rookie police officer in the New York Police Department. Spano told his friend that he (Spano) had taken a terrific beating from the murder victim, and, because he was dazed, he did not know what he was doing when he shot the victim. The officer relayed this information to his superiors. Spano was brought in for questioning, but his attorney advised him not to answer any questions. The department called in the rookie friend and told him to inform Spano that his telephone call had caused the officer a lot of trouble. The officer was instructed to win sympathy from Spano for the sake of his wife and children. Spano refused to cooperate, but after his friend's fourth try, he finally agreed to tell the police about the shooting. Spano was convicted and appealed.

The Court said that the use of deception as a means of psychological pressure to induce a confession was a violation of the defendant's constitutional rights and therefore excluded the evidence.

Rogers v. Richmond, 365 U.S. 534 (1961): Confession Not Voluntary–Not Valid The defendant was charged with murder and found guilty by a jury. While in jail pending trial, Rogers was questioned about the killing. The interrogation started during the afternoon of the day of his arrest and continued through the evening. During the interrogation, Rogers was allowed to smoke and was given a sandwich and some coffee. At no time was he ever subjected to violence or threat of violence by the police. Six hours after the start of the interview, Rogers still refused to give any information. The police then indicated that they were about to have Rogers's wife taken into custody, whereupon Rogers indicated his willingness to confess. The confession was introduced as evidence during the trial, and Rogers was convicted.

The Court held that the confession by Rogers was involuntary, and therefore not admissible, on the grounds that the accused did not have complete freedom of mind when making his confession.

Escobedo v. Illinois, 378 U.S. 748 (1964): Suspect Denied Counsel at the Police Station–Confession Not Valid Escobedo was arrested for murder and interrogated for several hours at the police station, during which time he was persuaded to confess. During the interrogation, Escobedo repeatedly asked to see his lawyer, who was also at the police station at that time and who demanded to see him. The police refused both requests and proceeded to interrogate Escobedo. He eventually confessed, was tried, and was convicted.

On appeal, the Court held that Escobedo was denied his right to counsel, so no statement taken during the interrogation could be admitted against him at the trial. The Court said that "where, as here, the investigation is no longer a general inquiry into the unsolved crime but has begun to focus on a particular suspect . . . no statement elicited by the police during the investigation may be used against him at a criminal trial."

This was an easy case for the Court to decide because the police had indeed grossly violated Escobedo's right to counsel. However, the *Escobedo* case left two issues unsettled: (1) Did the right to counsel apply only when the facts were similar to those in *Escobedo* (the suspect was accused of a serious offense, was being questioned at the police station, and had asked to see his lawyer, and the lawyer was present and demanded to confer with his client)? and (2) What did the Court mean when it said that the right to counsel could be invoked when the investigation had begun to "focus" on a particular suspect? Did it refer to when a suspect was under investigation, had been arrested, had been charged with an offense, or had been arraigned? Because of its unique facts, the *Escobedo* case raised more questions than it answered. Trial courts disagreed on the meaning of *Escobedo*, particularly the interpretation of the term *focus*, leading to conflicting decisions. Further guidance from the Court became necessary. *Escobedo* therefore set the stage for *Miranda* and, in fact, made *Miranda* necessary because the confusion had to be cleared up.

After *Miranda:* The Three-Question Test for Admissibility

In *Miranda,* the Court rejected voluntariness as the sole test to determine whether statements from suspects are admissible in court. Voluntariness is still required today, but it is assumed from a "yes" answer to all three questions the trial court must ask:

1. Were the *Miranda* warnings given?
2. If they were given, was there a waiver?
3. If there was a waiver, was it intelligent and voluntary?

Miranda, in effect, establishes a three-question test for admissibility.

1. If the statement was voluntary but the *Miranda* warnings were not given when they should have been (because there was a custodial interrogation), the evidence cannot be admitted in court.
2. Even if the statement was voluntary and the *Miranda* warnings were given, the statement is not admissible if the government cannot establish that there was a waiver.
3. If the statement was voluntary, the *Miranda* warnings were given, and there was a waiver, but the waiver was not intelligent and voluntary, the evidence obtained is not admissible in court.

These three situations can be illustrated as follows:

- *Question 1: Were the Miranda warnings given?* Example: Assume that after her arrest and in response to questions asked without the *Miranda* warnings, Suspect X gives the police a confession that is 100 percent voluntary. The evidence cannot be used in court because X was not given her *Miranda* warnings.
- *Question 2: If they were given, was there a waiver?* Example: Assume that Suspect Y was given the *Miranda* warnings. However, the prosecutor could not prove in court that Y in fact waived his rights prior to giving a confession. The evidence is not admissible.
- *Question 3: If there was a waiver, was it intelligent and voluntary?* Example: Assume that Suspect Z gave a voluntary statement to the police after being given the *Miranda* warnings. During the trial, however, the prosecutor could not prove that M's waiver was intelligent and voluntary. The evidence is not admissible.

For trial court judges, the importance of *Miranda* lies in the shift from the old voluntariness test to a new and clear standard that is easier to apply. Instead of determining voluntariness on a case-by-case basis, which took a lot of time, after *Miranda,* judges only need to ascertain the answers to the three questions. If the answers are yes to all three questions, then the evidence is admissible; conversely, if at least one of the answers is a no, the evidence is not admissible.

Voluntariness is still a requirement for admissibility, but it is no longer the sole focus of the trial court's initial inquiry. Involuntary confessions are not admissible under *Miranda,* but voluntariness is assumed if the answers to the three questions are all yes. Trial courts no longer need to investigate specific facts in each case to determine if the statement was in fact voluntary.

Missouri v. Seibert (2004)

The Court summarized these rules in *Missouri v. Seibert* (542 U.S. 600 [2004]) when it said:

> *Miranda* conditioned the admissibility at trial of any custodial confession on warning a suspect of his rights; failure to give the prescribed warnings and obtain a waiver of rights before custodial questioning generally requires exclusion of any statements obtained. Conversely, giving the warnings and getting a waiver has generally produced a virtual ticket of admissibility.

The Basics of *Miranda v. Arizona*

Although many in the public are familiar with the words in the *Miranda* warnings, fewer know the details of the case that brought them into everyday law enforcement language. In this section, we look at the *Miranda* case, the warnings, the constitutional requirements, when *Miranda* warnings must be given, a comparison with right to counsel, when the *Miranda* rights may be waived, and what is required to make a waiver stand up in court.

The Case

Miranda v. Arizona (1966)

Miranda v. Arizona (384 U.S. 436 [1966]), decided in a 5-to-4 vote, is undoubtedly the best-known and arguably the most significant law enforcement case ever to be decided by the U.S. Supreme Court. Because of its importance, the case deserves detailed discussion. We will look at the facts of the case, the legal issues, the Court's decision, and its significance.

The Facts
Ernesto Miranda was arrested at his home in Phoenix, Arizona, and taken to a police station for questioning in connection with a rape and kidnapping. Miranda was then twenty-three years old, poor, and a ninth-grade dropout. The officers interrogated him for two hours, after which they emerged from the interrogation room with a written confession signed by Miranda. The confession was admitted as evidence during the trial. Miranda was convicted of rape and kidnapping and sentenced to twenty to thirty years' imprisonment on each count. The Arizona Supreme Court affirmed the conviction; Miranda appealed to the U.S. Supreme Court.

The Legal Issue
Must the police inform a suspect who is subject to a custodial interrogation of his or her constitutional rights involving self-incrimination and counsel prior to questioning for the evidence to be admissible in court during the trial?

The Court's Decision Evidence obtained by the police during custodial interrogation of a suspect cannot be used in court during the trial unless the suspect was first informed of the right not to incriminate himself or herself and of the right to counsel. The Court said:

> We hold that when an individual is taken into custody or otherwise deprived of his freedom by the authorities and is subject to questioning, the privilege against self-incrimination is jeopardized. Procedural safeguards must be employed. . . .
>
> He must be warned prior to any questioning that he has a right to remain silent, that anything he says can be used against him in a court of law, that he has a right to the presence of an attorney, and that if he cannot afford an attorney one will be appointed for him prior to any questioning if he so desires. Opportunity to exercise these rights must be afforded to him throughout the interrogation.

Case Significance *Miranda v. Arizona* has had a huge impact on day-to-day crime investigation. It has drawn a "bright-line" rule for admissibility of confessions and admissions and has led to changes that have since become an accepted part of routine police work. No other law enforcement case initially generated more controversy within and outside police circles. Supporters of the *Miranda* decision hailed it as properly protective of individual rights, whereas critics accused the Court of being soft on crime and of coddling criminals. The 5-to-4 split among the justices served to fan the flames of the controversy in its early stages, with opponents of the ruling hoping that a change in Court composition would hasten its demise. But that has not happened, nor is it likely to happen in the near future.

Miranda is unusual because in a Court decision the Court seldom tells the police exactly what the police should do. In *Miranda,* the Court did not simply say that a constitutional right was violated; it went further and prescribed in no uncertain terms what the police should do. In clear language, the Court mandated that a suspect "must be warned prior to any questioning that he has a right to remain silent, that anything he says can be used against him in a court of law, that he has a right to the presence of an attorney, and that if he cannot afford an attorney one will be appointed for him prior to any questioning if he so desires." Seldom has the Court been as specific in its instructions about what it wanted the police to do.

Miranda also clarified some of the ambiguous terms used in *Escobedo.* "By custodial interrogation," said the Court, "we mean questioning initiated by law enforcement officers after a person has been taken into custody or otherwise deprived of his freedom of action in any significant way." It then added this footnote, "This is what we meant in *Escobedo* when we spoke of an investigation which had focused on an accused." Yet the "focus" test used in *Escobedo* was abandoned by the Court in later cases; in its place, the "custodial interrogation" test was used to determine whether the *Miranda* warnings needed to be given. The *Escobedo* case brought the right to counsel to the police station prior to trial; the *Miranda* case went beyond the police station and brought the right to counsel out into the street if custodial interrogation was to take place.

The *Miranda* Warnings

Miranda mandates that the following warnings must be given to a suspect or accused prior to custodial interrogation:

- You have a right to remain silent.
- Anything you say can be used against you in a court of law.
- You have a right to the presence of an attorney.
- If you cannot afford an attorney, one will be appointed for you prior to questioning.

Just about all law enforcement departments in the United States add a fifth warning: "You have the right to terminate this interview at any time." This additional statement, however, is not constitutionally required under the *Miranda* decision.

Most police departments direct officers to issue the warnings as given here (taken directly from the *Miranda* decision). However, in some cases, warnings that are not worded exactly as given here may still comply with *Miranda*, provided the defendant is given adequate information concerning the right to remain silent and to have an attorney present. In *Duckworth v. Eagan* (492 U.S. 195 [1989]), the police gave the following warnings: "You have a right to talk to a lawyer for advice before we ask you any questions, and to have him with you during questioning. "You have the right to the advice and presence of a lawyer even if you cannot afford to hire one. "We have no way of giving you a lawyer, but one will be appointed for you, if you wish, if and when you go to court." The last part of that warning—"if you wish, if and when you go to court"—was challenged as ambiguous and therefore inadequate.

Duckworth v. Eagan (1989)

In a 5-to-4 vote, the Court disagreed, saying that the warning, although ambiguous, was sufficient to inform the suspect of his rights. The Court added that this does not require that lawyers always be available. It is enough that the suspect is informed of his or her right to an attorney and to appointed counsel, and that, if the police cannot provide appointed counsel, they will not question the suspect until and unless there is a valid waiver. (See the waiver form in Figure 11.1.)

The Court also stated, "If the individual indicates in any manner any time prior to or during questioning that he wishes to remain silent, the interrogation must cease." If it does not cease, any information obtained by the police is not admissible as evidence in court unless the government can prove that the defendant knowingly and intelligently waived that right. As for access to a lawyer, the Court said:

> If the individual states that he wants an attorney, the interrogation must cease until an attorney is present. At that time, the individual must have an opportunity to confer with the attorney and to have him present during any subsequent questioning. If the individual cannot obtain an attorney and he indicates that he wants one, before speaking to the police, they must respect his decision to remain silent.

Statement of Miranda Rights

1. You have the right to remain silent.

2. Anything you say can and will be used against you in a court of law.

3. You have the right to talk to a lawyer and have him present with you while you are being questioned.

4. If you cannot afford to hire a lawyer, one will be appointed to represent you before any questioning, if you wish.

5. You can decide at any time to use these rights and not answer questions or make a statement.

Waiver of Rights

I have read the above statement of my rights and I understand each of those rights, and having these rights in mind I waive them and willingly make a statement.

SIGNED _____ Age _____

Address _____

Date _____ Time _____ Location _____

Witnessed by _____ Department _____

Witnessed by _____ Department _____

Witnessed by _____ Department _____

Remarks:

GO-WRITE FORM: 710/75/MF

Figure 11.1 Statement of *Miranda* Rights and Waiver of Rights

The *Miranda* Warnings: Required by the Constitution, Not Just by Judges

United States v. Dickerson (4th Cir. 1999)

In what was described as the most serious challenge to the *Miranda* rule since the decision came out in 1966, a three-judge panel in the federal Court of Appeals for the Fourth Circuit held, by a 2-to-1 vote in 1999, that voluntary confessions given without the *Miranda* warnings do not have to be excluded in federal court prosecutions and that congressional law overrules *Miranda* in federal courts (*United States v. Dickerson*, No. 97-4750 [4th Cir. 1999]). That ruling generated extensive publicity and was promptly appealed to the U.S. Supreme Court. The Court resolved that issue, holding that *Miranda v. Arizona* governs the admissibility in federal and state courts of confessions and admissions given during custodial interrogation by the police. It is required by the Constitution, and therefore any law passed by Congress that seeks to overturn the *Miranda* decision is unconstitutional (*Dickerson v. United States*, 530 U.S. 428 [2000]).

Dickerson v. United States (2000)

The facts in *Dickerson v. United States* (2000) are that Dickerson was arrested and made incriminating statements to police. Before his trial, he moved that the statements be suppressed because he had not received his *Miranda* warnings prior to being interrogated. His statements were voluntary, but they were made without having been given the *Miranda* warnings. The federal District Court granted the motion to suppress, but the Court of Appeals overturned it, stating that 18 U.S.C. Section 3501, passed by Congress in response to the *Miranda* decision, prevailed and only required a finding by a court that the confession was given voluntarily.

Note that 18 U.S.C. Section 3501 was part of a law passed by Congress in 1966 right after the *Miranda* decision came out, but a decision on the constitutionality of that law was never reached by the U.S. Supreme Court because it was not enforced by the federal government—until *Dickerson*. That law sought to overturn the Court decision in *Miranda* by providing that the admissibility of confessions and admissions in federal court is determined by whether or not they were voluntarily made, not by whether or not they complied with the *Miranda* warnings. Rejecting the constitutionality of 18 U.S.C. Section 3501, the Court said: "In sum, we conclude that Miranda announced a constitutional rule that Congress may not supersede legislatively."

Dickerson is a significant case because it settled an important issue: Can the *Miranda* decision be overruled by laws passed by Congress or state legislatures? The Court answered that *Miranda* is not just a rule of evidence; therefore, it cannot be undone by legislation, as Congress had tried to do. Only a constitutional amendment can do away at present with the *Miranda* warnings. Because of this decision, the *Miranda* warnings are here to stay unless the Court, in future years, changes its mind about it being required by the Constitution. Had the decision been different, federal cases immediately would have been governed by the provisions of the federal law. Some state legislatures probably would have passed similar legislation, leading to the admissibility of confessions and admissions being governed by different rules.

Decided in the year 2000 by a 7-to-2 vote, *Dickerson* is arguably the most important decision on the *Miranda* warnings since *Miranda v. Arizona* came out in 1966. The Court said that *Miranda v. Arizona* governs the admissibility in federal and state courts of confessions and admissions given during custodial interrogations. *Dickerson* reaffirms *Miranda* and places the *Miranda* warnings on a high pedestal as a constitutional rule beyond the reach of legislatures. The *Miranda* warnings are here to stay, unless the Court changes its mind.

The *Miranda* Warnings: Must Be Given for All Offenses Except Routine Traffic Stops

Berkemer v. McCarty (1984)

Should the *Miranda* warnings be given for all offenses or only for some? The Court answered this important question in *Berkemer v. McCarty* (468 U.S. 420 [1984]). The Court's answer can be summarized as follows:

- *The rule.* A person subjected to custodial interrogation must be given the *Miranda* warnings regardless of the nature or severity of the offense and whether the person goes to jail or not. This includes felonies, misdemeanors, and petty and traffic offenses.
- *The only exception.* The roadside questioning of a motorist detained pursuant to a routine traffic stop does not require the *Miranda* warnings.

In *McCarty,* an officer of the Ohio State Highway Patrol observed a driver weaving in and out of a highway lane. The officer stopped the car and forced McCarty to get out. Noticing that McCarty had difficulty standing, the officer asked him if he had been using intoxicants and requested that he take a field sobriety test. McCarty replied that he had consumed two beers and had smoked marijuana a short time before. The officer then arrested him and drove him to the county jail, where a blood test was performed. Questioning was resumed, and McCarty again gave incriminating statements. Convicted of driving while under the influence of alcohol and/or drugs, he sought exclusion of his incriminating statements, saying that at no point in the whole proceeding was he given the *Miranda* warnings. The state of Ohio countered that the warnings were unnecessary because McCarty was charged with a misdemeanor traffic offense.

The Court agreed with McCarty, saying, "We therefore hold that a person subjected to custodial interrogation is entitled to the benefit of the procedural safeguards enunciated in *Miranda,* regardless of the nature or severity of the offense of which he is suspected or for which he was arrested." The Court went on to say that the only exception is routine questioning of a motorist detained pursuant to a routine traffic stop. This is because a routine traffic stop is usually brief, and the motorist expects that, although he or she may be given a citation, in the end he or she most likely will be allowed to continue.

Contrary to McCarty's allegations, there is no deprivation of freedom in a significant way in a routine traffic stop. The Court said that there is no custodial interrogation in these cases, because the typical traffic stop is public; such exposure to public view reduces the opportunity for unscrupulous police officers to use illegitimate means to solicit self-incriminating statements and diminishes the motorist's fear of being subjected to abuse unless he or she cooperates. The Court further noted, "A motorist's expectations, when he sees a policeman's light flashing behind him, are that he will be obliged to spend a short period of time answering questions and waiting while the officer checks his license and registration, that he may then be given a citation, but that in the end he most likely will be allowed to continue on his way." (Read the Case Brief to learn more about *Berkemer v. McCarty.*)

Four years later, the Court reiterated this principle, saying that the curbside stop of a motorist for a traffic violation, although representing a Fourth

---

CASE BRIEF: The Leading Case on the Types of Offenses that Require *Miranda* Warnings

Berkemer v. McCarty, 468 U.S. 420 (1984)

Facts: After observing McCarty's car weaving in and out of a highway lane, Officer Williams of the Ohio State Highway Patrol forced McCarty to stop and get out of the car. Noticing that McCarty was having difficulty standing, the officer concluded that he would be charged with a traffic offense and would not be allowed to leave the scene, but McCarty was not told that he would be taken into custody. When McCarty could not perform a field sobriety test without falling, Officer Williams asked if he had been using intoxicants, whereupon McCarty replied that he had consumed two beers and had smoked marijuana a short time before. The officer then formally arrested McCarty and drove him to a county jail, where a blood test failed to detect any alcohol in his blood. Questioning was resumed, and McCarty again made incriminating statements, including an admission that he was "barely" under the influence of alcohol. At no point during this sequence was McCarty given the *Miranda* warnings. He was subsequently charged with operating a motor vehicle under the influence of alcohol and drugs, a misdemeanor under Ohio law. He pleaded "no contest" but later filed a writ of habeas corpus, alleging that the evidence obtained should not have been admitted in court.

Issue: *Was evidence obtained by the police without giving the suspect the* Miranda *warnings admissible in a prosecution for a misdemeanor offense? No.*

Supreme Court Decision: The Court decided that (1) a person subjected to custodial interrogation must be given the *Miranda* warnings regardless of the nature or severity of the offense of which the person is suspected or for which he or she was arrested, but that (2) the roadside questioning of a motorist detained pursuant to a routine traffic stop does not constitute "custodial interrogation," so there is no need to give the *Miranda* warnings.

Case Significance: This case settled two legal issues that had long divided lower courts. It is

---

clear now that once a suspect has been placed under arrest for any offense, whether it is a felony or a misdemeanor, the *Miranda* warnings must be given before interrogation. This rule is easier for the police to follow than the requirement of determining if the arrest was for a felony or a misdemeanor before giving the warning. The Court said that the purpose of the *Miranda* warnings, which is to ensure that the police do not coerce or trick captive suspects into confessing, is applicable equally to misdemeanor and felony cases.

The second part of the decision is equally important; it identifies a particular instance when the warnings do not need to be given. There is no custodial interrogation in a traffic stop because it is usually brief and the motorist expects that, although a citation may be forthcoming, in the end he or she will probably be allowed to continue on his or her way. However, if a motorist who has been detained is thereafter subjected to treatment that renders him or her "in custody" for practical purposes, then he or she is entitled to be given the *Miranda* warnings.

Excerpts from the Decision: Two features of an ordinary traffic stop mitigate the danger that a person questioned will be induced "to speak where he would not otherwise do so freely," First, detention of a motorist pursuant to a traffic stop is presumptively temporary and brief. The vast majority of roadside detentions last only a few minutes. A motorist's expectations, when he sees a policeman's light flashing behind him, are that he will be obliged to spend a short period of time answering questions and waiting while the officer checks his license and registration, that he may then be given a citation, but that in the end he most likely will be allowed to continue on his way. In this respect, questioning incident to an ordinary traffic stop is quite different from stationhouse interrogation, which frequently is prolonged, and in which the detainee often is aware that questioning will continue until he provides his interrogators the answers they seek.

Second, circumstances associated with the typical traffic stop are not such that the motorist feels completely at the mercy of the police. To be sure, the aura of authority surrounding an armed, uniformed officer and the knowledge that the officer has some discretion in deciding whether to issue a citation, in combination, exert some pressure on the detainee to respond to questions. But other aspects of the situation substantially offset these forces. Perhaps most importantly, the typical traffic stop is public, at least to some degree. Passersby, on foot or in other cars, witness the interaction of officer and motorist. This exposure to public view both reduces the ability of an unscrupulous policeman to use illegitimate means to elicit self-incriminating statements and diminishes the motorist's fear that, if he does not cooperate, he will be subjected to abuse. The fact that the detained motorist typically is confronted by only one or at most two policemen further mutes his sense of vulnerability. In short, the atmosphere [468 U.S. 420, 439] surrounding an ordinary traffic stop is substantially less "police dominated" than that surrounding the kinds of interrogation at issue in *Miranda* itself, and in the subsequent cases in which we have applied *Miranda*.

Pennsylvania v. Bruder (1988)

Amendment seizure of the person, is not sufficiently custodial to require the *Miranda* warnings (*Pennsylvania v. Bruder,* 488 U.S. 9 [1988]). However, traffic offenses that involve more than roadside questioning pursuant to a routine traffic stop need the *Miranda* warnings. In general, the arrest of a driver in connection with a traffic offense triggers the *Miranda* warnings, because this is no longer a case of roadside questioning pursuant to a routine traffic stop.

These rules can be illustrated as follows:

- *Example 1.* Y is stopped by an officer for driving while intoxicated. State law or local ordinance allows the officer to arrest the driver for this traffic offense, so he arrests Y and takes her to the police station for booking. If the officer asks anything other than preliminary questions (such as name and address), Y must be given the *Miranda* warnings. Otherwise, statements Y makes will not be admissible in court.
- *Example 2.* Z is stopped by an officer for failure to stop at a stop sign. The officer asks Z questions and then issues a citation or releases Z. The officer does not have to give Z the *Miranda* warnings even if she asks Z questions.

In sum, the *Miranda* warnings must be given when the suspect is interrogated for any type of offense—whether it is a felony, misdemeanor, or petty traffic offense. The only exception is roadside questioning of a motorist detained pursuant to a routine traffic stop.

Distinguishing the *Miranda* Warnings from the Right to Counsel

Although often associated with a suspect's right to counsel, *Miranda v. Arizona* is in fact based on the Fifth Amendment right to protection against self-incrimination, not on the Sixth Amendment right to counsel. *Miranda* warnings 1 and 2, as noted previously, protect the right not to incriminate oneself. Warnings 3 and 4 are right-to-counsel warnings, but they are there primarily to protect suspects against compulsory self-incrimination. In other words, a suspect is entitled to a lawyer during interrogation so that the right against self-incrimination may be protected. *Miranda* is but a small slice of the big right-to-counsel pie, although it is more often used in police work. Even if the proper *Miranda* warnings are given, the evidence is not admissible if the right to counsel under the Sixth Amendment is violated.

HIGHLIGHT

A Version of the Miranda *Warnings a Police Officer Should Never, Ever Give**

1. You have the right to remain silent—if you can stand the pain.

2. Anything you say can and will be used against you in a court of law. Our local judge, however, was a police officer and worked with us before going on to law.

3. You have the right to a lawyer, but if I were you I'd plead guilty and get it over with.

4. If you can't afford a lawyer, one will be assigned to you. He should be competent because he just passed the bar examination, although barely.

5. You have the right to end this interview at any time, but if I were you I'd go on confessing. It's good for your conscience—if you have one.

*On the lighter side—from the author.

In *Massiah v. United States* (377 U.S. 201 [1964]), the Court held that incriminating statements are not admissible in court if the defendant was questioned without an attorney present after the defendant was charged with a crime and had obtained an attorney. This case was decided two years before *Miranda* (1966) but has since been reiterated by courts in subsequent cases involving the right to counsel.

In a subsequent case, *United States v. Henry* (447 U.S. 264 [1980]), the Court held that the government violates a defendant's Sixth Amendment right to counsel by intentionally creating a situation likely to induce the accused to make incriminating statements without the presence of a lawyer. In *Henry*, Henry was indicted for armed robbery. While Henry was in jail, government agents contacted one of his cell mates, who was an informant, and instructed him to be alert to any statements Henry made but not to initiate any conversations regarding the robbery. After the informant was released, he was contacted by the agents and paid for the information he provided concerning Henry's incriminating statements about the robbery. Convicted, Henry appealed, saying that the testimony of the informant should have been excluded.

The Court agreed, holding the informant's testimony inadmissible. The Court believed it probable that the informant used his position to secure incriminating information and therefore probably acted beyond "mere listening" for information. The Court added that, although the government agent told the informant not to initiate any questioning of Henry, the agent must have known that the informant was likely to do so anyway. More important, in *Henry*, the basis for the appeal was a violation of the right to counsel, not the right to protection against self-incrimination—as was the case in *Miranda*.

In a more recent case, *Fellers v. United States* (540 U.S. 519 [2004]), the Court held that the proper standard to use when determining whether statements made by a defendant after an indictment are admissible in court is the Sixth Amendment right to counsel, not the Fifth Amendment right against self-incrimination. In this case, the defendant claimed that his Sixth Amendment right to counsel and his Fifth Amendment *Miranda* rights were both violated when the statement he made at his home and then later at the jail were used against him during the trial. The defendant, Fellers, was under indictment when both questionings took place.

If his Fifth Amendment right against self-incrimination had been used as the standard for admissibility, then his statements while in jail would have been admissible because he was given the *Miranda* warnings and had waived his Fifth Amendment right before giving the confession. However, he claimed that the jail statement was inadmissible because it violated his Sixth Amendment right to counsel in that it was the "fruit" of an unlawful interrogation at his home (after indictment and when he had a lawyer) and therefore should have been excluded even if he was given the *Miranda* warnings.

The Court agreed, saying that in previous cases "this Court has consistently applied the deliberate-elicitation standard in subsequent Sixth Amendment cases . . . and has expressly distinguished it from the Fifth Amendment custodial-interrogation standard." It then added that "there is no question here that the officers "deliberately elicited information from petitioner at his home." Because the officers interrogated the defendant at his home without counsel after he had been indicted, the absence of his lawyer made his statement in his home inadmissible. His subsequent statement in jail was also inadmissible because it was "fruit of the poisonous tree."

In cases involving confessions and admissions, the Fifth Amendment protection against compulsory self-incrimination and the Sixth Amendment right to counsel, although different, are closely intertwined and can be tricky for police officers. Giving the *Miranda* warnings may make the statement admissible under the Fifth Amendment right against self-incrimination, but that same statement may be inadmissible under the Sixth Amendment if the defendant has been assigned or obtained a lawyer for his or her defense. Thus, in some cases, in addition to giving the *Miranda* warnings, the police must ascertain whether or not the suspect already has or has been assigned a lawyer for that case.

In sum, the *Miranda* warnings and the right to counsel are not one and the same right. Some cases primarily involve the *Miranda* warnings and are self-incrimination cases; others, like *Henry,* involve the right to counsel before or after indictment. The rule is that, after a suspect has obtained counsel and is in custody, interrogation about any offense that is likely to elicit incriminating answers—in the absence of a lawyer—violates the suspect's right to counsel.

The differences between the *Miranda* rules and the right to counsel may be summarized as follows:

Miranda Warnings	Right to Counsel
Come under the Fifth Amendment right against self-incrimination	Comes under the Sixth Amendment
Apply only during custodial interrogation	Applies in many proceedings—before trial, during trial, and during an appeal of a conviction
Given by the police	Lawyer is either retained by the suspect or assigned by a judge
Given in the absence of a lawyer	Once defendant has a lawyer, defendant cannot be questioned in the absence of a lawyer unless the right is waived
Must be given every time there is a custodial interrogation about any offense except routine traffic stops	Once given, is violated only if the interrogation deals with the same offense but not if it is about other offenses, even if closely related

The *Miranda* Rights: May Only Be Waived Knowingly and Intelligently

In *Miranda,* the Court said, "After . . . warnings have been given, and such opportunity [to exercise these rights] afforded him, the individual may knowingly and intelligently waive these rights and agree to answer questions or make a statement." A **waiver** is an intentional relinquishment of a known right or remedy. The rights under *Miranda* may be waived expressly or implicitly, but the Court said that "a heavy burden rests on the government to demonstrate that the defendant knowingly and intelligently waived his privilege against self-incrimination and his right to retained or appointed counsel."

Certain aspects of a valid waiver warrant further discussion. Among these are (1) the meaning of the requirement that a waiver must be "intelligent and voluntary"; (2) whether a waiver can be presumed from the suspect's silence after receiving the *Miranda* warnings; (3) the validity of waivers made by mentally unstable defendants; (4) how long an interrogation can be delayed after a waiver before the warnings must be given again; and (5) why a valid waiver exists if a suspect asks to see anyone other than his or her lawyer after being given the warnings.

The Waiver: Must Be Intelligent and Voluntary The *Miranda* decision specifically states that the prosecution must prove that the defendant intelligently and voluntarily waived his or her right to silence and to retained or court-appointed counsel. An **intelligent waiver** means one given by a suspect who knows what he or she is doing and is sufficiently competent to waive his or her rights. In cases involving a suspect who is drunk, under the influence of drugs, or in a state of trauma or shock or who has been seriously injured, is senile, or is too young, intelligent waiver is difficult for the prosecution to prove. There is no definite guidance from the courts in these cases; the best policy is for the police either to wait until the suspect's competency is restored (even if temporarily) or to be certain that the suspect understands the warnings.

An **intelligent and voluntary waiver** is one that is not the result of any threat, force, or coercion and is made of the suspect's own free will. It is determined based on a totality of circumstances. In one case, a suspect in the killing of an undercover officer, who was in the intensive care unit of the hospital and under heavy sedation, was asked by the police if he had shot anyone. The suspect replied, "I can't say, I have to see a lawyer." The Court said that the statements obtained by the police were not "the product of his free and rational choice" and could not be used even for impeachment purposes (*Mincey v. Arizona*, 437 U.S. 385 [1978]). The Court added:

Mincey v. Arizona (1978)

> It is hard to imagine a situation less conducive to the exercise of a "rational intellect and a free will" than Mincey's. He had been seriously wounded just a few hours earlier, and had arrived at the hospital "depressed almost to the point of coma," according to his attending physician. Although he had received some treatment, his condition at the time of . . . interrogation was still sufficiently serious that he was in the intensive care unit. He complained to [the detective] that the pain in his leg was "unbearable." He was evidently confused and unable to think clearly about the events of that afternoon or the circumstances of his interrogation, since some of his written answers were on their face not entirely coherent.

Moreover, the waiver must be shown on the record. Quoting from an earlier case, the Court in *Miranda* said, "Presuming waiver from a silent record is impermissible. The record must show, or there must be an allegation and evidence which shows, that an accused was offered counsel but intelligently and understandingly rejected the offer. Anything less is not a waiver." The waiver does not have to be written or expressed, but it must be proved by the prosecution.

"Intelligent and voluntary" must be proved by prosecution The Court in *Miranda* held that the prosecution has a "heavy burden . . . to demonstrate that the defendant knowingly and intelligently waived his privilege against self-incrimination and his right to a retained or appointed counsel." If that burden is not met, the evidence obtained is inadmissible even if it is voluntary. Although a written waiver is not constitutionally required, most police departments have a written waiver form that suspects are asked to sign. The written waiver may be a part of the written confession, either before or after the statement by the accused, or be attached to it. If witnesses to the waiver are available (such as police officers, other police personnel, or private persons), they should be asked to sign the waiver to strengthen the showing of voluntariness (see Figure 11.1). If the confession is typewritten, it is a good practice to have the defendant read it and, in his or her own handwriting, correct any errors. This procedure reinforces the claim of a valid waiver. In the absence of a written waiver, the issue boils down to the testimony of the suspect against the testimony of the police officer that the waiver was in fact voluntary. A written waiver makes the claim of voluntariness by the police more credible.

In juvenile cases, the waiver of rights is usually governed by state law. In many states, there is a minimum age below which a juvenile cannot waive his or her rights. In other states, the waiver is valid only if signed by a parent or guardian and/or signed in the presence of a lawyer.

Signed waiver not required A signed waiver is not required. Refusal by the suspect to sign the waiver form (used by most police departments) does not necessarily mean that there is no valid waiver. The Court has said that "the question is not one of form but rather whether the defendant in fact knowingly and voluntarily waived the rights delineated in *Miranda*" (*North Carolina v. Butler*, 441 U.S. 369 [1979]). A written waiver, however, makes it easier to prove a valid waiver in court.

North Carolina v. Butler (1979)

Express waiver not required An express waiver is not required. The failure to make an explicit statement regarding the waiver does not determine whether the evidence is admissible. Instead, the trial court must look at all the circumstances to determine whether a valid waiver in fact has been made. An express waiver, although easier to establish in court, is not required (*North Carolina v. Butler*, 441 U.S. 369 [1979]). The court will most likely take into account a variety of considerations, such as the age of the suspect, whether the suspect was alone with the officers at the time of interrogation or was in the presence of other people, the time of day, and the suspect's mental condition at the time of questioning.

The Validity of a Presumption of a Waiver from Silence after the Warnings

The Court in *Miranda* said that a waiver cannot be presumed from silence after the defendant has been warned of his or her rights. The trial court cannot presume a waiver from the failure of the accused to complain after being given the warning or from the fact that the accused spoke with the police after the warnings were given (*Teague v. Louisiana*, 444 U.S. 469 [1980]). The Court has not decided authoritatively whether a nod or a shrug constitutes a valid waiver.

Teague v. Louisiana (1980)

The Validity of a Waiver "Following the Advice of God"

The admissibility of statements made when the mental state of the suspect interferes with his or her "rational intellect" and "free will" is governed by state rules of evidence rather than by Supreme Court decisions on coerced confessions. Such statements are therefore not automatically excluded; admissibility instead depends on state rules (*Colorado v. Connelly*, 479 U.S. 157 [1986]).

Colorado v. Connelly (1986)

In *Colorado v. Connelly* (1986), Connelly approached a uniformed Denver police officer and confessed that he had murdered someone in Denver in 1982 and wanted to talk to the officer about it. The officer advised Connelly of his *Miranda* rights. Connelly indicated that he understood his rights and wanted to talk about the murder. After a homicide detective arrived, Connelly was again advised of his *Miranda* rights and again indicated that he wanted to speak with the police. Connelly was then taken to the police station, where he told officers that he had come from Boston to confess to the murder. When he became visibly disoriented, he was sent to a state hospital. In an interview with a psychiatrist, Connelly revealed that he was "following the advice of God" in confessing to the murder. He sought exclusion of the evidence during trial, saying that the confession was, in effect, coerced.

The Court rejected the challenge, saying that confessions and admissions are involuntary and invalid under the Constitution *only if the coercion is exerted by the police*, not if exerted by somebody else—in this case, allegedly, by God. The police did not act improperly or illegally, so the confession was constitutionally admissible.

The Validity of a Waiver after a Prolonged Interruption before Questioning

In *Miranda,* the Court hinted that, even if there is a waiver, if there is a prolonged interruption before an interrogation is resumed, it is best to give the *Miranda* warnings again. Although no time has been specified, "prolonged interruption" should be taken to mean an interruption of several hours. The longer the time lapse, the greater is the need to give the warnings again. For example, suppose a suspect is give the *Miranda* warnings and waives his rights. The police interrogate him but then go on a lunch break. Fours hours later, when the officers resume their interrogation, he should be given the *Miranda* warnings again.[1] But what if the interruption is only for one, two, or three hours? There is no clear answer for a time lapse before the warnings must be given again. The better practice is to give the warnings whenever there is a significant lapse of time and when in doubt.

Ernesto Miranda was later retried (under an assumed name to avoid publicity) for the same offenses of rape and kidnapping. There is no double jeopardy when a defendant is retried after a successful appeal; the appeal is considered a waiver of the right against double jeopardy. His original confession was not used in the second trial, but he was reconvicted on the basis of other evidence. After serving time in prison, Miranda was released on parole. He was killed in 1972 in a skid-row card game in Phoenix, Arizona. The police gave his alleged assailant, an illegal alien, the *Miranda* warnings.

The Validity of a Waiver that the Suspect Has Withdrawn A suspect may withdraw a waiver once given. If the waiver is withdrawn, the interrogation must stop immediately. However, evidence obtained before the waiver is withdrawn is admissible in court. For example, suppose a suspect waives her rights and agrees to talk to the police. She gives incriminating information but changes her mind after fifteen minutes of questioning. The interrogation must cease immediately, but any statements she made prior to changing her mind are admissible.

A Waiver?: When the Suspect Requests Someone Other than a Lawyer The request by the suspect for somebody other than a lawyer constitutes a valid waiver of the right to counsel. For example, the request of a juvenile on probation to see his probation officer instead of a lawyer (after having been given the *Miranda* warnings by the police and asked if he wanted to see a lawyer) was considered by the Court to be a waiver of the juvenile's right to a lawyer, because a probation officer and a lawyer perform two different functions (*Fare v. Michael C.*, 442 U.S. 707 [1979]).

Fare v. Michael C.
(1979)

Custodial Interrogation: When the *Miranda* Warnings Must Always Be Given

When must the *Miranda* warnings be given? The simple but sometimes difficult-to-apply answer is, whenever there is a "custodial interrogation." Courts assume that custodial interrogations are inherently coercive; therefore, the *Miranda* warnings are needed to ensure that suspects' statements given are voluntary. The next question is, When is there a custodial interrogation? In *Escobedo v. Illinois* (discussed previously), the Court stated that the warnings must be given as soon as the investigation has "focused" on the individual as a suspect. In *Miranda*, the Court abandoned the "focus of the investigation" test and replaced it with the "custodial interrogation" standard. In other words, a person who is the focus of an investigation is entitled to the *Miranda* warnings if that person is under **custodial interrogation**. That phrase, in turn, means that *the suspect is (1) in custody and (2) under interrogation.*

Both factors must be true, or there is no custodial interrogation. Here are examples:

- *Situation 1.* Suspect A is in custody but is not being questioned—there is no need for the *Miranda* warnings.
- *Situation 2.* Suspect B is being interrogated but he or she is not in custody—there is no need for the *Miranda* warnings.

Next, we will discuss each term, *custodial* and *interrogation,* separately.

Custody

A suspect is in **custody** in two general situations: when the suspect is *under arrest* or is not under arrest but is *"deprived of freedom in a significant way."* According to the Court, the test that determines whether a person is in custody for *Miranda* purposes is "whether the suspect has been subjected to a formal arrest or to equivalent restraints on his freedom of movement" (*California v. Beheler,* 463 U.S. 1121 [1983]). Moreover, whether a person is in custody is determined not by just one fact but by the totality of circumstances. Each of these situations deserves an extended discussion.

California v. Beheler (1983)

Situation 1: When the Suspect Is under Arrest
The rule is clear that, when a person is under arrest, the *Miranda* warnings must be given prior to an interrogation. It makes no difference whether the arrest is for a felony or a misdemeanor. When, then, is a suspect under arrest? The answer is, whenever the four elements of arrest are present: intent, authority, custody, and understanding (as discussed in Chapter 6).

- *Example 1.* A suspect is arrested by virtue of a warrant. En route to the police station, the officer questions the suspect about the crime. The suspect must first be given the *Miranda* warnings.
- *Example 2.* A suspect is arrested without a warrant because the police have probable cause to make a warrantless arrest (as when a crime is committed in the presence of the police). If the suspect is questioned at any time by the police, the suspect must first be given the *Miranda* warnings.

The brief questioning of a person by the police is not an arrest if the police officer intends to let the person go after the brief detention. Also, stopping a motor vehicle for the purpose of issuing the driver a ticket or citation is not an arrest, so the *Miranda* warnings are not needed even if the police ask questions.

Situation 2: When the Suspect Is Not under Arrest but Is Deprived of Freedom in a Significant Way
This is the more difficult situation. The question is, When is a person **deprived of freedom in a significant way** so as to be considered in custody for purposes of *Miranda*? The answer is, when the person's freedom of movement is limited by the police and a reasonable person

in the same circumstances would feel he or she is in custody. Therefore, even if the investigation has focused on a person, the *Miranda* warnings need not be given unless the defendant will not be allowed to leave after the questioning. "Focus of the investigation" is no longer the test (as it was under *Escobedo v. Illinois* in 1964) to determine if the *Miranda* warnings must be given; "custodial interrogation" is now the test.

Whose perception determines whether a suspect has been deprived of freedom—that of the police or of the suspect? In *Berkemer v. McCarty* (468 U.S. 420 [1984]), the Court said that a "policeman's unarticulated plan has no bearing on the question whether a suspect was 'in custody' at a particular time; the only relevant inquiry is how a reasonable man in the suspect's position would have understood his position." In a subsequent case, *Thompson v. Keohane* (516 U.S. 99 [1995]), the Court was more specific when it said: "Two discrete inquiries are essential to the determination (whether a person is under custody): first, what were the circumstances surrounding the interrogation; and second, given those circumstances, would a reasonable person have felt he or she was not at liberty to terminate the interrogation and leave?" In the words of one writer, "To trigger the *Miranda* safeguards, it is not sufficient that the suspect have a subjective belief that he is not free to go, nor that unknown to him, the officers intend to restrain him if he tries to leave. The test is whether a reasonable person in the suspect's position would conclude that he is not free to go."[2] This is based on the totality of the circumstances and is therefore determined on a case-by-case basis. Some factors to be considered are the location of the encounter and the nature and tone of the officer's questions.[3]

A 1994 case clarifies what the Court means by "in custody." In *Stansbury v. California* (511 U.S. 318 [1994]), the Court rejected the "subjective test" by the officer and adopted instead the "objective test" in determining whether a person is in custody. The Court said that "an officer's subjective and undisclosed view concerning whether the person being interrogated is a suspect is irrelevant to the assessment of whether the person is in custody," adding that "in determining whether an individual was in custody, a court must examine all of the circumstances surrounding the interrogation, but the ultimate inquiry is simply whether there [was] a 'formal arrest or restraint on the freedom of movement' of the degree associated with a formal arrest." Therefore, the Court remanded the case for further proceedings.

The fact that the police denied that the suspect was "in custody" at the time some of the incriminating statements were made did not determine whether the suspect was in fact in custody. The Court admitted, however, that "an officer's knowledge or beliefs may bear upon the custody issue if they are conveyed, by word or deed, to the individual being questioned. Those beliefs are relevant only to the extent that they would affect how a reasonable person in the position of the individual being questioned would gauge the breadth of his or her 'freedom of action.'"

In sum, police intent is less important than the circumstances surrounding the interrogation when determining whether a person is in custody. A person may be in custody even if he or she is at home, in the office, or on the street. The *objective test* (meaning whether a reasonable person under the same circumstances would conclude that he or she was not free to go) determines whether a person actually is in custody.

Thompson v. Keohane (1995)

Stansbury v. California (1994)

In 2004, in *Yarborough v. Alvarado* (541 U.S. 652 [2004]), the Court held that a police officer did not need to consider a suspect's age or previous history with law enforcement to determine whether the suspect was in custody for purposes of the *Miranda* warnings. In that case, the police interviewed seventeen-year old Michael Alvarado at the police station as a suspect in a crime. He was not under arrest, and he was not given the *Miranda* warnings. He confessed to the crime, was prosecuted, and was convicted of second-degree murder and attempted robbery. In a habeas corpus case, he sought exclusion of his confession saying that although he was "in custody" he was not given the *Miranda* warnings.

In a 5-to-4 decision, the Court held that "determining whether a suspect is actually in custody has always been based on objective criterion like whether he had been brought to the police station by police or had come of his own accord." The Court then added that "requiring officers to consider individual characteristics of a suspect when determining whether he is in custody, such as the suspect's age or previous history with law enforcement, would make the test a subjective one that would be more difficult for officers to understand and abide by."

Here are some specific issues related to Situation 2 (where the suspect is not under arrest but is deprived of freedom in a significant way).

- *Questioning at the police station.* For example, suppose the police invite a suspect to come to the police station "to answer a few questions." This type of interrogation requires the *Miranda* warnings because a police station lends a "coercive atmosphere" to the interrogation. The exceptions to this general rule are (1) if the suspect on his or her own goes to the police station and knows that he or she is free to leave at any time and (2) if the suspect goes to the police station upon invitation of the police but is told that he or she is not under arrest and is free to leave at any time.

  In *Oregon v. Mathiason* (429 U.S. 492 [1977]), the police suspected a parolee of involvement in a burglary. The suspect came to the police station in response to an officer's message that the officer would "like to discuss something with you." It was made clear to the suspect that he was not under arrest but that the police believed he was involved in the burglary. The suspect confessed, but he later sought to exclude the evidence. The Court said that the *Miranda* warnings are necessary only if the suspect is in custody "or otherwise deprived of freedom in a significant way." Since those things had not occurred, the confession was admissible.

- *Questioning in a police car.* Questioning in police cars generally requires the *Miranda* warnings because of its custodial nature. The warnings must be given even if the suspect has not been placed under arrest. The reason is that questionings in police cars tend to be inherently coercive—the suspect is being deprived of freedom in a significant way.

- *Questioning when the suspect is not free to leave.* When the police will not allow the suspect to leave their presence, will not leave the suspect alone, or will not leave if asked to do so by the suspect, then the *Miranda* warnings *must be given.* If the police consider the suspect's attempt to leave or his or her refusal to answer questions as reason enough to stop the suspect from leaving or to arrest him or her formally, then the *Miranda* warnings must be given. Clearly, under these conditions, the suspect is being deprived of freedom in a significant way.

- *Questioning in the home.* Whether the *Miranda* warnings must precede questioning in a suspect's home depends upon the circumstances of the case. The Court has held that the questioning of a suspect in his bedroom by four police officers at four o'clock in the morning required the *Miranda* warnings (*Orozco v. Texas,* 394 U.S. 324 [1969]). In a later case, however, the Court held that statements obtained by Internal Revenue Service agents during a noncustodial, noncoercive interview with a taxpayer under criminal tax investigation, conducted in a private home where the taxpayer occasionally stayed, did not require the *Miranda* warnings as long as the taxpayer had been told that he was free to leave (*Beckwith v. United States,* 425 U.S. 341 [1976]).

Orozco v. Texas (1969)

Beckwith v. United States (1976)

  Note that, in both the *Orozco* and *Beckwith* cases, the investigation had already focused on the suspect. Under the old *Escobedo* standard, therefore, the warnings ought to have been given in both cases. The key consideration under *Miranda,* however, is whether the suspect's freedom of movement has been limited in a significant way—whether the suspect is truly free to leave after the questioning. In *Orozco,* aside from the coercive nature of the questioning, the suspect was not free to leave after the questioning, whereas in *Beckwith* the suspect was free to go.

- *Questioning a person who is in custody for another offense.* Any time the suspect being questioned for another offense is in jail or prison, the *Miranda* warnings must be given because the suspect is in custody. For example, suppose a prison inmate serving a state sentence is questioned by federal agents regarding a completely separate offense. The suspect is entitled to the *Miranda* warnings even though no federal criminal charges are contemplated at the time of questioning. Failure to give the *Miranda* warnings when the suspect is in jail or prison means that the evidence obtained cannot be used in a criminal trial. However, there is no need for jail or prison officials to give the *Miranda* warnings in prison disciplinary cases, as these are administrative proceedings. A defendant who is in custody for another offense is not under arrest, at least for this second offense, but is certainly being deprived of freedom in a significant way. A safe policy in situations involving the issue of "deprived of freedom in a significant way" is: When in doubt, give the *Miranda* warnings so as not to jeopardize the admissibility of any evidence obtained.

Interrogation

There are two situations in which a suspect is under **interrogation**: When the police ask questions that tend to incriminate and when the police ask no questions but, through their actions, create the "functional equivalent" of an interrogation.

When the Police Ask Questions that Tend to Incriminate

Most interrogations fall into this category. These questions are aimed at obtaining what may be an admission or confession from the suspect: "Did you kill her?" "Where is the gun?" "Why did you do it?" Note, however, that there is no need to give the *Miranda* warnings when asking identification or routine booking questions: "What is your name?" "Where do you live?" "Do you have a driver's license?" "What is your Social Security number?" Such questions are not self-incriminatory, so no warning is necessary.

When the Police Create the Functional Equivalent of an Interrogation

There are instances when no questions are actually being asked by the police, but the circumstances are so conducive to making a statement or giving a confession that the courts consider them to be the **functional equivalent of an interrogation**. In *Rhode Island v. Innis* (446 U.S. 291 [1980]), the Court said:

Rhode Island v. Innis (1980)

> A practice that the police should know is reasonably likely to evoke an incriminating response from a suspect thus amounts to interrogation. But since the police surely cannot be held accountable for the unforeseeable results of their words or actions, the definition of interrogation can extend only to words or actions on the part of the police officers that they would have known were reasonably likely to elicit an incriminating response.

In specific cases, the Court has made clarifications related to the following scenarios.

Brewer v. Williams (1977)

When police appeal to the defendant's religious interests

In one case, *Brewer v. Williams* (430 U.S. 387 [1977]), the suspect in a murder case turned himself in to the police. His lawyer told him he would not be interrogated or mistreated. On the drive from Davenport, Iowa (where he had turned himself in), to Des Moines, Iowa (where he was facing the charge), the officer gave the suspect the now-famous "Christian burial" speech. The officer called the suspect "Reverend" and indicated that the parents of the missing girl should be entitled to give a Christian burial to the poor child who had been snatched away from them on Christmas Eve. The defendant then showed the officers where the body was to be found.

The Court said that the evidence obtained was not admissible because of a violation of the suspect's right to counsel. The defendant had clearly asserted this right, and there was no evidence of knowing and voluntary waiver. Moreover, although there was no actual interrogation, the Court held that an interrogation nonetheless occurred when the police, knowing the defendant's religious interests, made remarks designed to appeal to those interests and thus induce the defendant to confess. Although *Brewer* is a right-to-counsel case, it illustrates the type of police behavior that is considered the functional equivalent of an interrogation.

When two officers converse between themselves Compare the *Brewer* case with *Rhode Island v. Innis.* In *Innis,* the officers were conversing between themselves while they had the suspect in the back of the car. The suspect had been arrested in connection with the shotgun robbery of a taxicab driver. The officers talked about the fact that it would be a terrible thing if one of the handicapped students from the school near the crime scene were to find a loaded shotgun and get hurt. The conversation, although held by fellow officers, was within the hearing of the suspect. The suspect then interrupted the police and told them the location of the shotgun. The Court held that this did not constitute interrogation, so the volunteered evidence was admissible (*Rhode Island v. Innis,* 446 U.S. 291 [1980]). What the police did was not the functional equivalent of an interrogation.

When a conversation between a suspect and his wife is recorded by an officer In *Arizona v. Mauro* (481 U.S. 520 [1987]), the police received a call that a man had just entered a store claiming that he had killed his son. When officers reached the store, the man admitted to committing the act and directed officers to the body. He was then arrested and advised of his *Miranda* rights. He was taken to the police station, where he was again given the *Miranda* warnings. The suspect then told the officers that he did not wish to make any more statements until a lawyer was present. At that time, the police stopped questioning him. The suspect's wife was in another room, and when the police questioned her, she insisted on speaking with the suspect. The police allowed the meeting on the condition that an officer be present to tape the conversation. The tape was later used to impeach the suspect's contention that he was insane at the time of the murder. During the trial, the suspect sought the exclusion of the recording, saying that he should have been given the *Miranda* warnings prior to the recording.

Arizona v. Mauro
(1987)

The Court disagreed, saying that a conversation between a suspect and his or her spouse that is recorded by and in the presence of an officer does not constitute the functional equivalent of an interrogation under *Miranda,* so the evidence was admissible. The Court added that what the police did was merely "arrange a situation" in which there was a likelihood that the suspect would say something incriminating.

Other Situations and Decisions on the *Miranda* Warnings

Leading decisions after *Miranda* (other than those already discussed) may be divided into three general categories: (1) those requiring the *Miranda* warnings, (2) those not requiring the *Miranda* warnings or not fully applying *Miranda,* and those never requiring the *Miranda* warnings.

Situations in which the *Miranda* Warnings Are Required

The cases discussed first are cases holding that the evidence obtained was not admissible, thus requiring that the *Miranda* warnings should have been given.

Further Questioning about the Same Offense after a Suspect Asks for a Lawyer

Edwards v. Arizona (1981)

In *Edwards v. Arizona* (451 U.S. 477 [1981]), a suspect was charged with robbery, burglary, and murder. At his first interrogation, he asked for a lawyer. The interrogation was stopped. The next day, the suspect still had not seen a lawyer, but he talked to two detectives and implicated himself in the crimes. The confession, admittedly voluntary, was ruled inadmissible in court because it had not been established that the suspect had waived his right to counsel "intelligently and knowingly." The Court said that, once a suspect invokes the right to remain silent until he or she consults a lawyer, the suspect cannot be questioned again for the same offense unless he or she initiates further communication, exchanges, or conversations with the police. This is known as the ***Edwards* rule**.

In *Edwards,* the suspect did not initiate further communication. Instead, the police came back the next morning and gave the suspect his *Miranda* warnings a second time. Because Edwards had learned by that time that another suspect had already implicated him in the crime, he gave an incriminating statement. The Court held the evidence obtained was inadmissible.

Minnick v. Mississippi (1991)

In a subsequent case, *Minnick v. Mississippi* (498 U.S. 146 [1991]), the Court held that, once the suspect requests a lawyer, the interrogation must stop—whether the defendant confers with the lawyer or not. The Fifth Amendment is violated when the suspect requests a lawyer, is given an opportunity to confer with the lawyer, and then is forced to talk to the police without the lawyer being present. Prior consultation with the lawyer is not enough. The lawyer must be present at all subsequent questionings; otherwise, the evidence obtained is not admissible.

Further Questioning about an Unrelated Offense after a Suspect Asks for a Lawyer

Arizona v. Roberson (1988)

Following the *Edwards* rule, the Court said in *Arizona v. Roberson* (486 U.S. 675 [1988]) that invoking the *Miranda* rights in one offense also invokes the *Miranda* rights for an unrelated offense. In that case, Roberson, after having been given his *Miranda* warnings, advised the police that he wanted an attorney. The police stopped questioning him. Three days later, however, while Roberson was still in custody, another police officer, who did not know that Roberson had previously invoked his right to an attorney, again advised him of his *Miranda* rights and then interrogated him about an unrelated burglary. Roberson incriminated himself. During the trial, he sought exclusion of the evidence, relying on the *Edwards* rule.

The Court agreed, saying that this case came under the "bright-line rule" enunciated in *Edwards,* so the evidence could not be admitted. The rule is now clear: Once the *Miranda* rights are invoked by a suspect in one offense, that suspect cannot be interrogated further for that or an unrelated offense.

Questioning about a Second Offense When the Suspect Has a Lawyer for a Different but Related Offense

In *Texas v. Cobb* (532 U.S. 162 [2001]), the Court held that the police may question a suspect about a second offense while the suspect has a lawyer for a different, although factually related, offense. Although *Cobb* is a right-to-counsel case, it has significance for police questioning of suspects and deserves discussion in this chapter and section.

Texas v. Cobb (2001)

Cobb was indicted for burglary in Huntsville, Texas, and was assigned a lawyer to represent him. He confessed to the burglary but denied involvement in the brutal killing of a woman and a child during that burglary. While free on bond in the burglary case and having moved to Odessa, Texas, Cobb had a conversation there with his father in which he confessed to the killings. On his own, the father told the Huntsville police by telephone about his son's confession. The Huntsville police told the father to go to the Odessa police station. He did and gave a statement. A warrant was issued; the Odessa police arrested Cobb and gave him the *Miranda* warnings before interrogating him. Cobb confessed to the murders, saying he committed them in the course of the burglary.

Charged with and convicted of capital murder, Cobb appealed, saying his right to counsel was violated when he was interrogated by the Odessa police for the murders without securing the permission of his lawyer for the burglary case. The Court rejected his appeal, saying that the Sixth Amendment right to counsel is "offense specific," meaning it applies only to that particular offense for which a lawyer has been assigned and not to other offenses even if they are closely "factually related." Because the offenses of burglary and murder are different offenses in Texas, as elsewhere, the assignment of a lawyer for the burglary did not mean that lawyer's permission had to be sought by the police before asking the suspect about the murders, which were committed during the burglary.

To avoid possible confusion, the *Roberson* and *Cobb* cases must be clearly distinguished. First, in the *Roberson* case, the suspect, after having been given the *Miranda* warnings, asked for an attorney. In the *Cobb* case, the suspect did not ask for an attorney even after receiving the *Miranda* warnings. Second, in the *Roberson* case, the questioning was for an unrelated offense, whereas in the *Cobb* case, the questioning was for a factually related, although different, offense.

Questioning a Defendant without a Lawyer after an Indictment

When a defendant is questioned by police agents without a lawyer present after an adversarial judicial proceeding (such as an indictment) has been started, the evidence is not admissible. The Court ruled in *United States v. Henry* (447 U.S. 264 [1980]) that incriminating statements made to a government informant sharing a suspect's jail cell were not admissible in evidence, because they violated the suspect's right to a lawyer.

In *Henry*, the defendant was indicted for armed robbery of a bank. While the defendant was in jail pending trial, government agents contacted an informant who was confined in the same cell block as Henry. An FBI agent instructed the informant to be alert to any statements Henry made but not to initiate conversations with or question him regarding the charges against him. After the informant was released from jail, he reported to the FBI agent that he and Henry had engaged in conversation and that Henry had made incriminating statements about the robbery. The informant was paid for giving the information. The Court excluded the evidence, saying that the government had violated Henry's Sixth Amendment right to a lawyer by intentionally creating a situation likely to induce the accused to make incriminating statements in the absence of a lawyer. The right was violated even if the defendant was not explicitly questioned, because the incriminating information was secured in the absence of a lawyer and after the defendant had been indicted.

Suspect Asking for a Lawyer during the Reading of *Miranda* Warnings
Once a suspect has clearly invoked his or her right to counsel, nothing the suspect says in response to further interrogation may be used to cast doubt on that invocation. An invocation of rights may be made very early in the process, such as *during* the interrogator's reading of the suspect's *Miranda* rights. Therefore, the questioning of an in-custody suspect may have to end even before it starts (*Smith v. Illinois,* 469 U.S. 91 [1984]).

Smith v. Illinois (1984)

In *Smith v. Illinois* (1984), the defendant was interrogated by the police. They informed him that they wanted to talk about a particular robbery and then began to advise him of his rights. As they read the suspect each right, they asked if he understood. They gave him warnings on the right to silence and on the state's right to use what he might say. Then they gave him the right to counsel warning as follows: "You have a right to consult a lawyer and to have a lawyer present with you when you're being questioned. Do you understand that?"

The suspect responded, saying, "Uh, yeah. I'd like to do that."

The officer continued with the rest of the *Miranda* warnings. When the suspect was asked whether he wanted to talk without a lawyer, he replied, "Yeah and no, uh. I don't know what's that, really."

The officer replied, "Well, you either have to talk to me this time without a lawyer being present, and if you do agree to talk with me without a lawyer being present you can stop at any time you want to."

The suspect agreed to talk and made some incriminating statements before cutting off the questioning with a request for counsel. The Court held that the evidence obtained could not be admitted in court because the suspect had invoked the right to counsel even before the giving of the *Miranda* warnings was completed.

Interrogation during Detention When Detention Is the Functional Equivalent of an Arrest
In *Kaupp v. Texas* (538 U.S. 626 [2003]), the Court held that a confession must be suppressed if obtained during a detention when officers did not have probable cause for an arrest and where the detention amounted to the functional equivalent of an arrest.

Kaupp v. Texas (2003)

In *Kaupp*, officers investigating the disappearance of a girl had Kaupp and the girl's half-brother as the main suspects. The half-brother confessed to the killing and implicated Kaupp. The brother had failed a polygraph test three times, but Kaupp had passed his polygraph. Given these, the officers did not feel they had probable cause to obtain an arrest warrant based solely on the brother's confession. Subsequently, officers went to Kaupp's home at three o'clock in the morning and, after his father let them in, went to his bedroom, awakened him with a flashlight, and told him "We need to go and talk." Kaupp was then hand-cuffed and taken to a patrol car. After going to the scene where the body had been recovered, officers took Kaupp to the sheriff's office. Kaupp was taken to an interview room; the handcuffs were removed and he was read his *Miranda* warnings. After initially denying any involvement in the crime, Kaupp admitted to having some part, but did not confess to the murder for which he was later tried.

During the trial, he sought exclusion of his confession, but the trial court rejected his motion, saying that Kaupp had consented to go with the officers when he answered "Okay" when the officer told him, "We need to go and talk." The trial court also said that the handcuffs were placed on Kaupp not because he was under arrest but for officer safety. The court added that handcuffing was routine and that Kaupp did not resist its use or act in other uncooperative ways.

On appeal the Court upheld Kaupp's contention, saying that the officers had created a situation where a reasonable person would not have felt free to leave and that Kaupp's detention, although not declared by the officers as such, in fact amounted to the "functional equivalent" of an arrest for which there was no probable cause. His arrest was invalid and the confession obtained by the police was ruled inadmissible.

Giving the *Miranda* Warnings Only after the Police Obtain an Unwarned Confession

In 2004, in *Missouri v. Seibert* (542 U.S. 600 [2004]), the Court held that giving the *Miranda* warnings but only after the police obtain an unwarned confession violates the *Miranda* rule; therefore, statements made after the *Miranda* warnings are given are not admissible even if these statements repeat those given before the *Miranda* warnings were read to the suspect. *Seibert* is important because it declares invalid a questionable practice in some law enforcement departments (see the Case Brief).

The facts in *Seibert* are tragic and the then-existent police practice in Missouri highly irregular. Seibert's son had cerebral palsy. When the son died in his sleep, Seibert feared she would be charged with neglect because the son died with bed sores. Together, Seibert, her two teenaged sons, and two of their friends planned to burn the family mobile home to cover up what she thought was a crime. They planned to leave a mentally ill teenager, who was living with the family in the mobile home, to avoid the appearance that the son who had cerebral palsy was left alone. The mentally ill teenager died in the fire. Days later, the police awoke Seibert at three o'clock in the morning. She was in the hospital where one of her sons was being treated for burns. She was arrested and taken to the police station.

The officer who made the arrest was told not to read her the *Miranda* warnings. Seibert was left in an interrogation room for about twenty minutes and then was interrogated for about forty minutes without being read her *Miranda* rights. She admitted she knew the mentally ill teenager was meant to die in the fire. After that admission, she was given a twenty-minute break. The officer then turned on a tape recorder, gave Seibert the *Miranda* warnings, obtained a signed waiver of rights, and resumed the interrogation. At the beginning of the interrogation, the officer confronted Seibert with her pre-*Miranda* warning statements and reacquainted her with those statements.

At a suppression hearing to exclude the statements, the officer admitted he made a conscious decision to withhold the *Miranda* warnings based on an interrogation technique he was taught by the police department. That technique was to question the suspect first, give the warnings after the confession, then repeat the questioning "until I get the answer she's already provided once."

On appeal after Seibert's conviction, the Court held that giving the *Miranda* warnings after an interrogation and an unwarned confession has first been obtained by the police violates *Miranda,* even if it repeats the same statements made before the warnings were given. The statements obtained could not be used in court.

CASE BRIEF: The Leading Case on Admissibility of Physical Evidence from an Unwarned Confession

Missouri v. Seibert, 542 U.S. 600 (2004)

Facts: Seibert's son had cerebral palsy. When he died in his sleep, Seibert feared charges of neglect because of bed sores on his body. In her presence, two of her teenaged sons and two of their friends planned to burn the family's mobile home to conceal the death of the son. They also planed to leave a mentally ill teenager who was living with the family in the mobile home to avoid the appearance that the son had been left alone. In the fire, the mentally ill teenager died. Five days later, the police awoke Seibert at 3 A.M. in the hospital where one of her sons was being treated for burns. She was arrested and taken to the police station.

The officer making the arrest was told not to read her the *Miranda* warnings. At the station, Seibert was left in an interrogation room for about twenty minutes, then she was interrogated for about forty minutes without being read her *Miranda* warnings. After she admitted she knew the teenager was meant to die in the fire, she was given a twenty-minute break. The office then turned on a tape recorder, gave Seibert the *Miranda* warnings, obtained a signed waiver of rights, and then resumed the interrogation. At the beginning of the interrogation, the officer confronted Seibert with her unwarned statements and essentially reacquainted her with the statements she had made prior to her *Miranda* warnings.

At a suppression hearing to exclude the statements, the officer admitted he made a conscious decision to withhold the *Miranda* warnings based on an interrogation technique he was taught by the police department—which was to question first, give the warnings, then repeat the questioning "until I get the answer she's already provided once."

Issue: *Are statements made after a suspect is given the* Miranda *warnings that repeat unwarned statements he or she made admissible in court? No.*

Supreme Court Decision: Giving the *Miranda* warnings after an interrogation and an unwarned confession has first been obtained by the police does not effectively comply with *Miranda's* constitutional requirement even if it repeats the statements made before the warnings were given; therefore, statements obtained are not admissible in court.

Case Significance: The Court in this case struck down an established practice in some police departments. In an earlier case, *Oregon v. Elstad,* the Court admitted a confession obtained after the police gave the *Miranda* warnings—even though the suspect had previously made statements before the warnings were given. This practice was subsequently used by police training organizations, such as the Police Law Institute, in what became known as a "question-first" technique of interrogation. This procedure first interrogates a person without the *Miranda* warnings. Once a confession is obtained, the *Miranda* warnings are then given. The officer resumes the interrogation and obtains a warned confession similar to the unwarned confession that has been given. In *Seibert,* the Court held this practice violative of *Miranda* and therefore held the evidence inadmissible.

The Court said that there are several distinctions between this case and *Elstad* (where the evidence obtained was admissible despite a prior unwarned statement). These include "the completeness and detail of the questions and answers in the first round of interrogation, the overlapping content of the two statements, the timing and setting of the first and the second statements, the continuity of police personnel, and the degree to which the interrogator's questions

treated the second round as continuous with the first." The overriding consideration in these types of "two-interrogation" cases is whether the two interrogations (the unwarned and the warned) can be seen as separate and distinct interrogations where a reasonable person would believe he or she is free to disregard the first and assert his or her rights on the second. In the *Seibert* case, the Court stated, "At the opposite extreme are the facts here [as opposed to the facts in the *Elstad* case], which by any objective measure reveal a police strategy adapted to undermine the *Miranda* warnings. The unwarned interrogation was conducted in the station house, and the questioning was systematic, exhaustive, and managed with psychological skill. When the police were finished there was little, if anything, of incriminating potential left unsaid. The warned phase of questioning proceeded after a pause of only fifteen to twenty minutes, in the same place as the unwarned segment. When the same officer who had conducted the first phase recited the *Miranda* warnings, he said nothing to counter the probable misimpression that the advice that anything Seibert said could be used against her also applied to the details of the inculpatory statement previously elicited. In particular, the police did not advise that her prior statement could not be used."

Therefore, the issue whether or not a subsequent warned admission or confession is admissible after the suspect has given an unwarned admission or confession depends on the facts and circumstances of the case. If the facts and circumstances are closer to *Elstad,* the statement is admissible, but if they are closer to *Seibert,* then the statement is not admissible.

Excerpts from the Decision: "The object of question-first is to render *Miranda* warnings ineffective by waiting for a particularly opportune time to give them, after the suspect has already confessed. . . . The threshold issue when interrogators question first and warn later is thus whether it would be reasonable to find that in these circumstances the warnings could function effectively as *Miranda* requires. Could the warnings effectively advise the suspect that he had a real choice about giving an admissible statement at that juncture? Could they reasonably convey that he could choose to stop talking even if he had talked earlier? For unless the warnings could place a suspect who has just been interrogated in a position to make such an informed choice, there is no practical justification for accepting the formal warnings as compliance with *Miranda,* or for treating the second state of interrogation as distinct from the first, unwarned and inadmissible segment. . . ."

There is no doubt about the answer that proponents of question-first give to this question about the effectiveness of warnings given only after successful interrogation, and we think their answer is correct. By any objective measure, applied to circumstances exemplified here, it is likely that if the interrogators employ the technique of withholding warnings until after interrogation succeeds in eliciting a confession, the warnings will be ineffective in preparing the suspect for successive interrogation, close in time and similar in content. After all, the reason that question-first is catching on is as obvious as its manifest purpose, which is to get a confession the suspect would not make if he understood his rights at the outset; the sensible underlying assumption is that with one confession in hand before the warnings, the interrogator can count on getting its duplicate with trifling additional trouble. Upon hearing warnings only in the aftermath of interrogation and just after making a confession, a suspect would hardly think he had a genuine right to remain silent, let alone persist in so believing once the police began to lead him over the same ground again. A more likely reaction on a suspect's part would

be perplexity about the reason for discussing rights at that point, bewilderment being an unpromising frame of mind for knowledgeable decision. What is worse, telling a suspect that "anything you say can and will be used against you," without expressly excepting the statement just given, could lead to an entirely reasonable inference that what he has just said will be used, with subsequent silence being of no avail. Thus, when *Miranda* warnings are inserted in the midst of coordinated and continuing interrogation, they are likely to mislead and "depriv[e] a defendant of knowledge essential to his ability to understand the nature of his rights and the consequences of abandoning them." By the same token, it would ordinarily be unrealistic to treat two spates of integrated and proximately conducted questioning as independent interrogations subject to independent evaluation simply because *Miranda* warnings formally punctuate them in the middle.

"The contrast between Elstad (470 U.S. 298 [1986]) and this case reveals a series of relevant facts that bear on whether the *Miranda* warnings delivered midstream could be effective enough to accomplish their object: the completeness and detail of the questions and answers in the first round of interrogation, the overlapping content of the two statements, the timing and setting of the first and the second, the continuity of police personnel, and the degree to which the interrogator's questions treated the second round as continuous with the first. In Elstad, it was not unreasonable to see the occasion for questioning at the station house as presenting a markedly different experience from the short conversation at home; since a reasonable person in the suspect's shoes could have seen the station house questioning as a new and distinct experience, the *Miranda* warnings could have made sense as presenting a genuine choice whether to follow up on the earlier admission."

Situations Not Requiring or Not Fully Applying the *Miranda* Warnings

In the next cases, the Court held that the evidence obtained was admissible despite the absence of the *Miranda* warnings, thus rejecting *Miranda* or not applying it in full.

Questioning on an Unrelated Offense after the Suspect Indicates a Wish to Remain Silent

Suppose a suspect indicates a desire to remain silent (as opposed to asking for a lawyer) after being given the *Miranda* warnings. May that suspect be interrogated again? The answer is yes as long as five conditions are present: (1) The suspect is given the *Miranda* warnings prior to the first interrogation; (2) the first interrogation stops right after the defendant indicates a desire to remain silent; (3) the questioning is resumed only after a significant period of time has lapsed (although the Court has not specified how long); (4) the suspect is again given the *Miranda* warnings; and (5) the second questioning is about crimes not covered in the first interrogation (*Michigan v. Mosley,* 423 U.S. 96 [1975]).

Michigan v. Mosley (1975)

In *Michigan v. Mosley* (1975), Mosley was arrested in connection with certain robberies and was given the *Miranda* warnings. He declined to discuss the robberies but did not indicate any desire to consult with a lawyer. More than two hours later, another detective, after again giving the *Miranda* warnings, questioned Mosley about an unrelated offense—a murder. Mosley gave an incriminating statement, which was used in his murder trial. Convicted, he appealed, saying that he should not have been asked any questions after he exercised his right to remain silent. The Court disagreed, admitting the evidence and saying that Mosley's second interrogation about another offense took place only after a significant time lapse and after a fresh set of warnings was given.

This scenario, in which a suspect indicates a *desire to remain silent,* should be distinguished from one in which the suspect indicates a *desire to see a lawyer*—as was the case in *Edwards v. Arizona* (discussed earlier). In *Edwards,* decided six years after *Mosley,* the Court held that, once a suspect indicates a desire for a lawyer, law enforcement agents must not question the suspect again—unless the suspect initiates the conversation. The Court apparently does not consider the desire to remain silent as highly protected as the desire to see a lawyer, and therefore the evidence is admissible as long as the five conditions listed are present. *Mosley* is a *Miranda* warning case, whereas *Edwards* is considered by the Court to be a right to counsel case; hence, the rules are different.

After a Knowing and Voluntary Waiver, Questioning until the Suspect Clearly Requests a Lawyer

Davis v. United States (1994)

The Court held in *Davis v. United States* (512 U.S. 452 [1994]) that the statement "I think I want a lawyer before I say anything else" by a suspect, after a knowing and voluntary waiver of his or her *Miranda* rights, does not constitute an invocation of the right to counsel because it is merely an ambiguous request for a lawyer.

In *Davis,* a navy sailor who was charged with the murder of another sailor had earlier waived his rights to remain silent and to counsel, both orally and in writing. Ninety minutes into the interrogation, however, Davis said, "Maybe I should talk to a lawyer." When agents inquired if he was asking for an attorney, Davis replied that he was not. The interrogation continued, and Davis's statements were used to convict him of murder. At his court-martial hearing, Davis moved to suppress the statements obtained after he suggested that he might need a lawyer. The Court admitted the evidence, saying that, unless a suspect makes a statement that a reasonable interrogator under the circumstances would interpret as an unambiguous request for counsel, the right to counsel under *Miranda* is not considered invoked.

Davis was decided on a 5-to-4 split. The justices who dissented did not think the preceding phrase, "I think," made that much of a difference in the tone of the request. It was clear to them that the suspect wanted a lawyer. The majority disagreed, holding that the request for counsel must be clear and unambiguous, judged from the perspective of a reasonable interrogator, before the *Edwards* rule applies. The Court said:

> To recapitulate: We held in *Miranda* that a suspect is entitled to the assistance of counsel during custodial interrogation even though the Constitution does not provide for such assistance. We held in *Edwards* that if the suspect invokes the right to counsel at any time, the police must immediately cease questioning him until an attorney is present. But we are unwilling to create a third layer of prophylaxis to prevent police questioning when the suspect *might* want a lawyer. Unless the suspect actually requests an attorney, questioning may continue.

The Court added that, in cases in which the suspect's statement is unclear, it is entirely proper for law enforcement officers to clarify whether the suspect, in fact, wants to see a lawyer. Seeking clarification from the suspect does not violate *Miranda*.

Using a Voluntary, but Inadmissible, Statement to Impeach a Defendant's Credibility

Trustworthy statements taken in violation of *Miranda* may be used to impeach the credibility of a defendant who takes the witness stand. The jury must be instructed that the confession may not be considered as evidence of guilt but only as a factor in determining whether the defendant is telling the truth (*Harris v. New York,* 401 U.S. 222 [1971]). Note, however, that the admission or confession cannot be used in court for any purpose whatsoever if it was obtained involuntarily.

Harris v. New York (1971)

For example, suppose a suspect confesses to the police even though she was not given the full *Miranda* warnings (she may have been warned that she has a right to remain silent but not of her right to a lawyer). The evidence is not admissible in court to prove her guilt. But suppose further that she takes the witness stand during the trial and testifies that she knew nothing at all about the crime. The confession may be used by the prosecutor to challenge her credibility as a witness. In this case, the confession is voluntary. But if the confession is involuntarily obtained (for example, through threats by the police), it cannot be used for any purpose, not even for impeachment.

Using an Inadmissible Statement to Obtain Collateral Derivative Evidence

Trustworthy statements obtained in violation of *Miranda* may be used to obtain *collateral derivative evidence* (meaning evidence of a secondary nature that is related to the case but not directly a part of it). For example, in *Michigan v. Tucker* (417 U.S. 433 [1974]), the police interrogated a suspect without giving the *Miranda* warnings. In the process, they obtained from the suspect the name of a person (the collateral derivative evidence) who eventually became a prosecution witness. The Court held that, although the defendant's own statements could not be used against him because they were obtained in violation of *Miranda*, the prosecution witness's testimony had been purged of its original taint and was therefore admissible.

Michigan v. Tucker (1974)

Interrogating without Informing the Suspect of All Crimes

A suspect's waiver of *Miranda* rights is valid even if he or she believes the interrogation will focus merely on minor crimes but the police bring up a different and more serious crime (*Colorado v. Spring*, 479 U.S. 564 [1987]).

Colorado v. Spring (1987)

In *Colorado v. Spring* (1987), Spring and a companion shot a man during a hunting trip in Colorado. An informant told federal agents that Spring was engaged in interstate trafficking in stolen firearms and that he had participated in the murder. Spring was arrested in Kansas City and advised of his *Miranda* rights. He signed a statement that he understood and waived his rights. He was asked about the firearms transaction (which had led to his arrest) and also whether he had ever shot a man. Spring answered yes but denied the shooting in question. He confessed to the murder later, however, after having been given the *Miranda* warnings. Tried and convicted, he appealed, saying that he should have been informed of all crimes about which he was to be questioned before there could be a valid waiver of his *Miranda* rights.

The Court rejected his challenge, saying that the Constitution does not require that a suspect know and understand every possible consequence of a waiver of a Fifth Amendment privilege. There was no allegation here that Spring failed to understand that privilege or that he did not understand the consequences of speaking freely.

Oral Confessions Admissible

An oral confession is admissible even if the suspect tells the police he will talk with them but will not make a written statement without a lawyer present (*Connecticut v. Barrett*, 479 U.S. 523 [1987]).

Connecticut v. Barrett (1987)

In *Connecticut v. Barrett* (1987), Barrett was arrested in connection with a sexual assault. Upon his arrival at the police station, he was advised of his *Miranda* rights and signed a statement saying he understood his rights. Barrett then said that he would not give a written statement in the absence of counsel but would talk to the police about the incident. In two subsequent interrogations, Barrett was again advised of his rights and signed a statement of understanding. On both occasions, he gave an oral statement admitting his involvement in the sexual assault but refused to make or sign a written statement. After being convicted of sexual assault, he appealed, alleging that his oral statements should not be admissible in court.

The Court rejected his challenge, saying that refusal by a suspect to put his or her statement in writing does not make an admission or confession inadmissible, as long as the police can establish that the *Miranda* warnings were given and the waiver was intelligent and voluntary. Note, however, that the admissibility of oral statements may be the subject of limiting rules in some states. For example, state law might provide that oral confessions are admissible only if corroborated by other evidence indicating guilt, such as a weapon or eyewitnesses.

Confession Admissible despite Failure to Inform the Suspect of a Retained Attorney

Moran v. Burbine (1986)

In *Moran v. Burbine* (475 U.S. 412 [1986]), the Court held that a suspect's waiver of the Fifth Amendment right to remain silent and to have counsel present during custodial interrogation is not nullified either by the failure of police officers to inform the suspect that the attorney retained on his or her behalf by a third party is attempting to reach the suspect or by misleading information given to the attorney by the police regarding their intention to interrogate the suspect at that time.

In that case, the failure of police officers to inform a suspect that the attorney retained for him by his sister was attempting to reach him did not make the evidence obtained inadmissible. If the officer knows, however, that the defendant has retained a lawyer, and the lawyer wants to be present during interrogation, that wish must be respected.

The Physical Fruits of an Unwarned but Voluntary Statement

United States v. Patane (2004)

In an important 2004 case, *United States v. Patane* (543 U.S. 630 [2004]), the Court held that failure to give the *Miranda* warnings to a suspect does not require the suppression of the physical fruits of a suspect's unwarned but voluntary statements.

In *Patane*, Patane was arrested for harassing his ex-girlfriend. He was released on bond, subject to a restraining order that prohibited him from contacting her. Patane violated the restraining order by telephoning her. A police investigating officer was given information by a probation officer that Patane had an illegal pistol. The officer went to Patane's home, inquired about his attempts to contact his ex-girlfriend, and then arrested Patane for violating the restraining order. When another officer tried to read Patane his *Miranda* warnings, Patane interrupted and said he knew his rights. After that, they made no further attempts to read Patane his *Miranda* rights. They then asked him about the pistol, and Patane told them where the pistol was located. Patane was arrested for being a felon in possession of a firearm. Tried and convicted, he appealed saying that the failure of the officers to give him the *Miranda* warnings required suppression of the pistol, which was the physical "fruit" of his unwarned but voluntary statements. The Court disagreed, saying that Patane's constitutional right against self-incrimination was not violated because the evidence involved (the pistol) was physical, not testimonial (spoken).

Table 11.1 A Summary of Cases after *Miranda v. Arizona*

Case	How Was Evidence Obtained?	Evidence Admissible?
United States v. Henry (1980)	Questioning after indictment	No
Edwards v. Arizona (1981)	No valid waiver of right to counsel	No
Smith v. Illinois (1984)	Interrogation after invocation of right to counsel during questioning	No
Arizona v. Roberson (1988)	Interrogation about second offense after invoking *Miranda* for first offense	No
Minnick v. Mississippi (1991)	Questioning after request for lawyer	No
Kaupp v. Texas (2003)	Detention without probable cause that amounted to the functional equivalent of an arrest	No
Missouri v. Seibert (2004)	Giving *Miranda* warnings but only after the police obtain an unwarned admission	No

Note that in this case, the focus was on the admissibility of the pistol that was obtained without the suspect being given the *Miranda* warnings and after he had asserted that he knew his rights. The statement itself was deemed voluntary. Given the suspect's statement that he knew his rights and the fact that what was recovered was a pistol, the Court concluded that the suspect's right against self-incrimination was not violated. The Court refused to apply the "fruit of the poisonous tree" doctrine (which holds that evidence obtained resulting from another evidence that is illegally obtained is not admissible in court) could not be used in this case, because that doctrine applies only to violations of the Fourth Amendment guarantee against unreasonable searches and seizures and is unrelated to the *Miranda* rule, which is based on the Fifth Amendment.

Situations in which the *Miranda* Warnings Are Not Needed

When are the *Miranda* warnings not required? The easy and quick answer is *whenever there is no custodial interrogation.* The *Miranda* case itself and subsequent Court decisions have identified a number of situations in which there is no need to give the *Miranda* warnings.

When the Officer Does Not Ask Any Questions
The *Miranda* warnings are unnecessary when the police do not ask questions of the suspect. *Miranda* applies only if the police interrogate the suspect; if they do not ask questions, no warnings need to be given. For example, suppose X is arrested by the police because of an arrest warrant. If the police do not question X during the time he is in police custody, the *Miranda* warnings do not need to be given. In many states, the magistrate gives the *Miranda* warnings when the arrested person is brought before him or her for initial appearance or presentment.

■ Table 11.2 Cases Either Rejecting *Miranda* or Not Applying *Miranda* in Full—Statements Are Admissible

Case	How Was Evidence Obtained?	Evidence Admissible?
Harris v. New York (1971)	Impeachment of credibility	Yes
Michigan v. Tucker (1974)	Collateral derivative evidence	Yes
Michigan v. Mosley (1975)	Questioning on an unrelated offense	Yes
New York v. Quarles (1984)	Threat to public safety	Yes
Berkemer v. McCarty (1984)	Roadside questioning of motorist pursuant to routine traffic stop	Yes
Oregon v. Elstad (1985)	Confession obtained after warnings given following earlier voluntary but unwarned admission	Yes
Moran v. Burbine (1986)	Failure of police to inform suspect of attorney retained for him	Yes
Kuhlmann v. Wilson (1986)	Informant in same cell	Yes
Colorado v. Connelly (1986)	Confession following advice of God	Yes
Connecticut v. Barnett (1987)	Oral confession	Yes
Colorado v. Spring (1987)	Shift to another crime	Yes
Arizona v. Mauro (1987)	Conversation with defendant's wife recorded	Yes
Pennsylvania v. Bruder (1988)	Curbside stop for traffic violation	Yes
Duckworth v. Eagan (1989)	Variation in warning	Yes
Michigan v. Harvey (1990)	Impeachment of testimony	Yes
Illinois v. Perkins (1990)	Officer posing as inmate	Yes
Pennsylvania v. Muniz (1990)	Routine questions and videotaping for DWI	Yes
Arizona v. Fulminante (1991)	Harmless involuntary confessions	Yes
Davis v. United States (1994)	No clear request to see attorney	Yes
Texas v. Cobb (2001)	Interrogation for closely related offense while having lawyer for first offense	Yes
United States v. Patane	Obtained physical evidence after failure to give the *Miranda* warnings	Yes

During General On-the-Scene Questioning *Miranda* warnings do not have to be given prior to **general on-the-scene questioning**, meaning questioning at the scene of the crime for the purpose of gathering information about the people involved. In the words of the Court in *Miranda*: "General on-the-scene questioning as to facts surrounding a crime is not affected by our holding. It is an act of responsible citizenship for individuals to give whatever information they may have to aid in law enforcement. In such situations the compelling atmosphere inherent in the process of in-custody interrogation is not necessarily present."

A distinction must be made, however, between general on-the-scene questioning and questioning at the scene of the crime after the police have focused on an individual, which requires the *Miranda* warnings. Consider these two examples:

- *Example 1.* Z has been stabbed fatally in a crowded bar. A police officer arrives and questions people at the scene of the crime to determine whether anyone saw the actual stabbing. This is considered general on-the-scene questioning, for which there is no need to give the *Miranda* warnings.

- *Example 2.* Assume instead that upon arrival at the bar the officer sees X with a bloody knife in his hands. The officer's suspicion will doubtless be focused on X. Therefore, any questioning of X requires the *Miranda* warnings even though such questioning is at the scene of the crime.

When the Statement Is Volunteered A person who volunteers a statement does not have to receive *Miranda* warnings before speaking. A **volunteered statement** is one given by a suspect without interrogation. For example, suppose X enters the police station and announces, "I just killed my wife." The statement is admissible in court because it was volunteered. A volunteered statement is different from a **voluntary statement**, which is a statement given without coercion and of the suspect's own free will. For example, Suspect X confesses to a burglary after having been given the *Miranda* warnings and consenting to a valid waiver. A volunteered statement is always voluntary, but a voluntary statement is not often volunteered.

When Asking a Suspect Routine Identification Questions When asking questions about a suspect's identification—"What is your name?" "Where do you live?" "How long have you lived here?"—the *Miranda* warnings are not required (*Pennsylvania v. Muniz,* 496 U.S. 582 [1990]).

Pennsylvania v. Muniz (1990)

In *Pennsylvania v. Muniz* (1990), Muniz was arrested for driving while under the influence of alcohol. He was taken to a booking center and was told that his actions and voice would be videotaped. He was asked seven questions regarding his name, address, height, weight, eye color, date of birth, and current age, which he answered. He later sought exclusion of his answers, saying he was not given the *Miranda* warnings before those questions were asked.

The Court disagreed, saying that Muniz's answers were admissible because these questions fall within a "routine booking question" exception to the *Miranda* rule. The Court agreed with the state court that "the first seven questions were requested for record-keeping purposes only." No possible self-incrimination was involved; hence, the *Miranda* warnings were not needed.

When Questioning Witnesses Who Are Not Suspects When the person being interrogated is merely a witness to a crime, not a suspect, the *Miranda* warnings are not needed. However, if the officer suspects during the questioning that the witness might be involved in the offense, then the warnings must be given. For example, assume that Officer X interviews Y about the rape of a neighbor committed the previous night. In the course of the interrogation, Officer X decides that Y is a suspect because of his inconsistent answers, nervous behavior, and a prior sexual record. At that stage, Y must be given his *Miranda* warnings because the situation has shifted from Y being a witness to his being a suspect in the crime.

In Stop and Frisk Cases

There is no need to give the *Miranda* warnings if a person is stopped by the police and asked questions to determine if criminal activity is about to take place or has taken place. In this brief encounter, which is preceded by a casual type of questioning, the suspect is not deprived of freedom in a significant way. The purpose of a stop is to determine whether criminal activity is about to take place, and the purpose of a frisk is to protect the officer. In neither case is custodial interrogation involved. Note, however, that once a stop and frisk situation turns into an arrest, the *Miranda* warnings must be given if the suspect is interrogated.

During Lineups, Showups, or Photographic Identifications

No *Miranda* warnings need to be given during lineups, showups, or photographic pretrial identifications. The reason is that these pretrial identification procedures are not protected by the Fifth Amendment guarantee against self-incrimination because the evidence obtained is physical in nature and does not constitute testimonial self-incrimination.

When the Statement Is Made to a Private Person, Not a Law Enforcement Officer

Miranda does not apply to statements or confessions made to private persons. Protection against compulsory self-incrimination applies only to interrogations initiated by law enforcement officers. Incriminating statements made by the accused to friends or cell mates while in custody are admissible even if made without the *Miranda* warnings. This is because the Bill of Rights does not apply to the actions of private persons as long as they are purely private.

When a Suspect Testifies before a Grand Jury

In an interrogation of a potential criminal defendant before a grand jury, the *Miranda* warnings are not required, even if the prosecutor intends to charge the witness with an offense. This is because grand jury questioning does not constitute custodial interrogation. The theory is that such interrogation does not present the same opportunities for abuse as custodial interrogation by the police. Questioning in a grand jury room is different from custodial police interrogation (*United States v. Mandujano,* 425 U.S. 564 [1976]). The evidence obtained may be held inadmissible, however, if state law requires the giving of the *Miranda* warnings even in grand jury proceedings. State laws that give more rights to suspects than the Constitution does are binding on government agencies in that state.

*United States v.
Mandujano* (1976)

When There Is a Threat to Public Safety

In *New York v. Quarles* (467 U.S. 649 [1984]), the Court carved out a **public safety exception** to the *Miranda* rule, saying that, when questions asked by police officers are reasonably prompted by

*New York v.
Quarles* (1984)

concern for public safety, the responses are admissible in court even though the suspect was in police custody and not given the *Miranda* warnings.

In the *Quarles* case, a woman approached two police officers who were on patrol, told them that she had just been raped, described her assailant, and said that the man had just entered a nearby supermarket and was carrying a gun. One officer entered the store and spotted Quarles, who matched the description given by the woman. Quarles ran toward the rear of the store but was finally subdued. The officer noticed that Quarles was wearing an empty shoulder holster. After handcuffing the suspect, the police asked where the gun was; Quarles nodded toward some empty cartons, where the gun was found. The suspect was given the *Miranda* warnings only after the gun was recovered. The Court said that the gun was admissible as evidence under the public safety exception.

The public safety exception is best limited to cases in which there is immediate danger to the public; otherwise, it might be abused. It must be limited to danger arising from a criminal act that has just been committed, as in this situation involving a firearm. It should not apply to cases in which the danger to public safety is not immediate or serious.

When an Undercover Officer Poses as an Inmate and Asks Questions

Illinois v. Perkins (1990)

In *Illinois v. Perkins* (496 U.S. 292 [1990]), the Court decided that an undercover law enforcement officer posing as a fellow inmate did not need to give the *Miranda* warnings to a suspect in jail before asking questions that might produce an incriminating response.

In this case, the police placed undercover agent Parisi in a jail cell block with the suspect Perkins, who had been detained on charges unrelated to the murder that Parisi was investigating. When Parisi asked Perkins if he had ever killed anybody, Perkins made statements incriminating himself in the murder. He was subsequently charged, tried, and convicted. On appeal, he sought to exclude the evidence, claiming that he should have been given the *Miranda* warnings before being asked the incriminating question by the agent.

The Court disagreed, saying that the doctrine must be enforced strictly but only in situations in which the concerns underlying that decision are present. These concerns were not present here, because the essential ingredients of a police-dominated atmosphere and compulsion were absent. The Court said that a coercive

HIGHLIGHT

Police Acceptance of Miranda

Despite their initial reaction of dismay, the police seem to have adjusted to *Miranda* fairly well. Under these the circumstances, the Court is probably willing to "live with" a case that has become part of American culture, especially if it continues to view the case as a serious effort to strike a proper balance between the need for police questioning and the need to protect a suspect against impermissible police pressure.

SOURCE: Yale Kamisar, in *The Oxford Companion to the Supreme Court of the United States*, ed. Kermit L. Hall (New York: Oxford University Press, 1992), p. 555.

atmosphere is "not present when an incarcerated person speaks freely to someone whom he believes to be a fellow inmate and whom he assumes is not an officer having official power over him." The Court then added that in such circumstances *Miranda* does not forbid mere strategic deception by taking advantage of a suspect's misplaced trust.

The Harmless Error Rule and *Miranda* Cases on Appeal: *Arizona v. Fulminante*

Arizona v. Fulminante (1991)

The **"harmless error" rule** provides that harmless errors during trial in civil or criminal cases do not require a reversal of the judgment by an appellate court. Conversely, if the error is *harmful,* the judgment must be reversed. In *Arizona v. Fulminante* (499 U.S. 279 [1991]), the Court ruled that the harmless error rule is applicable to cases involving involuntary confessions. But the burden of proving harmless error rests with the prosecution and must be established "beyond a reasonable doubt." This is significant because prior to *Fulminante* the rule was that the erroneous admission into evidence by the trial court of an involuntary confession led to an automatic reversal of the conviction on appeal regardless of whether the admission was harmless or harmful. That has now changed.

The facts of the case are sad, and the Court decision was complex, with three issues decided by the Court on close votes. Fulminante was suspected by police of having murdered his stepdaughter, but no charges were filed against him. He left Arizona for New Jersey, where he was later convicted on an unrelated charge of firearms possession. While incarcerated in a federal prison in New York on that charge, Fulminante was befriended by a fellow inmate, a certain Sarivola, who was serving a sixty-day sentence for extortion. Sarivola later become an informant for the FBI. Sarivola offered Fulminante protection from the other inmates (which Fulminante needed because of the rumor that he was a child murderer) in exchange for the truth. Fulminante admitted to Sarivola that he had driven his stepdaughter to the desert on his motorcycle, choked and sexually assaulted her, and made her beg for her life before shooting her twice in the head. After his release from prison, Fulminante also confessed to Sarivola's wife about the same crime. Indicted for first-degree murder, Fulminante sought exclusion of his confessions to Sarivola and Sarivola's wife. The trial court admitted the confession; Fulminante was convicted and sentenced to death.

On appeal, the Court addressed three issues raised by *Fulminante:*

- Should the harmless error rule apply to *Miranda* confessions on appeal? Yes.
- Was Fulminante's confession voluntary? No, it was coerced.
- Was the admission of Fulminante's confession by the trial court a harmless error in his conviction? No, because the government failed

to establish beyond a reasonable doubt that the admission was a harmless error.

The Court decision meant that Fulminante was to be given a new trial, but the involuntary confession could not to be admitted.

Under the *Fulminante* rule, the reversal of a conviction on appeal in *Miranda*-type cases involves two steps. The first step is determining whether the confession is voluntary or involuntary. If the confession is voluntary, then the admission by the trial court of the evidence is proper. If it is involuntary, the second step becomes necessary—determining whether the admission of such evidence by the trial court was a harmless error. The burden of proof rests with the prosecution. If the admission constitutes a harmless error (as determined by the appellate court), the conviction is affirmed. Conversely, the conviction is reversed (1) if the error is deemed harmful by the appellate court or (2) if the prosecution fails to establish beyond a reasonable doubt that the error was harmless (as was the situation in *Fulminante*).

Summary

The *Miranda* warnings:

- You have a right to remain silent.
- Anything you say can be used against you in a court of law.
- You have a right to the presence of an attorney.
- If you cannot afford an attorney, one will be appointed for you prior to questioning.
- You have the right to terminate this interview at any time.

The *Miranda* issues:

- *Importance. Miranda* sets the standard for admissibility of admissions or confessions.
- *Standard for admissibility before* Miranda. Voluntariness.
- *Standard for admissibility after* Miranda. Were the *Miranda* warnings given? Was there a waiver? If so, was the waiver intelligent and voluntary? The answer to all three questions must be yes.
- *When must the* Miranda *warnings be given?* Whenever there is a custodial interrogation.
- *When is a person in custody?* When under arrest or deprived of freedom in a significant way.

- *When is a person under interrogation?* When being asked questions or when the police create a situation that is likely to elicit a confession or admission.
- *For what offenses must the* Miranda *warnings be given?* All offenses—felonies or misdemeanors—except routine traffic stops.
- *Can the* Miranda *rights be waived?* Yes, but the government must prove that the waiver was intelligent and voluntary.
- *What is the rule for* Miranda *cases on appeal?* Conviction is reversed if the admission of excludable evidence by the trial court is harmful; conviction is not reversed if the admission of excludable evidence is harmless.

The *Miranda* warnings are not needed:

- When no questions are asked by the officer
- During general on-the-scene questioning
- When the statement is volunteered
- When questioning a suspect about identification
- When questioning witnesses
- In stop and frisk cases

- During lineups, showups, or photographic identifications
- When the statement is made to a private person
- When the suspect appears before a grand jury
- When there is a threat to public safety

Review Questions and Hypothetical Cases

1. Voluntariness was the old standard for the admissibility of confessions and admissions. Explain why that standard was difficult to apply.

2. How did *Miranda v. Arizona* change the standard for admissibility of confessions and admissions? In your personal opinion, is it a change for the better? Why? If yes, how is it better?

3. Assume that the state legislature of Kansas passes a law providing that confessions are admissible in state court criminal cases as long as they are voluntary, even without the *Miranda* warnings. Is that law constitutional? Cite a case precedent and reasons for your answer.

4. Explain what the term *custodial interrogation* means.

5. "The Miranda warnings must be given every time the police interrogate a suspect in connection with an offense." Is that statement true or false? Discuss your answer.

6. What is meant by the *functional equivalent of an interrogation*? Give an example.

7. Distinguish between the subjective test and the objective test used in determining whether a person is in custody for purposes of the *Miranda* warnings. If you are a police officer, which test would you prefer the courts use and why?

8. Based on Court decisions, give four situations when the *Miranda* warnings are not needed and why.

9. What is the harmless error rule on appeal? Give an example of its application in *Miranda* cases.

10. X robbed an apartment and kidnapped its sole occupant. Charged with both offenses, X was assigned a lawyer for the robbery but not for the kidnapping. Discuss whether X may be questioned by the police for the kidnapping in the absence of his lawyer.

11. S, a university student, ran a red light and was stopped by the police. He was asked to get out of his car and asked questions about why he ran a red light and was speeding. S gave unsatisfactory answers. The police looked around the car and saw a suspicious package. They asked if they could open it; S said yes. The package turned out to contain drugs. The police asked S for the source of the drugs. S said he got it from his dormitory roommate. The police then went to S's room and found more drugs. During the trial, S claimed he should have been given the *Miranda* warnings by the police. Based on the officer's failure to give the *Miranda* warnings, are any of the drugs confiscated admissible in evidence? Justify your answer.

12. Officer P went to G's house, a juvenile gang member. G's family knew Officer P because he lived in the same neighborhood and was a family friend. Officer P talked to G's parents and told them he had information about G's involvement in a murder. The officer asked the parents to appeal to their son to cooperate with the police. The parents called G and asked him to "tell Officer P the truth." At first G denied involvement, but after repeated questioning by his parents, G admitted his part in the murder, which he committed with two other gang members. During the trial, G sought exclusion of his statement, saying he should have been given the *Miranda* warnings by Officer P. You are the judge. Will you exclude or admit the statement? Why or why not?

Key Terms

Go to the Criminal Procedure 7e website for flash cards that will help you master the definitions of these terms.

admission, 400
confession, 400
custodial interrogation, 418
custody, 419
deprived of freedom in a significant way, 419
Edwards rule, 425

functional equivalent of an interrogation, 423
general on-the-scene questioning, 437
"harmless error" rule, 441
intelligent waiver, 415
intelligent and voluntary

waiver, 415
interrogation, 423
Miranda rule, 399
public safety exception, 439
voluntary statement, 438
volunteered statement, 438
waiver, 415

Holdings of Key Cases

See Appendix C for information on how to find cases in this chapter on FindLaw.com.

***Arizona v. Fulminante,* 499 U.S. 279 (1991)**
The harmless error rule is applicable to cases on appeal involving confessions.

***Arizona v. Mauro,* 481 U.S. 520 (1987)** A conversation between a suspect and his or her spouse that is recorded by and in the presence of an officer does not constitute the functional equivalent of an interrogation under *Miranda,* so the evidence obtained is admissible.

***Arizona v. Roberson,* 486 U.S. 675 (1988)**
Invoking the *Miranda* rights to one offense also invokes the *Miranda* rights to an unrelated offense.

***Beckwith v. United States,* 425 U.S. 341 (1976)**
Statements obtained by Internal Revenue Service agents during a noncustodial, noncoercive interview with a taxpayer under criminal tax investigation, conducted in a private home where the taxpayer occasionally stayed, did not require the *Miranda* warnings as long as the taxpayer had been told he was free to leave at any time.

***Berkemer v. McCarty,* 468 U.S. 420 (1984)** A person subjected to custodial interrogation must be given the *Miranda* warnings regardless of the nature or severity of the offense. Exception: The roadside questioning of a motorist detained pursuant to a routine traffic stop does not constitute custodial interroga-

tion; therefore, there is no need to give the *Miranda* warnings.

***Brewer v. Williams,* 430 U.S. 387 (1977)**
Interrogation takes place and therefore *Miranda* warnings are needed when the police officers, knowing of the defendant's religious interest, make remarks designed to appeal to that interest and thus induce a confession.

***Brown v. Mississippi,* 297 U.S. 278 (1936)**
Confessions obtained as a result of utter coercion and brutality by law enforcement officers violate the Due Process Clause of the Fourteenth Amendment and therefore are inadmissible.

***California v. Beheler,* 463 U.S. 1121 (1983)**
The ultimate determinant of whether a person is "in custody" for *Miranda* purposes is whether the suspect has been subjected to a formal arrest or to equivalent restraints on his or her freedom of movement.

***Chambers v. Florida,* 309 U.S. 227 (1940)**
Protracted questioning of defendants held in jail without contact with the outside world violates the defendants' right to due process of law under the Fourteenth Amendment, so the evidence thereby obtained is inadmissible.

***Colorado v. Connelly,* 479 U.S. 157 (1986)**
The admissibility of statements made when the mental state of the suspect interferes with

his or her rational intellect and free will is governed by state rules of evidence rather than by Supreme Court decisions on coerced confessions. Confessions and admissions are involuntary and invalid under the Constitution only if the coercion is exerted by the police, not if the suspect was "following the advice of God."

Colorado v. Spring, 479 U.S. 564 (1987) A suspect's waiver of *Miranda* rights is valid even if the suspect believes the interrogation will merely focus on minor crimes but the police actually cover a different and more serious crime.

Connecticut v. Barrett, 479 U.S. 523 (1987) An oral confession is admissible even if the suspect tells the police he or she will talk with them but will not make a written statement without a lawyer present.

Davis v. United States, 512 U.S. 452 (1994) After a knowing and voluntary waiver of the *Miranda* rights, law enforcement officers may continue questioning until and unless the suspect clearly requests an attorney.

Dickerson v. United States, 530 U.S. 428 (2000) *Miranda v. Arizona* governs the admissibility in federal and state courts of confessions and admissions given during custodial interrogation by the police. The *Miranda* warnings are a constitutional rule; therefore, any law passed by Congress that seeks to overturn it is unconstitutional.

Duckworth v. Eagan, 492 U.S. 195 (1989) The *Miranda* warnings do not need to be given exactly as worded in the *Miranda* case. What is required is that the wording reasonably convey to a suspect his or her rights. Informing a suspect that an attorney will be appointed "if and when you go to court" does not render the *Miranda* warnings inadequate.

Edwards v. Arizona, 451 U.S. 477 (1981) Once the suspect has invoked the right to remain silent until he or she consults a lawyer, the suspect cannot be questioned again for the same offense unless the suspect initiates further communication, exchanges, or conversations with the police.

Escobedo v. Illinois, 378 U.S. 748 (1964) A confession obtained from a defendant is inadmissible, even though an adversarial judicial proceeding has not yet been started, when he or she requested and was denied an opportunity to consult with a lawyer even though the lawyer was present and available to consult with him or her.

Fare v. Michael C., 442 U.S. 707 (1979) The request of a juvenile on probation to see his probation officer instead of a lawyer is considered a waiver of the juvenile's right to a lawyer, because a probation officer and a lawyer perform two different functions.

Fellers v. United States, 540 U.S. 519 (2004) The proper standard to be used when determining whether statements made by a defendant after an indictment are admissible in court is the Sixth Amendment right to counsel, not the Fifth Amendment right against self-incrimination.

Harris v. New York, 401 U.S. 222 (1971) Trustworthy statements taken in violation of *Miranda* may be used to impeach the credibility of a defendant who takes the witness stand, as long as the statements are voluntary.

Illinois v. Perkins, 496 U.S. 292 (1990) An undercover law enforcement officer posing as a fellow inmate does not need to give the *Miranda* warnings to a suspect in jail before asking questions that may produce an incriminating response.

Kaupp v. Texas, 538 U.S. 626 (2003) A confession must be suppressed if obtained during a detention where officers did not have probable cause and where the detention amounted to the functional equivalent of an arrest.

Massiah v. United States, 377 U.S. 201 (1964) When a police informer carries into the suspect's home an electronic device that transmits the conversation to the police outside, the evidence obtained is not admissible if the defendant was questioned without his lawyer by police after being charged and obtaining a lawyer.

Michigan v. Mosley, 423 U.S. 96 (1975) A suspect who indicates a desire to remain silent (as opposed to asking for a lawyer) after being given the *Miranda* warnings may be interrogated again as long as five conditions are present: (1) the suspect is given the *Miranda* warnings prior to the first interrogation; (2) the first interrogation stops right after the defendant indicates a desire to remain silent; (3) the questioning is resumed only after a significant period of time has lapsed; (4) the suspect must again be given the *Miranda* warnings;

and (5) the second questioning must be about crimes not covered in the first interrogation.

Michigan v. Tucker, 417 U.S. 433 (1974) Trustworthy statements obtained in violation of *Miranda* may be used to obtain collateral derivative evidence.

Mincey v. Arizona, 437 U.S. 385 (1978) Statements given by a suspect to the police that are not the product of free and rational choice are not admissible.

Minnick v. Mississippi, 498 U.S. 146 (1991) Once a suspect asks for a lawyer, interrogation must stop—whether the defendant confers with the lawyer or not.

Miranda v. Arizona, 384 U.S. 436 (1966) Law enforcement officers must give suspects the following warnings during custodial interrogation:
- You have a right to remain silent.
- Anything you say can be used against you in a court of law.
- You have a right to the presence of an attorney.
- If you cannot afford an attorney, one will be appointed for you prior to questioning.
- You may terminate this interview at any time.

Missouri v. Seibert, 542 U.S. 600 (2004) Giving the *Miranda* warnings but only after the police obtain an unwarned confession violates the *Miranda* rule; therefore, statements made after the *Miranda* warnings are given are not admissible even if these statements repeat those given before the *Miranda* warnings were read to the suspect.

Moran v. Burbine, 475 U.S. 412 (1986) A suspect's waiver of the Fifth Amendment rights to remain silent and to have counsel present during custodial interrogation is not nullified either by the failure of police officers to inform the suspect that the attorney retained on his or her behalf by a third party is attempting to reach him or her or by misleading information given to the attorney by the police regarding their intention to interrogate the suspect at that time.

New York v. Quarles, 467 U.S. 649 (1984) When questions asked by police officers are reasonably prompted by concern for public safety, the responses are admissible in court even though the suspect was in police custody and was not given the *Miranda* warnings.

North Carolina v. Butler, 441 U.S. 369 (1979) Failure to make an explicit statement regarding the waiver does not determine whether the evidence is admissible. Instead, the trial court must look at all the circumstances to determine if a valid waiver has, in fact, been made. Although an express waiver is easier to establish in court, it is not required.

Oregon v. Mathiason, 429 U.S. 492 (1977) The *Miranda* warnings are necessary only if the suspect is interrogated while in custody or otherwise deprived of freedom in a significant way. In this case, the suspect came to the police station in response to an officer's message that the officer would "like to discuss something with you." It was made clear to the suspect that he was not under arrest. The confession made without the *Miranda* warnings was admissible.

Orozco v. Texas, 394 U.S. 324 (1969) The questioning of a suspect in his or her home by police officers at four o'clock in the morning requires the *Miranda* warnings.

Pennsylvania v. Bruder, 488 U.S. 9 (1988) The curbside stop of a motorist for a traffic violation, although representing a Fourth Amendment seizure of the person, is not sufficiently custodial to require the *Miranda* warnings.

Pennsylvania v. Muniz, 496 U.S. 582 (1990) The police may validly ask routine questions of persons suspected of driving while intoxicated and videotape their responses without giving them the *Miranda* warnings.

Rhode Island v. Innis, 446 U.S. 291 (1980) Conversation between police officers while in a police car discussing the danger that one of the handicapped children from a school near the scene of the crime might find a loaded shotgun did not constitute interrogation, even though it was within hearing of the suspect.

Rogers v. Richmond, 365 U.S. 534 (1961) A confession obtained as a result of interrogation that continues for more than a day, accompanied by a threat that the suspect's spouse will be taken into custody if the suspect does not confess, is involuntary and therefore not admissible in court.

Smith v. Illinois, 469 U.S. 91 (1984) Once a suspect has clearly invoked his or her right to counsel during questioning, nothing the suspect says in response to further interrogation may be used to cast doubt on that invocation. Moreover, an invocation of rights may be made very early in the process—even during the interrogator's recitation of the suspect's rights. Therefore, the questioning of an in-custody suspect may have to end even before it starts.

Spano v. New York, **360 U.S. 315 (1959)** The use of deception as a means of psychological pressure to induce a confession violates a defendant's constitutional rights, so the evidence obtained is not admissible in court. The trial court's mistaken admission of a confession leads to an automatic reversal of the conviction.

Stansbury v. California, **511 U.S. 318 (1994)** A police officer's subjective and undisclosed view whether the person being interrogated is a suspect does not determine whether the person is, in fact, in custody for purposes of the *Miranda* warnings.

Teague v. Louisiana, **444 U.S. 469 (1980)** The trial court cannot presume a waiver from the failure of the accused to complain after receiving the *Miranda* warnings or from the fact that the accused spoke with the police after the warnings were given.

Texas v. Cobb, **562 U.S. 162 (2001)** The police may question a suspect about a second offense while the suspect has a lawyer for a different, although factually related, offense.

Thompson v. Keohane, **516 U.S. 99 (1995)** "Two discrete inquiries are essential to the determination (whether the suspect is in custody): first, what were the circumstances surrounding the interrogation; and second, given those circumstances, would a reasonable person have felt he or she was not at liberty to terminate the interrogation and leave."

United States v. Dickerson, **No. 97-4750 (4th Cir. 1999)** A three-judge panel in the U.S. Court of Appeals for the Fourth Circuit held, by a 2-to-1 vote, that voluntary confessions given without the *Miranda* warnings do not have to be excluded in federal court prosecutions and that congressional law overruled *Miranda* in federal courts. This ruling was overturned by the U.S. Supreme Court a year later.

United States v. Henry, **447 U.S. 264 (1980)** The government violates a defendant's Sixth Amendment right to counsel by intentionally creating a situation likely to induce the accused to make incriminating statements without the presence of a lawyer *(http://laws.findlaw.com/us/447/264.html)*.

United States v. Mandujano, **425 U.S. 564 (1976)** Grand jury investigations do not require the *Miranda* warnings, because the answers given are not statements in response to custodial interrogation.

United States v. Patane, **543 U.S. 630 (2004)** Failure to give the *Miranda* warnings does not require the suppression of the physical fruits of a suspect's unwarned but voluntary statements.

Yarborough v. Alvarado, **541 U.S. 652 (2004)** In determining whether a suspect is "in custody" for purposes of giving the *Miranda* warnings, a police officer does not have to consider a suspect's age or previous history with law enforcement.

 ## You Be the Judge . . .

In the United States Court of Appeals for the Ninth Circuit

In 1998, FBI Special Agent Bowdich received information from an unnamed source that a person named "Ralphy Rabbit" had participated in an armed robbery of a Bank of America branch on Ulrich Street. At some time before July 2000, Agent Bowdich had come to believe that Crawford was "Ralphy Rabbit" and learned that he was on state parole. He arranged with Crawford's parole officer to do a parole search of Crawford's residence with the intention of using the search to talk to Crawford about the Ulrich Street bank robbery.

During the search, which was conducted by four California state officers, Agent Bowdich pulled Crawford aside and tried to gain his confidence. He said he just wanted to talk about an old bank robbery. It was obvious that during the search the state officers found no evidence of any crime, but until that point Crawford was held in the apartment.

Crawford indicated he would feel more comfortable talking somewhere away from his home where the state officers were conducting the search. Bowdich offered his office, and Crawford agreed. He, Crawford, and San Diego Police Detective Gutierrez drove together to the FBI field office in San Diego. During the twenty-minute ride Crawford was not asked any questions.

At the FBI offices, Agent Bowdich asked Crawford to sign a *Miranda* waiver form, "Just to make things as clean as possible."

Crawford exclaimed, "So I'm under arrest?" Agent Bowdich and Detective Gutierrez assured him he was not under arrest and that he was free to leave. No further attempt to discuss Crawford's *Miranda* rights was made by either agent. At no point was Crawford threatened or made any promises. They questioned him for more than an hour, and eventually Crawford admitted both to participating in the Ulrich Street bank robbery and to carrying a gun in the course of that robbery. The officers ended the interview by returning Crawford to his home. He was indicted by a federal grand jury a few weeks later for the Ulrich Street bank robbery.

How will you decide this legal issue? Was Crawford's confession illegally obtained because it violated *Miranda* or because it was involuntary?

The Court's decision The U.S. Court of Appeals for the Ninth Circuit decided that Crawford's confession to the bank robbery was legally obtained; his confession was neither in conflict with his *Miranda* rights nor was it involuntarily obtained. He was not in police custody while in the FBI office. It was clear that he was free to leave. The atmosphere may have been a bit coercive, because of his presence in a police building and the presence of the two senior law enforcement officers, but this was not enough. The search of his house, assuming it was illegal, was separate enough in time to have no effect on the voluntary nature of his statements in the FBI office. If the search was to have any effect, it was to show Crawford that they had no physical evidence linking him to the robbery. *U.S. v. Crawford,* 372 F.3d 1048 (9th Cir. 2004).

In the United States Court of Appeals for the Second Circuit

In New York City, senior New York State Parole Officer Flot got a troubling call from a social worker. The worker reported that the mother of Newton, a parolee, had complained that Newton threatened to kill both his parents and kept a gun in the house where he lived with them. Newton had been paroled only nine months earlier from state incarceration on two convictions of robbery and one for drug trafficking. Officer Flot contacted Newton's supervising officer, Davis. Davis decided to make a "safety search" with two other parole officers of the apartment where Newton lived with his parents, and arrest Newton if they found a gun. He called the local precinct of the NYPD to ask for backup.

Accompanied by two other parole officers, and three NYPD officers, Officer Davis arrived at Newton's residence at about 8 A.M. After knocking for a long time, Newton opened the door in his underwear. Officer Davis asked Newton to step into the hallway, where Davis handcuffed him and told him he was not under arrest but was being restrained for his own safety and that of the officers. He was not read his *Miranda* rights.

Davis moved Newton in handcuffs back into the apartment, sat him in a chair, and asked him where his mother was. Newton said she was in the back of the apartment, where officers located her with his father and girlfriend. A parole officer asked Newton if there was any contraband in the apartment: he stated "only what's in the box" by the front door. The parole officer found a .22 caliber handgun and ammunition. Newton said the gun was for protection. He was placed under arrest within a minute of the officers' initial entry.

How will you decide this legal issue? Was the questioning by Davis an improper interrogation because Newton was handcuffed and not read his *Miranda* rights?

The Court's decision The U.S. Court of Appeals for the Second Circuit decided that the questioning of Newton about contraband was not "custodial" for the purposes of *Miranda*. Newton was held very briefly—just while a search was conducted that lasted less than a minute. He was told why he was being held, and he was held in his home. Although he was not free to leave during that minute, the "free to leave" test is not the complete inquiry. The coercive nature of the situation and its similarity to an arrest are also relevant. This was not similar enough to an arrest, in duration, location, or purpose to trigger the requirements of *Miranda*. *U.S. v. Newton*, 369 F.3d 659 (2nd Cir. 2004).

Recommended Readings

Criminal procedure—Application of the harmless error rule to Miranda (Miranda v. Arizona, *86 S.Ct. 1602) violations.* Western New England Law Review 109–144 (1992).

Steven A. Drizin and Beth A. Colgan. *Let the cameras roll: Mandatory videotaping of interrogations is the solution to Illinois' problem of false confessions.* 32 Loyola University Chicago Law Journal 337–424 (2001).

Karen L. Guy and Robert G. Huckabee. *Going free on a technicality: Another look at the effect of the* Miranda *decisions on the criminal justice process.* 4 Criminal Justice Research Bulletin 1, 3 (1988).

Fred E. Inbau. *Law and police practice: Restrictions on the law of interrogation and confessions.* 89 Journal of Criminal Law and Criminology 1393, 1403 (1999).

Charles D. Weisselberg. *Saving* Miranda (Miranda v. Arizona, *86 S.Ct. 1602 [1966]).* Cornell Law Review 109–192 (1998).

David A. Wollin. *Policing the police: Should* Miranda (Miranda v. Arizona, *86 S.Ct. 1602 [1996]) violations bear fruit?* 53 Ohio State Law Journal 805–868 (1992).

Notes

1. Lloyd L. Weinreb and James D. Whaley, *The Field Guide to Law Enforcement* (Westbury, NY: Foundation Press, 1999), p. 79.

2. G. M. Caplan, *Modern Procedures for Police Interrogation* (Washington, D.C.: Police Executive Research Forum, n.d.), p. 2.

3. Ibid.

Chapter **12** Constitutional Rights of the Accused during the Trial

What You Will Learn

- There are ten basic rights given to an accused during a trial.

- Defendants have the right to trial by jury in all serious offenses; jurors cannot be disqualified because of race or gender.

- Defendants need counsel during trials. There is a process for appointing lawyers, and defendants are entitled to "effective counsel."

- A defense lawyer's loyalty is to the client, not to society.

- Due process requires that evidence favorable to the accused must be disclosed by the prosecution; otherwise, the conviction is unconstitutional.

- The privilege against self-incrimination has different meanings for the accused and for witnesses, and it applies only to testimonial, not physical, self-incrimination.

- Double jeopardy applies to "same offense" and "lesser included offense."

- Defendants have the right to confront witnesses and to be present at all stages of the trial.

- The right to a fair trial may be controlled by the court in a number of ways.

The Top **5** Important Cases on the Rights of the Accused during Trial

***Gideon v. Wainwright* (1963)** The Sixth Amendment right to counsel is applicable to state proceedings through the Due Process Clause of the Fourteenth Amendment. The right to counsel applies every time an accused is charged with a felony offense.

***Batson v. Kentucky* (1986)** A prosecutor's use of peremptory challenges to exclude members of the defendant's race from the jury solely on racial grounds violates the equal protection rights of both the defendant and the excluded jurors.

***Lockhart v. McCree* (1986)** Persons who are unwilling to vote for the death penalty under any circumstances may be disqualified from a capital offense jury.

***J. E. B. v. Alabama* (1994)** The Equal Protection Clause prohibits discrimination based on gender in the selection of jurors.

***Apprendi v. New Jersey* (2000)** Judges may not alone determine a finding of fact that increases the level of punishment for the defendant beyond the prescribed statutory maximum. Any fact, other than the fact of prior conviction, must be submitted to a jury and proved beyond a reasonable doubt. A finding of fact cannot be made by the judge alone, based on a lower degree of certainty.

The Right to Proof of Guilt beyond a Reasonable Doubt
What Must Be Proved
Reasonable Doubt

Introduction

It is better that ten guilty persons escape than that one innocent suffer.
—Sir William Blackstone (1723–1780)

The individual rights guaranteed in the Bill of Rights are most carefully protected during the trial stage of a criminal proceeding. This is when the adversarial proceeding is at its peak. The government is represented by the prosecutor, and the accused's rights are championed by the defense counsel, who has been either retained by the accused or appointed by the state. The judge, a neutral party, presides over the trial, setting the rules for the lawyers to follow. In bench trials, the judge also determines the facts; in jury trials, that function is performed by the jury. The Constitution guarantees the accused fundamental rights during trial, the most important of which are discussed in this chapter. The ten constitutional rights discussed in this chapter cannot be diminished or taken away by federal or state laws. On the other hand, states and the federal governments may, by law or court decisions, grant *more* rights than those given in the Constitution. In sum, states and the federal government cannot diminish the rights given in the Constitution, but they can add more rights. Three examples illustrate this.

■ *Example 1.* There is no constitutional right to a twelve-member jury trial, but the federal government and most states provide for twelve-member juries by statute or by provision in the state constitution.
■ *Example 2.* The Constitution does not guarantee a defendant the right to appeal a criminal conviction, but the federal government and all states provide for the right to appeal, by either state law or a provision of the state constitution.
■ *Example 3.* There is no constitutional right to a jury trial in juvenile proceedings, but a jury hearing may be given by state law.

The Right to a Trial by Jury

Article III, Section 2, Clause 3 of the Constitution provides that "[t]he Trial of all Crimes, except in cases of Impeachment, shall be by Jury." The Sixth Amendment also provides that "In all criminal prosecutions, the accused shall enjoy the right to a speedy and public trial, by an impartial jury of the State and district wherein the crime shall have been committed."

We will look at issues surrounding trial by jury, including (1) the size of the jury; (2) unanimous versus nonunanimous verdicts; (3) serious versus petty offenses; (4) waivers; (5) the selection of the jury; (6) disqualification based on race or gender; (7) the constitutionality of death-qualified juries; and (8) the strengthening of the role of juries in sentencing.

Jury Size

Williams v. Florida (1970)

See Appendix C for information on how to find cases in this chapter on FindLaw.com.

Ballew v. Georgia (1978)

A jury of twelve is not required by the Sixth Amendment in criminal or civil trials; that number, however, is often required by state or federal law. In *Williams v. Florida* (399 U.S. 78 [1970]), the Supreme Court upheld a Florida law providing for a six-member jury in all state criminal cases except those involving capital offenses. The minimum number of jurors is six. Juries of fewer than six members are unconstitutional, because there would be too few jurors to provide for effective group discussion and it would diminish the chances of drawing from a fair, representative cross-section of the community—thus, impairing the accuracy of fact-finding (*Ballew v. Georgia,* 435 U.S. 223 [1978]). Although most juries are composed of either twelve or six members, any number between six and twelve is constitutional. Whether death penalty cases can be decided by juries of fewer than twelve is an issue the Court has not addressed. Given the severity of the punishment involved, the Court probably would not approve a jury of fewer than twelve people in death penalty cases.

Unanimous versus Nonunanimous Verdicts

Apodaca v. Oregon (1972)

Johnson v. Louisiana (1972)

The Constitution does not require that guilty verdicts in criminal cases be unanimous. In federal criminal cases, a unanimous jury verdict is required, but a **nonunanimous verdict** suffices in some state trials. For example, in *Apodaca v. Oregon* (406 U.S. 404 [1972]), the Court held that a 10-to-2 vote for conviction is constitutional. And in *Johnson v. Louisiana* (406 U.S. 356 [1972]), the Court upheld the constitutionality of a 9-to-3 vote for conviction. The Court has not decided whether an 8-to-4 or a 7-to-5 vote for conviction would also be constitutional.

What this means is that a state can provide for a less-than unanimous verdict for conviction (usually by law) and that such a procedure is constitutional. Currently, forty-five states require unanimity in criminal cases, but twenty-nine states do not require unanimity in civil trials. The vote needed to convict varies among jurisdictions that do not require unanimity, ranging from two-thirds in Montana to five-sixths in Oregon. All states require a unanimous verdict in capital cases. The Court prohibits a finding of guilty by less than a six-person majority; therefore, in a six-person criminal trial, the jury must always be unanimous in finding guilt.[1]

The Court has rejected the argument that permitting a nonunanimous verdict violates the reasonable doubt standard for conviction in criminal cases, saying that disagreement among jurors would not in itself establish that there was a reasonable doubt as to the defendant's guilt. Reasonable doubt refers to the thinking of an individual juror, not to a split vote among the jurors. A **hung jury** is a jury that cannot come to a unanimous agreement (in jurisdictions where unanimity is required) to convict or to acquit. When this happens, the defendant can be tried again at the discretion of the prosecutor. There is no constitutional limit to the number of times an accused can be tried again after a hung jury. This decision is left to the discretion of the prosecutor.

Serious versus Petty Offenses

Despite the wording of Article III, Section 2, Clause 3 of the Constitution, which states that "the Trial of all Crimes . . . shall be by Jury," the Court has ruled that the Constitution guarantees a jury trial only when a *serious offense* is charged. Such offenses must be distinguished from mere "petty" offenses. For purposes of the constitutional right to a trial by jury, a **serious offense** is one for which more than six months' imprisonment is authorized (*Baldwin v. New York,* 399 U.S. 66 [1970]). In making this determination, courts look at the maximum possible sentence that may be imposed. An offense is considered serious if the maximum punishment authorized by statute is imprisonment for more than six months, regardless of the penalty actually imposed; therefore, the accused is entitled to a jury trial. For example, suppose X is tried for theft, the maximum penalty for which is one year in jail. If X is denied a jury trial, convicted, and sentenced to five months in jail, the conviction must be reversed because it violates X's right to a trial by jury even though the actual penalty imposed was less than six months.

Baldwin v. New York (1970)

By contrast, an offense whose maximum penalty is six months or less is **"petty"** for purposes of the right to trial by jury (regardless of how that offense is classified by state law); therefore, the defendant has no constitutional right to a jury trial. The Court has ruled that when a state treats drunk driving as a petty offense, no jury trial is needed even if other peripheral sanctions (such as a fine and automatic loss of one's driver's license) may also be imposed (*Blanton v. North Las Vegas,* 489 U.S. 538 [1989]). Some states classify drunk driving as a serious offense for which the maximum penalty is more than six months of confinement. In those states, a jury trial is constitutionally required. In a 1996 case, the Court held that a defendant who is prosecuted in a single case for more than one petty offense does not have a constitutional right to a trial by jury even if the total penalty exceeds six months (*Lewis v. United States,* 59 CrL 2206 [1996]).

Blanton v. North Las Vegas (1989)

In *Lewis,* the defendant was charged in a single proceeding with two counts of mail obstruction. Each charge carried a penalty of six months' imprisonment. The defendant argued that he was entitled to a jury trial because he faced a total imprisonment of up to one year for the two petty offenses. On appeal, the Court disagreed, saying that the "scope of the Sixth Amendment does not change just because a defendant faces multiple charges" and that "the maximum penalty is an

Lewis v. United States (1996)

objective criterion that reveals the legislature's judgment about the offense's severity." The Court added, "Where we have a judgment by the legislature that an offense is petty, we do not look to the potential prison term faced by a particular defendant who is charged with more than one such petty offense."

In sum, the maximum authorized penalty for one offense determines whether a defendant is entitled to a jury trial, not the total penalty the defendant faces in cases of multiple charges. If no punishment is prescribed by statute, the offense is considered petty when the actual sentence imposed is six months or less.

Waiver of a Jury Trial

Singer v. United States (1965)

The right to a trial by jury may be waived by the accused, provided the waiver is *express* and *intelligent*. In some cases, however, the prosecution has the right to demand a jury trial even if the defendant waives it. This is because criminal defendants have no constitutional right to waive a jury trial and have their cases tried before a judge alone (*Singer v. United States,* 380 U.S. 24 [1965]). For example, in states where the death penalty may be imposed only by a jury, the prosecutor may insist on a jury trial even if the defendant waives that right and chooses to be tried by a judge in an effort to escape the death penalty. In these cases, the prosecution may demand a jury trial. The prosecutor's demand takes precedence over an accused's waiver of a jury trial.

The Selection of a Jury of Peers

Taylor v. Louisiana (1975)

The Supreme Court interpretation of the Sixth Amendment requires that trial juries in both federal and state criminal trials be selected from "a representative cross-section of the community." It also guarantees trial by a **jury of peers**. That phrase does not mean that, say, a student facing criminal charges must have a jury of students or that female defendants must have an all-female jury. What it does mean is that *jury service cannot be consciously restricted to a particular group.* For example, excluding women from juries or giving them automatic exemptions, with the result that jury panels are almost totally male, is invalid (*Taylor v. Louisiana,* 419 U.S. 522 [1975]). Likewise, the exclusion of persons because of race, creed, color, or national origin is unconstitutional.

The Disqualification of Jurors Based on Race

Batson v. Kentucky (1986)

A prosecutor's use of **peremptory challenges**—challenges for which no reason is stated, as opposed to **challenges for cause**, for which legal reasons for the challenge must be stated—to exclude members of the defendant's race from a jury solely on racial grounds violates the equal protection rights of both the defendant and the excluded jurors (*Batson v. Kentucky,* 476 U.S. 79 [1986]). In *Batson v. Kentucky* (1986), a trial judge in Kentucky conducted the examination of the jury and excused certain jurors for cause. After that, the prosecutor used his peremptory challenges to strike all four black persons from the jury pool, resulting in an all-white jury. On appeal, the Court reaffirmed the principle announced in an 1880 case (*Strauder v. West Virginia*, 100 U.S. 303 [1880]), saying that "the State denies a black defendant equal protection of the laws when it puts him on trial before a jury from which members of his race have been purposefully excluded." Interestingly, however, the prosecution's racially motivated use of peremptory challenges to exclude people from the trial jury does not violate the defendant's Sixth Amendment right to a trial by an impartial jury (*Holland v. Illinois*, 493 U.S. 474 [1990]). But the Court did hint that such a challenge could have been raised as a violation of the constitutional right to equal protection under the Fourteenth Amendment. Because that challenge was not raised in this case, the result was different from that of *Batson*.

Strauder v. West Virginia (1880)

Holland v. Illinois (1990)

In *Batson*, the Court outlined the three steps courts must follow in resolving cases of peremptory jury disqualification based on race:

- *Step 1.* The side making the allegation must establish a *prima facie* (meaning at first sight) case of discrimination based on race or other forbidden grounds.
- *Step 2.* If Step 1 is established, then the burden shifts to the side that made the peremptory strike to come up with a race-neutral explanation for the strike.
- *Step 3.* The trial court is then required to decide whether the side opposing the peremptory challenges has proved purposeful discrimination.

To illustrate the three-step process, suppose defendant X is tried and convicted by an all-white jury. X alleges that potential African American jurors were scratched from the jury pool by the prosecutor because of race. If X establishes a prima facie case that race was, in fact, the reason for their disqualifications (admittedly difficult to do in peremptory challenges because no reason is given), then the burden shifts to the prosecutor to establish that race was not the basis for removing them from the jury pool. The trial court then must decide whether X has, in fact, proved discrimination based on race.

Johnson v. California (2005)

In a 2005 case, *Johnson v. California* (125 S.Ct. 2410 [2005]), the Court held that "permissible inferences of discrimination were sufficient to establish a prima facie case of discrimination under *Batson*, shifting the burden to the state to explain adequately the racial exclusion by offering permissible race-neutral justifications for the strikes." These "permissible inferences of discrimination" make it easier for defendants to challenge racial discrimination during peremptory challenges (where no reason needs to be given by either side when striking a juror from the list, which often results in disqualification of racial minorities).

Georgia v. McCullum (1992)

The Court has also held that the Constitution prohibits a criminal defendant, as well as the prosecution, from engaging in purposeful discrimination on the grounds of race in the exercise of peremptory challenges (*Georgia v. McCullum*, 505 U.S. 42 [1992]). In that case, several white defendants were charged with assaulting two African Americans. Before the jury selection process began, the trial judge denied the prosecution's motion to prohibit defendants from exercising their peremptory challenges in a racially discriminatory manner, as the prosecution expected the defendants would do.

On appeal, the Court said that in previous cases it had held that the exercise of racially discriminatory peremptory challenges violates the Equal Protection Clause of the Fourteenth Amendment when the offending challenges are made by the state and, in civil cases, when they are made by private litigants. Using a four-factor analysis, the Court held that the prohibition should also be extended to discriminatory challenges made by criminal defendants.

May a white defendant object to the exclusion of black jurors from the jury through the use of a peremptory challenge, and vice versa? The answer is yes. The defendant does not need to be a member of the group excluded to invoke successfully the Equal Protection Clause (*Powers v. Ohio,* 499 U.S. 400 [1991]). In *Powers v. Ohio* (1991), Powers, a white man, objected to the prosecution's use of peremptory challenges to remove seven African Americans from the jury. The Court upheld his challenge on appeal, saying that under the Equal Protection Clause a defendant may object to the race-based exclusion of jurors through peremptory challenges even though the defendant and the excluded jurors are not of the same race. And, in a 1998 case, the Court extended that decision, ruling that a white defendant had reason to complain of discrimination against blacks in the selection of the grand jury (*Campbell v. Louisiana,* 523 U.S. 392 [1998]).

Powers v. Ohio (1991)

Campbell v. Louisiana (1998)

The Disqualification of Jurors Based on Gender

J. E. B. v. Alabama (1994)

In an important case decided in 1994, *J. E. B. v. Alabama* (511 U.S. 127 [1994]), the Court held that the Constitution forbids discrimination in the selection of jurors based on "gender" or "on the assumption that an individual will be biased in a particular case solely because the person happens to be a woman or a man." This case involved a paternity and child support trial in which the state used nine of its ten peremptory challenges to remove male jurors, resulting in an all-female civil jury. The state assumed that male jurors would be biased in favor of a man in a child support–paternity lawsuit.

In holding that the disqualifications violated the Equal Protection Clause, the Court said that "the conclusion that litigants may not strike potential jurors solely on the basis of gender does not imply the elimination of all peremptory challenges," as some had feared, adding that "so long as gender does not serve as a proxy for bias, unacceptable jurors may still be removed, including those who are members of a group or class that is normally subject to 'rational basis' review and those who exhibit characteristics that are disproportionately associated with one gender." Although this case involved peremptory challenges in a civil case, there is every reason to believe that it also applies to criminal cases in terms of both peremptory challenges and challenges for cause. (To learn more about this case, read the Case Brief.)

The principles and cases involving challenges based on race and gender represent an attempt by the Court to ensure that all juries are selected in a nondiscriminatory manner and that race and gender are not factors, whether in challenges for cause or in peremptory challenges. However, because peremptory challenges are made without giving reasons, it is difficult to determine whether a peremptory challenge is based on race—unless the results are clear, obvious, and can be proved, or one party admits to such bias.

The controversy over peremptory challenges based on race and gender may extend to similar challenges based on other grounds. Although discrimination based on race and gender has generated the most heat and attention in recent years, factors such as lifestyle, mental disability, religion, class, ethnicity, national origin, occupation, economics, and physical status may gain prominence in an era of inclusion and increasing diversity. Although some of these issues have been raised in lower courts, the U.S. Supreme Court has thus far not addressed them, continuing instead to focus on race and gender.

CASE BRIEF: Leading Case on Gender Discrimination in Jury Trials
J. E. B. v. Alabama, 511 U.S. 127 (1994)

Facts: The state of Alabama filed a complaint for paternity and child support against J. E. B. on behalf of the mother of a minor child. The trial court assembled a panel of 36 potential jurors—12 males and 24 females. Three jurors were excused for cause, leaving 10 males and 23 females in the jury pool. The state of Alabama used nine out of its ten peremptory challenges to remove male jurors; the petitioner used nine strikes to remove female jurors. The result was an all-female jury. Even before the jury was impaneled, the petitioner objected to the peremptory challenges by the state, saying that they were exercised against male jurors solely on the basis of gender. Trial was held, and the jury found the petitioner to be the father of the child; he was ordered to pay child support. He appealed.

Issue: *Does the Constitution prohibit discrimination in jury selection based on gender? Yes.*

Supreme Court Decision: "The Equal Protection Clause of the Constitution prohibits discrimination in jury selection on the basis of gender, or on the assumption that an individual will be biased in a particular case solely because that person happens to be a woman or a man."

Case Significance: This case extends the *Batson* ruling, which prohibits discrimination based on race on jury peremptory challenges, to discrimination based on gender, hence proscribing both types of discrimination. The petitioner in this case was a man who alleged that his equal protection rights were violated because the state of Alabama used its peremptory challenges to strike males from the jury, the result being an all-female jury that found him to be the father of the child and required him to pay child support. The Court upheld the challenge, saying that gender discrimination in jury selection is unconstitutional. The Court added, however, that "[t]he conclusion that litigants may not strike potential jurors solely on the basis of gender does not imply the elimination of all peremptory challenges. So long as gender does not serve as a proxy for bias, unacceptable jurors may still be removed, including those who are members of a group or class that is normally subject to 'rational basis' review and those who exhibit characteristics that are dis-

---

proportionately associated with one gender." What is prohibited are challenges based on bias simply because a potential juror is a male or a female and is therefore expected to vote in a certain way. Peremptory challenges based in gender bias are usually difficult to prove because they are made without reasons given. There are cases such as this one, however, in which the obvious reason for the strikes was gender bias. In these types of cases, the constitutional prohibition applies.

Excerpts from the Decision: Discrimination in jury selection, whether based on race or on gender, causes harm to the litigants, the community, and the individual jurors who are wrongfully excluded from participation in the judicial process. The litigants are harmed by the risk that the prejudice which motivated the discriminatory selection of the jury will infect the entire proceedings. The community is harmed by the State's participation in the perpetuation of invidious group stereotypes

and the inevitable loss of confidence in our judicial system that state sanctioned discrimination in the courtroom engenders.

When state actors exercise peremptory challenges in reliance on gender stereotypes, they ratify and reinforce prejudicial views of the relative abilities of men and women. Because these stereotypes have wreaked injustice in so many other spheres of our country's public life, active discrimination by litigants on the basis of gender during jury selection "invites cynicism respecting the jury's neutrality and its obligation to adhere to the law." The potential for cynicism is particularly acute in cases where gender related issues are prominent, such as cases involving rape, sexual harassment, or paternity. Discriminatory use of peremptory challenges may create the impression that the judicial system has acquiesced in suppressing full participation by one gender or that the "deck has been stacked" in favor of one side.

The Constitutionality of "Death-Qualified Juries"

The so-called **death-qualified juries** are "conviction prone" juries, meaning they are more likely to convict and impose the death penalty because potential jurors whose opposition to the death penalty is so strong it prevents or impairs the performance of their duties at the sentencing phase are disqualified from it. In death penalty cases, the Court has held that death-qualified juries do not violate a defendant's right to a jury trial and are constitutional (*Lockhart v. McCree,* 476 U.S. 162 [1986]).

Lockhart v. McCree (1986)

In *Lockhart v. McCree* (1986), McCree was charged with capital felony murder after being arrested when he was found driving a car that matched an eyewitness's description of a vehicle seen driving away from the scene of a robbery and murder. McCree admitted to being in the shop at the time of the crime but claimed a stranger had done the killing using McCree's rifle. During the jury selection, the judge removed for cause (meaning as allowed by law) prospective jurors who stated that they could not vote for the imposition of the death penalty under any circumstances. McCree was convicted and given life imprisonment without parole. He appealed his conviction, saying the removal of jurors who were strongly opposed to the death penalty violated his right to trial by jury. (Read the Case Brief to learn more about this case.)

The Court disagreed, holding instead that a death-qualified jury does not violate the "fair section" requirement of the Sixth Amendment as long as the jury reflected the composition of the community at large. Note, however, that potential jurors cannot be excluded from a death penalty trial simply because they oppose the death penalty (*Witherspoon v. Illinois,* 391 U.S. 510 [1968]).

Witherspoon v. Illinois (1968)

CASE BRIEF: The Leading Case on Death-Qualified Juries

Lockhart v. McCree, 476 U.S. 162 (1986)

Facts: McCree was charged with capital felony murder. He was arrested when found driving a car that matched an eyewitness's description of a vehicle seen driving away from a gift shop/gas station where a robbery and murder of the owner had just taken place. McCree admitted to being in the shop at the time of the murder but claimed that a stranger had done the killing, using McCree's rifle. McCree said that the stranger then rode in McCree's car for a short time, got out, and walked away with the rifle. This story was refuted by eyewitnesses who had seen only one person in the car during the time when McCree claimed he had a passenger. The rifle was located and ballistics tests identified it as the murder weapon.

During jury selection in McCree's trial, the judge removed for cause prospective jurors who stated that they could not vote for the imposition of the death penalty under any circumstances. The jury convicted McCree of capital felony murder but did not impose the death penalty as the state had requested. Instead, McCree was given life imprisonment without parole.

Issue: *Does the Constitution allow the removal for cause, during the guilt phase of a capital trial, of prospective jurors whose opposition to the death penalty is so great as to substantially impair their performance as jurors at the sentencing phase of the trial? Yes.*

Court Decision: Persons who are unwilling to vote for the death penalty under any circum-

stances may be disqualified from a capital offense jury.

Case Significance: Prospective jurors whose opposition to the death penalty is so strong as to prevent or impair the performance of their duties as jurors at the sentencing phase of a trial may be removed for cause from jury membership. In an earlier case, *Witherspoon v. Illinois* (391 U.S. 510 [1968]), the Court said that an Illinois law that allowed prosecutors to exclude potential jurors who had conscientious scruples against capital punishment or were merely opposed to it violated the defendant's right to due process because it stacked the jury in favor of the death penalty. *McCree* goes beyond that kind of a law, because the judge had removed for cause prospective jurors who stated that they could not vote for the imposition of the death penalty under any circumstances. The Court said that such disqualification was constitutional (a practice that led to "death qualified" juries). The difference between *Witherspoon* and *McCree* is this: The law at issue in *Witherspoon* (which allowed the disqualification of potential jurors who had conscientious scruples or were merely opposed to the death penalty) violated the defendant's right to a neutral jury, whereas the practice used in *McCree* (which allowed the disqualification of jurors whose opposition to the death penalty was so great as to substantially impair their performance as jurors at the sentencing stage of the trial) nonetheless preserved the defendant's right to a neutral jury in that a jury member could not be neutral if he or she would in essence refuse to vote for a death sentence regardless of circumstances. This principle was first articulated by the Supreme Court in *Adams v. Texas*, 448 U.S. 38 (1980). *McCree* followed the precedent set in that case.

Excerpts from the Decision: "Death qualification" of a jury does not violate the fair cross-section requirement of the Sixth Amendment, which applies to jury panels or venires but does not require that petit juries actually chosen reflect the composition of the community at large. Even if the requirement were extended to petit juries, the essence of a fair cross-section claim is the systematic exclusion of a "distinctive group" in the community—such as blacks, women, and Mexican-

Americans—for reasons completely unrelated to the ability of members of the group to serve as jurors in a particular case. Groups defined solely in terms of shared attitudes that would prevent or substantially impair members of the group from performing one of their duties as jurors, such as the "Witherspoon-excludables" at issue here, are not "distinctive groups" for fair cross-section purposes. "Death qualification" is carefully designed to serve the State's legitimate interest in obtaining a single jury that can properly and impartially apply the law to the facts of the case at both the guilt and sentencing phases of a capital trial.

SOURCE: This case brief also appears in Rolando V. del Carmen et al., *Briefs of Leading Cases in Corrections*, 4th ed. (Anderson Publishing, 2005), pp. 214–215.

The Strengthening of the Role of Juries in Sentencing

Apprendi v. New Jersey (2000)

The role of juries in criminal trials has been greatly strengthened by the Court in recent decisions. In *Apprendi v. New Jersey* (530 U.S. 466 [2000]), the Court held that judges may not alone determine a finding of fact that increases the level of punishment for the defendant beyond the prescribed statutory maximum. Moreover, a finding of fact cannot be based on a lower degree of certainty; any fact, "other than the fact of prior conviction, must be submitted to a jury and proved beyond a reasonable doubt."

Reaffirming that "the jury tradition . . . is an indispensable part of our criminal justice system," the Court held unconstitutional a New Jersey statute that allowed a judge to impose a punishment for second-degree offenses that was similar to that for first-degree crimes on a finding "by a mere preponderance of the evidence, that the defendant's purpose was to intimidate his victim based on the victim's particular characteristic." This meant that in New Jersey at that time the judge could increase the sentence beyond the maximum imposed by law for that particular offense if he or she found that the criminal act constituted a "hate crime." The Court said that "the Fourteenth Amendment right to due process and the Sixth Amendment right to trial by jury, taken together, entitle a criminal defendant to a jury determination that he is guilty of every element of the crime with which he is charged, beyond a reasonable doubt."

Two years later, the *Apprendi* decision was extended by the Court to death penalty cases, holding that it is unconstitutional for judges to make findings of aggravating factors that increase the penalty from life in prison to the death penalty

Ring v. Arizona (2002)

(*Ring v. Arizona*, 536 U.S. 584 [2002]). The Court concluded that a finding by the judge of an aggravating circumstance (which the judge was authorized to do under Arizona death penalty law) after a jury trial was "the functional equivalent of an element of a greater offense than the one covered by the jury's guilty verdict," and therefore violated the defendant's right to a jury trial.

The Right to Counsel

The Sixth Amendment to the Constitution provides that "in all criminal prosecutions, the accused shall enjoy the right . . . to have the Assistance of Counsel for his defence." This right has been held applicable to the states since the 1963 decision in *Gideon v. Wainwright* (372 U.S. 335 [1963]). A defendant has the right to be represented by counsel at "every critical stage" of the criminal proceeding. The meaning of the term *critical stage* has been determined by the Court on a case-by-case basis. One source states that a "stage is critical if the defendant is compelled [because of the nature of the proceedings] to make a decision which may later be formally used against him."[2]

Gideon v. Wainwright (1963)

The right to counsel is available throughout the criminal justice process but is constitutionally required in the following proceedings:

- Custodial interrogations (the *Miranda* warnings)
- Lineups, if formal charges have been filed
- Preliminary examination

- Arraignment
- Trial (discussed in this chapter)
- Sentencing
- Appeal from a conviction, if available to others

A lawyer is not required by the constitution in the following proceedings but may be by state or federal law:

- Criminal investigation
- Arrest, unless the suspect is interrogated
- Grand jury proceedings
- Habeas corpus proceedings
- Probation or parole revocation

HIGHLIGHT

*The Full Extent of the Constitutional Right to a Lawyer in Criminal Proceedings**

Type and Sequence of Proceedings[†]	Right to a Lawyer?
1. Criminal investigation	No
2. Arrest	No, unless interrogated
3. Custodial interrogation	Yes (*Miranda* warnings required)
4. Lineups	Yes, if formal charges have been filed No, if formal charges have not been filed
5. Preliminary examination	Yes
6. Grand jury (in states where required)	No
7. Arraignment	Yes
8. Trial	Yes, except for offenses that do not involve jail or prison time
9. Sentencing	Yes, except for offenses that do not involve jail or prison time
10. Appeal from conviction	Yes, if available to others
11. Habeas corpus (after appeal is exhausted)	No, but may be given by state or federal law
12. Probation revocation	No, but may be given by state law
13. Parole revocation	No, but may be given by state law

*BASIS: The Sixth Amendment right to counsel. The lawyer is either retained by the defendant or provided by the state if the defendant is indigent. No clear guidelines have been set as to whom is indigent. Trial court judges make that decision.

[†]The standard the U.S. Supreme Court uses to determine whether the right to a lawyer is given by the Constitution is: Is the proceeding a "critical stage"? That is, is the defendant "compelled to make a decision which may later be formally used against him or her"?

This chapter discusses only a small, but the most important, slice of the right to counsel pie—the right to counsel during trial. We will examine why counsel is needed; how it is obtained; the responsibility of the defense lawyer; the right to a court-appointed attorney during trial; the difficulty of proving ineffective counsel and claims of ineffective counsel during death penalty cases; and the right to act as one's own counsel.

Why Counsel Is Needed

Powell v. Alabama (1932)

In a celebrated case of long ago, the Court stated the justification for the right to counsel in criminal proceedings in the case of *Powell v. Alabama* (287 U.S. 45 [1932]). The *Powell* case was one of the two famous "Scottsboro cases" (the other was *Norris v. Alabama,* 294 U.S. 587 [1935]), in which nine black youths were charged with the rape of two white girls. Justice Sutherland wrote this often-quoted statement on why an accused needs counsel during the trial:

> Even the intelligent and educated layman has small and sometimes no skill in the science of the law. Left without aid of counsel, he may be put on trial without a proper charge, and convicted upon incompetent evidence irrelevant to the issue or otherwise inadmissible against him. Without counsel, though he may not be guilty, he faces the danger of conviction because he does not know how to establish his innocence.

Iowa v. Tovar (2004)

Despite the importance of the assistance of a lawyer during trial, as this quotation indicates, the Court in 2004 held that if a defendant says that he or she wishes to plead guilty without the assistance of counsel, the trial judge need not spell out all the possible consequences before accepting the plea (*Iowa v. Tovar,* 541 U.S. 77 [2004]). For the waiver of the right to counsel during the plea stage to be "full knowing, intelligent, and voluntary," it is enough that the trial court inform the accused of the nature of the charges filed, the right to have counsel, and the possible range of penalties the court can impose. There is no need for the accused to be informed that his defense will be jeopardized or that he or she will lose the opportunity to get an independent opinion of whether it is prudent to plead guilty.

How Counsel Is Obtained

The term *right to counsel* refers to either retained counsel or court-appointed counsel. Most of the discussion here is limited to the right to court-appointed counsel, because most criminal cases deal only with that issue. However, we begin with a discussion of retained counsel.

Retained Counsel
Retained counsel is *an attorney chosen and paid by the accused.* According to two noted legal authorities, Wayne LaFave and Jerold Israel, "the state has no Sixth Amendment obligation to allow representation by retained counsel in a proceeding as to which it has no Sixth Amendment obligation to appoint counsel for the indigent." They add, however, that jurisdictions usually

allow retained counsel to be present even in proceedings involving misdemeanors punishable only by a fine—offenses for which the Constitution does not require states to provide counsel to indigents.[3]

A defendant's right to hire an attorney of his or her own choosing (as opposed to an attorney provided by the state for an indigent) may be limited by the trial court to avoid a possible conflict of interest (*Wheat v. United States,* 486 U.S. 153 [1988]). In *Wheat v. United States* (1988), the defendant and others were charged with conspiracy to distribute drugs. Two days before trial, one of the defendants asked to replace his counsel with an attorney who represented two of the other alleged co-conspirators. These two co-conspirators had either already pleaded guilty to the charges or were getting ready to do so. The prosecution objected to the change of counsel, alleging conflict of interest if the same defense lawyer represented all three defendants because, for some reason, that would have limited cross-examination by the prosecutor.

Wheat v. United States (1988)

The trial court refused to allow the change of counsel by the defendant, saying that it would indeed create a conflict of interest, a decision upheld by the Court on appeal. In sum, a defendant's right to hire his or her own lawyer may be limited by the trial court if there is a compelling justification for it, such as a conflict of interest.

Court-Appointed Counsel Court-appointed counsel is an attorney appointed by the judge and paid by the county or state to represent an "indigent" accused at a "critical stage" in the criminal proceedings. More than half of felony defendants are classified as indigents, yet the Court has not set a uniform rule to determine indigency. In general, however, a defendant is **indigent** if he or she is too poor to hire a lawyer. Standards used by judges include being unemployed, not having a car, not having posted bail, and not having a house. The judge enjoys wide discretion in determining indigency, and that determination is rarely reversed on appeal. Indigency therefore varies from one jurisdiction or judge to another. The American Bar Association recommends the following standard: "Counsel should be provided to any person who is financially unable to obtain adequate representation without substantial hardship to himself or his family." It adds that a lawyer should not be denied "to any person merely because his friends or relatives have resources adequate to retain counsel or because he has posted or is capable of posting bond."[4]

The method of appointing counsel for an indigent defendant also varies. In some jurisdictions, judges use a list containing the names of available and willing attorneys, who are then assigned to cases on a rotational basis. In others, judges make assignments at random, assigning any lawyer who may be available in the courtroom at the time of the appointment. Still other jurisdictions employ full-time public defenders to handle indigent cases. The decision to create a public defender's office is usually driven by considerations of cost-effectiveness. From an economic perspective, the bigger the city or county, the more attractive the public defender model becomes.

An indigent defendant has no right to designate an attorney of his or her choice. The selection of a defense lawyer is made purely at the discretion of the court, although the judge may allow the accused some input in the process. Some states provide counsel to defendants but specify as a condition of probation or

Fuller v. Oregon
(1974)

parole that the defendant reimburse the state or county for the fees of the appointed lawyer. Such laws are valid as long as they exempt indigents who cannot afford to pay (*Fuller v. Oregon,* 417 U.S. 40 [1974]).

The Responsibility of the Defense Lawyer

It may surprise and disappoint many victims of crime to learn that, in the American system of justice, the loyalty of a defense lawyer is not to the public but solely to the client. This means that a lawyer is not an agent of the state but instead is obligated to give the client the best possible defense, whether the client is innocent or guilty. In the American system of justice, lawyers have an obligation to defend the guilty. Some lawyers do not even want to know whether their client is innocent or guilty, believing that guilt or innocence should not affect the way they do their job. This loyalty to the client comes from the adversarial model of criminal justice, in which both sides in a criminal case (the prosecution and the defense) are adversaries expected to fight fairly before a neutral judge or jury. Out of this fight, the truth is supposed to emerge. That does not always happen, but the system is supposed to work that way.

The limitations on the conduct of lawyers when defending a client come from two sources: a professional code of ethics and the penal code. A defense lawyer cannot do that which is *unethical* or *illegal*. Working for the good of the community is not among the responsibilities expected of a lawyer when defending an accused. To put it crudely, the welfare of the client is paramount; other considerations are unimportant. The conduct of lawyers is monitored by state bar associations and by the judiciary. The American Bar Association has promulgated Model Rules of Professional Conduct. States' codes of professional responsibility vary, although most codes or rules are based on the Model Rules of the ABA. The interpretation and enforcement of these rules may not conform to what the public expects, adding to the battered public image of the legal profession.

The Right to Court-Appointed Counsel during the Trial

Although the Sixth Amendment extends to "all criminal prosecutions," the Court has held that the right to court-appointed counsel applies only in the following types of criminal cases:

- The crime charged is a serious offense (*Gideon v. Wainwright,* 372 U.S. 335 [1963]).
- The crime charged is a misdemeanor for which the defendant faces a possible jail sentence (*Argersinger v. Hamlin,* 407 U.S. 25 [1972]).

Argersinger v. Hamlin (1972)

To illustrate these two decisions, suppose Y is charged with robbery, a serious offense in that jurisdiction. Y, if indigent, is entitled to court-appointed counsel during the trial. Y would also be entitled to a lawyer if indigent and charged with a misdemeanor for which he faced a possible jail sentence. However, if Y is charged with a traffic violation for which no jail sentence is attached, Y is not entitled to a lawyer.

Despite *Gideon* and *Argersinger,* the Court, in a 5-to-4 decision, later held that the state is not required to appoint counsel for an indigent defendant charged with a nonpetty offense that is punishable by imprisonment if the defendant is not, in fact, sentenced to prison (*Scott v. Illinois,* 440 U.S. 367 [1979]).

Scott v. Illinois (1979)

In *Scott,* the defendant was tried without a lawyer for the crime of theft (shoplifting). The maximum penalty prescribed by state law for the offense was a fine of $500 or a year in prison or both. Scott was convicted and sentenced to pay a fine of $50. On appeal, the Court affirmed the conviction, saying that the "federal Constitution does not require a state trial court to appoint counsel for a criminal defendant such as petitioner." Under *Scott,* the state is arguably not required to provide counsel, whether an indigent defendant is charged with a serious offense or a misdemeanor, if the defendant is not sentenced to prison (for example, when the judge assigns the defendant to community service or imposes a fine). Some observers note, however, that "states have the option of providing appointed counsel for all misdemeanor defendants, and many states follow that policy—at least where the misdemeanors are not punishable only by fine."[5] Although juvenile proceedings are not criminal in nature, a juvenile is nonetheless entitled to court-appointed counsel if the proceeding can lead to commitment in an institution in which the juvenile's freedom is restricted (*In re Gault,* 387 U.S. 1 [1967]).

In re Gault (1967)

The Difficulty of Proving Ineffective Assistance of Counsel

A defendant may challenge his or her conviction on the grounds that the lawyer at trial was so incompetent as to deprive the defendant of effective assistance of counsel. Although this claim is frequently raised, it is difficult to prove and therefore seldom succeeds. The meaning of "effective assistance of counsel" bothered lower courts for years because of the absence of a clear standard. However, in two 1984 cases, the Court clarified the issue by specifying the following criteria:

United States v. Cronic (1984)

- A claim of ineffective assistance of counsel can be made only by pointing out specific errors made by the trial counsel. It cannot be based on an inference drawn from the defense counsel's inexperience or lack of time to prepare, the gravity of the charges, the complexity of the defense, or the accessibility of witnesses to counsel (*United States v. Cronic,* 466 U.S. 648 [1984]).

- The Court assumes that effective assistance of counsel is present unless the adversarial process is so undermined by counsel's conduct that the trial cannot be relied upon to have produced a just result. An accused who claims ineffective counsel must show the following: (1) deficient performance by counsel and (2) a reasonable probability that but for such deficiency the result of the proceeding would have been different (*Strickland v. Washington,* 466 U.S. 668 [1984]).

Strickland v. Washington (1984)

Lockhart v. Fretwell (1993)

In a 1993 case, *Lockhart v. Fretwell* (506 U.S. 364 [1993]), however, the Court made the standard for reversal of conviction even more difficult: "To show prejudice under *Strickland,* a defendant must demonstrate that *counsel's errors are so serious as to deprive him of a trial whose result is fair or reliable, not merely that the outcome would have been different.*"

Under these standards, mere generalizations about the quality of the lawyer or the inadequacy of his or her efforts will not suffice. Specificity is required, and the burden is on the defendant to show a reasonable probability that if the lawyer's performance had not been deficient the results would have been different. This is difficult to establish, and, in most cases, the accused needs another lawyer who knows enough law to be able to prove this. For example, suppose that, after conviction, defendant X alleges that he had ineffective counsel because the lawyer assigned by the court to defend him (as an indigent) had limited experience handling criminal cases and finished last in his law school class. This will not suffice to establish ineffective counsel. Instead, X must specify the errors the defense lawyer committed that contributed to his conviction. Likewise, a mere error of law in advising a defendant to enter a guilty plea does not in itself constitute the denial of effective counsel. The test is whether the mistake was "within the range of competency" of most criminal defense lawyers. However, if the lawyer fails to follow state procedural rules, resulting in the dismissal of the appeal, this represents ineffective assistance of counsel.

Wiggins v. Smith (2003)

In a case involving a capital offender, the Court held that the defendant's Sixth Amendment right to effective counsel was violated by his lawyer's failure to conduct a reasonable investigation into his social history and mitigating factors (*Wiggins v. Smith,* 539 U.S. 510 [2003]). The Court said that the evidence that the lawyer failed to discover and present was "powerful" and could have made a difference in the sentence that was imposed (death); therefore, the defendant was prejudiced by the lawyer's poor performance. In another case, the Court held that the lawyer's closing argument in a case, in which he admitted some of the defendant's shortcomings, did not deprive the defendant of effective assistance of counsel, because the summation brought out several key points (*Yarborough v. Gentry,* 540 U.S. 1 [2003]).

Yarborough v. Gentry (2003)

Claims of Ineffective Counsel in Death Penalty Cases

Three death penalty cases illustrate claims of ineffective counsel: a sleeping lawyer, a silent lawyer, and a lawyer who had the victim as a client at the time he was murdered.

Burdine v. Johnson (5th Cir. 2001)

A Sleeping Lawyer In *Burdine v. Johnson* (No. 99–21034 [5th Cir. 2001]), which generated mass national publicity, a defense lawyer for a capital offense defendant in Texas kept falling asleep during the trial. Convicted and sentenced to death, the defendant, Calvin Burdine, appealed, claiming he was denied the constitutional right to effective counsel. A panel of the Fifth Circuit Court of Appeals first rejected Burdine's claim, but the full appeals court agreed to heard the case, concluded that Burdine did not have the benefit of effective counsel, and therefore ordered a new trial. The U.S. Supreme Court refused to hear the case on appeal; thus the decision to give Burdine a new trial was upheld. (In the meantime, the original defense lawyer who slept during the trial had died.)

HIGHLIGHT
It Is Difficult to Prove the Defense Lawyer Was Ineffective

An accused who claims ineffective counsel must establish the following: (1) deficient performance by counsel and (2) a reasonable probability that but for such deficiency the result of the proceeding would have been different. In a 1993 case, *Lockhart v. Fretwell* (506 U.S. 364 [1993]), the Court made the standard for reversal of conviction even more difficult when it said: "To show prejudice . . . a defendant must demonstrate that counsel's errors were so serious as to deprive him of a trial whose result is fair or reliable, and not merely that the outcome would have been different." This is a difficult barrier for defendants to overcome.

A Silent Lawyer In a second case, *Bell v. Cone* (505 U.S. 685 [2002]), the Court allowed a death sentence to stand even though the defendant's lawyer failed to make an argument to the jury to save his life. In this case, Cone was tried and found guilty of capital murder. During the sentencing stage, the sequence was for the prosecution to argue first, then the defense lawyer, and then the prosecutor again. A junior prosecutor argued first for the prosecution. The defense lawyer then decided to waive his argument because under court rules the prosecutor could not argue a second time if the defense lawyer waived the argument. This was done by the defense lawyer as a strategy so that the senior prosecutor, who was a highly effective lawyer and who was going to give the second prosecution argument, could not say a word. The jury gave the defendant the death penalty anyway even without the second argument by the prosecution. Cone appealed, claiming ineffective counsel. The Court upheld the sentence, saying that Cone's constitutional right was not violated because what the defense lawyer did as a strategy was reasonable.

A Lawyer Who Had the Victim as a Client In a third case, Mickens was convicted of murder and sentenced to death. He claimed ineffective assistance of counsel because he discovered, after trial, that his attorney had represented the victim Mickens had killed on unrelated charges, which were pending at the time of the murder. This was never revealed to Mickens by the lawyer or by the court, although the court had knowledge of the representation. This, Mickens argued, created a conflict of interest that resulted in ineffective representation.

The Court rejected his claim, saying that a defendant who claims that the right to counsel was violated because of a conflict of interest must show that the conflict had a negative effect on the attorney's representation and that there was a reasonable probability that the result would have been different. The Court concluded that "dual representation" in and of itself merely represents a "theo-

retical division of loyalties" and did not require a reversal of the results (*Mickens v. Taylor*, No. 00-9285 [2002]).

The Right to Act as One's Own Counsel

Under certain conditions, an accused has a constitutional right to waive counsel and represent himself or herself in a criminal proceeding (*Faretta v. California*, 422 U.S. 806 [1975]). In *Faretta v. California* (1975), the defendant had a high school education, had represented himself before, and did not want a public defender to represent him, because of the public defender's heavy caseload. The right to self-representation does not require legal skills, but in cases in which the defendant is ignorant or too inexperienced, the request to act as his or her own counsel will probably be denied by the court.

New Trial Is Denied to Man Whose Lawyer Slept in Court—Court Rules He Wasn't Deprived of Counsel Because His Other Attorney Stayed Awake

Austin—A capital murder defendant whose lawyer took daily naps throughout his trial should not get a new trial because he had another lawyer who stayed awake, the Court of Criminal Appeals said Wednesday.

The court unanimously denied George McFarland's claims of ineffective counsel during his 1992 trial for the robbery and killing of grocer Kenneth Kwan.

"We conclude that, although one of his attorneys slept through portions of his trial, applicant was not deprived of the assistance of counsel under the Sixth Amendment because his second attorney was present and an active advocate at all times," wrote Judge Cathy Cochran.

The issue resonates because of the earlier, infamous case of Calvin Burdine. In August 2001, the 5th U.S. Circuit Court of Appeals ordered a new trial, ruling that his sleeping lawyer denied Burdine his right to effective representation.

That case spurred an effort among Harris County judges to set standards for appointments in capital murder cases and led to passage of the Fair Defense Act, a state law requiring a systematic approach to selecting attorneys for poor people.

McFarland had hired 72-year-old John Benn. The trial judge appointed Sanford Melamed to serve as co-counsel.

The court opinion said that Benn first was observed sleeping during jury selection and the napping got worse as the trial progressed. At times the bailiff would nudge Benn's chair to awaken him, and the judge admonished Benn.

At a hearing on a motion for new trial, Benn explained, "I'm 72 years old. I customarily take a short nap in the afternoon."

Cochran said the court agreed that McFarland "did not have Mr. Benn's active assistance during his postprandial naps and that those naps occurred during 'critical stages' of this trial." However, she wrote that Melamed, although inexperienced in capital cases, was "an awake, active and zealous advocate" for McFarland.

Source: *Houston Chronicle*, May 19, 2005, p. 5. Copyright 2005 *Houston Chronicle* Publishing Company. Reprinted with permission. All rights reserved.

Before an accused can be permitted to waive counsel and represent himself or herself, the following constitutional requirements must be met:

- *Awareness of the right to counsel.* The court must fully advise the accused of his or her right to be represented by counsel.
- *Express waiver.* The accused's waiver of counsel cannot be inferred from his or her silence or from his or her failure to request the appointment of counsel.
- *Competency of the accused.* The trial judge must determine whether the accused is (1) competent to waive the right to counsel and (2) competent to make an intelligent choice in the case. In determining the defendant's competency to make an intelligent choice, the court must make the defendant aware of the dangers and disadvantages of self-representation. An accused who elects to represent himself or herself cannot later claim ineffective counsel.

The Right to Due Process

There are two Due Process Clauses in the U.S. Constitution. The Fifth Amendment (applicable to federal prosecutions) provides that "No person shall be held to answer for a capital, or otherwise infamous crime, . . . nor be deprived of life, liberty, or property, without due process of law; nor shall private property be taken for public use, without just compensation." A second Due Process Clause is found in Section 1 of the Fourteenth Amendment (applicable to state prosecutions), which provides that "No state shall make or enforce any law which shall abridge the privileges or immunities of citizens of the United States; nor shall any state deprive any person of life, liberty, or property, without due process of law; nor deny to any person within its jurisdiction the equal protection of the laws."

Due process means "fundamental fairness," but it has no fixed meaning. What process is due varies from one proceeding to another, depending upon the type of proceeding and what is at stake. For example, due process during a criminal trial is different from due process in probation or parole revocation proceedings or in prison disciplinary proceedings. What rights are due in a particular proceeding is ultimately decided by the courts. Any time fundamental fairness is an issue, due process can likely be raised in a criminal case. This is illustrated by the *Brady* rule. We will look at what the rule says and how it affected cases that came after the ruling.

The *Brady* Rule on Disclosure of Evidence to the Accused

Due process is protected to the utmost during criminal trials. In a criminal proceeding, the prosecutor has a duty to disclose evidence favorable to a defendant; failure to disclose violates a defendant's constitutional right to due process. This

Mooney v. Holohan
(1935)

obligation was first declared in *Mooney v. Holohan* (294 U.S. 103 [1935]), when the Court said that the "due process requirement is not satisfied by mere notice and hearing if the state, through prosecuting officers acting on state's behalf, has contrived conviction through pretense of trial which in truth is used as a means of depriving defendant of liberty through deliberate deception of court and jury by presentation of testimony known to be perjured."

Brady v. Maryland
(1963)

The *Holohan principle* was reiterated almost three decades later in *Brady v. Maryland* (373 U.S. 83 [1963]). *Brady* involved a case in which the defendant admitted participating in the crime but claimed that his companion did the actual killing. Prior to the trial, Brady's lawyer requested that the prosecutor allow him to examine the companion's extrajudicial statements. The prosecutor showed these to Brady's lawyer but withheld the statement in which the companion admitted doing the actual killing. The defense did not know about that statement until after Brady had been tried, convicted, and sentenced.

On appeal, the Court reversed Brady's conviction, saying that "the suppression by the prosecution of evidence favorable to an accused upon request violates due process where the evidence is material either to guilt or to punishment, irrespective of the good faith or bad faith of the prosecution." This holding, better known as the **Brady** rule, has been interpreted and refined by the Court in subsequent cases.

Cases after *Brady*

United States v. Agurs (1976)

One of the cases that interpreted *Brady* was *United States v. Agurs* (427 U.S. 97 [1976]). In *Agurs,* the Court said that the defendant's failure to request that favorable evidence be shown to the defense did not free the government of all obligation, but that the prosecutor's failure in this particular case did not violate the defendant's right to due process.

In *Agurs,* the Court distinguished three situations that can give rise to a *Brady* claim:

1. [W]here previously undisclosed evidence revealed that the prosecution introduced trial testimony that it knew or should have known was perjured
2. [W]here the Government failed to accede to a defense request for disclosure of some specific kind of exculpatory evidence
3. [W]here the Government failed to volunteer exculpatory evidence never requested, or requested only in a general way.

In this case, however, the Court stated:

> [The] prosecutor's failure to tender [defendant's] criminal record to the defense did not deprive respondent of a fair trial . . . where it appears that the record was not requested by defense counsel and gave rise to no inference of perjury, that the trial judge remained convinced of respondent's guilt beyond a reasonable doubt after considering the criminal record in the contest of the entire record, and that the judge's firsthand appraisal of the entire record was thorough and entirely reasonable.

In essence, the Court in *Agurs* limited the defendant's right to discovery procedure under the circumstances described in that case.

United States v. Bagley (1985)

In *United States v. Bagley* (473 U.S. 667 [1985]), the Court held that, "regardless of request, favorable evidence is material, and constitutional error results from its suppression by the government, if there is reasonable probability that, had the evidence been disclosed to the defense, the result of the proceeding would have been different."

Kyles v. Whitley (1995)

Another case on disclosure of evidence and the right of an accused to due process is *Kyles v. Whitley* (514 U.S. 419 [1995]). In *Kyles,* the Court held that, because the effect of the state-suppressed evidence favorable to the defendant raised a reasonable probability that its disclosure would have produced a different result at trial, the conviction had to be reversed.

In that case, Kyles was convicted of first-degree murder in Louisiana and sentenced to death. Later, it was revealed that the state had failed to disclose certain evidence favorable to the accused, including the following: (1) contemporaneous eyewitness statements taken by the police following the murder, (2) various statements made to the police by an informant who was never called to testify, and (3) a computer printout of license plate numbers of cars parked at the crime scene on the night of the murder, which did not contain the number of Kyles's car. The Court held that this evidence, taken together, raised a reasonable probability that its disclosure would have produced a different result at trial; hence, the conviction was reversed.

In a 1999 case, *Strickler v. Greene* (527 U.S. 263 [1999]), the Court held that the prosecution's failure to disclose evidence, in the form of interview notes from a detective that seriously undermined the truthfulness of the only eyewitness's testimony in a murder case, did not violate the *Brady* rule because the evidence was not material to the issue of guilt or innocence. In this case, the only eyewitness to the crime testified at trial that she had an exceptionally good memory and that she had absolutely no doubt that she had identified the defendant correctly. But it was later learned that the notes of her interview with a detective showed that she could not identify the defendant during that first interview.

On appeal, the Court held that the failure by the prosecution to disclose the detective's notes did not require a reversal of the conviction because the defendant had not shown by reasonable probability that disclosure of the notes would have changed the results of the trial.

In sum, the rule concerning an accused's right to disclosure of evidence by the prosecution has undergone refinement since the Court first held in *Holohan* that the presentation by prosecutors in court of testimony known to be perjured violated a defendant's right to due process. The latest rule states that if the circumstances surrounding the nondisclosure raise a "reasonable probability" that the disclosure would have made a difference in the trial's result, the defendant's due process right has been violated and the conviction must be reversed. But undisclosed favorable evidence that is not material to the issue of guilt or innocence does not lead to a reversal of the conviction.

The Right against Self-Incrimination

The prohibition against compulsory self-incrimination springs from the Fifth Amendment provision that "no person . . . shall be compelled in any criminal case to be a witness against himself." This guarantee is designed to restrain the government from using force, coercion, or other such methods to obtain any statement, admission, or confession that might be used by the police to take the place of other evidence. The right applies to criminal, civil, or administrative proceedings if the answer sought tends to incriminate the witness in a subsequent criminal case.

This section focuses on the scope of the provision, the privleges of both the accused and witnesses during a trial, immunity, and how the right against self-incrimination is waived.

The Scope of the Provision: Testimonial, Not Physical

The prohibition against self-incrimination extends only to testimonial (or communicative) self-incrimination; it does not prohibit **physical self-incrimination**, *which involves real or physical evidence.* For example, the accused can be forced to submit to reasonable physical or psychiatric examinations, and the prosecution may introduce the evidence obtained—such as fingerprints, footprints, blood or urine samples, or voice identifications. Also, a defendant can be forced to stand up for identification in the courtroom, to put on certain items of clothing, or to give a handwriting sample (*Gilbert v. California,* 388 U.S. 263 [1967]).

Gilbert v. California (1967)

In contrast, **testimonial or communicative self-incrimination** is that which in itself explicitly or implicitly relates a factual assertion or discloses information. It is in the form of verbal or oral communication. For example, a question that asks whether the defendant killed the deceased is testimonially self-incriminating because it asks for a factual assertion or disclosure of information of a nonphysical nature.

The Fifth Amendment's protection extends only to natural persons, meaning human beings. Corporations or partnerships (which are considered persons by law) cannot claim the privilege, so the records of such entities cannot be withheld on these grounds. For example, suppose a corporation faces charges of violating labor and anti-monopoly laws. The corporation may be required to produce its official books and records even if they contain incriminating evidence. The search and seizure of a person's private papers in accordance with a legal process, with or without a warrant, does not violate the right to protection against self-incrimination—at least if the information on the papers was written voluntarily, not obtained by testimonial compulsion. This is because the protection given to books and papers under the Fifth Amendment is very limited. Although they are perhaps the products of a mental process (such as a diary), the books or documents themselves constitute physical evidence.

Another aspect of the right to protection against self-incrimination is discussed in *South Dakota v. Neville* (459 U.S. 553 [1983]). That case involved a South Dakota law that permitted a person suspected of driving while intoxicated to refuse to submit to a blood alcohol test but also authorized revocation of the driver's license of anyone who refused to take the test. The statute permitted such a refusal to be used against the driver as evidence of guilt during the trial.

South Dakota v. Neville (1983)

The Supreme Court held that the admission into evidence of a defendant's refusal to submit to a blood alcohol test does not violate the defendant's Fifth Amendment right to protection against compulsory self-incrimination. A refusal to take the test, after a police officer has lawfully requested it, is not an act coerced by the officer and therefore is not protected by the Fifth Amendment. This case legalized the practice used in some states of giving DWI suspects a choice to take or refuse a blood alcohol test and then using a refusal as evidence of guilt later in court. The Court said that any self-incrimination resulting from a blood alcohol test is physical in nature, not testimonial or communicative, so it is not protected by the Fifth Amendment.

Two Separate Privileges during Trials: The Accused and the Witness

The privilege against compulsory self-incrimination during trials guarantees two separate privileges: the privilege of the accused and the privilege of a witness.

The Privilege of the Accused The defendant in a criminal case has a **privilege of the accused** not to take the stand and not to testify. The Court has ruled that the accused "may stand mute, clothed in the presumption of innocence." Moreover, prosecutors cannot comment on a defendant's assertion of the right not to testify. No conclusion of guilt may be drawn from the failure of the accused to testify during the trial. Therefore, the prosecutor is not permitted to make any comment or argument to the jury suggesting that the defendant is guilty because he or she refused to testify (*Griffin v. California*, 380 U.S. 609 [1965]).

Griffin v. California (1965)

However, this rule has been modified by the concept of **fair response**, which provides that a prosecutor's statement to the jury, during closing arguments, that the defendant could have taken the witness stand but refused to do so is proper as long as it is in response to defense counsel's argument that the government did not allow the defendant to explain his or her side of the story (*United States v. Robinson*, 485 U.S. 25 [1988]). Unless it is in the context of a fair response, the comments of a prosecutor suggesting that the defendant must be guilty because he or she refused to take the stand will lead to a reversal of the conviction.

United States v. Robinson (1988)

The privilege to remain silent and not to take the stand applies in all stages of a criminal proceeding, starting when the suspect is first taken into custody. It applies in criminal prosecutions or contempt proceedings but not in situations in which there is no prosecution and no accused, such as grand jury investigations or legislative or administrative hearings. Once an accused takes the witness stand in his or her own defense, he or she waives the privilege not to testify. Therefore, the accused must answer all relevant inquiries about the crime for which he or she is on trial. This is one reason defense lawyers may not want the accused to take the witness stand, particularly if the accused has a bad record or a background that is better kept undisclosed.

The Privilege of a Witness Any witness, other than an accused on the witness stand, has the **privilege of the witness** to refuse to disclose any information that may "tend to incriminate" him or her. The reason for this is that the witness is not on trial; he or she is in court merely to provide information about what happened. A question tends to incriminate a witness if the answer would directly or indirectly implicate that witness in the commission of a crime. The privilege does not apply if the answer might expose the witness to civil liability; but if the facts involved would make the witness subject to both civil and criminal liability, the privilege can be claimed. However, the privilege cannot be claimed merely because the answer would hold the witness up to shame, disgrace, or embarrassment.

The answer to the question does not need to prove guilt to give rise to the privilege. All that is needed is a reasonable possibility that the answer would "furnish a link in the chain of evidence needed to prosecute." In one case, the Court held that a witness, an immigrant from Lithuania, could be forced to testify in a case in the United States even if the testimony given might subject that witness to prosecution (for Nazi war crimes) in a foreign country—Lithuania (*United States v. Balsys*, 524 U.S. 666 [1998]).

United States v. Balsys (1998)

The witness's privilege protects only against the possibility of prosecution, so if a witness could not be or can no longer be prosecuted, he or she can be compelled to testify. Several examples will help illuminate this provision.

- *Example 1.* If the **statute of limitations**—a law providing that a crime must be prosecuted within a certain period of time—has run out on the crime, the witness can be forced to answer the question.
- *Example 2.* If the witness has been acquitted and therefore cannot be reprosecuted, he or she can be forced to answer the question.
- *Example 3.* If the witness is assured of immunity, he or she can be forced to answer the question.

The decision whether a witness's answer tends to incriminate him or her is made by the hearing officer or judge immediately after the question is asked and the opposing lawyer objects on the grounds that the question is self-incriminatory. The decision is appealable only after the trial, so the witness must testify if so ordered or face contempt proceedings.

The following list summarizes the distinctions between these two privileges:

Accused	**Witness**
An accused cannot be forced to testify.	A witness can be forced to testify if ordered by the court.
A refusal cannot be commented on by the prosecution.	A refusal can result in a contempt citation.
An accused who testifies cannot refuse to answer incriminating questions because the privilege at that stage is considered waived.	A witness who testifies can refuse to answer questions that might result in criminal prosecution.

The Grant of Immunity

There are many situations in which the government grants immunity to a witness or a codefendant in return for his or her testimony. **Immunity** in criminal cases means that the person granted immunity will not be prosecuted in a criminal case, either fully or partially—depending upon the type of immunity granted—for testimony given before a grand jury, in court, or in some other proceeding from which prosecution could otherwise have resulted. Immunity is usually given when the testimony of the witness is crucial to proving the government's case or when the government needs further information for investigative purposes, particularly in cases involving organized crime.

A witness who is granted immunity from prosecution may be forced to testify because the reason for the privilege (protection from self-incrimination) no longer exists. Once immunity is granted, a witness who still refuses to testify can be held in contempt of court.

The authority to grant immunity varies from one jurisdiction to another, but it is generally granted by law (which usually lists a category of witnesses who may be granted immunity), a grand jury, judges, or prosecutors. In a growing number of cases, such as gambling or drug possession, the same act may constitute a crime under both federal and state laws. The question then arises whether a grant of immunity from prosecution in one jurisdiction, state or federal, disqualifies the witness from claiming the privilege in another jurisdiction. The rules governing the grant of immunity are as follows:

Murphy v. Waterfront Commission (1964)

- If a state has granted the witness valid immunity, the federal government is not permitted to make use of the testimony (or any of its "fruits") in a federal prosecution against the witness (*Murphy v. Waterfront Commission,* 378 U.S. 52 [1964]). Therefore, the witness may be forced to testify in the state proceedings.
- The Supreme Court has not decided whether a state should be allowed to use compelled testimony given in federal court under a grant of federal immunity. However, its use would probably be prohibited under the reasoning of the *Murphy* case.
- Testimony given under a grant of immunity in a state court cannot be used as evidence against the witness in the court of another state.

Comparison between Transactional Immunity and Use and Derivative Use Immunity

Does the grant of immunity to a witness exempt the witness in full from further criminal prosecution? Not necessarily; instead, it depends on the type of immunity that is given. There are two types of immunity: transactional and "use and derivative use." With **transactional immunity**, the witness can no longer be prosecuted for any offense whatsoever arising out of that act or transaction. In contrast, **use and derivative use immunity** means that the witness is assured only that *his or her testimony and evidence derived from it* will not be used against him or her in a subsequent prosecution. But the witness can be prosecuted on the basis of evidence other than his or her testimony, if the prosecutor has such independent evidence.

Kastigar v. United States (1972)

In sum, transactional immunity is full immunity, whereas use and derivative use immunity is partial immunity. In *Kastigar v. United States* (1972), the Court decided that prosecutors only have to grant use and derivative use immunity to compel an unwilling witness to testify. The witness is not constitutionally entitled to transactional immunity before he or she can be compelled to testify.

In the *Kastigar* case, the witness refused to testify under a grant of use and derivative use immunity, claiming that the Fifth Amendment guarantee against compulsory self-incrimination requires that transactional immunity be given before a witness can be forced to testify. The Court disagreed, saying that use and derivative use immunity is sufficient for purposes of Fifth Amendment protection; the granting of transactional immunity is not required.

How the Right Is Waived

A witness's right to protection against self-incrimination may be waived through the following actions:

- *Failure to assert.* The witness is the holder of the privilege, and only the witness (or his or her lawyer) can assert it. If the witness fails to assert the privilege at the time an incriminating question is asked, the privilege is waived.
- *Partial disclosure.* When the witness discloses a fact that he or she knows to be self-incriminating, the witness also waives his or her privilege with respect to all further facts related to the same transaction.
- *Taking the witness stand.* When the witness is also the accused and voluntarily takes the stand, he or she must answer all relevant inquiries about the charge for which he or she is on trial. The accused is therefore "fair game" on all such matters during the cross-examination.

The Right to Protection against Double Jeopardy

The Fifth Amendment to the U.S. Constitution provides that "no person shall be . . . subject for the same offense to be twice put in jeopardy of life or limb." In this section, we look at what *double jeopardy* means, when it starts, and what happens when it is waived; what *same offense* and *lesser included offense* mean; and the constitutionality of prosecution for a higher offense after conviction for a lesser included offense and prosecution for the same offense by two states.

What *Double Jeopardy* Means

North Carolina v. Pearce (1969)

Double jeopardy is defined as the successive prosecution of a defendant for the same offense by the same jurisdiction. In the words of the Court in *North Carolina v. Pearce* (395 U.S. 711 [1969]), "It protects against a second prosecution for the same offense after acquittal. It protects against a second prosecution for the same offense after conviction. And it protects against multiple punishments for the same offense." Like most other constitutional rights, the prohibition against double jeopardy has been extended to state criminal proceedings.

This definition has three elements, all of which must be present for double jeopardy to occur:

- *Successive prosecution.* This means two criminal proceedings; if one case is criminal and the other civil, there is no double jeopardy. For example, there was no double jeopardy in the O. J. Simpson trials, because the first case was criminal (for double murder) and the second case was civil (it sought monetary compensation for wrongful death).
- *Same offense.* The two cases must be for the same criminal offense. If the elements of the two criminal prosecutions are different, there is no double jeopardy. Thus, if a police officer is criminally charged with abuse of authority and then with illegal detention, there is no double jeopardy if the two offenses require different elements for conviction.

■ *Same jurisdiction.* There can be two criminal prosecutions essentially for the same offense, but if they take place in different jurisdictions there is no double jeopardy. For example, the four police officers charged in the Rodney King beating in Los Angeles in 1991 were first tried and acquitted under California law and in state court. They were then charged with essentially the same offense under federal law and in federal court. Two were acquitted; the other two were convicted and sentenced to a federal prison. There was no double jeopardy, because the two criminal proceedings were in different jurisdictions—one state and the other federal.

When Double Jeopardy Starts

A person who has committed a criminal act can be subjected to only one prosecution or punishment for the same offense. Accordingly, when a defendant has been prosecuted for a criminal offense and the prosecution has resulted in either a conviction or an acquittal, or the proceeding has reached a point at which dismissal would be equivalent to an acquittal, any further prosecution or punishment for the same offense is prohibited.

The prohibition against double jeopardy applies (and the defendant cannot be retried for the same offense) when the trial has reached the following stage: (1) in a *jury trial,* when a competent jury has been sworn, or (2) in a *nonjury (bench) trial,* when the first witness has been called and sworn. If the charge is dismissed before either stage is reached, the defendant may be charged and tried again.

Smith v. Massachusetts (2005)

In a 2005 case, *Smith v. Massachusetts* (543 U.S.____[2005]), the Court held that a judge's acquittal of a defendant midway through a trial by jury prohibited him from reconsidering that acquittal later in the trial. In this case, defendant Smith was tried for illegal possession of firearms. The prosecutor failed to introduce direct evidence of the gun's length during trial, so the judge acquitted Smith because under state law the prosecutor could not meet the statutory definition of a firearm. The prosecutor later convinced the trial judge, however, that "testimony that a gun was a pistol or revolver was sufficient evidence to allow a firearm charge to go to the jury." A witness had testified during the trial that Smith's gun was a pistol. The judge then reversed the acquittal and allowed the jury trial to continue. On appeal, the Court held that reconsideration by the judge of Smith's acquittal and proceeding with the jury trial constituted double jeopardy.

When Double Jeopardy Is Waived

Double jeopardy is considered waived in the following instances:

1. *In mistrials.* When a new trial is ordered before a verdict on a motion by the defendant or otherwise with the defendant's consent, the defendant waives his or her right to protection against double

jeopardy. Thus, if in the course of a trial the defendant moves for a mistrial because of what a prosecutor or a witness has done, and the motion is granted by the judge, the case can be tried again.

2. *When a verdict of conviction is set aside on a defendant's motion or appeal.* The general view is that a defendant asking for a new trial or appealing a guilty verdict waives his or her right to protection against double jeopardy, so the defendant can be tried again for the same offense for which he or she was convicted in the first trial. If the convicted defendant is serving time, he or she will be released from prison and freed on bail or will be detained in jail pending another trial for the same or a related offense. The prosecutor may choose not to reprosecute, but there is no double jeopardy if the same or a similar charge is again filed.

In the celebrated *Miranda* case (discussed earlier in Chapter 11), the defendant, Ernesto Miranda, appealed his original conviction for rape on the grounds that his confession was obtained in violation of the guarantee against compulsory self-incrimination. His conviction was reversed by the Court, but he was tried again (under an assumed name) for the same offense in Arizona and was reconvicted on the basis of other evidence. There was no double jeopardy because, by appealing his first conviction, he waived his right not to be retried for the same offense.

However, at a second trial for the same offense following a successful appeal, a defendant cannot be tried on or convicted of charges that are more serious than the ones for which he or she was originally tried and convicted. For example, suppose a defendant is charged with second-degree murder but is convicted of negligent homicide (a lesser offense). If the defendant appeals the conviction and obtains a new trial, he or she cannot be charged with first-degree murder in the second trial (*Green v. United States,* 355 U.S. 184 [1957]). Also, a defendant whose conviction is reversed because the evidence is insufficient as a matter of law to sustain the conviction cannot be retried; the reversal amounts to an acquittal (*Burks v. United States,* 437 U.S. 1 [1978]).

Green v. United States (1957)

Burks v. United States (1978)

If the jury cannot agree on conviction or acquittal, the judge can declare a hung jury, and the defendant may be tried again before another jury. How soon this is declared is a matter of the judge's discretion. Some courts will declare a hung jury after several days of deadlocked jury deliberations; others require a longer period of stalemate.

3. *In habeas corpus cases.* Habeas corpus cases are filed by defendants who are serving time in prison or jail and who seek release on the grounds that their conviction is unconstitutional or invalid. They are different from appeals in that habeas corpus is filed after the appellate process has been exhausted and is a separate civil proceeding seeking

the defendant's release. If a habeas corpus case succeeds, the defendant can be tried again, because the filing is considered a waiver of the right to protection against double jeopardy, as the defendant is essentially saying, "Give me a new trial because there was something wrong with the first one."

What *Same Offense* Means

Blockburger v. United States (1932)

Double jeopardy applies only to prosecution for the "same offense." Once double jeopardy attaches, a defendant cannot be prosecuted a second time for the same offense involved in the first trial or for any other offense included in the act charged in the first trial, nor can the defendant be punished more than once for the same offense. In a 1932 case, *Blockburger v. United States* (284 U.S. 299 [1932]), the Court held that a second prosecution is barred if the two prosecutions reveal that the offenses have identical statutory elements or that one is a "lesser included offense" of the other.

To illustrate:

Illinois v. Vitale (1980)

- *Example 1*. In *Illinois v. Vitale* (447 U.S. 410 [1980]), the Court said that a conviction for failure to reduce speed to avoid an accident does not necessarily prohibit a second charge of involuntary manslaughter, because vehicular manslaughter does not always require proof of failure to reduce speed.

Brown v. Ohio (1977)

- *Example 2*. In contrast, a conviction for joyriding prohibits a second charge of motor vehicle theft, because no additional facts are needed for the second charge (*Brown v. Ohio,* 432 U.S. 161 [1977]).

The current test to determine what **same offense** means is the *Blockburger* standard: double jeopardy applies if the two offenses for which the defendant is being punished come under the "same elements" test. The key is whether one offense contains the same elements as the other. If it does, then double jeopardy applies; but if one offense requires an element not needed in the other offense, then double jeopardy does not apply.

What *Lesser Included Offense* Means

Double jeopardy attaches when the second prosecution is for a lesser included offense. **Lesser included offense** is defined as an offense that is "composed of some, but not all, of the elements of the greater crime, and which does not have any element not included in the greater offense."[6] For example, suppose X is charged with murder and is acquitted. She cannot be prosecuted again for homicide arising out of the same act, because homicide is a lesser included offense in that it contains all the elements of murder and does not contain any element that is not included in murder. Note that if X is charged with murder, most states will allow her to be convicted of homicide in the same proceeding. Consequently, prosecutors usually charge an accused with the highest possible offense warranted by the facts. If the higher charge fails, the accused may still be convicted of a lesser offense. In contrast, an accused can never be convicted of an offense higher than that with which he or she was charged; that would be a violation of an accused's constitutional rights.

To summarize:

- A person accused of murder can be convicted of homicide (a lesser included offense) in the same criminal proceeding, but a person accused of homicide cannot be convicted of murder (a higher offense) in the same criminal proceeding.
- A person accused and acquitted of murder can no longer be charged with homicide, because it is a lesser included offense.

Rutledge v. United States (1996)

In a 1996 case, *Rutledge v. United States* (517 U.S. 292 [1996]), the Court unanimously held that there cannot be two punishments for two offenses if one is a lesser included offense. In this case, Rutledge was convicted in federal court of conspiracy to distribute cocaine and of operating a continuing criminal enterprise. He received life sentences for each conviction. On appeal, he argued that the double jeopardy clause prohibits him from being convicted of both offenses, because conspiracy is a lesser included offense of the continuing offense of criminal enterprise.

The Court reversed the conviction but not based on double jeopardy. Instead, the Court relied on the "merger rule" for lesser included offenses. According to the merger rule, a lesser offense is merged with a more serious offense so that the offense becomes one and can be prosecuted only once. The Court added that the test to determine if a defendant is being punished twice for the same crime is the "same elements" test. In the *Rutledge* case, the "in concert" element of the continuing criminal enterprise offense was the same element that formed the basis of the conspiracy charge; hence, the "same elements" test was met and multiple punishment was disallowed.

The Constitutionality of Prosecution for a Higher Offense after Conviction for a Lesser Included Offense

Suppose X is tried for a lesser included offense (homicide) and is convicted, but circumstances later reveal or develop that could hold X liable for a higher offense

HIGHLIGHT

Double Jeopardy and Government Appeals

In the course of the debates over the Bill of Rights, there was no suggestion that the Double Jeopardy Clause imposed any general ban on appeals by the prosecution. . . . Nor does the common law background of the clause suggest an implied prohibition against state appeals. . . . The development of the Double Jeopardy Clause from its common law origins thus suggests that it was directed at the threat of multiple prosecutions, not at government appeals, at least where those appeals would not require a new trial.

(murder). Can X be charged and convicted again for the higher offense? The answer is yes, if the government cannot be blamed for the inadequacy of the first charge. This can happen in two ways: (1) "if the facts needed to prove the higher offense had not yet been discovered at the time of the first trial, despite the prosecution's due diligence," and (2) "if at the time the first case is tried, events have not yet occurred that are needed for the second crime."[7]

These may be illustrated as follows:

- *Example 1*. Suppose that D has been convicted of kidnapping V, but, at the time of conviction, the prosecutor did not know whether V was still alive. While D is serving time, the prosecutor learns and obtains evidence that V was, in fact, killed in the course of the kidnapping and that the body has been found. D can now be tried again for the higher crime of kidnapping with murder. There is no double jeopardy because the murder, although it had already occurred, was undiscovered at the time of the first trial.

- *Example 2*. Suppose Z is charged with and convicted of inflicting serious bodily injury and is now in prison. Months later, the victim dies as a result of these injuries. Z can now be charged with and convicted of homicide or murder. There is no double jeopardy, because death had not yet occurred at the time Z was tried for the lesser included offense. However, although constitutionally there is no double jeopardy, state law or policy may prohibit a second prosecution for a higher offense if the defendant has already been convicted of a lesser included offense.

The Constitutionality of Prosecution for the Same Offense by Two States

Heath v. Alabama (1985)

In a 1985 case, *Heath v. Alabama* (474 U.S. 82 [1985]), the Court decided that, under the dual sovereignty doctrine, successive prosecutions by two states for the same offense do not violate the double jeopardy clause of the Fifth Amendment. In *Heath,* the defendant hired two men to kill his wife. The hired men kidnapped the woman from her home in Alabama. Her body was later found on the side of a road in Georgia. The defendant pleaded guilty to murder "with malice" in a Georgia court, in exchange for a sentence of life imprisonment. Subsequently, he was tried and convicted of murder during a kidnapping (arising out of the same act) by an Alabama trial court and was sentenced to death. His claim of double jeopardy was rejected by the Alabama court, so he appealed his conviction to the U.S. Supreme Court.

In rejecting the double jeopardy claim, the Court said that, according to the dual sovereignty doctrine, when a defendant in a single act violates the "peace and dignity" of two sovereigns by breaking the laws of each, the defendant has committed two distinct offenses for double jeopardy purposes. The crucial question is whether the two entities that seek to prosecute a defendant successively for the same course of conduct can be termed separate sovereigns. If they are, no double jeopardy occurs. The states of Georgia and Alabama are separate from the federal government and from each other, so there is no double jeopardy. For purposes of criminal law and criminal procedure, therefore, there are, in effect, fifty-one different sovereigns in the United States: the fifty states and the federal government.

The Right to Confront Witnesses

The Sixth Amendment provides that "in all criminal prosecutions, the accused shall enjoy the right . . . to be confronted with the witnesses against him." The right to confrontation exists in all criminal proceedings—including trials, preliminary hearings, and juvenile proceedings in which the juvenile is suspected of having committed a crime. The right does not apply to purely investigative proceedings, such as grand jury proceedings, coroner's inquests, and legislative investigations. The right to confrontation includes the following rights: to cross-examine witnesses, to be physically present, to physically face witnesses at trial, and to know the identity of prosecution witnesses.

The Right to Cross-Examine Opposing Witnesses

The opportunity to cross-examine all opposing witnesses is an important right of the accused and is guaranteed by the Sixth Amendment. It is through skillful cross-examination that any falsehood or inaccuracy in a witness's testimony can be detected and exposed, and it is then that a skillful lawyer can elicit testimony that can be helpful to his or her client. Probably because this right is strictly observed during trials, there are only a few cases on the scope and meaning of the right. Any limitations on the right to cross-examine a witness are imposed by the judge during trial.

Crawford v. Washington (2004)

In *Crawford v. Washington* (541 U.S. 36 [2004]), the Court held that the use by the prosecution of a wife's statement obtained during police interrogation violated the defendant's constitutional right because the wife could not testify during the trial. In *Crawford,* the prosecution sought to introduce a recorded statement that the defendant's wife made during police interrogation saying that the stabbing of another person by her husband was not in self-defense. The wife could not testify during the trial because the marital privilege policy in the state of Washington prohibited her from testifying against her husband in a criminal case. The defendant argued that admitting his wife's statement obtained earlier by the police violated his Sixth Amendment right to "be confronted with the witnesses against him."

On appeal, the Court agreed, saying that "where testimonial statements are at issue, the only indicium of reliability sufficient to satisfy constitutional demands is confrontation." Because the wife could not testify during the trial and could not be cross-examined, her previous statement was not admissible.

The Right to Physical Presence during the Trial

The right to confrontation also includes the opportunity for the accused to be physically present in the courtroom at the time any testimony against him or her is offered. However, the right to be present may be waived under certain circumstances, such as a deliberate absence or disruptive behavior in the courtroom.

Deliberate Absence If an accused is present at the start of the trial but later voluntarily absents himself or herself, the Court has held that the trial may continue because the accused is considered to have waived his or her right to be present (*Taylor v. United States,* 414 U.S.17 [1973]). But the issue of whether a defendant can be tried in absentia if he or she was not present at the start of the trial has not been authoritatively decided by the Court. Some states allow criminal trials in absentia under certain circumstances; others provide that the accused must be present in court for the trial to be held.

Taylor v. United States (1973)

Disruptive Conduct in the Courtroom Likewise, an accused who persists in disorderly or disrespectful conduct in the courtroom can be held to have waived his or her right to be present and be excluded from his or her own trial. The Court has approved the following methods for dealing with a disruptive defendant: (1) holding the defendant in contempt of court, (2) binding and gagging the defendant in the courtroom, and (3) removing the defendant from the courtroom until he or she promises to behave properly (*Illinois v. Allen,* 397 U.S. 337 [1970]).

Illinois v. Allen (1970)

The Right to Face Witnesses at Trial

Coy v. Iowa (1988)

The Court decided in *Coy v. Iowa* (487 U.S. 1012 [1988]) that the right to confrontation also includes the right to physically face witnesses at trial. Therefore, a state law that allows testimony via closed circuit television or behind a screen violates a defendant's Sixth Amendment rights.

In *Coy,* the trial court allowed a semitransparent screen to be erected in court between the defendant and two youthful complainants in a child sex abuse trial so that the children could not see the defendant when they testified. The Court rejected this method, saying that face-to-face confrontation is the "core" of the constitutional right to confrontation.

Maryland v. Craig (1990)

Two years later, however, in *Maryland v. Craig* (497 U.S. 836 [1990]), the Court carved out an exception to this rule: Face-to-face confrontation may be dispensed with "when preventing such confrontation is necessary to further important public policy and the reliability of the testimony is otherwise assured." In that case, Craig was tried in a Maryland court for sexual abuse of a six-year-old child. In accordance with Maryland law, the judge permitted the child to testify in a different room, saying that courtroom testimony would result in the child's suffering such serious emotional distress that she could not reasonably communicate. This procedure allows the child, the prosecutor, and the defense counsel to withdraw from the courtroom to another room, where the child is examined and cross-examined. The judge, jury, and defendant remain in the courtroom, where the testimony is seen and heard via one-way, closed-circuit television. Craig claimed that the Maryland law violated his right to confrontation. The Court rejected the challenge, saying that although face-to-face confrontation forms the "core" of this constitutional right, it is not an indispensable element thereof.

The Right to Know the Identity of Prosecution Witnesses

United States v. Owens (1988)

Any witness who testifies against the accused must reveal his or her true name and address. Such information may be crucial to the defense in investigating and cross-examining the witness for possible impeachment. However, the Court concluded in *United States v. Owens* (484 U.S. 554 [1988]) that the admission into evidence of a prior, out-of-court identification of a witness, who was unable (due to loss of memory) to explain the basis for the identification, was not a violation of the right to confrontation. The Court added that the confrontation clause is satisfied if the defendant had a full and fair opportunity to bring up the witness's lapse of memory and other facts that consequently would tend to discredit the testimony.

The Right to Compulsory Process to Obtain Witnesses

Webb v. Texas (1972)

The Sixth Amendment expressly provides that the accused in a criminal prosecution shall have the right to compulsory process for obtaining witnesses in his or her favor. The right to obtain witnesses includes (1) the power to require the appearance of witnesses and (2) the right to present a defense, which in turn includes the defendant's right to present his or her own witnesses and his or her own version of the facts. The essence of this principle is that the defendant is given the same right as the prosecutor to present witnesses in state and federal proceedings. Thus, if the trial judge makes threatening remarks to the only defense witness, in effect driving the witness from the stand, the accused is deprived of the right to present a defense (*Webb v. Texas*, 409 U.S. 95 [1972]).

Chambers v. Mississippi (1973)

If the trial court excludes evidence crucial to the defense that bears substantial assurances of trustworthiness, this violates the right to present a defense—even when the evidence is technically not admissible under local rules of evidence. For example, in *Chambers v. Mississippi* (410 U.S. 284 [1973]), a defendant offered evidence of oral confessions to the crime by another witness. The trial court excluded the evidence because it constituted inadmissible hearsay under the local rules of evidence. This ruling was held to violate the defendant's right to present a defense, because the confessions bore substantial assurances of trustworthiness.

The Right to a Speedy and Public Trial

The Sixth Amendment provides that "in all criminal prosecutions the accused shall enjoy the right to a speedy and public trial." Two separate rights are guaranteed by this provision: a speedy trial and a public trial.

A Speedy Trial

A **speedy trial** is a trial free from unnecessary and unwanted delay. The Sixth Amendment applies only after a person becomes an "accused," meaning after the person has been formally charged with a crime or placed under arrest and detained to answer to a criminal charge. Most jurisdictions hold that, once a person is arrested, he or she is deemed an accused and is entitled to a speedy trial, even if later released on bail.

Violation of the constitutional right to a speedy trial is not established by delay alone. Instead, the determination of whether a case must be dismissed for lack of a speedy trial requires a balancing test. The conduct of both the prosecution and the defense are weighed, and the following factors are considered: (1) the length of the delay, (2) the reason for the delay, (3) the defendant's assertion or nonassertion of rights, and (4) any prejudice to the defendant. Any one factor alone is usually not sufficient either to justify or to condemn the delay in the trial (*Barker v. Wingo*, 407 U.S. 514 [1972]). If the delay is due to willful delay tactics by the accused, the accused will be deemed to have waived the right to a speedy trial. If the defendant's constitutional right to a speedy trial is violated, the only remedy is dismissal of charges. Dismissal prevents any further prosecution of the accused for the same offense.

Barker v. Wingo (1972)

In *Doggett v. United States* (505 U.S. 647 [1992]), a defendant was indicted on federal drug charges in 1980 but left the country before the Drug Enforcement Agency (DEA) could arrest him. The DEA knew the defendant was later imprisoned in Panama, but after requesting that he be returned to the United States, the DEA never followed up on the case. The DEA knew that the defendant had left Panama for Colombia but made no further attempt to locate him. The DEA was not aware that the defendant had reentered the United States in 1982 and that he had "subsequently married, earned a college degree, found steady employment, lived openly under his own name, and stayed within the law." He was eventually located during a simple credit check on individuals with outstanding warrants and was arrested in September 1988, eight and a half years after his original indictment. He objected to his prosecution, saying that it violated his Sixth Amendment right to a speedy trial.

Doggett v. United States (1992)

On appeal, the Court held that the extraordinary lag of eight and a half years between his indictment and arrest violated the defendant's right to a speedy trial. The Court concluded that the defendant could have faced trial six years earlier (when he reentered the United States) "but for the Government's inexcusable oversights."

In addition to the constitutional provision for a speedy trial, some statutes also provide for dismissal of an action when there have been unjustified delays in filing charges or bringing the defendant to trial. An example is the **Federal**

Speedy Trial Act of 1974, whose goal is to bring all federal criminal cases to trial within one hundred days following arrest. The act requires that an information or indictment be filed within thirty days after arrest, that arraignment follow within ten days thereafter, and that the trial commence within sixty days after arraignment. Similarly, many states require a trial begin within a given number of days after the filing of charges against the accused; otherwise, the charges are dismissed. Whether the charges can later be filed again in court depends upon the provisions of the state statute. Many statutes require, however, that the time limitation apply only after a request for a trial is initiated by the defendant.

A Public Trial

The accused has a right to a **public trial**—one that can be seen and heard by persons interested in ensuring that the proceedings are fair and just. The right, however, is not absolute. The trial judge, at his or her discretion, may exclude some or all spectators during particular parts of the proceedings for good cause, but under almost no circumstances may the friends and relatives of the accused be excluded from the trial. Spectators are frequently excluded if necessary to spare a victim extreme public embarrassment or humiliation, as in certain rape cases. Likewise, a judge may properly exclude certain persons if it can be shown that they are likely to threaten witnesses.

Criminal defendants also have a constitutional right to have their pretrial hearings conducted in public. However, the Court has not decided whether the public and the press have a right to attend pretrial hearings when the defendant wants them conducted in secret.

Authorities split on the issue of who may object to exclusions. Some courts hold that only the accused has the right to object. Others have indicated that the right also belongs to the public and that members of the public, such as the press, may therefore properly object to being excluded.

Juveniles have no constitutional right to a public trial. Many states still provide for closed juvenile adjudication proceedings and either limit or prohibit press reports. These practices are justified by the *parens patriae doctrine* (a doctrine by which the government supervises children or other persons who suffer from legal disability), which diminishes the constitutional rights of juveniles and protects them from unnecessary public exposure.

The Right to a Fair and Impartial Trial

The Due Process Clauses of the Fifth and Fourteenth Amendments guarantee the accused a fair trial by an impartial jury. What this guarantee basically means is that the circumstances surrounding the trial must not be such that they unduly influence the jury. Undue influence usually takes the form of publicity so massive that it becomes prejudicial to the accused.

The Prohibition of Prejudicial Publicity

Two basic principles of the U.S. system of criminal justice are that (1) a person must be convicted by an impartial tribunal and (2) a person must be convicted solely on the basis of evidence admitted at the trial. The publicity given to a notorious case before or during a trial may bias a jury or create a significant risk that the jury will consider information other than the evidence produced in court. Here are two examples:

- *Example 1.* Headlines announced that D had confessed to six murders and twenty-four burglaries, and reports were widely circulated that D had offered to plead guilty. Ninety percent of the prospective jurors interviewed expressed an opinion that D was guilty, and eight out of twelve jurors finally seated, familiar with the material facts, held such a belief. The Court held that D had been denied due process, stressing that this was a capital case (*Irvin v. Dowd,* 366 U.S. 717 [1961]).

Irvin v. Dowd (1961)

- *Example 2.* Police arranged to have B's prior confession shown several times on local television. The Court held that B had, in effect, been "tried" thereby—and that no actual prejudice needed to be shown to establish a denial of due process under such circumstances (*Rideau v. Louisiana,* 373 U.S. 723 [1963]).

Rideau v. Louisiana (1963)

Controlling Prejudicial Publicity

In an effort to control prejudicial publicity, the judge has the power to take several steps: change the venue, sequester the jury, grant a continuance, issue a gag order, or control the press.

Change of Venue A defendant claiming undue pretrial publicity or other circumstances that would endanger his or her right to a fair and impartial trial locally can move to have the *venue* (place) of the trial changed to another county, from which more impartial jurors can be drawn. This is allowable in both felony and misdemeanor cases.

Sequestration If there is a danger that jurors will be exposed to prejudicial publicity during the trial, some states permit **sequestration**—keeping jurors together during the trial and strictly controlling contact with the outside world—at the judge's discretion immediately following jury selection and continuing for the duration of the trial. A few states automatically sequester the jury throughout the trial, but most states sequester jurors only for serious cases and then only after the case is given to the jury for deliberation.

Continuance If the prejudice is severe, a *continuance* (postponement) may be granted to allow the threat to an impartial trial to subside.

Issuance of a Gag Rule The judge may impose a gag rule prohibiting the various parties in the trial from releasing information to the press or saying anything in public about the trial. Gag orders usually include the participating attorneys, witnesses, the police, and members of the jury. These orders are valid for the duration of the trial. However, the validity of a gag order beyond the duration of the trial is suspect because it may run afoul of constitutional rights.

Control of the Press This is a very difficult problem for the judge because of the First Amendment guarantee of freedom of the press. The press has a right to attend a criminal trial, but the media may be excluded if specific findings indicate that closure is necessary for a fair trial. The media do not have a Sixth Amendment right to attend a pretrial hearing in a criminal case. Generally, it is difficult to justify attempts to control the kinds of news items the news media can report in connection with a criminal case—even where such items may create a "clear and present danger" of an unfair trial for the accused. Courts usually prohibit the taking of photographs or the televising of courtroom proceedings. In a number of states, however, the televising of courtroom proceedings is left to the discretion of the trial judge.

Sheppard v. Maxwell (1966)

If the judge allows the televising of court proceedings, care must be taken not to create a "carnival atmosphere" inside the courtroom. The Supreme Court reversed the conviction in *Sheppard v. Maxwell* (384 U.S. 333 [1966]) because press coverage was too intrusive. The Court found the coverage so distracting to the judge, jurors, witnesses, and counsel that it created a "carnival atmosphere" and denied the defendant a fair trial.

The Right to Proof of Guilt beyond a Reasonable Doubt

The requirement that guilt be proved beyond a reasonable doubt derives from the Due Process Clause of the Constitution. The Bill of Rights contains no specific provisions on the degree of certainty needed for conviction, but the assumption is that it would be fundamentally unfair to convict anyone if there was any reasonable doubt that he or she had committed the crime.

What Must Be Proved

In every criminal case, the prosecution must prove the following beyond a reasonable doubt: (1) the question of guilt and (2) every element of the crime. Failure to prove both results in an acquittal of the accused.

For example, in a crime of theft, the element of intent and the fact that the property belongs to another person must be proved beyond a reasonable doubt. However, only elements of the crime that have to do with the defendant's guilt must be established beyond a reasonable doubt. Other issues are decided at a lower level of proof. Questions relating to the admissibility of evidence, such as whether the evidence was obtained by a lawful search or whether the defendant's confession was voluntary, need only be proved by a preponderance of the evidence.

Reasonable Doubt

Reasonable doubt is difficult to define. One court has defined it as follows:

> It is such a doubt as would cause a juror, after careful and candid and impartial consideration of all the evidence, to be so undecided that he cannot say that he has an abiding conviction of the defendant's guilt. It is such a doubt as would cause a reasonable person to hesitate or pause in the graver or more important transactions of life. However, it is not a fanciful doubt nor a whimsical doubt, nor a doubt based on conjecture. (*Moore v. United States*, 345 F.2d 97 [D.C. Cir. 1965]).

Moore v. United States (D.C. Cir. 1965)

This and other definitions used in various jurisdictions are unclear and do not provide a bright-line rule to guide jurors in their deliberations. In some states, reasonable doubt is defined by law; in other states, the term is defined by case law; and in a few states, there is no definition at all—leaving each court in the state to come up with its own definition. Federal courts do not prescribe a single definition.

In reality, despite instructions from the judge (couched in terms similar to those in the definition), an individual juror really determines what is meant by reasonable doubt. Definitions such as those given here are too legalistic and difficult to apply. In most cases, they merely provide a general framework for decision making. Ultimately, jurors define the term subjectively. Quantifying the term (such as defining reasonable doubt as comparable to 95 percent certainty of guilt) removes a lot of confusion, but such quantification is frowned upon by the legal community.

Cage v. Louisiana (1990)

In a 1990 case, *Cage v. Louisiana* (498 U.S. 976 [1990]), the Supreme Court invalidated a conviction in which the instructions of the trial court defined reasonable doubt as "such doubt as would give rise to grave uncertainty" and contrasted it with "a moral certainty" rather than "an absolute or mathematical certainty." These terms require a higher degree of doubt than reasonable doubt.

Sullivan v. Louisiana (1993)

Despite the absence of a clear and workable definition, the Court in 1993 said that a constitutionally deficient reasonable-doubt instruction by a judge to a jury can never be harmless error (that is, be automatically harmful) and therefore leads to a reversal of the conviction on appeal (*Sullivan v. Louisiana*, 508 U.S. 275 [1993]). In a later case, the Court held that references to "moral evidence," "moral certainty," and "substantial doubt" in the jury instructions given by a Nebraska trial court did not violate the due process requirement of the Fourteenth Amendment (*Victor v. Nebraska*, 511 U.S. 1 [1994]). The Court added that the Constitution does not prescribe any particular phrasing to be used when giving the jury instructions, as long as "taken as a whole, the instructions correctly convey the concept of reasonable doubt." The Court refrained, however, from saying what *reasonable doubt* really means.

Victor v. Nebraska (1994)

Summary

The Right to Trial by Jury

- *Source of the right.* Sixth Amendment.
- *Size of the jury.* The jury may number from six to twelve.
- *Unanimous verdict.* Not required by the Constitution.
- *When is a jury trial required?* When more than six months' imprisonment is authorized for the offense.
- *What is a jury of peers?* A jury whose membership is not consciously restricted to a particular group.
- *What is unconstitutional in jury selection?* Disqualification of jurors based on race, gender, creed, color, national origin, and other prohibited categories.

The Right to Counsel

- *Source of the right.* Sixth Amendment.
- *Why counsel is needed.* The defendant's lack of skill in the law might result in a wrongful conviction.
- *Two types of counsel.* Retained by defendant and court-appointed (if indigent).
- *Proceedings to which the right to counsel applies.* All serious offenses, as well as misdemeanors for which the defendant faces a possible jail sentence.
- *Right to effective assistance of counsel.* Guaranteed but difficult to establish ineffective counsel on appeal.
- *Right to act as one's own counsel.* Allowed but only if the accused is aware of his or her right to counsel, if there is an express waiver, and if the accused is competent.

The Right to Protection against Self-Incrimination

- *Source of the right.* Fifth Amendment.
- *Scope of the right.* Applies only to testimonial, not physical, self-incrimination.

- *Two separate privileges during trial.* The privilege of an accused and the privilege of a witness.
- *Effect of a grant of immunity.* The person can be forced to testify.
- *Types of immunity.* Transactional and use and derivative use.

The Right to Protection against Double Jeopardy

- *Source of the right.* Sixth Amendment.
- *Definition.* Successive prosecution of a defendant for the same offense by the same jurisdiction.
- *When does it attach?* In a jury trial, when a competent jury has been sworn; in a trial before a judge, when the first witness has been called and sworn.
- *What same offense means.* Two or more offenses have the same elements.
- *What lesser included offense means.* An offense that "is composed of some, but not all, of the elements of the greater crime, and which does not have any element not included in the greater offense."

The Right to a Speedy and Public Trial

- *Source of the right.* Sixth Amendment.
- *Speedy trial.* A trial free from unnecessary and unwanted delay. If the delay is due to willful delay tactics by the accused, the accused will be deemed to have waived the right.
- *Public trial.* A trial that can be seen and heard by persons interested in ensuring that the proceedings are fair and just.

The Right to a Fair and Impartial Trial

- *Source of the right.* Due Process Clauses of the Fifth and Fourteenth Amendments.
- *What it means.* The circumstances surrounding the trial must not be such that they unduly influence the judge or jury.

- *Ways a judge may control prejudicial publicity.* Change of venue, sequestration, continuance, issuance of a gag rule, control of the press.

The Right to Proof of Guilt beyond a Reasonable Doubt

- *Source of the right.* No specific constitutional provision but inferred from the Due Process Clauses of the Fifth and Fourteenth Amendments.

- *Definition.* Difficult to define with precision. The definition varies from one state to another and even from court to court within a state. No specific definition is constitutionally required as long as "taken as a whole, the instructions correctly convey the concept of reasonable doubt" (whatever that means).

- *What must be proved beyond a reasonable doubt?* The question of guilt and every element of the crime charged.

Review Questions and Hypothetical Cases

1. Suppose the state of Nebraska passes a law providing that all crimes are to be tried by a six-member jury. Is that law constitutional? Assume that the same law also provides that a 5-to-1 vote for conviction results in conviction. Will the law be valid? Explain your answer.

2. X, a man accused of rape, was tried and convicted by a jury made up of all women. Was his constitutional right to trial by a jury of peers violated? Justify your answer.

3. Discuss the responsibility of a defense lawyer in the American system of justice.

4. What is the meaning of the phrase *effective assistance of counsel*? Discuss why it is hard for prisoners to establish that their counsel during trial was ineffective.

5. Compare and contrast the protection against compulsory self-incrimination of an accused and of a witness.

6. Assume you are a lawyer for Defendant W in a prosecution for bribery against a high government official. Your client, a co-defendant, is given a choice by the prosecutor between transactional immunity and use and derivative use immunity. Which immunity would you advise your client to take and why?

7. P, a witness, is given immunity to testify in a state criminal proceeding in Arizona. Can P be prosecuted in nearby New Mexico in a subsequent criminal trial arising out of the same act? Justify your answer.

8. Q was charged with negligent homicide after she supposedly shot her neighbor accidentally. She was acquitted in that case. Two years later, however, prosecutors came across strong evidence establishing that Q in fact intended to kill that neighbor because of jealousy and made it appear like the killing was accidental. Can Q now be prosecuted for murder, a higher offense? Explain.

9. What is meant by *guilt beyond a reasonable doubt*? Why is it difficult for jurors or judges to apply?

10. Assume that H, an indigent Hispanic male, was charged in Colorado with a misdemeanor. The offense carries a maximum ten-month jail sentence, if convicted. He was tried without a lawyer before a jury of six white women. He was convicted on a 5-to-1 jury vote; the jury gave him a two-month sentence in the local jail. Explore all possible constitutional issues in the case, and state how the Court will likely decide each issue if brought to it on appeal.

11. J, a prison inmate in Texas, is serving the first six months of a five-year sentence for robbery. He seeks release, claiming that he had ineffective counsel because the lawyer assigned to him during the trial graduated from an unaccredited law school (although he passed the bar examination), was last in his class of seventy-five students, never had a defendant acquitted in five years of law practice, and was sometimes under

the influence of drugs during the trial. Assume all these are true. You are a federal judge hearing the case. Is J's claim of ineffective counsel valid or not? Support your decision.

12. Assume you are a judge in state court presiding over a high-profile criminal case where the governor, who is married and has five children, killed his campaign manager (who was also his mistress) because she wanted to break off their relationship. The case has generated tremendous publicity in the local and national media. Questions: (a) Discuss what constitutional issues might arise during the trial, given the nature of the case; and (b) as the trial judge, what you can do to avoid the conviction being reversed by the U.S. Supreme Court on those issues if raised on appeal.

Key Terms

Go to the Criminal Procedure 7e website for flash cards that will help you master the definitions of these terms.

Brady rule, 472
challenge for cause, 455
death-qualified juries, 459
double jeopardy, 479
fair response, 476
Federal Speedy Trial Act of 1974, 488
hung jury, 454
immunity, 477
indigent defendant, 465
jury of peers, 455

lesser included offense, 482
nonunanimous verdict, 453
peremptory challenge, 455
petty offense, 454
physical self-incrimination, 474
privilege of a witness, 476
privilege of the accused, 475
public trial, 489
reasonable doubt, 492
retained counsel, 464
same offense, 482

sequestration, 490
serious offense, 454
speedy trial, 488
statute of limitations, 477
testimonial (or communicative) self-incrimination, 475
transactional immunity, 478
use and derivative use immunity, 478

Holdings of Key Cases

See Appendix C for information on how to find cases in this chapter on FindLaw.com.

Apodaca v. Oregon, 406 U.S. 404 (1972) A 10-to-2 vote for conviction is constitutional.

Apprendi v. New Jersey, 530 U.S. 466 [2000]) Judges may not alone determine a finding of fact that increases the level of punishment for the defendant beyond the prescribed statutory maximum. Any fact, other than the fact of prior conviction, must be submitted to a jury and proved beyond a reasonable doubt. A finding of fact cannot be made by the judge alone based on a lower degree of certainty.

Argersinger v. Hamlin, 407 U.S. 25 (1972) The right to counsel applies even in misdemeanor cases if the accused faces the possibility of imprisonment, however short.

Baldwin v. New York, 399 U.S. 66 (1970) An offense is considered serious if the maximum punishment authorized by statute is imprisonment for more than six months, regardless of the actual penalty imposed. Therefore, the accused is entitled to a jury trial.

Ballew v. Georgia, 435 U.S. 223 (1978) The minimum number of jurors is six. Juries of five or fewer members are unconstitutional because they have too few to provide for effective group discussion. Juries of fewer than six members would also diminish the chances of drawing from a fair, representative cross-section of the community, thus impairing the accuracy of fact-finding.

Barker v. Wingo, **407 U.S. 514 (1972)** Violation of the right to a speedy trial is not established by delay alone. Rather, the determination requires a balancing test.

Batson v. Kentucky, **476 U.S. 79 (1986)** A prosecutor's use of peremptory challenges to exclude members of the defendant's race from a jury solely on racial grounds violates the equal protection rights of both the defendant and the excluded jurors.

Bell v. Cone, **505 U.S. 685 (2002)** A death sentence stands even though the defendant's lawyer failed to make an argument to the jury to save the defendant's life.

Blanton v. North Las Vegas, **489 U.S. 538 (1989)** When a state treats drunk driving as a petty offense, no jury trial is needed, even if other peripheral sanctions (such as a fine and automatic loss of a driver's license) may also be imposed.

Blockburger v. United States, **284 U.S. 299 (1932)** A second prosecution is barred if the two prosecutions are for offenses that have identical statutory elements or if one is a lesser included offense of the other.

Brady v. Maryland, **373 U.S. 83 (1963)** Due process is violated when the prosecution suppresses evidence favorable to an accused upon request where the evidence is material either to guilt or to punishment. This applies whether the prosecution acted in bad faith or in good faith in suppressing the evidence.

Brown v. Ohio, **432 U.S. 161 (1977)** Prosecution for joyriding prohibits a second trial for theft of a vehicle because no additional facts are needed for the second charge.

Burdine v. Johnson, **No. 99-21034 (5th Cir. 2001)** A capital defendant whose defense lawyer slept during the trial did not have effective counsel and therefore deserved a new trial.

Burks v. United States, **437 U.S. 1 (1978)** A defendant whose conviction is reversed because the evidence is insufficient as a matter of law to sustain the conviction cannot be retried; such a reversal amounts to an acquittal.

Cage v. Louisiana, **498 U.S. 976 (1990)** A trial court's jury instructions on reasonable doubt that equates it with "grave uncertainty" and "actual substantive doubt" is invalid because these terms require a higher standard of doubt than reasonable doubt.

Campbell v. Louisiana, **523 U.S. 392 (1998)** A white defendant has standing to complain of discrimination against blacks in the selection of a grand jury.

Chambers v. Mississippi, **410 U.S. 284 (1973)** The defendant offered evidence of an oral confession to the crime by another witness. The trial court excluded the evidence because it constituted inadmissible hearsay under the local rules of evidence. This ruling violated the defendant's right to present a defense because the confessions bore substantial assurances of trustworthiness.

Coy v. Iowa, **487 U.S. 1012 (1988)** The right to confrontation includes the right to physically face witnesses at trial. Hence, a state law that allows testimony via closed-circuit television or behind a screen violates a defendant's Sixth Amendment rights.

Crawford v. Washington, **541 U.S. 36 (2004)** The use by the prosecution of a wife's statement obtained during a police interrogation violates the defendant's constitutional rights, because the wife could not testify during the trial.

Doggett v. United States, **505 U.S. 647 (1992)** The delay of eight and a half years between a defendant's indictment and arrest, caused by government negligence, can violate the Sixth Amendment even if no actual prejudice to the defendant is shown.

Faretta v. California, **422 U.S. 806 (1975)** An accused has a constitutional right to waive counsel and represent himself or herself in a criminal proceeding.

Fuller v. Oregon, **417 U.S. 40 (1974)** A system that provides counsel to defendants but specifies as a condition of probation or parole that the defendant reimburse the state or county for the fees of the appointed lawyer is valid as long as it exempts indigents who cannot afford to pay.

Georgia v. McCollum, **505 U.S. 42 (1992)** The Constitution prohibits a criminal defendant from engaging in purposeful discrimination based on race in the exercise of peremptory challenges.

Gideon v. Wainwright, **372 U.S. 335 (1963)** The Sixth Amendment right to counsel is applicable to state proceedings through the Due Process Clause of the Fourteenth Amendment.

The right to counsel applies every time an accused is charged with a felony offense.

Gilbert v. California, 388 U.S. 263 (1967) A defendant can be forced to stand up for identification in the courtroom, to put on certain items of clothing, or to give a handwriting sample.

Green v. United States, 355 U.S. 184 (1957) A defendant who appeals a conviction and obtains a new trial cannot be charged with an offense that is greater than that for which he or she was originally convicted.

Griffin v. California, 380 U.S. 609 (1965) The prosecutor is not permitted to make any comment or argument to the jury suggesting that the defendant is guilty because he or she refused to testify; making such comments will lead to a reversal of the conviction on appeal.

Heath v. Alabama, 474 U.S. 82 (1985) Under the dual sovereignty doctrine, successive prosecutions by two states for the same conduct do not violate the Double Jeopardy Clause of the Fifth Amendment.

Holland v. Illinois, 493 U.S. 474 (1990) The prosecution's racially motivated use of peremptory challenges to exclude people from the trial jury does not violate the defendant's Sixth Amendment right to trial by an impartial jury.

Illinois v. Allen, 397 U.S. 337 (1970) The following methods for dealing with a disruptive defendant are approved: (1) holding the defendant in contempt of court, (2) binding and gagging the defendant in the courtroom, and (3) removing the defendant from the courtroom until he or she promises to behave properly.

Illinois v. Vitale, 447 U.S. 410 (1980) A conviction for failure to reduce speed to avoid an accident does not necessarily prohibit a second charge for involuntary manslaughter, because vehicular manslaughter does not always require proof of failure to reduce speed.

In re Gault, 387 U.S. 1 (1967) A juvenile proceeding is civil in nature, but a juvenile is nonetheless entitled to appointed counsel if the proceeding can lead to commitment in an institution where the juvenile's freedom will be restricted.

Iowa v. Tovar, 541 U.S. 77 (2004) If a defendant says that he or she wishes to plead guilty without the assistance of counsel, the trial judge does not need to spell out all the possible consequences before accepting the plea.

Irvin v. Dowd, 366 U.S. 717 (1961) Headlines announced that the defendant had confessed to six murders and twenty-four burglaries, and reports were widely circulated that the defendant had offered to plead guilty. Ninety percent of the prospective jurors interviewed expressed an opinion that the defendant was guilty, and eight out of twelve jurors finally seated held such a belief. All these circumstances denied the defendant his due process right, particularly because this was a capital punishment case.

J. E. B. v. Alabama, 511 U.S. 127 (1994) The Equal Protection Clause prohibits discrimination based on gender in the selection of jurors.

Johnson v. California, 125 S.Ct. 2410 (2005) "Permissible inferences of discrimination were sufficient to establish a prima facie case of discrimination under *Batson,* shifting the burden to the state to explain adequately the racial exclusion by offering permissible race-neutral justifications for the strikes."

Johnson v. Louisiana, 406 U.S. 356 (1972) A 9-to-3 jury verdict for conviction is constitutional.

Kastigar v. United States, 406 U.S. 441 (1972) Prosecutors need only grant use and derivative use immunity to compel an unwilling witness to testify. The witness is not constitutionally entitled to transactional immunity before he or she can be compelled to testify.

Kyles v. Whitley, 514 U.S. 419 (1995) Because the effect of the state-suppressed evidence favorable to the defendant raised a reasonable probability that its disclosure would have produced a different result at trial, the conviction had to be reversed.

Lewis v. United States, 59 CrL 2206 (1996) A defendant who is prosecuted in a single case for more than one petty offense does not have a constitutional right to trial by jury even if the total penalty exceeds six months.

Lockhart v. Fretwell, 506 U.S. 364 (1993) To show prejudice in appeals based on ineffective counsel, the defendant must demonstrate that counsel's errors were so serious as to result in a trial whose result was unfair or unreliable—not merely that the outcome would have been different.

Lockhart v. McCree, 476 U.S. 162 (1986) Persons who are unwilling to vote for the death penalty under any circumstances may be disqualified from a capital offense jury.

Maryland v. Craig, 497 U.S. 836 (1990) Despite defendants' Sixth Amendment rights, face-to-face confrontation may be dispensed with when it is necessary to further important public policy and the reliability of the testimony is otherwise assured.

Mickens v. Taylor, No. 00-9285 (2002) A capital defendant whose lawyer represented the victim on unrelated charges that were pending at the time of the murder had effective counsel.

Mooney v. Holohan, 294 U.S. 103 (1935) In a criminal proceeding, the prosecutor has a duty to disclose evidence favorable to a defendant; failure to disclose violates a defendant's constitutional right to due process.

Moore v. United States, 345 F.2d 97 (D.C. Cir. 1965) Reasonable doubt is defined as follows: "It is such a doubt as would cause a juror, after careful and candid and impartial consideration of all the evidence, to be so undecided that he cannot say that he has an abiding conviction of the defendant's guilt."

Murphy v. Waterfront Commission, 378 U.S. 52 (1964) If a state has granted a witness valid immunity from prosecution, the federal government is not permitted to make use of the testimony (or any of its "fruits") in a federal prosecution against the witness.

North Carolina v. Pearce, 395 U.S. 711 (1969) The constitutional right to protection against double jeopardy "protects against a second prosecution for the same offense after acquittal; it protects against a second prosecution for the same offense after conviction; and it protects against multiple punishments for the same offense."

Powell v. Alabama, 287 U.S. 45 (1932) The trial in state court of nine youths for a capital offense without a defense lawyer violated their right to due process.

Powers v. Ohio, 499 U.S. 400 (1991) A criminal defendant may object to a race-based exclusion of jurors through peremptory challenges even though the defendant and the excluded jurors are not of the same race.

Rideau v. Louisiana, 373 U.S. 723 (1963) Police arranged to have the defendant's prior confession shown several times on local television. The Court held that the defendant had, in effect, been "tried" thereby and that no actual prejudice needed to be shown to establish a denial of due process under such circumstances.

Ring v. Arizona, 536 U.S. 584 (2002) A finding by the judge of an aggravating circumstance (which the judge was authorized to do under Arizona death penalty law) after a jury trial was "the functional equivalent of an element of a greater offense than the one covered by the jury's guilty verdict," and therefore violated the defendant's right to a jury trial.

Rutledge v. United States, 517 U.S. 292 (1996) There cannot be two punishments for two offenses if one is a lesser included offense.

Scott v. Illinois, 440 U.S. 367 (1979) The state is not required to appoint counsel for an indigent defendant charged with a nonpetty offense that is punishable by imprisonment if the defendant is not, in fact, sentenced to imprisonment.

Sheppard v. Maxwell, 384 U.S. 333 (1966) A courtroom television process that is so distracting to the judge, jurors, witnesses, and counsel that it creates a "carnival atmosphere" denies the defendant a fair trial.

Singer v. United States, 380 U.S. 24 (1965) The prosecution has the right to demand a trial by jury even if the defendant waives it. Criminal defendants have no constitutional right to have their cases tried before a judge alone.

Smith v. Massachusetts, 543 U.S.____(2005) A judge's acquittal of a defendant midway through a trial by jury prohibits the judge from reconsidering that acquittal later in the trial.

South Dakota v. Neville, 459 U.S. 553 (1983) A law that allows the accused to refuse to take a blood alcohol test and provides that such refusal may be admitted in evidence against him or her is constitutional.

Strauder v. West Virginia, 100 U.S. 303 (1880) "The State denies a black defendant equal protection of the laws when it puts him on trial before a jury from which members of his race have been purposely excluded."

Strickland v. Washington, 466 U.S. 668 (1984)
The Court assumes that effective assistance of counsel is present unless the adversarial process is so undermined by counsel's conduct that the trial cannot be relied upon to have produced a just result. An accused who claims ineffective counsel must show (1) deficient performance by counsel and (2) a reasonable probability that, but for such deficiency, the result of the proceedings would have been different.

Strickler v. Greene, 527 U.S. 263 (1999) The prosecution's failure to disclose evidence in the form of interview notes from a detective that seriously undermined the truthfulness of the only eyewitness's testimony in a murder trial did not violate the *Brady* rule, because the evidence was not material to the issue of guilt or innocence.

Sullivan v. Louisiana, 508 U.S. 275 (1993) A constitutionally deficient reasonable-doubt instruction cannot be harmless error and therefore requires a reversal of a conviction.

Taylor v. Louisiana, 419 U.S. 522 (1975)
Excluding women from juries, or giving them automatic exemptions with the result that jury panels are almost totally male, is invalid.

Taylor v. United States, 414 U.S. 17 (1973) If an accused is present at the start of the trial but later voluntarily absents himself or herself, the trial may continue in the absence of the accused; the accused is considered to have waived his or her right to be present.

United States v. Agurs, 427 U.S. 97 (1976) A defendant's failure to request that favorable evidence be shown to the defense does not leave the government free of all obligation, but the prosecutor's failure in this particular case to show the favorable evidence did not violate the defendant's right to due process.

United States v. Bagley, 473 U.S. 667 (1985) Whether the evidence is requested or not, evidence favorable to the accused is material, and therefore it is constitutional error when it is suppressed by the government.

United States v. Balsys, 524 U.S. 666 (1998) A witness's fear that the testimony he is ordered to give in a proceeding in the United States will subject him to prosecution in another country is not a valid basis for asserting his Fifth Amendment right to protection against self-incrimination.

United States v. Cronic, 466 U.S. 648 (1984) A claim of ineffective assistance of counsel can be made only by pointing out specific errors of trial counsel. It cannot be based on an inference drawn from the defense counsel's inexperience or lack of time to prepare, the gravity of the charges, the complexity of the defense, or the accessibility of witnesses to counsel.

United States v. Owens, 484 U.S. 554 (1988) It does not violate a defendant's right to confrontation if the court admits into evidence a prior out-of-court identification of the accused by a witness who is unable, due to loss of memory, to explain the basis for the identification.

United States v. Robinson, 485 U.S. 25 (1988) A prosecutor's statement to the jury during closing arguments that the defendant could have taken the witness stand but refused to do so is proper as long as it is in response to the defense counsel's argument that the government had not allowed the defendant to explain his or her side of the story.

Victor v. Nebraska, 511 U.S. 1 (1994) References to "moral evidence," "moral certainty," and "substantial doubt" in the jury instructions do not violate the Due Process Clause.

Webb v. Texas, 409 U.S. 95 (1972) If the trial judge makes threatening remarks to the only defense witness, in effect driving the witness from the stand, the accused is deprived of the right to present a defense.

Wheat v. United States, 486 U.S. 153 (1988) A defendant's right to hire an attorney of his or her own choosing may be limited by the trial court to avoid a conflict of interest.

Wiggins v. Smith, 539 U.S. 510 (2003) The defendant's Sixth Amendment right to effective counsel in a death penalty case was violated by his lawyer's failure to conduct a reasonable investigation into his social history and mitigating factors.

Williams v. Florida, 399 U.S. 78 (1970) A Florida law providing for a six-member jury in all criminal cases except those involving capital offenses is constitutional.

Witherspoon v. Illinois, 391 U.S. 510 (1968) It is unconstitutional to exclude for cause potential jurors who have reservations about the death penalty.

***Yarborough v. Gentry,* 540 U.S. 1 (2003)** The lawyer's closing argument in a case, in which he admitted some of the defendant's shortcomings, did not deprive the defendant of effective assistance of counsel, because the summation brought out several key points.

You Be the Judge . . .

In the Court of Appeals of New York State

In New York, Lewis was on trial for possessing and selling cocaine. There was one key witness against Lewis, a person who had made a cocaine purchase from him. This witness returned with the police when they went to execute a search warrant on Lewis's residence for drugs and other items evidence of drug trafficking.

The witness made a written statement about his knowledge of the defendant's drug trafficking, which was what he was to be called to testify about by the prosecution. The prosecution gave Lewis's lawyer a copy of this statement shortly after jury selection. Within one hour, the witness received a threatening phone call: an unknown male told him that he had better not testify, saying that he knew where the witness's family lived.

The next day the witness called the police to let them know that he had been threatened and therefore refused to testify out of fear. He told a state police investigator that he would rather go to jail than testify. The law was clear: the prosecution could use the witness's written statement as evidence without the witness being present to testify, *unless* the witness was absent because of threats made by Lewis. The court then had a hearing to determine whether Lewis was behind the threats.

The state police investigator testified as to what the witness had told him, including the timing, which fixed the time of the telephone threat at just an hour after Lewis's lawyer got the written statement. Lewis then testified, admitting that his lawyer had shown him the statement right after the prosecution had handed it over, but he said it did not worry him. He said he told only one person, his friend Dale, and had not told Dale who the witness was. Dale could not have made the threats without knowing who to threaten.

This left open the possibility that Lewis's lawyer had told someone else about the statement who had decided to make the threatening phone call. The prosecution then made a highly unusual move: they called Lewis's lawyer to the witness stand to help make their case against Lewis. He did not object and willingly took the stand.

Lewis's lawyer testified that he had told no one else but Lewis about the witness's statement. The Judge decided that Lewis was behind the threats, and so allowed the prosecution to use the witness's written statement. Lewis was convicted of drug trafficking.

How will you decide this legal issue? Did the willing testimony of Lewis's lawyer for the prosecution constitute ineffective assistance of counsel?

The Court's decision The Court of Appeals for the state of New York decided that Lewis was denied effective assistance of counsel by his lawyer's testimony. In an adversarial system, each party's lawyer must be only that party's advocate. It is improper for a lawyer to "switch sides." A lawyer may never testify against his client. If the lawyer is called to do so, he must object. If the Court overrules the lawyer's objection, then the lawyer must withdraw from representing the defendant. Here, in failing to do so, the lawyer betrayed his client in a very significant way and could no longer be "effective." *People v. Lewis,* N.Y.3d 224 (N.Y. App. Div 4th Dept., 2003).

In the United States Court of Appeals for the Sixth Circuit

In Guernsey County, Ohio, Stumpf and Wesley stopped their car beside I-70 and walked to a nearby house, belonging to Mr. and Mrs. Stout. Stumpf and Wesley came to the Stouts' door and asked to use the telephone. The Stouts graciously let the two men use the phone. After using the phone, Stumpf and Wesley produced pistols and told the Stouts they were being robbed. Stumpf herded the couple back into their bedroom, while Wesley ransacked the house for something to steal. Mr. Stout moved toward Stumpf, who shot him between the eyes. The wounded Stout pushed Stumpf into the next room. He was pistol-whipped and shot again. Though then only semiconscious, he heard four shots being fired: these were the four shots that killed his wife.

Stumpf and Wesley fled in the Stouts' car and were picked up a few days later. Stumpf admitted to being involved in the robbery and shooting. He was indicted for the capital murder of Mrs. Stout. Investigators determined that the same weapon, a chrome Raven, had fired seven shots and another, the black .25, had fired just one based on the casings recovered. Which rounds had hit Mr. Stout were a mystery, but all four bullets that killed Mrs. Stout came from the same gun. So both men could have shot Mr. Stout, or only one. Ballistics determined that the black .25 tended to jam after firing just one shot.

Stumpf pled guilty to the murder but argued during sentencing that it was Wesley, and not he, who had shot and killed Mrs. Stout. He said that he shot Stout once with the chrome Raven, then dropped the gun and ran out. The prosecutor argued for death, saying that Stumpf shot both the Stouts. Stumpf's story was consistent with some of the evidence: If Stumpf shot once and dropped his pistol, the chrome Raven, and Wesley's black .25 had jammed after shooting Mr. Stout, then it would make sense that Wesley would have picked up the other gun if he wanted to kill Mrs. Stout. The three-judge panel that heard the arguments on sentencing, though, sentenced Stumpf to death.

When Wesley's trial came up, seven months later, his cell mate testified that Wesley had confided that Stumpf's version of the shooting was the truth, and that Wesley had therefore been the killer. The same prosecutor then argued that in fact Wesley had been the shooter, the opposite of what he had argued to convince the court to sentence Stumpf to death seven months earlier.

How will you decide this legal issue? Was the use of two contradictory versions of the facts by the same prosecutor to convict two different persons of being the actual killer improper?

The Court's decision The U.S. Court of Appeals for the Sixth Circuit decided that the prosecutor's behavior was in fact improper, and sent Stumpf back to be retried or released. Although new evidence came to light in Wesley's cell mate's testimony, the prosecutor could have then not supported his previously obtained death sentence. It is fundamentally unfair for two persons to be convicted of the same act, based on a prosecutor's arguing both sides of a factual issue. *Stumpf v. Mitchell*, 367 F.3d 594 (6th Cir. 2004). The story is not over; the U.S. Supreme Court has agreed to hear this case. *Mitchell v. Stumpf*, 125 S.Ct. 824 (2005).

Recommended Readings

William V. Dorseano III. *Reexamining the right to trial by jury.* SMU Law Review (Special Issue) 1695, 1737 (2001).

Charles Geyth. *The testimonial component of the right against self-incrimination.* Catholic University Law Review 611–642 (1987).

Anthony Lewis. *Keynote address (Symposium on indigent criminal defense in Texas).* South Texas Law Review 1050–1057 (2001).

James S. Montana Jr. *Right to counsel: Courts adhere to bright-line limits.* 16 Criminal Justice 4 (2001).

Kimberly A. Mottley, David Abrami, and Daryl K. Brown. *An overview of the American criminal jury.* St. Louis University Public Law Review 99, 122 (2002).

Notes

1. Bureau of Justice Statistics, *Report to the Nation on Crime and Justice,* 2nd ed. (Washington, D.C.: U.S. Government Printing Office, 1988), p. 84.

2. Steven L. Emanuel and Steven Knowles, *Emanuel Law Outlines: Criminal Procedure* (Larchmont, NY: Emanuel, 1998–99), p. 321.

3. Wayne R. LaFave and Jerold H. Israel, *Criminal Procedure,* 2nd ed. (St. Paul, MN: West, 1992), p. 523.

4. ABA Standards, Providing Defense Services, Sec. 6.1.

5. Supra note 3, at 535.

6. Henry C. Black, *Black's Law Dictionary,* 6th ed. (St. Paul, MN: West, 1990), p. 812.

7. Supra note 2, p. 365.

Chapter 13

Legal Liabilities and Other Consequences of Police Misconduct

What You Will Learn

- Being sued is an occupational hazard in modern-day policing.

- Legal liabilities in police work fall into two categories: under federal law and under state law.

- Legal liabilities under federal and state laws further fall into three sub-categories: administrative, civil, and criminal.

- An officer can be prosecuted under state and federal criminal laws for the same act, and the protection against double jeopardy does not apply.

- Civil liability under federal law (Section 1983) and under state law (state tort cases) have different requirements.

- Good faith (in federal law) and official immunity (in state tort cases) are the defenses often used in civil liability cases.

- In a civil liability case, plaintiffs often sue the officer, the supervisor, and the agency. The bases for liability for these defendants are different.

- Other consequences of police misconduct besides civil liabilities are criminal prosecutions, exclusion of evidence illegally obtained, administrative investigation, and revocation of law enforcement license.

The Top 5 Important Cases on Legal Liabilities and Other Consequences of Police Misconduct

Harlow v. Fitzgerald, 457 U.S. 800 **(1982)** Government officials performing discretionary functions are shielded from liability for civil damages as long as their conduct does not violate clearly established statutory or constitutional rights of which a reasonable person would have known.

Saucier v. Katz, 533 U.S. 194 **(2001)** A ruling on qualified immunity in Section 1983 cases is not linked to a ruling on the violation of a constitutional right. It should be made early in the proceedings so that, if established, the cost and expense of a trial are avoided.

Groh v. Ramirez, 540 U.S. 551 **(2004)** An officer is not entitled to qualified immunity if "it would be clear to a reasonable officer that his conduct was unlawful in the situation he confronted."

Brosseau v. Haugen, 543 U.S.____ **(2004)** "Because the focus is on whether the officer had fair notice that her conduct was unlawful, reasonableness is judged against the backdrop of the law at the time of the conduct. If the law at that time did not clearly establish that the officer's conduct would violate the Constitution, the officer should not be subject to liability, or indeed, even the burdens of litigation."

Town of Castle Rock v. Gonzales, 545 U.S.____ **(2005)** The wrongful failure by the police to arrest a husband who violated a domestic relations court restraining order does not amount to a violation of a constitutional right under the Fourteenth Amendment Due Process Clause and therefore does not result in liability under federal law.

CASE BRIEFS

Town of Castle Rock v. Gonzales (2005)
Groh v. Ramirez et al. (2004)

Introduction

One of the realities of modern-day policing is the threat of civil lawsuit. American society is litigation prone, and the police are a popular target because they exercise immense authority and are involved in highly charged, often emotional, confrontations with the public. The police are generally loved and respected because they provide a needed service to the community, but they are also sometimes reviled because some officers behave in a manner that reflects poorly on the departments and the other officers. Lawsuits have become so pervasive that there is probably no major police department in the country whose

Table 13.1 An Illustrative Chart of Police Liabilities

Conduct Involved	Possible Types of Liability			
	Ethics Violation	Administrative Liability	Civil Liability	Criminal Liability
Being negative about policing in general	No	No	No	No
Not giving 100% effort to the job	Probably	Generally, no	No	No
Accepting a free meal while on the job	Probably	Probably	No	No
Being rude or discourteous to a crime victim	Probably	No, unless specifically prohibited	No	No
Stopping drivers for minor traffic violations despite prohibition by agency policy	No	Yes	No	No
Making stops, seizures, or arrests based on racial profile	Yes	Yes	Yes	No, unless specifically prohibited by law
Using excessive force on a suspect	Yes	Yes	Yes	Yes
Accepting bribes	Yes	Yes	Yes	Yes
Fatally shooting a suspect without justification	Yes	Yes	Yes	Yes

officers and supervisors have not been sued in state or federal court. Liability lawsuits are here to stay; hence, this chapter must be learned well.

This chapter focuses on lawsuits the public usually files against police officers. First, we need to look at the wider liability picture. Legal liabilities (referring to lawsuits) are but a part of the wider liability picture that consists of the following actions: ethics violations, administrative violations (meaning violations of agency rules), violations that lead to civil liabilities, and violations that lead to criminal liabilities. Ethics and criminal violations can lead to reprimands or dismissal from the job; civil liabilities lead to monetary payments for damages and attorney's fees, while criminal liabilities result in the usual criminal sanctions such as fines, probation, or incarceration in a prison or jail. The wider liability picture is illustrated in Table 13.1. In general, the more serious the conduct, the greater is the likelihood that all of the liabilities will be imposed if what happened violates ethics, agency rules, civil statutes, and criminal laws.

Lawsuits against the Police: An Occupational Hazard

The Liability Reporter, published by the police-oriented Americans for Effective Law Enforcement, Inc., and other publications that monitor police liabilities, have featured the following headlines in recent years:

- "New York Will Pay $50 Million in 50,000 Illegal Strip-Searches."[1]
- "The City of Los Angeles Agreed to Pay $15 Million to a Man Who Said Police Officers Shot Him in the Head and Chest and then Framed Him in the Attack."[2]
- "Jury Assesses Damages of $256 Million for Motorist's Collision with Off-Duty Police Officer Which Left One Child Dead, One Quadriplegic, and One Paralyzed On One Side with a Damaged Brain."[3]
- "Chicago Reaches $18 Million Settlement with Family of Unarmed Woman Shot and Killed by Officer at the Conclusion of a 31-Block Pursuit of the Vehicle in Which She Was Riding."[4]
- "Oregon Jury Awards $8 Million, Including $4.5 Million in Punitive Damages, against State Trooper Who Allegedly Attacked Female Motorist After Stopping Her for Speeding and Then Shot Her in the Shoulder After She Attempted to Drive Away."[5]
- "Illinois Jury Awards $11 Million to 17-Year-Old Passenger Injured in Car Allegedly Pursued at 70 MPH by Officers Who Wanted Driver Because of Outstanding Warrant on Drug Charges."[6]
- "Passenger Injured in High-Speed Pursuit of Car in Which She Was Riding Is Awarded $11 Million by Illinois Jury."[7]

Lawsuits against officers, supervisors, and agencies have become a part of modern-day policing. Most officers, however, will not be sued in the course of their careers. But although the fear of a lawsuit is often exaggerated and unwarranted, the effect on police officers can be constant and real. One study of police trainees at a regional law enforcement academy concludes that law enforcement candidates have real concerns about work-related lawsuits, fostering an "us versus them" attitude among officers.[8] Others believe that the courts have handcuffed law enforcement officers and made police work unattractive and dangerous. According to one publication, "70 percent of officers involved in a shooting leave police work within five years due to the emotional strain and lack of departmental support."[9] Whatever the reaction, liability lawsuits are a presence in police work that is difficult to ignore.

A widely publicized case involving a New York City police officer shows how brutal some police cases can be and why huge damage awards are sometimes imposed. In what was perhaps the most highly publicized police brutality case in recent years, one newspaper ran this headline: "I sodomized . . . Abner Louima."[10] In that case, Officer Justin Volpe, along with "a ring of white cops," was charged with beating and brutalizing Abner Louima, a Haitian immigrant, after a fight outside a Brooklyn nightclub. The officers were subsequently tried

Slain Immigrant's Family Awarded $3 Million

On January 7, 2003, the Associated Press reported that the City of New York agreed to pay $3 million to the family of Amadou Diallo, a West African immigrant. Diallo was killed by undercover police in a "hail of 41 bullets" outside his home in 1999. He was unarmed. The immigrant was shot to death by four officers who said they "mistook his wallet for a gun." Diallo's parents had filed an $81 million lawsuit against the City of New York, but agreed to settle the case for $3 million. The mayor of New York and the police department expressed deep regret over the incident and extended their sympathies to the family.

SOURCE: *Houston Chronicle*, January 7, 2003, p. 11A.

The police officers involved in this case were investigating a rape case and said Diallo fitted the description of the alleged rapist. They fired a total of 41 shots during this incident and in the process also hit an innocent street vendor from Guinea 19 times. The shooting generated extensive publicity and led to massive protests in New York City. The officers were criminally prosecuted in New York State Court, but were acquitted. The federal government subsequently decided not to file federal criminal charges.

in federal court. At first, Volpe denied all charges. During the trial, however, he changed his mind and decided to plead guilty to ramming a stick into Louima's rectum, causing severe internal injuries and violating Louima's civil rights. In a hushed voice, Volpe told the federal judge that, "in the bathroom of the precinct house, I sodomized Mr. Abner Louima and threatened to kill him if he told anybody." Despite his guilty plea, Volpe was sentenced by a federal judge to thirty years in prison. Observers believe that the Louima case represents one of those uncommon instances when fellow police officers break the "blue wall of silence" in police brutality and corruption cases and inform on one another.

An Overview of Police Legal Liabilities

Police legal liabilities (as opposed to nonlegal liabilities, such as ethics violations) come from varied sources, but the whole arena of legal liabilities can be classified as in Table 13.2. As the table shows, police legal liability cases can be divided into liabilities under federal law and liabilities under state law. Each of these two categories can also be subclassified as civil liability, criminal liability, or administrative liability.

Can an officer be liable under all of the above? The answer is yes, if all the elements for liability are present. For example, an act of an officer that leads to the wrongful death of a suspect may subject the officer to liability under state and federal laws. Under each, the officer may be held liable civilly, criminally, and administratively. The double jeopardy defense does not work in these cases because it applies only if there are successive prosecutions for the same offense by the same jurisdiction. Civil and criminal penalties may result from a single act,

	Federal Law	State Law
Civil Liabilities	1. Title 42 of U.S. Code, Section 1983—Civil Action for Deprivation of Civil Rights	State tort law
	2. Title 42 of U.S. Code, Section 1985—Conspiracy to Interfere with Civil Rights	
	3. Title 42 of U.S. Code, Section 1981—Equal Rights under the Law	
Criminal Liabilities	1. Title 18 of U.S Code, Section 242—Criminal Liability for Deprivation of Civil Rights	1. State penal code provisions specifically aimed at public officers for crimes such as:
	2. Title 18 of U.S. Code, Section 241—Criminal Liability for Conspiracy to Deprive a Person of Rights	a. Official oppression
		b. Official misconduct
	3. Title 18 of U.S. Code, Section 245—Violations of Federally Protected Activities	c. Violation of the civil rights of prisoners
		2. Regular penal code provisions punishing such criminal acts as assault, battery, false arrest, serious bodily injury, and homicide
Administrative Liabilities	1. Federal agency rules or guidelines vary from one agency to another	Agency rules or guidelines on the state or local level vary from one agency to another

because "successive prosecution" requires that both cases be criminal; hence, it does not apply if one case is criminal and the other civil. Criminal prosecutions may also take place in state court and federal court for the same act. There is no double jeopardy, because of the "same jurisdiction" requirement. Federal and state prosecutions take place in different jurisdictions; therefore, there is no double jeopardy. There is no double jeopardy if an officer is dismissed from employment and then prosecuted later or held civilly liable for the same act. This is because dismissal by the agency is administrative in nature and is neither a civil nor a criminal proceeding.

An example of how these laws apply is what happened to the police officers in the infamous Rodney King beating in Los Angeles that was caught on video. In that case, the officers were first suspended and then dismissed from employment by the agency (administrative liability). They were then tried for criminal acts (in Simi Valley) in state court but were all acquitted. After acquittal, they were tried again for criminal acts (in Los Angeles) in federal court. Two of the four defendants were acquitted, but the other two were convicted and served time in a federal institution. The officers raised the double jeopardy defense on appeal, but that did not succeed, because they were tried by two different jurisdictions. The officers were also held liable for civil damages in addition to the administrative and criminal proceedings.

Although various legal remedies are available, plaintiffs usually sue for civil liabilities under federal or state tort law. The discussion in this chapter therefore focuses on those two types of liability: civil liability under federal law and civil liability under state tort law.

Civil Liability under Federal Law—Section 1983 Cases

For purposes of police liability, a **Section 1983 case** (also referred to as a civil rights case) is defined as a lawsuit filed under federal law that seeks damages from a police officer, supervisor, and/or department on the ground that these defendants, acting under color of law, violated the plaintiff's constitutional rights or rights given by federal law. Section 1983 and state tort cases (discussed later in this chapter) are not mutually exclusive; in fact, plaintiffs are likely to sue under both laws and in the same lawsuit. For example, suppose Officer P tries to arrest a suspect, but the suspect flees. Officer P shoots the suspect, killing him instantly. In addition to a criminal case, Officer P will also likely be charged civilly (1) under Section 1983 for violating the suspect's constitutional right to due process and (2) under state tort law for wrongful death.

The Federal Law

Liability under federal law is based on the provisions of Title 42 of the U.S. Code, Section 1983, Civil Action for Deprivation of Rights. That law provides:

> Every person who, under color of any statute, ordinance, regulation, custom, or usage, of any State or Territory, subjects, or causes to be subjected, any citizen of the United States or other persons within the jurisdiction thereof to the deprivation of any rights, privileges, or immunities secured by the Constitution and laws, shall be liable to the party injured in an action at law, suit in equity, or other proper proceeding for redress.

This law, commonly referred to as the civil rights law or Section 1983, is the most frequently used provision among the legal liability statutes available to plaintiffs. The law, originally passed by Congress in 1871, was then known as the Ku Klux Klan law because it sought to control the activities of state officials who were also members of that organization. For a long time, the courts interpreted the law in a limited manner and seldom applied it. In 1961, the Court adopted a much broader interpretation, thus opening wide the door for liability action in federal courts.

Among the reasons for the popularity of Section 1983 cases among plaintiffs are that they are usually filed in federal court, where discovery procedures are more liberal. Moreover, the plaintiff, if successful, may recover attorney's fees in accordance with the Attorney's Fees Act of 1976. A police officer or agency can be held liable for damages as well as for plaintiff's attorney's fees. As noted previously, the same act by the police may be the basis of both a Section 1983 lawsuit and an action under state tort law. For example, arrest without probable cause may constitute false arrest under state tort law and a violation of the arrestee's Fourth Amendment right to protection against unreasonable search and seizure, compensable under Section 1983. In such cases, a plaintiff may combine his or her claims and sue under multiple legal theories in federal court.

The Elements of a Section 1983 Lawsuit

The plaintiff must prove two elements in a Section 1983 lawsuit: (1) the defendant was acting under color of law, and (2) there was a violation of a right given by the Constitution or by federal law. Unless these two elements are proved by the plaintiff, the liability lawsuit will fail.

Acting under Color of Law

The phrase **acting under color of law** refers to the use of power possessed by virtue of law and made possible only because the officer is clothed with the authority of the state. The problem is that, although it is usually easy to identify acts that are wholly within the color of law (as when an officer makes a search or an arrest while on duty), some acts are not as easy to categorize.

- *Example 1.* Suppose a police officer working during off hours as a private security guard in a shopping center shoots and kills a fleeing shoplifter. Is he acting under color of law?
- *Example 2.* Suppose an officer arrests a felon during off hours when she is not in uniform. Is she acting under color of law?

The answer usually depends on job expectations. Many police departments (by state law, judicial decision, or agency regulation) require police officers to act in their official capacity twenty-four hours a day. In these jurisdictions, any arrest made, whether on or off duty, is made under color of law. In the case of police officers who "moonlight," courts have held that wearing a police uniform while acting as a private security agent, carrying a gun issued by the department, and informing department authorities of the second job combine to indicate that the officer is acting under color of law.

Courts have interpreted the term *color of law* broadly to include state laws, local ordinances, and agency regulations. It is not required that the act was authorized by law. It suffices that the act appeared to be lawful even if it was not authorized. Therefore, an officer acts under color of law even if he or she exceeds lawful authority. Moreover, the concept includes clearly illegal acts committed by the officer by reason of position or opportunity. For example, suppose an officer arrests a suspect without probable cause or brutalizes a suspect in the course of an arrest. These acts are clearly illegal, but they come under color of law.

Violation of a Right Given by the U.S. Constitution or by Federal Law

The second element a plaintiff must prove in a Section 1983 case is that the right violated is a constitutional right or a right given by federal law. Violations of rights given by state law cannot lead to liability under Section 1983. For example, neither the Constitution nor federal law gives the right to have a lawyer during a police lineup prior to being charged with an offense. Therefore, if an officer forces a suspect to appear in a lineup without a lawyer (assuming that right is given by state law), the officer is not liable under Section 1983. If the right is given by state law, its violation may be actionable under state law or agency regulation, but not under Section 1983.

The constitutional rights usually used by plaintiffs in cases against police officers are as follows:

- The Fourth Amendment right to protection against unreasonable searches and seizures. Example: Officer V is sued because she allegedly arrested a suspect without probable cause.
- The Fifth Amendment right to protection against self-incrimination and the right to due process. Example: A defendant sues Officer W because she allegedly interrogated a suspect and threatened to "blow your head off" if he did not "tell the truth."
- The Sixth Amendment right to assistance of counsel. Example: Officer X is sued because she allegedly continued to interrogate a suspect even after the suspect informed her that he had a lawyer and had been instructed by the lawyer not to answer any questions asked by the police.
- The Fourteenth Amendment rights to due process and to equal protection of the laws. Example: Officer Y is sued by a suspect because he allegedly used unreasonable force when arresting the suspect and engaged in racial profiling.

It is not hard for a plaintiff to file a Section 1983 lawsuit based on alleged violation of a constitutional right by the police. This is because the rights given in the Bill of Rights and the other constitutional amendments are "elastic" and may accommodate many alleged violations. For example, a violation of the Fourth Amendment protection against unreasonable searches and seizures can be alleged just about any time an arrest or a search or seizure of things takes place. Violation of due process can be charged any time a person feels that he or she has suffered unfairness at the hands of the police. The constitutional right to equal protection has traditionally been applied to discrimination based on race, but some courts have applied it to gender, lifestyle, and other types of discriminatory treatment. The right to privacy may include a host of violations that can form the basis of a Section 1983 lawsuit, ranging from search and seizures to interception of electronic communication. The scope of these constitutional rights makes it quite easy to file a Section 1983 lawsuit against police officers. Proving these allegations, however, is an entirely different matter.

Chavez v. Martinez (2004)

See Appendix C for information on how to find cases in this chapter on FindLaw.com.

In *Chavez v. Martinez* (538 U.S. 760 [2004]), the Court reemphasized the requirement that a Section 1983 case succeeds only if there is a proven violation of a constitutional right or of a right guaranteed by federal law. The suspect filed a Section 1983 case alleging that his constitutional right against self-incrimination was violated when he was not given the *Miranda* warnings and the interrogation continued despite his telling the police that "I am not telling you anything until they treat me." The Court held that "failure to read *Miranda* warnings to Martinez did not violate Martinez's constitutional rights and cannot be grounds for a Section 1983 action." An important fact in this case, however, was that the statements given to the police were not used in a criminal trial. The Court held that "statements compelled by police interrogation may not be used against a defendant in a criminal case, but it is not until such use that the Self-Incrimination Clause is violated." The officer could possibly have been held liable administratively for violating agency policy (if agency rules prohibited such practice) but could not be held liable under Section 1983. The Court would likely have decided differently if the statement had been used against the accused in a criminal trial because then the right against self-incrimination would have been violated.

Town of Castle Rock v. Gonzales (2005)

In a 2005 case, *Town of Castle Rock v. Gonzales* (545 U.S.____[2005]), the Court held that the wrongful failure by the police to arrest a husband who violated a domestic relations court restraining order does not amount to a violation of a constitutional right under the Fourteenth Amendment Due Process Clause and therefore does not result in civil liability under federal law (Section 1983). This case is discussed further in the Case Brief.

CASE BRIEF: The Leading Case on Police Liability for Failure to Arrest

Town of Castle Rock v. Gonzales, 545 U.S.___(2005)

Facts: Gonzales, a mother, lived with her three daughters in Castle Rock, Colorado, where she had a divorce pending. She obtained a restraining order against her estranged husband. The order provided that Gonzales' husband was to stay 100 yards away from the house where Gonzales lived with the children, except for specified visitation. The order commanded all law enforcement officials this:

> You shall use every reasonable means to enforce this restraining order. You shall arrest, or, if an arrest would be impractical under the circumstances, seek a warrant for the arrest of the restrained person when you have information amounting to probable cause that the restrained person has violated or attempted to violate any provision of this order. . . .

Three weeks after the order was issued, the husband took his daughters from where they were playing in the front yard of their house at about 5 or 5:30 P.M. He did this undetected by Gonzales, and without her notice or permission. Gonzales later noticed the girls were missing and called the Castle Rock Police Department at 7:30 P.M., which dispatched two officers. She showed them the restraining order, and she asked them to enforce it and return her children. They said there was nothing they could do about the order, but that she should call the Police Department again if her children had not been returned by 10 P.M. Gonzales called her husband on his mobile phone at 8:30 P.M., and he said he had the children at a Denver amusement park with him. Gonzales called the Police Department back, and requested that they "have someone check for" her husband's truck at the amusement park, or "put out an [all points bulletin]" for him. She was again told to wait until 10 P.M. to see if the girls were returned; she called at 10 P.M. and was told to call back at midnight; she called at midnight; she went to the husband's apartment at 12:10 A.M. and told the dispatcher her husband and girls were missing and was told to wait for an officer to arrive. No officer arrived, and at 12:50 A.M. she went to the Police Department and filed an incident report. The officer receiving the report took no action. At 3:20 A.M., the husband went to the police station, opened fire with a pistol purchased that evening, and was killed when police shot back. Police found in the husband's truck the bodies of his three daughters, who he had previously killed.

Issue: *Is a town civilly liable under federal law (Section 1983) for having a custom or policy that tolerates nonenforcement by its police department of court restraining orders? No.*

Supreme Court Decision: A town cannot be held civilly liable under federal law (Section 1983) for wrongfully and intentionally having a custom or policy that tolerates nonenforcement of court restraining orders. Such a town practice does not amount to a violation of plaintiff's due process rights and therefore does not result in civil liability.

Case Significance: This case is significant because it further clarifies when a government agency might be held civilly liable under federal law (Section 1983). The Court rejected the plaintiff's claim that the town was liable because it "tolerated the non-enforcement of restraining orders by its police officers."

The plaintiff in this case did not sue the police officers or their supervisors; instead, she sued the town for having "an official policy or custom of failing to respond properly to complaints of restraining order violations." She alleged in her complaint that "the town's actions 'were taken either willfully, recklessly or with such gross negligence as to indicate wanton disregard and deliberate indifference'" to her constitutional rights. The town admitted that her allegation was true, but claimed her constitutional right to due process was not violated by such a policy despite such horrendous results.

The facts in this case are absolutely tragic—three children killed by their estranged father, killings that could perhaps have been prevented had the police acted promptly and responded to their mother's complaint. The court's restraining order was blunt and specific—violation of a restraining order is criminal and law enforcement officials were ordered to "use every reasonable means to enforce this restraining order." Police officials clearly did not heed these warnings, but their refusal was justified by town custom or police. Because of this, the plaintiff sued the town instead of the officers.

Despite the terrible tragedy, the Court held that there was no civil liability because the mother's constitutional rights were not violated. Federal law (Section 1983) requires that for civil liability to ensue, the plaintiff must prove that her constitutional right or a right guaranteed by federal law was violated. The mother claimed her constitutional right to due process was violated by the town's "official policy and custom" of tolerating the nonenforcement of restraining orders by its police officers. The Court disagreed, saying that no such right existed based on the facts of this case and therefore there was no basis for a federal civil liability lawsuit.

The mother, however, was not left without recourse. Toward the end of its decision, the Court said: "This result reflects our continuing reluctance to treat the Fourth Amendment as a 'font of tort law,' but it does not mean States are powerless to provide victims with personally enforceable remedies. Although the framers of the Fourteenth Amendment and the Civil Rights Act of 1871, the original source of Section 1983, did not create a system by which police departments are generally held financially accountable for crimes that better policing might have prevented, the people of Colorado are free to craft such a system under state law." The Court in essence told the plaintiff to look for redress under state law, not under federal law.

Excerpts from the Decision: We conclude, therefore, that respondent did not, for purposes of the Due Process Clause, have a property interest in police enforcement of the restraining order against her husband. It is accordingly unnecessary to address the Court of Appeals' determination (366 F. 3d, at 1110–1117) that the town's custom or policy prevented the police from giving her due process when they deprived her of that alleged interest. See *American Mfrs. Mut. Ins. Co.* v. *Sullivan,* 526 U.S. 40, 61 (1999).

In light of today's decision and that in *DeShaney,* the benefit that a third party may receive from having someone else arrested for a crime generally does not trigger protections under the Due Process Clause, neither in its procedural nor in its "substantive" manifestations. This result reflects our continuing reluctance to treat the Fourteenth Amendment as "a font of tort law," but it does not mean States are powerless to provide victims with personally enforceable remedies. Although the framers of the Fourteenth Amendment and the Civil Rights Act of 1871, did not create a system by which police departments are generally held financially accountable for crimes that better policing might have prevented, the people of Colorado are free to craft such a system under state law.

NOTE: This case brief is a modified version of a brief of the same case in *Briefs of Leading Cases in Law Enforcement* by Rolando V. del Carmen and Jeff Walker, 6th ed. (Anderson Publishing/LexisNexis), 2005.

Defenses in Section 1983 Cases

Several defenses are available in Section 1983 cases. Two are discussed here because they are the defenses most often used by defendants in police civil liability cases. These are the "good faith" defense and the probable cause defense.

The Good Faith Defense ("Qualified Immunity")

The **good faith defense** (also known in legal circles as "qualified immunity") **in Section 1983 cases** holds that an officer is not civilly liable unless he or she violated a clearly established statutory or constitutional right of which a reasonable person would have known (*Harlow v. Fitzgerald,* 457 U.S. 800 [1982]). The Court in this case said:

Harlow v. Fitzgerald (1982)

> We therefore hold that government officials performing discretionary functions generally are shielded from liability for civil damages insofar as their conduct does not violate a clearly established statutory or constitutional right of which a reasonable person would have known. . . . The judge appropriately may determine, not only the currently applicable law, but whether that law was clearly established at the time an action occurred. If the law at that time was not clearly established,

an official could not reasonably be expected to anticipate subsequent legal developments, nor could he fairly be said to "know" that the law forbade conduct not previously identified as unlawful.

As this excerpt indicates, the good faith defense has two requirements: (1) that an officer has violated a clearly established statutory or constitutional right and (2) of which a reasonable person would have known. Both must be proved by the plaintiff; otherwise, no liability is imposed. When is a right considered to be "clearly established"? The U.S. Court of Appeals for the Fifth Circuit set this standard: "A plaintiff must show that, when the defendant acted, the law established the contours of a right so clearly that a reasonable official would have understood his acts were unlawful." The court then added that "[i]f reasonable public officials could differ on the lawfulness of the defendant's actions, the defendant is entitled to qualified immunity" (*Fraire v. City of Arlington*, 957 F.2d 1268 [5th Cir. 1992]).

Fraire v. City of Arlington (5th Cir. 1992)

The right violated must be a constitutional right or a right given by federal law. Therefore, if the right violated by the police is a right given by state law, there is no liability under Section 1983. For example, suppose that state law provides that a juvenile may be kept in custody by the police for no longer than ten hours, but Officer X takes a juvenile into custody and keeps him under detention for more than ten hours. Officer X may be held liable under departmental policy or state law but not in a federal Section 1983 case, because no constitutional right was violated. Instead, the right violated by the officer was a right given by state law.

Although the *Harlow* case did not involve police officers (it involved two White House aides under former President Nixon), the Court later said in *Anderson v. Creighton* (483 U.S. 635 [1987]) that the *Harlow* standard applies to police officers who are performing their duties. In a 2004 case, *Brosseau v. Haugen* (125 S.Ct. 596 [2004]), the Court shed more light on the meaning of the good faith defense (qualified immunity) when it said:

Anderson v. Creighton (1987)

Brosseau v. Haugen (2004)

> Because the focus is on whether the officer had fair notice that her conduct was unlawful, reasonableness is judged against the backdrop of the law at the time of the conduct. If the law at that time did not clearly establish that the officer's conduct would violate the Constitution, the officer should not be subject to liability, or indeed, even the burdens of litigation.

Groh v. Ramirez (2004)

However, in *Groh v. Ramirez* (540 U.S. 551 [2004]), also decided in 2004, the Court held that an officer was not entitled to qualified immunity because "it would be clear to a reasonable officer that his conduct was unlawful in the situation he confronted." In *Groh*, an agent of the Bureau of Alcohol, Tobacco, and Firearms (ATF) prepared an application for a search warrant based on information that weapons and explosives were located on Ramirez's farm. The application was supported by a detailed affidavit listing the items to be seized and describing the basis for his belief that the items were concealed on the property. Groh presented these documents, along with a warrant form he also completed, to a magistrate, who then signed the warrant form. The warrant itself did not incorporate any reference to the itemized list contained in the application or affidavit. The day after the magistrate signed the warrant, officers searched Ramirez's home but found no illegal weapons or explosives. No charges were filed against Ramirez, but he nonetheless later filed a lawsuit under Section 1983 claiming his Fourth Amendment right against unreasonable searches and seizures was violated.

On appeal, the Court agreed with Ramirez, saying that the warrant was "plainly invalid." The Court then held that for purposes of civil liability, the officer was "not entitled to qualified immunity . . . because it would be clear to a reasonable officer that his conduct was unlawful in the situation he confronted." The Court added, "Given that the particularity requirement is stated in the Constitution's text, no reasonable officer could believe that a warrant that did not comply with that requirement was valid." (Read the Case Brief to learn more about this case.)

Saucier v. Katz (2001)

In *Saucier v. Katz* (533 U.S. 194 [2001]), the Court ruled that a ruling by a trial court on the good faith defense is separate from a ruling on whether a constitutional right was violated and should be made as early as possible in the proceedings so that, if established, the cost and expense of trial are avoided. This decision is good news for police officers who are sued in Section 1983 cases because it spares them the burden of having to go through the whole trial if good faith (meaning the officer establishes that he or she did not violate a clearly established constitutional right of which a reasonable person would have known) is proved early in the case, usually in a motion to dismiss. Before this decision, some courts went through the whole trial and then determined whether the officer acted in good faith.

The good faith defense has three important implications for police officers and agencies. First, officers must know the basic constitutional and federal rights of the public they serve. Although officers should be familiar with these rights from college courses and police academy training, their knowledge needs constant updating in light of new court decisions in criminal procedure and constitutional law. Second, police agencies have an obligation to inform their officers constantly of new cases that establish constitutional rights. Third, agencies must update their manuals or guidelines regularly to reflect cases decided not only by the U.S. Supreme Court but also by federal courts in their jurisdiction.

 CASE BRIEF: The Leading Case on Police Liability for an Unconstitutional Search Warrant

Groh v. Ramirez et al., 540 U.S. 551 (2004)

Facts: Groh, an agent of the Bureau of Alcohol, Tobacco, and Firearms (ATF), prepared an application for a search warrant based on information that weapons and explosives were located on Ramirez's farm. The application was supported by a detailed affidavit listing the items to be seized and describing the basis for his belief the items were concealed on the property. Groh presented these documents, along with a warrant form he also completed, to a magistrate. The magistrate signed the warrant form. Although the application and affidavit described the contraband expected to be discovered, the warrant form only indicated that the place to be searched was Ramirez's home. The warrant did not incorporate any reference to the itemized list contained in the application or affidavit. The day after the magistrate signed the warrant, officers searched Ramirez's home but found no illegal weapons or explosives. Groh left a copy of the warrant at the home but did not leave a copy of the application. The following day, in response to a request from Ramirez's attorney, Groh faxed a copy of the application. No charges were filed against Ramirez, but he later filed suit, claiming his Fourth Amendment rights were violated by the nonspecific warrant.

Issue: *Does a search warrant that does not particularly describe the persons or things to be seized, but has those in the application that was filed with the judge, violate the Fourth Amendment? Yes.*

Supreme Court Decision: A search and seizure warrant that does not contain a particular description of the things to be seized is unconstitutional even if the application for the warrant contains such descriptions. An officer is not entitled to qualified immunity (meaning the good faith defense) if "it would be clear to a reasonable officer that his condition was unlawful."

Case Significance: The application for a warrant submitted by the officer to the judge in this case clearly specified the items to be seized. However, the warrant itself did not specify those items, neither did the warrant incorporate by reference the application's itemized list. The Court concluded that the warrant was "plainly invalid." The purpose for the specificity requirement is to have "written assurance" that the judge "actually found probable cause for a search as broad as the affiant requested." The Court also said that "the particularity requirement's purpose is not limited to preventing general searches; it also assures the individual whose property is searched and

seized of the executing officer's legal authority, his need to search, and the limits of his power to do so."

For purposes of civil liability, the Court held that the officer was "not entitled to qualified immunity despite the constitutional violation because it would be clear to a reasonable officer that his conduct was unlawful in the situation he confronted." It added, "Given that the particularity requirement is stated in the Constitution's text, no reasonable officer could believe that a warrant that did not comply with that requirement was valid." The Court, however, refused to specifically address two other issues involved in the case: (1) whether the warrant would have been valid if the warrant itself mentioned that the application clearly listed the items to be seized but without the list being available during the search, and (2) whether orally describing the items to the defendant during the search complies with the specificity requirement.

Excerpts from the Decision: *The warrant was plainly invalid.* The Fourth Amendment states unambiguously that "no Warrants shall issue, but upon probable cause, supported by Oath or affirmation, and *particularly describing* the place to be searched, and *the persons or things to be seized*" (emphasis added). The warrant in this case complied with the first three of these requirements: It was based on probable cause and supported by a sworn affidavit, and it described particularly the place of the search. On the fourth requirement, however, the warrant failed altogether. Indeed, petitioner concedes that "the warrant . . . was deficient in particularity because it provided no description of the type of evidence sought." . . .

The fact that the application adequately *described the "things to be seized"* does not save the *warrant* from its facial invalidity. The Fourth Amendment by its terms requires particularity in the warrant, not in the supporting documents. ("*The Fourth Amendment requires that the warrant* particularly describe the things to be seized, not the papers presented to the judicial officer . . . asked to issue the warrant"). And for good reason: "The presence of a search warrant serves a high function," and that high function is not necessarily vindicated when some other document, somewhere, says something about the objects of the search, but the contents of that document are neither known to the person whose home is being searched nor available for her inspection. We do not say that the Fourth Amendment forbids a warrant from cross-referencing other documents. Indeed, most Courts of Appeals have held that a court may construe a warrant with reference to a supporting application or affidavit if the warrant uses appropriate words of incorporation, and if the supporting document accompanies the warrant. But in this case the warrant did not incorporate other documents by reference, nor did either the affidavit or the application (which had been placed under seal) accompany the warrant. Hence, we need not further explore the matter of incorporation.

NOTE: This case brief is a modified version of a brief of the same case in *Briefs of Leading Cases in Law Enforcement*, by Rolando V. del Carmen and Jeff Walker, 6th ed. (Anderson Publishing/LexisNexis), 2005.

The Probable Cause Defense but Only in Search and Seizure Cases The second defense in Section 1983 discussed in this chapter is the **probable cause defense**, in which the officer is not liable in cases in which probable cause is present. It is a limited type of defense because it applies only in Fourth Amendment cases, in which probable cause is required for the police to be able to act legally, such as in arrests and search and seizure cases. It cannot be used in cases alleging violations of other constitutional rights, such as the First, Fifth, Sixth, or Fourteenth Amendments.

Rodriguez v. Jones (5th Cir. 1973)

One court has said that, for purposes of a legal defense in Section 1983 cases, probable cause simply means "a reasonable good faith belief in the legality of the action taken" (*Rodriguez v. Jones,* 473 F.2d 599 [5th Cir. 1973]). That expectation is lower than for the Fourth Amendment concept of probable cause, which is defined as

HIGHLIGHT

The Good Faith (Qualified Immunity) Defense in Section 1983 Cases

The good faith defense in federal (Section 1983) cases holds that an officer is not civilly liable in federal court unless there is a violation of *a clearly established statutory or constitutional right of which a reasonable person would have known.* The good faith defense has three important implications for officers and agencies. First, officers must know the basic constitutional and federal rights of the public they serve. Second, police agencies have an obligation to regularly inform their officers of new cases that establish constitutional and federal rights. Third, police agencies must update their manuals or guidelines to include cases decided not only by the U.S. Supreme Court but also by federal courts within their jurisdiction.

"more than bare suspicion; it exists when the facts and circumstances within the officers' knowledge and of which they had reasonably trustworthy information are sufficient in themselves to warrant a man of reasonable caution in the belief that an offense has been or is being committed" (*Brinegar v. United States*, 338 U.S. 160 [1949]). For example, suppose Officer X makes an arrest that is later determined to be without probable cause. According to *Rodriguez*, Officer X may be exempt from liability if he or she reasonably and in good faith believed at the time of the arrest that it was legal.

Brinegar v. United States (1949)

Civil Liability under State Tort Law

A second type of civil liability is liability under state tort law. **Tort** is defined as a civil wrong in which the action of one person causes injury to the person or property of another, in violation of a legal duty imposed by law. Tort law is primarily a product of judicial decisions, so it is not as precise as criminal law, which is neatly laid out in a state's penal code. State tort actions are the second most common form of lawsuit against police (Section 1983 cases are the most common). But more plaintiffs may be using the "state tort route" in the future if the Court continues to limit the use of Section 1983 cases as a remedy for violations of rights.

Types of State Tort Cases

There are two types of state tort cases: *intentional tort* and *negligence tort*. Negligence tort cases deserve extended discussion, because each type is often used by plaintiffs in police liability cases that are filed in state courts. We will look separately at intentional and negligence tort.

Intentional Tort

An **intentional tort** occurs when there is an intention on the part of the officer to bring some physical harm or mental coercion upon another person. Intent is mental and thus difficult to establish. However, courts and juries generally are allowed to infer the existence of intent from the facts of the case. For example, suppose an officer takes a person to the police station in handcuffs for questioning. When charged with false arrest, the officer denies that he intended to place the person under arrest. The judge or jury probably will decide that intent to arrest was, in fact, present because the person was handcuffed and obviously not free to leave.

Next, we discuss six of the more common kinds of intentional tort that are brought against police officers:

- False arrest and false imprisonment
- Assault and battery
- Excessive use of nondeadly force
- Excessive use of deadly force
- Wrongful death
- Intentional infliction of mental or emotional distress

False arrest and false imprisonment In a tort case for **false arrest**, the plaintiff alleges that the officer has made an illegal arrest. A claim of false arrest also arises if the officer arrests the wrong person named in the warrant. An officer who makes a warrantless arrest bears the burden of proving that the arrest was, in fact, based on probable cause and that an arrest warrant was not necessary because the arrest came under one of the exceptions to the warrant rule. If the arrest is made with a warrant, the presumption is that probable cause exists, unless the officer obtained the warrant with malice, knowing that there was no probable cause (*Malley v. Briggs*, 475 U.S. 335 [1986]). An arrest with a warrant is therefore unlikely to result in civil liability for false arrest unless the officer serves a warrant that he or she knows to be illegal or unconstitutional. For example, if Officer M serves an unsigned warrant or one that is issued for the wrong person, M will be liable for false arrest despite the issuance of a warrant.

Malley v. Briggs
(1986)

False arrest is a different tort from **false imprisonment**, but in police tort cases the two are virtually identical. This is because arrest necessarily means confinement, which is in itself an element of imprisonment. In both cases, the individual is restrained or deprived of freedom without legal justification. The cases do differ, however, in that a false arrest leads to false imprisonment, but false imprisonment is not necessarily the result of a false arrest. For example, a suspect may be arrested with probable cause (a valid arrest) but may be illegally detained in jail for several days without the filing of charges (false imprisonment). If an officer makes an arrest based on probable cause but later finds out that the person is innocent, continuing to hold the person constitutes false imprisonment even though the arrest was valid.

Assault and battery Although sometimes used as one term, assault and battery represent two separate acts. **Assault** is the intentional causing of an apprehension of harmful or offensive conduct; it is the attempt or threat (accompanied by the ability) to inflict bodily harm on another person. An assault is committed if the officer causes another person to think that he or she will be subjected to harmful or offensive contact. **Battery** is the intentional infliction of harmful or offensive body contact. Given this broad definition, the potential for battery exists every time an officer uses force on a suspect or arrestee. The main difference between assault and battery is that assault is generally menacing conduct that results in a person's fear of imminently receiving battery, whereas battery involves unlawful, unwarranted, or hostile touching—however slight. In some jurisdictions, assault is attempted battery.

Excessive use of nondeadly force Any discussion of the use of force by police must be separated into use of *nondeadly force* and use of *deadly force.* Lumping the two together confuses the issue because different rules govern them. Excessive use of force, nondeadly or deadly, leads to liability under state tort law and also under Section 1983. The police are often charged with "brutality" or use of "excessive force." The general rule is that nondeadly force may be used by police in various situations as long as such force is reasonable.

Reasonable force is force that a prudent and cautious person would use if exposed to similar circumstances; it is limited to the amount of force necessary to achieve legitimate results.

Lewis v. Downs (6th Cir. 1985)

In *Lewis v. Downs* (774 F.2d 711 [6th Cir. 1985]), a court found that the police used excessive force on a family when responding to a call to settle a neighborhood dispute. The father was not physically strong and was already being subdued by his brother when the police kicked him in the groin and struck him on the head with a nightstick. The officers also allegedly kicked the mother in the back and buttocks after she was handcuffed and lying face down in the mud. The son was injured as well during the arrest process. The police were ordered to pay $10,000 because the court said they used excessive force.

For the purpose of day-to-day policing, it is best to think of nondeadly force as either reasonable or punitive, rather than as reasonable or unreasonable. This is because it is often hard for an officer to distinguish between what is reasonable force and what is unreasonable force, particularly when making split-second decisions when emotions are running high and personal safety (the officer's and other people's) is at risk. In contrast, an officer is more likely to know when he or she is using **punitive force**, which is force that is meant to punish rather than merely bring the situation under control. In police work, the use of reasonable force is always legal, whereas the use of punitive force is always illegal and exposes the officer, his or her supervisors, and the city to lawsuits.

Excessive use of deadly force **Deadly force** is defined as force that, when used, would lead a reasonable officer objectively to conclude that it poses a high risk of death or serious injury to its target. The general rules for the use of deadly force may be summarized as follows: In misdemeanor cases, the safest practice is for officers to refrain from using deadly force except for self-defense or the defense of the life of a third person. The use of deadly force in misdemeanor cases to prevent an escape raises questions of disproportionality, because the designation of the offense as a misdemeanor denotes that the state does not consider it serious. Therefore, using deadly force to prevent the escape of a misdemeanant may be a disproportionate sanction.

In felony cases, the safest rule is to use deadly force only when the life of the officer or another person is in danger and the use of such force is immediately necessary to preserve that life. The use of deadly force is usually governed by specific departmental rules that must be followed strictly. If there are no departmental rules, state law must be followed. Author Isidore Silver summarizes the current case law on the use of deadly force to prevent the commission of a felony as follows: "There is no dispute that such force may be used to prevent the commission of a felony which threatens the life or safety of a human being, including the burglary of a dwelling house. . . . As to felonies which involve no such danger, the tendency in the modern cases is to say that the use of deadly force is unreasonable in proportion to the offense."[11]

Wrongful death The question of **wrongful death** arises whenever death occurs as a result of an officer's action or inaction. An officer has a duty to use not merely ordinary care but a high degree of care in handling a weapon, or else he or she can become liable for wrongful death. Sometimes an officer is held liable because of failure to follow good police procedure. In one case, a police officer was held liable for $202,295.80 in a wrongful death action for shooting and killing a man suspected of buying marijuana, even though the officer thought he was shooting in self-defense.

The district judge, relying on the testimony of an expert witness on police procedures, found that the police officer had acted negligently and contrary to sound police procedure in the following respects:

■ Failing to utilize a backup unit

■ Placing his patrol car in a dangerous cutoff position

■ Ordering the two men to exit their car rather than issuing an immobilization command to remain in the car with their hands in plain view

■ Increasing the risk of an incident by having the two suspects get out of a car

■ Abandoning a covered position and advancing into the open, where the odds of overreacting would be greater

The judge concluded that the officer's fault in not following sound police procedure not only placed the officer in a position of greater danger but also imperiled the deceased suspect by creating a situation in which a fatal error was more likely (*Young v. City of Killeen,* 775 F.2d 1349 [5th Cir. 1985]).

Young v. City of Killeen (5th Cir. 1985)

Infliction of mental or emotional distress Tort liability for **infliction of mental or emotional distress** arises when an officer inflicts severe emotional distress on a person through intentional or reckless extreme and outrageous conduct. Physical harm need not follow. For example, suppose a plaintiff who is arrested illegally suffers psychological dysfunction and trauma because the officer pointed a loaded gun at her during the arrest. This tort may be alleged any time an officer's conduct is so extreme and outrageous as to cause severe emotional distress. However, what is extreme and outrageous is difficult to determine, and the effect of an act may vary according to the plaintiff's disposition or state of mind. The plaintiff must allege and prove some kind of pattern of behavior or practice by the officer over a period of time, rather than merely isolated incidents.

Negligence Tort The second type of tort in state tort cases is **negligence tort**, which may be defined as the breach of a common law or statutory duty to act reasonably toward those who may foreseeably be harmed by one's conduct. This definition may be modified or superseded by specific state law providing for a different type of conduct, usually making it more restrictive than this definition. Negligence tort applies in many aspects of police work, five of which we will briefly discuss here:

- Liability for failing to protect a member of the public
- Liability for negligent use by police of motor vehicles
- Liability for injury caused by a fleeing motorist-suspect
- Liability for failure to respond to calls
- Liability for failure to arrest drunk drivers

Liability for failing to protect a member of the public The general rule is that there is no liability on the part of police officers for failing to protect a member of the public. This is because of the **public duty doctrine**, which holds that government functions are owed to the general public but not to specific individuals. Therefore, police officers who fail to prevent crime while acting within the scope of their official capacity are not liable to specific individuals for injury or harm that may have been caused by a third party. For example, the police would not be liable if X was sexually assaulted, Y was murdered, Z was robbed, or McDonald's™ was burglarized.

There is one major but multifaceted exception to the public duty doctrine: **special relationship**. It means that if a duty is owed to a particular person rather than to the general public, then a police officer or agency that breaches that duty can be held liable for damages. Special relationship has many meanings, depending

HIGHLIGHT

The General Rule in Negligence Tort

The general rule is that there is no liability on the part of police officers for failing to protect a member of the public. This is because of the *public duty doctrine,* which holds that government functions are owed to the general public but not to specific individuals. Therefore, police officers who fail to prevent crime while acting within the scope of their official capacity are not liable to specific individuals for injury or harm that may have been caused by a third party.

on state law, court decisions, and agency regulations. Liability might be imposed in the instances noted next based on the special relationship exception to the public duty doctrine. What these situations have in common is that the duty of the police has shifted from protecting the public in general to protecting a particular person, so a special relationship has been established.

- *When the police deprive an individual of liberty by taking him or her into custody.* For example, in a Florida case, a person was arrested for possession of a lottery ticket. He was handcuffed by the police but then was stabbed by another person. The court ruled that once the suspect was handcuffed and taken into custody, a special relationship was created in which the city was responsible for his safety, just as though he had been incarcerated in the city jail. In this case, however, the court did not find the officers liable, because there was no negligence in their handling of the suspect. They were just as surprised as the arrestee when a woman ran up and stabbed him (*Sanders v. City of Belle Glade,* 510 So.2d 962 [Fla. App. 1987]).

    In a 1989 case, the Court held that a person who is not in the custody of the state has no constitutional right to protection under the Due Process Clause of the Fourteenth Amendment, but liability may nonetheless arise under state court decisions or under state tort law—if state law so provides (*DeShaney v. Winnebago County Department of Social Services,* 489 U.S. 189 [1989]).

- *When the police assume an obligation that goes beyond police duty to protect the general public.* For example, a certain Schuster provided New York City police officers with information that led to the arrest of a fugitive. The incident received considerable media attention, exposing Schuster as the individual who had assisted in the fugitive's capture. When Schuster received life-threatening phone calls, he notified the police. Several weeks later, Schuster was shot and killed. Schuster's family brought suit, alleging that the city police had failed to provide him with adequate protection and that New York City thereby had breached a special duty owed to individuals who provide the police with information about a crime.

    A New York court rejected a motion to dismiss, saying that "in our view the public (acting in this instance through the City of New York) owes a special duty to use reasonable care for the protection of persons who have collaborated with them in the arrest or prosecution of criminals" (*Schuster v. City of New York,* 154 N.E. 2d 534 [N.Y. 1958]).

- *When protection is required by law.* Some states enact laws expressly protecting special groups or individuals. In other states, judicial decisions regard certain laws as protecting special groups or individuals even though they are not specifically protected by law. For example, in a case in Massachusetts, the police were found liable for failing to arrest a drunk driver who subsequently caused injury to

Sanders v. City of Belle Glade (Fla. App. 1987)

DeShaney v. Winnebago County Department of Social Services (1989)

Schuster v. City of New York (N.Y. 1958)

the plaintiff. A special relationship was considered to have been created by the legislature in a state statute that prohibited drunk driving. The court reasoned that "statutes which establish police responsibility in such circumstances evidence a legislative intent to protect both the intoxicated persons and users of the highway" (*Irwin v. Town of Ware*, 467 N.E. 2d 1292 [Mass. 1984]). This case does not necessarily mean that an automatic special relationship exists every time there is a DWI statute. What it means is that the Massachu-setts court interpreted the statute to have established a special relationship sufficient to hold the police liable.

Irwin v. Town of Ware (Mass. 1984)

- *When protection is ordered by the court.* This is illustrated in *Sorichetti v. City of New York* (482 N.E. 2d 70 [1985]), a much-publicized case. The New York Court of Appeals upheld a judgment for $2 million against the New York police for failure to protect a child who was under an order of protection issued by the court. The mother had obtained the order curtailing her husband's access to their child because of his violent tendencies. One weekend, the mother agreed to permit the husband to keep the child if he met her at the police station. At the station, the husband yelled to the wife that he was going to kill her and then pointed to the daughter and said, "You better do the sign of the cross before this weekend is up." The wife immediately asked the police to arrest her husband; the police replied that there was nothing they could do. The wife went to the police the next day and again demanded that they return her daughter and arrest her husband, but the police denied her request. That same weekend, the child was attacked by the father and suffered severe wounds. The appellate court upheld the huge damages award, saying that the court-issued protective order created a special relationship that required the police to take extra steps to protect the daughter from harm from a known source.

Sorichetti v. City of New York (1985)

- It is important to note, however, that *Sorichetti* was a state tort case filed in New York. If the same case were filed today under Section 1983 (not under state tort law, as here), the results would likely have been different because in 2005, the U.S. Supreme Court held that the wrongful failure by the police to arrest a husband who violated a domestic relations court restraining order does not amount to a violation of a constitutional due process right under the Fourteenth Amendment and therefore does not result in civil liability under federal law, Section 1983 (*Town of Castle Rock v. Gonzales*, 545 U.S.___[2005], which was discussed earlier under Section 1983). The special relationship doctrine does not apply in Section 1983 cases because of the requirement that there must be a violation of a constitutional right or a right given by federal law.

- *In some domestic abuse cases.* The rule is that the police do not have any liability in domestic abuse situations, because the duty to protect an abused spouse comes under the public duty doctrine. In some instances, however, a special relationship has been established, so failure to protect would lead to liability. For example, suppose a state passes legislation authorizing courts to issue protective orders to spouses in domestic abuse situations; an order is issued (creating a special relationship), and the police fail to enforce the order. Or suppose police behavior shows discrimination against a group in society (usually women) in protecting them against domestic abuse, thereby violating their constitutional right to equal protection.

■ In these cases, liability might result if police actions or departmental policy disproportionately disadvantaged that group and if intent to discriminate were proved. For example, a police department would be liable if its policy mandated no arrest in cases involving abused wives on the grounds that these cases usually do not result in charges being pressed against the offender.

In a 2003 case, a woman in Tennessee "claimed that the county and sheriff's deputies failed to adequately protect her against her estranged husband, who allegedly set fire to her home while divorce proceedings were pending." The claim was based on the allegation that the deputies failed to arrest the husband for violating a protection order and therefore left him free to commit the arson. She was awarded $30,000 in damages against the county and $130,000 in damages against the two deputy sheriffs. Violation of the protection order created the special relationship that led to liability.

Negligent Use of Police Vehicles As in other state tort negligence cases, the general rule is that there is no liability for police use of motor vehicles. If liability is imposed at all, it is usually based on police conduct that "shocks the conscience of the court" rather than on a lower standard. Liability under state law may also arise if there are violations of state law or departmental policy. Police departments have rules that officers must follow during vehicular chases. Failure to abide by departmental policy might establish a level of negligence that can lead to liability in a state tort action for the officer.

Injury Caused by a Fleeing Motorist-Suspect Some cases have been filed by third parties against police officers and departments, seeking damages for injuries caused by a fleeing motorist-suspect who, in the course of the pursuit, hits and injures a pedestrian. Most states hold that the police are not liable for injuries or harm caused by a fleeing violator, because the proximate cause of the injury was not the conduct of the police in making the chase but the negligent behavior of the fleeing violator.

Failure to Respond to Calls Numerous cases have been filed against the police based on alleged negligent failure to respond to calls for police help, including

911 calls. Most police departments encourage the public to call 911 in cases of emergency, and some have assured the public that such calls will be given priority and responded to promptly—even stating the number of minutes it will take the police to respond. The general rule, based on court decisions, is that the police cannot be held liable for either slow or improper response to calls for police help, including 911 calls, except when a special relationship exists between the police and the caller. It is not a good policy for police departments to ensure the public that they will respond within, say, five, ten, or fifteen minutes after a 911 call. Such a policy exposes the department to liability in the event that the police are unable to live up to that promise.

Failure to Arrest a Drunk Driver Most states hold that police officers are not liable for injuries inflicted on the public by drunk drivers whom the police fail to arrest. Illustrative of this rule is a Maryland Court of Appeals decision (*Ashburn v. Ann Arundel County,* 510 A.2d 1078 [Md. 1986]). In that case, a police officer found a certain Millham, intoxicated, sitting behind the wheel of a pickup truck in the parking lot of a 7-11 store. The officer told Millham to pull his truck to the side of the lot and to refrain from driving that evening, but he did not make an arrest. As soon as the officer left, Millham drove off and soon collided with the plaintiff, a pedestrian. After losing his left leg and suffering other injuries, the plaintiff brought suit.

Ashburn v. Ann Arundel County (Md. 1986)

On appeal, the Maryland Court of Appeals held as follows:

- The officer was acting in a discretionary capacity and was therefore immune from liability.
- The officer was not in a special relationship with pedestrians and therefore did not have a duty to prevent a driver from injuring pedestrians.
- The law that requires officers to detain and investigate a driver does not impose any duty on the police to prevent drivers from injuring pedestrians.

The public duty doctrine, although alive and well in cases of police failure to arrest drunk drivers, has started to erode. Some states now impose liability based on the concept of duty as a mandatory function or on the special relationship exception to the public duty rule. An example is the Massachusetts case of *Irwin v. Town of Ware* (467 N.E. 2d 1292 [1984]), mentioned earlier, in which the police were found liable for failing to arrest a drunk driver who subsequently caused injury to the plaintiff. The special relationship in that case was considered by the court to have been created by the legislature in a state statute that prohibited drunk driving. Although only a few states thus far have imposed liability, it is probable—given the impetus of the victims' rights movement—that other states might follow suit and create exceptions to the public duty doctrine that would make police officers liable (through the special relationship route) for failure to arrest drunk drivers.

Official Immunity Defense Most Often Used in State Tort Cases

A number of defenses are available in state tort cases, but the one most often used in state tort litigation is official immunity. Some states call it *qualified immunity* or *partial immunity*. Its meaning varies slightly from state to state. Despite variations, common elements of the official immunity defense can be identified. One state court states that government employees are entitled to **official immunity** from lawsuits if the act involves the performance of their "discretionary duties, in good faith, as long as they are acting within the scope of their authority" (*City of Lancaster v. Chambers*, 883 S.W. 2d 650 [Tex. 1994]). This definition requires that, for the official immunity defense to succeed, three elements must be proved by the officer in court: (1) that the act performed was discretionary, not mandatory; (2) that the officer acted in good faith; and (3) that the officer acted within the scope of his or her authority. What do these terms mean?

City of Lancaster v. Chambers (Tex. 1994)

Discretionary Acts An act is **discretionary** if it involves personal deliberation, decision, and judgment. Actions that require obedience to orders or performance of duties about which the officer has no choice are not discretionary; they are instead *mandatory* (*City of Pharr v. Ruiz*, 944 S.W. 2d 709 [Tex. Cr. App. 1997]). The opposite of a discretionary act is a mandatory act. For example, the decision to arrest a suspect for a minor offense usually is left to the discretion of the officer; hence, it is discretionary. But using lawful force when making an arrest is mandatory in that the police are required by the Constitution to respect the rights of arrested suspects. Using lawful force is mandatory; so is obeying the law or following departmental policy.

City of Pharr v. Ruiz (Tex. Cr. App. 1997)

The Officer Acted in Good Faith There are differences between the meaning of *good faith defense* in federal Section 1983 cases and in state tort cases. In state tort cases, **good faith** means that the officer "acted in the honest belief that the action taken or the decision was appropriate under the circumstances." For example, making an arrest without a warrant on the reasonable belief that the suspect would otherwise flee would be acting in good faith. On the other hand, making a warrantless arrest without probable cause is not acting in good faith, because every officer knows that a valid warrantless arrest can be made only if there is probable cause.

HIGHLIGHT
The Official Immunity Defense in State Tort Cases

The official immunity defense means that police officers are not liable for damages under state tort law if the following three elements are established: (a) that the act is discretionary, meaning it involves personal deliberation, decision, and judgment; (b) that the officer acted in good faith, meaning that the officer acted in the honest belief that the action taken or the decision was appropriate under the circumstances; and (c) that the officer acted within the scope of authority, meaning that the officer was discharging the duties generally assigned.

The Officer Acted within the Scope of Authority

City of Lancaster v. Chambers (Tex. 1994)

Acting within the scope of authority means that the officer is discharging the duties generally assigned (*City of Lancaster v. Chambers*, 883 S.W. 2d 650 [Tex. 1994]). For example, an officer serving a search warrant or making an arrest by virtue of a warrant is acting within the scope of authority. The same is true of an officer who makes an arrest based on probable cause or who uses reasonable force in making an arrest. In contrast, an officer who beats up a suspect or who makes a vehicle stop without any justification is clearly acting outside the scope of authority.

Comparison between Federal (Section 1983) and State Tort Cases

The following summary highlights the differences between federal (Section 1983) and state tort cases.

Federal (Section 1983) Cases	State Tort Cases
Based on federal law	Based on state law
Law passed in 1871	Developed in court cases
Usually filed in federal court	Usually filed in state court
Only public officials can be sued	Public officials and private persons can be sued
Basis for liability is violation of a constitutional right or a right given by federal law	Basis for liability is injury to a person or the property of another in violation of a duty imposed by state law
Good faith defense means the officer did not violate a clearly established constitutional or federal right which a reasonable person should have known	Good faith defense usually means the officer acted in the honest belief that the action taken was appropriate under the circumstances

Defendants in Civil Liability Cases: Legal Representation and Indemnification

What happens when police officers and the city are sued? If they lose, who pays? This section examines these questions as we study what happens when the police officer, supervisor, and city or county are defendants.

The Police Officer as Defendant

The officer is an obvious liability target because he or she allegedly committed the violation. The rule is that if what happened can be blamed on the officer alone and on nobody else, the officer alone is liable. For example, suppose an officer, despite excellent training, brutalizes a suspect. If what happened is solely the fault of the officer, then the officer alone is liable. If sued, an officer has two immediate concerns: (1) Who will represent him or her? and (2) If the jury finds liability, who will pay the damages?

Who Will Represent the Officer in a Lawsuit?

Most state agencies, by law or official policy, provide representation to state law enforcement officers in civil actions. Such representation is usually undertaken by the state attorney general. The situation is different in local law enforcement agencies, where representation usually is decided on a case-by-case basis. This means that the local agency is under no obligation to provide a lawyer if an officer is sued, although most agencies will provide some form of representation unless what the officer did constitutes gross abuse of authority. If the agency provides a lawyer, it will probably be the district attorney, the county attorney, or another lawyer who works with the government in some capacity. In some cases, the officer is allowed to choose a lawyer, whose fees are then paid by the agency. This is ideal for the officer but unpopular with agencies because of the high cost. It is cheaper to use somebody already employed by the municipality (such as a county attorney or a district attorney) to represent an officer than to hire an outside lawyer.

Who Will Pay If the Officer Is Held Liable?

A majority of states provide some form of indemnification (meaning the reimbursement of any damages paid by the officer) for state employees. The amount varies considerably; some states set no limit, but most states do. If the court awards the plaintiff an amount larger than the maximum allowed by the agency, the employee pays the difference. Although most state agencies provide some form of indemnification, it does not follow that the agency will automatically indemnify every time liability is imposed. Most agencies will pay if the officer acted within the scope of employment, but the agency will not indemnify if the officer's act was gross, blatant, or outrageously

HIGHLIGHT

Police Accountability

The truth is, police brutality has been with us forever. So has corruption. The two feed on each other. We don't recruit from the Planet Perfect. We recruit from society. But things are vastly better than they were. . . . Police departments must map brutality and corruption complaints the same way we mapped murders and shootings. Then commanders must be held accountable to prevent their recurrence. Stings of every kind must be run for theft, brutality and discourtesy. Once caught, serious offenders should be interrogated like any criminal so we can make more cases on other bad cops.

SOURCE: Jack Maple (former New York Police Department Deputy Commissioner), "Police Must Be Held Accountable," *Newsweek*, June 21, 1999, p. 67.

violative of individual rights or of agency regulations, as determined by the court. However, local agencies' practices vary from full indemnification to no indemnification whatsoever. Many state and local agencies will not pay for punitive damages (as opposed to token or actual damages) against a public employee, because the imposition of punitive damages indicates that the employee acted outside the scope and course of employment. Therefore, it would be against public policy for the agency to reimburse him or her.

The Supervisor as Defendant

The term *police supervisors* includes anybody who supervises somebody in the hierarchy of that organization. It therefore includes police sergeants, lieutenants, captains, majors, sheriffs, and police chiefs. Supervisors can be held liable in three general ways: (1) If the supervisor was personally involved in the act (personal liability); (2) if the supervisor was not personally involved but what happened can be linked to his or her negligence (vicarious liability); and (3) if the supervisor violates the rights of subordinates (direct liability).

The Supervisor Was Personally Involved in the Act
A police supervisor may be held liable if he or she participated in the act, ratified the act, directed the act, or was present at the time the act was committed and could have stopped it but did not. In these cases, the supervisor was personally involved in the act. Examples:

- *Participated in the act.* A police chief takes part in the beating of a suspect.
- *Ratified the act.* A sheriff knew about the beating of a detainee after it took place but approves of it.
- *Directed the act.* A captain tells a subordinate to arrest a suspect even without probable cause.
- *Was present when the act was committed.* A superior officer who is present when a suspect is beaten but does not do anything to stop it. For example, Sergeant Stacey Koon of the Los Angeles Police Department was present during the Rodney King beating. Although the court found that Koon did not participate in the beating, he could have stopped it; therefore, he was held liable.

What Happened Can Be Linked to Negligence by the Supervisor
This is called *vicarious liability,* meaning indirect liability because, although the supervisor did not have a direct hand in or intent to violate the right of the plaintiff, through negligence the act took place. A supervisor is liable if the illegal act by a subordinate comes under any of the following seven categories of supervisory negligence:

- Negligent failure to train
- Negligent failure to direct
- Negligent failure to supervise

- Negligent hiring
- Negligent failure to discipline
- Negligent assignment
- Negligent entrustment

City of Canton v. Harris (1989)

The level of negligence needed for supervisory liability in state tort cases varies from state to state. Most states, however, use **deliberate indifference** as the standard for negligence by supervisors. The Court has also ruled that in cases based on federal law (Section 1983), supervisory liability based on failure to train is based on "deliberate indifference" (*City of Canton v. Harris,* 489 U.S. 378 [1989]). There is no generally accepted definition of what deliberate indifference means. It is, however, a higher form of negligence than "mere indifference," but it is lower than "conduct that shocks the conscience." On a scale of one to ten, one being the slightest form of negligence, deliberate indifference would likely be a seven or eight. Conduct that shocks the conscience is a ten.

The defense that "I did not know what my subordinate did and therefore I should not be held liable," is not valid in legal liability cases against supervisors. Courts do not use the standard of actual knowledge for supervisor liability; instead, they use the standard of "should the supervisor have known" what their subordinates did? This requires supervisors to know what goes on in their departments and not simply tell subordinates: "Go ahead, do what you want to do, but don't tell me about it."

If the Supervisor Violates the Rights of Subordinates (Direct Liability) This type of supervisory liability does not come from the general public but from their own subordinates. Law enforcement officers have constitutional rights that supervisors must respect. These rights emanate from various sources: the Constitution, federal law, state law, court decisions, agency policies, and collective bargaining agreements. Supervisory liability arises if the supervisor violates any of these rights.

For example, a police chief is liable if he or she violates a police officer's freedom of religion. Similarly, a sheriff is liable if he or she discriminates against women in the agency or sexually harasses a subordinate—both of which are violations of the Civil Rights Act of 1964. Federal and state laws prohibit discrimination on the basis of national origin.

Many police departments are unionized and have collective bargaining agreements. Violations of collective bargaining agreements can result in liability. This area of personnel law is complex and beyond the scope of this chapter. It is mentioned here only for the purpose of presenting the total picture of supervisory liability. Violating the rights of subordinates, however, is a frequent source of liability in law enforcement and has resulted in an increasing number of lawsuits feted by police officers. It is a topic with which supervisors must be familiar.

The City or County as Defendant

The inclusion of the city or county as defendant is rooted in the **deep pockets theory**, which means that, whereas officers and supervisors may have limited financial resources to pay the plaintiff, police agencies have a broader financial base. States and state agencies generally cannot be sued and held liable under Section 1983, because they enjoy sovereign immunity under the Eleventh Amendment to the Constitution. This does not mean, however, that state officials are immune to liability. Sovereign immunity extends only to the state itself and its agencies; state officials may be sued and held liable just like local officials. Although states are generally immune from liability in Section 1983 cases, the same is not true in state courts. Many states have waived their sovereign immunity by law or court decisions. In these states, a liability lawsuit may be brought against the state itself.

The rule is different in cases involving cities and counties because these are local governments. The Court held that a municipality can be held liable if an unconstitutional action taken by an employee is caused by a **municipal policy or custom** (*Monell v. Department of Social Services,* 436 U.S. 658 [1978]).

Monell v. Department of Social Services (1978)

In *Webster v. City of Houston* (735 F.2d 838 [5th Cir. 1984]), the U.S. Court of Appeals for the Fifth Circuit defined "policy or custom" as follows:

Webster v. City of Houston (5th Cir. 1984)

1. *Policy.* A policy statement, ordinance, regulation, or decision that is adopted officially and promulgated by the municipality's lawmaking officers or by an official to whom the lawmakers have delegated policy-making authority.
2. *Custom.* A persistent widespread practice of city officials or employees that, although not authorized by officially adopted and promulgated policy, is so common and well settled as to constitute a custom that fairly represents municipal policy.

The distinction is that a policy is usually written, whereas a custom is unwritten.

There are instances when an officer or a supervisor will not be held liable for damages but the agency or municipality may be. In *Owen v. City of Independence* (445 U.S. 622 [1980]), the Court said that a municipality sued under Section 1983 cannot invoke the good faith defense if its policies violate constitutional rights. In that case, a police chief was dismissed by the city manager and city council for certain misdeeds while in office. The police chief was not given any type of hearing or due process rights, because the city charter under which the city manager and city council acted did not grant him any rights prior to dismissal. The Court held that the city manager and members of the city council acted in good faith based on the provisions of the city charter but that the city itself could not invoke the good faith defense.

In a 1985 decision, *Brandon v. Holt* (469 U.S. 464 [1985]), the Court ruled that a monetary judgment against a public officer "in his official capacity" imposes liability upon the agency that employs him or her, regardless of whether the agency is named as a defendant in the suit. In *Brandon,* the plaintiff alleged that, although the director of the police department had no actual notice of the police officer's violent behavior, administrative policies were such that he should have known. The Court added that, although the director could be shielded by qualified immunity, the city could be held liable.

And in a 1986 case, *Pembauer v. City of Cincinnati* (475 U.S. 469 [1986]), the Court decided that municipalities can be held liable in a civil rights case for violating constitutional rights on the basis of a single decision (rather than a "pattern of decisions") made by an authorized municipal policy maker. In *Pembauer,* the county prosecutor made official policy and thereby exposed his municipal employer to liability by instructing law enforcement officers to forcibly enter a doctor's office without a search warrant to serve certain writs on persons thought to be there. The officers were trying to arrest two of the doctor's employees, who had failed to appear before a grand jury. The Court held that this action violated the Fourth Amendment rights of the office owner and concluded that the City of Cincinnati could be held liable.

In a later case, the Court ruled that a county cannot be held liable under Section 1983 for a single hiring decision made by a county official (*Board of County Commissioners of Bryan County, Oklahoma v. Brown,* 520 U.S. 397 [1997]).

Other Consequences of Police Misconduct

The discussion in this chapter focuses primarily on the civil liabilities of the police. There are other sanctions, however, for improper police conduct. Four sanctions are discussed briefly in this section: criminal prosecution of police officers, exclusion of evidence illegally obtained, administrative sanctions for violations of department rules, and loss of law enforcement license.

Can the Police Sue Back?

Can the police retaliate by suing those who sue them? The answer is yes, and some departments have, in fact, struck back. The Fifth Circuit Court of Appeals has held that a city can criminally prosecute individuals for knowingly filing false complaints against the police (*Gates v. City of Dallas,* 729 F.2d 343 [5th Cir. 1984]). New York City has adopted a policy of countersuing individuals who have brought civil suits accusing police officers of brutality, asserting that it was the complainant who attacked the police. Nonetheless, the number of civil cases actually brought by the police against members of the public remains comparatively small.

The reality is that, although police officers may file tort lawsuits against arrestees or suspects, there are disincentives to doing that. For example, the officer will have to hire his or her own lawyer, a financial outlay that the officer is unlikely to recover from the defendant. Even if the officer wins the case, most of those who have encounters with the police are too poor to pay damages anyway. Thus, officers may prefer to get back at the suspect in a criminal case. States have criminal laws penalizing such offenses as assaulting a peace officer, resisting arrest or a search, hindering apprehension or prosecution, refusing to obey a police order, and committing aggravated assault. These offenses can be added to the original criminal charges filed against the person, thereby increasing the total penalty that may be imposed. Some officers also feel that the antagonistic treatment they sometimes get from the public is simply part of police work, to be accepted without retaliation. In sum, alternatives to suing plaintiffs civilly exist that police might find more effective and convenient.

Criminal Liabilities under Federal and State Penal Codes

Police officers are subject to criminal liabilities, which may be classified as follows:

Federal

1. Title 18 of U.S. Code, Section 242—Criminal Liability for Deprivation of Civil Rights

2. Title 18 of U.S. Code, Section 241—Criminal Liability for Conspiracy to Deprive a Person of Rights

3. Title 18 of U.S. Code, Section 245—Violations of Federally Protected Activities

State

1. State penal code provisions specifically aimed at public officers for crimes such as:
   a. Official oppression
   b. Official misconduct
   c. Violation of the civil rights of prisoners

2. Regular penal code provisions punishing such criminal acts as assault, battery, false arrest, serious bodily injury, and homicide

In serious violations, criminal prosecution of police officers is always an option. As discussed earlier, officers can be prosecuted in both federal and state courts for the same act. Because they are not the same jurisdiction, the prohibition against double jeopardy does not apply. Why do plaintiffs prefer to file civil cases instead of filing criminal cases so the officer can be prosecuted in criminal court? The answer probably lies in three realities: money, easier access to court, and higher chances of winning or getting a conviction. Here is a comparison of civil and criminal cases against the police:

Civil Cases	Criminal Cases
If the plaintiff wins, he or she gets a monetary award in the form of damages.	No monetary award is given to the victim even if the defendant is convicted.
The plaintiff can recover attorney's fees from the defendant. These fees can exceed the monetary award for damages.	No attorney's fees are involved.
The cases may be filed by the victim in court at any time, using his or her own lawyer.	Only the prosecuting attorney can file these cases. If he or she refuses to file, the prosecution does not take place.
Preponderance of the evidence is needed to win.	Guilt beyond a reasonable doubt is needed to convict.
If tried before a jury, unanimity usually is not required.	If tried before a jury, unanimity is required for conviction.

This list shows that civil cases are easier to win than criminal cases and financially benefit the plaintiff, which explains why plaintiffs often prefer the civil route in legal liability cases.

Exclusion of Illegally Obtained Evidence

This topic is discussed extensively in Chapter 4, "The Exclusionary Rule." That rule provides that any evidence obtained by the police in violation of the Fourth Amendment guarantee against unreasonable searches and seizures is not admissible in a criminal prosecution to prove guilt. Its main purpose is to deter police misconduct, the assumption being that there will be a strong disincentive for the police to misbehave if the evidence obtained thereby is not admitted. Its underlying philosophy is that, in a democratic society, it is better for nine guilty persons to go free than for one innocent person to be convicted.

Whether or not the exclusionary rule is an effective deterrent to police misconduct is debatable. There are studies to support both sides of the debate. The controversy has become academic anyway because at no time soon will the exclusionary rule be abandoned by the Court. Instead, the rule has been refined over the years.

The consequences of obtaining excludible evidence through improper conduct are not well defined. Although the evidence itself is excluded, the officer is usually left unpunished except in cases involving gross civil rights violations or in high-profile cases, where civil liabilities or criminal prosecutions might follow. The benefit of the doubt is usually resolved in favor of the police, perhaps with good reason.

In some cases, the police do not know that what they are doing is wrong unless it is later declared illegal by a trial court. This may sometimes be a product of poor officer training, and therefore the fault is systemic rather than personal. There are proposals to admit the evidence during trial but criminally punish the officer who obtained the evidence illegally. This, however, is unrealistic. For example, what jury would convict an officer in a subsequent criminal case for improper seizure of evidence in a major drug trial that resulted in the conviction of the accused?

Administrative Investigations and Sanctions

Internal police investigations result from a variety of officer misbehavior ranging from charges of unethical conduct to allegations of criminal wrongdoing. Among the categories of sanctions discussed earlier—civil, criminal, and administrative—the sanction that is imposed first and fastest is administrative. A major police misconduct results in immediate suspension, with or without pay, while the department investigates. Smaller departments leave the issue of discipline to supervisors, whereas large departments have internal affairs divisions that conduct investigations and recommend sanctions. Conduct that does not result in civil liability may nonetheless lead to an administrative sanction, particularly if it violates departmental policy.

The use of civilian review boards has long been advocated as a way to discipline officers. This approach, however, has been tried without much popularity or success. Although the use of civilian review boards is viewed by the public as an impartial way to investigate misconduct, police officers consider them selective and discriminatory. Their reaction is "Why us and not other public officials as well?" On the other hand, the public is wary of police departments investigating their own. Investigation by peers is suspect in any professional organization; it is worse when it involves the police, who have long had the reputation of drawing a "blue curtain" and a wall of secrecy between themselves and the public.

Revocation of Law Enforcement License

Law enforcement officers are professionals licensed by the state. Improper police conduct may result in loss of license, which disqualifies an officer from law enforcement work. Like other forms of sanction, loss of license may be imposed with other punishments, particularly after a criminal conviction. It is an administrative sanction, but its effects can be permanent and far-reaching.

Loss of license can result from a violation of professional ethics as well as from other serious forms of misconduct. *Ethical behavior* is a generic term that covers a wide range of police conduct, from not accepting free coffee to not committing a criminal act. Most police departments and organizations subscribe to a code of ethics that prescribes professional expectations. Such codes resemble a code of ideal behavior rather than a criminal code. Sanctions for violations vary—from simple censure to firing from the department. In some cases, however, a serious violation of professional ethics results in criminal prosecution. Examples are accepting bribes

As a law enforcement officer, my fundamental duty is to serve the community; to safeguard lives and property; to protect the innocent against deception, the weak against oppression or intimidation, and the peaceful against violence or disorder; and to respect the constitutional rights of all to liberty, equality, and justice.

I will keep my private life unsullied as an example to all and will behave in a manner that does not bring discredit to me or my agency. I will maintain courageous calm in the face of danger, scorn, or ridicule; develop self-restraint; and be constantly mindful of the welfare of others. Honest in thought and deed in both my personal and official life, I will be exemplary in obeying the law and the regulations of my department. Whatever I see or hear of a confidential nature or that is confided to me in my official capacity will be kept ever secret unless revelation is necessary in the performance of my duty.

I will never act officiously or permit personal feelings, prejudices, political beliefs, aspirations, animosities, or friendships to influence my decisions. With no compromise for crime and with relentless prosecution of criminals, I will enforce the law courteously and appropriately without fear or favor, malice or ill will, never employing unnecessary force or violence and never accepting gratuities.

I recognize the badge of my office as a symbol of public faith, and I accept it as a public trust to be held so long as I am true to the ethics of police service. I will never engage in acts of corruption or bribery, nor will I condone such acts by other police officers. I will cooperate with all legally authorized agencies and their representatives in the pursuit of justice.

I know that I alone am responsible for my own standard of professional performance and will take every reasonable opportunity to enhance and improve my level of knowledge and competence. I will constantly strive to achieve these objectives and ideals, dedicating myself before God to my chosen profession—law enforcement.

---

or lying during police investigations. The code of ethics for law enforcement officers constitutes a broad umbrella that covers a host of misconduct. It differs from other means of police control in that it expects the officer to behave properly and professionally and is more prescriptive than punitive.

A frequent complaint from certain segments of society is that some police officers lie. Although no reliable data or studies are available, most officers will likely concede that lies (white lies and the more serious types of lies) are told by some officers in the course of police work. The results can be devastating for a suspect or defendant. As one source notes, the police usually win "swearing contests." The same source adds: "Defendants' claims that they were coerced into talking often turn into swearing contests, with the police contending that everything was honest and above board."[12] One former prosecutor who is currently a defense lawyer shares this insight about lying by the police: "The cops have hard jobs. Often they are frustrated. There is a great temptation to cross the line. You've got to restrict them to a right to search only when they have a reason to believe a crime is going on. And a busted taillight is not enough to allow the search of a car. Neither is an illegal left turn. Neither is speeding. Or being black."[13] Whatever the justification or excuse, lying by the police is not only unethical; it is also criminal (perjury, if under oath) and should never happen in law enforcement.

Summary

Civil Liability under Federal (Section 1983) Cases

- *Definition.* A Section 1983 case is a case usually filed in federal court in which the plaintiff seeks monetary damages and/or an injunction from a government official who, while acting within the scope of authority, violated the plaintiff's constitutional rights or a right given by federal law.

- *Two elements for a Section 1983 lawsuit to succeed.* (1) The defendant must have been acting under color of law, and (2) there must have been a violation of a constitutional right or a right given by federal law.

- *Defenses. Good faith (also known as qualified immunity) defense.* An officer is not civilly liable unless he or she violated a clearly established statutory or constitutional right of which a reasonable person would have known.

Civil Liability under State Tort Law

- *Definition.* Tort is a civil wrong in which the action of one person causes injury to the person or property of another in violation of a legal duty imposed by law.

- *Types of state tort cases.* (1) *Intentional tort:* Occurs when there is an intention on the part of the officer to bring some physical harm to or mental coercion upon another person. (2) *Negligence tort.* Occurs when there is a breach of a common law or statutory duty to act reasonably toward those who may foreseeably be harmed by one's conduct.

- *Liability in negligence tort.* Generally, there is no liability under negligence tort for failing to protect a member of the public, because the officer is protected by the public duty doctrine, which holds that government functions are owed to the general public but not to specific individuals.

- *Defense often used in state tort cases.* Official immunity, which means that the officer is not liable if performing a discretionary duty in good faith and is acting within the scope of authority.

- When are defendants liable? (1) *Police officer*—When what happened can be blamed solely on the officer and on nobody else. (2) *supervisor*—When what happened can be linked to one or all of the seven areas of supervisor negligence. Deliberate indifference is the usual standard in supervisor negligence cases. (3) *City or county*—When what happened was the result of policy or custom.

Other Consequences of Police Misconduct

- Criminal prosecution
- Exclusion of evidence illegally seized
- Administrative investigations
- Revocation of law enforcement license

Review Questions and Hypothetical Cases

1. Give an overview of the types of legal liabilities to which police officers may be exposed in connection with their work.

2. What two elements are needed for civil cases under Section 1983 to succeed? Explain what each means.

3. What is the public duty doctrine? Explain its main exception.

4. What is the good faith defense in Section 1983 cases? Give examples.

5. Police officers are not liable in Section 1983 cases "unless they violate a clearly established constitutional or federally given right of which a reasonable person would have known." Using decided cases, explain what is meant by a "clearly established constitutional right."

6. Give five differences between Section 1983 and state tort cases.

7. When are police chiefs held liable for the acts of their subordinates? Give examples.

8. Why do plaintiffs prefer to file civil cases rather than criminal cases against police officers?

9. Give reasons why police officers prefer not to sue those who have falsely accused them.

10. Assume a police officer brutally beats up a high school student who was suspected of dealing dope. Lawsuits are filed against the officer. Could the officer be liable under state tort law? On what basis? Could the officer also be liable under Section 1983? On what basis? Could the officer be prosecuted successively in criminal cases in state court and then in federal court? Would the constitutional protection against double jeopardy apply to the officer? Explain your answers.

11. Officer X, a police officer in Kansas, violated a court order by refusing to arrest Y, a husband against whom a restraining order had been issued by the court. His refusal resulted in serious injury to Y's wife and daughter. A case is brought against Officer X alleging a violation of Section 1983 (federal law) and a violation of Kansas state tort law. Will Officer X be liable under one or both of these laws? Justify your answer.

12. Z, a university student, was arrested by the campus police because they had information from her roommate that she was selling drugs in the dormitory and had drugs in her car. Based on this information and without obtaining a warrant, university police officers arrested Z, bodily searched her, and also searched her car. The searches yielded no drugs. The police later learned that the information from the roommate was completely false and that the roommate intensely disliked Z. Questions: (a) Who will Z's lawyer likely include in a lawsuit and why? (b) What defenses, if any, are available to the officers? and (c) Will these defenses succeed? Justify your answers.

Key Terms

Go to the Criminal Procedure 7e website for flash cards that will help you master the definitions of these terms.

acting under color of law, 510
acting within the scope of authority, 529
assault, 520
battery, 520
deadly force, 521
deep pockets theory, 533
deliberate indifference, 532
discretionary act, 528
false arrest, 520

false imprisonment, 520
good faith defense in Section 1983 cases, 514
good faith defense in state tort cases, 528
infliction of mental or emotional distress, 522
intentional tort, 519
municipal policy or custom, 533
negligence tort, 523

official immunity, 528
probable cause defense, 518
public duty doctrine, 523
punitive force, 521
reasonable force, 521
Section 1983 case (or civil rights case), 509
special relationship, 523
tort, 519
wrongful death, 522

Holdings of Key Cases

See Appendix C for information on how to find cases in this chapter on FindLaw.com.

Anderson v. Creighton, 483 U.S. 635 (1987)
The *Harlow* standard, which affords immunity from acts that the official could have reasonably believed were lawful, applies to police officers in the performance of their responsibilities.

Ashburn v. Ann Arundel County, 510 A.2d 1078 (Md. 1986) Police officers are not liable for injuries inflicted on the public by drunk drivers whom the police fail to arrest.

Board of the County Commissioners of Bryan County, Oklahoma v. Brown, 520 U.S. 397 (1997) A county cannot be held liable under Section 1983 for a single hiring decision made by a county official.

Brandon v. Holt, 469 U.S. 464 (1985) A monetary judgment against a public officer in his or her official capacity imposes liability upon the agency that employs him or her, regardless of whether the agency was named as a defendant in the suit.

Brinegar v. United States, 338 U.S. 160 (1949) Probable cause is defined as more than bare suspicion; it exists when the facts and circumstances within the officers' knowledge and of which they had reasonably trustworthy information are sufficient in themselves to warrant a man of reasonable caution in the belief that an offense has been or is being committed.

Brosseau v. Haugen, 125 S.Ct. 596 (2004) "If the law at that time [of the incident] did not clearly establish that the officer's conduct would violate the Constitution, the officer should not be subject to liability, or indeed, even the burdens of litigation."

Chavez v. Martinez, 538 U.S. 760 (2004) A Section 1983 case succeeds only if there is a proven violation of a constitutional right or of a right guaranteed by federal law.

City of Canton v. Harris, 489 U.S. 378 (1989) Inadequate police training may serve as the basis for municipal liability under Section 1983 if the failure to train amounts to "deliberate indifference" to the rights of people with whom the police come into contact and the deficiency in the training program is closely related to the injury suffered.

City of Lancaster v. Chambers, 883 S.W. 2d 650 (Tex. 1994) Government employees are entitled to official immunity from lawsuits arising from the performance of their discretionary duties in good faith as long as they are acting within the scope of their authority.

City of Pharr v. Ruiz, 944 S.W. 2d 709 (Tex. Cr. App. 1997) An act is discretionary if it involves personal deliberation, decision, and judgment. Actions that require obedience to orders or performance of duties about which the officer has no choice are not discretionary; they are instead ministerial.

DeShaney v. Winnebago County Department of Social Services, 489 U.S. 189 (1989) A person who is not under the custody of the state has no constitutional right to protection under the Due Process Clause of the Fourteenth Amendment, but there may be liability under state court decisions or state tort law.

Fraire v. City of Arlington, 957 F.2d 1268 (5th Cir. 1992) A right is "clearly established" when, at the time the defendant acted, the law established the contours of a right so clearly that a reasonable official would have understood that his or her acts were unlawful.

Gates v. City of Dallas, 729 F.2d 343 (5th Cir. 1984) A city can criminally prosecute individuals for knowingly filing false complaints against the police.

Groh v. Ramirez, 540 U.S. 551 (2004) An officer is not entitled to qualified immunity if it would be clear to a reasonable officer that his or her conduct was unlawful in the situation he or she confronted.

Harlow v. Fitzgerald, 457 U.S. 800 (1982) Government officials performing discretionary functions are generally shielded from liability for civil damages insofar as their conduct does not violate clearly established statutory or constitutional rights of which a reasonable person would have known.

Irwin v. Town of Ware, 467 N.E. 2d 1292 (Mass. 1984) Statutes that establish police responsibility in DWI cases show a legislative intent to protect both the intoxicated person and the users of the highway and therefore create a special relationship that can lead to police liability.

Lewis v. Downs, 774 F.2d 711 (6th Cir. 1985) Police who used excessive force on a family when responding to a call to settle a neighborhood dispute were liable for damages under state tort law.

Malley v. Briggs, 475 U.S. 335 (1986) A police officer, when applying for an arrest warrant, is entitled only to qualified immunity, not absolute immunity, in Section 1983 cases. This means that, even if a warrant is issued by a magistrate as a result of the officer's complaint, the officer could be held liable if it is established that the complaint was made maliciously and without probable cause.

Monell v. Department of Social Services, 436 U.S. 658 (1978) Local units of government may be held liable in a civil rights lawsuit if the allegedly unconstitutional action was taken by the officer as a part of an official policy or custom.

Owen v. City of Independence, 445 U.S. 622 (1980) A municipality sued under Section 1983 cannot invoke the good faith defense, which is available to its officers and employees, if its policies violate constitutional rights.

Pembauer v. City of Cincinnati, 475 U.S. 469 (1986) Municipalities can be held liable in a civil rights case for violating constitutional rights on the basis of a single decision (rather than a pattern of decisions) made by an authorized municipal policy maker.

Rodriguez v. Jones, 473 F.2d 599 (5th Cir. 1973) Probable cause as a defense in civil rights cases simply means a reasonable good faith belief in the legality of the action taken.

Sanders v. City of Belle Glade, 510 So.2d 962 (Fla. App. 1987) Once a suspect is handcuffed and taken into custody, a special relationship is created that makes the city responsible for his or her safety as though he or she were incarcerated in the city jail.

Saucier v. Katz, 533 U.S. 194 (2001) A ruling on qualified immunity in Section 1983 cases is separate from a ruling on whether a constitutional right was violated. It should be made early in the proceedings so that, if established, the cost and expense of a trial are avoided.

Schuster v. City of New York, 154 N.E. 2d 534 (N.Y. 1958) The police have a special duty to use reasonable care to protect people who have collaborated with them in the arrest or prosecution of criminals.

Sorichetti v. City of New York, 482 N.E. 2d 70 (1985) The police may be civilly liable for failure to protect if a special relationship has been created—for example, if a judicial order has been issued for the police to protect a child, but they fail to do so.

Town of Castle Rock v. Gonzales, 545 U.S.____(2005) The wrongful failure by the police to arrest a husband who violated a domestic relations court restraining order does not amount to a violation of a constitutional right under the Fourteenth Amendment Due Process Clause and therefore does not result in civil liability under federal law.

Webster v. City of Houston, 735 F.2d 838 (5th Cir. 1984) "Official policy or custom" means "(a) a policy statement, ordinance, regulation, or decision that is officially adopted and promulgated by the municipality's lawmaking officers or by an official to whom the lawmakers have delegated policy-making authority; or (b) a persistent widespread practice of city officials or employees that, although not authorized by officially adopted and promulgated policy, is so common and well settled as to constitute a custom that fairly represents municipal policy."

Young v. City of Killeen, 775 F.2d 1349 (5th Cir. 1985) The court found a police officer liable for $202,295.80 in a wrongful death action for shooting and killing a man suspected of buying marijuana. The officer was liable even though he thought he was shooting in self-defense. The judge, relying on the testimony of an expert witness on police procedures, found that the officer had acted negligently and contrary to good police procedure. The officer's actions not only placed him in a position of greater danger but also imperiled the deceased suspect by creating a situation in which a fatal error was likely.

You Be the Judge . . .

In the United States Court of Appeals for the Eighth Circuit

At 10 P.M. on August 11, 1998, in Kansas City, Missouri, the Kansas City Police executed a search warrant for the home of Doran, searching for drugs and other contraband in a suspected methamphetamine lab. They were to use the law enforcement technique of "dynamic entry" to enter the house before the occupants had a chance to react. Officer Grant, the "ram officer," yelled "Police, search warrant!" as they struck the door with a battering ram. The door gave way on the third strike, and Officer Sumpter rushed in first, acting as "point man." Sumpter had just entered the doorway when he saw a man running toward him pointing a handgun. He yelled, "Police, search warrant, get down!" When Doran did not lower his weapon, Sumpter fired, hitting Doran twice, and wounding him seriously. They found no lab in the house, and only 1 oz. of marijuana. Doran sued Sumpter, Grant, their supervisor Sgt. Greenwell, and the Kansas City Police Commissioners under 42 USC §1983.

Sgt. Greenwell led the team executing the search warrant. The team's function was executing high-risk search warrants on suspected drug houses. The investigating officer, Detective Williamson, had received an anonymous tip stating:

- Methamphetamine was being manufactured in the Doran house.

- Doran sold methamphetamine and crack cocaine from the front door every day.

- Drugs were in dresser drawers and guns were in the bedroom.

- Doran's adult son living there had just been arrested for carrying a sawed-off shotgun.

Detective Williamson collected trash from in front of the house containing the Dorans' fifty plastic bags with the corners cut (a common manner of packaging drugs), bags with methamphetamine residue, and an empty package of "Dristan," a product used in making methamphetamine. Based on these facts, Detective Williamson obtained a search warrant.

Sgt. Greenwood read it, spoke to the detective, and drove by the house to determine "tactical considerations" of the entry. He believed they were facing a methamphetamine lab and armed occupants; he ordered a dynamic entry, wearing gas masks in case of fumes from the lab, and for a fire truck and ambulance to stand by in case of a fire or explosion in the "lab."

How will you decide this legal issue? Was Sgt. Green justified in serving the warrant using a "no-knock" method?

The Court's decision The U.S. Court of Appeals for the Eighth Circuit decided that Sgt. Greenwood was justified in serving the warrant as a "no-knock" warrant. It was reasonable for him to rely on the contents of the warrant and his conversations with Detective Williamson and assume that there was a methamphetamine lab and armed occupants in the Doran house. Detective Williamson could have done more to investigate the allegations, but this does not affect the liability of Sgt. Greenwood and his team. [Note, both the trial court and later a panel of the 8th Circuit Court of Appeals found the opposite, that there was not enough to justify Sgt. Greenwood's use of a "no-knock" entry without some corroboration, such as surveillance, or checking of the facts in the inherently unreliable anonymous tip (such as the allegation about Doran's son, which was false).] *Doran v. Echold,* 8th Cir. No. 03-810 (En Banc, 6/6/2005).

In the United States Court of Appeals for the Eleventh Circuit

In Coweta County, Georgia, a high-speed pursuit was underway. Sheriff's Deputy Scott heard on the radio that the suspect would not stop, and he joined in the chase. Harris, the driver, did not stop for the police, ran red lights, passed cars on a double yellow line, and drove between 70 and 90 mph. He maintained control of his vehicle, however, signaling his passing and turns.

Scott called his supervisor on the radio, requested permission to use a "Precision Intervention Technique," and was given permission to do so. In a PIT procedure, an officer strikes a fleeing vehicle in a specific way that makes it spin and stops it. It should be employed at low speeds, at a maximum of 35 mph.

When Scott was given permission to PIT Harris's car, he determined they were going too fast to perform a PIT, and so instead he rammed Harris's car at high speed. Harris lost control of his vehicle, careened down an embankment, and crashed. The wreck rendered him a quadriplegic.

Neither Scott nor his supervisor had heard what offense Harris had originally been pursued for: the deputy had clocked Harris going 73 mph in a 55 mph zone. The originally pursuing deputy never relayed this information, and no one asked him.

How will you decide this legal issue? Could Scott be held personally liable for Harris's injuries?

The Court's decision The U.S. Court of Appeals for the Eleventh Circuit decided that Scott could be held liable for violating Harris's civil rights through an excessive use of force. Whether an automobile is an instrument of deadly force may depend on the circumstances. Clearly, in a high-speed ramming Scott's car qualifies as deadly force. The use of deadly force is legal when the suspect is reasonably believed to threaten the officer or others with such force or to have just committed a crime involving such force, and force is necessary to prevent his escape *and* the suspect has been warned when feasible. Here Harris had not committed a serious crime, was in no danger of escaping, and could be found to not have threatened others with serious harm. [Note that these facts are in dispute, but the court accepted them as all true for the purposes of keeping the case open until a jury could hear it and decide the truth of all allegations.] *Harris v. Coweta*, 406 F.3d 1307 (11th Cir. 2005).

Recommended Readings

Andrew M. Ayers. *The police can do what? Making local governmental entities pay for unauthorized wiretapping.* 19 New York Law School Journal of Human Rights 651–696 (Spring 2003).

Erwin Chemerinsky. *High-speed chases.* 37 Trial 24–27 (2001).

Jeremy D. Kernodle. Note. *Policing the police: Clarifying the test for holding the government liable under 42 U.S.C. (section) 1983 and the state-created danger theory.* Vanderbilt Law Review 165–203 (2001).

Viola King. Note. Robinson v. City of Detroit: *When does liability attach in police pursuits?* Thomas M. Cooley Law Review 409–428 (2001).

Steve Ryals. *Problems concerning litigation custom and practice cases.* Touro Law Review 841–851 (2000).

Brian J. Serr. *Turning Section 1983's protection of civil rights into an attractive nuisance: Extra-textual barriers to municipal liability under Monell (Monell v. Department of Social Services of the City of New York, 98 S.Ct. 2018 [1978]).* Georgia Law Review 881–902 (2001).

Gregory A. Wix. Note. *Tort law—government immunity—during a police chase, police do not owe a duty of care to wrongdoers who are drivers or passengers.* University of Detroit Mercy Law Review 323–329 (2002).

Notes

1. *New York Times,* March 21, 2001, p. 1.
2. "Los Angeles Settles Lawsuit against Police," *New York Times,* November 22, 2000, final edition, sec. A.
3. *Liability Reporter,* November 2001, p. 168.
4. *Liability Reporter,* July 2001, p. 102.
5. *Liability Reporter,* February 2001, p. 22.
6. *http://www.aele.org/civilsample.html.*
7. Ibid.
8. F. Scogins and S. Brodsky, "Fear of Litigation among Law Enforcement Officers," 10 *American Journal of Police* 45.
9. *Training Aids Digest,* December 1992, p. 2.
10. *USA Today,* May 26, 1999, p. A3.
11. Isidore Silver, *Police Civil Liability* (New York: Matthew Bender, 1985), pp. 5–7.
12. Paul Bergman and Sara J. Berman-Barrett, *The Criminal Law Handbook,* 4th ed. (Berkeley, CA: Nolo, 2002), p. 119.
13. Leslie Abramson, *The Defense Is Ready* (Simon & Schuster, 1997), p. 89.

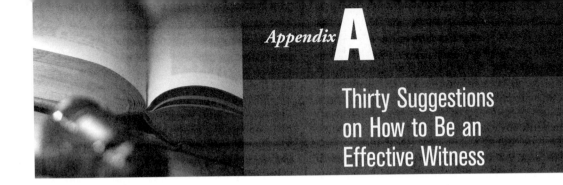

Thirty Suggestions on How to Be an Effective Witness

Note: *This appendix is based on the work of John Scott Blonien, senior assistant attorney general of the state of Washington, with additions and modifications by the author.*

As a witness, you have an important job to do. In order for the court to make a correct and wise decision and for justice to be served, the evidence in a case must be presented by all the parties in a truthful manner. Otherwise, the administration of justice becomes tainted and flawed.

All witnesses are required to take an oath "to tell the truth, the whole truth and nothing but the truth." There are two ways, however, to tell the truth. One is ineffectively—in a halting, stumbling, hesitant manner—which makes the court and the jury doubt your testimony. The other is effectively—in a confident, straightforward, and candid manner—which makes you a more credible and useful witness.

Here is a list of thirty suggestions to help you become a more effective witness. Go over this list before testifying.

1. **Be prompt.** Never keep the court and the jury waiting.
2. **Dress properly and be neat.** Do not wear gaudy or "loud" clothing or dark glasses. If your work requires a uniform, ask your attorney whether wearing a uniform for the occasion is appropriate.
3. **When taking the oath, stand upright, pay attention, and say "I do" clearly.**
4. **Be serious.** Avoid laughing, giggling, or talking about the case in the hallway or restrooms of the courthouse.
5. **Be sincere and candid; do not bluff.** It is better to admit a mistake than to try to bluff your way through.
6. **Testify from memory, but do not try to memorize what you are going to say.** If you do that, your testimony will sound "pat" and "rehearsed" and will not be as believable. You are allowed to consult the notes you made concerning the event about which you are testifying. Ordinarily, however, these notes are also available to the opposing attorney and will probably be referred to during cross-examination. Remember your notes well.
7. **Prior to your testimony, try to picture the scene, the objects there, the distances, and what happened.** This will make your recollection more

accurate. If the question is about distances or time, and your answer is only an estimate, be sure to say so.

8. **Speak clearly and loudly.** The person farthest away in the courtroom should be able hear you. Remember to glance at the judge and the jury and to talk to them honestly and openly, as you would to a friend or neighbor. Direct your answers mostly to the jury rather than to the opposing lawyer, your own lawyer, or the judge.

9. **Listen carefully to the questions asked.** Do not appear too eager to respond. Pause briefly before answering, and then give a well-considered answer.

10. **Never try to answer a question you do not understand.** If you do not understand a question, politely ask the person posing the question to repeat it.

11. **Explain your answer, if necessary.** Do not be afraid to ask the judge to allow you to explain your answer, particularly if the question cannot be answered truthfully with a simple "yes" or "no."

12. **Answer simply and directly, and answer only the question asked.** Do not volunteer information not actually sought by the questioner.

13. **Keep your answer short and to the point.** Avoid long narration.

14. **If you feel you did not answer the question correctly, make your correction immediately.** If your answer was not clear, clarify it.

15. **If you can, give categorical, definite answers.** Avoid saying, "I think," "I believe," or "In my opinion." If you do not know, say so. If asked about details that a person is not likely to remember, it is best simply to say, "I do not remember." Do not bluff, guess, or speculate.

16. **Do not give conclusions or opinions, unless asked.** In a court of law, only expert witnesses are usually allowed to give conclusions or opinions. The court and jury are interested only in the facts, not in an opinion or conclusion. For example, "X's death was caused by stab wounds" is stating an opinion. On the other hand, saying that you saw Y stab X is stating a fact, assuming that was what you saw happen.

17. **Avoid saying, "That is all of the conversation," or "Nothing else happened."** Instead say, "That is all I recall," or "That is all I remember happening." It is possible that after some thought you might remember something else.

18. **Be polite and courteous.** This suggestion applies even if the attorney questioning you behaves otherwise. Do not be cocky or antagonistic, or else you will lose credibility with the judge and jury.

19. **Remember that you are sworn to tell the truth; tell it.** Admit every material truth even if it is not to the advantage of your side. Do not stop to figure out whether your answer will help or hurt your cause. Just answer the questions truthfully and to the best of your recollection.

20. **Be aware that you are likely to be asked about earlier statements you made, if any, related to the case.** This would include any statements you may have made in an affidavit, deposition, or earlier testimony. Listen carefully to what is being read or repeated, and give a truthful answer.

21. **Do not be afraid to admit that you made an earlier statement.** As much as possible, your answer should be consistent with your previous statement. However, if there are discrepancies between your earlier statement and your current testimony, admit them and, if you can, explain them.

22. **Try not to appear nervous.** Avoid mannerisms (such as touching your nose or eyeglasses, wiping your eyebrow, or covering your mouth), which convey the impression that you are scared or are not telling the truth.

23. **Never lose your temper or show irritation.** The opposing attorney may try to agitate or aggravate you on cross-examination, in hopes that you will lose your temper and say things that will hurt your cause. Keep your cool at all times.

24. **If you do not want to answer a question, do not ask the court whether you must answer it.** This might make the judge or jury think you have something to hide. If the court wants you to answer the question, do so.

25. **Do not look at the attorney for your side or at the judge for help.** If the question is improper, the attorney for your side will probably object to it or have your answer stricken from the record after it is given. Give the attorney for your side an opportunity to react to or object to the question asked. Pause before giving an answer.

26. **Do not argue with the opposing attorney.** It is the job of the lawyer for your side to do that.

27. **Do not nod your head for a "yes" or "no" answer.** Speak clearly so that the court reporter or a recording device can hear or pick up your answer.

28. **Do not be intimidated by questions about whether you have conferred with your lawyer.** The opposing attorney might ask you the following question: "Have you talked to anybody about this case?" If you say, "No," the court will know that is probably not true, because good attorneys try to talk to a witness before he or she takes the stand. If you say, "Yes," the defense lawyer might imply that you have been told what to say. Be honest and say that you have talked with whomever you have talked with—an attorney, the victim, other witnesses—and that you simply told them what the facts were. Suppose the opposing lawyer asks, in a loud and mocking voice, "Do you mean to tell this honorable court that you discussed your testimony in this case with the district attorney?" If you did, simply answer, "Yes." Remember, there is nothing wrong with your discussing the facts of the case with your attorney; that is expected. What is wrong is your lawyer telling you what to say.

29. **Avoid any discussion of any kind with a juror or potential juror in or out of the courthouse.** Do not discuss the case with anyone at the courthouse other than your attorney, particularly if somebody is listening.

30. **When you leave the witness stand after testifying, act confident.** Do not smile, appear downcast, or exude an air of triumph.

The Constitution of the United States

WE THE PEOPLE OF THE UNITED STATES, IN ORDER TO FORM A MORE PERFECT UNION, ESTABLISH JUSTICE, INSURE DOMESTIC TRANQUILITY, PROVIDE FOR THE COMMON DEFENCE, PROMOTE THE GENERAL WELFARE, AND SECURE THE BLESSINGS OF LIBERTY TO OURSELVES AND OUR POSTERITY, DO ORDAIN AND ESTABLISH THIS CONSTITUTION FOR THE UNITED STATES OF AMERICA.

Article I

Section 1. All legislative Powers herein granted shall be vested in a Congress of the United States, which shall consist of a Senate and House of Representatives.

Section 2. The House of Representatives shall be composed of Members chosen every second Year by the People of the several States, and the Electors in each State shall have the Qualifications requisite for Electors of the most numerous Branch of the State Legislature.

No Person shall be a Representative who shall not have attained to the Age of twenty five Years, and been seven Years a Citizen of the United States, and who shall not, when elected, be an Inhabitant of that State in which he shall be chosen.

Representatives and direct Taxes shall be apportioned among the several States which may be included within this Union, according to their respective Numbers, which shall be determined by adding to the whole Number of free Persons, including those bound to Service for a Term of Years, and excluding Indians not taxed, three fifths of all other Persons. The actual Enumeration shall be made within three Years after the first Meeting of the Congress of the United States, and within every subsequent Term of ten Years, in such Manner as they shall by Law direct. The Number of Representatives shall not exceed one for every thirty Thousand, but each State shall have at Least one Representative; and until such enumeration shall be made, the State of New Hampshire shall be entitled to chuse three, Massachusetts eight, Rhode-Island and Providence Plantations one, Connecticut five, New-York six, New Jersey four, Pennsylvania eight, Delaware one, Maryland six, Virginia ten, North Carolina five, South Carolina five, and Georgia three.

When vacancies happen in the Representation from any State, the Executive Authority thereof shall issue Writs of Election to fill such Vacancies.

The House of Representatives shall chuse their Speaker and other Officers; and shall have the sole Power of Impeachment.

Section 3. The Senate of the United States shall be composed of two Senators from each State, chosen by the Legislature thereof, for six Years; and each Senator shall have one Vote.

Immediately after they shall be assembled in Consequence of the first Election, they shall be divided as equally as may be into three Classes. The Seats of the Senators of the first Class shall be vacated at the Expiration of the second Year, of the second Class at the Expiration of the fourth Year, and of the third Class at the Expiration of the sixth Year, so that one third may be chosen every second Year; and if Vacancies happen by Resignation, or otherwise, during the Recess of the Legislature of any State, the Executive thereof may make temporary Appointments until the next Meeting of the Legislature, which shall then fill such Vacancies.

No person shall be a Senator who shall not have attained to the Age of thirty Years, and been nine Years a Citizen of the United States, and who shall not, when elected, be an Inhabitant of that State for which he shall be chosen.

The Vice President of the United States shall be President of the Senate, but shall have no Vote, unless they be equally divided.

The Senate shall chuse their other Officers, and also a President pro tempore, in the Absence of the Vice President, or when he shall exercise the Office of President of the United States.

The Senate shall have the sole Power to try all Impeachments. When sitting for that Purpose, they shall be on Oath or Affirmation. When the President of the United States is tried, the Chief Justice shall preside: And no Person shall be convicted without the Concurrence of two thirds of the Members present. Judgment in Cases of Impeachment shall not extend further than to removal from Office, and disqualification to hold and enjoy any Office of honor, Trust or Profit under the United States: but the Party convicted shall nevertheless be liable and subject to Indictment, Trial, Judgment and Punishment, according to law.

Section 4. The Times, Places and Manner of holding Elections for Senators and Representatives, shall be prescribed in each State by the Legislature thereof; but the Congress may at any time by Law make or alter such Regulations, except as to the Places of chusing Senators.

The Congress shall assemble at least once in every Year, and such Meeting shall be on the first Monday in December, unless they shall by Law appoint a different Day.

Section 5. Each House shall be the Judge of the Elections, Returns and Qualifications of its own Members, and a Majority of each shall constitute a Quorum to do Business; but a smaller Number may adjourn from day to day, and may be authorized to compel the Attendance of absent Members, in such Manner, and under such Penalties as each House may provide.

Each House may determine the Rules of its Proceedings, punish its Members for disorderly Behaviour, and, with the Concurrence of two thirds, expel a Member.

Each House shall keep a journal of its Proceedings, and from time to time publish the same, excepting such Parts as may in their Judgment require Secrecy; and the Yeas and Nays of the Members of either House on any question shall, at the Desire of one fifth of those Present, be entered on the Journal.

Neither House, during the Session of Congress, shall, without the Consent of the other, adjourn for more than three days, nor to any other Place than that in which the two Houses shall be sitting.

Section 6. The Senators and Representatives shall receive a Compensation for their Services, to be ascertained by Law, and paid out of the Treasury of the United States. They shall in all Cases, except Treason, Felony and Breach of the Peace, be privileged from Arrest during their Attendance at the Session of their respective Houses, and in going to and returning from the same; and for any Speech or Debate in either House, they shall not be questioned in any other Place.

No Senator or Representative shall, during the Time for which he was elected, be appointed to any civil Office under the Authority of the United States, which shall have been created, or the Emoluments whereof shall have been encreased during such time; and no Person holding any Office under the United States, shall be a Member of either House during his Continuance in Office.

Section 7. All Bills for raising Revenue shall originate in the House of Representatives; but the Senate may propose or concur with Amendments as on other Bills.

Every Bill which shall have passed the House of Representatives and the Senate, shall, before it become a Law, be presented to the President of the United States; If he approve he shall sign it, but if not he shall return it, with his Objections to that House in which it shall have originated, who shall enter the Objections at large on their Journal, and proceed to reconsider it. If after such Reconsideration two thirds of that House shall agree to pass the Bill, it shall be sent, together with the Objections, to the other House, by which it shall likewise be reconsidered, and if approved by two thirds of that House, it shall become a Law. But in all such Cases the Votes of both Houses shall be determined by yeas and Nays, and the Names of the Persons voting for and against the Bill shall be entered on the Journal of each House respectively. If any Bill shall not be returned by the President within ten Days (Sundays excepted) after it shall have been presented to him, the Same shall be a Law, in like Manner as if he had signed it, unless the Congress by their Adjournment prevent its Return, in which Case it shall not be a Law.

Every Order, Resolution, or Vote to which the Concurrence of the Senate and House of Representatives may be necessary (except on a question of Adjournment) shall be presented to the President of the United States; and before the Same shall take Effect, shall be approved by him, or being disapproved by him, shall be repassed by two thirds of the Senate and House of Representatives, according to the Rules and Limitations prescribed in the Case of a Bill.

Section 8. The Congress shall have Power To lay and collect Taxes, Duties, Imposts and Excises, to pay the Debts and provide for the common Defence and general Welfare of the United States; but all Duties, Imposts and Excises shall be uniform throughout the United States.

To borrow Money on the Credit of the United States;

To regulate Commerce with foreign Nations, and among the several States, and with the Indian Tribes;

To establish an uniform Rule of Naturalization, and uniform Laws on the subject of Bankruptcies throughout the United States;

To coin Money, regulate the Value thereof, and of foreign Coin, and fix the Standard of Weights and Measures;

To provide for the Punishment of counterfeiting the Securities and current Coin of the United States;

To establish Post Offices and post Roads;

To promote the Progress of Science and useful Arts, by securing for limited Times to Authors and Inventors the exclusive Right to their respective Writings and Discoveries;

To constitute Tribunals inferior to the supreme Court;

To define and punish Piracies and Felonies committed on the high Seas, and Offences against the Law of Nations;

To declare War, grant letters of Marque and Reprisal, and make rules concerning Captures on Land and Water;

To raise and support Armies, but no Appropriation of Money to that Use shall be for a longer Term than two Years;

To provide and maintain a Navy;

To make rules for the Government and Regulation of the land and naval Forces;

To provide for calling forth the Militia to execute the Laws of the Union, suppress Insurrections and repel Invasions;

To provide for organizing, arming, and disciplining, the Militia, and for governing such Part of them as may be employed in the Service of the United States, reserving to the States respectively, the Appointment of the Officers, and the Authority of training the Militia according to the discipline prescribed by Congress;

To exercise exclusive Legislation in all Cases whatsoever, over such District (not exceeding ten Miles square) as may, by Cession of particular States, and the Acceptance of Congress, become the Seat of the Government of the United States, and to exercise like Authority over all Places purchased by the Consent of the Legislature of the State in which the Same shall be, for the Erection of Forts, Magazines, Arsenals, dock-Yards, and other needful Buildings;—And

To make all Laws which shall be necessary and proper for carrying into Execution the foregoing Powers, and all other Powers vested by this Constitution in the Government of the United States, or in any Department or Officer thereof.

Section 9. The Migration or Importation of such Persons as any of the States now existing shall think proper to admit, shall not be prohibited by the Congress prior to the Year one thousand eight hundred and eight, but a Tax or duty may be imposed on such Importation, not exceeding ten dollars for each Person.

The Privilege of the Writ of Habeas Corpus shall not be suspended, unless when in Cases of Rebellion or Invasion the public Safety may require it.

No Bill of Attainder or ex post facto Law shall be passed.

No Capitation, or other direct, Tax shall be laid, unless in Proportion to the Census or Enumeration herein before directed to be taken.

No Tax or Duty shall be laid on Articles exported from any State.

No Preference shall be given by any Regulation of Commerce or Revenue to the Ports of one State over those of another; nor shall Vessels bound to, or from, one State, be obliged to enter, clear, or pay Duties in another.

No money shall be drawn from the Treasury, but in Consequence of Appropriations made by Law; and a regular Statement and Account of the Receipts and Expenditures of all public Money shall be published from time to time.

No Title of Nobility shall be granted by the United States: And no Person holding any Office of Profit or Trust under them, shall, without the Consent of the Congress, accept of any present, Emolument, Office, or Title, of any kind whatever, from any King, Prince, or foreign State.

Section 10. No State shall enter into any Treaty, Alliance, or Confederation; grant Letters of Marque and Reprisal; coin Money; emit Bills of Credit; make any Thing but gold and silver Coin a Tender in Payment of Debts; pass any Bill of Attainder, ex post facto Law, or Law impairing the Obligation of Contracts, or grant any Title of Nobility.

No State shall, without the Consent of the Congress, lay any Imposts or Duties on Imports or Exports, except what may be absolutely necessary for executing its inspection Laws; and the net Produce of all Duties and Imposts, laid by any State on Imports or Exports, shall be for the Use of the Treasury of the United States; and all such Laws shall be subject to the Revision and Controul of the Congress.

No State shall, without the Consent of Congress, lay any Duty of Tonnage, keep Troops, or Ships of War in time of Peace, enter into any Agreement or Compact with another State, or with a foreign Power, or engage in War, unless actually invaded, or in such imminent Danger as will not admit of delay.

Article II

Section 1. The executive Power shall be vested in a President of the United States of America. He shall hold his Office during the Term of four Years, and, together with the Vice President, chosen for the same Term, be elected, as follows

Each State shall appoint, in such Manner as the Legislature thereof may direct, a Number of Electors, equal to the whole Number of Senators and Representatives to which the State may be entitled in the Congress: but no Senator or Representative, or Person holding an Office of Trust or Profit under the United States, shall be appointed an Elector.

The Electors shall meet in their respective States, and vote by Ballot for two Persons, of whom one at least shall not be an Inhabitant of the same State with themselves. And they shall make a List of all the Persons voted for, and of the Number of Votes for each; which List they shall sign and certify, and transmit sealed to the Seat of the Government of the United States, directed to the President of the Senate. The President of the Senate shall, in the Presence of the Senate and House of Representatives, open all the Certificates, and the Votes shall then be counted. The Person having the greatest Number of Votes shall be the President, if such Number be a Majority of the whole Number of Electors appointed; and if there be more than one who have such Majority, and have an equal Number of Votes, then the House of Representatives shall immediately chuse by Ballot one of them for President; and if no Person have a Majority, then from the five highest on the List the said House shall in like Manner chuse the President. But in chusing the President, the Votes shall be taken by States, the Representation from each State having one Vote; A quorum for this Purpose shall consist of a Member or Members from two thirds of the States, and a Majority of all the States shall be necessary to a Choice. In every Case, after the Choice of the President, the Person having the greatest Number of Votes of the Electors shall be the Vice President. But if there should remain two or more who have equal Votes, the Senate shall chuse from them by Ballot the Vice President.

The Congress may determine the Time of chusing the Electors, and the Day on which they shall give their Votes; which Day shall be the same throughout the United States.

No Person except a natural born Citizen, or a Citizen of the United States, at the time of the Adoption of this Constitution, shall be eligible to the Office of President; neither shall any Person be eligible to that Office who shall not have attained to the Age of thirty five Years, and been fourteen Years a Resident within the United States.

In Case of the Removal of the President from Office, or of his Death, Resignation, or Inability to discharge the Powers and Duties of the said Office, the Same shall devolve on the Vice President, and the Congress may by Law provide for the Case of Removal, Death, Resignation or Inability, both of the President and Vice President, declaring what Officer shall then act as President, and such Officer shall act accordingly, until the Disability be removed, or a President shall be elected.

The President shall, at stated Times, receive for his Services, a Compensation, which shall neither be increased nor diminished during the Period for which he shall have been elected, and he shall not receive within that Period any other Emolument from the United States, or any of them.

Before he enter on the Execution of his Office, he shall take the following Oath or Affirmation:—"I do solemnly swear (or affirm) that I will faithfully execute the Office of President of the United States, and will to the best of my Ability, preserve, protect and defend the Constitution of the United States."

Section 2. The President shall be Commander in Chief of the Army and Navy of the United States, and of the Militia of the several States, when called into the actual Service of the United States; he may require the Opinion, in writing, of the principal Officer in each of the executive Departments, upon any Subject relating to the Duties of their respective Offices, and he shall have Power to grant Reprieves and Pardons for Offenses against the United States, except in Cases of Impeachment.

He shall have Power, by and with the Advice and Consent of the Senate, to make Treaties, provided two thirds of the Senators present concur; and he shall nominate, and by and with the Advice and Consent of the Senate, shall appoint Ambassadors, other public Ministers and Consuls, Judges of the supreme Court, and all other Officers of the United States, whose Appointments are not herein otherwise provided for, and which shall be established by Law: but the Congress may by Law vest the Appointment of such inferior Officers, as they think proper, in the President alone, in the Courts of Law, or in the Heads of Departments.

The President shall have Power to fill up all Vacancies that may happen during the Recess of the Senate, by granting Commissions which shall expire at the End of their next Session.

Section 3. He shall from time to time give to the Congress Information of the State of the Union, and recommend to their Consideration such Measures as he shall judge necessary and expedient; he may, on extraordinary Occasions, convene both Houses, or either of them, and in Case of Disagreement between them, with Respect to the Time of Adjournment, he may adjourn them to such Time as he shall think proper; he shall receive Ambassadors and other public Ministers; he shall take Care that the Laws be faithfully executed, and shall Commission all the Officers of the United States.

Section 4. The President, Vice President and all civil Officers of the United States, shall be removed from Office on Impeachment for, and Conviction of, Treason, Bribery, or other high Crimes and Misdemeanors.

Article III

Section 1. The judicial Power of the United States shall be vested in one supreme Court, and in such inferior Courts as the Congress may from time to time ordain and establish. The Judges, both of the supreme and inferior Courts, shall hold their Offices during good Behaviour, and shall, at stated Times, receive for their Services a Compensation, which shall not be diminished during their Continuance in Office.

Section 2. The judicial Power shall extend to all Cases, in Law and Equity, arising under this Constitution, the Laws of the United States, and Treaties made, or which shall be made, under their Authority;—to all Cases affecting Ambassadors, other public Ministers and Consuls;—to all Cases of admiralty and maritime Jurisdiction;—to Controversies to which the United States shall be a Party;—to Controversies between two or more States;—between a State and Citizens of another State;—between Citizens of different States;—between Citizens of the same State claiming Lands under Grants of different States, and between a State, or the Citizens thereof, and foreign States, Citizens or Subjects.

In all Cases affecting Ambassadors, other public Ministers and Consuls, and those in which a State shall be Party, the supreme Court shall have original Jurisdiction. In all the other Cases before mentioned, the supreme Court shall have appellate Jurisdiction, both as to Law and Fact, with such Exceptions, and under such Regulations as the Congress shall make.

The Trial of all Crimes, except in Cases of Impeachment, shall be by Jury; and such Trial shall be held in the State where the said Crimes shall have been committed; but when not committed within any State, the Trial shall be at such Place or Places as the Congress may by Law have directed.

Section 3. Treason against the United States shall consist only in levying War against them, or in adhering to their Enemies, giving them Aid and Comfort. No Person shall be convicted of Treason unless on the Testimony of two Witnesses to the same overt Act, or on Confession in open Court. The Congress shall have Power to declare the Punishment of Treason, but no Attainder of Treason shall work Corruption of Blood, or Forfeiture except during the Life of the Person attainted.

Article IV

Section 1. Full Faith and Credit shall be given in each State to the public Acts, Records, and judicial Proceedings of every other State. And the Congress may by general Laws prescribe the Manner in which such Acts, Records and Proceedings shall be proved, and the Effect thereof.

Section 2. The Citizens of each State shall be entitled to all Privileges and Immunities of Citizens in the several States.

A Person charged in any State with Treason, Felony, or other Crime, who shall flee from Justice, and be found in another State, shall on Demand of the executive Authority of the State from which he fled, be delivered up, to be removed to the State having Jurisdiction of the Crime.

No person held to Service or Labour in one State, under the Laws thereof, escaping into another, shall, in Consequence of any Law or Regulation therein, be discharged from such Service or Labour, but shall be delivered up on Claim of the Party to whom such Service or Labour may be due.

Section 3. New States may be admitted by the Congress into this Union; but no new State shall be formed or erected within the Jurisdiction of any other State; nor any State be formed by the Junction of two or more States, or Parts of States, without the Consent of the Legislatures of the States concerned as well as of the Congress.

The Congress shall have Power to dispose of and make all needful Rules and Regulations respecting the Territory or other Property belonging to the United States; and nothing in this Constitution shall be so construed as to Prejudice any Claims of the United States, or of any particular State.

Section 4. The United States shall guarantee to every State in this Union a Republican Form of Government, and shall protect each of them against Invasion;

and on Application of the Legislature, or of the Executive (when the Legislature cannot be convened) against domestic Violence.

Article V

The Congress, whenever two thirds of both Houses shall deem it necessary, shall propose Amendments to this Constitution, or, on the Application of the Legislatures of two thirds of the several States, shall call a Convention for proposing Amendments, which, in either Case, shall be valid to all Intents and Purposes, as Part of this Constitution, when ratified by the Legislatures of three fourths of the several States, or by Conventions in three fourths thereof, as the one or the other Mode of Ratification may be proposed by the Congress; Provided that no Amendment which may be made prior to the Year One thousand eight hundred and eight shall in any Manner affect the first and fourth Clauses in the Ninth Section of the first Article; and that no State, without its Consent, shall be deprived of its equal Suffrage in the Senate.

Article VI

All Debts contracted and Engagements entered into, before the Adoption of this Constitution, shall be as valid against the United States under this Constitution, as under the Confederation. This Constitution, and the Laws of the United States which shall be made in Pursuance thereof; and all Treaties made, or which shall be made, under the Authority of the United States, shall be the supreme Law of the Land; and the Judges in every State shall be bound thereby, any Thing in the Constitution or Laws of any State to the Contrary notwithstanding.

The Senators and Representatives before mentioned, and the Members of the several State Legislatures, and all executive and judicial Officers, both of the United States and of the several States, shall be bound by Oath or Affirmation, to support this Constitution; but no religious Test shall ever be required as a Qualification to any Office or public Trust under the United States.

Article VII

The Ratification of the Conventions of nine States, shall be sufficient for the Establishment of this Constitution between the States so ratifying the Same.

Done in Convention by the Unanimous Consent of the States present the Seventeenth Day of September in the Year of our Lord one thousand seven hundred and Eighty seven and of the Independence of the United States of America the Twelfth *In witness whereof We have hereunto subscribed our Names,*

Amendments to the Constitution

(The first ten Amendments were ratified December 15, 1791, and form what is known as the "Bill of Rights.")

Amendment 1

Congress shall make no law respecting an establishment of religion, or prohibiting the free exercise thereof; or abridging the freedom of speech, or of the press; or the right of the people peaceably to assemble, and to petition the Government for a redress of grievances.

Amendment 2

A well-regulated Militia, being necessary to the security of a free State, the right of the people to keep and bear Arms, shall not be infringed.

Amendment 3

No Soldier shall, in time of peace be quartered in any house, without the consent of the Owner, nor in time of war, but in a manner to be prescribed by law.

Amendment 4

The right of the people to be secure in their persons, houses, papers, and effects, against unreasonable searches and seizures, shall not be violated, and no Warrants shall issue, but upon probable cause, supported by Oath or affirmation, and particularly describing the place to be searched, and the persons or things to be seized.

Amendment 5

No person shall be held to answer for a capital, or otherwise infamous crime, unless on a presentment or indictment of a Grand Jury, except in cases arising in the land or naval forces, or in the Militia, when in actual service in time of War or public danger; nor shall any person be subject for the same offence to be twice put in jeopardy of life or limb; nor shall be compelled in any criminal case to be a witness against himself, nor be deprived of life, liberty, or property, without due process of law; nor shall private property be taken for public use without just compensation.

Amendment 6

In all criminal prosecutions, the accused shall enjoy the right to a speedy and public trial, by an impartial jury of the State and district wherein the crime shall have been committed, which district shall have been previously ascertained by law, and to be informed of the nature and cause of the accusation; to be confronted with the witnesses against him; to have compulsory process for obtaining witnesses in his favor, and to have the Assistance of Counsel for his defence.

Amendment 7

In Suits at common law, where the value in controversy shall exceed twenty dollars, the right of trial by jury shall be preserved, and no fact tried by a jury, shall be otherwise re-examined in any Court of the United States, than according to the rules of the common law.

Amendment 8

Excessive bail shall not be required, nor excessive fines imposed, nor cruel and unusual punishments inflicted.

Amendment 9

The enumeration in the Constitution, of certain rights, shall not be construed to deny or disparage others retained by the people.

Amendment 10

The powers not delegated to the United States by the Constitution, nor prohibited by it to the States, are reserved to the States respectively, or to the people.

Amendment 11
(Ratified February 7, 1795)

The Judicial power of the United States shall not be construed to extend to any suit in law or equity, commenced or prosecuted against one of the United States by Citizens of another State, or by Citizens or Subjects of any Foreign State.

Amendment 12
(Ratified July 27, 1804)

The Electors shall meet in their respective states and vote by ballot for President and Vice President, one of whom, at least, shall not be an inhabitant of the same state with themselves; they shall name in their ballots the person voted for as President, and in distinct ballots the person voted for as Vice President, and they shall make distinct lists of all persons voted for as President, and of all persons voted for as Vice President, and of the number of votes for each, which lists they shall sign and certify, and transmit sealed to the seat of the Government of the United States, directed to the President of the Senate;—The President of the Senate shall, in the presence of the Senate and House of Representatives, open all the certificates and the votes shall then be counted;—The person having the greatest number of votes for President, shall be the President, if such number be a majority of the whole number of Electors appointed; and if no person have such majority, then from the persons having the highest numbers not exceeding three on the list of those voted for as President, the House of Representatives shall choose immediately, by ballot, the President. But in choosing the President, the votes shall be taken by States, the representation from each State having one vote; a quorum for this purpose shall consist of a member or members from two-thirds of the states, and a majority of all the states shall be necessary to a choice. And if the House of Representatives shall not choose a President whenever the right of choice shall devolve upon them, before the fourth day of March next following, then the Vice President shall act as President, as in case of the death or other constitutional disability of the President.—The person having the greatest number of votes as Vice President, shall be the Vice President, if such number be a majority of the whole number of Electors appointed, and if no person have a majority, then from the two highest numbers on the list, the

Senate shall choose the Vice President; a quorum for the purpose shall consist of two-thirds of the whole number of Senators, and a majority of the whole number shall be necessary to a choice. But no person constitutionally ineligible to the office of President shall be eligible to that of Vice President of the United States.

Amendment 13
(Ratified December 6, 1865)

Section 1. Neither slavery nor involuntary servitude, except as a punishment for crime whereof the party shall have been duly convicted, shall exist within the United States, or any place subject to their jurisdiction.

Section 2. Congress shall have power to enforce this article by appropriate legislation.

Amendment 14
(Ratified July 9, 1868)

Section 1. All persons born or naturalized in the United States, and subject to the jurisdiction thereof, are citizens of the United States and of the State wherein they reside. No State shall make or enforce any law which shall abridge the privileges or immunities of citizens of the United States; nor shall any State deprive any person of life, liberty, or property, without due process of law; nor deny any person within its jurisdiction the equal protection of the laws.

Section 2. Representatives shall be apportioned among the several States according to their respective numbers, counting the whole number of persons in each State, excluding Indians not taxed. But when the right to vote at any election for the choice of Electors for President and Vice President of the United States, Representatives in Congress, the Executive and Judicial officers of a State, or the members of the Legislature thereof, is denied to any of the male inhabitants of such State, being twenty-one years of age, and citizens of the United States, or in any way abridged, except for participation in rebellion, or other crime, the basis of representation therein shall be reduced in the proportion which the number of such male citizens shall bear to the whole number of male citizens twenty-one years of age in such State.

Section 3. No person shall be a Senator or Representative in Congress, or elector of President and Vice President, or hold any office, civil or military, under the United States, or under any State, who, having previously taken an oath, as a member of Congress, or as an officer of the United States, or as a member of any State legislature, or as an executive or judicial officer of any State, to support the Constitution of the United States, shall have engaged in insurrection or rebellion against the same, or given aid or comfort to the enemies thereof. But Congress may by a vote of two-thirds of each House, remove such disability.

Section 4. The validity of the public debt of the United States, authorized by law, including debts incurred for payment of pensions and bounties for services in suppressing insurrection or rebellion, shall not be questioned. But neither the United States nor any

State shall assume or pay any debt or obligation incurred in aid of insurrection or rebellion against the United States, or any claim for the loss or emancipation of any slave; but all such debts, obligations and claims shall be held illegal and void.

Section 5. The Congress shall have power to enforce, by appropriate legislation, the provisions of this article.

Amendment 15
(Ratified February 3, 1870)

Section 1. The right of citizens of the United States to vote shall not be denied or abridged by the United States or by any State on account of race, color, or previous condition of servitude.

Section 2. The Congress shall have power to enforce this article by appropriate legislation.

Amendment 16
(Ratified February 3, 1913)

The Congress shall have power to lay and collect taxes on incomes, from whatever sources derived, without apportionment among the several States, and without regard to any census or enumeration.

Amendment 17
(Ratified April 8, 1913)

The Senate of the United States shall be composed of two Senators from each State, elected by the people thereof, for six years; and each Senator shall have one vote. The electors in each State shall have the qualifications requisite for electors of the most numerous branch of the State legislatures. When vacancies happen in the representation of any State in the Senate, the executive authority of such State shall issue writs of election to fill such vacancies: *Provided*, That the legislature of any State may empower the Executive thereof to make temporary appointments until the people fill the vacancies by election as the Legislature may direct.

This amendment shall not be so construed as to affect the election or term of any Senator chosen before it becomes valid as part of the Constitution.

Amendment 18
(Ratified January 16, 1919. Repealed December 5, 1933, by Amendment 21)

Section 1. After one year from the ratification of this article the manufacture, sale, or transportation of intoxicating liquors within, the importation thereof into, or the exportation thereof from the United States and all territory subject to the jurisdiction thereof for beverage purposes is hereby prohibited.

Section 2. The Congress and the several States shall have concurrent power to enforce this article by appropriate legislation.

Section 3. This article shall be inoperative unless it shall have been ratified as an amendment to the Constitution by the Legislatures of the several States, as provided in the Constitution, within seven years from the date of the submission hereof to the States by the Congress.

Amendment 19
(Ratified August 18, 1920)

The right of citizens of the United States to vote shall not be denied or abridged by the United States or by any State on account of sex.

Congress shall have power to enforce this article by appropriate legislation.

Amendment 20
(Ratified January 23, 1933)

Section 1. The terms of the President and the Vice President shall end at noon on the 20th day of January, and the terms of Senators and Representatives at noon on the 3d day of January, of the years in which such terms would have ended if this article had not been ratified; and the terms of their successors shall then begin.

Section 2. The Congress shall assemble at least once in every year, and such meeting shall begin at noon on the 3d day of January, unless they shall by law appoint a different day.

Section 3. If, at the time fixed for the beginning of the term of the President, the President elect shall have died, the Vice President elect shall become President. If a President shall not have been chosen before the time fixed for the beginning of his term, or if the President elect shall have failed to qualify, then the Vice President elect shall act as President until a President shall have qualified; and the Congress may by law provide for the case wherein neither a President elect nor a Vice President shall have qualified, declaring who shall then act as President, or the manner in which one who is to act shall be selected, and such person shall act accordingly until a President or Vice President shall have qualified.

Section 4. The Congress may by law provide for the case of the death of any of the persons from whom the House of Representatives may choose a President whenever the right of choice shall have devolved upon them, and for the case of the death of any of the persons from whom the Senate may choose a Vice President whenever the right of choice shall have devolved upon them.

Section 5. Sections 1 and 2 shall take effect on the 15th day of October following the ratification of this article.

Section 6. This article shall be inoperative unless it shall have been ratified as an amendment to the Constitution by the legislatures of three-fourths of the several States within seven years from the date of its submission.

Amendment 21
(Ratified December 5, 1933)

Section 1. The eighteenth article of amendment to the Constitution of the United States is hereby repealed.

Section 2. The transportation or importation into any State, Territory, or possession of the United States for delivery or use therein of intoxicating liquors, in violation of the laws thereof, is hereby prohibited.

Section 3. This article shall be inoperative unless it shall have been ratified as an amendment to the Constitution by conventions in the several States, as provided in the Constitution, within seven years from the date of the submission hereof to the States by the Congress.

Amendment 22
(Ratified February 27, 1951)

Section 1. No person shall be elected to the office of the President more than twice, and no person who has held the office of President, or acted as President, for more than two years of a term to which some other person was elected President shall be elected to the office of President more than once. But this Article shall not apply to any person holding the office of President when this Article was proposed by Congress, and shall not prevent any person who may be holding the office of President, or acting as President, during the term within which this Article becomes operative from holding the office of President or acting as President during the remainder of such term.

Section 2. This article shall be inoperative unless it shall have been ratified as an amendment to the Constitution by the Legislatures of three-fourths of the several States within seven years from the date of its submission to the States by the Congress.

Amendment 23
(Ratified March 29, 1961)

Section 1. The District constituting the seat of Government of the United States shall appoint in such manner as Congress may direct:

A number of electors of President and Vice President equal to the whole number of Senators and Representatives in Congress to which the District would be entitled if it were a State, but in no event more than the least populous State; they shall be in addition to those appointed by the States, but they shall be considered, for the purposes of the election of President and Vice President, to be electors appointed by a State; and they shall meet in the District and perform such duties as provided by the twelfth article of amendment.

Section 2. The Congress shall have power to enforce this article by appropriate legislation.

Amendment 24
(Ratified January 23, 1964)

Section 1. The right of citizens of the United States to vote in any primary or other election for President or Vice President, for electors for President or Vice President, or for Senator or Representative in Congress, shall not be denied or abridged by the United States or any State by reason of failure to pay poll tax or any other tax.

Section 2. Congress shall have power to enforce this article by appropriate legislation.

Amendment 25
(Ratified February 10, 1967)

Section 1. In case of the removal of the President from office or of his death or resignation, the Vice President shall become President.

Section 2. Whenever there is a vacancy in the office of the Vice President, the President shall nominate a Vice President who shall take office upon confirmation by a majority vote of both Houses of Congress.

Section 3. Whenever the President transmits to the President pro tempore of the Senate and the Speaker of the House of Representatives his written declaration that he is unable to discharge the powers and duties of his office, and until he transmits to them a written declaration to the contrary, such powers and duties shall be discharged by the Vice President as Acting President.

Section 4. Whenever the Vice President and a majority of either the principal officers of the executive departments or of such other body as Congress may by law provide, transmit to the President pro tempore of the Senate and the Speaker of the House of Representatives their written declaration that the President is unable to discharge the powers and duties of his office, the Vice President shall immediately assume the powers and duties of the office as Acting President.

Thereafter, when the President transmits to the President pro tempore of the Senate and the Speaker of the House of Representatives his written declaration that no inability exists, he shall resume the powers and duties of his office unless the Vice President and a majority of either the principal officers of the executive department or of such other body as Congress may by law provide, transmit within four days to the President pro tempore of the Senate and the Speaker of the House of Representatives their written declaration that the President is unable to discharge the powers and duties of his office. Thereupon Congress shall decide the issue, assembling within forty-eight hours for that purpose if not in session. If the Congress, within twenty-one days after receipt of the latter written declaration, or, if Congress is not in session within twenty-one days after Congress is required to assemble, determines by two-thirds vote of both houses that the President is unable to discharge the powers and duties of his office, the Vice President shall continue to discharge the same as Acting President; otherwise, the President shall resume the powers and duties of his office.

Amendment 26
(Ratified July 1, 1971)

Section 1. The right of citizens of the United States, who are eighteen years of age or older, to vote shall not be denied or abridged by the United States or by any state on account of age.

Section 2. The Congress shall have power to enforce this article by appropriate legislation.

Amendment 27
(Ratified May 7, 1992)

No law varying the compensation for the services of the Senators and Representatives shall take effect, until an election of Representatives shall have intervened.

Information on How to Search FindLaw

FindLaw.com, a free case-law source service offered by Thomson, contains all of the cases mentioned in this book.

When looking for a case on FindLaw, first determine the jurisdiction and level of case you're searching for. Is it a Federal Court of Appeal or a State Supreme Court or Appellate Court decision?

To find a **Federal Case** from the Legal Professional homepage (*www.findlaw.com*), follow these steps:

1. Click on the "Cases & Codes" link under the "Research the Law" section;
2. Scroll down to the "Case Law" section;
3. Click on the appropriate court in which the case was decided, e.g., U.S. Court of Appeals 9th Cir.;
4. Fill in a search window with the case's Docket No. or a Party Name, then click "Search" (note that you may only search using the terms in one window);
5. Find the case in the search results list, and click on the highlighted link to view the full-text version of the case.

To find a **State Case** from the Legal Professional homepage, follow these steps:

1. Click on the "States" link beneath the "Cases & Codes" link, which is in the "Research the Law" section;
2. Browse the list of states and click on the state in which the case was decided;
3. Scroll down the page to the "State" section and click on the "Supreme Court Cases from FindLaw" link (this is usually the first link listed in the "State" section);
4. In the search window, enter the case's Case Number or a Party Name, then hit the "Submit" button or the "Enter" key;
5. Find the case in the search results list, and click on the highlighted link to view the full-text version of the case.

Glossary

abandonment: The giving up of a thing or item absolutely, without limitation as to any particular person or purpose. It implies the giving up of possession or ownership or of any reasonable expectation of privacy.

acting under color of law: The use of power possessed by virtue of law and made possible only because the officer is clothed with the authority of the state.

acting within the scope of authority: The situation in which an officer is discharging the duties generally assigned to him or her.

actual seizure: A seizure accomplished by taking the person into custody with the use of hands or firearms or by merely touching the individual without the use of force.

administrative searches: Searches conducted by government inspectors to determine whether there are violations of government rules and regulations.

admission: Owning up to something related to an act that one may not have committed.

affirmation (of a decision): The situation in which a decision of the lower court from which the case came is upheld by the appellate court.

Alford plea: A guilty plea by a defendant who claims innocence.

anticipatory search warrant: A warrant obtained based on probable cause and an expectation that seizable items will be found at a certain place at a certain time.

apparent authority principle: The principle that a search is valid if consent was given by a person whom the police reasonably believed to have authority to give such consent, even if that person turns out not to have such authority.

area of immediate control: The area from which an arrested person might be able to obtain a weapon or destroy evidence.

arraignment: A procedure by which, at a scheduled time and after prior notice, the accused is called into court, informed of the charges against him or her, and asked how he or she pleads.

arrest: The taking of a person into custody against his or her will for the purpose of criminal prosecution or interrogation.

arrest warrant: A "writ issued by a magistrate, justice, or other competent authority, addressed to a sheriff, constable, or other officer, requiring him or her to arrest the person it names and bring the person before the magistrate or court to answer, or to be examined, concerning some offense that he or she is charged with having committed."

assault: An intentional tort in which an officer causes apprehension of harmful or offensive conduct; it is the attempt or threat of bodily harm on another person, accompanied by the ability to inflict it.

bail: The security required by the court and given by the accused to ensure that the accused appears before the proper court at the scheduled time and place to answer the charges brought against him or her.

battery: An intentional tort in which an officer inflicts harmful or offensive body contact on another person. It usually involves unlawful, unwarranted, or hostile touching—however slight.

beeper: An electronic device sometimes used by the police to monitor the movement and location of a motor vehicle.

bench warrant: A writ "from the bench," used to arrest and bring nonappearing defendants before the court. "A procedure issued by the court itself or 'from the bench' for the attachment or arrest of a person."

bifurcated procedure: A trial in which the determination of guilt or innocence and sentencing are separate.

bill of indictment: A document submitted to the grand jury by the prosecutor, accusing a person of a crime.

Bill of Rights: The first ten amendments to the U.S. Constitution.

booking: The making of an entry in the police blotter or arrest book, indicating the suspect's name, the time of arrest, and the offense involved. If the crime is serious, the suspect may also be photographed or fingerprinted.

***Brady* rule:** The rule that "the suppression by the prosecution of evidence favorable to an accused upon request violates due process where the evidence is material either to the guilt or punishment, irrespective of the good faith or bad faith of the prosecution."

brain fingerprinting: "A real-time psychophysiological assessment of a subject's response to stimuli in the form of words or pictures presented on a computer monitor."

CALEA: See **Communications Assistance for Law Enforcement Act of 1994.**

capias: Literally, "you take"; a warrant issued by a judge, requiring an officer to take a named defendant into custody.

case-by-case incorporation: An approach that looks at the facts of a specific case to determine whether there is an injustice so serious as to justify extending the provisions of the Bill of Rights to that state case.

case citation: Information indicating the printed or Internet source where a case may be found.

case law: The law as enunciated in cases decided by the courts.

challenge for cause: A challenge to the fitness of a person for jury membership on the basis of causes specified by law.

***Chimel* rule:** The rule that after an arrest the police may search the areas within a suspect's immediate control, meaning the area from which the suspect might be able to obtain a weapon or destroy evidence.

citation: An order issued by a court or law enforcement officer commanding the person to whom the citation is issued to appear in court at a specified time to answer certain charges.

citizen's arrest: An arrest made by a citizen without a warrant; usually limited to situations in which a felony has actually been committed and

the citizen has probable cause to believe that the person arrested committed the offense.

common law: Law that originated from the ancient and unwritten laws of England.

Communications Assistance for Law Enforcement Act of 1994 (CALEA): Contains provisions regarding three techniques of lawfully authorized surveillance devices: pen registers, trap-and-trace devices, and content interceptions.

complaint: A charge made before a proper officer, alleging the commission of a criminal offense.

confession: Saying that one has committed an act.

constructive seizure: A seizure accomplished without any physical touching, grabbing, holding, or use of force; occurs when the individual peacefully submits to the officer's will and control.

contemporaneous search: A search made at the same time as, or very close in time and place to, the arrest.

criminal procedure: The process followed by the police and the courts in the apprehension and punishment of criminals—from the filing of a complaint by a member of the public or the arrest of a suspect by the police, up to the time the defendant is sent to jail or, if convicted, to prison.

curtilage: "The area to which extends the intimate activity associated with the 'sanctity of a man's home and the privacies of life.'"

custodial interrogation: Interrogation that takes place (1) when the suspect is under arrest or (2) when the suspect is not under arrest but is deprived of his or her freedom in a significant way.

custody: When the suspect is *under arrest* or is not under arrest but is "*deprived of freedom in a significant way.*"

***Daubert* doctrine:** Holds that expert testimony pertaining to scientific, technical, or other specialized knowledge that will assist the trier of fact to understand the evidence or to determine whether a fact in issue is admissible as evidence. Used in federal courts, it replaces the stricter *Frye* doctrine, which requires that, for scientific evidence to be admissible, the procedures used must be sufficiently established to have gained general acceptance in the particular scientific field to which they belong.

deadly force: Force that, when used, would lead a reasonable officer objectively to conclude that it poses a high risk of death or serious injury to its human target.

death-qualified juries: "Conviction prone" juries, meaning juries that are more likely to convict and impose the death penalty because potential jurors whose opposition to the death penalty is so strong as to prevent or impair the performance of their duties at the sentencing phase are disqualified from it.

deep pockets theory: The theory that individual officers may lack resources to pay damages, but the government agency has a broader financial base, so plaintiffs include government agencies in their lawsuits.

deliberate indifference: A standard for negligence by supervisors. It is a higher form of negligence than "mere indifference," but it is lower than "conduct that shocks the conscience." On a scale of one to ten, one being the slightest form of negligence, deliberate indifference would likely be a seven or eight. Conduct that shocks the conscience is a ten.

Department of Homeland Security: Created by law in 2002, as another response to the events of September 11, 2001. Its general purpose is to "mobilize and organize our nation to secure the homeland from terrorist attacks."

deprived of freedom in a significant way: Limitation by the police of one's freedom of movement.

discovery: A procedure used by either party in a case to obtain necessary or helpful information that is in the hands of the other party.

discretionary act: An act that involves personal deliberation, decision, and judgment.

DNA testing: A procedure that matches the suspect's DNA with the DNA found in semen or blood recovered from the scene of the crime.

double jeopardy: The successive prosecution of a defendant for the same offense by the same jurisdiction; being punished more than once for the same offense.

drug courier profile: A set of identifiers developed by law enforcement agencies indicating the types of individuals who are likely to transport drugs.

dual court system: The two court systems of the United States, one for federal cases and the other for state cases.

dual sovereignty: The concept that federal and state governments are each sovereign in their own right.

Due Process Clause: The provision in the Fourteenth Amendment of the Constitution stating that no state shall deprive any person of life, liberty, or property without due process of law.

ECPA: See **Electronic Communications and Privacy Act of 1986.**

Edwards **rule:** A rule stating that a suspect who invokes the right to consult a lawyer cannot be questioned again for the same offense unless the suspect initiates further communication, exchanges, or conversations with the police.

Electronic Communications and Privacy Act of 1986 (ECPA): An act passed by Congress modifying and supplementing Title III of the Omnibus Crime Control and Safe Streets Act of 1968.

electronic surveillance: The use of electronic devices to monitor a person's activities or whereabouts.

en banc decision: A decision made by an appellate court as one body, not in divisions.

exclusionary rule: The exclusion in court of evidence illegally obtained; the rule of evidence providing that any evidence obtained by the government in violation of the Fourth Amendment's guarantee against unreasonable search and seizure is not admissible in a criminal prosecution to establish the defendant's guilt.

exigent circumstances: Emergency circumstances that make obtaining a warrant impractical, useless, dangerous, or unnecessary and that justify warrantless arrests or entries into homes or premises.

factory survey: A practice in which immigration officials pay surprise visits to factories and ask employees questions to determine if they are illegal aliens.

fair response: A prosecutor's statement to the jury during closing arguments that the defendant could have taken the witness stand but refused to do so is proper as long as it is in response to defense counsel's argument that the government did not allow the defendant to explain his or her side of the story.

false arrest: A tort case that may result if an officer makes an illegal arrest or if the officer arrests the wrong person named in a warrant.

false imprisonment: A tort case that may result when one person unlawfully detains another.

Federal Speedy Trial Act of 1974: A law that specifies time standards for each stage in the federal court process. Thirty days are allowed from arrest to the filing of an indictment or an information; seventy days are allowed between information or indictment and trial.

felony: A criminal offense punishable by death or by imprisonment of more than one year.

fishing expedition: A search conducted by law enforcement officers with no definite seizable contraband or items in mind in hopes of finding some usable evidence.

formally charged with an offense: Indictment, information, preliminary hearing, or arraignment of the suspect.

frisk: The pat-down of a person's outer clothing after a stop to see if he or she has a weapon or something that feels like a weapon, which can be seized by the officer. A frisk is performed for the protection of the officer and of others.

fruit of the poisonous tree doctrine: The doctrine holding that once the primary evidence (the "tree") is shown to have been unlawfully obtained any secondary evidence (the "fruit") derived from it is also inadmissible.

Frye doctrine: Holds that, before the results of scientific tests will be admissible as evidence in a trial, the procedures used must be sufficiently established to have gained general acceptance in the particular field to which they belong.

functional equivalent of interrogation: Instances in which no questions are actually asked by the police but in which the circumstances are so conducive to making a statement or confession that the courts consider them to be the equivalent of interrogation.

general on-the-scene questioning: Questioning at the scene of the crime for the purpose of gathering information that might enable the police to identify the criminal. _Miranda_ warnings are not needed.

good faith defense in Section 1983 cases: In civil liability cases, the concept that an officer should not be held liable if he or she did not violate a clearly established constitutional right of which a reasonable person would have known.

good faith defense in state tort cases: The situation in which an officer "acted in the honest belief that the action taken or the decision was appropriate under the circumstances."

good faith exceptions: Exceptions to the exclusionary rule holding that evidence obtained by the police is admissible in court even if there was an error or mistake as long as the error or mistake was not committed by the police or, if committed by the police, was honest and reasonable.

grand jury: A jury, usually composed of from twelve to twenty-three members, that determines whether a suspect should be charged with an offense. A grand jury indictment is required in some states only for serious offenses.

habeas corpus: Literally, "you have the body"; a remedy used if a person seeks release from an allegedly illegal or unconstitutional confinement.

harmless error: An error made during a trial that does not result in the reversal of a conviction on appeal.

harmless error rule: A rule stating that an error made by the trial court in admitting illegally obtained evidence does not lead to a reversal of the conviction if the error is determined to be harmless. The prosecution has the burden of proving that the error is in fact harmless.

hot pursuit exception (to the warrant rule): A policy that authorizes peace officers from one state, through a uniform act adopted by most states, to enter another state in fresh pursuit to arrest a suspect for a felony committed in the first state.

hung jury: A jury that cannot agree unanimously (in jurisdictions where unanimity is required) to convict or acquit the defendant.

immunity: Exemption from prosecution granted to a witness in exchange for testimony against a suspect or an accused.

inadvertence: The concept that to come under the plain view doctrine the evidence must be discovered by the officer accidentally; the officer must have had no prior knowledge that the evidence was present in the place. Inadvertence is no longer required by the plain view doctrine.

incorporation controversy: The issue of whether the Bill of Rights of the U.S. Constitution protects against violations of rights by the federal government only or also limits what state government officials can do.

independent source exception: An exception to the exclusionary rule holding that evidence obtained is admissible, despite its initial illegality, if the police can prove that it was obtained from an independent source that is not connected to the illegal search or seizure.

indictment: A written accusation filed against the defendant by a grand jury, usually signed by the jury foreperson.

indigent defendant: A defendant who is too poor to hire his or her own lawyer.

inevitable discovery exception: An exception to the fruit of the poisonous tree doctrine holding that the evidence is admissible, despite its initial illegality, if the police can prove that they would inevitably have discovered the evidence by lawful means, regardless of their illegal action.

infliction of mental or emotional distress: A form of intentional tort consisting of the infliction of severe emotional distress on a person through intentional or reckless extreme and outrageous conduct.

information: A written accusation of a crime, prepared by the prosecuting attorney without referring the case to a grand jury.

in loco parentis: Literally means "in place of parents"; the concept is cited by the Court as a reason high schools should be given certain search and seizure powers over students during school hours.

intelligent and voluntary waiver: A waiver given by a suspect who knows what he or she is doing and who is sufficiently competent to waive his or her rights.

intelligent waiver: One given by a suspect who knows what he or she is doing and is sufficiently competent to waive his or her rights.

intentional tort: A type of tort that occurs when an officer intends to bring some physical harm or mental coercion to bear upon another person.

interrogation: The asking of questions by the police. For purposes of the *Miranda* rule, however, *interrogation* means not only express questioning but also words or actions (other than those attendant to arrest and custody) on the part of the police that they should have known are reasonably likely to elicit an incriminating response from the suspect.

John Doe warrant: A warrant in which only the name John Doe appears, because the real name of the suspect is not known to the police. It is valid only if it contains a description of the accused by which he or she can be identified with reasonable certainty.

judicial precedent: The concept that decisions of courts have value as precedent for future cases similarly circumstanced.

judicial review: "The power of any court to hold unconstitutional and hence unenforceable any law, any official action based on a law, or any other action by a public official that it deems to be in conflict with the Constitution."

jurisdiction: The power of a court to try a case.

jury nullification: The situation in which a jury decides a case contrary to the weight of the evidence presented during a trial.

jury of peers: A jury that is not consciously restricted to a particular group.

***Kirby* rule:** A suspect is not entitled to have a lawyer present in a lineup or other face-to-face confrontation before being formally charged with a crime.

lesser included offense: An offense that is "composed of some, but not all, of the elements of the greater crime and which does not have any element not included in the greater offense."

level of proof: The degree of certainty required by law for an act or happening to be legal.

lineup: "A police identification procedure by which the suspect in a crime is exhibited, along with others with similar physical characteristics, before the victim or witness to determine if he or she can be identified as having committed the offense."

man of reasonable caution: Not a person with training in the law, but rather an average "man on the street" who, under the same circumstances, would believe that the person being arrested had committed the offense or that items to be seized would be found in a particular place.

Miranda **rule:** A rule stating that evidence obtained by the police during custodial interrogation of a suspect cannot be used in court during the trial unless the suspect was first informed of the right not to incriminate himself or herself and of the right to counsel.

Miranda **warnings:** Warnings informing suspects of their right to remain silent, that anything they say can be used against them in a court of law, that they have a right to counsel, and that, if they are indigent, counsel will be provided by the state.

misdemeanor: A crime punishable by a fine or imprisonment for less than one year; not as serious as a felony.

motion: A request made orally or in writing by a party in a case, asking the judge for a legal ruling on a matter related to a case.

motion for a directed verdict of acquittal: A motion by the defendant at the close of the presentation of evidence in a jury trial, asking the court for an acquittal on the grounds that the prosecution failed to introduce sufficient evidence concerning the offense charged.

motion for a mistrial: A motion filed by the defense seeking dismissal of the charges because of improper conduct on the part of the prosecution, judge, jury, or witnesses during the trial.

multiple voir dire: A voir dire in which the judge chooses several juries for future trials.

municipal policy or custom: A policy statement, ordinance, regulation, or decision (usually in writing) that is officially adopted by the municipality's lawmaking officers (or those delegated by them) or a persistent practice of city employees that, although not formally authorized in writing, is so common that it is the equivalent of municipal policy.

negligence tort: A tort arising from the breach of a common law or statutory duty to act reasonably toward those who may foreseeably be harmed by one's conduct.

neutral and detached magistrate: A magistrate (issuing a warrant) who is not unalterably aligned with the police or the prosecutor's position in a case.

new concept of electronic surveillance: The idea that electronic surveillance constitutes a search under the Fourth Amendment if the police activity violates a person's "reasonable expectation of privacy."

no-knock searches: Searches without announcement, authorized by state statutes, particularly in drug cases.

nolle prosequi: A motion, filed by the prosecutor, that seeks dismissal of the charges.

nolo contendere plea: Literally, "no contest"; a plea made when the defendant does not contest the charges. The effect is the same as that of a guilty plea, except that the plea cannot be used against the defendant as an admission in any subsequent civil proceeding arising out of the same offense.

nondeadly force: Force that, when used, is not likely to result in serious bodily injury or death.

nonunanimous verdict: A verdict for conviction that is not the product of a unanimous vote by jury members. A 9-to-3 vote for conviction in a state court has been declared constitutional by the Court.

official immunity: The concept that officers are not liable when they perform discretionary duties in good faith and are acting within the scope of their authority.

old concept of electronic surveillance: The idea that electronic surveillance does not violate the Fourth Amendment unless there was "some trespass into a constitutionally protected area."

open fields doctrine: The doctrine that items in open fields are not protected by the Fourth Amendment guarantee against unreasonable searches and seizures, so they can properly be seized by an officer without a warrant or probable cause.

open view: The phrase used to describe the circumstances of an officer who is out in open space (such as out on the streets) but sees an item within an enclosed area.

original jurisdiction: The case is heard in a court for the first time, not on appeal.

pen register: An electronic device that records the numbers dialed from a particular telephone; installed on the property of the telephone company rather than at the place where a suspect has access to the telephone.

peremptory challenge: A challenge to a prospective juror without stating a reason; the challenge is made entirely at the discretion of the challenging party. This is the opposite of challenge for cause, in which a reason for the challenge, usually specified by law, must be stated. Disqualification of a juror, by the defense or the prosecution, for which no reason is given.

petty offense: An offense whose maximum penalty is six months or less.

photographic identification (rogue's gallery): A procedure in which photographs of possible suspects are shown to the victim or witness.

physical self-incrimination: A form of self-incrimination, not protected under the Fifth Amendment, that stems from real or physical evidence. Examples are footprints, fingerprints, blood, and urine samples.

plain feel doctrine: See **plain touch doctrine.**

plain odor doctrine: The doctrine that if an officer smells something that is immediately recognizable as seizable, that object can be seized as long as such knowledge amounts to probable cause.

plain touch (plain feel) doctrine: The doctrine that if an officer touches or feels something that is immediately recognizable as seizable, the object can be seized as long as such knowledge amounts to probable cause. "[I]f the officer, while staying within the narrow limits of a frisk for weapons, feels what he has probable cause to believe is a weapon, contraband, or evidence, the officer may expand the search or seize the object."

plain view doctrine: The doctrine that items within the sight of an officer who is legally in the place from which the view is made, and who had no prior knowledge that the items were present may properly be seized without a warrant—as long as the items are immediately recognizable as subject to seizure.

plea: An accused's response in court to the indictment or information that is read to him or her in court.

plea bargain: A process in which a defendant is induced to plead guilty to an offense in exchange for a lower charge, a lower sentence, or other considerations favorable to the defendant.

preliminary examination (or hearing): A hearing held before a magistrate to determine whether there is probable cause to support the charges against the accused. This takes place before the grand jury hearing.

pretextual stops: Stops used as pretexts for motor vehicle searches.

preventive detention: The detention of an accused person not for purposes of ensuring his or her appearance in court but to prevent possible harm to society by dangerous individuals.

prima facie case: A case established by sufficient evidence; it can be overthrown by contrary evidence presented by the other side.

privilege of a witness: The Fifth Amendment right not to be forced to answer incriminating questions while on the witness stand.

privilege of the accused: The Fifth Amendment right not to answer incriminating questions or to take the witness stand. If the accused takes the witness stand, he or she must answer incriminating questions.

probable cause: More than bare suspicion; it exists when "the facts and circumstances within the officers' knowledge and of which they have reasonably trustworthy information are sufficient in themselves to warrant a man of reasonable caution in the belief that an offense has been or is being committed." In searches and seizures (in contrast to arrests), the issue of probable cause focuses on whether the property to be seized is connected with criminal activity and whether it can be found in the place to be searched.

probable cause defense: In Section 1983 cases, an officer's reasonable good faith belief in the legality of the action taken.

protective sweep: Entry made by the police into places or areas other than where an arrest or seizure is taking place for purposes of personal protection.

public duty doctrine: A doctrine holding that government functions are owed to the general public but not to specific individuals. Therefore, police officers who fail to prevent crime while acting within the scope of their official capacity are not liable to specific individuals for injury or harm that may have been caused by a third party.

public safety exception: The concept that responses to questions asked by police officers if reasonably prompted by concern for public safety are admissible in court even though the suspect was in police custody and not given the *Miranda* warnings.

public trial: A trial open to all persons interested in ensuring that the proceedings are fair and just.

punitive force: Force that is meant to punish rather than merely to bring the situation under control.

purged taint exception: An exception to the fruit of the poisonous tree doctrine, applicable when the defendant's subsequent voluntary act dissipates the taint of the initial illegality. A defendant's intervening act of free will is sufficient to break the causal chain between the tainted evidence and the illegal police conduct, so that the evidence becomes admissible.

racial profile stops: Stops of motor vehicles based on the driver's race.

racial profiling: Stopping a person solely on the basis of racial or ethnic identity.

reasonable doubt: "Such a doubt as would cause a juror, after careful and candid and impartial consideration of all the evidence, to be so undecided that he or she cannot say that he or she has an abiding conviction of the defendant's guilt."

reasonable expectation of privacy: The degree of privacy that entitles a person by constitutional right to be protected from government intrusion in private or public places.

reasonable force: The kind of force that a prudent and cautious person would use if exposed to similar circumstances; it is limited to the amount of force that is necessary to achieve valid and proper results.

reasonable suspicion: That "quantum of knowledge sufficient to induce an ordinarily prudent and cautious man under similar circumstances to believe criminal activity is at hand. It must be based on specific and articulable facts, which, taken together with rational inferences from those facts, reasonably warrant intrusion." A degree of proof that is less than probable cause but more than suspicion. It is sufficient to enable a police officer to conduct a stop and frisk. Reasonable suspicion must be

anchored in specific, objective facts and logical conclusions based on the officer's experience. It represents a degree of certainty (around 20 percent) that a crime has been or will be committed and that the suspect is involved in it.

rebuttal evidence: Evidence introduced by one party in the case to discredit the evidence given by the other side.

release on recognizance (ROR): An arrangement in which the court on the basis of the defendant's promise to appear in court as required releases the defendant without requiring him or her to post money or securities.

retained counsel: A lawyer paid by the defendant, not by the state.

reversal (of a decision): The situation in which a decision of the lower court where the case came from is overthrown, vacated, or set aside by the appellate court.

reverse and remand decision: The situation in which a decision by the lower court is reversed but the lower court has an opportunity to hear further arguments and give another decision in the case.

right to privacy: The right to be let alone by others, including the government and its law enforcement agents.

roadblock: A law enforcement practice for halting traffic. It is not strictly a form of detention, but it limits a person's freedom of movement by blocking vehicular movement. It is used by the police for a variety of purposes, including spot checks of drivers' licenses and car registrations, violations of motor vehicle laws, and apprehension of fleeing criminals and suspects.

rule of four: A rule providing that the Supreme Court needs the votes of at least four justices to consider a case on its merits.

rule of law: Holds that no person is above the law, that every person, from the most powerful public official down to the least powerful individual, is subject to the law and can be held accountable in the courts of law for what he or she does.

same offense: Two offenses that have the same elements.

search: The exploration or examination of an individual's home, premises, or person to discover things or items that may be used by the government as evidence in a criminal prosecution.

search warrant: A written order issued by a magistrate, directing a peace officer to search for property connected with a crime and bring it before the court.

Section 1983 case (or civil rights case): A lawsuit, filed under federal law, seeking damages from a police officer, supervisor, and/or department on the grounds that these defendants, acting under color of law, violated a plaintiff's constitutional rights or rights given by federal law.

seizure: The exercise of dominion or control by the government over a person or thing because of a violation of law.

selective incorporation: An approach holding that the Fourteenth Amendment's Due Process Clause should be interpreted to incorporate only those rights granted in Amendments I–X of the Constitution that are considered fundamental; this is the position advocated by most Supreme Court justices.

sentencing: The formal pronouncement of judgment by the court or judge on the defendant after conviction in a criminal prosecution, imposing the punishment to be inflicted.

sequestration: The practice of keeping members of the jury together and in isolation during a jury trial, to prevent their decision from being influenced by outside factors.

serious offense: One for which more than six months' imprisonment is authorized.

showup: A "one-to-one confrontation between a suspect and a witness to a crime."

silver platter doctrine: A doctrine applied in federal courts from 1914 to 1960, under which evidence of a federal crime that had been illegally obtained by state officers was admissible in federal courts, although it would not have been admissible if it had been obtained by federal officers.

sobriety checkpoint: A checkpoint set up by the police at a selected site along a public road; all vehicles passing through the checkpoint are stopped and the drivers checked for signs of intoxication.

special needs beyond law enforcement exception: An exception to the requirements of a warrant and probable cause under the Fourth Amendment; it allows warrantless searches and searches on less-than-probable cause in cases where there are needs to be met other than those of law enforcement, such as the supervision of high school students, probationers, and parolees.

special relationship: An exception to the public duty doctrine (which exempts the police from liability for failure to protect), by which the police will be held civilly liable if a special relationship with a particular individual has been created.

speedy trial: A trial that is free from unnecessary and unwanted delay.

standing: The issue of whether a party in a case is the proper party to raise a legal issue.

stare decisis: Literally, "to abide by, or adhere to, decided cases."

stationhouse detention: A form of detention, usually in a police facility, that is short of arrest but greater than the on-the-street detention of stop and frisk. It is used in many jurisdictions for obtaining fingerprints or photographs, ordering police lineups, administering polygraph examinations, or securing other identification or nontestimonial evidence.

statute of limitations: A law providing that a crime must be prosecuted within a certain period of time or else it lapses and can no longer be prosecuted.

stop: The brief detention of a person when the police officer has reasonable suspicion, in light of his or her experience, that criminal activity is about to take place.

stop and frisk: A police practice that allows an officer, based on reasonable suspicion rather than on probable cause, to stop a person in a public place and ask questions to determine if that person has committed or is about to commit an offense and to frisk the person for weapons if the officer has reasonable concern for his or her own personal safety.

summons: A writ directed to the sheriff or other proper officer, requiring the officer to notify the person named that he or she is required to appear in court on a day named and answer the complaint stated in the summons.

testimonial (or communicative) self-incrimination: A form of self-incrimination, protected under the Fifth Amendment, that in itself explicitly or implicitly relates a factual assertion or discloses information. It is in the form of verbal or oral communication. Self-incrimination through oral testimony or communication; prohibited by the Fifth Amendment. It occurs when the suspect is required to "speak his guilt."

Title III of the Omnibus Crime Control and Safe Streets Act of 1968: The federal law that law enforcement officers nationwide, federal and state, cannot tap or intercept wire communications or use electronic devices to intercept private conversations, except if (1) a court order has authorized the wiretap or (2) consent is given by one of the parties.

tort: A civil wrong in which the action of one person causes injury to the person or property of another in violation of a legal duty imposed by law.

total incorporation: An approach holding that the Fourteenth Amendment's Due Process Clause should be interpreted to incorporate all the rights granted in Amendments I–VIII of the Constitution; this position is advocated by some Supreme Court justices.

total incorporation plus: An approach proposing that, in addition to extending all the provisions of the Bill of Rights to the states, other rights ought to be added, such as the right to clean air, clean water, and a clean environment.

totality of circumstances test (on information given by an informant): If a neutral and detached magistrate determines that, based on an informant's information and all other available facts, there is probable cause to believe that an arrest or a search is justified, then the warrant may be issued. This replaces the "separate and independent" two-pronged test of the *Aguilar* decision.

transactional immunity: A type of immunity that exempts the witness from prosecution for any offense arising out of an act or transaction.

USA Patriot Act: A comprehensive law passed after the events of September 11, 2001, that gives the government more power and resources to be able to respond to terrorism more effectively.

use and derivative use immunity: A type of immunity that assures the witness only that his or her testimony and evidence derived from it will not be used against him or her in a subsequent prosecution. However, the witness can be prosecuted on the basis of evidence other than his or her own testimony if the prosecutor has such independent evidence.

vehicle impoundment: The act of taking a vehicle into custody for such reasons as using it in a crime, impeding traffic, or being a threat to public safety.

vehicle inventory: The listing by the police of personal effects and properties found in the vehicle after impoundment.

venue: The place or territory in which a case is tried.

verdict: A jury or judge's pronouncement of guilt or innocence.

voir dire: Literally, "to tell the truth"; a process in which prospective jurors may be questioned by the judge or lawyers to determine whether there are grounds for challenge.

voluntary statement: A statement given without threat, force, or coercion and of the suspect's own free will.

volunteered statement: A statement made by a suspect without interrogation. *Miranda* warnings are not needed.

Wade-Gilbert rule: The rule that a suspect is entitled to have a lawyer present in a lineup or other face-to-face confrontation after being formally charged with a crime.

waiver: The intentional relinquishment of a known right or remedy. The waiver of *Miranda* rights must be intelligent and voluntary.

without unnecessary delay: When used in connection with arrests, the provision that an arrestee must be brought before a magistrate as soon as possible. However, its meaning varies from one jurisdiction to another, taking circumstances into account. Maximum limits are set by various jurisdictions.

wrongful death: A tort action in which the surviving family, relatives, or legal guardians of the estate of the deceased bring a lawsuit against an officer for death caused by the officer's conduct.

Index

Miranda warnings for, 409–412
passengers from vehicle, ordering, 288–289
plain view doctrine and, 290, 334
post-stop authority, 287–293
pretextual stops, 293–294
probable cause, authority based on, 291–292
questioning driver and passengers, 289–290
racial profiles, stops based on, 294–296
reasonable suspicion requirement, 283–284, 290–291
vehicle identification number (VIN), obtaining, 290
warrantless search of vehicle, 291–292
weapons, searching for, 291
Muehler v. Mena, 544 U.S. (2005), 255
Mug shot identification. *See* Photographic identification
Muhammad, John Allen, 11
Multiple prosecutions, 11
Municipal courts, 8
Municipalities, liability of, 533–535
Municipal policy or custom, 533
Murphy v. Waterfront Commission, 378 U.S. 52 (1964), 478, 498

Names, refusal to give, 149–151
Nardone v. United States, 302 U.S. 379 (1937), 258, 259, 273
National Academy of Sciences
on DNA testing, 384
on polygraph examinations, 386
National Institute of Justice Journal, 381
Nationalization of rights, 26
Negligence
by supervisor, 531–532
torts, 523–526
Neil v. Biggers, 409 U.S. 188 (1972), 360, 368, 372–373, 394
Neutral and detached magistrate, defined, 182
New concept of electronic surveillance, 259–260
New Jersey v. T.L.O., 469 U.S. 325 (1985), 253–254, 273
New trial motions, 61
New York v. Belton, 453 U.S. 454 (1981), 189, 217, 222, 239, 273, 281, 302–303, 305, 320
New York v. Burger, 482 U.S. 691 (1987), 252, 273
New York v. Class, 475 U.S. 106 (1986), 290, 320
New York v. Quarles, 467 U.S. 649 (1984), 437, 439–440, 446
Nichols, Terry, 11, 12
Night searches, 233
911 calls, failure to respond to, 526–527

9th Cir. v. United Airlines, No. 01-55319 (9th Cir. 2002), 153
Nix v. Williams, 467 U.S. 431 (1984), 121, 132
No contest pleas. *See* Nolo contendere plea
No information, 91
No-knock searches, 234
Nolle prosequi motion, 43
Nolo contendere plea, 46
withdrawal of, 47–48
Noncriminal proceedings, exclusionary rule in, 125
Nondeadly force, 204–205
excessive use of, 520–521
Noriega, Manuel, 12
Norris v. Alabama, 2924 U.S. 587 (1935), 464
North Carolina v. Alford, 400 U.S. 25 (1970), 47, 71
North Carolina v. Butler, 441 U.S. 369 (1979), 416, 446
North Carolina v. Pearce, 395 U.S. 711 (1969), 479, 498
Not guilty pleas, 46–47
Not guilty verdicts, 60
No trespassing signs and open fields doctrine, 340–341
Nullification by jury, 61–62

Objective reasonableness rule, 307
Odor, doctrine of plain, 336
Off-duty officers, search and seizure by, 256
Office of Technology Assessment, 388
Official immunity defense, 528–529
Ohio v. Robinette, 519 U.S. 33 (1996), 296, 320
Old concept of electronic surveillance, 258
Oliver v. United States, 466 U.S. 170 (1984), 326, 340–341, 342, 355
Olmstead v. United States, 277 U.S. 438 (1928), 110, 258, 259, 260, 273
Omnibus Crime Control and Safe Streets Act of 1968, Title III of, 261–264, 266
On Lee v. United States, 343 U.S. 757 (1952), 262, 273–274
Open fields doctrine, 336–344
abandonment and, 345
curtilage, 337–340
electronic beepers and, 343–344
excluded areas, 337
factors determining, 345–346
locked gate and, 340–341
plain view doctrine compared, 344
and sense-enhancement technology, 341–343
Opening statements, 55
Open view
comparison of plain view and, 335
plain view and, 333–334

Oral statements
confessions, admissibility of, 434–435
search warrants based on, 227–229
warrantless searches, consent to, 241–242
Oregon v. Elstad, 470 U.S. 298 (1986), 430–431, 437
Oregon v. Mathiason, 429 U.S. 492 (1977), 421, 446
Original jurisdiction of Supreme Court, 4
Ornelas et al. v. United States, 517 U.S. 690 (1996), 96, 99, 142, 164
Orozco v. Texas, 394 U.S. 324 (1969), 422, 446
Owen v. City of Independence, 445 U.S. 622 (1980), 533–534, 542

Padilla, Jose, 212
Palko v. Connecticut, 302 U.S. 319 (1937), 25, 31
Parent, consent to search by, 243
Parole
exclusionary rule in revocation proceedings, 125
right to counsel in revocation proceedings, 463
searches of parolees' homes, 246
Passengers. *See* Motor vehicle searches; Motor vehicle stops
Pat-down frisk. *See* Stop and frisk
Payton v. New York, 445 U.S. 573 (1980), 169, 180, 181–182, 217
Pembauer v. City of Cincinnati, 475 U.S. 469 (1986), 534, 542
Pennsylvania Board of Probation and Parole v. Scott, 524 U.S. 357 (1998), 125, 132, 246, 274
Pennsylvania v. Bruder, 488 U.S. 9 (1988), 411, 437, 446
Pennsylvania v. Mimms, 434 U.S. 106 (1977), 137, 159, 164, 171, 288, 289, 320
Pennsylvania v. Muniz, 496 U.S. 582 (1990), 437, 438, 446
Pen registers, 268
People v. Lewis, N.Y. 3d 224 (N.Y. App. Div 4th Dept., 2003), 500
Peremptory challenges. *See* Jury
Persons, seizure of, 171–174
Peterson v. City of Long Beach, 155 Cal Rptr 360 (1969), 13
Petit jury. *See* Jury
Petty offenses, jury trial for, 454–455
Photographic identification, 373
due process rights, 374–376
Justice Department guidelines, 380–381
Miranda warnings in, 439
reliability of, 377–378
right to counsel at, 374
search and seizure rights, 376
self-incrimination rights, 376